W9-ANH-598

HISTORY OF THE BYZANTINE STATE

Frontispiece: *Head of Constantine the Great.* Bronze with traces of gilding. 306–337. Found at Nissa in Yugoslavia, Constantine's birthplace. Ht. 14⅛". Belgrade, The National Museum. Photo: Hirmer Fotoarchiv, Munich.

GEORGE OSTROGORSKY

HISTORY OF THE
BYZANTINE STATE

Translated from the German by JOAN HUSSEY

With a Foreword by PETER CHARANIS

REVISED EDITION
1969

WITHDRAWN

RUTGERS UNIVERSITY PRESS
New Brunswick   *New Jersey*

MILSTEIN
DF
552.5
.08153
1969

Tenth paperback printing, 2009

Copyright © C. H. Beck'sche Verlagsbuchhandlung (Oscar Beck) München 1952

Copyright © 1969 by Rutgers, The State University of New Jersey

Library of Congress Cataloging-in-Publication Data
Ostrogorski, Georgije
   Geschichte des byzantinischen Staates. English
   Translation of Geschichte des byzantinischen
Staates.
   Includes bibliographical references.
   1. Byzantine Empire—History. I. Title.
II. Series.
DF552.5.08153 1969   949.5   71-83571
ISBN 0-8135-0599-2
ISBN 0-8135-1198-4 (pbk.)

Manufactured in the United States of America
All rights reserved

AUTHOR'S PREFACE

From the preface to the first edition (1940)

THIS book sets out to trace the development of the Byzantine State and to show how this was determined by the interaction of changing internal and external forces. For this reason the internal development of the State is given greater prominence than in previous general surveys of Byzantine history, and an attempt is made to bring out the essential interdependence of events at home and abroad, political, ecclesiastical and cultural. I have deliberately avoided any arrangement of material under special headings, such as 'the State', 'the Church', 'cultural history', 'eastern policy' or 'western policy', since this kind of presentation would have made it impossible to give a picture either of the continuous development of the polity as a whole over the centuries or of its general situation at any given moment, quite apart from the tedious repetition which it would necessarily have meant.

In conformity with the plan of this series[1] the account of the early Byzantine period is confined to a description of its main features, with only such detail as is essential for an understanding of the history of the medieval Byzantine State.

The survey of sources given for each section and the bibliography at the beginning of each chapter have made it possible to cut down the number of references to sources and secondary material in the text. . . .

From the preface to the second edition (1952)

The first edition of this book was exhausted far sooner than was expected and for some time a second edition has been needed. At the request of the publishers and at the insistence of my colleagues I therefore agreed to set about revising the book.

My first concern was to make good the failings which I myself had noticed and which my critics had brought to my attention. It is true that most of the reviews were far more favourable than I had dared to hope. All the same, and I am indeed most grateful for this,

---

[1] [The German editions appeared in the series *Handbuch der Altertumswissenschaft*, founded by I. von Müller, continued by W. Otto, XII, pt. I, vol. 2.]

various criticisms were made which could not be ignored, and the new edition has greatly profited from them. But above all, it was necessary to review and assess numerous recent contributions to the subject. In spite of the troubled times, very important advances have been made in Byzantine scholarship since the first edition came out. I have naturally tried to take these into account, and I have made full use of well-established conclusions and have given my own views on various reasonable hypotheses and on the more important controversial questions. In addition there was a further reason for a new edition, for it will be readily understood that an author may well find himself not entirely satisfied with what he has written ten years earlier. Some sections needed rearrangement, others expansion or supplementation, while much had to be re-written or differently emphasized. The book as it now stands is thus not only a revision, but an entirely new edition. . . .

From the preface to the third edition (1963)

Since the second edition of this book appeared in 1952, I have more than once had the opportunity of revising it. The first occasion was when it was translated into French (*Histoire de l'État byzantin*, trad. de Jean Gouillard, Paris, Payot, 1956) and into English (*History of the Byzantine State*, transl. by Joan Hussey, Oxford, Blackwell, 1956 and Rutgers University Press, New Brunswick, N.J., 1957). Not long afterwards a new edition was published in Serbo-Croat (*Istorija Vizantije*, Belgrade 1959) and then in Slovene (*Zgodovina Bizanca*, prev. Jože in Milena Zupančič, Ljubljana 1961). As a result of the rapid advance of knowledge in this field, the French and English translations contained many additions and corrections to the second German edition of 1952. The work which I carried out on the Serbo-Croat edition, besides further additions, also necessitated the rewording of certain passages.

This new edition does however differ considerably both from the second German edition of ten years ago and from the more recent editions in other languages. In the first place, the results of recent research have had to be taken into account. As in the earlier editions, I have made no attempt to cite everything which has been published, but I have drawn attention to what is of importance. Nevertheless, the steady advance of research has once again meant a large number of corrections and additions. In the once neglected field of Byzantine studies so much material is now being made available in so widely scattered a range of publications, that the author of a comprehensive study of Byzantine history is bound to be anxious as to whether he has succeeded in reading everything worthwhile and in avoiding unfortunate omissions. Moreover, while I was engaged on this revision I realized that it was necessary to make extensive changes in the text itself. There are of course limits to such alterations. For whatever the author may wish, the structure of a work cannot be altered when preparing a new edition. However this may be, the previous edition has been revised far more than might be assumed merely from the comparatively small increase in the number of pages....

Preface to the first English edition

My English colleagues have often expressed the wish for an English translation of this book. I am delighted that the fulfilment of this desire, so gratifying to me, has been made possible, thanks to the initiative of the Oxford publisher, Mr. Basil Blackwell, and that the book will now be available to a wide circle of English-speaking readers.

It gave me special pleasure and was indeed an honour when so distinguished a Byzantinist as Professor Joan Hussey agreed to undertake the translation. I should like to thank her most warmly for all the time and trouble she has so willingly devoted to this work.

Only a comparatively short time has elapsed between the publication of the second edition of the German original and the English translation, but nevertheless a good deal of work on Byzantine history has been published in the meantime, dealing with the most varied topics, and I was anxious to make some reference to the results of this latest research. Professor Hussey was most co-operative in meeting this wish, so that I have been able to make a considerable number of additions and corrections to the text and, more especially, to the footnotes, and I hope that this will add to the value of the book. The English edition, which is in all essentials a reproduction of the second German edition, has thus also taken into account the most recent advances in scholarship.

GEORGE OSTROGORSKY

Belgrade, December 1954

TRANSLATOR'S FOREWORD

Note to the first English edition

PROFESSOR OSTROGORSKY'S book is already an acknowledged classic. His masterly integration of the various strands of Byzantine history over a period of more than a thousand years has convincingly demonstrated both the organic nature of the Byzantine State and its links with Classical Antiquity. Here the beginner will get an excellent introduction to Byzantium, and the scholar will often find some bibliographical reference which has escaped his notice, while novice and expert alike will enjoy the penetrating and illuminating comments of a master of his subject.

I should like gratefully to acknowledge the constant help which I have had from Professor Ostrogorsky himself, particularly in personal discussions when he has given most generously of his time, thus making it possible to produce a version which has been revised in the light of recent research. I am much indebted to many other friends, particularly Dr. Janet Sondheimer, and I should also like to thank Miss Mary Dickson and Mr. Sumner Austin.

London, April 1955   J. M. HUSSEY

Note to the second English edition

PROFESSOR OSTROGORSKY'S *History of the Byzantine State* has become a valued and indeed an indispensable tool for medievalists. The third German edition was published in 1963 and the second English translation is based on this version.

It did not prove possible for the author to bring the bibliography of the new English translation up to 1967 when this book went to press. The only exception is the addition in the General Bibliography of one or two references to recent general works likely to be easily available to the English speaking readers for whom this book is intended.

It is a pleasure to acknowledge once again the generous help which I have received from Professor Ostrogorsky.

London, May 1968   J. M. HUSSEY

SERIES EDITOR'S FOREWORD

IN HIS preface to the third German edition of his *History of the Byzantine State*, Ostrogorsky makes it clear in what way that edition differs from the previous ones. The English version which we offer here is a translation of the third German edition made by Joan Hussey. At the suggestion of students we have appended three additional lists: one of the Patriarchs of Constantinople, another of the Popes, and one of the Despots of the Morea. We have also added to the illustrations, virtually doubling the number which appeared in our first edition.

May 1969

PETER CHARANIS
General Editor
Rutgers Byzantine Series

CONTENTS

ILLUSTRATIONS

Note: The illustrations for this new American edition were compiled with the gracious cooperation of the many institutions, archives, agencies, and individuals acknowledged in the photo captions. The staff of the Dumbarton Oaks Center for Byzantine Studies in particular provided invaluable assistance, and full use of the Library and Photograph Collection. Special thanks are also due to Dr. John W. Barker, Miss Susan A. Boyd, Dr. Demetrios J. Constantelos, Mrs. Caroline Gordon Dosker, Dr. Lillian Malcove, Dr. Cyril Mango, Dr. Marvin Ross, Dr. Robert L. Van Nice, and Dr. D. H. Wright, for their generous help and advice in assembling this material.

ABBREVIATIONS USED FOR FREQUENTLY
CITED WORKS AND PERIODICALS

AASS . . . . *Acta sanctorum,* Antwerp, 1643-.

'Actes de l'Athos' . . L. Petit, B. Korablev, V. Regel, E. Kurtz, 'Actes de l'Athos', VV Pril. 10 (1903), 12 (1906), 13 (1907), 17 (1911), 19 (1912), 20 (1913).

Adontz, 'Basile I' . . N. Adontz, 'L'âge et l'origine de l'empereur Basile I', B 8 (1933), 475–550; 9 (1934), 223–60.

Adontz, 'Samuel l'Arménien' N. Adontz, 'Samuel l'Arménien, roi des Bulgares', *Mémoires de l'Académie Royale de Belgique,* Classe des Lettres 38 (1938), 1–63.

Alexander, *Patr. Nicephorus* P. J. Alexander, *The Patriarch Nicephorus of Constantinople. Ecclesiastical Policy and Image Worship in the Byzantine Empire,* Oxford. 1958.

Andreev, *German i Tarasij* . I. Andreev, *German i Tarasij, Patriarchi konstantinopolskie* (Germanus and Tarasius, Patriarchs of Constantinople), Sergiev Posad, 1907.

Andreeva, *Očerki* . . M. Andreeva, *Očerki po kulture vizantijskogo dvora v XIII v.* (Studies in the culture of the Byzantine court in the thirteenth century), Prague, 1927.

B . . . . . *Byzantion,* Brussels, 1924-.

Babinger, *Beiträge* . . F. Babinger, *Beiträge zur Frühgeschichte der Türkenherrschaft in Rumelien (14.–15. Jahrhundert),* Südosteuropäische Arbeiten 34, Brno-Munich-Vienna, 1944.

Banescu, *Duchés byzantins* . *Les Duchés byzantins de Paristrion (Paradounavon) et de Bulgarie,* Bucarest, 1946.

Barišic, *Čuda Dimitrija Solun-* F. Barišic, *Čuda Dimitrija Solunkog kao*
skog *istoriski izvori* (The Miracles of S. Demetrius of Thessalonica as a historical source), Belgrade, 1953.

Baynes, *Byzantine Studies* . N. H. Baynes, *Byzantine Studies and Other Essays,* London, 1955.

Baynes-Moss, *Byzantium* . *Byzantium,* edd. N. H. Baynes and H. St. L. B. Moss, Oxford, 1948.

Beck, *Kirche* . . . H.-G. Beck, *Kirche und theologische Literatur im byzantinischen Reich* (Handbuch der Altertumswissenschaft XII, 2.1: Byzantinisches Handbuch II, 1), Munich, 1959.

Beneševič, 'Ranglisten' . V. N. Beneševič, 'Die byzantinischen Ranglisten nach dem *Kletorologion Philothei* und nach den Jerusalemer Handschriften', BNJ 5 (1926), 97–167; 6 (1928), 143–45.

BNJ . . . . . *Byzantinisch-Neugriechische Jahrbücher*, Berlin, 1920–1925, Athens 1926–.

Bon, Le Péloponnèse . A. Bon, *Le Péloponnèse byzantin jusqu'en 1204*, Paris, 1951.

Bratianu, *Études byz.* . G. I. Bratianu, *Études byzantines d'histoire économique et sociale*, Paris, 1938.

Bratianu, *Privilèges* . G. I. Bratianu, *Privilèges et franchises municipales dans l'Empire byzantin*, Paris-Bucarest, 1936.

Bréhier, *Schisme* . . L. Bréhier, *Le schisme oriental du XIᵉ siècle*, Paris, 1899.

Bréhier, *Vie et Mort* . L. Bréhier, *Vie et mort de Byzance. Le Monde Byzantin* I (L'évolution de l'humanité 32), Paris, 1947.

Bréhier, *Institutions* . L. Bréhier, *Les institutions de l'empire byzantin. Le Monde Byzantin* II (L'évolution de l'humanité 32, bis), Paris, 1948.

Bréhier, *Civilisation* . L Bréhier, *La civilisation byzantine. Le Monde Byzantin* III (L'évolution de l'humanité 32, ter), Paris, 1950.

Bréhier-Aigrain . . L. Bréhier et R. Aigrain, *Grégoire le Grand, les états barbares et la conquête arabe* (Histoire de l'église depuis les origines jusqu'à nos jours, publ. par A. Fliche et V. Martin, t. 5), Paris, 1938.

BS . . . . . *Byzantinoslavica*, Prague, 1929–.

Bury, *Later Rom. Empire*[1] . J. B. Bury, *A History of the Later Roman Empire from Arcadius to Irene* (395–800), 2 vols., London, 1889.

Bury, *Later Rom. Empire*[2] . J. B. Bury, *A History of the Later Roman Empire from the Death of Theodosius I to the Death of Justinian* (395–565), 2 vols., London, 1923.

Bury, *Eastern Rom. Empire* . J. B. Bury, *A History of the Eastern Roman Empire from the Fall of Irene to the Accession of Basil I* (802–67), London, 1912.

Bury, *Admin. System* . . J. B. Bury, *The Imperial Administrative System in the Ninth Century*, with a Revised Text of the *Kletorologion* of Philotheos, London, 1911.

Bury, *Constitution* . . J. B. Bury, *The Constitution of the Later Roman Empire*, Cambridge, 1909; reprinted in *Selected Essays of J. B. Bury*, ed. H. Temperley, Cambridge, 1930.

BZ . . . . . *Byzantinische Zeitschrift*, Leipzig, 1892–.

CAH . . . . *Cambridge Ancient History*, 12 vols., Cambridge, 1923–39.

CB . . . . *Corpus Scriptorum Historiae Byzantinae*, Bonn, 1828–97.

Chalandon, *Alexis I* . . F. Chalandon, *Essai sur le règne d'Alexis I Comnène* (1081–1118), Paris, 1900.

Chalandon, *Les Comnènes* II . F. Chalandon, *Les Comnènes II: Jean Comnène* (1118–43) *et Manuel Comnène* (1143–80), Paris, 1912.

Chalandon, *Domination normande* . F. Chalandon, *Histoire de la domination normande en Italie et en Sicilie*, 2 vols., Paris, 1907.

Chapman, *Michel Paléologue* . C. Chapman, *Michel Paléologue, Restaurateur de l'Empire byzantin*, Paris, 1926.

Charanis, 'Monastic Properties' . . . P. Charanis, 'The Monastic Properties and the State in the Byzantine Empire', *Dumbarton Oaks Papers* 4 (1948), 51–119.

Charanis, 'Palaeologi and Ottoman Turks' . . P. Charanis, 'The Strife among the Palaeologi and the Ottoman Turks, 1370–1402', B 16 (1942/43), 286–315.

Charanis, 'Short Chronicle' . P. Charanis, 'An Important Short Chronicle of the Fourteenth Century', B 13 (1938), 335–62.

Christophilopulos, Ἐπαρχικὸν βιβλίον . . . A. Christophilopulos, Τὸ ἐπαρχικὸν βιβλίον Λέοντος τοῦ Σοφοῦ καὶ αἱ συντεχνίαι ἐν Βυζαντίῳ, Athens, 1935.

CMH . . . . *Cambridge Medieval History*, 8 vols., Cambridge, 1924–36; IV, Pts I and II, *The Byzantine Empire*, 2 vols., new ed., Cambridge, 1966–67.

Dennis, *Manuel II* . . G. Dennis, *The Reign of Manuel II in Thessalonica* (1382–7), Rome, 1960.

Diehl, *Justinien* . . . Ch. Diehl, *Justinien et la civilisation byzantine au VIᵉ siècle*, Paris, 1901.

Dvornik, *Légendes*	F. Dvornik, *Les légendes de Constantin et de Méthode vues de Byzance* (*Byzantinoslavica supplementa* I), Prague, 1933.
Dvornik, *Les Slaves*	F. Dvornik, *Les Slaves, Byzance et Rome au IX⁰ siècle*, Paris, 1926.
Dvornik, *Photian Schism*	F. Dvornik, *The Photian Schism: History and Legend*, Cambridge, 1948.
Dujčev, *Proučvanija*	I. Dujčev, *Proučvanija vŭrchu bŭlgarskoto srednovekovie* (Essays on medieval Bulgaria), Sofia, 1943.
EB	*Études Byzantines*, vols. 1–4, Bucharest, 1943–6 (continued as REB).
EEBS	Ἐπετηρὶς Ἑταιρείας Βυζαντινῶν Σπουδῶν, Athens, 1924–.
EHR	*English Historical Review*, London, 1886–.
EO	*Échos d'Orient*, Paris, 1897–1939 (continued as EB).
Ferjančić, *Despoti*	B. Ferjančić, *Despoti u Vizantiji i južno-slovenskim zemljana* (Despots in Byzantium and in South Slav countries), Belgrade, 1960.
Ferluga, *Viz. uprava*	J. Ferluga, *Vizantiska uprava u Dalmaciji* (The Byzantine administration of Dalmatia), Belgrade, 1957.
Florinskij, 'Andronik i Kantakuzin'	T. Florinskij, 'Andronik Mladšij i Ioann Kantakuzin' (Andronicus the Younger and John Cantacuzenus), ŽMNP 204 (1879), 87–143, 219–51; 205 (1879), 1–48.
Fuchs, *Höhere Schulen*	F. Fuchs, *Die höheren Schulen von Konstantinopel im Mittelalter, Byz. Archiv* 8, Leipzig-Berlin, 1926.
Gardner, *The Lascarids*	A. Gardner, *The Lascarids of Nicaea, the Story of an Empire in Exile*, London, 1912.
Gay, *Italie*	J. Gay, *L'Italie méridionale et l'Empire byzantin depuis l'avènement de Basile I jusqu'à la prise de Bari par les Normands* (867–1071), Paris, 1909.
Gay, *Clément VI*	J. Gay, *Le pape Clément VI et les affaires d'Orient* (1342–52), Paris, 1904.
Geanakoplos, *Michael Palaeologus*	D. J. Geanakoplos, *The Emperor Michael Palaeologus and the West*, Cambridge, Mass., 1959.

Gelzer, 'Themenverfassung'. H. Gelzer, 'Die Genesis der byzantinischen Themenverfassung' (*Abh. d. Kgl. Sächs. Ges. d. Wiss.*, Phil.-hist. Kl., 18, Nr. 5), Leipzig, 1899.

Gerland, *Lat. Kaiserreich* . E. Gerland, *Geschichte des lateinischen Kaiserreiches von Konstantinopel*, I: *Geschichte der Kaiser Balduin I und Heinrich* 1204-16, Homburg v. d. Höhe, 1905.

Gibbon-Bury . . . E. Gibbon, *The History of the Decline and Fall of the Roman Empire*. Ed. in 7 vols. with introd., notes, appendices, and index by J. B. Bury, London, 1923.

Glykatzi-Ahrweiler, *Recherches* H. Glykatzi-Ahrweiler, *Recherches sur l'administration de l'Empire byzantin aux IXe– XIe siècles*, Bull. de correspondance hell. 84 (1960), 1-111 (and published separately).

Grabar, *Empereur* . . A. Grabar, *L'empereur dans l'art byzantin. Recherches sur l'art officiel de l'Empire de l'Orient* (Publications de la Faculté des Lettres de l'Univ. de Strasbourg 75), Paris, 1936.

Grafenauer, 'Nekaj vprašanj' B. Grafenauer, 'Nekaj vprašanj iz dobe naseljevanja južnih Slovanov' (Some problems relating to the period of the settlement of the South Slavs), *Zgodovinski časopis* (Zgodovinsk Review) 4 (1950), 23-126.

Grégoire, 'Inscriptions' . H. Grégoire, 'Inscriptions historiques byzantines. Ancyre et les Arabes sous Michel l'Ivrogne', B 4 (1927/28), 437-68.

Grégoire, 'Michel III' . . H. Grégoire, 'Michel III et Basile le Macédonien dans les inscriptions d'Ancyre', B 5 (1929/30), 327-46.

Grégoire, 'Neuvième siècle'.. H. Grégoire, 'Études sur le neuvième siècle', B 8 (1933), 515-50.

Grégoire, 'Épopée byzantine' H. Grégoire, 'Études sur l'épopée byzantine', *Revue des études grecques* 46 (1933), 29-69.

Grosse, *Röm. Militärgeschichte* R. Grosse, *Römische Militärgeschichte von Gallienus bis zum Beginn der byzantinischen Themenverfassung*, Berlin, 1920.

Grumel, *Reg.* . . . V. Grumel, *Les Regestes des Actes du Patriarchat de Constantinople*, Vol. I: *Les Actes des Patriarches*, fasc. I: 381-715; II: 715-1043; III: 1043-1206, Socii Assumptionistae Chalcedonenses 1932, 1936, 1947.

Grumel, *Chronologie* . . V. Grumel, *La Chronologie. Traité d'Etudes byzantines* I (*Bibliothèque byzantine*), Paris, 1958.

Halecki, *Un empereur* . . O. Halecki, *Un empereur de Byzance à Rome. Vingt ans de travail pour l'union des églises et pour la défense de l'Empire d'Orient*: 1355–75, Warsaw, 1930.

Hartmann, *Byz. Verwaltung* . L. M. Hartmann, *Untersuchungen zur Geschichte der byzantinischen Verwaltung in Italien* (540–750), Leipzig, 1889.

Heisenberg, 'Neue Quellen'. A. Heisenberg, 'Neue Quellen zur Geschichte des lateinischen Kaisertums und der Kirchenunion' I–III, *Sitz.-Ber. der Bayer. Akad. d. Wiss.*, Philos.-philol. u. hist. Kl., 1922, 5. Abh.; 1923, 2. Abh. 1923, 3. Abh., Munich, 1923.

Heisenberg, 'Palaiologenzeit' A. Heisenberg, 'Aus der Geschichte und Literatur der Palaiologenzeit', *Sitz.-Ber. der Bayer. Akad. d. Wiss.*, Philos.-philol. u. hist. Kl. 1920, 10. Abh., Munich, 1920.

Heyd, *Commerce du Levant* . W. Heyd, *Histoire du commerce du Levant au Moyen âge*, 2 vols., Leipzig, 1936 (2nd impression).

Honigmann, *Ostgrenze* . . E. Honigmann, *Die Ostgrenze des byzantinischen Reiches von 363 bis 1071 nach griechischen, arabischen, syrischen und armenischen Quellen* (*Corpus Bruxellense Hist. Byz.* 3), Brussels, 1935.

Hopf, *Geschichte* . . . K. Hopf, *Geschichte Griechenlands vom Beginn des Mittelalters bis auf die neuere Zeit* in Ersch-Gruber, *Allgem. Encyklopädie der Wiss. und Künste*, vol. 85/86, Leipzig, 1867–68.

Hussey, *Church and Learning* . J. M. Hussey, *Church and Learning in the Byzantine Empire 867–1185*, London, 1937.

HZ . . . . . *Historische Zeitschrift*, Munich and Berlin, 1859–.

IRAIK . . . . *Izvestija Russkogo Archeologičeskogo Instituta v Konstantinopole*, 1895–1914.

Jaffé . . . . . *Regesta Pontificum Romanorum*, 2nd ed. (ed. W. Wattenbach, S. Loewenfeld and others), 2 vols., Leipzig, 1885–8.

JHS . . . . . *Journal of Hellenic Studies*, London, 1880–.

Jireček, *Geschichte* . . K. Jireček, *Geschichte der Serben* I (to 1371) and II (to 1537), Gotha, 1911, 1918 (Geschichte der europäischen Staaten).

Jorga, *Geschichte* . . . N. Jorga, *Geschichte des osmanischen Reiches* I (to 1451) and II (to 1538), Gotha, 1908, 1909 (Geschichte der europäischen Staaten).

JRS . . . . . *Journal of Roman Studies*, London, 1911–.

Kap-Herr, *Kaiser Manuel* . H. v. Kap-Herr, *Die abendländische Politik Kaiser Manuels mit besonderer Rücksicht auf Deutschland*, Strassbourg, 1881.

Každan, *Derevnja i gorod* . A. P. Každan, *Derevnja i gorod v Vizantii IX–X vv.* (Country and town in Byzantium in the ninth and tenth centuries), Moscow, 1960.

Kolias, Ἡ ἀνταρσία Ἰωάννου Ζ´ . G. Kolias, Ἡ ἀνταρσία Ἰωάννου Ζ´ ἐναντίον Ἰωάννου Ε´ Παλαιολόγου (1390), Ἑλληνικά 12 (1951), 34–64.

Kornemann, *Doppelprinzipat* E. Kornemann, *Doppelprinzipat und Reichsteilung im Imperium Romanum*, Leipzig-Berlin, 1930.

Kornemann, *Weltgeschichte* . E. Kornemann, *Weltgeschichte des Mittelmeerraumes von Philipp II von Makedonien bis Muhammed*, 2 vols., Munich, 1948, 1949.

Kretschmayr, *Venedig* . . A. Kretschmayr, *Geschichte von Venedig*, 2 vols., Gotha, 1905, 1920 (Geschichte der europäischen Staaten).

Kulakovskij, *Istorija* . . J. Kulakovskij, *Istorija Vizantii* (History of Byzantium), I: 395–518; II: 518–602; III: 602–717, Kiev 1912, 1913, 1915.

Kyriakides, Βυζ. Μελέται . St. P. Kyriakides, Βυζαντιναί Μελέται II–V, Thessalonica, 1937.

Lampros-Amantos, Βραχέα   Σπ. Λάμπρου Βραχέα Χρονικά, ἐκδ. ἐπιμελείᾳ Κ. Ι.
  Χρονικά . . . . Ἀμάντου (Μνημεῖα τῆς ἑλληνικῆς Ἱστορίας I, 1), Athens, 1932.

Laskaris, *Viz. princeze* . M. Laskaris, *Vizantiske princeze u srednjevekovnoj Srbiji. Prilog istoriji vizantisko-srpskih odnosa od kraja XII do sredino XV veka*, Belgrade, 1926.

Laurent, 'Notes'. . . V. Laurent, 'Notes de chronographie et d'histoire byzantine', EO 36 (1937), 157–74.

Lemerle, *Philippes* . . P. Lemerle, *Philippes et la Macédoine orientale à l'époque chrétienne et byzantine* (Bibl. des Écoles françaises d'Athènes et de Rome 158), Paris, 1945.

Lemerle, 'Invasions' . . P. Lemerle, 'Invasions et migrations dans les Balkans depuis la fin de l'époque romaine jusqu'au VIII siècle', *Revue historique* 211 (1954), 265-308.

Lemerle, 'Histoire agraire' . P. Lemerle, 'Esquisse pour une histoire agraire de Byzance: les sources et les problèmes', *Revue historique* 219 (1958), 32-74, 254-84; 220 (1958), 43-94.

Lemerle, *L'Emirat d'Aydin* . P. Lemerle, *L'Emirat d'Aydin. Byzance et l'Occident. Recherches sur 'La Geste d'Umur Pacha'*, Paris, 1957.

Levčenko, 'Materialy' . . M. V. Levčenko, 'Materialy dlja vnutrennej istorii Vostočnoj Rimskoj imperii V–VI vv.' (Material for the internal history of the Eastern Roman Empire in the fifth and sixth centuries), *Vizantijskij Sbornik*, Moscow-Leningrad 1945, 12-95.

Levčenko, *Očerki* . . M. V. Levčenko, *Očerki po istorii russko-vizantijskich otnošenij* (Studies in the history of Russo-Byzantine relations), Moscow, 1956.

Lipšic, 'Viz. krest'janstvo . E. E. Lipšic, 'Vizantijskoe krest'janstvo i slavjanskaja kolonizacija' (The Byzantine peasantry and Slav colonization), *Vizantijskij Sbornik*, Moscow-Leningrad, 1945, 96-143.

Lipšic, *Očerki* . . . E. E. Lipšic, *Očerki istorii vizantijskogo obščestva i kul'tury, VIII—pervaja polovina IX veka* (Studies in the history of Byzantine society and culture from the eighth to the first half of the ninth century), Moscow-Leningrad, 1961.

Litavrin, *Bolgarija i Vizantija* G. G. Litavrin, *Bolgarija i Vizantija v XI–XII vv.* (Bulgaria and Byzantium in the eleventh and twelfth centuries), Moscow, 1960.

Loenertz, *Lettres de D.Cydonès* R.-J. Loenertz, *Les recueils de lettres de Démétrius Cydonès* (Studi e testi 131), Vatican, 1947.

Loenertz, 'M. Paléologue et D. Cydonès' . . .   R.-J. Loenertz, 'Manuel Paléologue et Démétrius Cydonès. Remarques sur leurs correspondances', EO 36 (1937), 271–87, 474–87; 37 (1938), 107–24.

Loenertz, 'Péloponèse' .   R.-J. Loenertz, 'Pour l'histoire du Péloponèse au XIVᵉ siècle' (1382–1404), REB 1 (1943), 152–96.

Longnon, *Empire latin* .   J. Longnon, *L'Empire latin de Constantinople et la principauté de Morée*, Paris, 1949.

Lot, *Fin du monde antique* .   *La fin du monde antique et le début du Moyen âge* (L'évolution de l'humanité, ed. H. Berr, 31), Paris, 1927.

Mansi . . . .   J. D. Mansi, *Sacrorum Conciliorum nova et amplissima collectio*, Florence, 1769–.

Manojlović, 'Peuple de C/ple'   G. Manojlović, 'Le peuple de Constantinople', B 11 (1936), 617–716 (= Carigradski narod, *Nastavni vijesnik* 12, 1904, 1 ff.).

Maricq, 'Partis populaires' .   A. Maricq, 'La durée du régime des partis populaires à Constantinople', *Bull. de l'Acad. Royale de Belgique*, Cl. des Lettres 35 (1949), 63–74.

Martin, *Iconoclastic Controversy*   E. J. Martin, *A History of the Iconoclastic Controversy*, London, n.d. [1930].

Mélanges Grégoire I–IV .   = *Annuaire de l'Institut de Philologie et d'Histoire orientales et slaves*, vols. 9–12, Brussels, 1949–52.

Meliarakes, Ἱστορία .   A. Meliarakes, Ἱστορία τοῦ Βασιλείου τῆς Νικαίας καὶ τοῦ Δεσποτάτου τῆς Ἠπείρου (1204–61), Athens, 1898.

Melioranskij, *Georgij Kiprjanin*   B. M. Melioranskij, *Georgij Kiprjanin i Ioann Ierusalimljanin, dva maloizvestnych borca za pravoslavie v VIII v.* (George of Cyprus and John of Jerusalem, two little known champions of Orthodoxy in the eighth century), St. Petersburg, 1901.

Meyendorff, *Palamas* .   J. Meyendorff, *Introduction à l'étude de Grégoire Palamas*, Paris, 1959.

MGH . . . .   *Monumenta Germaniae Historica*, edd. G. H. Pertz, T. Mommsen, and others. Hanover, 1826– (New eds. in progress).

Michel, *Kerullarios* .   A. Michel, *Humbert und Kerullarios*, 2 vols., Paderborn, 1925, 1930.

Mickwitz, *Geld u. Wirtschaft* . G. Mickwitz, *Geld und Wirtschaft im römi-schen Reich des 4. Jahrhunderts*, Helsingfors, 1932.

Mickwitz, *Zünfte*.   .   G. Mickwitz, *Die Kartellfunktionen der Zünfte und ihre Bedeutung bei der Entstehung des Zunftwesens*, Helsingfors, 1936.

Migne, PG   .   .   .   J. P. Migne, *Patrologiae cursus completus*, Series Graeco-latina, Paris, 1857-.

Migne, PL   .   .   .   J. P. Migne, *Patrologiae cursus completus*, Series Latina, Paris, 1884-.

Miklosich-Müller   .   .   F. Miklosich et J. Müller, *Acta et diplomata medii aevi sacra et profana*, 6 vols., Vienna, 1860-90.

Miller, *Latins*   .   .   W. Miller, *The Latins in the Levant. A History of Frankish Greece* (1204-1566), London, 1908.

Miller, *Essays*   .   .   W. Miller, *Essays on the Latin Orient*, Cambridge, 1921.

Monnier, 'Épibolé'   .   .   H. Monnier, 'Études de droit byzantin: l'épibolé', *Nouv. rev. hist. de droit français et étranger* 16 (1892), 125-64, 497-542, 637-72; 18 (1894), 433-86; 19 (1895), 59-103.

Moravcsik, *Byzantinoturcica* . Gy. Moravcsik, *Byzantinoturcica*, I: Die byzantinischen Quellen der Geschichte der Türkvölker, II: Sprachreste der Türkvölker in den byzantinischen Quellen, 2nd ed. Berlin, 1958.

Müller, FHG   .   .   .   C. Müller, *Fragmenta Historicorum Graecorum* IV and V, Paris, 1885, 1883.

Mutafčiev, *Istorija*   .   .   P. Mutafčiev, *Istorija na bŭlgarskija narod* (History of the Bulgarian nation), 2 vols., Sofia, 1943.

Mutafčiev, *Vojniški zemi*   .   P. Mutafčiev, *Vojniški zemi i vojnici v Vizantija prez XIII-XIV v.* (Military holdings and soldiers in Byzantium during the thirteenth and fourteenth centuries) (Spisanie na Bŭlg. Akad. na Naukite). [Publications of the Bulgarian Academy of Sciences, 27], Sofia, 1923.

Neumann, *Weltstellung* .   .   C. Neumann, *Die Weltstellung des byzantini-schen Reiches vor den Kreuzzügen*, Leipzig, 1894. French trans. in *Revue de l'orient Latin* 10 (1903-4), 56-171.

Niederle, *Manuel*. . . L. Niederle, *Manuel de l'Antiquité Slave*, Paris, 1926.

Nikov, 'Turskoto zavlade- P. Nikov, 'Turskoto zavladevane na Bŭl-
vane' . . . garija i sadbata na poslednite Šišmanovci' (The Turkish conquest of Bulgaria and the fortunes of the last Šišmanovici), *Izvestija na Istor. Družestvo* (Transactions of the Historical Society), 7/8 (1928), 41–112.

Norden, *Papsttum und Byzanz* W. Norden, *Das Papsttum und Byzanz. Die Trennung der beiden Mächte und das Problem ihrer Wiedervereinigung bis zum Untergange des byzantinischen Reiches*, Berlin, 1903.

OCP . . . . *Orientalia Christiana Periodica*, Rome, 1935–.

Ostrogorsky, *Bilderstreit* . G. Ostrogorsky, *Studien zur Geschichte des byzantinischen Bilderstreites*, Breslau, 1929.

Ostrogorsky, 'Querelle des G. Ostrogorsky, 'Les débuts de la Querelle
Images' . . . des Images', *Mélanges Ch. Diehl* I (1930), 235–55.

Ostrogorsky, 'Chronologie' . G. Ostrogorsky, 'Die Chronologie des Theophanes im 7. und 8. Jahrh.', BNJ 7 (1930), 1–56.

Ostrogorsky, 'Steuerge- G. Ostrogorsky, 'Die ländliche Steuer-
meinde' . . . gemeinde des byzantinischen Reiches im 10. Jahrh.', *Vierteljahrschr. f. Sozial- u. Wirtschaftsg.* 20 (1927), 1–108.

Ostrogorsky, 'Avtokrator' . G. Ostrogorsky, 'Avtokrator i Samodrzac' (Autocrator and Samodržac), *Glas Srpske Akad.* 164 (1935), 95–187.

Ostrogorsky, 'Agrarian G. Ostrogorsky, 'Agrarian Conditions in
Conditions' . . the Byzantine Empire in the Middle Ages,' *Cambridge Economic History of Europe* I (2nd ed., 1966), 205-234, 774-779.

Ostrogorsky, *La feodalité* . G. Ostrogorsky, *Pour l'histoire de la féodalité byzantine (Corpus Brux. Hist. Byz.*, Subsidia I), Brussels, 1954 = French trans. by H. Grégoire from the original Serbian work, *Pronija. Prilog istoriji feudalizma u Vizantiji i u južnoslovenskim zemljama* (Pronoia. A contribution to the history of feudalism in Byzantium and South Slav countries.) *Posebna izdanja Vizantološkog instituta Srpske akad. nauka* I (Occasional Publications of the Byzantine Institute of the Serbian Academy of Sciences, I), Belgrade, 1951; and from the Russian paper 'Vizantijskie piscovye knigi', (Byzantine Praktica), BS 9 (1948), 203–306.

Ostrogorsky, *Paysannerie* . G. Ostrogorsky, *Quelques problèmes d'histoire de la paysannerie byzantine* (Corpus Bruxellense Hist. Byz., Subsidia II), Brussels, 1956.

Pančenko, 'Krestjanskaja sobstvennost' . . . B. Pančenko, 'Krestjanskaja sobstvennost v Vizantii' (Peasant proprietorship in Byzantium), *Izv. Russk. Archeol. Inst. v K/pole* (Transactions of the Russian Archaeological Institute in Constantinople), 9 (1904), 1–234.

Papadopulos, *Genealogie der Palaiologen* . . A. Papadopulos, *Versuch einer Genealogie der Palaiologen*, (1259–1453), Diss. Munich, 1938.

Pernice, *Eraclio* . . . A. Pernice, *L'imperatore Eraclio, Saggio di storia bizantina*, Florence, 1905.

Piganiol, *Empire chrétien* . A. Piganiol, *L'Empire chrétien (325–95)* (*Histoire générale*, fondée par G. Glotz: *Histoire romaine* IV, 2), Paris, 1947.

PW . . . . . Pauly-Wissowa-Kroll's *Real-Encyclopädie der klassischen Altertumswissenschaft*, Stuttgart, 1894–.

REB . . . . Continuation of EO and EB as *Revue des Etudes Byzantines*, Bucharest, 1947–8, Paris, 1949–.

Rhalles and Potles . . G. A. Rhalles and M. Potles, Σύνταγμα τῶν θείων καὶ ἱερῶν κανόνων, 6 vols., Athens, 1852–59.

Rosen, *Bolgarobojca* . . V. R. Rosen, *Imperator Vasilij Bolgarobojca, Izvlečenija iz letopisi Jachji Antiochijskogo* (The Emperor Basil the Slayer of the Bulgarians, extracts from the chronicle of Jahja of Antioch), St. Petersburg, 1883.

Rostovtzeff, *Gesellschaft und Wirtschaft* . . . M. Rostovtzeff, *Gesellschaft und Wirtschaft im römischen Kaiserreich*, 2 vols., Leipzig [1930].

Runciman, *Romanus Lecapenus* S. Runciman, *The Emperor Romanus Lecapenus and his reign*, Cambridge, 1929.

Runciman, *Bulgarian Empire* . S. Runciman, *A History of the First Bulgarian Empire*, London, 1930.

Runciman, *Crusades* . . S. Runciman, *A History of the Crusades*, I–III, Cambridge, 1951, 1952, 1955.

Sathas, Μεσ. βιβλ. . . . K. N. Sathas, Μεσαιωνικὴ βιβλιοθήκη (*Bibl. graeca medii aevi*), 7 vols., Venice and Paris, 1872–94.

Schlumberger, *Nicéphore*   G. Schlumberger, *Un empereur byzantin au*
  Phocas . . . . *Xe siècle: Nicéphore Phocas*, Paris, 1890 (2nd
    impression, 1923).

Schlumberger, *Épopée byzan-* G. Schlumberger, *L'épopée byzantine à la fin*
  tine . . . . *du Xe siècle*, 3 vols., Paris, 1896 (2nd impres-
    sion, 1925), 1900, 1905.

Schwarzlose, *Bilderstreit* . K. Schwarzlose, *Der Bilderstreit. Ein Kampf
    der griechischen Kirche um ihre Eigenart und um
    ihre Freiheit*, Gotha, 1890.

Seeck, *Untergang* . . O. v. Seeck, *Geschichte des Untergangs der
    antiken Welt*, 6 vols., Stuttgart, 1920–3.

Sem. Kond. . . . *Seminarium Kondakovianum*, Prague, 1927–
    38, Belgrade, 1940.

Setton, *Crusades* . . K. M. Setton (gen. ed.), *A History of the
    Crusades*. I. *The First Hundred Years*, ed. M.
    W. Baldwin, Philadelphia, 1955; II. *The
    Later Crusades 1189-1311*, ed. R. L. Wolff
    and H. W. Hazard, Philadelphia, 1962.

Ševčenko, 'Cabasilas' . I. Ševčenko, 'Nicholas Cabasilas' "Anti-
    Zealot" Discourse: A Reinterpretation',
    DOP 11 (1957), 81–171.

Silberschmidt, *Das oriental.* M. Silberschmidt, *Das orientalische Problem
  Problem . . . . *zur Zeit der Entstehung des türkischen Reiches
    nach venezianischen Quellen. Ein Beitrag zur
    Geschichte der Beziehungen Venedigs zu Byzanz,
    Ungarn und Genua und zum Reiche von Kipt-
    schak* (1381-1400), Leipzig-Berlin, 1923.

Šišić, *Geschichte* . . F. Šišić, *Geschichte der Kroaten* I (to 1102),
    Zagreb, 1917.

Šišić, *Povijest* . . F. Šišić, *Povijest Hrvata u vrijeme narodnih
    vladara.* (The history of Croatia at the time
    of the national rulers), Zagreb, 1925.

Šišić, *Povijest* II . . F. Šišić, *Povijest Hrvata za kraljeva iz doma
    Arpadovića* (The history of Croatia under
    the kings of the Arpad dynasty), Zagreb,
    1944.

Skabalanovič, *Viz. gosudarstvo* N. Skabalanovič, *Vizantijskoe gosudarstvo i
    cerkov v XI v.* (The Byzantine State and
    Church in the eleventh century), St. Peters-
    burg, 1884.

Stadtmüller, *Michael Choniates* G. Stadtmüller, *Michael Choniates, Metropolit
    von Athen, Orientalia Christiana Analecta* 33,
    2 (1934), 128–324.

Stanojević, *Vizantija i Srbi* . St. Stanojević, *Vizantija i Srbi* (Byzantium and the Serbs), 2 vols. (Knjige Matice Srpske 7/8 u, 14/15), Novi Sad, 1903, 1906.

Stein, *Geschichte* . . . E. Stein, *Geschichte des spätrömischen Reiches* I. *Vom römischen zum byzantinischen Staate* (284–476), Vienna, 1928; French trans. 2 vols., Paris, 1959.

Stein, *Bas-Empire* . . E. Stein, *Histoire du Bas-Empire* II. *De la disparition de l'Empire d'Occident à la mort de Justinien* (476–565), Paris-Brussels-Amsterdam, 1949.

Stein, *Studien* . . . E. Stein, *Studien zur Geschichte des byzantinischen Reiches, vornehmlich unter den Kaisern Justinus II und Tiberius Constantinus*, Stuttgart, 1919.

Stein, 'Ein Kapitel' . . E. Stein, 'Ein Kapitel vom persischen und vom byzantinischen Staat', BNJ I (1920), 50–89.

Stein, 'Untersuchungen' . E. Stein, 'Untersuchungen zur spätbyzantinischen Verfassungs- und Wirtschaftsgeschichte', *Mitt. zur Osman. Gesch.* 2 (1923/25), 1–62.

Stein, 'Vom Altertum' . E. Stein, 'Vom Altertum im Mittelalter. Zur Geschichte der byzantinischen Finanzverwaltung', *Vierteljahrschr. f. Sozial- u. Wirtschaftsgesch.* 21 (1928), 158–70.

Stöckle, *Zünfte* . . . A. Stöckle, *Spätrömische und byzantinische Zünfte. Untersuchungen zum sog.* ἐπαρχικὸν βιβλίον *Leos des Weisen, Klio*, Beiheft 9, Leipzig, 1911.

Tafel and Thomas . . G. L. F. Tafel and G. M. Thomas, *Urkunden zur älteren Handels- und Staatsgeschichte der Republik Venedig*, Pts. I–III, Vienna, 1856/57 (*Fontes Rerum Austr.*, Abt. II, vols. 12–14).

Tafrali, *Thessalonique* . . O. Tafrali, *Thessalonique au XIVe siècle*, Paris, 1913.

Treitinger, *Kaiseridee* . . O. Treitinger, *Die oströmische Kaiser- und Reichsidee nach ihrer Gestaltung im höfischen Zeremoniell*, Jena, 1938.

Uspenskij, *Obrazovanie* . . F. I. Uspenskij, *Obrazovanie vtorogo bolgarskogo carstva* (The Formation of the Second Bulgarian Empire), Odessa, 1879.

Uspenskij, *Očerki* . . . F. I. Uspenskij, *Očerki po istorii vizantijskoj obrazovannosti* (Studies in the history of Byzantine civilization), St. Petersburg, 1891.

Uspenskij, 'Voennoe ustrojstvo' . . . F. I. Uspenskij, 'Voennoe ustrojstvo vizantijskoj imperii' (The Military Organization of the Byzantine Empire) *Izvestija Russk. Archeol. Inst. v K/pole* 6 (Transactions of the Russian Archeological Institute in Constantinople 6) (1900), 154-207.

Uspenskij, *Istorija* . . F. I. Uspenskij, *Istorija vizantijskoj imperii* I, II, 1, III (The History of the Byzantine Empire, I, II, 1, III), St. Petersburg, 1913, Leningrad, 1927, Moscow-Leningrad, 1948.

Vasiliev, *History* . . . A. A. Vasiliev, *History of the Byzantine Empire 324-1453*, Madison, 1952.

Vasiliev, *Byzance et les Arabes* I . . . . A. A. Vasiliev, *Byzance et les Arabes* I: *La dynastie d'Amorium* (820-67). Édition française préparée par H. Grégoire et M. Canard (*Corpus Bruxellense Hist. Byz.* I), Brussels, 1935.

Vasiliev, *Byzance et les Arabes* II, 2 . . . A. A. Vasiliev, *Byzance et les Arabes* II: *La dynastie macédonienne* (867-959). Edition française préparée par H. Grégoire et M. Canard. Deuxième partie: Extraits des sources arabes, trad. par M. Canard (*Corpus Bruxellense Hist. Byz.* II, 2), Brussels, 1950.

Vasiliev, *Vizantija i Araby* II A. A. Vasiliev, *Vizantija i Araby. Političeskie otnošenija Vizantii i Arabov za vreme makedonskoj dinastii* (867-959) (Byzantium and the Arabs. The political relations between Byzantium and the Arabs at the time of the Macedonian Dynasty (867-959)), St. Petersburg, 1902.

Vasiliev, 'Putešestvie Manuila' . . . A. A. Vasiliev, 'Putešestvie vizantijskogo imperatora Manuila II Paleologa po zapadnoj Evrope' (The Journey of the Byzantine Emperor Manuel II Paleologus in Western Europe), ZMNP N.S. 39 (1912), 41-78, 260-304.

Vasiliev, 'Foundation' . . . A. A. Vasiliev, 'The Foundation of the Empire of Trebizond', *Speculum* 11 (1936), 3-37.

Vasiljevskij, *Pečenegi* . . V. G. Vasiljevskij, *Vizantija i Pečenegi* (Byzantium and the Patzinaks) *Trudy* I (Works I) (1908), 1-175.

Vasiljevskij, 'Materialy'	. V. G. Vasiljevskij, 'Materialy k vnutrennej istorii vizantijskogo gosudarstva' (Materials for the internal history of the Byzantine State), ZMNP 202 (1879), 160–232 (= *Trudy* (Works) IV, 250–331), 368–438; 210 (1880), 98–170, 355–440.
Vizantiski izvori . .	. *Vizantiski izvori za istoriju naroda Jugoslavije* (Byzantine sources for the history of the South Slav peoples), I–II, Belgrade, 1955, 1959.
Vogt, *Basile I* . .	. A. Vogt, *Basile I, empereur de Byzance et la civilisation byzantine à la fin du IXe siècle*, Paris, 1908.
VV	. *Vizantijskij Vremennik* (Byzantina chronica), St. Petersburg, 1894–1927. New series, Moscow-Leningrad, 1947–.
Wittek, *Mentesche* .	. P. Wittek, *Das Fürstentum Mentesche, Studien zur Geschichte Westkleinasiens im 13.–15. Jahrh.*, Istanbul, 1934.
Wroth, *Byz. Coins* .	. W. Wroth, *Catalogue of the Imperial Byzantine Coins in the British Museum*, 2 vols., London, 1908.
Xanalatos, *Beiträge* .	. D. A. Xanalatos, *Beiträge zur Wirtschafts- und Sozialgeschichte Makedoniens im Mittelalter, hauptsächlich auf Grund der Briefe des Erzbischofs Theophylaktos von Achrida*, Diss. Munich, 1937.
Zachariae, *Jus* . .	. K. E. Zachariae a Lingenthal, *Jus Graeco-Romanum*, 7 vols., Leipzig, 1856–84.
Zachariä, *Geschichte* .	. K. E. Zachariä v. Lingenthal, *Geschichte des griechisch-römischen Rechtes*,³ Berlin, 1892.
Zakythinos, *Despotat* .	. D. Zakythinos, *Le despotat grec de Morée*, I and II, Paris, 1932–53.
Zakythinos, *Crise monétaire*	. D. Zakythinos, *Crise monétaire et crise économique à Byzance du XIII au XV siècle*, Athens, 1948.
Zepos, *Jus* . . .	. J. and P. Zepos, *Jus graecoromanum*, 8 vols., Athens, 1931.
Zlatarski, *Istorija* .	. V. Zlatarski, *Istorija na Bŭlgarskata Dŭržava prez srednite vekove* (The History of the Bulgarian State in the Middle Ages), I, 1 and 2, II, III, Sofia, 1918, 1927, 1934, 1940.

Zlatarski, 'Izvestijata' .   . V. Zlatarski, 'Izvestijata za Blŭgarite v
                                chronikata na Simeona Metafrasta i Logo-
                                teta' (Information on the Bulgarians in the
                                chronicle of Symeon Metaphrastes and
                                Logothete), *Sbornik za narodni umotvorenija,
                                nauka i knižnina* 24 (Collection on National
                                Folk-lore, Science and Literature 24)
                                (1908), 1–161.

ZMNP   .   .   .   . *Žurnal ministerstva naradnogo prosveščenija*
                                (Journal of the Ministry of Public Instruc-
                                tion), St. Petersburg, 1834–?1923.

ZRVI   .   .   .   . *Zbornik radova Vizantološkog instituta,*
                                Belgrade, 1952 ff.

HISTORY OF THE BYZANTINE STATE

Figure 1: *Diptych of Consul Rufinus Probianus.* Ivory, circa 400. Front leaf (left): the enthroned consul is flanked by two scribes; below stand two officials acclaiming him, with a writing table between them. Back leaf (right): the same composition, except that the consul holds a sealed scroll in his left hand, with his right hand raised in benediction. Each leaf, ht. 12⅛", w. 5". Tübingen, Preuss. Staatsbibliothek. Photo: Ann Münchow, Aachen.

Introduction

THE DEVELOPMENT OF BYZANTINE STUDIES

THE following summary can only indicate the main lines of development and refer to some of the more important individual works and scholars. Further surveys of the general development of Byzantine historical research may be found in V. G. Vasiljevskij, 'Obozrenie trudov po vizantijskoj istorii' (Survey of work on Byzantine history), ŽMNP 250 (1887), 222–65; 252 (1887), 113–47; 253 (1887), 97–153; 266 (1889), 380–92 (unfinished); L. Bréhier, 'Le développement des études d'histoire byzantine du XVIIe au XXe siècle', *Revue d'Auvergne*, Janvier-Février 1901; A. Vasiliev, *History of the Byzantine Empire* (1952), 3–42; E. Gerland, 'Das Studium der byzantinischen Geschichte vom Humanismus bis zur Jetztzeit', BNJ, Beiheft 12 (1934); D. Angelov, *Istorija na Vizantija I* (1959), 4–17; D. Zakythinos, Βυζαντιναὶ σπουδαί, Μεγάλη Ἑλληνικὴ Ἐγκυκλοπαιδεία, Συμπλήρωμα, τ. Β΄ (1959), 176–82. Surveys of work carried out in individual countries and on various periods are available in constantly increasing numbers in the specialist journals. A very complete list of these is given in Moravcsik, *Byzantinoturcica I* (2nd ed., 1958), 2–6. Only two important and purely bibliographical publications need be mentioned here: *Dix années d'études byzantines, Bibliographie internationale* 1939–48, Paris 1949, and F. Dölger-A. M. Schneider, *Byzanz* (Wissenschaftliche Forschungsberichte, Geisteswissenschaftliche Reihe, vol. 5), Berne 1952, for the period 1938–50. For the development of research in church history and in theology see Beck, *Kirche*, 7–23.

Scholarly research in Byzantine studies grew out of interest in the classical world. The road to ancient Greece led through Byzantium, for it was here that the classical heritage had been preserved and that the West at the time of the renaissance could find the means of satisfying its passionate desire to know more about Greek culture. As soon as scholars became interested in acquiring Greek manuscripts and in editing and commenting on classical texts, they were forced to turn to Byzantine resources, and it was Byzantine scholars such as Manuel Chrysoloras, John Argyropulus and Bessarion who inaugurated the study of Greek philology in the West. To begin with, Byzantium was regarded as the store-house in which the treasures of the classical world were to be found, while there was little interest in the schismatic Byzantine Empire itself. But as the Greek language became more widely known, travellers often visited the old centres of Byzantine culture, and classical literature was studied with the help of Byzantine commentators, all of which prepared the way for a genuine interest in Byzantium itself. Moreover since Byzantine history as yet occupied no place in its own right, there was often no distinction made between classical and Byzantine authors, and editors of classical texts sometimes included Byzantine works.

The first scholar to appreciate Byzantine history for its own sake and to recognize its distinctive quality was Melanchthon's pupil, Hieronymus Wolf (1516–80). He was librarian and secretary to the Fuggers in Augsburg and he was most keenly interested in Byzantine as well as in classical authors. With the help of Anton Fugger, he published the *Chronicle* of John Zonaras, the *History* of Nicetas Choniates and part of Nicephorus Gregoras' *History*. Wolf was the first to regard Byzantine history as occupying a special and independent province of its own, and he conceived the idea of a *Corpus byzantinae historiae*.

Wolf's work was continued by others. The new humanism stimulated the spirit of research and this was roused still further by political and ecclesiastical interests—by the problem of the struggle against the Ottoman Turks, by the movement for union among the Catholics, and by Protestant sympathy for an anti-papal Byzantium. In different places and in different ways western humanists at the end of the sixteenth and in the seventeenth century were impelled to investigate the sources for Byzantine history and law. The great pioneers in this work were: in Germany, Wolf's pupils Wilhelm Holzmann (Xylander) and David Hoeschel and the distinguished jurist Johannes Leunclavius; in France, the learned Jesuits, especially D. Petavius (Denis Petau); in the Netherlands, B. Vulcanius and above all in Holland Johannes Meursius; and in Italy the Greek Uniates, Nicolaus Alemannus and Leo Allatius.

In this initial stage Byzantine studies were usually limited to editing the sources and translating them into Latin, and the choice of authors selected was more or less a matter of chance. So far scholars had no idea of the wide range of available material and there was no clearly

defined plan of action. The beginnings were modest, though none
the less significant.

It was in the middle of the seventeenth century in France that
Byzantine studies really began to flourish. Intellectual activity at
Louis XIII's court, and even more so under Louis XIV, found an
increasing outlet in Byzantine history. Editing was no longer a
haphazard affair and individual efforts were co-ordinated in a united
and carefully organized plan which fostered and made use of the
lively and growing interest in scientific scholarship. Under the
patronage of Louis XIV and Colbert the famous printing-house of
the Louvre began to publish its great series of Byzantine historians.
The first to appear was the *History* of John Cantacuzenus in 1645.
In 1648 Constantine Porphyrogenitus' *Excerpta de legationibus* followed, and this was prefaced by an appeal by Ph. Labbe in which
he put forward plans for a *Corpus* of Byzantine historians, emphasizing the significance of Byzantine history and inviting the co-operation
of scholars of all countries. During the next decade this work was
eagerly followed up and for the first time something like a complete
edition of Byzantine historical sources was produced. These were
later reprinted in their entirety in the *Venice Corpus*, and the greater
part of them in the *Bonn Corpus*, together with certain additions.

Some of the most distinguished French scholars of the age
contributed to the *Paris Corpus*, such as the Jesuits Philippe Labbe
(1607–67) and Pierre Poussines (1609–86), the Dominicans Jacques
Goar (1601–53) and François Combéfis (1605–97), and the eminent
jurist Charles Annibal Fabrot (1580–1659). There were also valuable
collaborators outside France, and particularly in Rome, such as
Lucas Holstenius and Leo Allatius. Many Byzantine authors were
published for the first time in the Louvre edition, and works already
known were re-edited, so that the *Paris Corpus* with its better texts
and its particularly useful commentaries marked a real advance.

In addition to the *Paris Corpus* a good deal of progress was made
in the field of ecclesiastical and legal studies, as is evidenced by such
works as Labbe's *Concilia* (the basis of the later editions of Hardouin
and Mansi[1]), Goar's well-known Greek *Euchologium*, Combéfis'
edition of patristic writings and Fabrot's edition of the *Basilica*.

At first the *Paris Corpus* was particularly sponsored by Goar and
Fabrot, but at the height of its activity about 1670 the outstanding

---

[1] The editing of the *Acta* of the oecumenical councils has been placed on a new basis
by the monumental work of E. Schwartz, *Acta conciliorum oecumenicorum*, 1922– (cf.
below, p. 24 note 8).

figure of Du Cange appears. Charles Du Fresne, sieur Du Cange (1610–88) is the real founder of Byzantine historical studies and at the same time the greatest and most learned scholar in the history of Byzantine research. Du Cange edited the *History* of John Cinnamus, the *Chronicle* of John Zonaras and the *Paschal Chronicle*. He added detailed commentaries to these works, as well as to Poussines' editions of Anna Comnena and Nicephorus Bryennius. Moreover, with unquenchable energy Du Cange undertook pioneer research in an astonishingly wide range of subjects, including not only history, but the related fields of philology, genealogy, topography and numismatics. Even today many of his works are indispensable aids to research, particularly his *Histoire de l'empire de Constantinople sous les empereurs français* (1657) and his *Historia Byzantina duplici commentario illustrata*, a large work in two parts consisting of a topographical study (*Constantinopolis Christiana*) and an authoritative genealogical work (*De familiis byzantinis*). But Du Cange's greatest achievements are his dictionaries of medieval Greek and Latin; and of these, the *Glossarium ad scriptores mediae et infimae graecitatis*[1] is of special value to the Byzantinist. It is true that other dictionaries are now available, in particular the useful *Lexicon* of E. A. Sophocles,[2] but in spite of this Du Cange's *Glossarium* with its extensive references to original sources and its historical notes still remains one of the indispensable tools of Byzantine research.

Du Cange's work was continued by his younger contemporaries, Jean Mabillon (1632–1707) who laid the foundation of the scientific study of original documents and Bernard de Montfaucon (1655–1741) whose *Palaeographia graeca* initiated the study of Greek palaeography. They were followed by the Dominican Michel Lequien (1661–1733) with his *Oriens christianus* and the Benedictine Anselmo Banduri of Ragusa (1670–1743), the compiler of the *Imperium Orientale* which contains important topographical and archaeological material.

The seventeenth-century interest in Byzantium had had remarkable results, particularly in France. Byzantine studies, however, met with a most unfortunate setback in the eighteenth century. The enlightened age of rationalism was proud of its 'reason', its philosophical outlook and its religious scepticism, and it despised the

[1] This was reprinted by the Collège de France, Paris 1943.
[2] *Greek Lexicon of the Roman and Byzantine Periods*, new ed., Cambridge, Mass., 1914. Special reference must also be made to the large-scale comprehensive dictionary of D. Dimitrakos, Μέγα λεξικὸν τῆς ἑλληνικῆς γλώσσης, 9 vols., Athens 1949–50, which includes the development of the Greek language at all periods.

history of the whole medieval period. It was particularly contemptuous of the conservative and religiously minded Byzantine Empire whose history was merely 'a worthless collection of orations and miracles' (Voltaire), 'a tissue of rebellions, insurrections and treachery' (Montesquieu), or at best only a tragic epilogue to the glory of Rome. And so Byzantine history was shown as the thousand years' decline of the Roman Empire by Charles Lebeau in his *Histoire du Bas Empire* (Paris 1757–86) and by Edward Gibbon in his *Decline and Fall of the Roman Empire* (London 1776–88). Gibbon himself declared that his work described 'the triumph of barbarism and religion'.

Today there is no need to emphasize the unsoundness of the outlook of Lebeau or Gibbon: it is no longer necessary for Byzantine scholars to justify their choice of subject or indignantly to refute the assertions of Gibbon. The volumes of Lebeau and Gibbon have ceased to rouse such intense feelings and both their weaknesses and their great historical value can be assessed in a calmer atmosphere. For Gibbon and Lebeau were genuine historians—and Gibbon a very great one—and their works, in spite of factual inadequacy, rank high for their presentation of their material. For all their faults they are worth reading, often more so than some nineteenth-century Byzantine scholars whose work may be sounder philologically and historically. Moreover J. B. Bury's edition of Gibbon (1897–1900) is of particular value because of the editor's scholarly notes and appendices.

Gibbon's forceful presentation of his theme had a strongly deterrent effect on scholars and damped enthusiasm for Byzantine research for nearly a century. Even today the religious development of Byzantium is often seen through Gibbon's spectacles. Byzantine studies did not, however, entirely die out. J. A. Fabricius' *Bibliotheca graeca* provided an indispensable tool for the history of Byzantine literature (14 vols., Hamburg 1705–28, and a new edition in 12 vols., 1790–1809). The fortunate discovery of the Leipzig manuscript of the *De cerimoniis* and the commentary on it by John Jacob Reiske (1716–74) is without doubt one of the greatest events in the history of Byzantine studies, though it was characteristic of the age that the commentaries of this distinguished Greek and Arabic scholar remained unedited for several decades. K. B. Hase's edition of Leo the Deacon concluded the *Paris Corpus* of Byzantine historians in 1819 and gave further stimulus to Byzantine research. Soon after this in 1828 Niebuhr laid the foundation stone of the Bonn *Corpus scriptorum historiae byzantinae* with his edition of Agathias. For a man like Niebuhr neither prejudice nor general apathy could obscure the historical significance of Byzantium. The *Bonn Corpus* was to a great extent only a reprint of the *Paris Corpus*, but it was a much handier, and a fuller, collection and its importance is well known.

At the same time advances were being made in the presentation of Byzantine history. Byron's friend, the philhellene George Finlay (1799–1875), laid great stress on the Byzantine age in his extensive history of Greece. His work culminated in seven volumes covering the period 146 B.C. to A.D. 1864, *A History of Greece from the Conquest by the Romans to the Present Time* (London 1877). From France came the monographs of V. Parisot on John Cantacuzenus (1845) and of Berger de Xivrey on Manuel II (1853), both of which are still of value. In Germany G. L. F. Tafel (1787–1860) and G. M. Thomas (1817–87) were active; J. P. Fallmerayer (1790–1861) was producing his stimulating writings, and Karl Hopf (1832–73) his valuable work on Greece. His *Geschichte Griechenlands vom Beginn des Mittelalters bis auf unsere Zeit* (in Ersch und Gruber, Allg. Encycklopädie d. Wissensch. u. Künste 85/6, 1867–8) was based on careful study of the sources and on extensive work in archives; in spite of the author's tortuous mode of presentation which makes it heavy going and the fact that his statements are not always reliable, it is of permanent value as a collection of material and of great use for the period of the Latin domination and the still insufficiently explored age of the Palaeologi. Works based on Hopf and popular in their day, though no longer of much use, are G. F. Hertzberg's *Geschichte Griechenlands seit dem Absterben des antiken Lebens bis zur Gegenwart* (4 vols., Gotha, 1876–79) and his *Geschichte der Byzantiner und des Osmanischen Reiches bis gegen Ende des 16. Jahrhunderts* (Berlin 1883). A. F. Gfrörer's much read *Byzantinische Geschichten* (3 vols., Graz 1872–77) has a strong element of fantasy in it and is valueless today. On the other hand, Ferdinand Hirsch produced serious and scholarly work and his *Byzantinische Studien* (Leipzig 1876) can still offer a mine of instructive detail and comment.

The deeper appreciation of history which developed in the nineteenth century could not fail to modify the arrogant and unhistorical attitude of the age of enlightenment which had so discredited the world of Byzantium. An appreciation of the significance of historical development grew up. The influence of men like Ranke and Mommsen dispelled the legend of a long thousand-year-old decline, and in the last quarter of the nineteenth century interest in Byzantine history rapidly increased in the leading European countries. Alfred Rambaud, Vasilij G. Vasiljevskij, Karl Krumbacher, J. B. Bury were each able to establish Byzantine studies in their own countries as an independent branch of learning. The efforts of these men laid the foundations of modern Byzantine research and once prejudices and misrepresentations were cast aside there was a ready response. The study of Byzantine history no longer lagged behind other historical research but came to the front.

A. Rambaud (1842–1905) unfortunately soon deserted Byzantium and turned his attention to Russian history, producing work that was popular rather than scholarly. But he had already roused French interest in Byzantine history by his epoch-making book on the age of Constantine Porphyrogenitus and his work was carried on by Gustave Schlumberger and Charles Diehl.

Continuing the work of J. Sabatier (*Description des monnaies byzantines*, 2 vols., Paris 1862), G. Schlumberger (1844–1928) made extremely valuable contributions in the field of numismatics and particularly on seals. Out of the wide range of all his scholarly work, the Byzantine student of today prizes most highly his *Sigillographie de l'Empire byzantin* (Paris 1884). Even so, one must not forget the significance of his monumental *Épopée byzantine* and his many other works which spread an interest in Byzantium among the educated public far more widely than before. Ch. Diehl (1859–1944) was even more brilliant at popularization, and he became famous for the perfect artistry of his much admired essays, *Figures byzantines*. At the same time he was an amazingly versatile scholar who mastered all fields of Byzantine history and art and he combined rare gifts of vivid presentation with the most accurate scholarship. This is admirably illustrated by his comprehensive research on the Exarchate of Ravenna (1888), on Byzantine Africa (1896), and on Justinian (1901), as well as by several essays collected in his *Études byzantines* (1905). Few scholars have done so much to advance Byzantine research, or to stimulate others by their work, as Diehl who attracted many pupils both from his native land and from other countries. Thus tremendous impetus was given to Byzantine studies in France at the end of the nineteenth and in the early years of the twentieth centuries; Diehl's work was continued by a number of scholars, amongst whom Louis Bréhier, Ferdinand Chalandon and Jules Gay were outstanding, while at Bordeaux Henri Monnier was laying the foundations of the school which was to concentrate on legal history, an important field of Byzantine research.

In Germany it was Karl Krumbacher (1856-1909) who inaugurated systematic work on Byzantium. In 1891 he published his *Geschichte der byzantinischen Litteratur* and six years later he brought out a considerably enlarged second edition which had a section on theological literature by Albert Ehrhard and an outline of Byzantine history by Heinrich Gelzer. This work was the most magnificent effort of scholarship and industry in the Byzantine field which had appeared since Du Cange's time and it became an indispensable work of reference for all Byzantinists. In 1892 Krumbacher founded the *Byzantinische Zeitschrift*, a scholarly periodical which immediately became the centre of west European Byzantine studies and provided Byzantinists with an excellent bibliography, thus enabling them to keep in touch with contemporary research. At the same time Krumbacher's *Seminar für mittel- und neugriechische Philologie* in Munich became an international centre for work in Byzantine studies. And so in these various ways the great philologist made possible a marked advance in historical research in the Byzantine field.

Towards the end of the nineteenth century Byzantine historical studies in Germany were particularly promoted by Karl Neumann and Heinrich Gelzer. Neumann's stimulating work *Die Weltstellung des byzantinischen Reiches vor den Kreuzzugen* (1894) remains a masterpiece of research and presentation; he was also engaged on other important Byzantine studies and one can only regret that he so soon deserted Byzantium for the history of art. Gelzer's *Abriss der byzantinischen Kaisergeschichte* (Krumbacher, pp. 911-1067) is unfortunately not up to the standard of Krumbacher's work, but he made a contribution to Byzantine studies in a number of more specialized works, particularly in his *Genesis der byzantinischen Themenverfassung* (1899). Krumbacher's successor in Munich was August Heisenberg. Though primarily a philologist, he did not neglect history, and particularly the history of art, and he advanced the scientific study of Byzantine history by reprinting Byzantine authors in a critical edition and by publishing and commenting on new sources. Byzantine studies in Germany and Austria also profited from the work of historians and philologists of classical and medieval times who had an interest in Byzantium, such as L. M. Hartmann, O. Seeck, E. Schwartz. The work of the great legal historian K. E. Zachariä von Lingenthal (1812-94) was particularly important. His *Jus graeco-*

romanum (7 vols., Leipzig 1856-84) made available the most important Byzantine legal sources and his *Geschichte des griechisch-römischen
Rechtes* (3rd ed., Berlin 1892) laid firm foundations for research in
the history of Byzantine law.

The beginnings of Byzantine work in Russia were connected with
research into the early history of the country, and the Silesian Ernst
Kunick (1814-99) was one of the most important pioneers. He was a
member of the Imperial Russian Academy of Sciences in St. Petersburg and he did valuable work, both on medieval Russian history
and on the relevant Byzantine sources, thus helping on Byzantine
studies. With him must be mentioned the Swiss Eduard de Muralt
(1808-95) whose work on chronology, *Essai de chronographie byzantine*
(2 vols., St. Petersburg 1855 and 1871) still has its uses, though it is
now very out of date.

The real founder of Byzantine historical research in Russia was
V. G. Vasiljevskij (1838-99), while N. P. Kondakov (1844-1925)
inaugurated work on Byzantine archaeology and history of art.
Vasiljevskij's contribution is of permanent value and is distinguished
by its firm grasp of original material, its critical approach and the
stimulating nature of its inquiries. His research on the relations
between Russia and Byzantium, his fundamental treatment of Byzantium and the Patzinaks, and above all his pioneer investigation of the
internal history of the Byzantine Empire, are today still quite indispensable. In 1894 he founded the *Vizantijskij Vremennik*. Before
this Russian Byzantinists had been forced to rely on the hospitality
of other periodicals, particularly the *Žurnal Ministerstva Narodnogo
Prosveščenija*, but now they had their own, which, together with the
Byzantinische Zeitschrift founded two years earlier, rendered great
services to Byzantine studies. A year later F. I. Uspenskij as Director
of the recently founded Russian Archaeological Institute at Constantinople began the *Izvestija Russkogo Archeologičeskogo Instituta v
Konstantinopole*. After Vasiljevskij, it was Uspenskij (1845-1928)
who played the greatest part in promoting Byzantine studies in
Russia. He lacked Vasiljevskij's marked capacity for detailed
research and his critical approach, but his vast and scholarly output
decisively influenced Byzantine historical studies. There is scarcely
any important problem of Byzantine history with which he was not
concerned and there are many fundamental questions which he was
the first to consider. He was not only the most productive, but the

most many-sided, of Russian Byzantinists, and in contrast to Vasiljevskij he produced a comprehensive historical work, the monumental *Istorija vizantijskoj imperii* (*History of the Byzantine Empire*), the
most detailed modern general presentation of Byzantine history.
Owing to difficult times, the various volumes appeared at long
intervals (vol. 1 in 1913; vol. 2, part 1, in 1927; and vol. 3 in 1948),
and the work has still not yet been completely published.

The exceptional activity of Russian Byzantinists at the end of the
nineteenth and beginning of the twentieth centuries is mainly due to
scholars stimulated by Vasiljevskij and Uspenskij, particularly A. A.
Vasiliev, B. A. Pančenko, P. A. Jakovenko and P. V. Bezobrazov.
The Byzantine agrarian problem had been of special interest to Vasiljevskij and Uspenskij, and this continued to be a favourite subject
for research. Pančenko's book on peasant-holdings in Byzantium
(1904) challenged the views of his great predecessors, Zachariä von
Lingenthal, Vasiljevskij and Uspenskij, and broke new ground.
P. Bezobrazov and especially P. Jakovenko, like Pančenko, concentrated on the problems of the internal history of the Byzantine
Empire, and, like Vasiljevskij before them, did valuable research on
original documents. A. Vasiliev published a basic work on the
history of Byzantine and Muslim relations in the ninth and tenth
centuries (2 vols., 1900–2). J. A. Kulakovskij, who had begun by
specializing in the classical period, wrote a history of the Byzantine
Empire from 395 to 717 (3 vols., Kiev 1913–15), a dry, though
extremely sound and useful work. The great impetus given to
Russian research in Byzantine studies is shown by the establishment
in 1915 of another periodical in addition to the *Vizantijskij Vremennik*: this was the *Vizantijskoe Obozrenie* (*Revue Byzantine*) and three
volumes appeared, going down to 1917.

In England modern research in Byzantine studies was represented
from the late nineteenth century onwards by J. B. Bury (1861–
1927).[1] Bury was without doubt one of the most outstanding of
Byzantinists. He was a scholar of great range and unusual learning,
with a marked capacity for penetrating and critical analysis, and a
characteristically disciplined and austere approach. He left many
important specialist studies, as well as several general works covering long periods of Byzantine history. In 1889 his *History of the
Later Roman Empire* from 395 to 800 came out in two volumes;

---

[1] A penetrating assessment of Bury's scholarship and personality and a complete
bibliography of his works is to be found in N. H. Baynes, *A Bibliography of the Works of
J. B. Bury*, Cambridge 1929.

this was followed in 1912 by his valuable *History of the Eastern Roman Empire* which goes from the coronation of Charles the Great to the accession of the Macedonian Basil I. In 1923 he brought out a new edition of his earlier history under the same title, again in two volumes, but in a considerably expanded form so that it only covers the ground from 395 to the death of Justinian I. Special mention must be made of Bury's excellent commentary to his new edition of the *Cletorologion* of Philotheus in *The Imperial Administrative System in the Ninth Century* (1911). As the Russians had laid the foundations for work in Byzantine agrarian history, so Bury inaugurated that systematic research in Byzantine administrative history which was later so successfully developed by Ernst Stein and Franz Dölger. Bury found a worthy successor in Norman H. Baynes who particularly distinguished himself in the field of early Byzantine history. The history of the Byzantine Empire in the later middle ages, especially its relations with the Latins established in the Aegean, was dealt with in the important studies of William Miller.

Greece had long been concerned with Byzantine history, for to Greek scholars Byzantium was simply a part of their own national history. Considerable attention was paid to it in the work of the fiery patriot K. Paparrhegopulos, Ἱστορία τοῦ Ἑλληνικοῦ ἔθνους ἀπὸ τῶν ἀρχαιοτάτων χρόνων μέχρι τῶν νεωτέρων (5 vols., Athens 1860–77; new edition by Karolides, 1925; the main points are summarized in Paparrhegopulos' *Histoire de la civilisation hellénique*, Paris 1878). Sp. Lampros (1851–1919) contributed much to Byzantine research by his work on manuscripts and his numerous editions of texts; he also wrote a popular history of Greece from earliest times to 1453, Ἱστορία τῆς Ἑλλάδος μετ' εἰκόνων ἀπὸ τῶν ἀρχαιοτάτων χρόνων μέχρι τῆς ἁλώσεως τῆς Κωνσταντινουπόλεως (6 vols., Athens 1886–1908). In the same way A. Andreades (1876–1935) later on did great service by his research into Byzantine finances and economic history, the results of which appeared in a number of specialist studies and in his Ἱστορία τῆς ἑλληνικῆς Δημοσίας οἰκονομίας (Athens 1918). The special interest which Greeks took in Byzantine studies is reflected in the attention paid to them in Greek periodicals, particularly the Δελτίον τῆς Ἐθνολογικῆς Ἑταιρείας (Athens 1893–) and the Νέος Ἑλληνομνήμων whose editor and main contributor from 1904 to 1917 was the indefatigable Sp. Lampros.[1] A periodical solely for Byzantine

---

[1] The editorship of the periodical was taken over by K. Dyobuniotes who added seven further volumes (to 1927) to the fourteen already brought out by Lampros. An index to all twenty-one volumes was published by Charitakis in 1930.

studies was planned by N. Bees, the Βυζαντίς, only two volumes of which have appeared (1909 and 1911).

At the turn of the century Byzantine studies were making great strides in many other countries. Italy produced notable work, not only in the fields of history and philology, but in the history of law. In the Balkan countries, Byzantine research was bound up with work on their own national history, an interdependence which profited both. In Bulgaria, P. Mutafčiev (1883-1943) was working on Byzantine history side by side with the historians of medieval Bulgaria, V. Zlatarski (1866-1935) and P. Nikov (1884-1939). In Yugoslavia, Byzantine research benefited not only from the work of the Byzantinists D. Anastasijević (1877-1950) and F. Granić (1883-1948), but from the research on medieval Serbia and Croatia achieved by St. Stanojević (1874-1937), J. Radonić (1873-1956), N. Radojčic and F. Šišić (1869-1940). In Rumania, Byzantine studies were in full swing before the first world war, thanks to the astounding activity of N. Jorga (1871-1940), whose own remarkable works ranged over the fields of Byzantine history, Rumanian history and literature, as well as Ottoman and world history.

Byzantine studies depended on co-operative work on an international scale. Such collaboration was impossible during the two world wars, but gradually with much toil and labour the threads were picked up again and progress went on. In the breathing space between the two wars Byzantine studies leapt ahead. The scope of research and of editions of texts was widened and this expansion found a visible expression in International Byzantine Congresses, in the establishment of new specialist periodicals and the emergence of new centres of Byzantine research.

Byzantinists before 1914 had two journals of their own—the *Byzantinische Zeitschrift* and the *Vizantijskij Vremennik*, but a whole row of new periodicals appeared after the first world war as witness to the progress made. In 1925 *Byzantion* was begun and under the guidance of Henri Grégoire has done great work. Thanks to this periodical and to the amazing activity of its editor, Brussels has become an important centre for Byzantine research. Another periodical published in Brussels from 1932 onwards is also important for Byzantine studies: this is the *Annuaire de l'Institut de philologie et d'histoire orientales et slaves*. The *Byzantinisch-Neugriechische Jahrbücher* was another important Byzantine periodical which was edited by N. Bees, appearing first in Berlin in 1920, but after 1926 in Athens;

this came to a standstill towards the end of the second world war (a supplementary volume 18 for 1945-49 appeared in 1960). Above all, Greek activities in the Byzantine field have found their outlet from 1924 onwards in the Ἐπετηρὶς Ἑταιρείας Βυζαντινῶν Σπουδῶν and in Ἑλληνικά which first came out in 1928. Then there was *Studi Bizantini e Neoellenici* inaugurated by S. G. Mercati in Rome in 1924 which appeared at less regular intervals. *Byzantinoslavica* was begun in Prague in 1929; during the war it was forced to come to a standstill, but was afterwards revived under the editorships of M. Paulová, B. Havránek and N. L. Okunev and its original scope was considerably widened. It is no longer limited to Byzantino-Slav relations but is an important organ for the whole field of Byzantine studies. On the other hand, the *Seminarium Kondakovianum* (*Annales de l'Institut Kondakov*), established in 1926, has ceased publication after a period of varied and most fruitful activity. It was associated with the famous Kondakov Institute, an important centre of Byzantine and archaeological studies, established first in Prague, and from 1938 onwards in Belgrade until its destruction in 1941 in an air raid, with the loss of two of its most staunch collaborators.

The Institute of the learned order of Assumptionists was another important and an old established centre for Byzantine research; to begin with it was set up in Kadiköi, then in Bucharest, and today is in Paris where a vast spate of work is poured out. Its periodical, the *Échos d'Orient*, which was originally brought out in 1897 as a 'Revue trimestrielle d'histoire, de géographie et de liturgie orientales', has since concentrated more and more on Byzantine studies, thus reflecting the growing interest in this branch of learning. In 1943 it became the *Études byzantines*, and from 1946 (vol. 4 onwards) the *Revue des Études byzantines*, so that Byzantine studies were enriched by a new and very useful specialist journal. In America a new periodical *Byzantina Metabyzantina* has come out, though so far only one volume has appeared (in two parts, 1946 and 1949). In Paris the American Th. Whittemore established a Byzantine Institute which since 1946 has been associated with the *Bulletin of the Byzantine Institute*, a publication concentrating especially on archaeology and the history of art. In America the establishment of the Dumbarton Oaks Research Centre was of the greatest significance for work on the archaeology, art, and civilization of Byzantium; it publishes the fine *Dumbarton Oaks Papers* (1941—) and the *Dumbarton Oaks Studies* (1950—). A centre mainly for theological and ecclesiastical research has grown up at Scheyern, now assisted by a recently established offshoot at Ettal. In Vienna a Society for Byzantine Studies was formed after the second world war, whose activity is evidenced by the appearance from 1951 onwards of the *Jahrbücher der Österreichischen Byzantinischen Gesellschaft*. In Belgrade the Byzantine Institute of the Serbian Academy of Sciences is another modern foundation which promotes work on the history of Byzantino-Slav relations, and the first volume of its annual publication came out in 1952. Amongst recently founded centres for Byzantine studies special mention must be made of the Sicilian Institute for Byzantine and Modern Greek Studies in Palermo (Director: Bruno Lavagnini), the Greek Institute for Byzantine and post-Byzantine Studies in Venice (Director: Sophia Antoniadis), and the Byzantine Research Centre in Athens (Director: Dionysios Zakythinos). For the whole range of activities and the promising plans of this last Institute, see the *Report of the Byzantine Research Centre* (Athens 1962) by D. Zakythinos.

The immense advance made by this comparatively young branch of learning is thus evidenced by the development of a considerable number of centres for research as well as by the numerous periodicals devoted to its study. Even these do not give a complete picture of the growing interest in Byzantium, for there are an increasing number of periodicals in related fields which now tend more and more to include Byzantine subjects within their scope.[1]

Russia, the country which had once played so great a part in promoting Byzantine studies, for a long time lay dormant. After the first world war Russian work experienced a serious setback and it came to an almost complete standstill after the death of F. I. Uspenskij. Up to 1916 the *Vizantijskij Vremennik* had produced a regular series of twenty-two stout volumes, but the following decade saw only three slender numbers (1922, 1925 and 1927) followed by a long silence. Interest in Byzantine work in the U.S.S.R. did, however, gradually revive and the rebirth of this Russian research is clearly manifested in the *Vizantijskij Shornik* (1945). Soviet studies are now in full spate. The intense activity of Byzantine research in Moscow and Leningrad, as well as in many other cities in the Soviet Union, is shown today by the ever increasing flood of publications, and the new series of the *Vizantijskij Vremennik* now consists of 22 comprehensive volumes. As with Russian scholars of earlier gener-

[1] The bibliography published by the Association Internationale des Études byzantines for 1939–48 includes 2,800 entries drawn from about 280 different periodicals, series or collected works.

ations, so the main emphasis of present day work is on social and economic problems which are now interpreted in the light of a materialistic view of history.

Such marked progress in Byzantine studies would have been impossible but for the increasing availability of original material. Editorial activity brought to light new sources of various kinds, and it produced critical editions in place of the unsatisfactory older ones, although today there is an enormous amount waiting to be done in this direction, for we still depend on the defective old text of the *Bonn Corpus* for most of the histories and chronicles. Attempts to meet this need were made at the end of the nineteenth century by the *Bibliotheca Teubneriana*, and more recently by the *Collection byzantine de l'Association Guillaume Budé*, as well as in many important separate publications, so that many Byzantine historians and chronicles are now available in a critical edition which has superseded that of the *Bonn Corpus* (for details see the note on sources prefacing each section).

One important advance in Byzantine research was the publication of documentary material. The somewhat uncritical, though extensive, collection of F. Miklosich and J. Müller appeared during the years 1860–90. At the beginning of the present century an equally important and better edited collection of documents from Mt. Athos began to appear in the Supplements to the *Vizantijskij Vremennik*. The great progress made in this direction is evidenced by recent publications: G. Rouillard and P. Collomp, *Actes de Lavra I* (Archives de l'Athos I), Paris 1937; P. Lemerle, *Actes de Kutlumus* (Archives de l'Athos II), Paris 1945; F. Dölger, *Aus den Schatzkammern des Heiligen Berges*, Munich 1948; A. Guillou, *Les archives de Saint-Jean-Prodrome sur le mont Ménécée* (Bibliothèque Byzantine, Documents 3), Paris 1955 (see under 'Sources' for further details). These compare favourably with the older publications in many respects—they are produced with facsimiles of documents and seals, they give better texts and are accompanied by detailed expert notes as well as full indices.

This increasing concentration on documents reflects the tendency in modern research to reconstruct the internal life of the Byzantine state as accurately as possible and to build up a clearer picture of its administration and its social and economic development.[1] Byzantine

---

[1] A report on work in Byzantine economic and social history was given by G. I. Bratianu, 'Les études byzantines d'histoire économique et sociale', B 14 (1939), 497–511. Cf. also what is virtually a survey by P. Charanis, 'On the social structure of the Later

scholars have indeed far to go before they are anywhere near achieving the plan for a *Corpus der griechischen Urkunden des Mittelalters und der neueren Zeit* which Krumbacher laid before the Association Internationale des Académies as early as 1904, but a good deal of important material has been made available by now, and a number of significant specialist studies have also been published.[1] A particular debt is owed here to the pioneer work of F. Dölger, especially in the field of Byzantine diplomatic and palaeography, where we have his *Facsimiles byzantinischer Kaiserurkunden* (Munich 1931) as well as his *Regesten der Kaiserurkunden des oströmischen Reiches*, which has started off the planned *Corpus der griechischen Urkunden des Mittelalters und der neueren Zeit* (of the five parts envisaged, all have now come out, covering the years 556–1025, 1025–1204, 1204–82, 1282–1341 and 1341–1453 (Munich-Berlin 1924, 1925, 1932, 1960 and 1965)). This last work is a vital tool for any Byzantine historian, for it gives a complete register, with critical notes, of all imperial documents, both those which have actually survived and those which are only known from being mentioned in some other source. The period 311–476 is covered by O. Seeck, *Regesten der Kaiser und Päpste* (Stuttgart 1919). Documents from the Patriarchate of Constantinople are being dealt with by V. Grumel in *Les Régestes des Actes du Patriarchat de Constantinople*; three parts of this have appeared for the years 381–1206 (1932, 1936, 1947). A most important work at present available for the study of Byzantine church history and the history of dogma is the excellent reference book by H. G. Beck, *Kirche und theologische Literatur im byzantinischen Reich* (Handbuch der Altertumswissenschaft XII, 2. 1: Byzantinisches Handbuch II, 1), Munich, 1959.

Recent Byzantine historical research is giving increasing attention to epigraphic, and particularly numismatic and sphragistic, sources. The evidence of coins and seals has much to contribute towards the solution of all kinds of problems, especially those relating to the

---

[1] Cf. the excellent reports on research in the field of Byzantine diplomatic by G. Rouillard, 'La Diplomatique byzantine depuis 1905', B 13 (1938), 605–29, and F. Dölger, 'Bulletin diplomatique', REB 7 (1949), 69–90.

Roman Empire', B 17 (1944–5), 39–57. For recent research on legal history cf. the detailed report by B. Sinogowitz, 'Die byzantinische Rechtsgeschichte im Spiegel der Neuerscheinungen', *Saeculum* 4 (1953), 313–33 and see also the brief account of J. de Malafosse, 'Chronique de Droit byzantin', B 32 (1962), 605-19. For recently published documents see A. P. Každan, 'Novye materialy po vnutrennej istorii Vizantii X-XV vv.' (New material for the internal history of Byzantium from the tenth to the fifteenth centuries), VV 13 (1958), 302–13.

A   B   C   D

Figure 2: (ABOVE) *Gold Coins of Constantius III (421) and Galla Placidia.*
Actual size. (BELOW) *Gold Coins of Theodosius II (408–450).* Actual size.
Both groups from the Dumbarton Oaks Collections, Washington, D.C. Photos:
Dumbarton Oaks Collections.

A   B   C   D

A   B   C   D

Figure 3: (ABOVE) *Gold Coins (Solidi) of Justinian I (527–565)*. Actual size. (BELOW) *Gold Coins of Heraclius (610–641) and Heraclius Constantine (641)*. Actual size. Both groups from the Dumbarton Oaks Collections, Washington, D.C. Photos: Dumbarton Oaks Collections.

A   B   C   D

internal history of Byzantium, and is indeed often decisive. Numismatic material is indispensable for any study of the currency and economic history on the one hand, and of the symbolical representation of imperial authority on the other, and it would also be absolutely unthinkable today to investigate problems of administrative history without a thorough consideration of sigillographic evidence. All the same, in spite of remarkable progress, general knowledge of this important type of source material does indeed lag far behind the needs of scholarship. Thanks to the publication of a large collection of seals by V. Laurent, *Documents de sigillographie byzantine: La collection C. Orghidan* (Bibliothèque byzantine, ed. P. Lemerle, Documents 1), Paris 1952, a particularly significant step forward has recently been taken. This excellent work by the most distinguished modern expert on Byzantine seals and the older big collections of seals and coins (cf. below, pp. 26–7) can be supplemented by the invaluable and evergrowing body of material in individual publications, together with studies and separate reports on finds of coins and seals scattered in periodicals. The full reports on this subject by V. Laurent[1] have very much lightened the task of tracking down this material which is not always easy to come by. Nevertheless the publication of a *Corpus* of Byzantine coins and a *Corpus* of Byzantine seals remain most urgent *desiderata*.

The great importance attached in modern Byzantine studies to ancillary historical disciplines is shown by the inauguration in Paris of a series of publications devoted to these branches of study. This series of publications is directed by the distinguished French historian P. Lemerle and so far two valuable reference works have appeared: V. Grumel, *Chronologie* (Bibliothèque byzantine. Traité d'Études byzantines I, Paris 1958) and A. Bataille, *Les Papyrus* (ibid. II, Paris 1955).

Detailed discussion of the character of recent research in Byzantine studies is not our concern here. The periodicals specializing in this subject, with their detailed bibliographies and surveys on the research of individual scholars, as well as the activities in different countries, are an eloquent witness to recent progress. As they come out, current publications are admirably dealt with in the *Byzantinische Zeitschrift*; from its foundation in 1892 up to the present day (with the exception of several years break during and after the two world

---

[1] V. Laurent, 'Bulletin de sigillographie byzantine', B 5 (1929–30), 571–654, 6 (1931), 771–829, and 'Bulletin de numismatique byzantine 1940–49', REB 9 (1951), 192–251.

wars) this has systematically and carefully noted work in all branches of Byzantine studies, and all important studies are critically appraised, either by review in Part II or in the bibliographical indices in Part III. More recently, a similar systematic bibliography has been provided by *Byzantinoslavica*. Such are the invaluable aids to bibliographical information supplied by the various periodicals specializing in Byzantine studies. What follows is a very brief guide to the more comprehensive recent presentations of Byzantine history.

The early Byzantine period has been treated in detail by E. Stein in his *Geschichte des spätrömischen Reiches* I (1927) and *Histoire du Bas-Empire* II (1949).[1] These two substantial volumes by the great expert on Byzantine administration covering the years 284 to 565 take their place beside Bury's work as the safest guide to the history of this era and are fundamental for any understanding of the nature of the early Byzantine state.

The *Cambridge Medieval History* planned by J. B. Bury devotes part of volumes I (1911) and II (1913) to the Byzantine period and the whole of volume IV (1923) under the title of *The Eastern Roman Empire* (717–1453). As with all co-operative enterprises the chapters are not of equal merit, but on the whole it is an excellent and reliable work of reference and it has the great advantage of a detailed bibliography. An expanded and completely rewritten volume IV edited by J. M. Hussey has now appeared, *The Byzantine Empire*, Pt. I, *Byzantium and its Neighbours*, C.U.P., 1966, Pt. II: *Government, Church and Civilization*, C.U.P., 1967.

As early as 1919 the brilliant French Byzantinist Ch. Diehl brought out his little book *Histoire de l'Empire byzantin* briefly covering the ground from Constantine the Great to 1453 (new edition 1924; English translation 1925; Serbian translation 1933). In the *Histoire générale* begun under the general editorship of G. Glotz, Diehl contributed a detailed and comprehensive account of Byzantine history from 395 to 1081, while his colleague G. Marçais gave an excellent account of the history of the Arabs from Muhammed up to the twelfth century (Ch. Diehl and G. Marçais, *Le monde oriental de 395 à 1081*, Histoire générale, IIe section: Histoire du Moyen Âge, vol. III, Paris 1936). In a later volume Diehl dealt with the period 1081–1204 which R. Guilland continued to 1453, while R. Grousset completed the story by describing the Latin principalities

---

[1] A new edition of the first volume has been posthumously published in French by J.-R. Palanque (E. Stein, *Histoire du Bas-Empire*, I, 1959).

in the East (Ch. Diehl, L. Oeconomos, R. Guilland and R. Grousset, *L'Europe orientale de* 1081 à 1453, ibid. IX, 1, Paris 1945).

In 1917 the distinguished scholar A. A. Vasiliev wrote (in Russian) his history of the Byzantine Empire from its origin to the crusades, and in 1923–25 he brought out three smaller publications on the period of the crusades, the history of the Latin domination and the age of the Palaeologi. An enlarged edition of his work was published in English, *History of the Byzantine Empire* (2 vols., Madison 1928–9). This was followed by a revised and expanded version in French, *Histoire de l'Empire byzantin* (2 vols., Paris 1932), which has been translated into Spanish (*Historia del Impero Bizantino*, 2 vols., Barcelona 1948) and into Turkish (vol. 1 only, Ankara 1943—inaccessible to me). Now a still further revised edition, based on the French, has appeared in English in a single volume (Madison 1952). It is generally recognized that this valuable work provides a clear and reliable guide to the study of Byzantine history.

The many-sided Rumanian historian, N. Jorga, produced his stimulating, but somewhat hastily written, picture of Byzantine history under the title *Histoire de la vie byzantine* (3 vols., Bucharest 1934). The period to 1204 has been treated by the Greek historian K. Amantos, Ἱστορία τοῦ Βυζαντινοῦ Κράτους (2 vols., Athens 1939, 1947; new edition of vol. 1, Athens 1953). The first attempt to give a Marxist presentation of Byzantine history was made by M. V. Levčenko in his *Istorija Vizantii* (Moscow-Leningrad 1940), a short survey, uneven in quality and in treatment of various aspects of his material. It has been translated into Bulgarian (*Istorija na Vizantija*, Sofia 1948) and into French (*Byzance des origines* à 1453, Paris 1949). The Bulgarian historian D. Angelov has also begun a study of Byzantine history: the first volume has been published, dealing with the period from 395 to 867: *Istorija na Vizantija* I, Sofia 1959. A lucid though quite brief sketch of a popular nature is given by P. Lemerle, *Histoire de Byzance* ('Que sais-je?' Paris 1948).

Special recognition should be given to L. Bréhier's work, *Le monde byzantin* (L'évolution de l'humanité, ed. H. Berr, Nr. 32, 32b, 32c, Paris 1947, 1949, 1950). The late French historian to whom Byzantine studies owe so much has provided a detailed picture of the political history of the Byzantine Empire (*Vie et Mort de Byzance*), of its internal administration (*Les Institutions de l'Empire byzantin*), and of its civilization (*La Civilisation byzantine*). All three

volumes are characterized by thorough and careful treatment, but
the third is particularly outstanding for its individual approach to
the history of Byzantine culture and it gives a vivid picture of the
everyday life of the different classes of Byzantine society. Thus
Bréhier's *Civilisation byzantine* should be compared, not so much with
earlier presentations of Byzantine civilization, as with the great work
of Phaidon Kukules, Βυζαντινῶν βίος καὶ πολιτισμός (so far 5 vols.
in 8 books have appeared, Athens 1948–52), in which the distinguished Greek historian gives the results of his extensive investigations into the ordinary private lives of the Byzantines. In contrast,
other accounts of the history of Byzantine civilization seem to
represent certain aspects of Byzantine development, weaving the
different elements into a composite picture and usually placing the
main emphasis on public life. Presentations of this kind are Ch.
Diehl, *Byzance, Grandeur et Décadence* (Paris 1919); A. Heisenberg,
'Staat und Gesellschaft des byzantinischen Reiches', *Die Kultur der
Gegenwart II*, Abt. IV, 1² (Leipzig-Berlin 1923, pp. 364–414); N. H.
Baynes, *The Byzantine Empire* (London 1926; reprinted 1943); S.
Runciman, *Byzantine Civilization* (London 1933); J. M. Hussey, *The
Byzantine World*, London, 3rd ed. 1966; H. W. Haussig, *Kulturgeschichte
von Byzanz*, Stuttgart, 2nd ed. 1966. A brief but comprehensive
account is given in a collection of essays by various scholars, *Byzan-
tium. An Introduction to East Roman Civilization*, ed. by N. H. Baynes
and H. St. L. B. Moss (Oxford 1948). H. Hunger, *Byzantinische
Geisteswelt von Konstantin dem Grossen bis zum Fall Konstantinopels*,
Baden-Baden 1958, illustrates Byzantine cultural life by extracts from
the sources. His judicious choice of texts and excellent translations
make this little book very well worth reading.

Byzantine scholars are also particularly indebted to works dealing
with those peoples and countries having special links with the
Byzantine Empire, such as the Italian city states, the Persians,
Arabs, Turks and South Slavs. Works about these are often of
more value to the Byzantinist than studies specifically concerned
with Byzantium, as is the case with V. Zlatarski's *Istorija na Bŭlgarskata dŭržava prez srednite vekove* (*History of the Bulgarian state in the
middle ages*, 4 vols., Sofia 1918, 1927, 1934, 1940). Zlatarski treats
his subject very broadly and tends sometimes to theorize, but he
does valuable service in collecting all the material for the history of
Byzantino-Bulgarian relations from earliest times to the end of the
thirteenth century. Another book of this kind is K. Jireček's *Geschichte*

der Serben (2 vols., Gotha 1911, 1918) which is exceedingly compressed and austere almost to the point of dryness, but thanks to the author's critical approach is a reliable and penetrating work.

It is fitting to conclude this survey with the most important contribution of Gy. Moravcsik, *Byzantinoturcica* I–II, the first edition of which appeared in Budapest (1942–43) while the present definitive and much enlarged second edition was published in Berlin in 1958 by the Deutsche Akademie der Wissenschaften. The distinguished Hungarian scholar has now been through the whole range of Byzantine sources to collect material bearing on the history of the peoples of Turkic origin. His work is of the greatest practical value because he interprets his subject in the widest sense and therefore finds relevant material in practically every Byzantine historical writing. Moreover he gives a short but masterly description of each individual source consulted and adds invaluable information on manuscripts and editions, as well as the more important secondary authorities. It is no exaggeration to compare his work to Krumbacher's *Geschichte der byzantischen Litteratur*; it is, in fact, an invaluable supplement to the masterpiece which was first published over seventy years ago. Both are indispensable to the Byzantine scholar.

Figure 4: *Gold Medallion of Constantius II (323–361).* Actual size. Dumbarton Oaks Collections, Washington, D.C. Photo: Dumbarton Oaks Collections.

The Early Byzantine State: Its Development and Characteristics (324-610)

SOURCES

KNOWLEDGE of Byzantine history is derived from a variety of widely differing sources, both Byzantine and non-Byzantine. The general course of events in its main outline is supplied by the Byzantine historians and chroniclers who differ considerably in quality, detail and accuracy. The picture is then completed, and sometimes corrected, by information from western and oriental, and later on from Slav, sources, as well as by the evidence supplied by other types of Byzantine material. Various writings, reports of ambassadors, letters and speeches, can often make significant additions to, and help to clarify, the accounts given in the histories. In view of the important role of the Church in the development of Byzantium it is also essential for the historian to bear in mind theological works and especially the *acta* of the Councils. Lives of the saints are often of considerable value as historical sources, and for certain periods are no less important than the actual historical works themselves.[1]

But none of these writings supply much information on the economic life of the Empire or its legal and administrative organization, and material on such subjects is to be found in the various official and unofficial accounts of court life and administrative and military procedure and of economic conditions. In addition there are the legal works in which Byzantium was particularly rich, as well as the papyri, while for the later period there are above all the documents to which Byzantine scholars are now increasingly devoting their attention, and rightly so. It is not, however, until the second half of the eleventh century that Byzantine charters exist in any number, while only a few have survived for the age of the Macedonian dynasty and none for the earlier periods.

Finally, there is a special class of source material in archaeological evidence—monuments, inscriptions, coins, seals, and so on. In the

[1] For these writings now see Beck, *Kirche*.

22

Figure 5: *St. John Chrysostom*. Icon of miniature mosaic, set in wax; Constantinople, first half of the 14th century. Ht. 7″, w. 5″. Dumbarton Oaks Collections, Washington, D.C. Photo: Dumbarton Oaks Collections.

Figure 6: *St. Gregory and St. Basil the Great.* Detail of mosaic panel, Cappella Palatina, Palermo, Sicily; 12th century. Photo: Fratelli Alinari, Florence.

past Byzantine historians have made less use of this material than historians of ancient history, but at the present time Byzantinists are emphasizing more and more the value of such evidence.[1]

The survey of sources prefacing each section only attempts to indicate the most important evidence as briefly as possible. An exhaustive treatment of the literary sources will be provided in the history of Byzantine literature by F. Dölger in Pt. II of the *Byzantinisches Handbuch*.

What follows here in this section is merely introductory and is therefore necessarily limited to a few of the more important sources.

Byzantine historical writing begins with Eusebius, Bishop of Caesarea. As the author of a chronicle (in two books, to 325) he is one of the first representatives of the chroniclers whose works were to assume great importance in Byzantium, while his great ecclesiastical history[2] (in ten books, to 324) was a pioneer work breaking fresh ground. The famous *Life* of Constantine the Great also bears his name.[3] The most important historian of the fourth century is Ammianus Marcellinus, a broadminded pagan, whose *Res gestae*, written in Latin, was conceived as a continuation of Tacitus (only Books 14–31 for the period 353–78 have survived).[4] For the rest, works in Greek already predominate in the historiography of this period. Mention must be made of three pagan historians—Eunapius of Sardes (for 270–404, only surviving in fragments),[5] Olympiodorus of Thebes (fragments for 407–25)[6] and Zosimus (from Augustus to

[1] Cf. Moravcsik, *Byzantinoturcica* I, 165 ff., for a most instructive analysis of the characteristics of Byzantine sources.

[2] ed. E. Schwartz and T. Mommsen, 3 vols., Leipzig 1903–9; small edition by E. Schwartz, Leipzig 1914. Cf. also the notes by E. Schwartz, PW 6 (1907), 1370 ff.

[3] ed. I. A. Heikel, Leipzig 1902. H. Grégoire, B 13 (1938), 561 ff., has questioned the authenticity of the Vita and thinks that at any rate the material was worked over and interpolations made at the end of the fourth century. Most scholars reject this thesis. Cf. the forceful counter-arguments by N. H. Baynes, BZ 39 (1939), 46 ff.; J. Vogt, 'Berichte über Kreuzeserscheinungen aus dem 4. Jh. n. Chr.', *Mélanges Grégoire* I (1949), 593 ff. and *Constantin der Grosse und sein Jahrhundert* (1949), 164 ff.; A. Piganiol, 'Sur quelques passages de la *Vita Constantini*', *Mélanges Grégoire* II (1950), 513 ff., and *Empire Chrétien*, p. xiii; H. Dörries, *Das Selbstzeugnis Kaiser Konstantins*, Abh. d. Akad. d. Wiss. zu Göttingen, Phil-hist Kl., III Folge, No. 34 (1954); A. H. M. Jones, 'Notes on the Genuineness of the Constantinian Documents in Eusebius' Life of Constantine', *Journ. Eccl. Hist.* 5 (1954), 196 ff.; J. Moreau, 'Zum Problem der *Vita Constantini*', *Historia* 4 (1953), 234 ff.; K. Aland, 'Die religiöse Haltung Kaiser Konstantins', *Studia Patristica* I (1957), 549 ff. On the other hand, Grégoire's thesis is supported by P. Orgels, 'À propos des erreurs historiques de la *Vita Constantini*', *Mélanges Grégoire* IV (1953), 575 ff.

[4] ed. C. Clark, Berlin 1910, 1915.

[5] Müller, FHG IV, 7–56. Cf. also *Excerpta de legationibus*, ed. C. de Boor (1903), 591–9.

[6] Müller, FHG IV, 57–68.

410, in some detail from Diocletian onwards).[1] The historical work of Priscus[2] supplies valuable excerpts for the years 433–68, especially for Attila and the Huns. Following in the footsteps of Eusebius, church history was continued by Socrates (for 306–439),[3] by Sozomen (for 324–415),[4] and by Theodoret of Cyrrhus (for 325–428).[5] To these must be added Evagrius, whose work (from 431 to 593) is also of considerable value for secular history,[6] and the same is true of John of Ephesus' ecclesiastical history written in Syriac which has only survived in part and goes down to the time of the Emperor Maurice.[7] There is valuable historical material in the writings of the great church fathers of the period, particularly Athanasius of Alexandria, Gregory of Nazianzus, Basil of Caesarea, Gregory of Nyssa and John Chrysostom. The *acta* of the oecumenical councils[8] are very important for the historian, and the first five councils are relevant for the early Byzantine period covered in this section. There is a wide variety of rhetorical works and of these special mention must be made of the writings of the Emperor Julian,[9] and his contemporaries Themistius[10] and Libanius,[11] as well as Synesius whose activity extends into the fifth century.[12]

The outstanding historian of the age of Justinian is Procopius of Caesarea (in Palestine).[13] As secretary to Belisarius he had taken part in the wars against the Vandals, Goths and Persians, and he wrote

[1] ed. L. Mendelssohn, Leipzig 1887.

[2] Müller, FHG IV, 69–100; V, 24–6. *Excerpta de legationibus*, ed. C. de Boor (1903), 121–255, 575–91.

[3] Migne, PG 67, 28–842.

[4] Migne, PG 67, 843–1630.   [5] ed. L. Parmentier, Leipzig 1911.

[6] ed. J. Bidez and L. Parmentier, London 1898.

[7] Trans. J. M. Schönfelder, Munich 1862 and R. P. Smith, Oxford 1860. A new edition of the third and most important part of this work, with a Latin translation, is given by Brooks, *Corpus Script. Christ. Or. Scriptores Syri*, Series II, t. III. 1935, 1936 (inaccessible to me). Cf. the great monograph by A. P. Djakonov, *Ioann Efesskij i ego cerkovno-istoričesfie trudy* (John of Ephesus and his Ecclesiastical History), St. Petersburg, 1908, and idem 'Izvestija Joanna Efesskogo i sirijskich chronik o slavjanach VI–VII vv.', (Account of the Slavs in the sixth and seventh centuries in John of Ephesus and the syriac chronicles), *Vestnik drevnej istorii* 1946, 1, 20 ff.

[8] Complete edition in Mansi. For the Councils of Ephesus and Chalcedon there is the new critical edition by E. Schwartz, *Acta conciliorum oecumenicorum* vol. I, fasc. 1–5 (1922–30); vol. II, fasc. 1–6 (1922–30); vol. II, fasc. 1–4 (1933–6).

[9] ed. J. Bidez and F. Cumont, Paris 1922, 1924.

[10] ed. L. Dindorf, Leipzig 1832.

[11] ed. R. Förster, Leipzig 1903–27.

[12] Migne, PG 66, 1053–1616; French translation of the περὶ βασιλείας with a commentary, C. Lacombrade, *Le Discours sur la Royauté de Synésios de Cyrène à l'empéreur Arcadios*, Paris, 1951. For the work and the personality of this great rhetorician, cf. idem, *Synésios de Cyrène, Hellène et Chrétien*, Paris 1951.

[13] ed. J. Haury, Leipzig 1905, 1906, 1913.

an account of them in seven books, finished in 551, while a supple-mentary eighth volume appeared in 553. In addition to this impor-tant work, he wrote the famous *Secret History* in which Justinian and Theodora are blackened, and in 554 the *De aedificiis* in which Justianian's building activities are described.[1] Procopius was not always distinguished for his objectivity—in his writings on buildings, and to some extent in his history of the wars, he is a panegyrist, while in the *Secret History* he is a malicious pamphleteer—but all the same his works are of inestimable value as a source, and in style and presentation they rank very high indeed. Procopius found a succes-sor in his younger contemporary Agathias, who covers the history of the years 552–8 in his work on Justinian.[2] He in turn was followed by Menander Protector whose valuable work deals with the period 558–82, though only surviving in fragments.[3] Menander was succeeded by Theophylact Simocattes who wrote the history of the Emperor Maurice (582–602) in eight books.[4] Thus the complete period is covered by a series of accounts, the one carrying on where the other left off, a feature which also appears in later Byzantine historical writing. Equally characteristic of Byzantine historio-graphy at all periods is the tendency to take ancient Greek historians as models; an obvious instance in this particular epoch is found in Procopius, who avowedly set himself out to follow Thucydides. This awareness of the classical tradition is certainly one of the reasons why Byzantine historiography on the whole reaches a very high level and is far superior to that of the medieval West.

As well as histories properly speaking, there are also chronicles, a second and characteristic form of historical writing in Byzantium. John Malalas wrote a world chronicle which went to the last years of Justinian's reign.[5] John of Antioch produced another chronicle which has only survived in part and which apparently went to the year 610.[6] Theophanes and other later chroniclers whose works are

---

[1] On Procopius and his writings see the detailed study by B. Rubin, *Prokopios von Kaisareia*, Stuttgart 1954 (= RE, XXII, 2), in which all the earlier literature is listed. See also the bibliography in Moravcsik, *Byzantinoturcica* I, 496–500.

[2] ed. B. G. Niebuhr in CB. A Russian translation with a detailed introduction is given in M. V. Levčenko, *Agafij. O carstrovanii Justiniana* (Agathias, On the reign of Justinian), Moscow-Leningrad 1953.

[3] Müller, FHG IV, 220–69. *Excerpta de legationibus*, ed. C. de Boor (1903), 170–221, 442–77.

[4] ed. C. de Boor, Leipzig 1887. Russian translation: *Feofilakt Simokatta, Istorija*, Moscow 1957.

[5] Unless otherwise indicated, the Bonn Corpus of Byzantine historians (CB) is used.

[6] Müller, FHG IV, 535–622; V, 27–38.

also of some importance for this early period will be dealt with in the sections to which they belong.

The basic sources for law and administration in the early Byzantine age are above all the *Codex Theodosianus*[1] and the great legal work of Justinian, and for the historian the most important parts of this latter are the *Codex Justinianus* and the *Novels*.[2] The hierarchy of both military and civil officials in the early Byzantine state are described in the *Notitia dignitatum*[3] which dates from the first half of the fifth century and in the *De magistratibus* of John the Lydian from the middle of the sixth century.[4] The writings of Peter the Patrician who was *magister officiorum* from 539 to 565 have only survived in fragments.[5] His descriptions of court ceremonial, especially the imperial coronation during the fifth and sixth centuries, are particularly valuable and were incorporated by Constantine VII Porphyrogenitus into his *Book of Ceremonies* (I, ch. 84–95). The military treatise known as the *Strategicon* of Maurice, or the Pseudo-Maurice, belongs to the end of the sixth or the beginning of the seventh century; it is of significance, not only for the history of the art of war in Byzantium, but particularly for the history of other peoples, as the Persians, Turks, Avars, Slavs and Antae, Franks and Lombards, since it contains valuable information on their methods of warfare and other customs.[6]

The main works on numismatics and seals—and these are also relevant for the later sections—are J. Sabatier, *Description générale des monnaies*, 2 vols., Paris, 1862 (reprinted Leipzig 1930 and Graz 1955); W. Wroth, *Catalogue of the Imperial Byzantine Coins in the British Museum*, 2 vols., London 1908; I. Tolstoj, *Vizantijskie monety (Monnaies byzantines)*, fasc. 1–7, St. Petersburg 1912–14; N. Goodacre, *Handbook of the Coinage of the Byzantine Empire*, 3 vols., London 1928–33; G. Schlumberger, *La sigillographie byzantine*, Paris 1884; B. A. Pančenko, Katalog molivdovulov, *Izv. Russk. Archeol. Inst. v K/pole* 8 (1903), 199–246, 9 (1904) 341–96, 13 (1908) 78–151; K. Konstantopoulos, Βυζαντιακὰ μολυβδόβουλλα, Athens

[1] ed. T. Mommsen and P. M. Meyer, I, 1, 2, II, Berlin 1905; trans. C. Pharr, Princeton 1952.

[2] *Institutiones. Digesta*, ed. P. Krüger, 1911; II: *Codex Justinianus*, ed. P. Krüger, 1906; *Novellae*, ed. R. Schöll-G. Kroll, 1912.

[3] ed. O. Seeck, Berlin 1876.

[4] ed. R. Wünsch, Leipzig 1903. On the dating of the work see Stein, *Bas-Empire*, 729 ff., 838 ff.

[5] Cf. Stein, *Bas-Empire*, 723 ff.

[6] The only complete edition of this important work is by J. Scheffer, Upsala 1664. On the much disputed question of its date see Moravcsik, *Byzantinoturcica* I, 417 ff. and *Vizantiski izvori* I, 128.

1917; V. Laurent, *Documents de sigillographie byzantine*: *La collection C. Orghidan*, Paris 1952. Separate publications of coins and seals scattered in periodicals have increased with astonishing rapidity during recent years, and for these cf. the reports of V. Laurent already cited above on p. 17.

1. THE CHRISTIAN ROMAN EMPIRE

General bibliography: Stein, *Geschichte* I; Bury, *Later Roman Empire* I²; Piganiol, *Empire chretien*; H. St. L. B. Moss, 'The formation of the East Roman Empire', CMH IV, Pt I (2nd ed., 1966), 1–41; G. Mathew, 'The Christian background', ibid., 42–60; Seeck. *Untergang* I–IV; Lot, *Fin du Monde Antique*; F. Heichelheim, *Wirtschaftgseschichte des Altertums,* Leyden 1938, I 766–859, II 1191–1225; Rostovtzeff, *Gesellschaft und Wirtschaft*; Mickwitz, *Geld und Wirtschaft*; Kornemann, *Weltgeschichte* II; H. Bengtson, *Griechische Geschichte,* Munich 1960, 542 ff.; W. Ensslin, 'The Reforms of Diolcetian', CAH XII (1939), 383–408; J. Burckhardt, *Die Zeit Constantins des Grossen*⁵, *Gesamtausgabe* II, Stuttgart 1929; E. Schwartz, *Kaiser Constantin und die christliche Kirche*², Leipzig and Berlin 1936; N. H. Baynes, *Constantine the Great and the Christian Church*, London 1929; A. Piganiol, *L'Empereur Constantin*, Paris 1932; H. Grégoire, 'La "conversion" de Constantin', *Revue de l'Univ. de Bruxelles* 34 (1930–1), 231–72; idem, 'Nouvelles recherches constantiniennes', reprinted from B 13 (1938), 551–93; A. Alföldi, *The Conversion of Constantine and Pagan Rome*, Oxford 1948; J. Vogt, *Constantin der Grosse und sein Jahrhundert*, 2nd ed., Munich 1960; N. H. Baynes, 'Constantine's Successors to Jovian', CMH I (1911), 24–54; P. Allard, *Julien l'Apostat*, 3 vols., Paris 1900–3; G. Negri, *L'imperatore Giuliano l'Apostata*, Milan 1902; J. Geffcken, *Kaiser Julianus*, Leipzig 1914; J. Bidez, *La vie de l'empereur Julien*, Paris 1930, Munich 1940 (German translation).

Roman political concepts, Greek culture and the Christian faith were the main elements which determined Byzantine development. Without all three the Byzantine way of life would have been inconceivable. It was the integration of Hellenistic culture and the Christian religion within the Roman imperial framework that gave rise to that historical phenomenon which we know as the Byzantine Empire.[1] This synthesis was made possible by the increasing concern of the Roman Empire with the East which was necessitated by the crisis of the third century. Its first visible expressions were the recognition of Christianity by the *imperium romanum* and the foundation of the new capital on the Bosphorus. These two events— the victory of Christianity and the virtual transference of the political

[1] Cf. N. H. Baynes, *The Hellenistic Civilization and East Rome*, O.U.P. 1946 (reprinted in *Byzantine Studies*, pp. 1 ff.). On the hellenistic tradition of culture and education cf. the penetrating comments of R. J. H. Jenkins, *Byzantium and Byzantinism. Lectures in Memory of Louise Taft Semple*, The University of Cincinnati 1963, pp. 8 ff.

centre of the Empire to the hellenized East—mark the beginning of the Byzantine period.

Byzantine history is indeed only a new phase of Roman history, just as the Byzantine state is only a continuation of the old *imperium romanum*. The word 'Byzantine' is of course the expression of a later generation and was not used by the so-called 'Byzantines'. They always called themselves Romans ('Ρωμαῖοι) and their Emperor considered himself as a Roman ruler, the successor and heir of the old Roman Caesars. They remained under the spell of the name of Rome as long as the Empire lasted and to the end the traditions of Roman government dominated their political thought and purpose.[1] The Empire contained many different races all bound together by means of the Roman idea of the state, and the relation of the Empire to the outside world was determined by the Roman concept of universality.

As heir of the Roman *imperium* Byzantium aspired to be the sole Empire and claimed control of all lands which had originally belonged to the Roman *orbis* and now formed part of the Christian world (*oikoumene*). Hard reality thrust this claim further and further into the background, but the states which grew up within the Christian oecumenical jurisdiction on former Roman territory side by side with the Byzantine Empire were not regarded as being its equals. A complicated hierarchy of states developed and at its apex was the ruler of Byzantium as Roman Emperor and head of Christendom.[2] In the early Byzantine era imperial politics concentrated on maintaining direct control of the *orbis romanus*; in the middle and late Byzantine periods they were concerned with maintaining what was by then a theoretical supremacy.

However much Byzantium retained its awareness of its connection with Old Rome and however tenaciously it clung to its Roman heritage in the sphere of political theory as well as of practical politics, it is nevertheless true that as time went on it was continually travelling further away from the original characteristics of the Roman world. In culture and language Greek elements gained the day and at the same time the influence of the Church grew increasingly strong in Byzantine life. Economic, social and political

[1] Cf. F. Dölger, 'Rom in der Gedankenwelt der Byzantiner', *Zeitschr. f. Kirchengesch.* 56 (1937), 1 ff.; reprinted in Dölger, *Byzanz*, 70 ff.
[2] Cf. G. Ostrogorsky, 'Die byzantinische Staatenhierarchie', *Sem. Kond.* 8 (1936), 41 ff.; also F. Dölger, 'Die "Familie der Könige" im Mittelalter', *Hist. Jb.* 60 (1940), 397–420; reprinted in Dölger, *Byzanz*, 34 ff.

Figure 7: (ABOVE) *Triumphal Procession of a Christian Emperor.* Brown sardonyx cameo, 4th century; the emperor stands in a quadriga, while a winged victory crowns him with a wreath; once in the collection of Catherine II of Russia. Ht. 4½", w. 5⅞". (BELOW) *Large Gold Chain or Girdle.* Filigree medallion with 32 flat links and a small chain, circa 5th century. Length 34". Both objects from the University Museum Collections, Philadelphia. Photos: University Museum Collections.

Figure 8: *Diptych Panel of a Circus Scene*. Ivory, circa 425. One of the three sponsors seated at the top opens the games with a libation; below, a huntsman battles with stags, while 3 gameskeepers watch from the arena gates. Ht. 15″, w. 4¾″. Free Public Museum, Liverpool. Photo: D. H. Wright.

developments made inevitable the emergence of a new economic and social structure; by the early middle ages there had also developed what was in essence a new political entity and a new administrative system. In contrast to the views which used to be held, the development of the Byzantine state was something exceedingly dynamic. Everything was in constant flux, always being modified or built anew, and by the time that the Empire of the Byzantines had come to the end of its historical development it had nothing in common with the former Roman *imperium* except its name and the inherited claims which could no longer be put into practice.

In contrast to this, the Byzantine Empire in the early period was in actual fact still a Roman Empire and its whole life was riddled with Roman elements. This period can indeed be just as well called late Roman as early Byzantine, for it is as much concerned with Roman as with Byzantine development. The last three centuries of Roman, or the first three centuries of Byzantine, history cover a characteristic age of transition and bridge a gulf between the Roman Empire and the medieval Byzantine Empire. It was during this period that the old Roman life gradually gave way to the new Byzantine elements.

The beginning of Byzantine history can be traced back to the Roman Empire as it emerged from the crisis of the third century. The economic difficulties of this period had had particularly disastrous effects in the western half of the Empire. The East had greater powers of resistance—a factor which determined future development and accounted for the 'Byzantinizing' of the Roman Empire. Nevertheless the *pars orientalis* experienced the same crisis which was common to all parts of the late Roman Empire with its decadent economic and social structure, and was not spared economic collapse accompanied by severe social and political upheavals. It is true that the East did not suffer so noticeable a decline in population or so irreparable a decay of city life and economy as the West, but in common with the whole Empire its economic life was endangered by lack of labour and its trade and industry seriously threatened. The crisis of the third century marked the break with the life of the city of the ancient world.[1] Another widespread phenomenon was the continual growth of the great estate (*latifundium*). Throughout the Empire private estates steadily expanded at the expense of both

[1] Cf. Rostovtzeff, *Wirtschaft und Gesellschaft* II, 238 ff.; A. H. M. Jones, *The Greek City from Alexander to Justinian*, Oxford 1940, 85 ff.; and more recently H. Bengtson, *Griechische Geschichte*, 2nd ed. Munich 1960, 534 ff., especially 542 ff.

small-holder and imperial domain alike. A result of the decay of the small-holder was the increasing tying of the peasant to the soil, which was further accelerated by the pressing need for labour. The serfdom of the peasantry was, however, only a special instance of the general compulsory tying of the population to their occupation which with the third-century crisis began to be systematically enforced in the late Roman Empire. Compulsion in economic life paved the way for compulsion in political affairs.

With the disturbances of the crisis the Roman principate went under, and disappeared during Diocletian's absolute rule, out of which the Byzantine autocracy was to develop. The old municipal authorities of the Roman cities were in a condition of grave deterioration. The whole administration of the state was centred in the hands of the Emperor and his administrative officials, and after considerable expansion this civil service was to become the backbone of the Byzantine autocracy. The Roman system of magistrates gave place to the Byzantine bureaucracy. The Emperor was no longer the first magistrate, but an absolute ruler, and his power was derived not so much from earthly authorities as from the will of God. The time of crisis with its heavy trials and tribulations had inaugurated an age when men turned to religion and the world to come.

All the same, the concept of sovereignty as something rooted in the will of the people did not entirely disappear, and the senate, the city population organized in demes, and the army show themselves as political forces which imposed real limitations on the imperial power, particularly in the early Byzantine period.[1] The significance of these factors, rooted in the Roman past, subsequently dwindled before the all-embracing imperial authority. On the other hand, the Church, as the spiritual power in a Christian state, exercised an increasingly weighty influence as time went on. In the early Byzantine period the Emperor still had almost unlimited control over the Church and in accordance with Roman practice he treated the religion of his subjects as part of the *ius publicum*. But in the middle ages the Church established itself of necessity in Byzantium, as elsewhere, as a force to be reckoned with, and it was here that imperial authority received its most severe setback. Byzantium saw not infrequent clashes between the secular and spiritual powers in which the imperial side was by no means always the victor. But

---

[1] Cf. Bury, *Constitution*, 5 ff.

antagonism between the *imperium* and the *sacerdotium* was not characteristic of Byzantium, where there was on the whole a close and intimate relationship between State and Church, a fundamental interdependence of the Orthodox Empire and the Orthodox Church which together formed a single political and ecclesiastical entity. It was usual to find both powers with a common aim combining together against any danger which threatened the order of the divinely ordained world, whether by reason of internal or external enemies of the Emperor or of the undermining forces of the various heresies. But an understanding of this kind tended to bring the Church under the direct protection of the powerful Empire, and so the preponderance of the imperial over the ecclesiastical authority always remained characteristic and, as it were, the normal relationship in Byzantium.

The Emperor was not only the highest military commander, the supreme judge and the only legislator, but also the protector of the Church and of orthodoxy. He was chosen by God and he was therefore not only the lord and ruler but the living symbol of the Christian Empire which God had entrusted to him. Removed as it were from the earthly and human sphere, he stood in direct relationship to God and became the object of a special cult that was both political and religious. Day by day this cult was enacted in the impressive ceremonial of the imperial court in which both the Church and the whole court took part. It was reflected in the portraits of the Christ-loving Emperor, in the dignity surrounding his sacred person, in the words spoken by him or addressed to him in public.[1] His subjects were his servants. Whenever they were allowed to see his countenance they all, even the very highest in rank, greeted him by prostrating themselves to the ground in the *proskynesis*. But this splendid pomp of Byzantine court ceremonial and the imperial absolutism of which it was the reflection both had their roots in the Hellenistic and Roman worlds.[2] The peculiar

---

[1] Cf. A. Alföldi, 'Die Ausgestaltung des monarchischen Zeremoniells am römischen Kaiserhofe', *Mitt. d. Deutschen Archäol. Inst.*, Röm. Abt. 49 (1934), 1–118, and 'Insignien und Tracht der römischen Kaiser', ibid. 50 (1935), 1–171; Treitinger, *Kaiseridee*; cf. also the short summary: 'Vom oströmischen Staats- und Kaisergedanken', *Leipziger Vierteljahrschr. f. Südosteuropa* 4 (1940), 1 ff.; Graber, *Empereur*; F. Dölger, 'Die Kaiserurkunde der Byzantiner als Ausdruck ihrer politischen Anschauungen', HZ 159 (1939), 234 ff. (reprinted in Dölger, *Byzanz*); J. Straub, *Vom Herrscherideal in der Spätantike*, Stuttgart 1939; W. Ensslin, 'Gottkaiser und Kaiser von Gottes Gnaden', *S.B. d. Bayer. Akad. d. Wissensch.* 1943, vol. 6, Munich 1943; idem, 'Das Gottesgnadentum des autokratischen Kaisertums der frühbyzantinischen Zeit', *Studi biz. e neoell.* 5 (1939), 154 ff.; Bréhier, *Institutions*, 52 ff.

[2] Alföldi, op. cit.; Treitinger, *Kaiseridee*.

glory of the Byzantine imperial court thus developed from something which already contained many oriental elements, and these were to be still further accentuated by direct borrowing from the East, from the Sassanids, and later the Muslim Caliphate.[1]

Byzantine civilization was not only directly descended from late antiquity, but had the closest affinities with its way of life. As in the Hellenistic world, the various elements in Byzantium were bound together by a common cultural bond. Both worlds had something of an epigonic and eclectic character, especially Byzantium. Both lived on their heritage of great creative works, and their own productions were not so much original as in the nature of synthesis. The compiler was a type common to both ages. It is true that a predilection for compilation denoted a real intellectual aridity, that imitation skimmed over the meaning and content of the subject matter, and empty conventional rhetoric often missed the original beauty of form, but on the other hand a great deal is owed to Byzantium for its solicitous preservation of classical masterpieces and its careful attention to Roman law and Greek culture. The two high-lights and the two antipodes of the ancient world, Greece and Rome, grew together on Byzantine soil, the sphere of their greatest achievement: the Roman state and Greek civilization united to produce a new way of life inextricably bound up with that Christian religion which the old Empire and the old civilization had once so strongly repudiated. Christian Byzantium proscribed neither pagan art nor pagan learning. Roman law always remained the basis of its legal system and legal outlook, and Greek thought of its intellectual life. Greek learning and philosophy, Greek historians and poets, were the models of the most devout of Byzantines. The Church itself incorporated into its teaching much of the thought of the pagan philosophers and used their intellectual equipment in articulating Christian doctrine.

[1] Direct influences from the East were, however, of secondary importance; they were never determining factors in Byzantine civilization, unlike Roman, Hellenistic and Christian influences which not only moulded Byzantine development throughout, but were basic elements in its original make-up. It is impossible to assess rightly the individual quality and subtlety of Byzantine development if it is designated, as often happens, as a process of 'orientalization', as though Byzantium was simply an 'oriental' state. My stand in the first edition of my book against this widespread view gave a number of reviewers (cf. the excellent review of H. Gerstinger, *Wiener Zeitschr. f. d. Kunde d. Morgenlandes* 48, 1941, 312 ff.) the impression that I underestimated the oriental elements in Byzantine history, a misunderstanding due mainly to the ambiguity of the term 'oriental', and perhaps partly to the brevity of my remarks on this point which I have now tried to make clearer.

Figure 9: (ABOVE) *The Riha Paten*. Silver repoussé, with gilding and niello, Constantinople, 565–578. The Communion of the Apostles is depicted, with the figure of Christ shown twice. Diam. 13¾″. Dumbarton Oaks Collections, Washington, D.C. Photo: Dumbarton Oaks Collections. (BELOW) *Gold Bracelet*. One of a pair, middle or late 4th century. Carved in an overall open-work pattern, it is set with eight cabochon stones, alternately emeralds and sapphires. Diam. 4½″. Virginia Museum Collections, Richmond. Photo: Virginia Museum.

Figure 10: *Hanging Lamp in the Shape of a Foot in a Sandal*. Bronze, late 4th or early 5th century. The cone-shaped lid, with a dove finial, is engraved with a cross in front, and a tree and the Key of St. Peter on either side. Ht. 5½", w. 2½", l. 7". Malcove Collection, New York. Photo: Geoffrey Clements.

This tenacious awareness of the classical achievements was a special source of strength to the Byzantine Empire. Rooted in the Greek tradition, Byzantium stood for a thousand years as the most important stronghold of culture and learning; rooted in Roman concepts of government, its Empire had a predominant place in the medieval world. The Byzantine state had at its disposal a unique administrative machine with a highly differentiated and well-trained civil service, its military technique was superb, and it possessed an excellent legal system and was based on a highly-developed economic and financial system. It commanded great wealth and its gold coinage became increasingly the pivot of the state economy. In this it differed fundamentally from other states of late antiquity and the early medieval periods with their natural economy. The power and prestige of Byzantium were founded above all on its gold and in its heyday its credit seemed to be inexhaustible. On the other hand, the state pursued a harsh fiscal policy, subordinating all and sundry to its financial needs. Its first-rate administrative machinery was also an instrument for ruthless extortion.[1] The corruption and greed of the Byzantine civil service became proverbial and was always a most terrible scourge for the people. The wealth of the Empire and the high level of its culture were bought at the expense of the masses who lived in misery without means of redress and without freedom.

The important reforms of Diocletian were designed to meet the new situation which had been created during the disturbances of the third century. He used what was of value in the earlier system, but accepted or introduced necessary changes, so that the result of his work was a fundamental reorganization of the whole imperial administration. Constantine the Great was responsible for the further development and completion of Diocletian's work. Thus a new system grew up which was to be the basis of Byzantine administration.[2] In all essentials the arrangements of Diocletian and Constantine held throughout the early Byzantine period, and its basic characteristics—imperial autocracy, political centralization and bureaucratic government—remained as long as Byzantium survived.

[1] It is pointless to dispute this as is done by J. Karayannopulos, *Das Finanzwesen des frühbyzantinischen Staates*, Munich 1958. Cf. my review in *Vierteljahrsschr. f. Sozial-u. Wirtschaftsgesch.* 47, 2 (1960), 258 ff.

[2] On what follows see especially Seeck, *Untergang* II, 59 ff.; Bury, *Later Rom. Empire* I², 18 ff.; Lot, *Fin du Monde Antique*, 99 ff.; Rostovtzeff, *Gesellschaft und Wirtschaft* II, 210 ff.; Stein, *Geschichte* I, 98 ff., 168 ff.; W. Ensslin, 'The Reforms of Diocletian', CAH XII (1939), 383 ff.; Kornemann, *Weltgeschichte* II, 247 ff.; Piganiol, *Empire chrétien*, 275 ff.; Vogt, *Constantin der Grosse* (1949); 2nd ed. 1960, 95 ff.

The steps taken by Diocletian and Constantine were unmistakably directed towards strengthening imperial authority and prestige which had been shattered in the time of troubles. Hence the attempts to limit the power of the senate and of other factors dating from Rome's republican past, and also to define the competence of each department so as to prevent any dangerous accumulation of authority. Civil and military organization, central and provincial administration were carefully separated from each other. Individual departments were co-ordinated and controlled by the Emperor who stood at the apex of the hierarchically organized government, and the whole state machinery was directed from the centre.

The extent of the Empire was by now enormous and in order to maintain the efficacy of imperial control as far as possible its territory was subdivided for purposes of government. The early imperial period afforded the precedent of co-Emperors[1] and with this in mind Diocletian instituted a system of collegiate rule by four, that is, two Augusti and two Caesars. The Augusti were to control the eastern and the western halves of the Empire respectively, and each would have under him a Caesar who was bound to him not by ties of blood but by adoption and chosen solely for his personal qualities. As each Augustus retired, his Caesar would take his place, and a new Caesar would be created to fill the gap in the Tetrarchy. This scheme was all too logical in its conception and it caused endless civil wars. Constantine the Great emerged victorious from the fierce struggles and became the sole ruler, but set up again a number of joint rulers, and on his death-bed he divided the Empire afresh. He did not, however, resurrect Diocletian's artificial method of selection and he split up the Empire among his own offspring. But this family control also led to severe and bloody strife. Nevertheless, the principle of territorial division for administrative purposes survived and the system of co-Emperors was commonly employed.

Diocletian's reorganization of provincial government had put an end to the special position of Italy and did away with the distinction, by now pointless, between the imperial and senatorial provinces. From now on the administration of all provinces was under imperial control alone, and Italy, once the dominating country, was subdivided into provinces and subjected to taxation like the rest of the Empire. It was also significant that the larger provinces were split up into several smaller units. This made a considerable increase in

[1] Cf. Kornemann, *Doppelprinzipat*.

the number of provinces: under Diocletian there were getting on for
a hundred, and in the fifth century more than a hundred and twenty.
Diocletian also divided the Empire into twelve dioceses and by the
end of the fourth century these had been increased to fourteen.[1]
Finally, Constantine split up the Empire into prefectures, each consisting of several dioceses, while each diocese was made up of a
considerable number of provinces. Thus provinces were subordinated to dioceses, and dioceses to the prefectures, the whole
forming a centralized and hierarchically arranged system of government. To begin with the extent, and even the number, of the prefectures varied, and it was not until the end of the fourth century that
their boundaries took firm shape.

The enormous prefecture of the East (*Praefectura praetorio per
Orientem*) consisted of the five dioceses of Aegyptus, Oriens, Pontus,
Asiana and Thracia, thus including Egypt with Libya (Cyrenaica),
the Near East and Thrace. The Illyrian prefecture (*Praefectura
praetorio per Illyricum*) contained the dioceses of Dacia and Macedonia,
i.e. Greece and the central Balkans. The Italian prefecture (*Praefectura
praetorio Illyrici, Italiae et Africae*) was made up of Italy as well as the
greater part of Latin Africa on the one hand, and of Dalmatia,
Pannonia, Noricum and Rhaetia on the other. The prefecture of the
Gauls (*Praefectura praetorio Galliarum*) contained Roman Britain,
Gaul, the Iberian Peninsula and the neighbouring western part of
Mauretania. Each of the prefectures therefore covered an area
considerably larger than many modern states. At the head of each
pretorian complex there was a pretorian prefect, though occasionally
the office was divided between two colleagues. The pretorian prefect
of the East (who lived in Constantinople) and that of Italy were the
two highest ranking officials of the Empire, and they were followed
by their colleagues of Illyricum (whose seat was Thessalonica) and
of the Gauls.

A particularly important and characteristic mark of the administrative reforms of Diocletian and Constantine was the basic distinction
made between the military and civil authorities. The civil administration of a province was now the exclusive concern of its governor,
and military affairs rested with the *dux* who had command over one
or even more provinces. This system was carefully extended

[1] An independent *dioecesis Aegypti* was split off from the *dioecesis Orientis*, and the
dioecesis Moesiarum was separated into the two d. Dacia and Macedonia which then
made up the *Praefectura praetorio per Illyricum* (cf. below, p. 54). Cf. Bury, *Later Rom.
Empire* I², 28 ff.; E. Kornemann, 'Dioecesis' in PW 5 (1905), 727 ff., and *Weltgeschichte*
254 ff. (with good maps XIX and XXI appended).

throughout the whole provincial administration. Even the pretorian prefecture, which was the only instrument of government still to retain civil and military control under Diocletian, was deprived of its once military character by Constantine and became a purely civil authority, though even so it still had extraordinarily far-reaching powers during the early Byzantine period.[1]

The pretorian prefects attempted to increase still further this full authority which they possessed as the imperial representative by means of open competition with the organs of central administration. Their great authority is the outstanding characteristic of the administrative history of the early Byzantine period and to some extent it sets its mark on the whole system. The Emperor, on the other hand, was continually striving to reduce their power by limiting their spheres of influence and by trying to play off against them their vicars and diocesan governors, and above all by extending the competence of certain departments of the central administration. The real interest of the development of the administrative system of this period turns on the internal struggle between the different instruments of government.

Rome and Constantinople were removed from the control of the pretorian prefect and placed under their own city prefects, who ranked immediately after the pretorian prefects and took precedence of all other imperial officials. The city prefect was the first member of the senate and was to some extent the personification of whatever remained of the old republican tradition in the city life. He was the only official who did not wear military dress but kept the toga, the characteristic mark of the Roman citizen. The eparch of Constantinople (ὁ ἔπαρχος τῆς πόλεως) played a leading role in the life of the capital, both in the earlier and later Byzantine periods. In Constantinople he was in charge of the courts of justice, he was responsible for the maintenance of law and order, he had to see that the city was adequately provisioned; he controlled its trade and industry and indeed its whole economic life.

As both Constantinople and Rome were made separate administrative units, the powers of the pretorian prefects were considerably limited. They were still further restricted by the development of the departments of the central government under Constantine the Great. The most important official of the central administration was

---

[1] Cf. Stein, *Geschichte* I, 53 ff. and *Untersuchungen über das Officium der Prätorianerpräfektur seit Diokletian*, Vienna 1922; J. R. Palanque, *Essai sur la préfecture du prétoire au Bas-Empire*, Paris 1933.

now the *magister officiorum*.[1] From modest beginnings he had gradually built up his authority, particularly at the expense of the pretorian prefect. He had control over all the *officia* of the Empire, which in practice gave him authority over the whole administration, not excepting that within the competence of the pretorian prefect. For the *officia*, the bureaux of the different departments with their countless officials, were the essential elements in the bureaucratic administrative machine. His own *officium* consisted of *agentes in rebus* who acted both as imperial couriers and as informers (*curiosi*) throughout the provinces and reported on the doings and loyalty of civil servants and subjects alike. They were a vast body and in the middle of the fifth century there were more than 1,200 of them in the eastern half of the Empire alone. The *magister officiorum* was also responsible for the safety of the Emperor's person and he was therefore in command of the *scholae palatinae*, the imperial bodyguard. He was the chief Master of Ceremonies and as such presided over all the ceremonial of the imperial court, and in this capacity an important political function devolved upon him: he was responsible for receiving foreign ambassadors and also had to conduct negotiations with foreign powers. Finally, from the end of the fourth century he was in charge of the imperial postal service (*cursus publicus*) which had originally been under the pretorian prefects.

Next to the *magister officiorum*, the *quaestor sacri palatii* was the most important official of the central administration from Constantine the Great's day onwards. He was in charge of judicial affairs and his work included the drafting of laws and the countersigning of imperial decrees. Financial administration was under the two heads of the *fiscus* and the *res privatae*, who from Constantine's time were known as the *comes sacrarum largitionum* and the *comes rerum privatarum*. Their importance was, however, considerably limited, as the most important provincial tax, the *annona*, came directly under the pretorian prefect.

Everything that was connected with the person of the Emperor tended to grow in significance, hence the increase in the authority of the *sacrum cubiculum*, which was concerned with the administration of the imperial household, particularly the imperial camera (*sacra vestis*). The *praepositus sacri cubiculi* was one of the highest ranking and most influential office-holders. Indeed, when a weak ruler was on the throne the Grand Chamberlain was often the most powerful

[1] Cf. A. E. R. Boak, *The Master of the Offices in the Later Roman and Byzantine Empires*, New York 1914.

man in the Empire. Following oriental custom, the *praepositi sacri cubiculi* were almost always eunuchs, as were also most of the imperial bodyguard who were under their control.[1]

The senate of Constantinople as constituted under Constantine was above all an advisory body. In the days of the Roman Empire the senate had crumbled before the growing imperial absolutism and had lost its once far-reaching authority. Its influence dwindled still further in Byzantium. It did not, however, entirely surrender all constitutional and legislative functions at once, and it lingered on until its former glory gradually faded out. For several centuries the *synkletos* of Constantinople played a considerable role in the life of the Byzantine state, though but a shadow of the old Roman senate.[2]

Although entirely subordinate to the imperial will, the senate acted as an advisory body in legislation and sometimes promulgated the imperial decrees. It drew up resolutions (*senatus consulta*) to which the Emperor could give the force of law if he so desired. Many laws were read in the senate before they were promulgated. At the imperial command, the senate could act as the highest court of justice. Most important of all, when a change of government occurred the senate had the right of choosing the new Emperor and ratifying his election. The senate had little influence as long as there was an Emperor on the throne, but it did, however, sometimes come into its own when the imperial throne was vacant. It is true that the senate's views were not necessarily decisive every time a new ruler succeeded. The last Emperor might already have designated his successor and had him crowned as co-Emperor, and then the senatorial ratification was in the nature of a formality. But the decision lay with the senate and the military generals when the throne fell empty without any successor having been appointed or when there was no possibility of his being designated by some representative (whether man or woman) of the imperial house.

Members of the senate of Constantinople were the successors of the Roman senatorial class and, although they were not put on a legal equality with the Roman senate until Constantius, Constantine the Great had foreshadowed this by his success in enticing representatives of the old Roman aristocracy to Constantinople in great

---

[1] A. S. Dunlap, *The Office of the Grand Chamberlain in the Later Roman and Byzantine Empires*, New York 1924. R. Guilland, 'Les eunuques dans l'Empire byzantin', EB 1 (1943), 196 ff., and 'Fonctions et dignités des eunuques', EB 2 (1944), 185 ff., 3 (1945), 179 ff.

[2] On the Byzantine senate see the thorough study by E. Christophilopulu, 'Η σύγκλητος εἰς τὸ Βυζαντινὸν κράτος, Athens 1949.

numbers. But admission to the Byzantine senate became increasingly confined to the imperial officials of the three highest classes of the *illustres, spectabiles* and *clarissimi*. On the whole, whether they came from the old aristocracy or the new official nobility, senators were substantial landowners, and it was this, together with their position in the imperial service, which constituted the real authority of this highest class of society, and not their membership of the senatorial body. Most senators—and by about the middle of the fourth century they already numbered about 2,000—lived on incomes from their property. In actual practice it was only the members of the highest and most select group of the *illustres*, to which the most important imperial officials belonged, who were active members of the senate.

After the middle of the sixth century the highest office-holders were given the new title of *gloriosi*. Emperors had grown more and more generous in their bestowal of titles. Those already in existence naturally deteriorated in value, and when the class of the *clarissimi* became swollen with its increased numbers, its former members were promoted to the ranks of the *spectabiles*, and the old *spectabiles* were pushed up to join the *illustres*. Hence it became necessary to bestow a new and higher rank on the old *illustres* and they became the *gloriosi*. This 'devaluation' of Byzantine ranks was characteristic, and it became even more noticeable with the continual piling up of titles in the later middle ages.[1]

Besides the senate there was the *sacrum consistorium*, a development of the earlier *concilium principis*, which acted as a select advisory body to the Emperor. Its permanent members were the *comites consistorii* who came from the ranks of the highest officials of the central government. Senators who did not belong to the *consistorium* could be summoned to it in an advisory capacity. The pretorian prefects who used to be the most important members of the imperial council were excluded from it. It owed its name to the fact that the members of the council now had to stand (*consistere*) in the presence of the Emperor. And still more light was thrown on the relation between the council and its imperial master by the name of *silentium* which was given to its meetings—if senators took part in its 'sitting' it was called *silentium et conventus*. Later on this expressive term became the

---

[1] For a detailed discussion of the honorary titles of the early Byzantine period, especially the title *spectabilis*, cf. R. Guillard, 'Études sur l'histoire administrative de l'Empire byzantin. Les titres nobiliaires de la haute époque (IVe–VIe siècles)', ZRVI 8, 1 (1963), 117 ff.

proper name of the imperial council and indeed the later σιλέντιον was not a permanent body, but was summoned by the Emperor to deal with important affairs of the state, and also of the Church, as occasion demanded.[1] On the other hand, in medieval Byzantium κονσιστώριον stood for the purely ceremonial appearance of the higher officials at the imperial court on festive occasions.[2]

The reforms of Diocletian and Constantine had restored the administration and strengthened the authority of the state, but the vast majority of the people still found themselves as before in great poverty. The majority of the peasants were *coloni* and they were the mainstay of production in the countryside in the late Roman period, and were fast falling into hereditary serfdom. Diocletian's system of taxation still further penalized them and therefore hastened this development. The old taxes payable in gold had depreciated in value with the debasement of the coinage and payment in kind was therefore resorted to. These emergency levies during a time of troubles were converted into a regular system by Diocletian and established on a permanent basis. The *annona* which had developed in this way became the most important tax and the main source of revenue, but being a payment in kind it was levied only on the country population. Under Diocletian the *capitio-iugatio*, a combination of the poll tax and the land tax, appear as the constituent elements of the *annona*.[3] The unit of taxation consisted of the *iugum*, or piece of land of definite value and area, and the *caput*, or single individual who could manage to cultivate it. For purposes of assessment the *iuga* and the

---

[1] Cf. E. Christophilopulu, 'Σιλέντιον', BZ 44 (1951) (*Dölger-Festschrift*), 79 ff.

[2] Cf. J. Ebersolt, *Le Grand Palais de Constantinople et le Livre des cérémonies*, Paris 1910, p. 40, n. 2. A. Vogt, *Constantin Porphyrogénète. Le Livre des cérémonies, Commentaire I* (1935), 126, is not clear in his notes because he does not seem to have noticed that the expression ἵστανται κονσιστώριον (not κονσιστωρίῳ, as he gives in Text I, p. 90, 13) in chapter 16 also occurs in many other places in the *Book of Ceremonies*. He appears to have overlooked Ebersolt's notes.

[3] The question of Diocletian's system of taxation is much disputed. The most important works are: O. Seeck, 'Die Schatsordnung Diocletians', *Zeitschr. f. Sozial- u. Wirtschaftsgesch.* 4 (1896), 275 ff.; F. Leo, *Die* capitatio plebeia *und die* capitatio humana *im römisch-byzantinischen Straatsrecht* Berlin 1900; F. Thibault, 'Les impôts directs sous le Bas-Empire Romain', *Revue générale du droit* 23 (1899), 289 ff., 481 ff.; 24 (1900), 32 ff., 112 ff.; A. Piganiol, *L'impôt de capitation sous le Bas-Empire Romain*, Chambéry 1916; F. Lot, *L'impôt foncier et la capitation personelle sous le Bas-Empire et à l'époque franque*, Paris 1928; H. Bott, *Die Grundzüge der diokletianischen Steuerverfassung*, Diss. Frankfurt 1928; Stein, *Geschichte* I, 109 ff.; Rostovtzeff, *Gesellschaft und Wirtschaft* II, 221 ff.; W. Ensslin, 'The Reforms of Diocletian', CAH XII (1939), 399 ff.; A Déléage, *La Capitation du Bas-Empire*. Macon 1945; A. H. M. Jones, 'Capitatio et iugatio', JRS 47 (1957), 88 ff.; J. Karayannopulos, *Das Finanzwesen des frühbyzantinischen Staates*, Munich 1958, 28 ff. See also the following note.

Figure 11: *Steelyard Weight in the Form of a Bust of a Byzantine Empress.*
Bronze, late 4th or early 5th century. An unusually large example, hollow and
cast in the *cire perdu* process. Ht. 8½″, w. 4″. Malcove Collection, New York.
Photo: Geoffrey Clements.

Figure 12: *Crozier in the Shape of a* τ *(tau)*. Bronze, Coptic, 4th or 5th century. Headpiece pierced by 3 crosses set in circles, joined to a hollow stem by a 4-column "tabernacle" beneath an ornament pierced by 2 circles. Ht. 8¾", w. 4⅛", stem diam. ¾". Malcove Collection, New York. Photo: Geoffrey Clements.

capita were to be reckoned separately,[1] but a *iugum* could not be taxed unless it had a corresponding *caput* or vice-versa. So the treasury had therefore to create a balance between the *iugatio* and *capitatio* by providing a *caput* for each available *iugum*, which was exceedingly difficult by reason of the marked depopulation in the Empire and shortage of labour as the peasants were often driven to flight owing to want and unsettled conditions. Consequently the state authorities made every effort to bind the *caput*, once he had been produced, to the *iugum* assigned to him. Citizens who were not property-owners were not subject to the *annona*, and thus found themselves to begin with in a most advantageous position; but after Constantine the city population engaged in trade and industry were burdened with a heavy tax payable in gold, the *auri lustralis collatio*.

The shortage of agricultural labour also gave rise to a system of great importance to Byzantine finance, the ἐπιβολή (*adiectio sterilium*). This developed in Egypt where as early as the Ptolemies state-owned fallow land was assigned to private landowners for compulsory cultivation with the obligation of paying the appropriate tax. By the end of the third century this system was in use throughout the Empire, and was applied to the uncultivated land of private owners, as well as to the property of the state.[2]

By the third century the Roman monetary system had completely collapsed. The result was not only an extraordinary rise in prices, but a far-reaching reversion to barter and natural economy.[3] In the West this natural economy took such a strong hold that it remained the predominant feature of the economic life of the new medieval world, in spite of the tenuous survival of the currency system. The East with its greater economic resources swung back to a gold coinage which it maintained for centuries to come, although to some extent it also continued to use a natural economy. The stabilizing of the currency in the Byzantine Empire was clearly reflected in the increasing commutation of the *annona* and of other payments in kind

---

[1] That follows from the decree of 297. Cf. A. E. R. Boak, 'Early Byzantine Papyri from the Cairo Museum', *Études de papyrologie* II, 1 (1933), 4 ff.; A. Piganiol, 'La capitation de Dioclétien', *Revue Hist.* 176 (1935), 1 ff. The new information which is given in the text published by Boak, and in part reprinted by Piganiol and translated into French, really concerns the technical side of assessing taxes and does not in any way invalidate the conclusion, based on the rest of the source material, that the *capitatio-iugatio* stood for a uniform system of taxation. Cf. also the similar opinion of Stein, *Bas-Empire* 199, note 2.

[2] M. Rostovtzeff, 'Studien zur Geschichte des römischen Kolonates', *Archiv. f. Papyrusforsch.*, Beiheft 1 (1910), 57 f., 195, 329 f.; Monnier, 'Épibolé'.

[3] Rostovtzeff, *Gesellschaft und Wirtschaft* II, 177 ff.; Lot, *Fin du Monde Antique* 62 ff.

which were now assessed in gold.[1] Constantine the Great created a
new currency of unparalleled stability. The basis of this system was
the gold *solidus* with a normal gold content of 4.48 grammes, making
72 *solidi* to a pound of gold. With it was the silver *seliqua* of 2.24
grammes, representing one twenty-fourth of a *solidus*, since the value
of silver and gold was in the proportion of 1 : 12. This coinage had
a remarkably long life. For a full thousand years the *solidus* of
Constantine (the Greek νόμισμα, later the ὑπέρπυρον) formed the
basis of the Byzantine monetary system, and for many centuries was
the currency *par excellence* of international trade. It experienced
periods of instability,[2] but these were only temporary, and it was not
until the Empire itself began to disintegrate during the eleventh
century that there was any noticeable depreciation in its value.

Diocletian and Constantine introduced fundamental changes into
military organization.[3] During the early Empire the army had
really consisted of frontier units. Almost the whole of its strength
was split up and distributed along the unending length of the
Roman frontiers. There was a lack of mobile troops, and of strong
military reserves within the Empire. In this latter category there
was really only the Praetorian Guard in Rome to draw on. It had
long been clear that this system could not meet the increased military
demands, and during the troubles of the third century there was a
complete breakdown. Diocletian began by considerably strengthening the frontier defence. But what was particularly needed—and for
political as well as military reasons—was the creation of a strong
mobile force within the Empire which would serve both as a military
reserve to be used against external dangers and for the protection of
the imperial authority against any internal threats from usurpers.
The *exercitus comitatensis*, which was brought into being by Diocletian
and considerably developed by Constantine, was designed to serve
this double purpose. The troops of the *comitatenses* had a completely
different significance and influence from the old Praetorian Guard.
The latter were well known for their unreliability and their tendency

[1] A particularly important work full of information on this problem is H. Geiss,
*Geld- und naturalwirtschaftliche Erscheinungsformen im staatlichen Aufbau Italiens während der
Gotenzeit*, Diss. Breslau 1931. Cf. also Mickwitz, *Geld und Wirtschaft*, 147 ff.
[2] Cf. Mickwitz, *Geld und Wirtschaft*; Bratianu, *Études byz.*, 59 ff.; A. Segrè, 'Inflation
and its Implication in Early Byzantine Times', B 15 (1940–1), 249 ff.
[3] Cf. T. Mommsen, 'Das römische Militärwesen seit Diocletian', *Ges. Schr.* VI
(1889), 206 ff.; Grosse, *Röm. Militärgeschichte*; J. Maspéro, *Organisation militaire de
l'Égypte byzantine*, Paris 1912; W. Ensslin, 'Zum Heermeisteramt des spätrömischen
Reiches', *Klio* 23 (1929), 306–25; 24 (1930), 102–47, 467–502; Bury, *Later Rom. Empire*
I², 34 ff.; Stein, *Geschichte* I, 106 ff., 186 ff.

to support rival claimants to the throne; they were regarded with extreme distrust by Diocletian; and they were finally disbanded by Constantine after the battle of the Milvian Bridge. The new Imperial Guard soon became the real kernel of the Roman army, for Constantine did not hesitate to strengthen the *comitatenses* at the expense of the frontier units recently reinforced by Diocletian. This meant that the *exercitus comitatensis* lost its original character of a bodyguard, but its crack regiments were distinguished by the title of *palatini* and the real Imperial Guard now consisted of the *scholae palatinae* under the control of the *magister officiorum*.

From Constantine's day the supreme command of the army was in the hands of the *magistri militum*, although to begin with the *magister peditum* had control over all the infantry and the *magister equitum* over the cavalry. This division of authority was no doubt a precautionary measure to ensure that these two high military commanders were not too great a danger to imperial authority. But this unusual arrangement was soon given up and it was considered that security would be sufficiently ensured by having two commanders-in-chief equal in status, and both with the title of *magister equitum et peditum praesentalis* and resident at each capital. Besides these, there were also three generals in the *pars orientalis* with authority over the different zones assigned to them: these were the *magistri militum per Orientem, per Thracias* and *per Illyricum*. They had authority over the *comitatenses* stationed within their respective zones, as well as over the *duces* in charge of the frontier troops in the various provinces. The two *magistri militum praesentales* commanded the Palace Guards. Thus in the early Byzantine period control of the armed forces was divided between five commanders-in-chief; these were themselves directly responsible to the Emperor who in his own person represented the supreme military command.

With the establishment of a considerable mobile force in the *comitatenses*, the border troops, the *limitanei*, were able to develop a special character of their own which was connected with their function of defending the frontiers. These soldiers were given property in return for military service and they formed a class of military small-holders whose land provided their livelihood as well as the means of frontier defence, an arrangement which was to have a great future in the Byzantine Empire.

Both in Roman and Byzantine times the army was characterized by the increasing prevalence of barbarian elements, particularly

Germanic peoples, and within the Empire the Illyrians, and from the fourth century onwards the more able barbarians, were continually rising to positions of high rank as officers. It is also noticeable that the cavalry gained steadily in importance, due to the fact that military tactics had to be adapted to warfare against the Sassanid army whose strength in the field depended largely on mounted troops.

The removal of the Empire's centre of gravity to the East was due first and foremost to the greater economic resources of the more densely populated *pars orientalis*.[1] It was due also to new military problems which confronted the Empire here, particularly on the lower Danube where pressure was coming from the barbarians of the north, and in the Near East where the rejuvenated Persian Empire was proving a growing menace under the Sassanids. This Empire of the Sassanids was a much more formidable opponent than the vanquished Parthian kingdom had been. Just as the Byzantine Emperors regarded themselves as the heirs of the Roman Caesars, so the Sassanids claimed succession from the Achaemenids and the right to all the territory which once belonged to the old Persian Empire. The new Persian danger had already been felt from the third century onwards and it continued to harass the Empire throughout the whole early Byzantine period: the struggle with the Persian King of Kings presented one of the most serious political and military problems which the Byzantine state had to face.[2]

In order to meet the changed situation Diocletian had already reserved for himself the eastern half of the Empire, and he usually resided in Nicomedia. The western half was left for his co-Emperor Maximian. It remained for Constantine to give the Empire a really permanent centre in the East. He rebuilt the old Greek colony Byzantium on the Bosphorus and raised it to the status of a capital city. This was begun in November 324[3] immediately after his victory over Licinius had further extended his authority in the East, and on 11 May 330 the new capital was solemnly inaugurated. Few foundations have been destined to play so important a part in world

[1] On the distribution of population in the late Roman period: Lot, *Fin du Monde Antique*, 72 ff.; Stein, *Geschichte* I, 3 ff.

[2] Cf. A. Christensen, *L'Iran sous les Sassanides*, Copenhagen-Paris 1936; 'Sassanid Persia', CAH XII (1939), 109 ff.; E. Kornemann, 'Die römische Kaiserzeit', introd. in *Altertumswiss.* III³, 2 (1933), 139 ff. (Neurom und Neupersien); *Weltgeschichte* II, 276 ff.

[3] J. Maurice, *Numismatique Constantinienne* II (1911), 481 ff.; E. Gerland, 'Byzantion und die Gründung der Stadt Konstantinopel', BNJ 10 (1933), 93 ff.; R. Janin, *Constantinople byzantine*, Paris 1950, 29.

history.[1] The choice of site was brilliant. At the meeting point of two continents, washed by the Bosphorus on the east, the Golden Horn on the north, the Sea of Marmora on the south, accessible by land on only one front, the new capital occupied an unique strategic position. It controlled communications between Europe and Asia, as well as the sea-route from the Aegean into the Black Sea, and it rapidly became the most important centre of international trade and commerce. For a thousand years Constantinople was the political, economic and military centre of the Byzantine Empire, the focus of its intellectual and ecclesiastical life: it was also a factor of vital importance in international politics and cultural development.

The new capital made steady progress, while the importance of Rome diminished and its population steadily decreased. Within a century of her foundation Constantinople had more inhabitants than Rome and by the sixth century the figure was well over half a million.[2] It was New Rome that was destined to take the place of Old Rome and to supplant it as the new administrative centre of the Empire.[3] Even in planning the layout of the new city, Rome had

[1] Gregorovius remarked in his *Geschichte der Stadt Athen im Mittelalter* I (1889), 25: 'This was the most important city in the world to be established since the foundation of Rome'; and E. Schwartz, *Kaiser Constantin und die christliche Kirche²* (1936), 85, wrote: 'Since Alexander's creation of a cosmopolitan centre in Egypt, no other city has so changed the course of events as the great stronghold which arose on the ruins of a Greek town and today still bears witness to the commanding spirit of its founder'. A. Philippson, *Das byzantinische Reich als geographische Erscheinung* (1939), 26, compares the foundation of Constantinople with that of Alexandria and St. Petersburg. Cf. also Philippson, op. cit., 29 ff. and 214.
[2] Cf. Stein, *Geschichte* I, 195, note 6; A. Andréadès, 'La population de Constantinople', *Metron* 1 (1920), 5 ff. (cf. also idem, 'La population de l'Empire byzantin', *Bull. de l'Inst. archéol. bulgare* 9, 1935, 117 ff.). Andréadès' exaggerated estimate should be modified in the light of Stein's convincing remarks, and in Baynes-Moss, *Byzantium* (1949), 53 (Economic Life of the Byzantine Empire), Andréadès himself finally recognizes the view that Constantinople in its palmy days had 'not fewer than 500,000 inhabitants, and perhaps sometimes more'. Stein, *Bas-Empire*, 759 and 842, gives a minimum figure of 600,000 for the population of Constantinople in Justinian's day; cf. also Bréhier, *Civilisation*, 81 ff. on its size and ethnical composition. My agreement with Stein on this point is not in any sense an attempt to minimize the historical significance of Constantinople, as Stein does, following Seeck (cf. *Geschichte* I, 2 ff., and especially *Gnomon* 4 (1928), 410 ff.). On the other hand, Stein's estimate of the population of Constantinople should be reduced even more according to D. Jacoby, 'La population de Constantinople à l'époque byzantine: un problème de démographie urbaine', B 31 (1961), 81 ff. He puts it at less than 400,000 in the sixth century. But Jacoby's valuable discussion itself shows quite clearly that any estimate can only be very approximate.
[3] On the emergence of the conception 'New Rome' which soon supplanted that of a 'Second Rome' see F. Dölger, 'Rom in der Gedankenwelt der Byzantiner', *Zeitschrift f. Kirchengesch.* 56 (1937), especially pp. 13 ff. (reprinted in Dölger, *Byzanz*, 70 ff.). Constantine's regard for the tradition of Old Rome and the slow stages by which the old capital was pushed into the background are rightly stressed. Cf. especially A. Alföldi, *The Conversion of Constantine and Pagan Rome*, Oxford 1948, and 'On the Foundation of Constantinople', JRS 37 (1947), 10 ff.; J. M. C. Toynbee, 'Roma and Constantinopolis in Late-Antique Art', ibid. 135 ff.

been taken as a model and all the traditions associated with Old
Rome were transferred to it.[1] Constantinople was to share in the
privileges of Rome, and Constantine spared nothing in his attempt
to build up the wealth and splendour of the new capital. He enriched the city with magnificent buildings and with works of art
gathered from all parts of the Empire. He was particularly lavish in
building churches. From its earliest days Constantinople was marked
by its Christian character and the greater part of its population was
Greek-speaking. By the recognition of Christianity within the
Empire and by the foundation of a new capital on the Bosphorus
Constantine had doubly emphasized the victory of the East.

Few problems have been so controversial as the nature of Constantine's conversion to Christianity which has provoked bitter and
unending disputes amongst scholars.[2] Some consider that Constantine was indifferent to religion and only took Christianity under his
wing from political motives; others think that the change in the
imperial religious policy was due to a real conversion. There are
many arguments for both points of view, and evidence can be
found to support Constantine's genuine belief in Christianity as well
as his continued adherence to pagan practice, or indeed a combination of both. Political considerations alone would have been
sufficient to determine Constantine's policy. It was clear to all,
including even his most staunch supporter Galerius, that Diocletian
had failed in his policy of persecution and that the eastward orientation of the Empire was incompatible with continued hostility to the
Christian religion.[3] The evidence makes it equally certain that
Constantine himself had been through genuine religious experiences,

---

[1] Cf. R. Janin, *Constantinople byzantine*, Paris 1950, 30 ff.

[2] There is an exceedingly rich literature on this subject and only a selection of the more
important works can be cited: J. Burckhardt, *Die Zeit Constantins des Grossen*[5], Gestam-
tausgabe II, Stuttgart 1929; E. Schwartz, *Kaiser Constantin und die christliche Kirche*[2],
Leipzig-Berlin 1936; N. H. Baynes, *Constantine the Great and the Christian Church*, London
1929, and 'Constantine', CAH XII (1939), 678–99; A. Piganiol, *L'empereur Constantin*,
Paris 1932, and *Empire Chrétien*, 25 ff.; H. Grégoire, 'La "conversion" de Constantin',
Revue de l'Univ. de Bruxelles 34 (1930–1), 231 ff.; 'Nouvelles recherches constantiniennes',
B 13 (1938), 551 ff.; 'La vision de Constantin "liquidée" ', B 14 (1939), 341 ff.; J. Zeiller,
'Quelques remarques sur la "vision" de Constantin', ibid., 329 ff.; H. Lietzmann, 'Der
Glaube Konstantins des Grossen', *S.B. d. Preuss. Akad.* 28–9 (1937), 263 ff.; A. Alföldi,
'Hoc signo victor eris, Beiträge zur Bekehrung Konstantins des Grossen', *Pisciculi* (1939),
1 ff. and *The Conversion of Constantine and Pagan Rome*, Oxford 1948; J. Vogt, *Constantin
der Grosse und sein Jahrhundert*, Munich 1949, 2nd ed. 1960, 244 ff.

[3] 'Qui veut l'Orient doit être, sinon chrétien, du moins prochrétien', as H. Grégoire
admirably expresses it, B 13 (1938), 588. On the period before the victory of Christianity
see H. Grégoire, 'Les persécutions dans l'Empire romain', *Mémoires de l'Acad. de
Belgique*, Classe de Lettres 46, 1 (1951).

Figure 13: *The Virgin and Child Flanked by Constantine I and Justinian I.*
Mosaic lunette (detail) over the south door of the narthex, Hagia Sophia, Con-
stantinople; end of the 10th century. Constantine (right) presents the City of
Constantinople to the enthroned Virgin and Child, while Justinian (left) offers
the Church of Hagia Sophia. Photo: Byzantine Institute, Inc., Washington,
D.C.

Figure 14: *Large Paten with Engraved Chrismon.* Silver, with gilding and niello, Constantinople, circa 570. The large gilded chrismon (monogram of Christ) is encircled by an engraved and nielloed inscription, with a border of 24 cusps with gilded medallions in repoussé, rising to a flat rim, also in repoussé and gilded. Part of a large church treasure found near Antalya in southern Turkey. Diam. 23⅝″. Dumbarton Oaks Collections, Washington, D.C. Photo: Dumbarton Oaks Collections.

both as a Christian and as a pagan. Religious indifference is something which can certainly not be attributed to him, whether by way of praise or condemnation. He lived in an age when men were almost universally influenced by cults of one kind or another. Religions were indeed essentially eclectic, and it was quite normal to be a devotee of several cults simultaneously. In 312 Constantine ranged himself on the side of the Christian God, and from then onwards Christianity was assured of his unfailing protection which was continually strengthened as time went on. This did not mean however that he necessarily dedicated himself to Christianity alone and broke with all pagan traditions by becoming a Christian in the sense in which his Byzantine successors were. He continued to permit pagan practices, and even took part himself in some of these, particularly the cult of the Sun god. To regard Christianity as the one and only religion would have been entirely foreign and incomprehensible to an age of such strongly marked eclectic tendencies, and would have seemed equally strange to 'the first Christian Emperor'. It was many years before the spirit of exclusiveness prevailed in religious matters and the Roman world came to regard Christianity as the only true faith, possessing the absolute truth to the exclusion of all other beliefs. In the end the result of Constantine's policy was inevitable and the Christian faith alone was permitted in the Empire. This, however, came about some considerable time after Constantine (cf. p. 53), and the title of Pontifex Maximus was retained, not only by Constantine himself, but by his successors up to 379.[1]

Christianity was, however, of great influence in the Roman state of Constantine's day, and this was brought out when the Emperor summoned to Nicaea in 325 the first of those oecumenical Councils which were to define the doctrine and discipline of the Christian Church. The Emperor not only called the Council and took charge of its procedure, but he exercised considerable influence over its decisions. He himself was not yet a full member of the Church, for he did not receive baptism until he was on his death-bed, but in practice he acted as the leader of the Church, and in so doing set a

---

[1] See A. Alföldi, *A Festival of Isis in Rome under the Christian Emperors of the IVth Century, Dissertationes Pannonicae*, Ser. II, Fasc. 7 (1937), a short study packed with information on this question. He uses a rare series of Egyptian coins with the representation of Isis or Serapis belonging to the reigns of all the Emperors from Constantine to Gratian. The series only breaks off with Gratian who was the last to bear the title of Pontifex Maximus (Alföldi, p. 36, argues convincingly that he discarded this at the beginning of 379).

precedent which was followed by his Byzantine successors. The Council was mainly concerned with the teaching of the Alexandrian presbyter Arius whose monotheist views made it impossible for him to recognize the equality of the Father and the Son or the divinity of Christ. This Arian doctrine was condemned and it was acknowledged that the Son is of One Substance with the Father (ὁμοούσιος). It was in this way that the formulation of the creed began. It was added to at the second General Council of Constantinople (381) and was accepted as a statement of Christian belief.

The co-operation between Church and State which was inaugurated by Constantine's policy brought benefits to both partners: it also produced a completely new set of problems. The Christian religion gave a strong spiritual unity to the Byzantine state and equally strong moral support to imperial absolutism. The Church, for its part, received from the state generous material endowments, as well as firm backing in its missionary activities and in its struggle against its enemies, but this did also imply a measure of dependency on the state. On the other hand, once the state had thrown in its lot with the Church, it was drawn into all the endless disputes of the various ecclesiastical parties. Controversy over doctrine ceased to be the private concern of the Church, but was affected by political needs and became an important element in political as well as in ecclesiastical life. Moreover, secular and ecclesiastical interests were by no means always identical, and co-operation between the two authorities was often replaced by conflict. All this was obvious even in Constantine's day which saw the intervention of the state in Church disputes, the clash of secular and ecclesiastical aims, and the antagonism, as well as the co-operation, of Church and State. Arianism was not rooted out simply by being condemned at the Council of Nicaea. The Emperor, who had begun by underestimating the strength of his opponents, had to alter his tactics, and he forced the Church to receive Arius back again into the fold. This brought him into conflict with the orthodox clergy and particularly Athanasius, who had been Bishop of Alexandria since 328. This great churchman, though driven from exile to exile, continued to fight for orthodoxy until his death in 373.

The doctrinal dispute was also responsible for increasing the dissension between the sons of Constantine, at the same time emphasizing the rift between the two halves of the Empire. Constantius ruled the eastern half and declared for Arianism: Constantine who died early (340) and the young Constans controlled the West and acknowledged the Nicene creed. In the autumn of 343 a Council was held at Sardica on the borders of the two parts of the Empire, but it could find no means of reconciling the two views. The superior strength of the younger brother, who now ruled over all the West, forced Constantius to yield and to reinstate the orthodox bishops whom he had exiled. This move split Arianism into two camps: the semi-Arians who maintained that the Father and Son were of like substance (ὁμοιούσιος) but not of the same substance (ὁμοούσιος), and the out-and-out Arians under Eunomius who completely denied any kind of likeness. Meanwhile the position was reversed when Constans was killed in 350 fighting against the pagan usurper Magnus Magnentius. Constantius then defeated the usurper in an exceedingly fiercely contested battle in 351.

The victory of the eastern Emperor restored the supremacy of the *pars orientalis*. Like his father, Constantius was concerned to give Constantinople a constitutional position equal to that of Rome, which meant in practice that the new Christian capital was to supplant the old half-pagan Rome. When he visited Rome he had the altar of Victory removed from the curia of the Roman senate-house, an act which personified the passing away of the ancient world. But his supremacy also implied the triumph of Arianism. The will of the Emperor was to prevail without limitation in Church as well as State. He had to face opposition led by Athanasius of Alexandria, but he laid this low and had Arianism proclaimed as the state religion at the synods of Sirmium and Rimini in 359. There was a split in the ranks of the semi-Arians. The moderates went into opposition and began to come nearer to the Nicene position; the rest joined the Eunomians and under imperial leadership became the ruling party. It was at this time that the conversion of the Goths began, a fact of far greater historical significance than the temporary triumph of the Arians. Ulfila, who translated the Bible into Gothic, was consecrated bishop in 341 by the Arian Eusebius of Nicomedia, and long after the collapse of Arianism in the Empire many of the German tribes still held fast to its tenets.

The period of religious unrest under Constantius was followed by a pagan reaction led by the Emperor Julian (361–3).[1] This raised in acute form the question as to how far the old pagan culture was

---

[1] Cf. especially J. Bidez, *La vie de l'empereur Julien*, Paris 1930.

compatible with the new faith, always one of the fundamental problems of Byzantium. The last member of the house of Constantine was under the spell of the magic of a vanishing world and was passionately devoted to its art, culture and learning, and he was a keen and active opponent of the new faith. It looked as though the unending dissensions of the different parties in the Christian Church would play into his hand. The pagans were still numerically strong, especially in the western half of the Empire and particularly in Rome, while a considerable part of the predominantly barbarian army had not yet been converted to Christianity. Moreover, a fair number now apostasized from Christianity. But Julian never succeeded in working up a really formidable opposition to the Christians. In his efforts against them he remained primarily the leader of a cultured pagan aristocracy of neoplatonic philosophers and rhetoricians whose beliefs he himself shared. In the eastern part of the Empire, and especially in Antioch where he had fixed his residence, he experienced bitter disappointments. The essential weakness of his reactionary movement showed itself all too plainly by the very fact that in setting up his pagan clergy he was driven to copy the organization of the Christian Church. The pains which he took to revive pagan cults, even sacrificing to the gods himself in person, provoked scornful astonishment, and not only in Christian circles. Like all attempts to bolster up old ways simply because they are old and to oppose innovation because it is innovation, his attempts were doomed to failure. While on campaign against the Persians, he was, however, fatally wounded by a lance and he died in camp. His work died with him. His swift downfall had demonstrated that the triumph of Christianity was inevitable.

2. THE AGE OF THE MIGRATIONS AND THE CHRISTOLOGICAL CONTROVERSIES

General bibliography: Stein, *Geschichte* I; Bury, *Later Rom. Empire* I²; H. St. L. B. Moss, 'The formation of the East Roman Empire,' CMH IV, Pt. I (2nd. ed., 1966), 1–41; G. Mathew, 'The Christian backgound,' ibid., 42–60; Kulakovskij, *Istorija* I; Seeck, *Untergang* V and VI; E. Demougeot, *De l'unité à la division de l'Empire romain, 395–410. Essai sur le gouvernement impérial*, Paris 1951; L. Schmidt, *Geschichte der deutschen Stämme bis zum Ausgang der Völkerwanderung. Die Ostgermanen²*, Munich 1941; idem, *Geschichte der Wandalen²*, Munich 1942; F. Lot, *Les invasions germaniques*, Paris 1905; C. Courtois, *Les Vandales et l'Afrique*, Paris 1955; E. A. Thompson, *A History of Attila and the Huns*, Oxford 1948; F. Altheim,

Attila und die Hunnen, Baden-Baden 1951; A. Harnack, *Lehrbuch der Dogmengeschichte* II¹, Tübingen 1909; L. Duchesne, *Histoire ancienne de l'Église* III⁵, Paris 1911; H. Lietzmann, *Geschichte der Alten Kirche* IV², Berlin 1953; Ensslin, 'Die Religionspolitik des Kaisers Theodosius d. Gr.', *S. B. d. Bayer. Akad. d. Wiss.*, Phil.-hist. Kl., 1953, Heft 2; *Das Konzil von Chalkedon*, edd. A. Grillmeier and H. Bacht, I, Würzburg 1951; N. H. Baynes, 'The Dynasty of Valentinian and Theodosius the Great', CMH I (1911), 218–49; A. Güldenpennig, *Geschichte des oströmischen Reiches unter den Kaisern Arcadius und Theodosius* II, Halle 1885; W. Ensslin, 'Marcianus', PW XIV 2 (1930), 1514–29; idem, 'Leo I', PW XII, 1 (1924), 1947–61; W. Barth, *Kaiser Zeno*, Basle 1894; E. W. Brooks, 'The Emperor Zenon and the Isaurians', EHR 8 (1893), 209–38; idem, 'The Eastern Provinces from Arcadius to Anastasius', CMH I (1911), 457–86; A. Rose, *Kaiser Anastasius I. Die äussere Politik des Kaisers*, Halle 1882; idem, *Die byzantinische Kirchenpolitik unter Kaiser Anastasius I*, Wohlau 1888; P. Charanis, *The Religious Policy of Anastasius I*, Madison 1939; W. Ensslin, *Theoderich der Grosse*, 2nd ed., Munich 1959.

The religious struggles and endless civil wars which had drained the strength of the Roman army were bound to have a serious effect on the position of the Empire in relation to outside powers. In Constantius' day it was already clear that the Persians were the predominant influence in the Mesopotamian region. After the tragic death on campaign of Julian, the last pagan Emperor, Jovian (363–4) who was an ardent Christian signed a peace treaty with the Persians by which the Empire gave up its claims in Armenia, as well as considerable territory in Mesopotamia. In the North the Empire had to deal with the repercussions of the tribal migrations which presented a new problem of far-reaching consequences. The northern frontiers of the *pars orientalis* now became the scene of endless fighting. From this time onwards Byzantium was almost unceasingly engaged in defending a double front against the great powers that arose in the East and the continuous wave of invaders that bore down from the North and the West—a struggle which lasted as long as the Byzantine Empire stood.

The first Emperor to engage in this vital double warfare was the Arian Valens, and he lost his life in so doing. Like Constantius and Constans, the two brothers Valentinian I (364–75) and Valens (364–78) each held diametrically opposed religious views.[1] Valentinian who ruled in the West supported the Nicene doctrine, and

[1] A. Nagl, 'Valentinianus', PW, Reihe 2, 7A (1943), 2158 ff.; 'Valens', ib. 2097 ff.; A. Alföldi, 'Valentinien Ier, le dernier des grands Pannoniens', *Revue d'hist. comparée* 4 (1946), 7 ff.; idem, *A Conflict of Ideas in the Late Roman Empire. The Clash between the Senate and Valentinian I*, Oxford 1952.

Valens who controlled the East was an Arian. So once more the growing differences between the eastern and western halves of the Empire were reflected in their religious outlooks. In actual fact the links between the two halves were fast weakening, but for the moment all problems had to be shelved in face of pressing external dangers. The crisis had been heralded by the invasions of Britain by the Saxons, the Picts and Scots, and by the fierce battles with the Alemanni on the Rhine and Neckar, and the Sarmatae and Quadi in the Danube basin. It came to a head with the appearance of the Visigoths on the Danube. After being settled in the diocese of Thrace, they began to plunder neighbouring imperial lands. They were joined by the Ostrogoths and the Huns who had followed them, and soon the whole of Thrace was overrun by barbarians. Valens hurriedly returned from the Persian front to Constantinople and thence to Adrianople where he came face to face with the enemy. It was here on 9 August 378 that the historic battle was fought in which the Visigoths, with the help of the Ostrogoths, wiped out the Roman forces, including the Emperor who fell on the field.

The catastrophe had most significant results. Form now onwards Germanic migrations presented a major problem to the Roman State: the eastern half of the Empire had to wrestle with this for over a century, while the western half was to succumb to the invaders. To defeat the Goths by force of arms seemed an impossibility, and a peaceful settlement offered the only practical way out of the desperate situation in which the Empire found itself. This was the policy pursued by Theodosius the Great whom Gratian (375–83), the son and successor of Valentinian I, had proclaimed Augustus on 19 January 379 with authority over the eastern half of the Empire.

Once the Goths had been driven back behind the Balkan Mountains, the Emperor concluded an agreement (*foedus*) with them. The Ostrogoths were to settle in Pannonia, the Visigoths in the northern districts of the diocese of Thrace. They were granted complete autonomy, exemption from taxation and a high rate of pay for their military services; they were to be enlisted as *foederati* in the imperial service.[1] Many even chose to serve directly under the Emperor. Thus for the time being the danger of a violent Germanic irruption into the Empire was avoided. The invaders were pressed into service, and were particularly useful in the army where recent

---

[1] On the *foederati* in general see Mommsen, 'Das römische Militärwesen seit Diokletian', *Gesamm. Schriften* VI (1910), 225 ff.; Grosse, *Röm. Militärgeschichte*, 280 ff.

depletions were made good by the strong reinforcements of *foederati*. All the same this solution only meant that a hostile Germanic invasion had been converted into a peaceful one. The German element in the army became so predominant that the greater number of the troops came from this source, and the most important commanders were German.[1] Theodosius' policy towards the Goths had another side to it, for it entailed a considerable drain on the exchequer and a consequent increase in financial burdens. The plight of the people grew worse and worse, and the system of patronage (*patrocinium*), against which the predecessors of Theodosius had struggled in vain, flourished in every corner of the Empire. The peasants were ruined economically, crushed by heavy burdens, defenceless before the arrogance and abuse of the government officials. This was the reason why they placed themselves under the patronage of the great landowners, becoming their bondsmen and surrendering to their protectors a freedom which had become almost intolerable. So by the turn of the fourth century the *colonus* bound to the soil was a common phenomenon throughout the Empire.[2]

The fall of Valens also meant the final collapse of Arianism. In 381 the second General Council of Constantinople set its seal on the victory of orthodoxy that reaffirmed and expanded the doctrine of Nicaea, thus stating the Christian creed in its ultimate form. Theodosius ardently upheld the Nicene creed and supported orthodoxy with all his strength, bitterly opposing both pagans and heretical Christian sects. It was during his reign that Christianity became the state religion, thus gaining a position of monopoly, while other religions and beliefs were denied the right to exist.

After lengthy civil wars in the West, Theodosius succeeded in reuniting the whole Empire under his own rule shortly before he died. But on his death-bed he once more split up what had been so laboriously brought together. He himself came from stock originating in the farthest West, yet he clearly recognized the importance of the East. Whereas Constantine the Great had set his eldest son over Britain, the Gauls and Spain, and Valentinian I had reserved

---

[1] H. Delbrück, *Gesch. der Kriegskunst* II (1902), 219; Grosse, *Röm. Militärgeschichte,* 260 ff.
[2] Stein, *Geschichte* I, 301 ff.; M. Gelzer, *Studien zur byzantinischen Verwaltung Ägyptens* (1909), 63 ff.; P. Vinogradoff, 'Social and Economic Conditions of the Roman Empire in the Fourth Century', CMH I (1911), 542 ff.

the West for himself and given the East to his younger brother, Theodosius in contrast made his elder son Arcadius ruler of the East and assigned the West to the younger Honorius. Soon after this the disputed dioceses of Dacia and Macedonia were incorporated into the eastern half of the Empire, and they became part of the Prefecture of Illyricum with Thessalonica as its centre. Out of its former Illyrian possessions the West only kept Pannonia (from now onwards usually known as the diocese of Illyricum).[1] Thus historical events had drawn a frontier which became increasingly the dividing line between eastern and Byzantine, and western and Roman, spheres of influence.

Theodosius' division of the Empire did not in itself indicate any particularly new development. It is, however, significant that from now onwards until the final disintegration of the *pars occidentalis* the Empire remained thus divided. But the conception of imperial unity was tenaciously maintained: there were not two Empires, but one, divided into two halves, under the control of two Emperors. Decrees were often promulgated in the names of both Emperors and the edicts of either were valid throughout the Empire, provided that they were sent to the other colleague for publication. If one Emperor died or vacated the throne, the other had the right to designate his successor. But in actual practice there were no strong links between the two parts of the Empire: for one thing, events in East and West took a very different course, and relations between the two governments were usually anything but friendly. Under Theodosius' sons there was continual rivalry between the rapid succession of regents who governed for the weak Arcadius, and the powerful German Stilicho who controlled the West for more than ten years in the name of the young Honorius.[2]

A severe crisis threatened to undermine the policy towards the Goths which Theodosius had initiated. The Visigoths rose under Alaric and ravaged the entire Balkan peninsula to the walls of Constantinople and the southernmost regions of Greece. Dissension

---

[1] Stein, *Geschichte* I, 353; E. Demougeot, *De l'unité à la division de l'Empire Romain*, 395–410, Paris 1951, 143 ff.; idem, 'Les partages de l'Illyricum à la fin du IVᵉ siècle', *Revue hist.* 198 (1947), 16 ff., and 'À propos des partages de l'Illyricum en 386–95', *Actes du VIᵉ Congrès Intern. d'Études byz.* I (1950), 87 ff.; J.-R. Palanque, 'La préfecture du prétoire d'Illyricum au IVᵉ siècle', B 21 (1951), 5 ff.; V. Grumel, 'L'Illyricum de la mort de Valentinien Iᵉʳ à la mort de Stilicon', REB 9 (1951), 5 ff.

[2] A detailed description of this period is given by E. Demougeot, *De l'unité à la Division de l'Empire Romain*, Paris 1951, 93 ff. See also idem, 'Note sur la politique orientale de Stilicon', B 20 (1950), 27 ff.

Figure 15: (ABOVE) *Base of the Theodosian Obelisk.* Constantinople, the Hippodrome, circa 395. Relief sculpture depicting Theodosius I in the imperial box in the Hippodrome, with his court, guards, and other spectators. The base supports an Egyptian obelisk set up by Theodosius in the Hippodrome. (BE-LOW) *The Golden Gate.* Constantinople, circa 390. The triumphal gate in the Land Walls of Constantinople, with a triple-arched entrance and paved court guarded by two massive flanking towers, is believed to have been built by Theodosius I at approximately the same time he set up the obelisk base shown above. Photos: Hirmer Fotoarchiv, Munich.

Figure 16: (ABOVE and BELOW) *The Land Walls of Constantinople.* 5th century. Built in the reign of Theodosius II, these immense fortifications consist of a high inner wall with 96 towers (built in 413), a lower wall with 96 towers in the spaces between the towers of the higher wall, and a masonry-lined moat with a protective parapet on the inner side (both built in 447). The terraces behind the moat and between the two walls are each about 60 feet wide. Photos: (above) Robert L. Van Nice; (below) Cyril Mango.

between the two Roman governments prevented effective opposition, and peace was only bought at a price: the eastern government appointed Alaric as the imperial *magister militum per Illyricum* while the Goth Gainas received the office of *magister militum praesantalis* and entered Constantinople with his troops. This provoked an anti-German party in the Byzantine capital which grew steadily in strength,[1] and by the beginning of the fifth century had succeeded in gaining control of the situation. The Germans were excluded from the army and there was a radical reorganization of the Roman military forces.[2] Circumstances, however, made the rehabilitation of German troops inevitable, and down to the seventh century they continued to form the most important and most valuable element in the imperial army. But in contrast to Theodosius' provision for autonomous units of Gothic *foederati* under their own officers in the East, the Germans were now recruited individually as mercenaries and commanded by imperial officers. In the West the earlier arrangement remained unchanged, and finally brought about the submergence of the *pars occidentalis* by the German hordes. The success of the anti-German reaction in the East and the failure of many such attempts in the West revealed the differing conditions in the two halves of the Empire, and to some extent foreshadowed future developments. The eastern half was soon free of Alaric who withdrew with his army to Italy, and after three attempts at investing Rome took the city by storm in 410. In the West the position steadily deteriorated, but from the beginning of the fifth century onwards the East settled down to enjoy a considerable breathing space.

During this time of comparative peace the university of Constantinople was founded and the *Codex Theodosianus* drawn up. The weak Emperor Theodosius II (408–50) was at first under the guardianship of his energetic sister Pulcheria, and then in later years was much influenced by his wife Athenais-Eudocia, the daughter of a pagan professor of rhetoric in Athens. The personality of this Empress is a living instance of the way in which Christianity and classical learning were found side by side in Byzantium: she remained all her life true to the cultural tradition of her native city, and yet she was also a fervent follower of the new faith, and it was characteristic that she

---

[1] Synesius' writings are typical of the hostile attitude towards the Germanic element (Migne, PG 66, 1089 ff.).

[2] Grosse, *Röm. Militärgeschichte*, 262 ff.

composed both secular verse and church hymns. It may well have been her influence which was responsible in 425 for reorganizing and expanding the foundation established since Constantine the Great's day so that it was virtually a new university.[1] This institution, which became the most important centre of learning in the Empire, had ten Chairs of Greek and ten of Latin grammar, five for Greek and three for Latin rhetoric, with one for philosophy and two for law.

Another event of equal importance was the promulgation of the *Codex Theodosianus* in 438 which was a landmark in juristic development. It was the most significant work of legal codification before Justianian's *Corpus Juris* and was a collection of all the imperial edicts from Constantine the Great's day. This new Codex placed the imperial law on a firm foundation and eliminated the possibility of error in legal rulings through lack of an official collection for reference. The *Codex Theodosianus* was promulgated in East and West alike under the names of the two Emperors Theodosius II and Valentinian III, thus giving special emphasis to the unity of the Empire. This conception was not, however, reflected in everyday practice, as was borne out by the very different courses which legal developments took in the respective halves of the Empire. It is significant that after the promulgation of the *Codex Theodosianus* the ruler of the eastern part rarely sent his edicts to the West and generally speaking those of the western Emperor did not reach the East at all.[2] There was a long period of peace between the two halves after the eastern government had installed Valentinian III (425–55) in the West, but their mutual estrangement became daily more apparent. Politically and culturally they went their own ways and developed along very different lines. An obvious and significant sign of this growing rift was the increasing divergence in language. In the West, knowledge of Greek as good as vanished, and in the East, Latin steadily gave way to Greek, although it was still the official language of the Empire and therefore its existence was somewhat artificially prolonged. The Graecizing of the Empire went on apace and leapt ahead during the reign of Theodosius II and the

[1] Cod. Th. XIV 9, 3 and VI 21, 1. On this see Fuchs, *Höhere Schulen,* 1 ff.; L. Bréhier, 'Notes sur l'histoire de l'enseignement supérieur à Constantinople', B 3 (1926), 82 ff.
[2] In addition to the manuals of Roman law see especially Seeck, *Regesten der Kaiser und Päpste für die Jahre* 311–476 (1919); Stein, *Geschichte* I, 431 ff.; Bury, *Later Rom. Emp.* I², 232 ff.

Empress Athenais-Eudocia. Even in the newly-founded university there were more Greek than Latin professors.[1]

This same period saw native cultural stirrings in neighbouring Armenia which found means of self-expression through Christianity.[2] The Armenian alphabet was invented and the Bible was translated into Armenian. Since Theodosius the Great's day part of the country had been under Byzantine rule, though most of it remained under Persian overlordship. Byzantium had strongly supported this deepening sense of native self-consciousness which was so intimately connected with the establishment of the Christian Church in Armenia. But the Armenian problem, together with the intervention of the Byzantine government on behalf of the persecuted Christians in Persia, led to a fresh outbreak of hostilities between the two great powers. The war did not bring any territorial changes and in 422 a peace treaty was concluded designed to last for a century, though in fact it was observed for barely twenty years.

In the forties of the fifth century the eastern Empire again experienced another serious crisis in foreign policy, due to the Huns under Attila.[3] Destructive raids by the Huns alternated with short-lived treaties, each of which imposed on the Empire more severe and humiliating conditions. The entire Balkan peninsula was plundered and laid waste until finally Attila, having squeezed the East dry by his financial demands, departed to the West. He was attacking Gaul when he was defeated on the Catalaunian Fields in 451 by Aetius, the Roman general of the West. The next year the Huns made terrible inroads on Italy, but in 454 Attila suddenly died and soon after this his enormous empire broke up. But even the removal of the external threat of invasion by the Huns did not bring any real relief to the disintegrating western half of the Empire. The position rapidly deteriorated, and after the murder of Aetius (454) and Valentinian III (455) there was chaos in Italy. The most important provinces outside Italy remained in the hands of the Germanic

---

[1] On the question of language in general see H. Zilliacus, *Zum Kampf der Weltsprachen im oströmischen Reich*, Helsingfors 1935, and F. Dölger's comments on this (BZ 36 (1963), 108 ff.). For the language of administration and law in the fifth century see Stein, *Geschichte* I, 443 f. who gives convincing data for the advance of Greek as also for the tenacity of Latin. On the use of both languages in the papyri of the early Byzantine period see U. Wilcken, *Atti del IV. Congresso intern. di papirologia* (1936), 101 ff., also W. Otto, 'Zum heutigen Stand der Papyrusforschung', HZ 157 (1937), 312, note 1. Cf. also G. Bardy, *La question des langues dans l'église ancienne* I, Paris 1948.

[2] Cf. Stein, *Geschichte* I, 425; A. Ter-Mikelian, *Die armenische Kirche in ihren Beziehungen zur byzantinischen* (1892), 33 ff.

[3] Cf. Moravcsik, *Byzantinoturcica* I, 56 ff. (detailed bibliography).

tribes who now set up their own kingdoms, as for instance the Vandals in Africa and the Visigoths in Gaul and Spain.

The western half of the Roman Empire was perishing in confusion, but in the old imperial city, now the battleground of barbarian invaders, there was still the Roman Church, a power which was to make Rome the spiritual centre of the world. While the Hun invasions were in full swing and Rome was being plundered by the Vandals, in the midst of the hopeless confusion and political dis-integration, Pope Leo the Great (440–61) was emphasizing the primacy of the Roman Church as never before.[1] In the doctrinal conflicts of the fifth century, which were at the same time struggles for leadership among the great ecclesiastical centres, Rome played a significant part.

These important theological disputes influenced the whole course of events in the Byzantine Empire even more than the Arian contro-versy had done.[2] In response to the challenge of Arianism the Church formulated the doctrine of the complete Godhead of the Son and His consubstantiality with the Father; the question now at issue was the relation of the divine and human natures in Christ. The theological school of Antioch taught that there were two separate natures co-existent in Christ. The chosen vessel of the Godhead was Christ, the man born of Mary—hence the contention that Mary was not the Mother of God (θεοτόκος) but the Mother of Christ (χριστοτόκος). In sharp opposition to this rationalist con-ception was the mystical Alexandrian teaching of God made man in whom the divine and human natures were united. In 428 Nestorius, a follower of the school of Antioch, became Patriarch of Constantinople and used the authority of his position to propagate Antiochene Christology. But both as a theologian and as a politician he was far outmatched by his great opponent, Cyril, the Patriarch of Alexandria. The Egyptian monks, a formidable body, were behind Cyril to a man and Rome also ranged herself on his side. Nestorius had the support of the Emperor, but in spite of this he

[1] Cf. the well-known accounts of E. Caspar, *Geschichte des Papsttums* I (1930), 423 ff., and J. Haller, *Das Papsttum* I (1936), 142 ff., although the latter—in contrast to Caspar—does not attach as much importance to the personality of Leo I as is usually (and I think rightly) given to it. Cf. especially H. M. Klinkenberg, 'Papsttum und Reichskirche bei Leo dem Gr.', *Zeitschr. d. Savigny-Stiftung, Kan. Abt.* 38 (1952), 37 ff., where the signifi-cance of Leo in the development of the claim to primacy is particularly well brought out.

[2] In addition to the ecclesiastical and doctrinal histories see also E. Schwartz, 'Die Konzilien des 4. und 5. Jahrhunderts', HZ 104 (1910), 1 ff., and 'Zur Vorgeschichte des ephesinischen Konzils', HZ 112 (1914), 237 ff. Cf. also 'Die sog. Gegenanathematismen des Nestorius', *S.B. d. Bayer. Akad.* 1922, Abh. 1.

was worsted at the third General Council of Ephesus (431) and condemned as a heretic. Cyril had won a decisive victory, both as a theologian and as an ecclesiastical politican. He had triumphed over the Patriarch of the capital and over the imperial government which had upheld him. He had taken upon himself the leadership of the eastern Church, and even in secular affairs he imposed his authority on the local imperial officials. The Patriarchate of Alexandria had already been gaining in prestige ever since the days of Athanasius the Great, and now under Cyril it reached the height of its power.

Cyril died in 444, and at first the authority of Alexandria was maintained by his successor Dioscorus. The imperial government accepted its defeat and swam with the Alexandrian stream. The representative of the Alexandrian faction in Constantinople, Eutyches, was exceedingly powerful at court. But the sees of Constantinople and Rome soon made common cause against the over-powerful Alexandria. As church politicians, Dioscorus and Eutyches were certainly the faithful followers of Cyril, but they went even further than he did in their doctrinal teaching by maintaining that the two natures of Christ became a single divine nature at the incarnation. Thus Nestorius laid less stress on the divine nature, the Alexandrians, on the human nature, and in reaction against the Nestorians, the monophysite heresy was born. The standing patriarchal synod at Constantinople, the σύνοδος ἐνδημοῦσα, condemned Eutyches as a heretic, and Pope Leo I showed himself to be in agreement with the Patriarchate of Constantinople by declaring in his famous *Tome* that the incarnate Christ was a single Person in whom two perfect natures could be distinguished. Thus Rome found herself on the side of Constantinople in the struggle against the over-swollen power of Alexandria. The Alexandrine policy did score one more triumph at the so-called Robber Council of Ephesus in 449, when under the presidency of Dioscorus it beat down all opposition and declared for monophysitism. Then came a violent reaction, largely due to the fact that on the death of Theodosius II in 450 the able soldier Marcian became Emperor and married the energetic sister of his predecessor, the Augusta Pulcheria.[1]

In 451 the new Emperor (450-57) called the Council of Chalcedon, the fourth oecumenical Council, which formulated the doctrine of

[1] On Pulcheria's role in the preparations for the Council of Chalcedon see the interesting remarks of E. Schwartz, 'Die Kaiserin Pulcheria auf der Synode von Chalkedon', *Festgabe für A. Jülicher* (1927), 203 ff.

the two perfect and indivisible, but separate, natures of Christ. It condemned both the monophysites and the Nestorians. Its own dogma stood as it were midway between the two; salvation came through a Saviour who was at the same time Perfect God and perfect man.

Constantinople had emerged the victor, not only in the formation of dogma, but also in matters of ecclesiastical policy. The claims of New Rome and its leading position in the Eastern Church had already been recognized in the second oecumenical Council of 381: its third canon stated that after the Pope of Rome, the Bishop of Constantinople had the highest place in the Christian Church. Victory over Alexandria won with Rome's help showed that this claim was not merely a theoretical one; Constantinople now went a step further and completely destroyed its Roman ally's satisfaction in the common success which had been won. The famous 28th canon of Chalcedon did in fact recognize the Pope's primacy of honour, but otherwise laid down the complete equality of Old and New Rome.[1] Thus the underlying antagonism between the two ecclesiastical centres was foreshadowed. But the immediate result of the decrees of Chalcedon was to widen the rift between the Byzantine centre and the eastern provinces of the Empire. Not only Egypt, but also Syria, once the stronghold of the Nestorian heresy, supported monophysitism and repudiated the doctrine of Chalcedon. The conflict between the dyophysite Church of Constantinople and the monophysite Churches of the Christian East became the burning problem in ecclesiastical and secular politics of the early Byzantine Empire. Monophysitism served as an outlet for the political separatist tendencies of Egypt and Syria; it was the rallying cry of the Copts and Syrians in their opposition to Byzantine rule.

Besides these religious problems the Empire had to face the disorganizing effects of the barbarian immigrations, which in the fifth century were almost as decisive a factor in the Byzantine East as in the West. By 400 it looked as though the eastern half of the Empire had weathered the storm and had managed to deal with the invaders, but with the downfall of the empire of the Huns there was a fresh influx of Germanic tribes, and this element began once more to exercise considerable influence in Byzantine political and military affairs. So while the West was in the throes of its death struggle, the East was once again confronted with the problem of how to keep

---

[1] Mansi 7, 445.

the Germans under control. By about the middle of the fifth century Aspar the Alan was already exercising considerable influence over the government of Constantinople.[1] Marcian, and to a still greater extent his successor Leo I (457–74), owed their thrones to him.

Leo I seems to have been the first Emperor to receive his crown from the hands of the Patriarch of Constantinople.[2] His predecessors, for all their devotion to Christianity, had been content to follow the Roman tradition and accept it from some high official or general and be raised in the shield and acclaimed by the army, the people, and the senate.[3] The innovation is significant in the light of the powerful position which the Patriarchate of Constantinople had achieved at the last oecumenical Council. From now on all Byzantine Emperors were to be crowned by the Patriarch of the capital, and the coronation took on the character of a religious consecration. A religious ceremonial was thus added to the old Roman secular coronation with its military emphasis and gradually superseded the latter, and in the middle ages was thus regarded as the really essential act in the bestowal of the Byzantine crown.

Leo I determined to free himself from the tutelage of Aspar and the Ostrogoths, and he tried to do this by using the warlike native Isaurians. The Isaurian chieftain Tarasicodissa appeared in the capital with a strong force, took the Greek name of Zeno, and married the Emperor's elder daughter Ariadne (466).[4] This setback to Aspar resulted in a change of imperial policy. The eastern government no longer turned an obstinately deaf ear to pleas from the West for help, but dispatched a large expeditionary force against the Vandal kingdom in Africa. In spite of its overwhelmingly superior military strength, this venture, which cost the Empire 130,000 pounds of gold, was a lamentable failure, due partly to the

---

[1] Cf. G. Vernadsky, 'Flavius Ardabur Aspar', *Südost-Forschungen* 6 (1941), 38 ff.

[2] See the detailed account of his coronation by Peter the Patrician in *De cerim.* 410 ff. Relying on Theophanes I, 103 and Symeon Logothetes (Leo Gram. 111), W. von Sickel, 'Das byzantinische Krönungsrecht bis zum 10. Jahrh.', BZ 7 (1898), 517 f., 539 f., has inferred that Marcian was crowned by the Patriarch, and this view has been generally accepted (as by myself in the first edition of this book). A different view has been put forward by W. Ensslin, 'Zur Frage nach der ersten Kaiserkrönung durch den Patriarchen und zur Bedeutung dieses Aktes im Wahlzeremoniell', BZ 42 (1942), 101 ff. (completed, Wurzburg 1947); he has found a more conclusive interpretation of the relevant sources and I now concur in his conclusion that the first imperial coronation in which the Patriarch took an active part was that of Leo I who figures first on the list of the accounts of the old coronations in Constantine's *Book of Ceremonies*.

[3] Cf. W. Ensslin, 'Zur Torqueskrönung und Schilderhebung bei der Kaiserwahl', *Klio* 35 (1942), 268 ff.

[4] On chronology see E. W. Brooks, 'The Emperor Zenon and the Isaurians', EHR 8 (1893), 212 and note 16; Bury, *Later Rom. Emp.* I², 318 and note 2.

skill of the Vandal king Gaiseric, partly to the sheer incompetence of the imperial commander Basiliscus, the brother-in-law of Leo I.[1] Aspar's star once more rose and his son Patricius received the hand of the Emperor's second daughter, and in spite of his foreign origin and Arian belief was made the heir presumptive, and as such received the title of Caesar. But it was not long before anti-German feeling again broke out in Constantinople. In 471, Aspar and his son Ardabur were assassinated, while Patricius, who had escaped with severe wounds, was divorced from the Emperor's daughter and deprived of his position as Caesar. Zeno now took control of affairs and Isaurian influence became predominant.[2] When Leo I died early in 474 he was succeeded by his grandson Leo II, the son of Zeno and Ariadne, with Zeno as co-Emperor. In the autumn of the same year the child died, and Zeno the Isaurian became sole possessor of the throne of Constantinople.

From the cultural point of view there is no doubt that the Isaurians were on a much lower level than the Goths who had profited early on from their contact with the Graeco-Roman world. In contrast to the Germans, they were, of course, imperial subjects and therefore could not be called 'barbarians' in the Graeco-Roman sense of the word. All the same, they were counted as foreigners by the Byzantine populace, and the Isaurian régime produced just as much opposition as the German domination under Aspar. In January 475 there was a conspiracy which deprived Zeno of his throne, but as its promoter could find no better substitute than Basiliscus, the commander in the inglorious Vandal campaign of 468, Zeno was reinstated as Emperor after about twenty months, and in spite of endless plots and bitter civil war he kept his throne for fully fifteen years (476–91). The occasion of his second accession to power coincided with the final collapse of the western half of the Roman Empire. The government of Constantinople had no other choice but to accept the *fait accompli*, and it was all the easier to do this because Odoacer loyally and openly acknowledged the overlordship of the Emperor of East Rome. The new ruler of Italy was created the imperial *magister militum per Italiam* and he governed the country as the Emperor's viceroy. Thus outward appearances were saved,

---

[1] Cf. L. Schmidt, *Geschichte der Wandalen* (1942), 89 ff.; C. Courtois, *Les Vandales et l'Afrique*, Paris 1955, 201 ff.

[2] Cf. E. W. Brooks, 'The Emperor Zenon and the Isaurians', EHR 8 (1893), 216, with references to sources.

Figure 17: *The Empress Ariadne*. Ivory plaque, circa 500. The empress, presumed to be Ariadne, daughter of Leo I and wife first of Zeno (d. 491) and then of Anastasius, stands in a columned and domed niche, clad in full imperial regalia. An embroidered panel on her richly jeweled robe depicts a prince or emperor as consul. Two eagles, suspending a chain in their beaks, flank the cupola. Florence, Museo Nazionale. Ht. 14⅛″, w. 5⅛″. Photo: Hirmer Fotoarchiv, Munich.

Figure 18: *Church of St. John Studion.* Constantinople, circa 463. View from above, toward the apse. The church, erected by the Patrician Studios in 463, became a mosque about 1500, was severely damaged by fire in 1782, and had become a roofless ruin by 1900. Photo: Byzantine Institute, Inc., Washington, D.C.

though in reality Italy was lost to the Empire and, like most of the West, was under German rule.

On the other hand, in the eastern half of the Empire the German element was soon to be completely under control. The elimination of Aspar had only been the first step. There still remained strong forces of Ostrogoths in the Balkans, under Theodoric Strabo in Thrace and under Theodoric the Amal in the prefecture of Illyricum. At one moment the German chieftains would be serving in the imperial army and occupying the highest posts in the Empire, and at the next they would be in arms against the government, allowing their troops to plunder imperial territory. They took a hand in all civil wars and faction fights, and were often the deciding factor in the contest. The Empire was freed from Theodoric Strabo by his death in 484, and in 488 the Byzantine government devised a means of getting rid of Theodoric the Amal by suggesting that he should move westwards to eliminate Odoacer, who no longer enjoyed imperial support, and should govern Italy in his place. The fierce struggle between the two German leaders ended with the victory of Theodoric, who slew his rival with his own hand and took over the control of Italy (493). Thus was founded the Italian kingdom of Theodoric the Great.[1] Byzantium had avoided the necessity of having to make war itself against Odoacer, and at the same time was freed of the unruly Goths. As in the crisis of Alaric's day, the eastern half of the Empire was rid of the Germans by their departure to the West, and it so happened that at the very time when the East disembarrassed itself of these invaders, the whole of the West had fallen to them.

Freedom from the Germanic peoples did not, however, provide any final solution to the racial problem as long as Isaurian influence was predominant in the Empire. In its attempt to find relief from German pressure, the suffering Empire had swallowed the Isaurian antidote. This worked, but it was an overpowerful dose, and the body of the Empire was correspondingly affected. The Isaurian people felt themselves to be a state within a state, and the Empire became the scene of bloody struggles between the different Isaurian chieftains. When one of them became Emperor, the others attempted to deprive him of the crown, and for several years Zeno

---

[1] Cf. L. Schmidt, *Die Ostgermanen*, 88 ff., 337 ff.; W. Ensslin, *Theoderich der Grosse*, 2nd ed., Munich 1959.

waged a regular war against his former general, Illus, and his fellow-countryman Leontius, who had set himself up as rival Emperor.

The religious problem, too, remained unsolved. Monophysitism, condemned at Chalcedon, was steadily gaining ground in the East and widening the breach between the central and eastern provinces of the Empire. Basiliscus had thrown himself into the arms of the monophysites and on his own authority had condemned the canons of Chalcedon and the *Tome* of Leo in an imperial encyclical.[1] This roused bitter resentment in orthodox Byzantine circles and only hastened his downfall. On the other hand, Zeno attempted to reconcile the monophysite eastern Christians with the dyophysite Byzantines by introducing a compromise. With the approval of Acacius the Patriarch of Constantinople, Zeno published in 482 his famous *Henoticon*, or Edict of Union, in which the rulings of the first three oecumenical Councils were recognized, but the actual point at issue was evaded by avoiding the expression 'two natures' or 'one nature'.[2] But it soon became clear that any compromise in religious matters was impossible, because the *Henoticon* obviously satisfied neither the supporters of Chalcedon nor the monophysites. Instead of two, there were now three conflicting parties: the avowed monophysites, the avowed dyophysites, and the lukewarm from both camps who supported the imperial formula. The Pope for his part flatly repudiated the *Henoticon* and excommunicated the Patriarch of Constantinople. In return, the latter removed the papal name from the diptychs, thus causing a schism between Rome and Constantinople which lasted for more than thirty years.

Zeno died in 491, and when the election of a new Emperor was impending the crowds greeted the widowed Ariadne with cries of 'Give the Empire an orthodox Emperor! Give the Empire a Roman Emperor!'[3] The two burning questions of the day—the religious and the racial—still awaited solution and were to the forefront in all minds. In Constantinople men did not wish to be ruled any longer by upstart foreigners or by heretics. The choice fell on the elderly court official Anastasius (491–518), an able administrator who had done particularly good service in the departments of finance.[4] He

---

[1] The text of the imperial letter is in Evagrius, ed. Bidez-Parmentier, pp. 101–4. For the repudiation which Basiliscus was soon forced to make, but which could not save him, see ibid. 107.

[2] Evagrius, 111–14.

[3] *De cerim.* 418 and 419.

[4] Cf. E. W. Brooks, CMH I (1911), 484; Bury, *Later Roman Empire* I². 441 ff.; Stein, *Studien*, 146 and *Bas-Empire*, 192 ff.

had perfected the monetary system of Constantine the Great by attempting to stabilize the copper *follis*, whose rate fluctuated considerably, by relating its value to the gold coinage.[1] Above all he had reorganized the system of collecting taxes. He transferred the responsibility for collecting the city taxes from the impoverished and ineffective *curiales* to the *vindices* who were subordinate to the pretorian prefecture. Further, he abolished the so-called χρυσάργυρον, the old *auri lustralis collatio*, which had proved a burden to the industrial and business sections of the population, and thus afforded great satisfaction to the townsfolk and contributed considerably to a revival of trade and industry. On the other hand, this meant additional demands from the countryside, for when the χρυσάργυρον was abolished, the deficiency was made good by insisting on the payment of the *annona* in gold and not in kind.[2] The complete commutation of the land tax, the χρυσοτέλεια, showed that even the countryside was steadily returning to a gold economy. But at the same time the demand of the State for natural produce was shown by the use of the so-called *coemptio* (συνωνή), the compulsory sale of essential commodities at a low price fixed by the government.[3] So, while the pressure on trade and industry was considerably relieved by Anastasius, the agricultural classes had to face fresh and irksome demands, which accounts for the frequent disturbances and popular unrest. But all the same, by the time of his death the Emperor's careful financial policy had enriched the state treasury by the enormous sum of 320,000 pounds of gold.[4]

The accession of Anastasius I had meant the end of Isaurian influence, but the Emperor had to wage systematic warfare against the Isaurians before their resistance was broken (498). After this, considerable numbers of them were transported from their native land and settled in Thrace; their power was now crushed and the

[1] Cf. R. P. Blake, 'The Monetary Reform of Anastasius I and its Economic Implications', *Studies in the History of Culture* 1942, 84 ff.

[2] John Malalas 394: ἐποίησε χρυσοτέλειαν τῶν ἰούγων τοῖς συντελεσταῖς πᾶσι διὰ τὸ μὴ ἀπαιτεῖσθαι τὰ εἴδη καὶ διατρέφεσθαι ὑπὸ τῶν στρατιωτῶν. See also Evagrius, ed. Bidez-Parmentier, p. 144. Cf. the remarks of W. Ensslin, BZ 42 (1942), 260, whose interpretation is to be accepted in spite of the disagreement of Karayannopulos, 'Die Chrysoteleia der iuga', BZ 49 (1956), 72 ff.

[3] The *coemptio*-συνωνή became very widespread and resembled a tax in character, with the result that finally in the middle Byzantine period (as I was able to show in my 'Steuergemeinde' 50) it came to denote the land tax which was by then naturally paid in gold. Cf. also H. Geiss, *Geld- und naturalwirtschaftliche Erscheinungsformen im staatlichen Aufbau Italiens während der Gotenzeit*, Breslau 1931, 1 ff., and Stein, *Bas-Empire*, 200. This is not of course to maintain that the *coemptio* was not introduced until the reign of Anastasius I, as Karayannopulos, op. cit., 75 ff., wrongly maintains.

[4] Procopius, *Anecdota* (ed. Haury, *Opera* III, 1), 121.

racial crisis within the Empire at last surmounted. On the other hand, the religious problem grew daily more acute. When he came to the throne, Anastasius, at the Patriarch's request, had made a formal profession of orthodoxy, even though he was a warm supporter of the monophysites. To begin with, he took his stand on the *Henoticon*; but his ecclesiastical policy gradually became more and more monophysite in character, until finally he gave his full support to monophysitism. This was a source of great satisfaction to the monophysite Copts and Syrians, but was bitterly resented by the orthodox Byzantines. The reign of Anastasius became a series of revolts and civil wars, and the discontent was aggravated by administrative oppression. The people found themselves in a continual state of unrest and the strife between the demes became even more bitter than usual.

The Byzantine factions of the Blues and the Greens were organizations for political purposes and not merely for sports.[1] It is true that they associated themselves with the old Circus parties and took over their names and colours, but the Hippodrome of Constantinople, like the Forum of Rome and the Agora of Athens, was also the place where the political views of the people were voiced. The popular parties of the Greens and the Blues, whose leaders were appointed by the government, had important public functions, for they served as the city guard and they took part in repairing the city walls. Strictly speaking, the demes were that section of the urban population which was organized as the city militia.[2] The rest of the people ranged themselves behind these factions, joining either the Greens or the Blues, supporting the one and attacking the other. Thus in all the big cities of the Empire the Greens and the Blues played a very important part, since it was through them that the

[1] The demes are regarded merely as circus factions not only by Gibbon (ed. Bury), IV, 220, but also by Wilken, *Die Parteien der Rennbahn, vornehmlich im byzantinischen Kaiserthum, Abh. d. Preuss. Akad.* 1827, 217 ff., Rambaud, *De byzantino hippodromo et circensibus factionibus* (1870; French summary in *Revue des deux Mondes* 1871 = *Études sur l'hist. byz.*[2] [1919], 3 ff.) and even Monnier, 'Épibolé' 16 (1892), 504 f. It was Uspenskij ('Partii' 1 ff.) who first stressed their political significance and this view was soon adopted by scholars, but it is only recently that research on this subject has begun to make greater progress (see below).

[2] Cf. Bury's admirable phrase 'The demes were the urban populace organized as a local militia', *Admin. System*, 105, n. 2. Uspenskij, 'Partii', had already supported a similar view. In this respect it is characteristic that the number of the active members of the demes appears from the sources to have been small; the contemporary account of Theophylact Simocattes (ed. de Boor, 207) was based on official statistics and for the year 602 stated that there were 1,500 Greens and 900 Blues in Constantinople. According to the late account of Codinus (*De signis* 47) the two demes numbered 8,000 men at the time of Theodosius II, which would have been only a very small proportion of the population of Constantinople.

people voiced their political opinions. It is not true to maintain that the Blues were the aristocratic faction and the Greens the faction supported by the lower social classes.[1] On the whole the general masses were to be found in both parties, though the Blues tended to draw their leaders from members of the great landowners, the Graeco-Roman senatorial aristocracy, and the Greens from the representatives of trade and industry, as well as from those in court service or financial administration who often originated in the eastern lands of the Empire.[2] Thus the Blues usually supported Greek orthodoxy and the Greens favoured monophysitism and other eastern heresies. The antagonism between the two factions showed itself in severe and frequent clashes, and from the mid-fifth century the political life of the Empire was marked by a perpetual struggle between the Blues and the Greens. The central authority was forced to take the demes into account in its policy, favouring either the one or the other, so that as a rule one faction would support the government while the other joined the opposition. At times both demes made common cause against imperial rule in order to defend their liberties against the absolutism of the central administration. The organization of the demes was the means whereby something of the traditional liberty of the ancient cities survived.[3]

The economic policy of Anastasius I suited trade and industry, and in religion the Emperor was an avowed monophysite, so that he was the champion of the Greens and was therefore violently attacked by the Blues. Again and again public buildings were set on fire and the imperial statues were thrown down and dragged through the streets. In the Hippodrome there were hostile demonstrations against the sacred person of the Emperor; the aged ruler himself was insulted and even pelted with stones. In 512 a rebellion broke out in Constantinople against the monophysite version of the *Trisagion* (the 'Thrice-Holy' in the liturgy) which nearly cost Anastasius his throne. The crisis came to a head with the revolt of Vitalian, the commander-in-chief of Thrace, who since 513 had three times

---

[1] This is the view of Manojilović, 'Peuple de Constantinople'.

[2] See Djakonov, 'Viz. dimy', and also M. Levčenko, 'Venety i prasiny v Vizantii v V–VII vv.' (Greens and blues in Byzantium from the fifth to the seventh centuries), VV 26 (1947), 164 ff., who summarizes the results of Djakonov's important work.

[3] In addition to bibliography already cited see Bury, *Later Rom. Empire* I², 84 ff., and also Bratianu, *Privilèges*, 46 ff.; H. Grégoire, 'Le peuple de Constantinople ou les Bleus et les Verts', *Comptes rendus de l'Acad. des Inscr. et Belles Lettres* 1946, 568 ff.; F. Dvornik, 'The Circus Parties in Byzantium', *Byzantina-Metabyzantina* I (1946), 119 ff. Particularly important is the recent work by A. Maricq, 'La durée du régime des partis populaires à Constantinople', *Bull. de l'Acad. de Belgique* 35 (1949), 63 ff., and 'Factions du cirque et partis populaires', ibid. 36 (1950), 396 ff.

advanced with the army and fleet and had got as far as the walls of Constantinople. The Emperor was always prepared to come to terms in moments of great danger and to change his policy when the tension slackened, so that the affairs of the Empire continued to lack any stable guidance or continuity. Vitalian's rebellion was not solely, nor even primarily, inspired by religious motives, but he gained considerable additional support by being represented as the champion of orthodoxy against a monophysite Emperor. The reign of Anastasius had shown that a monophysite ecclesiastical policy was only a blind alley. It was highly doubtful whether the peace with far-off Egypt and Syria would last, and in any case it had only been achieved at the expense of continual unrest in the heart of the Empire.

3. JUSTINIAN'S WORK OF RESTORATION AND ITS COLLAPSE

General bibliography: Bury, *Later Rom. Empire* II²; Kulakovskij, *Istorija* II; H. St. L. B. Moss, 'The formation of the East Roman Empire,' CMH IV, Pt. I (2nd. ed., 1966), 1–41; G. Mathew, 'The Christian background,' ibid., 42–60; Stein, *Bas-Empire*; A. A. Vasiliev, *Justin the First. An introduction to the Epoch of Justinian the Great*, Cambridge, Mass. 1950; Diehl, *Justinien*; B. Rubin, *Das Zeitalter Justinians I*, Berlin 1960; P. Collinet, *Études historiques sur le droit de Justinien I*, Paris 1912; Z. V. Udalcova, *Italija i Vizantija v VI veke* (Italy and Byzantium in the sixth century), Moscow 1959; L. Schmidt, *Geschichte der Wandalen²*, Munich 1942; N. H. Baynes, 'The Successors of Justinian' CMH II (1913), 263–301; Stein, *Studien*; Hartmann, *Byz. Verwaltung*; Diehl, *Exarchat*; O. Adamek, *Beiträge zur Geschichte des byz. Kaisers Maurikios*, Graz 1890; P. Goubert, *Byzance avant l'Islam*. Vol. 1: *Byzance et l'Orient sous les successeurs de Justinien. L'empereur Maurice*, Paris 1953, Vol. II: *Byzance et l'Occident sous les successeurs de Justinien. Byzance et les Francs*, Paris 1956; M. J. Higgins, *The Persian War of the Emperor Maurice*, Washington 1939; R. Spintler, *De Phoca imperatore Romanorum*, Jena 1905; N. V. Pigulevskaja, *Vizantija i Iran na rubeže VI i VII vekov* (Byzantium and Iran at the end of the sixth and beginning of the seventh centuries), Moscow-Leningrad 1946; idem, *Vizantija na putjach v Indiju* (Byzantium on the routes to India), Moscow-Leningrad 1951.

The sounder polity of the *pars orientalis* with its greater economic resources and its more densely populated areas had survived the crisis which had wrecked the western half of the Empire. All the same, the East had not emerged from this experience unscathed: it had experienced the horrors of the barbarian invasions, and for more

Figure 19: *Gold Medallion of Justinian*. Constantinople, 534–548. Obverse: Three-quarter-face bust of Justinian in full armor and plumed helmet and carrying a spear. Reverse: Justinian, in full armor astride a richly caparisoned horse, preceded by a Victory figure bearing a palm branch and an arms trophy. Diam. 3⅜″. The gold original, from which this electrotype was made, was stolen from the Cabinet des Médailles, Paris, in 1831 and destroyed. Photo: Hirmer Foto-archiv, Munich.

Figure 20: (ABOVE) *Church of Hagia Irene*. Constantinople, circa 532. Exterior, viewed from Hagia Sophia; Topkapi Palace and Seraglio Point in the background, with the Golden Horn at left and the Bosphorus at right. This twin-domed basilica, the Church of the Holy Peace, was erected by Justinian to replace an earlier church destroyed in the Nika riots of 532. Following the Turkish conquest it was used as an armory. (BELOW) *Church of SS. Sergius and Bacchus*. Constantinople, 527–536. Exterior, from the east. The earliest of Justinian's churches, this centralized octagonal structure has survived as a mosque. Photos: Robert L. Van Nice.

than a century had wrestled with the menace of overpowerful foreign elements in the administration and the army. At the time when successive waves of barbarian invasions were swamping the West, Byzantium herself was sorely crippled and rarely able to be more than a passive onlooker. But by the beginning of the sixth century the East had at last solved its racial problems, and was now in a position to undertake a more active policy and to attempt to recover its lost territories in the West. The conception of the unity of the Empire firmly persisted, even though it was divided into two separate halves for administrative purposes; the universality of Roman rule persisted equally firmly, even in the face of the Germanic conquests in the West. The Roman Emperor was still regarded as the head of the *orbis romanus* and the Christian *oikoumene*. The lands which had once belonged to the Roman Empire were held to belong to her inalienably and in perpetuity, even though they were under the actual control of the Germanic kings. And indeed to begin with, these rulers themselves did at least acknowledge the overlordship of the Roman Emperor, and exercised their power as his delegates.[1] It was the natural obligation of the Roman Emperor to recover the Roman heritage. More than that, it was his sacred mission to free Roman lands from the yoke of barbarian invaders and Arian heretics, and to restore the ancient frontiers of a single Roman and orthodox Christian Empire. And it was towards this end that the whole of Justinian's policy was directed.

Justinian himself ruled from 527 to 565, but in actual fact he had already been responsible for much of the imperial policy of his uncle Justin I (518–27). The latter, born in the village of Tauresium (probably in the region of Naissus, had entered the imperial army, became an officer and finally commander of the *excubitores*. He was eventually chosen Emperor on the death of Anastasius I.[2] But it was Justinian who was responsible for the break with Anastasius' monophysite policy, and the restoration of ecclesiastical relations with the Church of Rome, which was an essential preliminary to the realization of his political ambitions in the West. Justinian, the son of a peasant from a Balkan province, was one of the most

---

[1] Like Odoacer, Theodoric the Great had the title of *magister militum* and his coins always showed the portrait and name of the Emperor. He never promulgated *leges*, only *edicta*, which was within the competence of the higher imperial officials, as for instance the pretorian prefects. Cf. Mommsen, 'Ostgotische Studien', *Ges. Schr.* IV, 334 ff.; Bury, *Later Rom. Empire* I², 453 ff.

[2] See the detailed work of A. A. Vasiliev, *Justin the First. An Introduction to the Epoch of Justinian the Great*, Cambridge, Mass. 1950.

cultured and learned men of his day, which is a striking testimony to the civilizing power of the Byzantine capital. The personal greatness of the man himself is shown by the breadth of his political aims and the extraordinary many-sidedness of his influence and interests. The grave weaknesses in his character pale before the quality of his all-embracing intellect. It is true that it was Belisarius, and after him, Narses, who led the victorious campaigns of reconquest, Tribonian who headed the commission responsible for the great codification of the laws, John of Cappadocia who bore the heaviest burdens of administration. But it was Justinian who inspired these great achievements of his famous reign. The restoration of a universal Roman Empire was the constant dream of Byzantium, and here Justinian's work of restoration found its finest expression. It afforded a magnificent example to posterity, even though it was not permanent and its collapse had disastrous results for the Empire.[1]

In 533 Belisarius sailed for Africa with a small expeditionary force of about 18,000 men.[2] The days of Gaiseric and the Vandal power were over. In contrast to the miserable failure of the great expedition of 468 (cf. above p. 62), Belisarius gained control of the Vandal kingdom in a very short time. After being decisively beaten at Decimum and Tricamarum, the Vandal king Gelimer was forced to surrender, and in 534 Belisarius made a triumphal entry into Constantinople. The conquest of the Vandal kingdom was, however, followed by long drawn-out guerrilla warfare with the local Berber tribes lasting until 548. Meanwhile in 535 Belisarius had commenced operations against the Ostrogoths in Italy. This campaign also began with a series of victories, for while one Byzantine army marched into Dalmatia, Belisarius took Sicily and penetrated into Italy. Naples and Rome fell in quick succession. But then the opposition hardened and in Rome Belisarius had to face a long siege, and it was with the greatest difficulty that he succeeded in breaking through and driving north, where he captured Ravenna and subdued Vitiges, the brave king of the Ostrogoths, whom he took as a prisoner to Constantinople (540), as he had earlier done with Gelimer. The Ostrogoths, however, rose again under the energetic leadership

---

[1] On Justinian's foreign policy and its effect see especially Bury, *Later Rom. Empire* II², 124 ff. Diehl, *Justinien* 173 ff.; Kulakovskij, *Istorija* II, 93 ff.; Stein, *Bas-Empire* 283 ff., 485 ff. On the Vandals see Diehl, *L'Afrique byzantine* (1896), and especially L. Schmidt, *Geschichte der Wandalen*² (1942), 122 ff.; C. Courtois, *Les vandales et l'Afrique*, Paris 1955, 353 ff.; on the Gothic wars see Hartmann, *Gesch. Italiens im Mittelalter* I (1897), 248 ff. and Hodgkin, *Italy and her Invaders* IV² (1896) and V (1895); Z. V. Udalcova, Italija i Vizantija v VI veke (Italy and Byzantium in the sixth century), Moscow 1959, 236 ff.

[2] Cf. L. Schmidt, *Geschichte der Wandalen* (1942), 125 f.

of Totila, and the position grew more serious. Belisarius suffered a number of reverses and it looked as though all his earlier successes would be imperilled; but Narses, a skilled strategist and crafty diplomat, broke the enemy's resistance after a hard struggle. The country lay at Justinian's feet, but only after the ups and downs of a a twenty years' war (555). The restoration of Byzantine authority was accompanied by a return to the previous social and economic structure. The great land-owning aristocracy, dispossessed by the Ostrogoths, received back again their property and their privileges.

The great conquests were rounded off by the war against the Visigoths in Spain. Intervening here too in disputes between local rulers, the Byzantines had landed an army in Spain and had occupied the south-east corner of the Iberian peninsula (554). It looked as though the old Empire was rising again. A good deal of the former Roman territory still remained to be recovered, but Italy, the greater part of North Africa, and part of Spain, with the Mediterranean islands, had been seized from the Germans and brought under the sceptre of the Roman Emperor of Constantinople. The Mediterranean was once more a Roman lake.

It soon became clear that these notable successes had been bought at a price. The wars in the West had meant neglect of the Danube frontiers and the slackening of the imperial struggle against the Persians. In Anastasius I's day, Martyropolis, Theodosiopolis, Amida and Nisibis had already fallen into Persian hands. In 532 Justinian and the Persian King of Kings, Chosroes I Anushirvan (531–79), signed a treaty which provided for an 'everlasting' peace together with the Byzantine payment of tribute to the Persian Empire. This made it possible for Justinian to concentrate on the West. But in 540 Chosroes violated this 'everlasting' peace, attacked Syria, destroyed Antioch and pressed on to the coast. In the North the Persians ravaged Armenia and Iberia and took possession of Lazica on the eastern shores of the Black Sea. By agreeing to pay more tribute Justinian succeeded in negotiating a five years' truce which was twice renewed. Then in 562 a peace treaty for fifty years was signed, again at the cost of an increased tribute, although the Byzantine Emperor did at least get the Persians to give up their claims on Lazica. But Persian power was in the ascendant and Byzantine influence in the Near East was on the wane.

In the Balkans events were taking place which had even more fateful consequences for the Byzantine Empire. Scarcely had the migrations of the Germanic peoples ended when new tribes appeared in the frontiers. The penetration of the Slavs was of particular significance. During Justin's day the Antae had attacked the Empire,[1] and in the early years of Justinian's reign the Slav tribes in alliance with the Bulgars made continual inroads on the Balkan lands. The great wars of conquest in Africa and Italy had drained the Empire of the resources needed for the defence of the Balkans. Justinian had built a powerful system of fortifications in Europe as well as in Asia, and in the Balkan peninsula he had erected a strong inner chain of forts behind the lines of defence on the Danube. But however good the fortifications, they were useless without sufficient troops to man them. The Slavs poured over the whole Balkan peninsula as far as the Adriatic, the Gulf of Corinth, and the shores of the Aegean, thus ravaging the very centre of the Empire, while Byzantine armies were celebrating their victories in the distant West. The invading barbarian hordes began by being content to plunder the countryside and then to retire beyond the Danube with their booty, but the full flood of the Slav migrations was beginning to spread over the Empire, and the time was not far distant when the Slavs would begin to settle permanently in the Balkans.

These external dangers were accompanied by severe internal disturbances. A bitter struggle arose between the autocratic central government and the political organizations of the people, and in 532 the terrible Nika revolt broke out in Constantinople.[2] During Justin I's reign Justinian had opposed the Greens, who had been favoured by Anastasius, and had declared for the Blues, who supported his political and ecclesiastical policies. But once he came to the throne, he tried to make himself entirely independent of the demes and took strong measures against these unruly popular factions. His punitive measures, inflicted on both parties alike, turned the Blues as well as the Greens against him, and this general hostility was aggravated by the heavy burdens imposed on the people by his expensive policy. The two demes united and made common cause against the central government. The Hippodrome echoed to the unusual cry of 'Long life to the merciful Greens and Blues'.[3] The revolt assumed alarming proportions, the capital was in flames, and a nephew of Anastasius I

---

[1] Niederle, *Manuel* 61 f.; Stein, *Bas-Empire* 222; Uspenskij, *Istorija* I, 464 f.; Jireček, *Geschichte* I, 81; Šišić, *Geschichte* 50; idem, *Povijest* 207 f.; Grafenauer, *Nekaj vprašanj* 28 ff.; *Vizantiski izvori* I, 45 ff.

[2] Bury, 'The Nika Riot', JHS 17 (1897), 98 ff., and *Later Rom. Empire* II², 39 ff.; Diehl, *Justinien* 455 ff.; Uspenskij, *Istorija* I, 499 ff.; Stein, *Bas-Empire* 449 ff.

[3] John Malalas 474, 10.

Figure 21: *Church of Hagia Sophia.* Constantinople, 532–537. (ABOVE)
Exterior from the south. (BELOW) Exterior, west façade. For many centuries the largest church in the world, Justinian's Church of the Holy Wisdom
was built in 5 years immediately after the Nika riots of 532. The minarets and
most of the surrounding buildings are Turkish additions. Photos: (above)
Hirmer Fotoarchiv, Munich; (below) Robert L. Van Nice.

Figure 22: *Church of Hagia Sophia.* Constantinople, 532–537. Interior, looking east toward the apse. The 260-foot nave of the Church of the Holy Wisdom
is revealed on the interior, with the great dome soaring above the central section
on pendentives, and two-story galleries along the sides, screened by columns.
Originally, mosaics entirely covered the areas above the polished marble walls.
Photo: Hirmer Fotoarchiv, Munich.

was acclaimed Emperor and invested with the purple in the Hippodrome. Justinian thought that all was lost and prepared for flight. He was prevented by the indomitable courage of the Empress Theodora, and the situation was saved by the resolution of Belisarius and the resourcefulness of Narses. By secretly negotiating with the Blues, Narses split the unity of the rebels, while Belisarius fell on the Hippodrome with some loyal troops and took the malcontents by surprise. A terrible massacre, costing thousands of lives, put an end to the revolt. Thus Byzantine autocracy had triumphed over the demes, the representatives of the last remnants of the old civic freedom. The Emperor's most prominent advisers, dismissed as a result of public pressure, were now recalled. Hagia Sophia arose in new splendour: in place of the old church which had been burnt down Justinian built a magnificent basilica with cupolas which marked an epoch in the development of Christian architecture. But the crushing of the revolt did not bring any real relief. Justinian's policy with its great military undertakings imposed a terrible burden on the people, and this was made almost intolerably heavy by the additional demand of his extensive building activity. His victories were bought at the price of the complete financial exhaustion of the whole Empire.

The pretorian prefect, John of Cappadocia, had the thankless task of producing the means for the Emperor's costly military undertakings, and he was bitterly hated by the people. Nevertheless, his work did make a positive contribution to the administration of Justinian's day. Most of Justinian's novels were addressed to him, and it was primarily due to his efforts that the government took energetic measures to curb the overpowerful nobles.[1] These measures were not, however, very effective, and the power of the great landowning magnates increased apace at the expense of the small-holders and the imperial domain. Justinian's administrative measures aimed at tightening up the control of the government, at abolishing the sale of offices, and above all at making certain that the taxes were properly collected. He abandoned the strict division of authority in the provinces between the civil and military authorities introduced by Diocletian and Constantine, though only in certain districts, where a measure of unity was secured by giving the supreme control sometimes to the military and sometimes to the civil power. These administrative reforms of Justinian were not

[1] Cf. E. Stein, 'Justinian, Johannes der Kappadozier und das Ende des Konsulats', BZ 30 (1929–30), 376 ff., and *Bas-Empire* 435 ff.

sufficiently decisive in character to be described as inaugurating any fundamental change. They were *interim* measures and formed a bridge between the clear-cut reorganization of Diocletian and Constantine and the equally clearly defined, but contrasting, system of Heraclius.

Justinian's government vigorously promoted industry and commerce. Constantinople was the halfway house controlling trade routes between Europe and Asia and it served as an entrepôt for the two continents. Mediterranean trade was completely in the hands of Greek and Syrian merchants. It was, however, not the economic traffic with the impoverished lands of the West which enriched the Byzantine Empire, but its trade with the East, with China and India. This was not entirely an import trade, because Byzantium itself exported to the East costly materials and goods from its Syrian workshops, although its own exports certainly did not balance the demand for oriental luxury imports, particularly silks. It was not always easy to carry on trade with China as this depended on a working arrangement with Persia, and even in times of peace this involved unnecessary expense, entailing an increasing flow of gold from the Empire, while during the frequent periods of hostility with the Sassanids the silk trade was altogether suspended. The land route to China went through Persian territory, and the sea traffic through the Indian Ocean was also controlled by Persian merchants who sailed from the Persian Gulf to Taprobane (Ceylon) to collect the goods which poured in from China.

Justinian tried to establish contact with China by a roundabout route, going by way of his satellites Cherson and Bosporus in the Crimea through Lazica and the Caucasus district. Here Byzantium carried on a lively trade with the peoples of the steppes north of the Black Sea, exchanging textiles, jewellery and wine for furs, leather and slaves, and the strengthening of its influence in the Crimea and region of the Caucasus was therefore of considerable importance. It was through the problem of the silk trade that Byzantium was first brought into contact with the Turks, whose power at that time extended to the northern Caucasian area. Like the Byzantines, they had fallen out with the Persians over the silk trade. Justinian's successor, Justin II, concluded a treaty with them, and they supported Byzantium against the Persian Empire.

Justinian was equally concerned to safeguard the sea route to India through the Red Sea; he tried to increase his own sea traffic with the East, and he established friendly relations with the Ethiopian kingdom of Axum. But neither Byzantine nor Ethiopian merchants could break Persian control of the Indian Ocean, and the alternative land-route from the Black Sea to Central Asia was difficult and dangerous. It was therefore a piece of good fortune for the Byzantine Empire when its agents succeeded in finding out the secret of manufacturing silk and smuggled some silkworms into the country. The Byzantine production of silk grew rapidly, particularly in Constantinople itself, in Antioch, Tyre and Beyrut, and later on in Thebes. It became one of the most flourishing industries in the Empire, and as a state monopoly provided an exceedingly important source of income.[1]

The most notable and enduring achievement of the age of Justinian was the codification of Roman law.[2] Under Tribonian's direction this was accomplished in a remarkably short time. First of all the valid imperial edicts since the time of Hadrian were collected together, a piece of work which owed much to the earlier *Codex Theodosianus* and the private collections of Diocletian's day, the *Codex Gregorianus* and the *Codex Hermogenianus*. This new collection was published in 529 as the *Codex Justinianus* and a completed edition appeared five years later. The appearance of the *Digest* (the *Pandects*) in 533 marked an even greater achievement. This was a collection of the writings of the classical Roman jurists and, together with the imperial edicts, it formed the main body of current law. The *Codex Justinianus* marks a distinct advance on previous collections of this kind, although it certainly drew on the work of earlier centuries. The *Digest*, however, broke fresh ground and was the first attempt to bring the innumerable and often contradictory rulings of Roman jurists into an ordered system. In addition to the *Codex* and *Digest*, there was the *Institutes*, a handbook for use in law schools which gave extracts from the two main works. A collection of the novels promulgated by Justinian since the appearance of the *Codex*

---

[1] Cf. Heyd, *Commerce du Levant* I, 2 ff.; R. S. Lopez, 'Silk Industry in the Byzantine Empire', *Speculum* 20 (1945), 1 ff.; N. V. Pigulevskaja, 'Vizantijskaja diplomatija i torgovlja šelkom' (Byzantine diplomacy and the silk trade), VV 26 (1947), 184 ff.; idem, *Vizantija na putjach v Indiju* (Byzantium on the routes to India), Moscow-Leningrad, 1951, 184 ff. Stein, *Bas-Empire* 769 ff., 843; Hennig, 'Die Einführung der Seidenraupenzucht ins Byzantinerreich', BZ 33 (1933), 295 ff. An important contribution to the history of the internal and foreign trade of Byzantium is the very thorough work based on a far-reaching use of sources by Hélène Antoniadis-Bibicou, *Recherches sur les douanes à Byzance*, Paris 1963. This is the first comprehensive investigation into the Byzantine customs system.

[2] In addition to works and textbooks on the history of Roman jurisprudence see especially P. Collinet, *Études historiques sur le droit de Justinien* I (1921).

completed the *Corpus Juris Civilis*. The *Codex*, the *Digest* and the *Institutes* were in Latin, but most of the novels were already in Greek. There rapidly appeared Greek translations of the more important parts of the *Corpus*, as well as abridged versions and commentaries.

This codification of Roman law supplied an underlying unity to the centralized state. With unsurpassed clarity and forcefulness, Roman law as presented by Byzantine jurists regulated all public and private affairs, the life of the state as well as the individual and his family, the relations of citizens to each other, their business doings and their private concerns. Nor was the *Corpus Juris Civilis* a merely mechanical and entirely faithful repetition of the old Roman law. Justinian's jurists abbreviated and often altered classical Roman law so that the code might be brought into line with the needs of contemporary society, and reconciled with the Christian commandments and the customs of the Hellenistic East. Under the influence of Christianity, it was often modified in the direction of greater humaneness, particularly with regard to the laws concerning the family. But the dogmatic exclusiveness of the Christian religion also meant that all other religions were proscribed and completely denied any legal protection. The law in Justinian's day might proclaim the freedom and equality of all mankind, but the practical application of this must not be pressed too far. It was only due in part to this high ideal, as well as to the influence of Christianity, that the position of slaves improved and their emancipation was made easier under Justinian.[1] A consideration of even greater importance was the fact that slave labour played only a subordinate part in the economic life of the sixth century, particularly in the country.[2] The *coloni* had long been the mainstay of production and the law in Justinian's day did nothing to improve their position. On the contrary, it emphasized that they were tied to the soil, and consequently the bondage of the majority of the rural population was once more given legal sanction.

The outstanding characteristic of Justinian's legislation was its strong emphasis on the powers of the Emperor. The *Corpus Juris*

[1] Cf. A. Hadjinicolaou-Marava, *Recherches sur la vie des esclaves dans le Monde Byzantin*, Athens 1950, 22 ff.

[2] Z. V. Udalcova, 'Nekotorye izmenenija v́ ekonomičeskom položenii rabov v Vizantii VI v. (po dannym zakonodatel'stva Justiniana)' (Some changes in the economic position of slaves in Byzantium in the sixth century—based on the legislation of Justinian), ZRVI 8, 1, 1963, 281 ff. also refers to the changes in the position of slaves, which came about with the collapse of the classical system of slavery in the early Byzantine period. The legislation cf Justinian took into account the existing situation and legalized the economic emancipation of slaves.

Civilis Justiniani gave legal support to monarchical authority, and it had a lasting influence on the development of political thought in the West, as well as in Byzantium. In the Byzantine Empire, Roman law remained the basis of legal development throughout its history, and Justinian's *Corpus* was the starting point for all future work in this field. It was not until the twelfth century that it returned to the West. Here, through the medium of the *Corpus*, the Reception was to play a great part in shaping legal and political thought, and Roman law as presented by Justinian's jurists was until very recently one of the main elements in the codes of all European countries.

Justinian was the last Roman Emperor to occupy the Byzantine throne. He was at the same time a Christian ruler filled with the consciousness of the Divine source of his imperial authority. His strivings towards the achievement of a universal Empire were based on Christian, as well as on Roman, conceptions. For him the *imperium romanum* was to be identified with the Christian *oikoumene*, and the triumph of Christianity was as sacred a mission as the restoration of Roman supremacy. No ruler since Theodosius the Great had made such an effort to convert the Empire and to root out paganism. Though numerically the pagans were not strong at this time, they still had considerable influence in learning and culture. Justinian therefore deprived them of the right to teach, and in 529 he closed the Academy in Athens, the centre of pagan neoplatonism. The scholars who were driven out found a refuge at the court of the Persian King of Kings, bringing with them the fruits of Greek learning. Thus in Byzantium the old religion was dead, and a long chapter of human history brought to a close.

In Justinian the Christian Church found a master as well as a protector, for though Christian, he remained a Roman to whom the conception of any autonomy in the religious sphere was entirely alien.[1] Popes and Patriarchs were regarded and treated as his servants. He directed the affairs of the Church as he did those of the state, and took a personal interest in details of ecclesiastical organization. Even in matters of belief and ritual the final decision rested with him, and he summoned church councils, wrote theological treatises and composed church hymns. In the history of the relations between Church and State, the age of Justinian is the high-watermark of imperial influence in religious matters, and no other

[1] Cf. H. Alivisatos, *Die kirchliche Gesetzgebung des Kaisers Justinian I*, Berlin 1913; Pargoire, *L'Église byzantine de 527 à 847* (1905), 11 ff.; Duchesne, *L'Église au VIe siècle* (1925), 256 ff.

Emperor either before or after had such unlimited authority over the Church.

The burning ecclesiastical problem was that of the Church's attitude towards the monophysites. The policy of expansion in the West made it essential to have an understanding with Rome, and hence there was an anti-monophysite orientation. This, however, only increased the hostility of Egypt and Syria towards the central government in Constantinople and gave fresh impetus to the separatist tendencies of the Copts and Syrians. It was clear that peace with the West could only be bought at the cost of increasing opposition in the East; similarly, any approach to the monophysite churches of Syria and Egypt would mean a break, not only with the West, but also with the central Byzantine provinces. Justinian tried in vain to find some way out of this dilemma. At the fifth oecumenical Council of Constantinople in 553, the so-called Three Chapters (the writings of Theodore of Mopsuestia, Theodoret of Cyrrhus and Ibas of Edessa, suspected of Nestorian tendencies) were condemned. But this did not pacify the monophysites, and Justinian's further attempts to do so only increased the tension in the Empire.

For all its shortcomings the Empire of Justinian undeniably exercised great authority. For the last time the old *imperium* displayed its full powers, and experienced its last great revival, both politically and culturally. Its boundaries were once more extended to take in the whole Mediterranean world. Its literature and art displayed to perfection the old classical heritage in a Christian framework, though this was soon followed by a period of cultural decline. Justinian had meant his reign to inaugurate a new era, but it really marked the close of a great age. He did not succeed in rebuilding the Empire. He had managed to expand its frontiers, but only for a short time, and to breathe fresh life into the worn-out state of the late Roman period was beyond his power. His territorial reconquests therefore could not be established on any sound foundations and the consequences of the sudden collapse of his work were doubly disastrous. In spite of magnificent successes, Justinian left his successors an Empire internally exhausted, and completely ruined financially and economically. They had to make good the great mistakes of a great man in order to save what still remained to be saved.

It was in Italy that the Empire suffered the hardest blow. This was the most important of the regained imperial lands, and its reconquest had made great demands on the Empire's resources and

Figure 23: *Church of San Vitale*. Ravenna, 526–547. Interior, looking east toward the sanctuary and apse. Similar in plan to the Church of SS. Sergius and Bacchus in Constantinople, this large octagonal church retains its original decoration in the sanctuary and apse, which are entirely covered with mosaics and marble paneling. (See Figure 24 for details.) Photo: Hirmer Fotoarchiv, Munich.

Figure 24: (ABOVE) *Justinian and His Retinue*. (BELOW) *Theodora and Her Attendants*. Details of mosaic panels, Church of San Vitale, Ravenna, 526–547. Set to the left and right of the apse, the large panels depict Justinian, with Archbishop Maximian at his left, and Theodora in full imperial regalia, both presenting gifts to the church. (See Figure 23 for location.) Photos: Hirmer Fotoarchiv, Munich.

had cost most bitter sacrifices. In 568 it was invaded by the Lombards, and in a short time most of the country was in their hands.[1] In Spain the Visigoths began a counter-offensive. The most important Byzantine base of Cordova, which had temporarily fallen to the Visigoths in 572, was finally lost to them in 584, and forty years later the last remaining remnant of Justinian's reconquests in Spain was in Visigothic hands.[2] In North Africa, however, the Empire stood its ground until the great Arab invasions, though only at the cost of long drawn-out and exhausting campaigns against the local Berber tribes. And even in Italy itself it managed to retain its hold on important areas for several centuries. Thus some remnants of Justinian's work of restoration remained to provide a base from which the Byzantines could exercise their influence in the West. But any attempt to establish universal authority was a thing of the past.

The balance of Byzantine policy of necessity now swung to the East again. Here the situation was most serious, and Justinian's successors had to set about rebuilding the shattered prestige of the Empire in the Near East. One of the main achievements of Byzantine foreign policy during the following years was the successful stand which was made against Persia. In spite of the internal exhaustion of the Empire, Justinian's nephew and successor, Justin II (565–78), boldly refused to pay the Persian King of Kings his usual tribute, and in so doing broke the peace treaty which Justinian had worked so hard to achieve. The result was a long and wearisome war which was mainly fought out over Armenia, strategically and economically so important, and for centuries a bone of contention between the two Empires. At this point, control of Armenia was more essential than ever for Byzantium. Originally the influx of Germanic peoples into the Empire had created an acute crisis, but with their migration elsewhere a crisis of a different kind arose, for their departure meant the drying-up of a very useful supply of mercenaries. Byzantium now had to rely more and more on its own people for military recruits, and in particular it wished to draw on the Armenians who made excellent soldiers.[3] For a full twenty years under the Emperors Justin II, Tiberius Constantine (578–82) and Maurice (582–602) the war was prosecuted unsparingly and with varying success. Internal troubles in the Persian Empire finally

---

[1] On the history of the Lombards see L. Schmidt, *Die Ostgermanen* (1941), 565 ff.

[2] There are important studies in the little explored field of Byzantine rule in Spain by P. Goubert, 'Byzance et l'Espagne wisigothique', EB 2 (1944), 5–78, and 'L'Espagne byzantine', ib. 3 (1945), 127–42; ib. 4(1946), 71–133.

[3] Cf. Stein, *Studien* 5 ff.

came to Byzantine assistance, and the energetic Maurice was able to take advantage of this to bring the war to a favourable conclusion. With his support the young Chosroes II Parviz, a grandson of the great Chosroes, gained possession of the throne, and at once signed a peace treaty with the Byzantine Empire in which a large part of Persian Armenia was ceded to the Byzantines (591).[1]

Maurice was one of the most outstanding of Byzantine rulers. His reign marks an important step forward in the transformation of the worn-out late Roman Empire into the new and vigorous organization of the medieval Byzantine Empire. The eastward orientation and the forced surrender of most of the western territory annexed by Justinian did not mean any fundamental surrender of imperial interests in the West. By the decisive measures which he took, Maurice did at least secure for the Empire a part of the western possessions for some time to come. He regrouped the remnants of Justinian's conquests and created the exarchates of Ravenna and of Carthage, and by means of a strictly military organization he tried to ensure their adequate defence. The lands in North Africa, and the territory salvaged from the Lombard invaders in the neighbourhood of Ravenna, were organized on military lines, and the entire civil administration, as well as the military, was under the authority of the exarchs.[2] These two exarchates became the outposts of Byzantine power in the West. Their organization pointed the way towards the militarization of Byzantine administration and foreshadowed Heraclius' introduction of the system of themes. Maurice was certainly not inclined to give up the western possessions, and this is shown by the will which he drew up when he was seriously ill in 597. It provided that his eldest son Theodosius should rule in Constantinople over the eastern lands, and his second son Tiberius in Rome over Italy and the western islands.[3] Rome as the second capital of the Empire was again to become an imperial city. The idea of an universal Empire still survived, as well as the conception of a

---

[1] Dölger, *Reg.* 104. Cf. P. Goubert, *Byzance et Orient sous les successeurs de Justinien: L'empereur Maurice*, Paris 1951; M. J. Higgins, *The Persian War of the Emperor Maurice*, Washington 1939. Byzantino-Persian relations are also considered in Higgins' interesting study, 'International Relations at the Close of the Sixth Century,' *Catholic Hist. Rev.* 27 (1941), 279–315.

[2] The exarchate of Ravenna is mentioned for the first time in 584. Cf. Diehl, *Exarchat* 6 ff.; Hartmann, *Byz. Verwaltung* 9 ff.; Gelzer, *Themenverfassung* 6 ff. The Exarchate of Carthage first appears in 591. Cf. Diehl, *L'Afrique Byzantine*, 478 ff.

[3] Theophyl. Simocattes 305 ff. (ed. de Boor), who adds that 'the remaining parts' of the Roman state were to be handed over to Maurice's two young sons, and Bury (*Later Roman Empire* II[1], 94, note 2) makes the possible suggestion that one was to have Illyricum and the other North Africa.

single *imperium romanum*, though this was divided for administrative purposes and governed by several rulers.[1]

There was now peace in Asia—even if only temporarily—and the remains of Justinian's proud work in Italy had been salvaged, but in the Balkans the situation was always critical. Ever since the Slav invasions there had been confusion in these lands, and this became still worse with the appearance of the Avars in Central Europe. A powerful federation of peoples came into being in the Pannonian plain, and from then on Byzantium was under increasing pressure from the Avars and from the Slavs on the middle Danube whom the Avars controlled. A violent struggle soon broke out over the Byzantine border fortresses which guarded the crossings of the Sava and the Danube. After a long and bitter siege the Khan of the Avars, Bajan, entered Sirmium in 582. Two years later Viminacium fell, and for a short time Singidunum[2] as well. The Byzantine system of defence was breached and the Avars and Slavs devastated the whole of the Balkan peninsula. At the same time the Slav tribes on the lower reaches of the Danube, who were independent of the Avars, penetrated further and further into the Byzantine provinces.[3] It was at this time that the first Slav and Avar-Slav attacks on Thessalonica took place (584 and 586).[4] More disconcerting still was the fact that from the last quarter of the sixth century onwards the Slavs had begun to settle permanently in the Balkans. No longer satisfied with mere plunder, these tribes began to establish themselves on Byzantine soil and took firm possession of the country.[5]

[1] Cf. Kornemann, *Doppelprinzipat* 161.

[2] Cf. F. Barišić, 'Vizantiski Singidunum', ZRVI III (1955) 10 ff.

[3] On the independence of the Slavs on the lower Danube cf. St. Stanojević, *Vizantija i Srbi* I, 171 ff. (with sources and bibliography); A. Djakonov, 'Izvestija Ioanna Efesskogo i sirijskich chronik o slavjanach VI–VII v.' (Information in John of Edessa and the Syriac chronicles on the Slavs in the sixth and seventh centuries), *Vestnik Drevnej Istorii* 1946, 1, 20 ff. See also Grafenauer, *Nekaj vprašanj* 87 ff.

[4] The so-called *Miracula S. Demetrii* describe these. Cf. *Vizantiski izvori* I, 175, 176 ff. F. Barišić, *Čuda Dimitrija Solunskog*, 49 ff., 56 ff.

[5] Cf. the account of John of Ephesus (VI 25, trans. Schönfelder, p. 255) where the Slavs are described as living in the Roman provinces at that time (i.e. 584) 'in freedom and without fear'; the statement that they inhabited the country 'until God ejected them', which seems to point in the opposite direction, is an error in Schönfelder's translation. Cf. A. Vasiliev, 'Slavjane v Grecii', VV 5 (1898), 409, note 3; K. J. Jireček, *Die Romanen in den Städten Dalmatiens* I (1901), 25; A. Djakonov, 'Izvestija Ioanna Efesskogo', op. cit., 1, 32, who says that the passage wrongly translated should read 'as long as God permits them'; R. Payne Smith (Oxford 1860) also translates it thus. The new edition by E. W. Brooks, *Corpus script. christ. orient. Scriptores Syri* III, 1935, with Latin trans., 1936, is unfortunately inaccessible to me; cf. E. Honigmann, B 14, 1939, 615 ff. Cf. also H. Grégoire, 'L'Origine et le Nom des Croates et des Serbes', B 17 (1944–5), 109 ff.

During the early Byzantine period no development due to external factors was of greater significance for posterity than the Slav penetration into the Balkans. All other barbarian inroads into the Empire at that time were temporary in character, and even the great Germanic invasions which had so seriously affected the course of events finally moved elsewhere. The Slavs, however, made a permanent home in the Balkans, and the outcome of this penetration was to be the later growth of independent Slav kingdoms on what had once been Byzantine soil.

The wars of reconquest in the West in Justinian's reign, and the long struggle with Persia under his successors, had compelled Byzantium to adopt a defensive policy in the Balkans. It was only with the victorious outcome of the Persian war that it was possible to make a real drive against the Slavs in the Danube regions. In fact, only an extensive and successful expedition against the headquarters of the Slavs beyond the Danube would protect the northern frontier from further hostile attacks and secure the Empire in its possession of the Balkans. The struggle which was to decide its fate began in 592.[1] At first the Byzantines seemed to be doing well; they repeatedly crossed the Danube and won several victories over the Slavs and Avars. But isolated successes of this kind made little impression on the powerful hordes of the Slavs and the war dragged on; it was difficult to control operations in these remote parts and the enthusiasm of the army cooled off.

After the collapse of Justinian's work, the government had suffered a marked decline in prestige. There was a natural reaction against Justinian's absolutism, and the senate recovered some of its political significance, while the people again voiced their opinions. The critical years at the end of the sixth and beginning of the seventh centuries saw a fresh outburst of activity from the demes. The continual deepening of social and religious dissension was reflected in the bitter internal clashes, and frequent fights between the Greens and the Blues in all the big cities. In the army there was a serious deterioration in discipline, which frequently resulted in open disaffection, and was aggravated by the cuts in pay imposed by the

---

[1] The chronological difficulties raised by the account of Theophylact Simocattes have often been discussed. For a recent and detailed study see G. Labuda, 'Chronologie des guerres de Byzance contre les Avars et les Slaves à la fin du VIᵉ siècle', BS 11 (1950), 167 ff., who maintains that the war did not begin until 596, and Grafenauer, *Nekaj vprašanj* 62 ff., who considers (rightly in my view) that the war lasted from 592 until 602. See also J. B. Bury, 'The Chronology of Theophylactus Simocatta', EHR 3 (1888), 210 ff.

financially straitened government. The deep unrest which had seized the Empire also took possession of the army, which was by now worn out and dispirited at the prospect of a war whose end was not in sight. When in 602 the troops were ordered to take up winter quarters on the far side of the Danube, a revolt broke out. Phocas, a junior officer and half-barbarian, was raised on the shield, and he advanced on Constantinople at the head of the mutinous soldiers. There was also a rising in the capital and both the Blues and the Greens revolted against the imperial government.[1] Maurice was overthrown, and with the approval of the senate Phocas was acclaimed Emperor.

After ten years' long struggle the campaigns on the Danube had proved fruitless. This decided the fate of the Balkans, which now fell uncontested to the Slavs, while it also brought the long suppressed internal crisis in the Empire to a head. During Phocas' reign in Constantinople (602-10) the aged and worn-out late Roman Empire was in the throes of its death struggle. Phocas' reign of terror provided the external framework within which the finishing touches were put to the slow disintegration of the state and society of late Roman times.

The revolutionary fever which had seized the Empire led to an uncontrollable reign of terror accompanied by fierce internal struggles. The deposed Maurice was executed after his sons had been cut down before his very eyes, and this was followed by a wave of indiscriminate slaughter which was particularly directed against members of the most distinguished families in order to forestall their opposition. The aristocracy answered this orgy of massacres with a series of conspiracies, all of which ended in further executions. From only one quarter did Phocas' actions meet with approval. A heated controversy had broken out between Constantinople and Rome at the end of the sixth century because of Gregory I's fierce protest against the title 'oecumenical Patriarch' which the

---

[1] The Greens were the favoured party under Maurice according to Y. Janssens, 'Les Bleus et les Verts sous Maurice, Phocas et Héraclius', B 11 (1936), 499 ff. This is warmly defended by H. Grégoire, 'L'empereur Maurice s'appuyait-il sur les Verts ou sur les Bleus?' *Annales de l'Inst. Kondakov* 10 (1938), 107 ff.; see also his illuminating notes, 'Sainte Euphémie et l'Empereur Maurice', *Mélanges Lefort* (1946), 295 ff. The opposite view is taken by F. Dölger, BZ 37 (1937), 542 f. and 38 (1938), 525 ff. Djakonov ('Viz. Dimy' 221.) considers that Maurice favoured the Blues, but adopted a conciliatory attitude towards the Greens.

Patriarchs of Constantinople had been using for nearly a century.[1] Maurice answered this protest with considerable coolness. Phocas, on the contrary, was ready to be more compliant. His markedly conciliatory policy towards Rome culminated in an edict addressed to Pope Boniface III in which he recognized the Apostolic Church of St. Peter as the head of all the churches.[2] A column erected in the Roman forum with an inscription praising the Byzantine tyrant showed the remarkable favour which Phocas enjoyed in Rome. In Byzantium itself he became more and more hated, particularly in the Near East where his orthodox ecclesiastical policy had shown itself in cruel persecution of the monophysites and Jews. The internal struggles daily increased and grew more bitter. The Greens, who had been behind him to begin with, turned against him with such hostility that their members were completely forbidden to hold any office,[3] while the Blues then supported his régime of terror. The clash between the demes now reached its most acute pitch and the flames of civil war spread over the Empire.[4]

[1] Cf. H. Gelzer, 'Der Streit über den Titel des ökumenischen Patriarchen', *Jahrb. f. protest. Theol.* 13 (1897), 549 ff.; E. Caspar, *Gesch. des Papsttums* II (1933), 367, 452 ff.; J. Haller, *Das Papsttum* I (1936), 285 ff.; V. Laurent, 'Le titre de patriarche oecuménique et la signature patriarcale', REB 6 (1948), 5 ff.

[2] Dölger, *Reg.* 155.

[3] Theophanes I 297, 4, ἐκέλευσε τοὺς πρασίνους μηκέτι πολιτεύεσθαι. Owing to the uncertainty and ambiguity of the sources it is not easy to decide when the party of the Greens abandoned Phocas. Y. Janssens, op. cit., 515 ff., makes a detailed attempt to argue that the Greens' break with Phocas was as early as 603. See also J. Kulakovskij, 'K kritike izvestij Feofana o poslednem gode pravlenija Foki' (a critical examination of Theophanes on the last year of Phocas' reign), VV 21 (1914), 9 f. On the other hand, most scholars put the proscription of the Greens towards the end of Phocas' reign. See also Bury, *Later Rom. Empire* II¹, 204; Pareti, 'Verdi e azzuri ai tempi di Foca', *Studi Italiani di Filol. class.* 19 (1912) 305 ff.; N. H. Baynes, 'The Successors of Justinian', CMH II (1913) 286; Dölger, *Reg.* 159. Djakonov, op. cit., 223 ff., has recently made an exhaustive attempt to show that the Greens were finally disbanded by Phocas in 609 (also M. Levčenko, 'Venety i prasiny v Vizantii v V–VII vv' (Blues and Greens in Byzantium from the fifth to the seventh centuries), VV 26 (1947), 177 ff., who repeats Djakonov's argument, often almost word for word). The important question is, however, not so much which year the break between Phocas and the Greens came, as the fact that it was the antagonism of the Greens which contributed decisively to Phocas' fall, for they turned against him with great bitterness at the critical point and decided for Heraclius. Also the orthodox and pro-Roman emphasis of Phocas' ecclesiastical policy, which is of more importance than Djakonov allows ('Viz. dimy' 225, likewise Levčenko, op. cit. 179 in almost identical words), does not argue for 'Green' sympathies.

[4] There are vivid descriptions in contemporary sources of the anarchical conditions in the Byzantine Empire at that time. Particularly significant is the description in the *Miracula S. Demetrii*, AASS, 8 Oct., IV, 132 (Migne, PG 116, 1261 f.): 'You all know only too well what a cloud of dust the devil has stirred up under the successor of Maurice of blessed memory, for he has stifled love and sown mutual hatred throughout the whole east, in Cilicia and Asia and Palestine and all the regions round, even up to the gates of the imperial city itself: the demes, not satisfied with shedding the blood of their fellow

Figure 25: (ABOVE) *Pectoral Cross*. Gold, 6th to 7th centuries. It is decorated in repoussé with a central cross and rosettes in the flaring arms. Ht. 2¼", including ring attachment, w. 1⁹⁄₁₆". Malcove Collection, New York. Photo: Geoffrey Clements. (BELOW) *Pressed Medallion Pendant*. Gold, 565–578. The central medallion, in repoussé, depicts a standing archangel; within the beaded borders are 12 small medallions, 4 displaying crosses and 8 the likeness of an emperor, all in repoussé. Diam. 3½". Virginia Museum Collections, Richmond. Photo: Virginia Museum.

Figure 26: *Oil Lamp on a Stand.* Bronze, 6th century or earlier. The lamp, with foliate spiral handles supporting a finial of a dove perched on a cross, and with a double-hinged lid, rests on a spiked stand with a claw-footed tripod base. Ht. 19½″; lamp, w. 6¾″, l. 9½″. Malcove Collection, New York. Photo: Geoffrey Clements.

At this point the very catastrophe which all the bitter wars of the previous years had tried to avert descended on the Empire. In the Balkans and in Asia there was a complete military breakdown. The Persian Chosroes II rose up to avenge the murdered Maurice and made a great drive against Byzantium. The Empire had been so shattered by its internal troubles that it had neither the resources nor the will to defend itself. It did at first put up some sort of a fight, but it experienced misfortune after misfortune. The Persian army broke through the frontier defences, took the fortress of Dara in 605, swiftly penetrated into Asia Minor itself and captured Caesarea. A detachment of Persian troops even got as far as Chalcedon. Meanwhile a flood of Slavs and Avars spread over the Balkans, despite Phocas' attempt to buy them off in 604 by raising the tribute paid them.[1] The whole Balkan peninsula was rapidly overrun. It looked as though the Empire was on the point of disintegrating.

The situation was saved by vigorous action at the periphery. The exarch of Carthage, Heraclius, rose against Phocas' tyrannical rule, and after Egypt had thrown in its lot with him he sent a fleet against Constantinople under the command of his son, also named Heraclius. On its way the ships had to put in at various islands and ports, and the younger Heraclius was enthusiastically received by the people and particularly by the party of the Greens. On 3 October 610 his fleet appeared before Constantinople. Here he was also hailed as a saviour, and he put a quick end to the bloody rule of Phocas. On 5 October he received the imperial crown from the hands of the Patriarch.[2] After the execution of the deposed tyrant, his statue in the Hippodrome was overturned and publicly burnt as a kind of symbolical *damnatio memoriae*, and with it the party colours of the Blues were also significantly consigned to the flames.[3]

The years of anarchy under Phocas were the last phase in the history of the late Roman Empire. During this time the old *imperium*

demesmen in the streets, have forced their way into each others' houses and mercilessly murdered those within, throwing down alive from the upper stories women and children, young and old, who were too weak to save themselves by flight; in barbarian fashion they have plundered their fellow-citizens, their acquaintances and relations, and have set fire to their houses. . . .'

[1] Dölger, *Reg.* 152.

[2] On the date see Ostrogorsky, 'Chronologie' 30, note 1.

[3] *Chron. Paschale* 701, 17. Insufficient attention has been given to this very informative document in the discussion as to which of the two parties Phocas was most closely associated with (cf. p. 84, n. 3 above).

finally went under and the late Roman, or early Byzantine, period
came to an end. Byzantium was to emerge from the crisis in an
essentially different form, able to throw off the heritage of decadent
political life and to draw on new and vigorous sources of strength.
Byzantine history properly speaking is the history of the medieval
Greek Empire, and it is now that it begins.

Figure 27: *Circular Polycandelon.* Silver, with niello, Constantinople, circa 570.
The circles in the elaborate openwork design of this polycandelon (lamp holder)
were intended to hold 14 glass lamps. The disk was suspended on 4 chains from
the ceiling. Part of a large church treasure found near Antalya in southern
Turkey. Diam. 21¾". Dumbarton Oaks Collections, Washington, D.C.
Photo: Dumbarton Oaks Collections.

II

The Struggle for Existence and the Revival of the Byzantine State (610–711)

SOURCES

In contrast to the flourishing literary activity under Justinian, the seventh century was in this respect a barren period. This is particularly true of the epoch after Heraclius, which by reason of the great paucity of sources has rightly been called the dark age of Byzantium.

The great deeds of Heraclius were sung by George of Pisidia who was deacon, skeuophylax and chartophylax of Hagia Sophia under the Patriarch Sergius (610–39). He was a remarkable poet whom the later Byzantines compared to Euripides and he wrote, amongst other works, several historical poems in iambic trimeter. Of special importance are the poems describing Heraclius' campaign against the Persians in the year 622 and the Avar attack on Constantinople in 626, as well as the laudatory *Heraclias* celebrating the final overthrow of the Persians.[1] The siege of Constantinople by the Avars and Slavs in the year 626 is dealt with in detail in a speech by Theodore Syncellus, who like George of Pisidia wrote under Heraclius and was skeuophylax and presbyter of Hagia Sophia.[2] The author of the so-called Paschal Chronicle was also a contemporary of Heraclius and one of Patriarch Sergius' circle. This work consists of chronological lists with some historical comment, and it extends from Adam to the year 628, though it is now only extant to the year 627. It is only the last part from the death of Maurice onwards which is of real value.

The most important sources for the age of Heraclius, and the only Greek historical sources for the period of his successors, are the two chronicles of Theophanes and the Patriarch Nicephorus. The chronicle of the monk Theophanes,[3] compiled between 810 and

---

[1] A new critical edition with an Italian translation and detailed commentary is given by A. Pertusi, *Giorgio di Pisidia Poemi* I. *Panegirici epici*, Ettal 1960.

[2] Ed. L. Sternbach, *Analecta avarica*, Cracow 1900. Cf. also *Vizantiski izvori* I, 159 ff.

[3] Ed. C. de Boor, 2 vols., Leipzig, 1883–5. The concluding section (717–813) has been translated into German, with an introduction by L. Breyer, *Bilderstreit und Arabersturm*, in *Byzantinische Geschichtsschreiber* VI. Graz 1957.

814, is a continuation of the unfinished world chronicle of George Syncellus; it begins where he left off, i.e. with Diocletian, and ends shortly after the accession of Leo V, thus extending from 284 to 813. Theophanes lacks depth of scholarship, historical insight and an objective approach, but his work is based on older sources and is of the greatest value, particularly for the seventh and eighth centuries. A special feature of his chronicle is the carefully worked out chronological system, which provides the main basis for Byzantine chronology during the two dark centuries. The narrative is arranged in the form of annals, and each individual year begins with chronological tables in which, side by side with the year since the creation and since the birth of Christ, is given the current year of the Byzantine Emperor, and also those of the Persian and Arab rulers, the Pope and the four Patriarchs. Theophanes not only gives the year, calculated after the Alexandrine reckoning, which put the birth of Christ 5492 years after the creation, but the number of the indiction cycle, although in most sections he does not explicitly indicate the year of the indiction. It should be noted that from the year of the creation 6102 (A.D. 609/10) to 6265 (A.D. 772/73)—with the exception of the brief period 6207 to 6218 (A.D. 714/15–725/26)—Theophanes' calculations, by reason of an error in the division of his material, fall a year behind the indiction number stated or implied. On the other hand he always works out the indictions correctly, so that when using his chronological information for the period in question one year should be added to the date given.[1] The chronicle of Theophanes enjoyed a high reputation in Byzantium and formed the basis of all later Byzantine annals. It became known in the West through the Latin translation made by the papal librarian

---

[1] Cf. Ostrogorsky, 'Chronologie' 1 ff., where the older work on the problem of the chronology of Theophanes is discussed; also my article, 'Theophanes', PW (Reihe 2) 10 (1934), 2127 ff. V. Grumel, EO 33 (1934), 319 ff., attempts to explain the inconsistency between the world years and the indictions by suggesting that Theophanes reckoned his year from 25 March and not from 1 September, but this is not very satisfactory as Dölger shows (BZ 35 (1935), 154 f.). Cf. also F. Dölger, 'Das Kaiserjahr der Byzantiner', S.B. der Bayer. Akad. d. Wissensch., 1949, Heft 1, p. 21, 38; D. Anastasijević, 'Carskij god v Vizanti' (The imperial year in Byzantium), Sem. Kond. 11 (1940), 147 ff. and esp. 170 ff., abandons Grumel's theory and accepts my conclusions, although he considers that the discrepancy between the indiction and world years which first appears in Theophanes' Chronicle for the year 609–10 did not continue up to 714–15, but righted itself in the last years of Constans II. The March reckoning theory has been recently defended by V. Mošin, 'Martovsko datiranje', Istor. Glasnik 1–2 (1951), 19–57. But cf. my review in BZ 46 (1953), 170 ff., where it is shown that the March reckoning was not so widespread as Mošin and Grumel would like to imply, and that it cannot explain the chronological peculiarities of Theophanes' chronicle, which, on the contrary, follows the September reckoning.

Anastasius in the seventies of the ninth century; this translation is also of value to modern Byzantinists since it derived from a text older than any of the surviving manuscripts.

Nicephorus, who was Patriarch of Constantinople from 806 to the outbreak of the iconoclast controversy in 815, wrote a number of theological works, and also a short history (ἱστορία σύντομος) which covers the period 602–769[1] and draws in part on the same unknown sources as Theophanes. Nicephorus' account is less detailed than that of Theophanes, but it is of almost equal historical significance and is on the whole distinguished by greater objectivity. On the other hand, Nicephorus' chronological epitome (χρονογραφικὸν σύντομον) from Adam to 829, the year of the author's death, is of very limited value.

Compensation for the paucity of the Greek sources is to some extent provided by the information given by oriental writers. The most important of these is the Armenian bishop Sebeos, who wrote a *History of Heraclius* in the sixties of the seventh century (probably in 661).[2] Heraclius and his great opponent Chosroes II form the central theme of the work, though not exclusively so, for it also contains a brief account of the preceding period, and continues to the elevation of Muawija as Caliph (661), besides dealing in some detail with ecclesiastical affairs in Armenia.

At the end of the seventh century Bishop John of Nikiu in Egypt wrote a world chronicle[3] which is very important, particularly for the early years of Heraclius; this has unfortunately only survived in a mutilated condition and in a later Ethiopic version. There are also several contemporary and later anonymous Syriac chronicles,[4] as well as the chronicle of the Metropolitan Elias of Nisibis[5] which

---

[1] ed. C. de Boor, Leipzig 1880. The London MS. British Museum Add. 19390 (ninth century) was not used by de Boor, but has recently been made known by L. Orosz, *The London Manuscript of Nikephoros 'Breviarium'*, Budapest 1948, who gives the text of the first part (to p. 15, 2, ed. de Boor), and for the second part, where the difference is much less, he collates with de Boor's text and gives the variant readings. For a full account of the literary work and personality of Nicephorus, see Alexander, *Patr. Nicephorus*.

[2] French trans. by F. Macler, *Histoire d'Héraclius par l'évêque Sebéos*, traduite de l'arménien et annotée, Paris 1904. Russian trans. by K. Patkanov, *Istorija imp. Irakla, perevod s armjanskogo* (History of the Emperor Heraclius, a translation from the Armenian), St. Petersburg 1862. On the much discussed question of the structure, the sources and the date of the work see S. S. Malchasjanc, 'Istorik Sebeos', VV 27 (1949), 94 ff.

[3] ed. with French trans. by H. Zotenberg, Chronique de Jean Evêque de Nikiou, *Notices et Extraits des MSS. de la Bibl. Nationale* XXIV (1883); English trans. by R. H. Charles, *The Chronicle of John, Bishop of Nikiu*, transl. from Zotenberg's Ethiopic text, London 1916.

[4] ed. with Latin trans. in the *Corpus Script. Christ. Orient., Scriptores Syri*, Ser. III, vol. IV, 1–3 (1903–5).

[5] ib. vol. VII (1910).

is based on earlier accounts, and the most valuable work of Michael the Syrian.[1]

For the history of the Slav invasions of the Balkans the *Miracula* of St. Demetrius are of considerable value; they describe the Slav attacks on Thessalonica with astonishing freshness and many vivid details.[2] The first part was written in the second decade of the seventh century by John, Archbishop of Thessalonica, and the second part by an unknown author in the eighties of the seventh century, while the third part, which was added later, is of no value.[3]

The *acta* of the sixth oecumenical Council and the Quinisextum,[4] together with the writings of Maximus the Confessor (Homologetes), are indispensable for the ecclesiastical history of the period.[5]

The seventh century is exceedingly poor in legal sources. There is, however, every reason to attribute the invaluable *Farmer's Law* (νόμος γεωργικός) to this epoch.[6] It is in fact only possible to say with absolute certainty that it was drawn up in either the seventh or the eighth century, but generally speaking, scholars are agreed that it can hardly be later than the first half of the eighth century, and it seems to fit best into the end of the seventh century, a probability which is strengthened by the fact that its inscription appears to indicate Justinian II.[7] The *Rhodian Sea Law* (νόμος ῥοδίων ναυτικός),

---

[1] ed. with French trans. by J. B. Chabot, *La chronique de Michel le Syrien*, 3 vols., Paris 1899–1904.

[2] AASS., Oct. 8, vol. IV, 104 ff., 162 ff. (= Migne, PG 116, 1204 ff., 1325 ff.); A. Tougard, *De l'histoire profane dans les actes grecs des Bollandistes*, Paris 1874.

[3] Cf. F. Barišić, *Čuda Dimitrija Solunskog kao istoriski izvor* (The Miracles of St. Demetrius of Thessalonica as an historical source), Belgrade 1954; P. Lemerle, 'La composition et la chronologie des deux premiers livres des Miracula S. Demetrii', BZ 46 (1953), 349–61. A. Burmov, 'Slavjanskite napadenija srešču Solun v "Čudesata na Sv. Dimitra" i tjachnata chronologija (The sieges of Thessalonica by the Slavs in the 'Miracles of St. Demetrius' and their chronology)', *Godišnik na Filos-istor. Fak.* II, Sofia 1952, 167–214.

[4] Mansi XI, 196 ff. and 929 ff.

[5] Migne, PG 90 and 91.

[6] The best ed. is by W. Ashburner, 'The Farmer's Law', JHS 30 (1910), 85–108; 32 (1912), 68–95, with *apparatus criticus*, detailed notes and English trans. The text is reprinted in Zepos, *Jus* II, 65–71.

[7] As the title shows, the *Farmer's Law* consists of extracts from a law-book of Justinian, and the problem has arisen as to whether they come from the legal works of Justinian I (despite the fact that they actually deal with what is predominantly new law, while the parallels which can be found in Justinian I's law appear to be comparatively insignificant: cf. W. Ashburner, op. cit., 32, p. 90 ff., and F. Dölger, 'Nomos Georgikos' 35 ff.), or whether they are extracts from an unknown law-book of Justinian II. The older research after Cujacius' time supported this latter view, but it was lost sight of when other views were championed. Mortreuil, *Histoire du droit byzantin* I (1843), 395, and C. W. E. Heimbach, 'Gesch. des griech.-römischen Rechts' in Ersch und Gruber, *Enzyklop. d. Wiss.* 86 (1868), 278 f., thought that the title of the *Farmer's Law* referred to the legal work of Justinian I. Of still greater influence were the views of Zachariä *Geschichte* 250 ff.; he was led by the close relationship of the *Farmer's Law* to the *Ecloga* o

Leo III and Constantine V to attribute it to these Emperors, but then he was particularly partial to the iconoclast rulers (his 'favourites', as Ashburner says, op. cit., vol. 32, p. 73) and gives them credit for a number of other works for which we now know that they could not have been responsible. As in many other problems, Zachariä's authoritative word secured the acceptance of his view for some time, in spite of the reasoned criticisms of such scholars as Pančenko, 'Krestjanskaja sobstvennost' (Peasant proprietorship), 24 ff., and Ashburner, op. cit., 32, p. 87 ff. The discussion took a new turn when G. Vernadsky, 'Sur l'origine de la Loi agraire', B 2 (1925), 127 ff., more recently put the case for attributing the work to Justinian II. His suggestions were supported by Stein, 'Vom Altertum' 162 and BZ 31 (1931), 355, Vasiliev, *Histoire* I (1932), 325 (cf. *History* (1952), 245), Bréhier, *Institutions* 176, Ostrogorsky, BZ 30 (1929–30), 396, and B 6 (1931), 240; cf. also H. Grégoire, B 12 (1937), 642. They were not accepted by F. Dölger, HZ 141 (1930), 112 f., and 'Nomos Georgikos' 21 ff., or by E. Lipšic, 'Vizantijskoe krestjanstvo i slavjanskaja kolonizacija' (The Byzantine peasantry and Slav colonization), *Viz. Sbornik* (1945), 100 ff. Of the manuscripts of the *Farmer's Law* so far known, only one (Paris. gr. 1367, twelfth century) gives a clear reference to the legal works of Justinian I, and here the title is somewhat peculiar and the copyist cites the *Digest* and *Institutes* as well as a number of unidentified writings. But the inscriptions in the other manuscripts, with some unimportant variations, read: Κεφάλαια νόμου γεωργικοῦ κατ' ἐκλογὴν ἐκ τοῦ 'Ιουστινιανοῦ βιβλίου, (on the MS. tradition see Ashburner, op. cit., 30, p. 85 ff., and J. de Malafosse, 'Les lois agraires à l'époque byzantine', *Recueil de l'Acad. de Législation* 19, 1949, 11 ff.). The use of the singular form βιβλίου is significant, for it precludes any reference to Justinian I which would have been followed by the plural βιβλίων. Of the six MSS. cited by Ashburner (in addition to the Paris. gr. 1367), only the twelfth-century Marc. gr. 167 gives the plural form, while the other five (including the three oldest, and probably independent, copies of the eleventh century) agree in reading βιβλίου (or βίβλου). This fact (as I stated in my first edition of this book and in my 'Agrarian Conditions' 198) seems to me to be a vital point in settling this much disputed question. Nevertheless Dölger, 'Nomos Georgikos' 30 f., does not recognize its force, although he cannot refute it. It could only be invalidated if we had a Byzantine legal work which showed from its title that it was obviously referring to Justinian I's *Corpus* and cited this as το 'Ιουστινιανοῦ βιβλίου. But the *Ecloga*, which is in all probability a near contemporary of the *Farmer's Law*, shows the usual way of making such reference in cases of citation from Justinian I's *Corpus*; it was in fact a selection from his legal works and the inscription clearly describes it as an ἐκλογή τῶν νόμων . . . ἀπὸ τῶν Ἰνστιτούτων, τῶν Διγέστων, τοῦ κώδικος, τῶν νεαρῶν τοῦ μεγάλου 'Ιουστινιανοῦ Διατάξεων. In opposition to Zachariä's view (*Geschichte* 250 ff.) that the *Farmer's Law* was an official work, Dölger, 'Nomos Georgikos', attempts to show that it was a private compilation. But whether the *Farmer's Law* which has come down to us was in origin official or unofficial, the 'Book of Justinian' from which these extracts regulating everyday peasant life are taken was certainly an official compilation, and evidence all points towards a legal work of Justinian II. The question of the date of the *Farmer's Law* is, however, more important than the question of authorship, and Dölger ('Nomos Georgikos' 48) finally concludes that it most probably belongs to the end of the seventh century or the first quarter of the eighth century. Cf. Dölger, 'Harmenopulos und der Nomos Georgikos', Τόμος Κ. 'Αρμενοπούλου (1951). See also Lemerle, 'Histoire agraire', 219 (i), p. 53 ff. The article by J. Karayannopulos, 'Entstehung und Bedeutung des Nomos Georgikos', BZ 51 (1958), 357 ff., which attempts to show that the *Farmer's Law* 'Keine Neuerungen ausweist' but 'nur älteres Recht wiedergibt' is a complete failure.

The unusually large number of MSS. of the *Farmer's Law* shows its importance and widespread use. Its significance is not confined to the limits of the Byzantine Empire, for it was soon translated into Slavonic and had a marked influence on legal developments among the South and East Slavs. Cf. A. Pavlov, 'Knigi zakonnye' (Lawbooks), *Shornik vtorogo otd. Imp. Ross. Akad. Nauk* 38 (1885). An Old Serbian translation has been published by Dj. S. Radojičić, *Srpski rukopis Zemljoradničkog zakona* (A Serbian manuscript of the *Farmer's Law*), ZRVI 3 (1955), 15 ff. In Serbia it formed an important part of the legal compilation known as 'the Law of the Tzar Justinian', and was normally found in MSS. together with the law-book of Stephen Dušan and the *Syntagma* of Matthew Blastares. Cf. Solovjev, *Zakonodavstvo Stefana Dušana* (The legal work of Stephen Dušan), Skoplje 1928, 49 ff.

a collection of maritime regulations, may also be noted here;[1] it is not, however, possible to assign a close date to this compilation and one can only say that it falls within the period 600–800.[2]

1. THE WARS WITH THE PERSIANS AND THE AVARS: HERACLIUS' WORK OF REORGANIZATION

General bibliography: Bury, *Later Rom. Empire* II[1] (also for the later chapters up to the year 800); H. St. L. B. Moss, 'The formation of the East Roman Empire', CMH IV, Pt. I (2nd. ed., 1966), (also for the later chapters up to 717); D. Obolensky, 'The Empire and its northern neighbours 565–1018', ibid.; Kulakovskij, *Istorija* III (also for the later chapters up to the year 717); Pernice, *Eraclio*; Stein, *Studien*; idem, 'Ein Kapitel'; Diehl, 'Régime des themes'; Gelzer, 'Themenverfassung'; G. Owsepian, *Die Entstehungsgeschichte des Monotheletismus*, Leipzig 1897; V. Grumel, 'Recherches sur l'histoire du monothélisme', EO 27 (1928), 6–16, 157–77, 28 (1929), 272–82, 29 (1930), 16–28; N. V. Pigulevskaja, *Vizantija i Iran na rubeže VI i VII vekov* (Byzantium and Iran at the end of the sixth and beginning of the seventh centuries). Moscow-Leningrad 1946.

The Empire lay in ruins when the government was taken over by Heraclius (610–41), one of the greatest rulers in Byzantine history. The country was economically and financially exhausted and the worn-out administrative machinery had come to a standstill. Military organization, based on mercenary recruitment, no longer functioned, for there was no money, nor were the old sources of man-power any longer available. The vital central provinces of the Empire were overrun by the enemy: Slavs and Avars were settling in the Balkans and the Persians were entrenching themselves in the heart of Asia Minor. Only internal regeneration could save the Empire from destruction.

But Byzantium had within itself the resources which were to provide a deep-rooted social, political and cultural revival. To begin with, the Empire was so enfeebled and poverty-stricken that it was powerless against the attacks of its enemies. For a time Heraclius

---

[1] ed. by W. Ashburner, *The Rhodian Sea Law*, Oxford 1909; trans. E. H. Freshfield, *A Manual of Later Roman Law* (Cambridge 1927).

[2] Cf. W. Ashburner, op. cit., pp. cxii ff.; Zachariä, *Geschichte* 316, also attributes this law to the iconoclast Emperor and likewise the *Tactica Leonis* (cf. his comments in 'Zum Militärgesetz des Leo', BZ 2 (1893), 606 ff., and 'Wissenschaft und Recht für das Heer', ib. 3 (1894), 437 ff.), although this belongs without doubt to Leo VI (see below, p. 215, note 5). On all this legal work see my comments in 'Über die vermeintliche Reformtätigkeit der Isaurier', BZ 30 (1929–30), 394 ff.

even thought of moving his headquarters to Carthage and organizing the counter-offensive from this base, as he had done before when he launched his attack against Phocas. He was prevented, however, by the deep despondency which this proposal roused in the populace of Constantinople and by the Patriarch Sergius' energetic opposition to the plan.[1] Nevertheless, the very fact that this could ever have been contemplated shows the exceeding precariousness of the position in the East and also the considerable importance attached to the western provinces.

By the end of the sixth century isolated groups of Slavs had already begun to settle in the Balkans. After the failure of Maurice's campaigns on the Danube at the beginning of the seventh century, the Slav occupation began on a grand scale. Innumerable hordes of Slavs and Avars swarmed over the whole peninsula from the shores of the Adriatic in the west to the Aegean Sea in the south and east. After terrible plundering and ravaging most of the Avars withdrew again to the territory north of the Danube, but the Slavs settled down in the Balkans and took possession of it, thus disrupting Byzantine control over this area. The newcomers were powerful enough to occupy the Danube regions as well as the whole of Macedonia, and they laid waste Thrace up to the walls of Constantinople itself. They made particularly fierce attacks on Thessalonica, which was repeatedly besieged and assailed by countless hordes of Slavs and Avars.[2] The city held its own, but all the country round fell to the Slavs, and the wave of Avars and Slavs poured on through Thessaly to central Greece and the Peloponnese beyond. From here the seafaring Slavs crossed to the Greek islands, and even made a landing in Crete. The invasion was equally severe in Dalmatia where its administrative centre, Salona, was destroyed in 614, an event which signalled the downfall of Byzantine control and influence in the western regions of the peninsula. Together with Salona and many other Dalmatian cities, most of the important towns of the interior also fell at this time, such for instance as Singidunum (Belgrade), Viminacium (Kostolac), Naissus (Niš) and Sardica (Sofia). Apart from Constantinople, the few remaining centres left in Byzantine hands in the Balkans were the important Thessalonica, and certain cities on the Adriatic coast, such as Jader (Zadar, Zara) and

---

[1] Nicephorus 12, 10.

[2] After the attacks in the ninth decade of the sixth century (cf. p. 81 above), described in the *Miracula S. Demetrii I*, the *Miracula II* tells of attacks in 616 and 618. Cf. Barišić, *Čuda Dimitrija Solunskog*, 81 ff.

Tragurium (Trogir) in the north, and Butua (Budva), Scodra (Skadar) and Lissus (Lješ) in the south.[1]

Throughout the whole region of the Balkans significant ethnic changes took place owing to the Slav migrations. The effects of these invasions were felt down to the most southerly point of the peninsula. But even though the Peloponnese itself was under Slav control for more than two hundred years,[2] there was no question of any permanent Slavonization of Greek territory.[3] Little by little the Byzantine authorities in Greece and the other coastal regions managed to regain lost ground and to preserve, or in some cases to recover, their Greek character for these areas. Under pressure of Slav invasion the original population everywhere had withdrawn towards the maritime districts and the neighbouring islands, and this partly accounts for the fact that the Greek element was strengthened again and gradually preponderated over the Slav on the southern and eastern coasts, while the Roman element reasserted itself on the western shores. Even so, these districts too were penetrated by Slavs. The greater part of the Balkan peninsula, the whole interior, became a completely Slav country and from now onwards is referred to in Byzantine sources as the region of 'Sclavinia'.

At the same time Persian penetration in the Near East continued.

---

[1] Cf. C. Jireček, *Die Romanen in den Städten Dalmatiens* I (1901), 21 ff., and *Geschichte* I, 93 ff.; Šišić, *Povijest* 232; Niederle, *Manuel* 65 f., 103 ff. On the ethnic changes that took place on Byzantine territory, and especially on the question of the Slavs in Greece, cf. the thorough discussion by R. J. H. Jenkins, *Byzantium and Byzantinism*, 21 ff.

[2] Cf. P. Charanis, 'The Chronicle of Monemvasia and the Question of the Slavonic Settlements in Greece', *Dumbarton Oaks Papers* 5 (1950), 141 ff. See also below, p. 193, and note 2.

[3] As was maintained by J. P. Fallmerayer, Geschichte der Halbinsel Morea während des Mittelalters, Stuttgart 1830. From Fallmerayer's day onwards this question has been much discussed in an extensive literature of unequal value, considerably swollen in recent years by the many Greek contributions. Mention should be made of D. A. Zakythinos, Οἱ Σλάβοι ἐν Ἑλλάδι, Athens 1945; A. N. Diomedes, Βυζαντιναὶ Μελέται Β': Αἱ σλαβικαὶ ἐπιδρομαὶ εἰς τὴν Ἑλλάδα καὶ ἡ πολιτικὴ τοῦ Βυζαντίου, Athens 1946; St. Kyriakides, Βυζαντιναὶ Μελέται VI: Οἱ Σλάβοι ἐν Πελοποννήσῳ, Thessalonica 1947. A penetrating and scholarly treatment of the problem will be found in A. A. Vasiliev, 'Slavjane v Grecii', VV 5 (1898), 404-38, 626-70, and M. Vasmer, *Die Slaven in Griechenland, Abh. d Preuss. Akad. d. Wiss.* 1941, Phil.-hist. Kl. 12. The criticisms of D. Georgakas, 'Beiträge zur Deutung als slavisch erklärter Ortsnamen', BZ 41 (1941), 351 ff., even in the cases where his attempted interpretations seem to be plausible or worth serious consideration, do not impair the value of Vasmer's work. Cf. A. Bon, *Le Péloponnèse byzantin jusqu'en* 1204, Paris 1951, which is distinguished by its thoroughness and marked objectivity, and P. Lemerle, 'Une province byzantine: Le Péloponnèse', B 21 (1951), 341 ff. Cf. also the very suggestive treatment by F. Dölger, 'Ein Fall slavischer Einsiedlung im Hinterland von Thessalonike im 10. Jahrhundert', *S.B. d. Bayer. Akad. d. Wiss.*, 1952, H. 1, Munich 1952 (cf. BZ 46 (1953) 210 f.—a reply to Kyriakides); A. Maricq, 'Notes sur les Slaves dans le Péloponnèse et en Bithynie', B 22 (1952), 337 ff.; P. Lemerle, 'Invasions et migrations dans les Balkans depuis la fin de l'époque romaine jusqu'au VIIIe siècle', *Rev. hist.* 211 (1954), 303 ff.

Figure 28: *The Virgin and Child, with Attendant Saints and Angels.* Encaustic icon, Monastery of St. Catherine, Mount Sinai, 6th to 7th centuries. The saints are probably SS. Theodore and George. Photo: University of Michigan.

Figure 29: *Large Footed Censer*. Bronze, 6th to 8th centuries. (ABOVE) Scenes of the Life of Christ surround the bowl; the Crucifixion is visible in the center. Beneath the 3 chain attachments are busts of saints. (BELOW) Encircling the foot is a band filled with 6 flying angels. Within the footed base, and on the bottom of the bowl, is an enthroned figure, possibly Christ. Diam. 4″, ht. 4½″. Malcove Collection, New York. Photos: Geoffrey Clements.

It is true that the enemy was forced to evacuate Caesarea in 611, but the attempted Byzantine counter-attack in Armenia and Syria was an utter failure. The imperial army was badly defeated at Antioch in 613 and as a result the Persians swiftly pushed forward on all fronts. They pressed south and took Damascus; they forced their way north to Cilicia and took the important fortress of Tarsus; and the Byzantines were also driven out of Armenia. A particularly heavy blow was struck at the morale of the Christians when the holy city of Jerusalem was captured by the Persians after a three weeks' siege. For several days the conquered city was given over to fire and massacre, and the church of the Holy Sepulchre, which Constantine had built, was destroyed by fire. This had a shattering effect on Byzantium, particularly as the most treasured of all relics, the Holy Cross, had fallen into Persian hands and been carried off to Ctesiphon. In 615 fresh inroads into Asia Minor were made and part of the Persian army again got as far as the Bosphorus. The enemy now advanced on the capital from two sides, the Persians from the east and the Avars and Slavs from the north. The Emperor himself nearly fell a victim to treachery during a meeting with the Khan of the Avars which took place in Heraclea in June 617.[1] The conquest of Egypt, the richest province of the Empire, began in the spring of 619 and was soon completed, thus seriously imperilling the corn supply of the Byzantine capital.

The Persians were therefore in control of almost the whole of the Near East and it looked as though the old empire of the Achaemenids would be revived, just as a few years earlier it had seemed that Justinian was on the point of restoring the old *imperium romanum*. But defeat came even more quickly to the Persians, and even greater was their downfall than in the case of Byzantium. The terrible years when the Slav and Avar hordes were pouring over the Balkans, and the Persians were penetrating the eastern provinces of the Empire, saw the beginning of the process of reorganization which was to bring fresh strength to Byzantium. Existing sources are too scanty to show more than the main outline of the profound changes which were set in motion at that period in the internal development of the Byzantine Empire. Everything suggests that it was during these critical years that a fundamental change took place in the structure of the Byzantine army and administration, which

---

[1] On the chronology see N. H. Baynes, 'The Date of the Avar Surprise', BZ 21 1912), 110 ff.

resulted in the organization of the Empire into 'themes'. The territory in Asia Minor which still remained untouched by the enemy was
divided into large military zones, called 'themes', and thus the foundations were laid of a system which was to characterize the provincial
administration of the medieval Byzantine state for centuries.[1] The
organization of the provinces into themes meant a final break with
the principles of the administrative system of Diocletian and Constantine, and carried forward a development which had begun with
the organization of the exarchates. Like the exarchates of Ravenna
and Carthage, the themes in Asia Minor were units of military
administration, and they were each under the control of a *strategus*,
who exercised the highest military and civil power in his district.
This did not mean the complete elimination of existing provincial
divisions and organization, which continued for some time within
the framework of the theme, while the proconsul of the theme,
the head of the civil administration, stood next in rank to the
strategus.[2] But is was clear from the outset that the *strategus* was in
supreme command, especially as a single theme included several
of the old provinces.

[1] On the themes see Gelzer, 'Themenverfassung'; Diehl, 'Régime des thèmes';
Uspenskij, 'Voennoe ustrojstvo' (Military organization); E. W. Brooks, 'Arabic Lists of
the Byzantine Themes', JHS 21 (1901), 67–77; Kulakovskij, *Istorija* III, 387–431. Stein,
Studien 117–40 and 'Ein Kapitel' 50–89 are particularly important. See also Honigman,
Ostgrenze 43 ff., 64 ff. During the last few years a considerable number of studies on the
origin of the organization of the themes have appeared, and particular attention has
been given to the question of the date when the first themes originated: A. Pertusi,
Constantino Porfirogenito De thematibus, Vatican City 1952 (commentary to his new
edition, see esp. p. 103 ff.); idem 'Nuova ipotesi sull origine dei "temi" bizantini',
Aevum 28 (1954), 126–50; idem, 'La formation des thèmes byzantines', *Berichte zum XI
Intern. Byzantinisten-Kongress* I, Munich 1958; N. H. Baynes, 'The Emperor Heraclius
and the Military Theme System', EHR 67 (1952), 380 f.; W. Ensslin, 'Der Kaiser
Heraklios und die Themenverfassung, BZ 46 (1953), 362–86; G. Ostrogorsky, 'Sur la
date de la composition du Livre des Thèmes et sur l'époque de la constitution des
premiers thèmes d'Asie Mineure', B 23 (1953), 31–66; idem, *Berichte zum XI. Intern.
Byzantinisten-Kongress*, Korreferate, p. 1–8, Munich 1958; H.-W. Haussig, 'Anfänge der
Themenordnung' in: Altheim-Stiehl, *Finanzgeschichte der Spätantike*, Frankfurt-am-
Main 1957, 82–114; J. Karayannopulos, *Die Entstehung der byzantinischen Themenordnung*,
Munich 1959 (cf. my review in *Vierteljahrschr. f. Sozial-u. Wirtschaftsgesch.* 47 (1960),
261 ff.). For the origin of the word 'theme' cf. S. Kyriakides, EEBS 23 (1953), 392–94
and Ἑλληνικά 13 (1954), 339; F. Dölger, 'Zur Ableitung des byzantinischen Ver-
waltungsterminus θέμα', *Historia* 41 (1955), 189–98. Charanis, 'Some Remarks on the
Changes in Byzantium in the seventh Century', ZRVI 8, 1 (1963), 71 ff., emphasizes the
changes undergone by the Byzantine Empire at the end of the sixth century and during
the seventh century. On the disputed question of the beginning of the establishment of
the themes, Charanis adopts the view put forward in this book. J. Karayannopulos,
'Über die vermeintliche Reformtätigkeit des Kaisers Herakleios', on the other hand,
has recently categorically defended his own quite different views (cf. above and p. 97,
note 1), in particular attempting to show that changes were introduced into the
Byzantine structure of government 'auf jeden Fall nicht unter Herakleios'.

[2] Cf. Stein, 'Ein Kapitel' 70 ff.

The word theme(θέμα) is the normal term for a division of troops and was transferred to the new military zones, which casts significant light on the origin of the new system. It was brought into being by the settlement of troops—the 'themes'—in districts of Asia Minor, and it was for this reason that these areas became themselves known as 'themes'. They were not merely administrative areas, but represented the districts settled by the troops. Inalienable grants of land (called in later sources στρατιωτικὰ κτήματα) were made to the soldiers on condition of hereditary military service.[1] Thus the new system of themes was a development of the older system of *limitanei*, soldiers settled on land in the *limes*, the frontier regions. The system of frontier defence had collapsed under the pressure of hostile invasion, the troops in the *limes* were withdrawn into the heart of Asia Minor, and were settled in the regions which remained under Byzantine rule.[2] Besides the soldiers from the *limes*, the crack regiments of the Byzantine army were also settled in Asia Minor. Thus as early as the reign of Heraclius, the themes of the Opsikion (*Obsequium*) the Armeniakon and the Anatolikon were brought into being, and it is possible that the maritime theme of the Carabisiani on the southern coast of Asia Minor was also set up at this time.[3] It is notable that the development of the system of themes was restricted during this

---

[1] The connection of the theme system with the settlement of troops and the introduction of soldiers' properties was first pointed out by Uspenskij, 'Voennoe ustrojstvo', 199 ff. Without knowing of Uspenskij's work, Stein, *Studien*, 134 ff., came to the same conclusion, and subsequent research on this development has been influenced by his important study. The recent doubts cast on this by Lemerle, 'Histoire Agraire' 219, p. 70 ff., 220, p. 43 ff., and Karayannopulos, op. cit., 15 ff., 72 ff., are quite unjustified. Cf. my comments in 'L'exarchat de Ravenne et l'origine des thèmes byzantins', *VII Corso di cultura sull'arte ravennate e byzantina*, 1960, fasc. 1, 105 ff. Cf. also the well founded criticism by A. P. Každan, VV 16 (1959), 92 ff.

[2] Cf. A. Pertusi, 'La formation des thèmes byzantines', 31, and my own article referred to in the previous note. In view of the obvious relationship between the theme system and the earlier organization of the Roman-Byzantine Empire I see no reason to suppose, as Stein does ('Ein Kapitel' 50 ff.), that Heraclius' system of themes was borrowed from the Persian Empire, however great the similarities may be. The same applies to Darkó's theory that the organization of the themes may be traced back to Turanian models, cf. E. Darkó, 'Influences touraniennes sur l'évolution de l'art militaire des Grecs, des Romains et des Byzantins', B 10 (1935), 443 ff., 12 (1937), 119 ff.; 'La militarizzazione dell'Impero bizantino', *Studi biz. e neoell.* 5 (1939), 88 ff.; 'Le role des peuples nomades cavaliers dans la transformation de l'Empire romain aux premiers siècles du Moyen Âge', B 18 (1948), 85 ff.

[3] The name of the theme Opsikion (Lat. *obsequium*) clearly shows that regiments of guards were settled here. A similar origin is revealed by the names of the themes Bucellarion and Optimaton, which were later formed by dividing the theme Opsikion. In the same way, the themes Armeniakon and Anatolikon are not geographical descriptions but the districts where troops of that name settled, especially as the theme Armeniakon was not in Armenian territory, while the theme Anatolikon lay in the western part of Asia Minor. Similarly the later theme Thracesion was the district where troops moved from Thrace to Asia Minor were settled (cf. p. 100, n. 3 below).

first stage to Asia Minor. In the Balkan peninsula the introduction of themes did not seem possible at that time, thus illustrating all too clearly the extent of the disasters which had befallen the Empire throughout this region. It was not until a good deal later on, and then only gradually, that Byzantine administration (including the theme system) could be reintroduced into certain areas of the Balkans, especially the coastal regions (cf. below, p. 132 ff. and p. 193 ff.).

The system of themes was the basis on which an effective native army was built up, and it freed the Empire from the expensive necessity of recruiting unreliable foreign mercenaries from a supply that was very often unequal to the demand. Besides the soldiers of the frontier army, besides the crack Byzantine regiments, drawn from the warlike races of Asia Minor and the Caucasian area, there were also a considerable number of Byzantine peasants who became soldier-farmers, endowed with small-holdings in return for under-taking military obligations. Many Slavs were later transplanted to Asia Minor by the government and settled in the themes as *stratiotai* (cf. below, p. 117 and p. 130). In this way a remedy was found for a method of recruitment whose uncertainties had often landed the Empire in great difficulties, and by making use of the influx of fresh blood vigorous development took place within the framework of sound military and administrative reorganization. The new army drawn from the themes consisted of soldier-farmers who were settled on their own land, and whose soldiers' farms provided the economic means whereby they were maintained and equipped. Later sources show that when they were called out for military service they had to appear armed and each with his horse.[1] It is true that they did also receive a very modest amount of fixed pay.[2] This new system afforded great relief to the treasury[3] and the granting of these soldiers' farms also helped to strengthen the position of the free small-holder (cf. below, p. 133 ff.).

Together with the reorganization of provincial government, important changes were taking place in the central administration which were to be of lasting significance for the Byzantine state and marked a clear break with the earlier tradition. The pretorian prefecture, which had been one of the main features of early Byzan-

[1] 'La vie de S. Philarète', B 9 (1934), 126.
[2] Ibn Hordadbeh, ed. de Goeje, pp. 84 and 85; cf. also *De cerim.* 654 ff. and 667 ff.
[3] It has been calculated that the total expenditure on the army in the middle Byzantine period was approximately 'half that paid out in the sixth century for an army which was not much larger but which was certainly worse', Stein, *Studien* 143.

tine administration, lost its importance, and from now on it was reduced to a mere figurehead. Its place was taken by the theme, and in those regions where it had not yet been possible to introduce the theme system hostile inroads had temporarily dislocated all law and order. As the Byzantine government gradually regained control over these districts, they too were organized into themes, so that eventually the prefecture ceased to exist even on paper (cf. below, p. 132 f. and p. 193 f.). The extensive financial system of the prefecture disintegrated and was replaced by a number of independent departments of finance. Generally speaking, this marked the beginning of a retrograde process in the central administrative system. The tremendous growth of the pretorian prefecture during the previous centuries (cf. above, p. 35 f.) had meant that the old departments of finance —the *comitiva sacrarum largitionum* and the *comitiva rerum privatarum*— had been allowed to decay, and in order to satisfy its own growing financial needs the prefecture had appropriated for itself the receipts of the *res privatae* and especially those of the *largitiones*.[1] The impoverished *comitiva sacrarum largitionum* had to be continually supplied from the imperial privy purse, the *sacellium*, and as a result at the beginning of the seventh century the *sacellarius* (the keeper of the privy purse) completely took over the function of the *comes sacrarum largitionum*, and apparently was also responsible for the work of the weakened *comitiva rerum privatarum*. With the collapse of the unwieldy and inflated financial department of the pretorian prefecture, fresh arrangements were made.[2] The various offices of its chancery—the στρατιωτικόν, the γενικὴ τράπεζα, and the ἰδικὴ τράπεζα—were given independent status, and their former heads appear as the logothetes τοῦ στρατιωτικοῦ, τοῦ γενικοῦ and τοῦ ἰδικοῦ in charge of these new boards of finance.[3] In addition to the logothetes on the financial side, there was later on the λογοθέτης τοῦ δρόμου, who really took

---

[1] This development has been elucidated by Stein, *Studien* 144 ff. Cf. also Stein's comments in *Ztschr. d. Savigny-Stift.*, Rom. Abt. 41 (1920), 239 ff.; *Rhein Mus.* 74 (1925), 389 ff.; *Geschichte* I, 340 f.

[2] Stein, *Studien* 147: 'The old financial departments, particularly the *largitiones*, were killed by malnutrition, but the pretorian prefecture shortly afterwards died of the opposite malady for it literally burst from gross overnutrition'.

[3] A logothete, whom Stein, 'Ein Kapitel' 74 f., establishes as the λογοθέτης τοῦ στρατιωτικοῦ, appears in the year 626 in *Chron. Paschale* 721. There is also evidence of the λογοθέτης τοῦ γενικοῦ at the end of the seventh century, cf. Theophanes 365, 367, 369 and Nicephorus 37. Cf. Bury, *Admin. System* 86. The last certain mention of a Praetorian Prefect of the East comes from the year 629: Zepos, *Jus* I, 37. Cf. Stein, 'Ein Kapitel' 72 ff. The τοῦ πραιτωρίου ἔπαρχος mentioned by Nicephorus 38, 15 in 695 was certainly not Praetorian Prefect of the East, but commander of the Praetorium in Constantinople.

over the work of the former *magister officiorum*, and gradually became the chief minister in the Empire.[1]

For centuries to come it was the themes in provincial administration and the logothetes in the central departments which characterized Byzantine government. The results of the extensive reforms were soon apparent. The militarization of imperial administration and the reorganization of the armed forces explain what otherwise appears to be an incredible change of fortune in the war with Persia in the twenties of the seventh century. Past defeats were redeemed by miraculous victories. The prostrate Empire rose again and the enemy which had been advancing so triumphantly now suffered an overwhelming defeat.

The powerful Byzantine Church contributed a good deal towards the imperial successes. For the impending struggle she had put her wealth at the disposal of the impoverished state, and the war opened in an atmosphere of religious fervour unknown in the earlier period. It may be described as the first characteristically medieval war and the forerunner of the later crusades. The Emperor placed himself in person at the head of his army, and during his absence from the capital he appointed the Patriarch Sergius and the Patrician Bonus as regents for his son, who was still a minor. In this respect, as in many others, he was following the example of the Emperor Maurice, who had personally led an expedition against the Avars. This was most unusual, and Heraclius, again like Maurice, had to face the vigorous opposition of his councillors,[2] for since the time of Theodosius I no Emperor before Maurice had taken the field in person.

At the price of heavy tribute Heraclius first signed a peace treaty with the Avars so that he might be able to transport his troops unharassed from Europe to Asia.[3] After attending a solemn celebration of the liturgy, he left the capital on Easter Monday, 5 April 622.[4] In

[1] The first known λογοθέτης τοῦ δρόμου fell in 759/60 in the Bulgarian war, Theophanes 431. Cf. Stein, *Studien* 144; Dölger, 'Kodikellos' 54.

[2] Cf. Theophyl. Sim. 218 and Theophanes 268 (for Maurice) and George Pisides, *Exped. Pers.* I, 104 ff. (for Heraclius).

[3] Theophanes 302 (under the year 621): μετήνεγκε τὰ στρατεύματα τῆς Εὐρώπης ἐπὶ τὴν Ἀσίαν. The founding of the later theme τῶν Θρακησίων, at that time a *turma*, i.e. a part of the theme Anatolikon, is clearly connected with the settling of the European troops in Asia Minor (as Kulakovskij, *Istorija*, III, 58, has already observed).

[4] For the Persian expeditions of Heraclius see Pernice, *Eraclio* 111 ff., and Kulakovskij, *Istorija* III, 57 ff., and also the detailed studies by Gerland, BZ 3 (1898), 330 ff., and especially N. H. Baynes, EHR 19 (1904), 694 ff., and 27 (1912), 287 ff., also BZ 26 (1926), 55 f., opposing A. Jülicher, *Harnack-Festgabe* (1921), 121–33. See also J. A. Manandjan, Maršruty persidskich pochodov imperatora Iraklija (The itineraries of the Persian campaigns of the Emperor Heraclius), VV 3 (1950), 133 ff. Summary by N. H. Baynes, CMH II (1913), 292 ff.

Asia Minor he set out for the district of the themes, and here he got together his army and spent the entire summer training the fresh troops.[1] He himself had concentrated on the study of military science and developed new tactical methods.[2] The use of cavalry in the Byzantine army became increasingly important, and Heraclius seemed to have attached special significance to the lightly-armed mounted archery.[3] The real campaign did not begin until the autumn when by skilful manœuvring the Emperor forced a way to Armenia. This compelled the Persians to abandon their positions in the mountain passes of Asia Minor, and they followed the imperial army 'like a dog on a chain'.[4] The two forces met on Armenian soil and the result was a decisive victory of the Byzantines over the great Persian general Šahrbarâz. The first goal was reached: Asia Minor was cleared of the enemy.

The threatening attitude of the Avar Khan made it essential for the Emperor to return to Constantinople. The tribute paid to the Avars was then raised and near relatives of the Emperor were sent to the Khan as hostages,[5] so that Heraclius was able to resume the war with Persia by March 623. In spite of the defeat of the previous year, Chosroes II refused to consider a truce, and he sent the Emperor a letter full of the most insulting expressions and blasphemous utter-

---

[1] Theophanes 303 (under the year 622): ἐντεῦθεν Δὲ ἐπὶ τὰς τῶν θεμάτων χώρας ἀφικόμενος, συνέλεγε τὰ στρατόπεδα καὶ προσετίθει αὐτοῖς νέαν στρατείαν. The expression 'the districts of the themes' shows that the process of establishing troops (themes) in specific areas of Asia Minor has already begun by this time. This extremely important passage, which Theophanes undoubtedly drew from a contemporary source, is characteristic of the initial stage of the organization of the themes. Soon afterwards the names of individual themes appear: in 626 the contemporary *Easter Chronicle* (*Chron. paschale* 715, 20) mentions a Comes of the Opsikon (for ὀψαρίου read Ὀψικίου: cf. C. Diehl, BZ 9, 677) and in January 627 the chronicle of Theophanes (Thoeph. 325, 3) mentions a *turmarch* of the Armeniakon. Thus the setting up of the system of themes was begun before the victory of Heraclius over Persia, and not after as Stein believed (also W. Ensslin in the article cited above, p. 96, n. 1), in contradiction to his entirely justifiable view that the setting up of the themes provides the only possible explanation for the 'ans Wunderbare grenzenden Umschwung' in the war between Byzantium and Persia (*Studien*, 133). Even less acceptable is the view of A. Pertusi and N. H. Baynes (in the works cited above, p. 96, n. 1), that the setting up of the theme system did not begin until the second half of the seventh century. For a more detailed discussion see my own articles referred to in the same note.
[2] Georg. Pisides, *Heraclias* II, 108 ff., ed. Pertusi, p. 256.
[3] Cf. E. Darkó, 'Die militärischen Reformen des Kaisers Herakleios', *Bull. de l'Inst. archéol. bulgare* 9 (1935), 110 ff.; 'Influences touraniennes sur l'évolution de l'art militaire des Grecs, des Romains et des Byzantins', B 10 (1935), 443 ff., 12 (1937), 119 ff.; 'Le rôle des peuples nomades cavaliers dans la transformation de l'Empire romain aux premiers siècles du Moyen Âge', ib. 18 (1948), 85 ff.
[4] Georg. Pisides, *Exped. Pers.* II, 357, ed. Pertusi, p. 114.
[5] Cf. Pernice, *Eraclio* 121. Also Kulakovskij, *Istorija* III, 65, note 4.

ances against the Christian faith.[1] Passing through Cappadocia, Heraclius again moved towards Armenia. Dvin was taken by storm and razed to the ground, and many other cities suffered the same fate. The Emperor then made a drive towards the south and marched on Ganzak, the capital of the first Sassanid Ardašir and an important religious centre for Persia. Chosroes was forced to fly from the city, which fell into the hands of the Byzantines, and the great Persian sanctuary, the fire-temple of Zoroaster, was destroyed in revenge for the plundering of Jerusalem. Heraclius then retired with countless prisoners to winter behind the Araxes. Here he got into touch with the Christian Caucasian tribes and was able to reinforce his army with Lazi, Abasgi and Iberians. The position, however, was difficult, and he spent the following year on Armenian territory in an exhausting struggle against the attacking Persians. He did not succeed in the attempt to break through to Persia. In 625 he tried to reach enemy soil by means of a détour through Cilicia, but again without any decisive result, and in spite of some victories he withdrew through Sebastea to the region of Pontus as winter approached.[2]

The Persians were now able to take the offensive again, and in 626 Constantinople had to face the terrible danger of a two-faced attack from the Persians and Avars. It was this which Heraclius had always feared and had tried to avert by buying off the Avars with humiliating concessions. Šahrbarâz pushed through Asia Minor at the head of a large army, occupied Chalcedon and encamped on the Bosphorus. Soon after this the Avar Khan and his hordes of Avars, Slavs, Bulgars and Gepids appeared before Constantinople and besieged the city by land and sea. The Patriarch Sergius kept up the religious fervour of the people by means of sermons, night vigils and solemn processions, while the valiant garrison beat back all enemy attacks. Byzantine superiority at sea finally decided the issue. During the final onslaught on 10 August the Slav fleet was defeated, and as a result their land forces were thrown back with heavy losses and forced to retreat in wild disorder.[3] The downfall of the Avars

[1] This has been preserved in Sebeos, trans. Macler 79. The inscription of the letter reads: 'Chosrov, chéri des dieux, maître et roi de toute la terre, fils du grand Armazd, à notre serviteur, imbécile et infâme, Héraclius'.
[2] Kulakovskij, *Istorija* III, 72 and 74, rightly stresses that this renewed retreat indicates that the campaigns of the years 624 and 625 were less successful for the Byzantine Emperor than would appear from the account of Theophanes 312 f.
[3] A full account of the siege of Constantinople, based on all available sources, is given by F. Barišič, 'Le siège de Constantinople par les Avares et les Slaves en 626', B 24 (1954), 371 ff.

meant the failure of the Persian invasion, and Šahrbarâz had to evacuate Chalcedon and retreat with his army to Syria, while Šahin, the second-in-command, was decisively beaten by the Emperor's brother, Theodore. The critical hour was past and the great Byzantine counter-attack could be launched.

At the time when his capital was in deadly peril, Heraclius and his army had been in distant Lazica. He now negotiated an alliance with the Khazars, as he had earlier done with the Caucasian peoples, and the resulting Byzantino-Khazar understanding became from now onwards one of the main features of imperial eastern diplomacy. As allies of the imperial troops the Khazars fought the Persians on Caucasian and Armenian soil. In the autumn of 627 the Emperor began his great advance south into the heart of the enemy's territory. Here he had to rely on his own resources, since the Khazars could not stand up to the rigours of the campaign and return home. In spite of this, at the beginning of December Heraclius stood before Nineveh. It was here that the deadly battle was fought which really decided the outcome of the conflict between the Persians and Byzantines. The Persian army was practically wiped out and Byzantium had won the war. Heraclius continued his victorious advance and at the beginning of 628 he occupied Dastagerd, the Persian king's favourite residence from which he had had to beat a hasty retreat. In the spring of 628 events occurred in Persia which made any further fighting unnecessary. Chosroes was deposed and murdered and his son Kavādh-Široe, who succeeded him, immediately came to terms with the Byzantine Emperor. As a result of their own successes and the total collapse of the Persians, the Byzantines secured the return of all territory which had formerly belonged to them, and Armenia, Roman Mesopotamia, Syria, Palestine and Egypt were restored. A few months later Široe on his death-bed named the Byzantine Emperor as his son's guardian: Chosroes II had once called the Emperor his slave, but the position was now reversed, and Široe declared his son and heir to be the slave of the Byzantine Emperor.[1]

After six years' absence Heraclius returned to his capital. His son Constantine, the Patriarch Sergius, the clergy, the senate and the people received him on the coast of Asia Minor with olive branches and lighted candles, with hymns and acclamations of joy. While the Roman provinces were being cleared of Persians, Heraclius went to

---

[1] According to Nicephorus 20 f. he wrote to Heraclius: 'In the same way as you say that your God was presented to the old man Symeon, so I present your slave, my son, into your hands'.

Jerusalem in the spring of 630. Here on 21 March amid great rejoicing he once more set up the Holy Cross won back from the Persians,[1] and by this solemn act symbolized the victorious conclusion of the first great holy war of Christendom.

The two foes before whom Byzantium had once trembled now lay prostrate. The struggle at Nineveh had crushed the Persian might, and the battle of Constantinople had brought the pride of the Avars to the dust. This latter victory had its repercussions far beyond the boundaries of the Byzantine Empire. It was a signal for the tribes who had been living under the domination of the Avar Khan, particularly the innumerable Slavs, to rise up and shake off the Avar yoke, and as a result of this revolt against the Avars the first real Slav empire was set up at this time under the leadership of Samo.[2] Some years later the Bulgar tribes north of the Black Sea and the Caspian Sea broke away from Avar control under their ruler Kuvrat. In his struggle against the Avars, Kuvrat had Byzantine support: he made an alliance with the Emperor Heraclius, was given the title of Patrician and received Christian baptism in Constantinople.[3] Among the various changes which took place at this time were the migrations of the Serbs and Croats of which Constantine Porphyrogenitus has left a detailed account.[4] They also came to an understanding with Byzantium and freed themselves from the control of the declining Avar power. They left their earlier home beyond the Carpathians and with the consent of the Emperor Heraclius they moved into the Balkan peninsula. After defeating the Avars, the Croats established themselves in the north-west regions of the Balkans. The neighbouring districts to the south-east were occupied by the Serbs.[5] Thus the Slav element in the Balkans received considerable reinforcement. The Emperor Constantine VII was fond of

[1] On the chronology see Kulakovskij, *Istorija* III, 367 ff. Cf. also A. Frolow, 'La Vraie Croix et les expeditions d'Heraclius en Perse', REB 11 (1953), 88 ff.

[2] On the problems concerning the rise of Samo's empire see B. Grafenauer, 'Novejša literatura o Samu in njeni problemi' (Recent literature on Samo and its problems), *Zgodovinski Časopis* 4 (1950), 151 ff.

[3] Nicephorus 24, 9, who also states (p. 12, 20) that Kuvrat's uncle Organa, the founder of the federation of Bulgarian tribes in the northern Caucasus, visited Constantinople in 619, accepted Christianity and was given the title of Patrician. Apparently Kuvrat was amongst his followers on that occasion and was left behind in Constantinople as a hostage; John of Nikiu (ed. Zotenberg, p. 460) records that Kuvrat grew up at the imperial court and accepted Christianity while he was still a child. Cf. G. Ostrogorsky, 'The Byzantine Empire in the World of the Seventh Century', DOP 13 (1959), 15 ff.

[4] *De adm. imp.*, c. 29–36, pp. 122–64 (ed. Moravcsik-Jenkins).

[5] The reliability of this account has been criticized by E. Dümmler, *S.B. d. Wiener Akad.* 20 (1856), 357 ff., by F. Rački, *Knijževnik* 1 (1864), 36 ff., and *Rad Jugosl. Akad.*

repeating that after their arrival in the Balkans the Serbs and Croats recognized the overlordship of the Byzantine Empire and in view of the situation after the Byzantine victory over the Avars and Persians this was not improbable. But too much importance should not, however, be attached to Byzantine claims of overlordship over the Slav tribes who were then establishing themselves in the Balkans, and there was in any case no question of any real restoration of Byzantine authority in these areas. But it is certainly true that the final disappearance of the Avar raids brought a very considerable measure of relief to Byzantium.

Brilliant as his military successes were, the significance of Heraclius' work does not lie in his foreign policy alone. A few years later

52 (1880), 141 ff., and especially by V. Jagić, *Archiv f. slav. Philol.* 17 (1895), 47 ff., with the result that it has been generally accepted—contrary to the account of Constantine Porphyrogentius—that the Croats and Serbs penetrated into the Balkans about the year 600 together with the other Slav tribes. In spite of the objections of certain scholars, notably K. Grot, *Izvestija Konstantina Bagrannorodnogo o Serbach i Chorvatach* (The evidence of Constantine Porphyrogenitus concerning the Serba and Croats) (1880), K. Klajic, *Povest Hrvata* I (History of Croatia) (1899), 30ff., and *Rad. Jugosl. Akad.* 130 (1897), 11 ff., N. Nodilo, *Historija serdnjega vijeka* (History of the Middle Ages), III (1905), 433 ff., this view had had the support of the highest authorities in the fields of Slav history and philology, including K. Jireček, L. Niederle, St. Stanojević, F. Šišić. Recently there has been a reaction and it has been pointed out that there are not sufficient grounds for rejecting the account of Constantine VII which, though embroidered with legendary details, is in essence thoroughly reliable. Cf. the informative article by D. Anastasijević in: S. Stanojević, *Narodna Enciklopedija* IV (1929) 81 ff., who himself defends the trustworthiness of Porphyrogenitus (cf. also his article in *Narodna Enciklopedija* III, 607 ff.). The study of the problem has been advanced by the important research of L. Hauptmann (cf. especially his article 'Seoba Hrvata i Srba' (The migration of the Croats and Serbs), *Jugosl. Istor. Časopis* 3 (1937), 30 ff.). Of particular value are the comments by B. Grafenauer, "Prilog kritici izveštaja Konstantina Porfirogenita o doseljenju Hrvata' (A contribution to the critical evaluation of the information given by Constantine Porphyrogenitus on the immigration of the Croats), *Hist. Zbornik* 5 (1952), 1–56, who in many respects follows Hauptmann, but who rightly rejects his theory of the Caucasian origin of the Serbs and Croats, and of the origin of the Croatian aristocracy. Cf. also F. Dvornik, *The Making of the Central and Eastern Europe*, London, 1949, 215 ff. and *The Slavs, their Early History and Civilization*, Boston, 1956, 62 ff., and also the stimulating discussion by H. Grégoire, 'L'origine et le nom des Croates et des Serbes', B 17 (1944/5), 88 ff., who provides a much fuller list of sources as the basis of the whole investigation, though one cannot agree with him when he tries to relate the name 'Croat' to 'Kuvrat', and certainly not when he would like to derive the word 'Serb' from 'servus', as does Constantine VII. Cf. instead Grafenauer, op. cit. and A. Maricq, B 22 (1952), 345 ff. Similar suggestions concerning the name Croat can also be found in Bury, *Later Rom. Empire* II (1st ed., 275 f.) and Howorth, *Journ. of the Anthropological Inst. of Great Britain and Ireland* II (1882), 224 ff. An excellent summary of the whole literature on this problem up to approximately 1925 is given by Šišić, *Povijest*, 236–65, though his criticisms are coloured by his own 'anti-Constantinian' point of view. Cf. also the bibliography in *Istorija naroda Jugoslavije* (A history of the peoples of Yugoslavia) I (1953), 101–3. A particularly important recent contribution is that of B. Ferjančić, *Vizantiski izvori* II, who translates everything Constantine Porphyrogenitus has to say concerning the South Slavs into Serbo-Croat, and gives an extensive commentary, in which he discusses all the previous literature. See also F. Dvornik in *Constantine Porphyrogenitus: De Administrando Imperio*, II, *Commentary*, London, 1962, 94 ff.

his conquests in the East were to be lost to the Arabs, but what did survive was his new military and administrative organization. It was indeed on these foundations that Byzantine power in the following centuries was built up, and it was only with the collapse of this system that the Byzantine polity began to disintegrate. The themes were the backbone of the medieval Byzantine state.

The age of Heraclius marked a cultural as well as a political turning point in the history of East Rome. It was now that the Roman period ended and Byzantine history properly speaking began. Emphasis on the Greek element and the strength of ecclesiastical influence combined to give the Empire a new appearance. The early Byzantine state had clung with astonishing tenacity to Latin as the official language and it only yielded slowly and reluctantly to the steady predominance of Greek, without making any open and decisive change. The existence of one language for administration and another as the vernacular was characteristic of the early Byzantine period, and in practically all government circles, as well as in the army, the official tongue was Latin which was not understood by the overwhelming majority of the people in the eastern provinces. Heraclius put an end to this state of affairs and Greek, the medium of the people and the Church, became the official language of the Byzantine Empire. Freed from any artificially imposed restraint, Hellenization developed even more rapidly, and by the next generation a knowledge of Latin was rare, even in educated circles.[1]

Under the influence of this Hellenization an important change, which was at the same time a simplification, was made in the imperial title in the Byzantine Empire. Heraclius gave up the complicated Latin form of address, and following popular Greek usage he took the title of βασιλεύς. Thus the royal title of the ancient Greek kings, which had hitherto only been used unofficially for the Byzantine Emperor, now replaced the Roman titles, *imperator, caesar, augustus*. In future the Byzantine Emperor was officially designated as Basileus and this was recognized as the actual imperial title.[2] It was this title

---

[1] Cf. H. Zilliacus, *Zum Kampf der Weltsprachen im oströmischen Reich*, Helsingfors 1935, 36 ff. See also above p. 57, note 1.

[2] The title of Basileus first appears in the novel of 629 whose inscription runs: Ἡράκλειος καὶ Ἡράκλειος νέος Κωνσταντῖνος, πιστοὶ ἐν Χριστῷ βασιλεῖς (Zepos, *Jus* I, 36). In the first years of his reign Heraclius used the old Roman title as his predecessors had done, and the designation then read: αὐτοκράτορες καίσαρες Φλάβιοι Ἡράκλειος καὶ Ἡράκλειος νέος Κωνσταντῖνος πιστοὶ ἐν Χριστῷ αὔγουστοι (ibid. 33, cf. also p. 27 under the year 612). The title of Basileus had thus replaced the titles αὐτοκράτωρ, καῖσαρ and αὔγουστος (i.e. *imperator, caesar* and *augustus*) and the designation Flavius had also lapsed. Cf. L. Bréhier, 'L'origine des titres impériaux à Byzance', BZ 15 (1906),

which Heraclius gave to his son and co-Emperor, Heraclius νέος Constantine, and then later to his second son, Heraclonas. From now on until the downfall of the Empire it was held by all Byzantine Emperors and co-Emperors, while the title of Caesar finally lost its imperial significance.

The institution of a system of co-Emperors in Byzantium was of special value in securing the succession. Here, as in Rome, this was not regulated by law, and so the Byzantine Emperors therefore adopted the practice of designating their desired successor as co-Emperor during their own lifetime. This co-Emperor wore the crown and was accorded the imperial title, his portrait often appeared on the coinage side by side with that of the senior Emperor, and he was often named in imperial edicts, while he was known unofficially among the people as the δεύτερος or μικρὸς βασιλεύς. When the senior ruler died, he succeeded to full powers as Emperor, and in this way the succession could be kept in the imperial family and the continuity of the dynasty assured. Nevertheless, it took some time before the hereditary system was finally established, and Heraclius himself introduced complications into the system by designating his second son, as well as his first, as co-Emperor and successor to the throne.[1]

The recovery of the eastern provinces once more confronted the Empire with the problem of monophysitism. The Patriarch Sergius had no delusions about the gravity of the situation and he made unceasing efforts to restore peace in the Church. He made use of the doctrine of a single energy in Christ which had arisen in the eastern provinces of the Empire, for the assumption that the divine and human natures of Christ had one active force (ἐνέργεια) seemed to offer a compromise between the dogma of Chalcedon and mono-

161 ff., and Ostrogorsky, *Avtokrator* 99 ff. The erroneous view exists amongst scholars that the change of title under Heraclius was originally connected with the overthrow of the Persian Empire and the conquest of the only ruler to whom the Byzantines had apparently conceded the title of Basileus, apart from their own Emperors. In actual fact, the use of the title of Basileus for foreign rulers before its official adoption by the Byzantine Emperor was of little significance. Basileus had at that time the same meaning as *rex* and in the early Byzantine period, when the Byzantine ruler had the official title of *Imperator*, it was used not only for the Persian monarch, but for such as Attila and the kings of Armenia and Ethiopia, and sometimes, alternating with other designations, for the Germanic rulers and even the leaders of the Abasgi and Zechi (R. Helm, *Archiv für Urkundenf.* 12 (1932), 383 f., note 2, has very skilfully set out the evidence). It was the Byzantine Emperor's official adoption of the title of Basileus that created the essential difference between *rex* and βασιλεύς, for the latter now had the same meaning as *Imperator*.

[1] On the co-Emperor in Byzantium cf. Bury, *Constitution* 12 ff., and my arguments in Kornemann, *Doppelprinzipat* 166 ff. On the titles of the co-Emperors cf. Dölger, BZ 33 (1933), 136 ff., and Ostrogorsky, *Avtokrator* 107 ff.

physitism.[1] Sergius therefore supported the teaching of a single energy, and he entered into negotiation with the eastern churches. The Patriarch's action seemed to be justified on political grounds, for there was no doubt that the longstanding doctrinal differences between Constantinople and the monophysite East had contributed considerably to Persian successes. Heraclius himself also adopted this same teaching. During his eastern campaigns he had already discussed the question of ecclesiastical union with various church-men in those areas, particularly in Armenia. After the reconquest of the monophysite provinces, negotiations were continued on a more extensive scale and with increased vigour, for the necessity of coming to terms now seemed even more urgent than before. A promising beginning was made, and union seemed assured, not only in Armenia, but in Syria, as well as in Egypt where Cyrus, Patriarch since 631, gave the project his strong support. Pope Honorius also gave his sanction to the policy pursued by Sergius and Cyrus. But disillusion-ment was not long delayed. In Syria, and more particularly in Egypt, the work of reconciliation had only been achieved under pressure, and the opposition from both orthodox and monophysites grew daily stronger. The champion of orthodox opposition was the monk Sophronius; he had become Patriarch of Jerusalem in 634 and was famous for his powers of oratory. He relentlessly scourged the new doctrine as a bastard form of monophysitism and a corruption of the orthodox doctrine of Chalcedon. Pressure from this opposition, and the views expressed by Pope Honorius, who showed that he had doubts about the teaching of the single energy, though he accepted, however, a single will in Christ, apparently led Sergius to modify his position. He relegated the single energy to the back-ground, and now propounded the doctrine of a single will (θέλημα) in Christ. This new monothelete formula, set out in an edict drafted by Sergius, was promulgated by the Emperor in 638 under the name of the *Ecthesis* and put up in the narthex of Hagia Sophia. The leaders of Church and State supported monotheletism, and with the death of Sergius on 9 December 638 the ardent monothelete Pyrrhus took his place as Patriarch of Constantinople. It was, however, clear that the *Ecthesis* was a futile effort. It was rejected both by the orthodox and by the monophysites and was strongly repudiated by Honorius'

[1] G. Owsepian, *Die Entstehungsgeschichte des Monotheletismus*, Leipzig 1897; Pargoire, *L'Église byzantine de 527 à 847* (1905), 157 ff.; Duchesne, *L'Église au VIe siècle* (1925), 381 ff.; V. Grumel, 'Recherches sur l'histoire du Monothélisme', EO 27 (1928), 6-16, 257-77, 28 (1929), 272-82, 29 (1930), 16-28; Beck, *Kirche*, 292 ff.

successors in Rome. As a means of reconciliation monotheletism had failed just as badly as the combined efforts of Church and State to produce a compromise in earlier centuries. As in the case of previous attempts at reconciliation, it had only produced fresh hostility and increased confusion. The situation was further complicated by the Arab conquest of Syria and Palestine, both of which had been occupied by the enemy by 638, while Egypt was soon to suffer the same inevitable fate. Thus monotheletism had failed in its political aim, and the religious ferment in the eastern provinces which had assisted the Persians was now to do the same in the cause of the Arabs.

Figure 30: *The Dome of the Rock.* Jerusalem. Originally built by the Caliph Abdalmalik at the end of the 7th century. Photo: Erica Cruikshank.

2. THE PERIOD OF THE ARAB INVASIONS
THE LAST YEARS OF HERACLIUS: CONSTANS II

General bibliography: G. C. Caetani, *Annali dell'Islam* I–VIII, Milan 1905–18; Cl. Huart, *Histoire des Arabes* I, Paris 1912; C. Becker, 'The Expansion of the Saracens', CMH II (1913), 329–64, 365–90; idem, *Vom Werden und Wesen der Islamischen Welt* I, Leipzig 1924; A. J. Butler, *The Arab Conquest of Egypt and the last thirty years of the Roman Dominion*, Oxford 1902; E. W. Brooks, 'The Successors of Heraclius to 717', CMH II (1913), 391–417; idem, 'The Arabs in Asia Minor (641–750), from Arabic Sources', JHS 8 (1898), 182 ff.; J. Wellhausen, 'Die Kämpfe der Araber mit den Romäern in der Zeit der Umajiden', *Nachr. d. Kgl. Ges. d. Wiss. Göttingen* 1901, pp. 414–47; H. Manandean, 'Les invasions arabes en Arménie', B 18 (1948), 163–95; T. Kaestner, *De imperio Constantini III (641–668)*, Leipzig 1907.

The very year in which the victories of the Byzantine Empire over the Persians began is the Muslim year of the Hijra. While Heraclius was defeating the Persian Empire, Muhammed was laying the foundations of the political and religious unity of the Arab world. His work was undeveloped and devoid of intellectual quality, but was full of primitive energy and dynamic in the extreme. A few years after his death the great Arab movement began and its elemental force drove the Arabs to leave their barren country. Their aim was not so much the conversion of men to the new faith as the subjugation of fresh territory and the establishment of their control over the unbeliever.[1] The first victims of this lust for conquest were the two neighbouring empires: Persia went under at the first attack and Byzantium lost her eastern provinces scarcely ten years after the death of the Prophet. The conflict between the Persians and the Byzantines had weakened both empires and so in a sense prepared the way for the Arabs. After Heraclius' victories, Persia had been left in a state of utter chaos; one usurper succeeded another and the backbone of the Sassanid empire was broken. But in spite of her successes, Byzantium too had exhausted her resources in the long exacting struggle. At the same time irreconcilable religious differences had raised up a wall of hatred between Constantinople and her eastern provinces, the separatist tendencies of the Syrians and Copts had been strengthened, and their willingness to defend the Empire finally undermined. Abuses in the military organization of these

---

[1] Cf. C. Becker, *Vom Werden und Wesen der Islamischen Welt* I (1924).

districts and disruption in administrative circles, due to the over-powerful influence of the big landowners, helped to ease the task of the conquerors, particularly in Egypt.[1]

Led by the great conqueror, Caliph Omar, by 634 the Arabs had broken into imperial territory and advanced with rapid success through the province so recently won back from the Persians. They completely routed the Byzantine army at the famous battle of Jarmuk on 20 August 636, and thus Byzantine resistance was broken and the fate of Syria decided. Antioch, the capital of Syria, and most of the other cities in the country, surrendered to the victorious enemy without putting up any fight. In Palestine resistance was stronger. Under the leadership of the Patriarch Sophronius, Jerusalem had long defied the invader, but the Holy City was finally compelled by the rigours of the siege to open its gates to Omar. Meanwhile the Persian Empire was subdued and Byzantine Mesopotamia taken (639–40). The Arabs followed this up by attacking Armenia and taking the great Armenian stronghold of Dvin (October 640).[2] At the same time they began their conquest of Egypt.

Heraclius had led all the expeditions against Persia in person, but in contrast to this he took no real part in the fighting against the Arabs. At first he had tried to direct operations from Antioch, but after the battle of Jarmuk he gave up the cause for lost and completely withdrew. His life's work collapsed before his eyes. The heroic struggle against Persia seemed to be utterly wasted, for his victories here had only prepared the way for the Arab conquest. Over the territory which he had won back from the Sassanids after incredibly heavy fighting, the Arab invasion now spread like an irresistible flood. The Holy Land which he had hoped to rescue for Christendom was again in the hands of the infidel. This cruel turn of fortune broke the aged Emperor both in spirit and in body. After his return from Syria he remained for some time in the palace of Hieria on the coast of Asia Minor. He dreaded the crossing to Constantinople for he had a phobia about looking at the sea, and it was not until a conspiracy had been discovered in the city that he pulled himself together and overcame his fear sufficiently to cross the Bosphorus to his capital on a ship's deck covered with sand and foliage.

---

[1] Cf. J. Maspero, *L'Organisation militaire de l'Égypte byzantine* (1912), 12 off.; M. Gelzer, *Studien zur byzantinischen Verwaltung Ägyptens* (1909), 82 ff.

[2] Cf. H. Manandean, 'Les invasions arabes en Arménie', B 18 (1948), 163 ff.

The private life of Heraclius had also turned out tragically. On the day of his coronation he had married Fabia-Eudocia, who bore him a daughter and a son, Heraclius νέος Constantine. She suffered from epilepsy and died a few months after the birth of her son (612), and a year later the Emperor married his niece Martina. This marriage roused great indignation and was regarded as incestuous by both Church and people, and a connection of this kind by reason of near consanguinity did in fact constitute an offence against both canon law and the law of the State. Martina was hated in Constantinople, but ignoring the attitude of his subjects, Heraclius lavished great affection on his second wife who shared his joys and sorrows and accompanied him on his hardest campaigns. It was, however, a great trial to him—and in the eyes of the people a clear mark of Divine displeasure—that of the nine children borne him by Martina four died in infancy and the two elder sons had physical disabilities. The enmity of the people towards Martina grew as this ambitious woman tried to secure the succession to the throne for her own offspring to the prejudice of Eudocia's son. From this a family feud arose which still further darkened the Emperor's embittered old age, and after his death plunged the Empire into sharp strife. Heraclius died on 11 February 641 after great suffering.

By bequeathing the Empire to his two elder sons, Heraclius tried to give Martina's offspring a share in the government without robbing his firstborn Constantine of his imperial rights. In spite of the great difference in age between them, for Constantine was then twenty-eight and Martina's son Heraclonas only fifteen years old, Heraclius expressly declared in his will that the half-brothers should share the sovereignty with equal status and rights. This is one of the best instances in Roman and Byzantine history of rule by co-Emperors.[1] In order to insure Martina a measure of direct influence in the affairs of state, Heraclius further declared in his will that she should be regarded by both rulers as 'mother and Empress'.[2]

But when Martina made her late husband's will public there was strong opposition to this provision and, in addition to the old hatred against the person of the Empress, certain questions connected with the general constitutional position were raised. The people acclaimed the two sons and former co-Emperors of Heraclius as their rulers

---

[1] Cf. Kornemann, *Doppelprinzipat* 162 f.

[2] Nicephorus 27, Διαθήκας οὖν ἐξετίθει, ὥστε Κωνσταντῖνον καὶ Ἡράκλειον τοὺς υἱοὺς αὐτοῦ βασιλεῖς ὁμοτίμους εἶναι, καὶ Μαρτῖναν τὴν αὐτοῦ γυναῖκα τιμᾶσθαι παρ' αὐτῶν ὡς μητέρα καὶ βασίλισσαν.

without any protest, but they would not hear of any participation in the government by Martina and rebuffed her with the argument that as a woman she could not represent the Roman Empire nor give audience to foreign ambassadors.[1] Martina had to yield, but she did not give up the game. The rift between the two branches of the ruling house widened visibly and the two factions, the one supporting Constantine and the other Martina and Heraclonas, faced each other as foes. Constantine III certainly had the larger following, but he suffered from a serious illness—apparently consumption[2]—and he died on 25 May 641 after reigning barely three months.

The boy Heraclonas now became the sole ruler,[3] though in actual fact Martina seized the reins of government and sent the most prominent supporters of the late Constantine into exile. With Martina's rise to power the Patriarch Pyrrhus gained fresh influence, and this meant a revival of the monothelete ecclesiastical policy which Constantine had wished to abandon.[4] The ardent monothelete Cyrus now received back the see of Alexandria, and like many of his predecessors he took over not only ecclesiastical, but also secular, control in Egypt. Acting upon instructions from the new government who considered any further resistance to the Arabs as useless, he opened negotiations with the victors and signed a treaty which to all intents and purposes gave the whole of Egypt to the Arabs. This treaty, however, involved protracted negotiations, and it did not come into force until early in November 641 after the fall of Martina and Heraclonas.[5]

From the very outset heavy clouds had gathered above the heads of Martina and Heraclonas. The more prominent elements in the Empire, the senatorial aristocracy, the military commanders and the orthodox clergy, turned against their government, and popular hatred of the Empress and the monothelete Patriarch persisted. They were represented as having caused the early death of Constantine by poisoning him, and people demanded the throne for his little son. One of Constantine III's followers, the Armenian Valentine Arsacidus (Aršakuni), incited the troops in Asia Minor against Martina and Heraclonas and appeared at their head before Chalcedon. Heraclonas yielded to pressure and crowned the son of

---

[1] Nicephorus 28.   [2] Cf. John of Nikiu, trans. Zotenberg 565.

[3] Nicephorus 29, αὐτοκράτωρ τῆς βασιλείας ἀναγορεύεται Ἡράκλειος. This is the first passage in which the word *autocrator* is used in the sense of sole ruler. Cf. Ostrogorsky, *Avtokrator* 102.

[4] Mansi 10, 703 and also Kulakovskij, *Istorija* III, 174. See also Bréhier-Aigrain 143 f.

[5] Dölger, *Reg.* 220.

Constantine III as co-Emperor, but this did not prevent his downfall at the end of September 641.[1] By order of the senate Martina and Heraclonas were deposed, and this decision was sealed by cutting off Martina's tongue and Heraclonas' nose. This is the first time that the oriental custom of mutilation by cutting off the nose is met with on Byzantine soil: it was regarded as a sign that the victim was no longer capable of holding office. Mother and son were banished to Rhodes and the Patriarch Pyrrhus shared their fate, while Paul, the former *oeconomus* of Hagia Sophia, ascended the patriarchal throne.

The senate conferred the sovereignty upon the son of Constantine III, then a boy of eleven years. Like his father, he had been baptized Heraclius, but he was given the name of Constantine at his coronation. The people called him Constans (Κώνστας), which was a diminutive of Constantine, just as Heraclonas was of Heraclius. Later he received the nickname of 'Pogonatus' (the bearded) because as he grew older he favoured a particularly long and luxuriant beard.[2]

The power of the senate had been shown in the deposition of Martina and Heraclonas, and this was also revealed when it took over the guardianship of the young Emperor Constans II. In a speech which he delivered before the assembled senate on his accession, Constans emphasized the fact that Martina and Heraclonas had been removed 'by decree of the senate with the help of God', because the senators 'who were well known for their outstanding piety could not endure lawlessness in the Empire of the Romans'. Moreover, he bade the senators to be 'the future advisers and executors of the common good of the subject'.[3] These words had of course been dictated to the young Emperor by the senators themselves, but they are none the less indicative of the high position and influence which the senate could command at that time.

The senate of Constantinople had been pushed right into the background by the absolutism of Justinian, but after his death it soon

---

[1] Cf. Ostrogorsky, 'Chronologie' 31. See also Kaestner, *De Imperio Constantini* III (1907), 27 f., who has rightly observed that Pyrrhus, whose successor ascended the patriarchal throne in October, had not been deposed during the reign of Heraclonas (Niceph. 31 f.), but simultaneously with the fall of Martina and Heraclonas (Theoph. 341 f. and John of Nikiu). Kaestner, however, did not arrive at the obvious conclusion that the fall of Heraclonas should not be placed at the end of November (Theoph. 341 length of reign given as 'six months'), but at the end of September, as Symeon Logothetes gives it (Leo Gram. 156, 15, length of reign 'four months'). As Brooks, BZ 4 (1895), 440, note 2, points out, this would also agree with Mansi 10, 864, where the Lateran Synod of October 649 took place in the ninth year of Constans II.

[2] Cf. Brooks, 'Who was Constantinus Pogonatus?' BZ 17 (1908), 455–62, and the coins given in Wroth, *Imp. Byz. Coins* I, p. xxx ff.

[3] The speech is given in Theophanes 342, 10–20; cf. also Symeon Log., Leo Gram. 157, 6–15.

began to regain its significance and experienced a real revival of its authority in the seventh century.[1] Under the Heraclian dynasty it exercised important functions as adviser to the crown and as the supreme court of justice (cf. below p. 119). With a change of sovereign senate was naturally much in evidence (cf. above p. 38), and it is not surprising that the young Constans had to confide himself to its protection and guidance to begin with. He did not, however, endure this tutelage for very long. Like most of the Heraclian family, he possessed a decidedly autocratic nature, and as he grew older became almost too self-willed.

The foreign policy of the Empire during the first half of Constans II's reign was dominated by the further advance of the Arabs. In accordance with the treaty which the Patriarch Cyrus of Alexandria had made with the Arabs at Martina's instigation, an agreed period was allowed for the evacuation of the country by the Byzantines and their troops left Alexandria on 12 September 642 and set sail for Rhodes. The victorious Arab general Amr then entered the city of Alexander the Great on 29 September, and from here he extended Arab rule along the North African coast, subjugated the Pentapolis and in 643 took the city of Tripolis on the Syrtis. After Omar's death in November 644, the new Caliph Othman recalled Amr, and this encouraged the Byzantines to make a counter-offensive. A strong fleet set out for Egypt under the Byzantine commander Manuel. He was able to take the Arab garrison by surprise and to recapture Alexandria, but his success did not last long. Amr was hurriedly sent back to Egypt and after defeating Manuel's force at Nikiu he entered Alexandria again in the summer of 646. Manuel was forced to take flight to Constantinople, while the Coptic population of Alexandria led by the monophysite Patriarch Benjamin willingly gave in to the Arabs and formally ratified their surrender, thus once again proving that they preferred the Arab yoke to the Byzantine. After the second fall of Alexandria Egypt remained permanently under Muslim rule, and the Byzantine Empire had lost once and for all her richest, and economically most valuable, province.[2]

Muawija, who was then governor of Syria, was an even greater general than Amr. When the Arabs had secured their position in Syria and Mesopotamia, they turned their thoughts to Armenia and Asia Minor. By 642–43 they had made fresh inroads into Armenian

---

[1] Cf. the weighty arguments of Ch. Diehl, 'Le sénat et le peuple byzantin aux VIIᵉ and VIIIᵉ siècles', B 1 (1924), 201 ff.

[2] A. J. Butler, *The Arab Conquest of Egypt* (1902), 194 ff.

territory.[1] In 647 Muawija invaded Cappadocia and took Caesarea. From there he turned to Phrygia, and although he did not succeed in capturing the strongly defended city of Amorium he traversed the wealthy province and returned to Damascus with valuable booty and many prisoners.

Penetration into the arena of Mediterranean politics necessitated the establishment of the Arabs as a sea-power. This was a completely new problem for a desert race, and even the famous conqueror Omar had no real appreciation of the value of a fleet. The creation of Muslim naval power was the great achievement of Muawija who was the first Arab statesman to realize that war against Byzantium necessitated a strong naval force. Soon after Omar's death he began to build a fleet, and in 649 the first naval expedition went to sea. Under the personal leadership of Muawija the Arab fleet sailed for Cyprus, one of the most important strategic bases of Byzantine sea-power in the East, and it took by storm the capital of the island, Constantia. It was of little avail for the Byzantine government to buy a three years' truce at considerable expense, for during these years Muawija made further additions to his fleet and when the temporary breathing space had expired he renewed his sea operations with increased strength. In 654 he ravaged Rhodes; and the statue of Helios, the famous Colossus, which was still counted as one of the seven wonders of the world, though it had been overthrown by an earthquake in 225 B.C., was sold to a Jewish merchant from Edessa, who had the mass of metal carried away by 900 camels. Soon after this the island of Cos fell to the Arabs and Crete had to endure their plundering inroads. There was no doubt even then that Muawija's goal was Constantinople: his route—Cyprus, Rhodes, Cos—clearly showed this. It was impossible for Byzantium to sit inactive while such obvious danger threatened, and Constans II himself took command of the Byzantine fleet and gave battle to the Arabs off the Lycian coast in 655. This first great sea fight between the two powers ended in the complete defeat of the Byzantines, and the Emperor himself was in the gravest danger and was only saved by the heroic self-sacrifice of a young Byzantine soldier.[2]

---

[1] Cf. H. Manandean, 'Les invasions arabes en Arménie', B 18 (1948), 177 ff.

[2] According to Theoph. p. 346, 9 f., the Emperor was saved by someone who changed clothes with him and thus enabled him to escape, while he died fighting the Arabs in his place. His saviour was one of the two sons of a *buccinator* (trumpeter, cf. Kulakovskij, *Istorija* III, 207, note 1), and his heroic and adventurous deeds are described by Theoph. p. 345, 10 ff., where elements of a popular historical heroic epic seem to be woven into the account.

Byzantine supremacy at sea was shattered, but the great victory had no immediate results owing to internal complications in the Caliphate. Even during the last years of Othman's reign there had been considerable unrest in the Arab empire, and this increased after his assassination (17 June 656). Bitter civil war broke out between Muawija, who had been proclaimed Caliph in Syria, and the ortho-dox Caliph Ali, the son-in-law of the Prophet, who had been elected in Medina, and the strife was only ended by the murder of Ali in 661. This situation had forced Muawija to come to an under-standing with the Byzantines and he therefore made peace with them in 659, even pledging himself to pay tribute to the Empire.[1] There was also a change of policy in Armenia and the most prominent Armenian families resumed relations with Byzantium.

Relieved of anxiety in the East, Constans was able to turn his attention to his European possessions. In 658 he undertook an expedition against the Slav-occupied Balkans and he attacked 'Sclavinia' where 'many were taken prisoner and brought under his control'.[2] The scanty sources do not give any details on the effects of this campaign, but they do make it clear that Constans II com-pelled some of the Slavs, probably those in Macedonia, to acknow-ledge Byzantine overlordship. This was the first considerable Byzantine offensive against the Slavs since Maurice's time. Constans II's campaign seems to have been accompanied by mass transporta-tion of Slavs to Asia Minor, and from now on Slavs are found in Asia Minor and in the imperial army. In 665 a Slav division of 5,000 men deserted to the Arabs and was settled by them in Syria.[3]

After his successes in the Balkans, Constans II turned his attention to imperial territory further west, where there was a very tricky

---

[1] Dölger, *Reg.* 230.

[2] Theoph. 347, ἐπεστράτευσεν ὁ βασιλεὺς κατὰ Σκλαυινίας καὶ ἠχμαλώτευσε πολλοὺς καὶ ὑπέταξεν. There seems no reason to doubt the accuracy of Theophanes' dates and put the campaign at an earlier date (Stanojević, *Vizantija i Srbi* II, 40 f., 215 f.) or later (Kaestner, *De imperio Constantini* III, 75). It is clear that this campaign could only have taken place after the disturbances in the Caliphate had broken out, which makes it impossible to accept the statement of Stanojević who, in agreement with Pančenko's dating of the lead seal of Bithynia (see below, p. 130, note 4) puts the campaign in 649. But there is also no reason to follow Kaestner in thinking that the campaign took place after the formal peace with Muawija (in the autumn of 659) because the out-break of the Arab troubles considerably eased the situation on the eastern frontier. It is true that Elias Nisib. (*Scriptores Syri* VII, 64) puts the campaign in the year of the Hijra 39 (29 May 659—16 May 660), but even so Elias, like Theophanes, places it before the peace with the Arabs, which he wrongly assigns to the year of the Hijra 42 (after 26 April 662).

[3] Theophanes 348, 18

situation, complicated by ecclesiastical controversy over the mono-thelete doctrine. The results of this religious discord were particu-larly disastrous in Latin North Africa which was in the utmost danger owing to the conquest of Egypt. Earlier on the hatred of the Syrian and Egyptian monophysites towards Byzantium had facili-tated the conquest of the eastern provinces, and now the defence of North Africa was hampered by the animosity of the western ortho-dox population. North Africa was at that time the refuge of ortho-doxy in the struggle against monotheletism, and it was here that Maximus the Confessor, the real leader of the orthodox party and the outstanding theologian of his age, worked for many years. It was at his instigation that synods were held in many North African cities early in 646, and the monothelete teaching which the Byzantine govern-ment supported was condemned as heretical. This opposition to the central Byzantine government soon took on a highly ominous political significance. The exarch of Carthage, Gregory, pro-claimed himself Emperor supported by both the population of the imperial province and the neighbouring Moorish tribes. It was the Arabs who saved the imperial central authority from the dangers which might have arisen from such a situation. After consolidating their conquests in Egypt, they organized an attack on the North African exarchate in 647, and the rival emperor Gregory was killed fighting against them. The Arabs sacked his capital, Sufetula, exacted heavy tribute and then withdrew.

Thus North Africa still remained in Byzantine possession, but these events struck a serious note which echoed loudly in Rome. Constans II realized the necessity for a reconciliation with the Church and he tried to find a compromise. In 648 he promulgated his famous *Type* which certainly authorized the removal of the *Ecthesis* from the narthex of Hagia Sophia, but the main issue was evaded even more effectively than in the case of Heraclius' edict, because under threat of heavy penalty he forbade any discussion of the problem of the divine will as well as that of the divine energy. He had thus taken up an attitude very like that of Zeno when he published his *Henoticon* on the two natures more than a hundred years earlier (cf. above, p. 64). The *Type* was just as impossible as the *Henoticon* as a basis of agreement, for it satisfied neither the convinced orthodox nor the convinced monotheletes, and it soon became obvious that it was useless to attempt to solve religious difference of opinion by ignoring the real problem at issue and suppressing freedom of speech.

Pope Martin, who had become Pope on 5 July 649 without the imperial exarch's sanction, held a large council in the Church of St. Saviour in the Lateran Palace in October. The majority of the 105 bishops who attended the council came from dioceses of the Roman see, but, theologically speaking, this Lateran synod was entirely under Greek influence and its whole procedure followed that of Byzantine oecumenical councils.[1] The Lateran synod condemned both the *Ecthesis* and the *Type*, but for political motives it threw the blame for these doctrinal edicts, not on the imperial government, but on the Patriarchs Sergius and Paul, who were excommunicated together with Pyrrhus. A pastoral letter from the Pope was sent to all the bishops and clergy of the Christian Church, and the Emperor received an exceedingly correct letter with a Greek translation of the minutes of the council.

Nevertheless, the manner of Martin I's elevation to the Papacy was sufficient to move Constans II to swift and autocratic intervention. Olympius, the exarch of Ravenna, was sent to Rome to arrest the Pope who had not obtained imperial recognition and to extort from all the Italian bishops their signature to the *Type*. He arrived in Rome before the end of the Lateran synod and he soon realized how difficult it would be for him to carry out his orders in such an atmosphere. Instead of obeying the imperial commands, he attempted to exploit Rome's strong feeling against Constantinople in order to detach Italy from the Empire and assume control of it himself. So in Italy, as in North Africa, the government's ecclesiastical policy had only succeeded in turning the local governors against the central authority. The usurper crossed to Sicily with his army and the Byzantine government seems to have done nothing to oppose him, which is perhaps explained by the fact that it was then fully occupied in the East with Muawija's first naval operation. With the death of Olympius in 652 the rebellion died a natural death.

The reckoning with Pope Martin came a year later. The new exarch appeared in Rome at the head of his army on 15 June 653, and after arresting the Pope, who was seriously ill at the time, he removed him by night from the rebellious city. Martin was taken to Constantinople and brought before the senate at the end of December. The trial assumed a distinctly political character. The charge was one of high treason, for Martin—perhaps with some justice—was accused of supporting Olympius. In the face of this, the

---

[1] E. Caspar, 'Die Lateransynode von 649', *Zeitschr. f. Kirchengesch.* 51 (1932), 75–137.

religious aspect sank into the background and the Pope's attempt to introduce the question of the *Type* was brusquely swept aside by his judges. His conviction had originally carried the death penalty, but at the personal command of the Emperor the sick old man was publicly maltreated and finally banished to far-off Cherson where he died in April 656, after enduring hunger and privation.[1] Soon after Martin's condemnation Maximus was extradited from Italy to Constantinople as a criminal, and he also had to stand his trial before the senate. Whereas Martin had been accused of conspiring with Olympius, Maximus was charged with supporting Gregory, the rebel exarch of North Africa, and more especially with refusing to recognize the imperial *Type*. Short work had been made of Martin and his religious convictions had been ignored, but Maximus was the real spiritual leader of the orthodox Greeks and the government therefore made every attempt to induce him to recant. But all its efforts were useless, though for many years Maximus was dragged from one place of exile to another and suffered much ill usage. His last place of banishment was the fortress Schemarium in Lazica (near the present-day Muri),[2] and here he died at the age of eighty on 13 August 662.

The doctrinal dispute had an important effect on the question of church policy, especially in the ecclesiastical struggle against the submission of the Church to imperial authority. Maximus announced the principle that as a layman the Emperor had no right to pronounce on questions of belief and that this was the concern of the Church alone.[3] This idea was not new; it had already been voiced by the church fathers of the early Byzantine period. But no one had fought for the freedom of the Church with such keenness as Maximus. He was the first real medieval Byzantine church father; it was he who had legitimatized the use of the mystical teaching of the pseudo-Dionysius within the Church and who had introduced medieval ecclesiastical ideas into conceptions surviving from the ancient world. In the person of the Emperor Constans and the monk Maximus two worlds stood in opposition to each other. And though Maximus had to submit to imperial omnipotence, the ideas

---

[1] Cf. P. Peeters, *Anal. Boll.* 51 (1933), 225 ff.

[2] Cf. A. Brilliantov, 'O meste končiny i pogrebenija sv. Maksima Ispovednika' (On the place of the death and burial of St. Maximus the Confessor), *Christ. Vostok* 6 (1917), 1–62.

[3] Cf., for instance, *Acta Maximi*, c. 4, Migne, PG 90, 117 BC.

for which he fought lived on in the religious struggles of the following centuries.

After ruling for twenty years on the Bosphorus, Constans came to a remarkable decision: he decided to leave Constantinople and remove his residence to the West. This did not mean that he abandoned the eastern imperial lands as lost; as long as war raged in the East he stuck to his post and it was only when the real crisis was over that he left the Byzantine capital. This westward move only shows what store the Byzantine Empire set on the retention of its possessions in the West, as being of as much importance as the eastern lands to the Empire of that day. If Constans II's move is compared with the earlier plans of Maurice and Heraclius (cf. above, p. 80 and p. 94 f.), continuity of imperial policy is apparent and it is evident that the Byzantines of that time certainly had no thought of limiting themselves to the East with the idea—as in the following century—of concentrating their resources there at the expense of the West.

The Emperor was finally driven to take this decision for reasons which the sources present as the only real motives for his removal to the West. Constans had lost the support of his orthodox Byzantine subjects because of his ecclesiastical policy and his cruel treatment of Martin and Maximus. Not content with this, in 660 he forced his brother Theodosius to be ordained priest and then had him murdered. He alleged that he was guilty of high treason but—as in the case of the sons of Heraclius and later on the sons of Constans himself—the real reason was that according to the custom of those days the brother of the Emperor had a claim to be co-Emperor, and Constans could not bear the thought of any such encroachment on his own imperial position. The immediate occasion of his conflict with Theodosius may have been the fact that as early as Easter 654 he had made his eldest son Constantine (IV) co-Emperor, and in 659 he followed suit with his two younger sons, Heraclius and Tiberius, thus again passing over his brother. The conflict, which ended with the murder of his brother, roused great resentment among the Byzantines, and the Emperor found himself pursued by the hatred of the people who called him another Cain.[1] This particular quarrel with the populace of his capital may have strengthened Constans' determination to leave Constantinople and it certainly had the effect

---

[1] *Chronica Minora, Scriptores Syri* IV, 55. Cf. also Scylitzes-Cedrenus I, 762.

of making his departure look like a deliberate break with the old capital.

To all appearances Constans was planning to visit the most important centres of his European possessions. He made his first stop in Thessalonica, then had a longer stay in Athens, and it was not until 663 that he arrived at Tarentum. Using this as his base, he began a campaign against the Lombards. At first he had many successes, a number of cities surrendered unconditionally to him, and soon he was besieging Beneventum. But neither the military nor the financial means at the Emperor's disposal were adequate for a long campaign, in spite of ruthless extortion from his Italian subjects. Constans was compelled to break off the siege and retire to Naples. Thus in spite of his initial victories he had failed to free Italy from the Lombards.[1]

From Naples Constans moved to Rome. There the Emperor, who had been responsible for the death of Pope Martin, was received by Pope Vitalian at the head of the Roman clergy six miles from the city walls and solemnly escorted to the ancient capital which was now but a shadow of its former self. Constans was the first Emperor to visit Rome since the fall of the western half of the Empire. His stay here was only a passing visit of twelve days and was given up to solemn processions and services. On 17 July 663 he left the Eternal City and soon after sailed from Naples to Sicily which needed to be defended against the Arab attacks. Here he made Syracuse his new capital, and he even thought of letting his family —his wife and sons—join him, only this was opposed in Constantinople where the plan of removing the imperial residence to the West was naturally frowned on.[2]

The site of his new headquarters was well chosen, for in Sicily, which the usurper Olympius had earlier on made the centre of operations, the Emperor could command the key position between his Italian territories threatened by the Lombards and North Africa exposed to Arab onslaught. Little is known about Constans' activities in Syracuse, but it is clear that the maintenance of the court and the imperial army imposed a very heavy burden upon the entire western dominions, while the despotic behaviour of the Emperor soon alienated everyone here, as elsewhere. This explains the catastrophe which brought Constans' stay in Syracuse to an end.

[1] Cf. Hartmann, *Geschichte Italiens im Mittelalter* II, 1 (1900), 248 ff.; Brooks, CMH II 1911), 394 ff.; Kulakovskij, *Istorija* III, 221 ff.
[2] Theophanes 348, 4; 351, 14.

A plot was hatched among his immediate entourage and on 15 September 668 he was murdered in his bath by a chamberlain. The conspiracy included many representatives of noble Byzantine and Armenian families, and it was an Armenian, Mezezius, who was proclaimed Emperor by the army after Constans' death. Meanwhile, at the beginning of 669 the rebellion was suppressed by the forces of the loyal exarch of Ravenna[1] and the usurper and several of the leading conspirators were executed. The body of the Emperor was brought to Constantinople and buried in the Church of the Holy Apostles.

3. THE SAVING OF CONSTANTINOPLE AND THE DEVELOPMENT OF THE HERACLIAN REFORMS: CONSTANTINE IV AND JUSTINIAN II

General bibliography: M. Canard, 'Les expéditions des Arabes contre Constantinople', *Journal Asiatique* 108 (1926), 61–121 (see also the bibliography on the history of the Arab invasions on p. 110 above); Zlatarski, *Istorija* I, 1; Mutafčiev, *Istorija* I; Runciman, *Bulgarian Empire*; Ch. Diehl, 'L'empereur au nez coupé', *Choses et gens de Byzance* (1926), 174–211; Ostrogorsky, 'Das byzantinische Kaiserreich in seiner inneren Struktur', *Historia Mundi* VI (1958), 445–73.

After the death of Constans II, his young son Constantine IV (668–85) came to the throne. This reign inaugurated a period of vital significance for world history as well as for Byzantium: it was a time during which the struggle between the Arabs and the Byzantines took a decisive turn.

While Constans II had been occupied in the West, Muawija had been settling the disputes in the Caliphate and he was now able to resume once more his attacks on the Byzantine Empire. In 663 the Arabs again appeared in Asia Minor and during the course of the next fifteen years they made annual raids.[2] The unfortunate countryside was ravaged and its inhabitants dragged off to slavery; on occasion the invaders even got as far as Chalcedon and they frequently wintered on imperial territory. But the fight for the possession of Constantinople itself, the really decisive battle on which the

---

[1] Theoph. 352 says that, after the murder of his father, Constantine IV led a force to Sicily in person and this is often accepted in modern works, but it has been pointed out that it is erroneous by E. W. Brooks, 'The Sicilian expedition of Constantine IV', BZ 17 (1908), 455–9; cf. also CMH II (1913), 395, and Kulakovskij, *Istorija* III, 235 and 358. H. Grégoire, B 13 (1938), 170, has attempted to justify Theophanes' account, but Brooks' view still seems to me to be the more probable.

[2] Cf. Kulakovskij, *Istorija* III, 232 f.

fate of the Empire hung, took place at sea. While he was governor of Syria, Muawija had been occupied with plans of conquest, and as Caliph he now resumed operations at the point where he had had to suspend them more than ten years before. The Arabs held Cyprus, Rhodes and Cos, and Muawija completed the chain of islands by the capture of Chios, and in 670 one of his generals seized the peninsula of Cyzicus in the immediate neighbourhood of the Byzantine capital, thus providing him with a useful base for an attack on Constantinople. Meanwhile, before delivering the final knock-out blow against the very heart of the Byzantine world, part of his fleet had captured Smyrna in 672 and another section of it had occupied the coasts of Lycia and Cilicia.

The main action began early in 674 when an imposing squadron appeared before the walls of Constantinople. The struggle went on all through the summer, and in the autumn the Arab fleet retired to Cyzicus. Next spring it appeared again, and throughout the summer the Byzantine capital was in a state of siege. The same proceeding was repeated during the following years, but all the efforts of the Arabs to take by storm the strongest citadel in the world were doomed to failure. They were forced to abandon the attempt, and in 678 they left Byzantine waters after having suffered severe losses in various naval actions fought beneath the walls of Constantinople.[1] Here one of the most useful Byzantine weapons was used for the first time. This was the famous Greek fire, invented by Callinicus, a Greek architect who had migrated to Byzantium from Syria; it was a mixture of explosives whose formula was known only to the Byzantines and by means of an instrument called a 'siphon' it could be hurled against enemy ships from a great distance, causing devastating fires to break out.[2] In retreating, the Arab fleet suffered still further losses in a storm which it encountered off the Pamphylian coast and at the same time the Arab forces in Asia Minor were heavily defeated. The aged Muawija therefore found himself compelled to conclude a thirty years' peace with Byzantium and he

[1] Thus the siege of Constantinople lasted five years (674–8). Theoph. 354 and Nicephorus 32 maintained that the struggle for Constantinople lasted seven years, although Theoph. himself (355 ff.) puts the peace treaty in the year 678. Apparently both the chroniclers reckoned from the capture of Cyzicus, as is pointed out by Gibbon, ed. Bury, VI 2, note 1.

[2] On Greek fire see C. Zenghelis, 'Le feu grégeois et les armes à feu des Byzantins', B 7 (1932), 265 ff. The older literature is given by Vasiliev, *History* 214, note 57. According to Zenghelis the main ingredient was saltpetre, so that Callinicus' discovery anticipated the later invention of gunpowder.

agreed to pay the Emperor 3,000 gold pieces annually and to send in addition fifty prisoners and fifty horses.[1]

The failure of the Arab attack made a deep impression far beyond the frontiers of the Byzantine Empire. The Khan of the Avars and the tribal leaders of the Slavs in the Balkan peninsula sent ambassadors to Constantinople who did homage to the Byzantine Emperor, asked for his peace and friendship and acknowledged the imperial suzerainty. 'And so,' as Theophanes wrote, 'undisturbed peace prevailed in both East and West.'[2]

And indeed the significance of the Byzantine victory of 678 cannot be overestimated. For the first time the Arab advance was really checked and the invasion which had swept forward as irresistibly as an avalanche was now halted. In the defence of Europe against the Arab onslaught this triumph of Constantine IV was a turning point of world-wide historical importance, like the later victory of Leo III in 718, or Charles Martel's defeat of the Muslims in 732 at Poitiers at the other end of Christendom. Of these three victories which saved Europe from being overwhelmed by the Muslim flood, that of Constantine IV was the first and also the most important. There is no doubt that the Arab attack which Constantinople experienced then was the fiercest which had ever been launched by the infidels against a Christian stronghold, and the Byzantine capital was the last dam left to withstand the rising Muslim tide. The fact that it held saved not only the Byzantine Empire, but the whole of European civilization.

In the Balkans new difficulties were created for the Empire by the arrival of the Bulgars, a people of Turkic origin. The great Empire of the Bulgars, or rather the Onogur-Bulgars, had maintained friendly relations with Byzantium in the days of Heraclius, but about the middle of the seventh century it had disintegrated under pressure from the westward-moving Khazars.[3] Some of the Bulgars submitted to the Khazars, but several Bulgar tribes left their former home. One of the larger hordes under Asparuch (the Isperich of the old Bulgarian list of rulers) migrated to the west and in the seventies

---

[1] Dölger, *Reg.* 239.

[2] Theophanes 356 (cf. Nicephorus 33). Cf. Šišić, *Povijest* 270 f., who is doubtless right in thinking that the words ἔξαρχοι τῶν πρὸς τὴν δύσιν ἐθνῶν refer to the leaders of the Slav tribes in the Byzantine West, and that ἐκύρωσε καὶ πρὸς αὐτοὺς δεσποτικὴν εἰρήνην implies Slav recognition of the authority of the Byzantine Emperor in return for which he confirmed their possession of the lands which they were occupying.

[3] Cf. J. Moravcsik, 'Zur Geschichte der Onoguren', *Ungarische Jahrb.* 10 (1930), 53 ff., and the full bibliography in *Byzantinoturcica* I, 2nd ed., 112 ff.

appeared at the mouth of the Danube. Constantine IV was not blind
to the fact that the presence of these warlike peoples on the northern
frontier constituted a serious threat to the Byzantine state. After
making peace with the Arabs he immediately made preparations
for an expedition against the Bulgars and by 680 war had broken
out.[1] A large squadron of ships under the personal command of the
Emperor crossed the Black Sea and disembarked north of the Danube
mouth, and at the same time cavalry were brought from Asia Minor
and they reached the Danube by way of Thrace and got to the
northern bank of the river. But the swampy ground made operations difficult for the Byzantines, while the Bulgars were able to
avoid any real encounter with the superior forces of their enemy.
The Byzantine army wasted their strength without success, and
finally had to withdraw after the Emperor himself had been compelled by illness to leave his troops. While they were crossing the
Danube they were attacked by the Bulgars and suffered heavy losses;
the Bulgars then followed the retreating enemy over the river and
broke into the district of Varna.[2] Thus Constantine IV's expedition
failed to stave off the disaster which he feared and indeed actually
facilitated the penetration of the enemy into his Empire.

   The territory which the Bulgars invaded was by then largely
slavonized and was inhabited by seven Slav tribes, in addition to the
Severi. These became tributary to the Bulgars[3] and seem to have
made common cause with them against the Byzantines.[4] Thus a
Slav-Bulgar kingdom grew up in the area of the former province of
Moesia between the Danube and the range of the Balkan mountains.
The Bulgar invasion of the north-eastern part of the Balkans, then

---

[1] Theophanes A.M. 6171 = 679/80 (not 678/9; corresponding to Ostrogorsky,
'Chronologie' 1 ff.).

[2] Theophanes 359, 7 ff.; Nicephorus 35, 15 ff.

[3] Theophanes 359, 7 ff., describes the seven Slav tribes as ὑπὸ πάκτον ὄντες, and
it is quite clear, especially from Theoph. 359, 20 (where the Byzantine Emperor is
compelled ἐτησία . . . πάκτα παρέχειν to the Bulgars) that πάκτον is not 'treaty', as
Zlatarski, *Istorija* I, 1 (1918), 142 ff., tries to show, but 'tribute', as rightly maintained by
J. Dujčev, 'Protobulgares et Slaves', *Sem. Kond.* 10 (1938), 145 ff., who also correctly
adds that according to Theophanes the obligation to pay tribute did not extend to the
Severi. Nevertheless, the latest history of Bulgaria, published by the Bulgarian Academy
(*Istorija na Bŭlgarija*, Sofia, 1954, p. 65), speaks of an alliance which the Protobulgars
are said to have made with the Slavs, and even with the Slav state. Cf. also D. Angelov
and M. Andreev, *Istorija na Bŭlgarskata dŭržava i pravo* (History of the Bulgarian state
and law), Sofia, 1955, 59.

[4] This struggle to establish the kingdom of the Bulgars was not concluded in a single
year 679–80 as Theophanes 356 ff. says, but probably lasted on into the summer of 681
(as noted by Kulakovskij, *Istorija* III, 249, from Mansi XI, 617). This passage is also
commented on by J. Trifonov, *Izvestija na Istorič. Družestvo* 11–12 (1931–2), 119 ff.,
who uses it, however, as the basis of a number of untenable hypotheses.

in possession of the Slavs, accelerated the formation of new principalities and led to the development of the first South Slav empire. It is of course true that the Bulgars and the Slavs belonged to two different racial groups and for a long while a clear distinction is drawn between them in Byzantine sources, but gradually the Bulgars were assimilated to the Slav majority.

The Byzantine Emperor was forced to recognize the *status quo* by concluding a formal treaty and pledging himself to pay annual tribute to the young Bulgarian empire, 'to the great disgrace of the Roman name'.[1] So for the first time an independent kingdom arose on Byzantine soil and was recognized as such by Byzantium. This fact is in itself of real significance, even though the actual territorial loss suffered by the Empire at the hands of the Bulgars was slight, for the districts occupied by them had already virtually been lost to the Byzantines by reason of the Slav invasions.

Developments in the East necessitated a reorientation of Byzantine ecclesiastical policy. With Byzantine reverses in the East, the provinces which had fallen to the Arabs had no longer to be reckoned with, and any further maintenance of monotheletism was therefore pointless. As a means of reconciling the eastern Christians this ecclesiastical policy had proved useless, and it had only brought about disastrous complications between Byzantium itself and the West. In consultation with Rome, Constantine IV summoned a Council to Constantinople to put an end to monotheletism. This was the sixth General Council of the Christian Church and it had the unusually large number of eighteen sessions, lasting from 7 November 680 to 16 September 681. The doctrines of the two energies and the two wills, which had been set aside not long before, were now reinstated as the orthodox teaching of the Church. Monotheletism was condemned, and the leaders of the monothelete party, together with its earlier champions, the Patriarchs Sergius, Pyrrhus and Cyrus and Pope Honorius, were excommunicated. The Emperor took a prominent part in the proceedings of the Council. He was present at the first eleven, and most important, sessions, as well as the last session, and he took the chair and led the discussions. At the formal closing session, after he had put his signature to the decisions of the Council, he was acclaimed by the ecclesiastical assembly as the protector, and even as the interpreter, of orthodox belief: 'Long life to the Emperor! You have revealed the meaning

[1] Theophanes 358, 19; Nicephorus 35, 24; Dölger, *Reg.* 243.

of the natures of Christ. Lord, preserve the Light of the world! Constantine, the new Marcian, live for ever! Constantine, the new Justinian, live for ever! You have destroyed all heretics!'[1]

Soon after the conclusion of the oecumenical Council a serious quarrel broke out in the imperial family which was almost a repetition of the bitter conflict between Constans II and his brother Theodosius. Like Constans II, Constantine IV wished for undivided sovereignty and he therefore decided to deprive his two younger brothers, Heraclius and Tiberius, of all imperial rights, though they had already been crowned during his father's lifetime. He met with stiff opposition from the senate, as well as from the army who supported the present arrangement[2] and even found in it a kind of mystical Christian significance. The protest against the Emperor's action was said to have been voiced by the Anatolikon theme in the words 'We believe in the Trinity, we want a trinity of rulers'.[3] But this opposition did not turn Constantine IV from his purpose. He began by depriving his brothers of the imperial titles which were their due,[4] and at the end of 681 he had the noses of both the unfortunate princes cut off.[5] The representatives of the Anatolikon theme who had tried to compel the Emperor to change his mind were executed. This *coup d'état* of Constantine IV had important repercussions on future constitutional development. After several generations of fierce family strife, the principle of a single supreme ruler seemed to be firmly established, and by limiting the right of succession to the eldest son of the ruler considerable progress was made in furthering the acceptance of an hereditary monarchy.[6] As a means of securing the succession to the throne the system of co-Emperors remained as important as ever, but from now on, provided

[1] Mansi XI, 656.
[2] By 670 Constantine IV had decreed that his two brothers were to share the imperial prerogatives equally with him and that the portraits of all three Emperors were to appear on the coins. Cf. Dölger, *Reg.* 236.
[3] Theophanes 352, 15.
[4] In the official dating of the *acta* of the sixth oecumenical Council Heraclius and Tiberius are not described as the co-Emperors of Constantine IV, but as his divinely protected brothers. Cf. Mansi XI, 208 E, 217 A, 221 CD, 229 AB, 316 DE, etc.
[5] Cf. Brooks, 'The Brothers of the Emperor Constantine IV', EHR 30 (1915), 42 ff.
[6] In spite of Dölger, BZ 33 (1933), 137 ff., I believe, as I have already indicated in Kornemann, *Doppelprinzipat* 166, that when he deposed his brothers Constantine IV's main concern was not to secure the succession for his son Justinian (II) but to safeguard the principle of undivided sovereignty. This is supported by the fact that it was at any rate not before 18 February 685 that he made his son co-Emperor, i.e. more than three years after the *coup d'état*, for Justinian II's letter of 17 February 687 to the Pope (as well as the inscription on the tomb of the father of Pope John VII) is dated the second year of the reign and the second year of the consulate of Justinian.

that the senior Emperor was of age and capable of governing, the co-Emperors had no further share in the actual exercise of authority. Complete sovereignty lay with the senior Emperor, the Autocrator.

The rule of Constantine IV left an indelible mark on the foreign and domestic policy of the Byzantine Empire as well as on affairs of Church and State. He was only thirty-three years old when he died in September 685 after a reign of seventeen years, and his early death brought his son Justinian II (685–95; 705–11) to the throne. Like his father, he was scarcely sixteen years old on his accession. He possessed neither the astute circumspection nor the balanced judgment of the true statesman, for he was by nature passionate and impulsive, taking after his grandfather in disposition. He also had the autocratic spirit which was characteristic of all the Heraclians and, as in the case of Constans II, this took the form of a ruthless despotism which could brook no opposition. He bore a name which carried with it great responsibilities but also great temptations. With the example of Justinian I before him, filled with ideas of the magnificence of the imperial office, this young, immature, unbalanced ruler was often led astray by his burning ambition and his unquenchable longing for fame. His unrestrained despotism and his extreme irritability drove him to acts which stained his reputation in the eyes of his contemporaries and have blinded modern historians to the significance of his reign. For all his faults, Justinian II was a true representative of the Heraclian dynasty and a gifted ruler with a clear perception of the needs of the state.

Thanks to the decisive victories of Constantine IV, the Empire was in a strong position in the East, while the Caliphate seemed to be crippled by internal troubles after the death of Muawija. Abdalmalik, who became Caliph in the year of Justinian II's accession, attempted to stabilize the situation by a new peace treaty with Byzantium. This agreement was exceedingly advantageous for the Empire: the tribute which the Arabs had pledged themselves to pay Constantine IV was increased and a settlement was reached with regard to Cyprus on the one hand, and Armenia and Iberia on the other, whereby the revenue from these countries was to be divided between the two signatories.[1] For several centuries Cyprus remained under a kind of *condominium* of the two powers without belonging to either.[2]

Peace in the East gave to Justinian II the opportunity to turn

[1] Dölger, *Reg.* 257.
[2] Cf. the important comments of R. J. H. Jenkins, 'Cyprus between Byzantium and Islam. A.D. 688–965', *Studies presented to D. M. Robinson* II (1953), 1006 ff.

his attention towards the Balkans. As early as 687/88 he transferred cavalry from Asia Minor to Thrace, in order, as Theophanes says, 'to subjugate the Bulgars and the Sclavinias'.[1] At the head of this army he set off in the year 688/89 on a lengthy campaign principally directed against the Slavs. After a clash with the Bulgars he advanced upon Thessalonica and 'subjected a great number of Slavs'.[2] The course of this campaign is a striking comment on the situation in the Balkans at the period: in order to reach Thessalonica from Constantinople, the Emperor had to fight his way through country occupied by the Slavs, with a powerful force assembled for that very purpose. His break-through to Thessalonica was regarded as a great victory. He celebrated his triumph by a solemn entry into the city and by gifts to the Church of St. Demetrius, the patron of Thessalonica.[3] Justinian made the conquered Slavs migrate to Asia Minor and settled them as *stratiotai* in the theme Opsikion.[4] Thus the

---

[1] Theophanes 364, 8.

[2] Theophanes 364, 13.

[3] Justinian II's edict of 688/9 (indiction 2) doubtless refers to this campaign. In it the Emperor grants a saltpan exempt from taxes to the Church of St. Demetrius in Thessalonica as a thank-offering for the help given him in battle by St. Demetrius, and the Emperor's visit to Thessalonica is also mentioned here (new ed. by A. Vasiliev, 'An Edict of the Emperor Justinian II, September 688', *Speculum* 18(1943), 1 ff., and H. Grégoire, 'Un Edit de l'Empereur Justinien II, daté de septembre 688', B 17 (1944–5), 119 ff. See also A. Vasiliev, 'L'entrée triomphale de l'empereur Justinien II à Thessalonique en 688', OCP 13 (1947), 352 ff.). I do not understnd why these two learned editors maintain that the edict was issued in 688, while in reality line 10 of the edict actually states that the Church of St. Demetrius's possession of the saltpan presented to it dated from September 'of the present second indiction', i.e. that the revenue from it was reckoned from the beginning of the year. A similar parallel is found in the *pittakion* of Michael VII Ducas of February 1073, which ordered certain property to be handed over to Andronicus Ducas and ruled that the income should be paid to the recipient as from the beginning of the current indiction, i.e. from September 1072 (Miklosich-Müller VI, 4 ff.). It is then clear that the edict of Justinian II (corresponding to indiction 2) fell in the year 688–9 and it was in precisely this year that Justinian II's campaign took place, according to Theophanes, since the world year 6180 was the equivalent here of 688/9 (cf. Ostrogorsky, 'Chronologie'). St. Kyriakides, Ἱστορικὴ τοιχογραφία τῆς ἐκκλησίας τοῦ ἁγίου Δημητρίου: Τρεῖς Διαλέξεις, Thessalonica 1953, 5 ff., has published the edict in a lecture on the representation of the triumphal entry of Justinian II in the Church of St. Demetrius (cf. also Vasiliev cited above). On this representation cf. also Kantorowicz, 'The King's Advent', *The Art Bulletin* 26 (1944), 216, note 63, and for another view J. D. Breckenridge, 'The Long Siege of Thessalonica', BZ 48 (1955), 116 ff.

[4] Theophanes 364, 15. An interesting lead seal connected with this migration of the Slavs is published by Pančenko, Pamjatnik Slavjan v Viñnii' (Evidence of the Slavs in Bithynia), *Izv. Russk. Archeol. Inst. v K/le* 8 (1902), 15 ff. On the obverse the legend runs ΑΠΟ ΥΠΑΤωΝ, and on the reverse, as amended by G. Schlumberger, BZ 12 (1903), 277, ΤωΝ ΑΝΔΡΑΠΟΔΟΝ (*sic*) ΤωΝ ΣΚΛΑΒΟωΝ ΤΗΕ ΒΙΘΥΝωΝ ΕΠΑΡΧΙΑΣ. The seal can therefore be dated 694/5 (indiction 8) and the Emperor represented on it would thus be Justinian II. It belonged to the imperial official who was placed as administrator over the Slav soldiers settled in Bithynia and who had the title of an ἀπὸ ὑπάτων. Kulakov-skij, *Istorija* III, 360, had already suggested assigning it to Justinian, and had shown that Pančenko's dating to the year 650 was based on false hypotheses. Kulakovskij is however wrong in placing the seal in the year 710/11 (more correctly 709/10); the youthful

colonization of Asia Minor by Slavs, begun under Constans II, was continued, though on a much greater scale. The Slav tribes who were now settled in the Opsikion had to produce a military levy of thirty thousand men,[1] and the extra forces so obtained meant not only a considerable increase in the size of the Byzantine army, but undoubtedly brought about the economic regeneration of the countryside, which had been devasted by hostile attacks.

Justinian II's policy of colonization was not limited to the resettlement of the Slavs in Asia Minor, important as this was. It was also applied to the Mardaites, a Christian tribe of bandits living in the region of Amanus who had once served the Byzantines well in the struggle against the Arabs but were now gradually drifting over to the Muslims. They were reclaimed for the Empire and settled as sailors in the Peloponnese, the island of Cephalonia and the port of Nicopolis in Epirus, and most probably also in the region of Attaleia on the southern coast of Asia Minor.[2] In addition, Justinian II transferred the inhabitants of Cyprus to the district of Cyzicus which had suffered greatly during the siege of Constantinople and badly needed experienced seamen.

This removal of the Cypriots to some extent conflicted with the interests of the Caliphate, but Justinian II in the knowledge of his own superiority disdainfully rejected the Caliph's protests, thus provoking a clash of arms in 691/92. Meanwhile, the new Slav troops went over to the enemy with the result that the Byzantines met with a severe defeat at Sebastopolis in Armenia (the present-day Sulu-saray),[3] and Byzantine Armenia again came under the control of the Caliphate. The Arabs settled the Slav deserters in Syria after the Byzantine manner, and used them as soldiers in the subsequent wars against Byzantium. It is not of course possible to credit Theophanes when he says that in revenge Justinian II ordered

appearance of the Emperor points against this, and in addition in the period of his second reign Justinian is usually found represented with his son and co-Emperor Tiberius (cf. Wroth, *Byz.* Coins II, 354 ff. and pl. XLI). P. Charanis, 'The Slavic Element in Byzantine Asia Minor', B 18 (1948), 70, returns to Pančenko's dating of 650, because, strangely enough, he takes at its face value the report of Theophanes that in 692 Justinian exterminated the Slavs who had settled in the Opsikion after 688 (see below). But cf. the objections of A. Maricq, 'Notes sur les Slaves dans le Péloponnèse et en Bithynie', B 22 (1952), 348 ff., who supports my dating to the year 594/5. This dating is also supported by A. Vasiliev, op. cit., 366, and H. Grégoire, op. cit. 123 (cf. the previous note). Cf. also *Vizantiski izvori* I, 245.

[1] Theophanes 366, 1.

[2] Cf. Honigmann, *Ostgrenze* 41.

[3] On the identification of the site of the battle, cf. A. Maricq, 'Notes sur les Slaves dans le Péloponnèse et en Bithynie', B 22 (1952), 350 ff.

all the Slavs in Bithynia to be massacred[1] and that the transportation
of the Mardaites meant a pointless exposure of the Byzantine eastern
frontier, while the resettlement of the Cypriots was a total failure
with the loss of the greater number of them en route.[2] It is true that
the Cypriots appear to have returned home later on,[3] but in the
tenth century Slavs are still found in the Opsikion theme, and
Mardaites both in the Cibyraeot theme, where their commander,
the κατεπάνω τῶν Μαρδαϊτῶν, held an important position next to the
strategus of the Cibyraeots, and also in the theme of Hellas, where
they had an effective force of 5,087, or 4,087 men.[4] Thus Justinian's
policy of colonization had proved to be practicable, and, whatever
the hardship for the individual, it served a vital need of the Byzantine
State. A new lease of life was given to the Empire when Heraclius
began to settle *stratiotai* in the themes. In continuing his work, his
successors gave a strong impetus to the process of rejuvenation, and
those districts of the Empire which had been drained of their
manpower were recolonized from outside by settlers who were to
be both soldiers and farmers.

The organization of the system of themes is one of the most
important problems of Byzantine development in the early middle
ages. Byzantine historical sources do not go into this question in
any detail, but from the second half of the seventh century increasing
mention of the districts of the themes is found, thus indicating the
extent to which this administrative arrangement was steadily taking
root in the Byzantine polity.[5] A document of Justinian II of 17
February 687 names, in addition to the two exarchs of Italy and
Africa, the *stratiotai* of five themes, the Opsikion, Anatolikon and
Armeniakon themes, the maritime theme of the Carabisiani, and the
theme of Thrace.[6] The themes of Asia Minor went back to the time
of Heraclius, and the theme of Thrace was set up by Constantine IV
to afford protection against the Bulgars.[7] The theme of Hellas was
created by Justinian II in central Greece.[8] Apparently Justinian II

---

[1] Theophanes 366, 1.   [2] Theophanes 364, 5 and 365, 9.
[3] Cf. *De adm. imp.*, cap. 47, 24, ed. Moravcsik and Jenkins.
[4] For the Slavs see: *De cerim.* 662, 22; 666, 15; 669, 10. For the Mardaites: ibid. 654,
1 *et passim*.
[5] Cf. Diehl, 'Régime des thèmes' 276 ff.; Gelzer, 'Themenverfassung' 19 ff.
[6] Mansi XI, 737.
[7] *De thematibus* 44. Cf. Kyrakides, Βυζ. Μελέται 117 ff.; Lemerle, *Philippes* 120 f.
[8] The first *strategus* of Hellas is mentioned in 695: Theophanes 368, 20; Nicephorus
38, 1. Cf. G. Ostrogorsky, 'Postanak tema Hellada i Peloponez' (The origin of the
themes of Hellas and the Peloponnese), *Zbornik radova Viz. Inst.* 1 (1952), 64 ff., where
it is shown that, contrary to the usual belief, this theme consisted of central Greece,
and not almost the whole of present-day Greece.

also set up certain elements of a military administrative organization in the region of the Strymon, once again by settling Slav *stratiotai* there.[1] The authority of the Byzantine state did not however extend over by far the greater part of the Balkan peninsula which remained in the hands of the Bulgarians and individual Slav tribes. The former Illyrian prefecture was effectively limited to Thessalonica and the land in its vicinity. Although it was never officially abolished, the Illyrian prefecture gradually disappeared, and the prefect of Illyricum became prefect of the city of Thessalonica.[2]

The system of themes, which became more and more highly developed in Asia Minor and was also gradually established in certain regions in the Balkan peninsula, forms the framework in which the regeneration of the Byzantine Empire took place. Over a long period the Byzantine government endeavoured with striking consistency to bring the greatest possible number of Slavs within the territory of the Empire and to settle them in the newly created themes as *stratiotai* and small farmers, in order to increase the military force at the Empire's disposal and to strengthen the country economically. The internal revival experienced by the Byzantine Empire from the seventh century onward was in fact due more than anything else to the rise of a large class of peasants and the formation of a new army of *stratiotai*. This meant an increase in the number of smallholders, for the *stratiotai*, who were settled on the land, were at the same time small landowners. The *stratiotes'* obligation of military service usually passed to his eldest son, who also inherited the 'soldiers' property' to which obligatory military service was attached.[3] The rest of his offspring represented a surplus of free peasant labour which was naturally interested in cultivating the existing surplus of fallow land, and these peasants could similarly be enrolled amongst the numbers of the *stratiotai*. The free peasants and the *stratiotai* form a single class and it was this class which from

---

[1] Cf. *De thematibus*, c.3, ed. Pertusi. See also M. Rajković, 'Oblast Strimona i tema Strimon' (The region of the Strymon and the theme Strymon'), ZRVI 5 (1958), 1 ff.

[2] Cf. Lemerle, 'Invasions', 269 ff. It may be left an open question here as to whether the Illyrian prefecture, as Lemerle is inclined to believe, ceased to exist in the mid-seventh century, i.e. in the period between the composition of Book I and Book II of the *Miracula S. Demetrii*. In any case, it is tempting to suppose that the well-known passage in the only letter of Theodore the Studite mentioning an eparch still in Thessalonica in 796 (Migne, PG99, col. 917) really refers to the city eparch of Thessalonica. This would do away with the obviously difficult assumption that the Illyrian prefecture continued into the ninth century, i.e. until the establishment of the theme of Thessalonica (cf. Gelzer, 'Themenverfassung' 35 ff.; Bury, *Eastern Rom. Empire* 223 f., followed by later scholars).

[3] *Basilica* V, p. 190 (ed. Heimbach).

henceforth provided the force that sustained the Byzantine Empire.

The large estates which had dominated the early Byzantine period were considerably reduced in number after the crisis at the end of the sixth and the beginning of the seventh centuries and they suffered severely under the hostile attacks which followed. It is scarcely conceivable that the old landed estates could have survived to any significant extent the assaults of the Avars and Slavs on the one hand, and the Persians and then the Arabs on the other. As far as can be seen, they did in fact largely disappear, and were replaced by smallholders, i.e. free peasants who took possession of the fallow land and the *stratiotai* who formed the new army of the themes.

Thus within the Byzantine state a great change took place in the countryside which placed the social structure of the Empire upon a new foundation and directed its development along new paths. By contrast, the pattern of city life in Byzantium displays a high degree of permanence.[1] City life within the Byzantine state was never interrupted like that of the West. All the same, numerous cities, particularly in the Balkans, were destroyed by enemy attacks,

[1] Research into the history of the Byzantine city in relation to the ancient *polis* is still at an early stage. Apart from the important work of Bratianu, *Privilèges*, it is only in the last few years that a number of studies on this problem have appeared. See especially E. Kirsten, 'Die byzantinische Stadt', *Berichte zum XI. Internationalen Byzantinisten-Kongress*, Munich 1958; F. Dölger, 'Die frühbyzantinische und byzantinisch beeinflusste Stadt', *Atti dei 3° Congresso internazionale di studi sull' alto medioevo*, Spoleto 1958, 1 ff.; G. Ostrogorsky, 'Byzantine Cities in the Early Middle Ages', DOP 13 (1959), 45 ff. Important contributions have been made by Byzantine scholars in the U.S.S.R. In particular there is first the stimulating discussion by A. P. Každan, 'Vizantijskie goroda v VII–XI vekach' (Byzantine cities from the seventh to the eleventh centuries), *Sovetskaja archeologija* 21 (1954), 164 ff., and *Derevnja i gorod*, in which he argues for an extensive decline in Byzantine cities in the early Middle Ages, while E. E. Lipšic, 'K voprosu o gorode v Vizantii VIII–IX vv.' (On the question of the city in Byzantium from the eighth to the ninth centuries), VV 6 (1953), 113 ff. and *Očerki*, 87 ff., M. J. Sjuzjumov, 'Rol' godorov-emporiev v istorii Vizantii' (The role of market-towns in Byzantine history), VV 8 (1956), 26 ff., both accept, in my view correctly, the unbroken continuity of Byzantine cities. Cf. also the comprehensive account of city and village in Byzantium by N. V. Pigulevskaja, E. E. Lipšic, M. J. Sjuzjumov and A. P. Každan, 'Gorod i derevnja v Vizantii v IV–XII vv.' (Town and country in Byzantium from the fourth to the twelfth centuries), *Actes du XIIe Congrès Intern. des Ét. byz.*, Ochrida, 1961, I (Belgrade, 1963). Against Každan's view that the numismatic material is evidence for a sharp decline in Byzantine city life in the seventh century onward, cf. my discussion, op. cit. 48 ff. and I. V. Sokolova, 'Klady vizantijskich monet kak istočník dlja istorii Vizantii VIII–XI vv' (Hoards of Byzantine coins as a source for the history of Byzantium from the eighth to the eleventh centuries), VV 15 (1959), 50 ff. See also the important observations by P. Grierson, 'Commerce in the Dark Ages: a Critique of Evidence', *Transactions of the Royal Historical Society*, 5th series, vol. 9 (1959), 123 ff., and G. L. Kurbatov, *Rannevizantijskij gorod (Antiochija v IV veke)* (An early Byzantine city—Antioch in the fourth century), Leningrad, 1962. On the continuity of urban life in early medieval Byzantium see also S. Vryonis, 'An Attic Hoard of Byzantine Gold Coins (668–741) from the Thomas Whittemore Collection and the Numismatic Evidence for the Urban History of Byzantium', ZRVI 8, 1 (1963), 291 ff.

so that in the greater part of the Balkan peninsula, which passed out of Byzantine control, city life came to an end for a considerable period. On the other hand, in Asia Minor, which remained under Byzantine rule, the cities persisted and their numbers did not significantly decrease. However deficient our knowledge of Byzantine city life in the early Middle Ages may be, there is nevertheless no doubt that many Byzantine cities retained their importance as centres of trade and commerce, which also explains the fact that Byzantium continued to practise a money economy. City life is the real element of continuity in the development of Byzantium. It ensured the continuance of the traditional pattern of the state and the survival of the intellectual and material civilization of the ancient world.

The new pattern of the Byzantine village is most clearly reflected in the famous *Farmer's Law* (νόμος γεωργικός),[1] which gives a picture of the daily life of the Byzantine peasantry in the early Middle Ages. It would seem that the *Farmer's Law* principally has in view new settlements arising from the colonization of a deserted countryside. One gets the impression of village settlements lying in wooded country, for there is repeated mention of the clearing of woodland and the bringing into cultivation of fallow land.[2] The peasants whose legal relationships are regulated by the *Law* are free land-owners. They have no obligations to any landlord but only to the state, as taxpayers. There are no restrictions on their freedom of movement. This does not mean that there were no serfs at all in this period, but it does imply that the free peasantry formed a large class and that the word 'farmers' (γεωργοί) referred at that time particularly to free landowners. Significantly, the *Farmer's Law* speaks of them as masters (κύριοι) of their property. In addition, they possessed not only land and cattle, but occasionally slaves who still played a not unimportant role in Byzantine rural economy. The *Farmer's Law* pays particular attention to the maintenance of the individual's title to his personal property.

Nevertheless, the inhabitants of a village formed a community (κοινότης),[3] a relationship which was shown in many different ways.

---

[1] On the date of the *Farmer's Law* see above p. 90 and note 7.

[2] This is correctly pointed out by Lipšic, '*Viz. krest'janstvo*' 105 ff., and *Očerki*, 57 ff.

[3] This village community had nothing to do with the type of community organization distinguished by common cultivation and periodical redistribution of land which was once thought to have existed in Byzantium and whose origin was attributed to the influence of the 'primitive' Slav community life introduced by Slav migration. This

Arable land and fields, vineyards, orchards and vegetable gardens were the entire and personal possession of the farmer or his family, and individuals occasionally even owned woodland. But the individual holding resulted originally from the division of territory taken over by the village community and if necessary it could be supplemented by new divisions of land. At the same time, certain parts of the land possessed by the village continued to be held in common by the whole community. Pasture land was used in common and the cattle of the village were guarded by cow-herds who were paid by the community. The government regarded the village as an administrative unit for fiscal purposes. The members of the community were jointly responsible for the correct payment of taxes and had to make good the deficits of their insolvent neighbours. The late

theory was put forward by Zachariä and developed by Vasilijevskij and more particularly by Uspenskij. It is based on false hypotheses; its supporters had constructed their supposed primitive Slav communities after the model of the Russian *mir* system which is now recognized as a product of a later period. Community organization of this kind among the Slavs at the time of their settlement in the Balkans is on the contrary at least unknown and unrecorded. To sum up—Byzantium had never had a community organized on the basis of common cultivation, and, if we rely on the sources, we can find no such community among the early Slavs either. Byzantium certainly had communities of the kind described above, and these were found long before the Slav settlement, as was also the case elsewhere.

It is to the great credit of Pančenko, 'Krest'janskaja sobstvennost', that he was not led astray by the authority of Zachariä or of his great Russian predecessors, and as a result of a careful analysis of sources he showed that the property of the Byzantine peasant was his individual, unrestricted and hereditary possession. Unfortunately, he went too far in the opposite direction. Like his predecessors, he always thought of a community in terms of an agricultural community with periodical redistribution of land, and since he rightly found no trace of this in Byzantine sources, he simply concluded that Byzantium had no village communities at all. This was in complete contradiction to the sources which certainly did recognize and frequently mentioned them.

There is no doubt that the Slavs played an extremely important part in the revival of the Byzantine Empire in the seventh century. This was not because they imported a specifically Slav type of community organization, as has been argued by means of a whole chain of false conclusions, but because they brought new energy and strength into the enfeebled state; both the farmer-soldiers and the free peasants in the Byzantine themes undoubtedly contained a large proportion of the Slavs who had penetrated into the Empire. The importance of the Slavs in the development of Byzantium is especially emphasized by Byzantine scholars in the U.S.S.R. Cf. especially Lipšic, 'Viz. Krest'-janstvo'. Lemerle, 'Histoire Agraire', 219, p. 63 ff., emphasizes the importance of the 'demographic revolution' (bouleversement démographique) which began in Byzantium with the appearance of the Slavs in the seventh century. The theory of a Slav community organization imported into Byzantium, on the other hand, is increasingly being given up by Soviet Byzantine scholars who originally supported it. Cf. Levčenko, 'Materialy', 28 ff., 37 and especially M. J. Sjuzjumov, 'Bor'ba za puti razvitija feodal'nych otnošenij v Vizantii' (The dispute about the development of feudal relationships in Byzantium), *Vizantijskie očerki*, Moscow, 1961, 41 ff. But see also Z. V. Udalcova and A. P. Každan, 'Nekotorye nerešennye problemy social'no-economičeskoj istorii Vizantii' (Some unsolved problems in the social and economic history of Byzantium), *Voprosy istorii* 1958, 10, 83 ff., and the objections put forward by M. J. Sjuzjumov, 'Nekotorye problemy istorii Vizantii' (Some problems in the history of Byzantium), ibid. 1959, 3, 101 ff., which I consider to be justified.

Roman system of the ἐπιβολή had provided for the compulsory conveyance of waste land to the owner of cultivated acres and consequent liability for the appropriate tax on this additional land (cf. above, p. 41). This had now been altered, for the tax on the fallow land was laid on the neighbouring farmers, who at the same time acquired the right to enjoy the use of the extra ground. This new regulation making the community liable for the taxes is first met with in the *Farmer's Law* and appears later on under the designation of ἀλληλέγγυον.[1] The transference of the land becomes merely a consequence of the transference of the tax which is the factor of primary concern. The fundamental Byzantine axiom that the owner is the tax-payer now receives its full recognition.

Towards the end of the seventh century the system of assessing the main taxes seems to have undergone an important change. The connection between the poll tax and land tax, which was an essential feature of the system of the *capitatio-iugatio* instituted by Diocletian, had survived up to the beginning of Justinian II's reign,[2] but this now disappeared. The poll tax was levied apart from the land tax and was applied to all tax-payers alike, so that in future liability for poll tax did not depend on land tenure. The fixed regulations of the early Byzantine period had meant that the tax-payers had been systematically bound to the soil in order to ensure payment of taxes at a time when labour was scarce, but with the alteration in the system, the main reason for this fell to the ground, and the reform of the methods of taxation therefore encouraged a rise in the numbers of the free-moving peasants.[3]

[1] The relationship between the provisions of the *Farmer's Law* on this matter (§ 19) and the *allelengyon* regulations is also referred to by Lipšic, *Viz. Krest'janstvo* 104, while Každan, *Gorod i derevnja*, 169 ff., and 'K voprosu ob osobennostjach feodal' noj sobstvennosti v Vizantii VIII–X vv.' (On the question of the characteristics of feudal holdings in Byzantium from the eighth to the tenth centuries), VV 10 (156), 63 ff., denies it.

[2] *Vita Johannis* V, c. 2 and *Vita Cononis* c. 3. Cf. Hartmann, *Byz. Verwaltung* 90, 171, and Stein, 'Vom Altertum' 150, 152.

[3] Ostrogorsky, 'Das Steuersystem im byzantinischen Altertum und Mittelalter', B 6. (1931), 229 ff., where the ἐπιβολή-ἀλληλέγγυον problem is also dealt with. Cf. N. A, Constantinescu, 'Réforme sociale ou réforme fiscale?' *Bulletin de l'Acad. Roumaine.* Section Hist. 11 (1924), 94 ff., but he incorrectly expounds the nature of the tax reform in question by assuming a capitation tax levied only upon the non-property-owning population. He also goes too far in the assumption that the tax reform not only developed, but even created, the peasants' freedom of movement, and by reviving the old theme of Zachariä, Paparrhegopulos, Vasiljevskij and Uspenskij he assumes that serfdom entirely disappeared from the seventh to the eleventh centuries, without realizing that during this period πάροικοι who are serfs are frequently met with. An attempt has recently been made to deny the fundamental difference between ἐπιβολή and ἀλληλέγγυον by J. Karayannopulos, 'Die kollektive Staatsverantwortung in der frühbyzantinischen Zeit', *Vierteljahrschr. f. Sozial u. Wirtschaftsgesch.* 43 (1956), 289 ff. But cf. Lemerle, 'Histoire Agraire', 219, 37 ff.

There was also the steady growth of ecclesiastical and monastic estates which were constantly being enlarged by the gifts of devout Byzantines of all classes, from the Emperor down to the humblest peasant. This process, together with the rapid increase of monasticism, reveals the rising power of the Church. A clear picture of the extent to which monastic life had spread in Byzantium is found in the account given later on by Patriarch John of Antioch at the end of the eleventh century, which in spite of its obvious exaggeration seems to be fairly characteristic. This important representative of the eastern clergy and determined advocate of the validity of monastic claims to property maintained that the population of the Byzantine Empire before the outbreak of the iconoclast controversy fell into two almost evenly balanced groups—monks and laity.[1] The increase in monastic possessions corresponded to the increase in the numbers of monasteries and monks.[2]

Justinian II was an exceedingly devout ruler. In the legends on his coinage he called himself the *servus Christi* and he was the first Byzantine Emperor to have the figure of Christ stamped on the reverse side of his coins.[3] During his reign in 691-2 a Council was held which is known as the Quinisextum, since its many disciplinary canons supplemented the doctrinal decrees of the last two oecumenical Councils, the fifth of 553 and the sixth of 680-1; it is also sometimes called the Council *in Trullo* because it was held in the domed room in the imperial palace, the Trullian Hall. The 102 canons of the Council laid down rulings for ecclesiastical administration and ritual and particularly emphasized the need to raise and strengthen the Christian morale of the people and clergy. Certain customs and usages were condemned, partly by reason of their pagan origin and partly on moral grounds, but they afford interesting insight into the folklore of the time. It is evident that pagan festivals were still observed; at the Brumalia men and women, disguised and masked, danced in the streets, at the wine harvest songs were sung in honour of Dionysus, and at the new moon funeral pyres were erected in front of the houses and young men jumped over the fire. These and many other customs dating from pagan times were now forbidden,

---

[1] Migne, PG 132, 1117 ff.

[2] Cf. Vasiljevskij, 'Materialy', *Trudy* IV, 319 ff. There is also a detailed study by M. Levčenko, 'Cerkovnye imuščestva V–VII vv. v Vostočno-Rimskoj imperii' (Ecclesiastical property from the fifth to the seventh centuries in the East Roman Empire), VV 27 (1949), 11 ff.

[3] Wroth, *Byz. Coins* II, 333 ff. and pl. XXXVIII ff.; Grabar, *Empereur* 164, and *Iconoclasme*, 36ff.

and amongst the various rulings there was also one which laid down that the students of the university of Constantinople were not to take part in theatrical shows.[1] From the historical point of view the most significant decrees of the Quinisextum Council were those revealing differences in matters of discipline in the eastern and western Churches, as for instance the permission for priests to marry, or the express rejection of the Roman fast on Saturdays. Scarcely ten years after agreement on doctrinal problems had been reached at the sixth General Council fresh disputes now broke out between Rome and Byzantium. This time the conflict did not arise over matters of faith, but over questions which revealed the divergent developments of the two world centres.

It is not surprising that the Pope refused to accept the decrees of the Quinisextum. Justinian II thought that he could act in the manner of his grandfather and bring this dispute to a speedy conclusion. He sent his representative to Rome to arrest the Pope and bring him to Constantinople to stand his trial before the Emperor. But times had changed since Martin's day. The Emperor no longer had the same authority in Italy, while the papal position had been considerably strengthened. The militia of both Rome and Ravenna took such exception to the demands of the imperial representative that he had to throw himself on the Pope's generosity in order to escape with his life. This was indeed a revenge for the humiliation which the Papacy had suffered at the hands of the Byzantine Emperor forty years earlier. But this time the humiliation inflicted on the Emperor was to go unavenged, for shortly afterwards Justinian II was dethroned.

The Heraclians' policy of making the military small-holders and the free peasantry the backbone of the Empire was hardly likely to commend itself to the Byzantine nobles. Under Justinian II the policy of the government took on a markedly anti-aristocratic emphasis, and the abrupt provocative manner of the young Emperor, who never shrank from violent measures, drove the opposition to a head. Well-informed oriental sources tell us that Justinian's proceedings threatened the aristocracy with complete destruction. Nor indeed were his measures exactly calculated to win popular support. His policy of colonization might be essential for the needs of state, but it was very hard on those whom it affected, who were forcibly

---

[1] The effectiveness of such prohibitions should not be overestimated. For instance, the festival of the Brumalia is met later on, and even held at the imperial court; cf. Philotheus (ed. Bury), 175.

torn from their homeland and transplanted to an unknown and unfamiliar country. Moreover Justinian's rule involved his subjects in heavy financial burdens, especially as the Emperor, in imitation of his great namesake, had a passion for indulging in building activity on a most extravagant scale.[1] His merciless extortion filled the people with particular bitterness against the officials in charge of the financial departments, Stephen the σακελλάριος and Theodotus the λογοθέτης γενικοῦ, who seem to have been distinguished by unusual brutality and ruthlessness. Towards the end of 695 a revolt broke out against Justinian II's government, and Leontius, the *strategus* of the new theme of Hellas, was raised to the throne by the party of the Blues.[2] Both Justinian's chief officials, the *sacellarius* Stephen and the logothete Theodotus, were sacrificed to the fury of the mob, while Justinian himself had his nose cut off. The deposed Emperor was exiled to Cherson where Pope Martin had once ended his life.

4. THE DOWNFALL OF THE HERACLIAN DYNASTY

The changes of 695 introduced great uncertainty into Byzantine affairs and inaugurated a time of troubles which was to last for more than twenty years. This period of internal confusion exposed the Empire to fresh dangers and brought new and heavy losses. The first severe blow came with the failure to keep imperial possessions in North Africa. For some time previously Arab attacks on the exarchate of Carthage had died down, but its fall was only a question of time after the failure of Constans II's plan to find an effective means of defending the western territories. In 697 the Arabs broke

---

[1] For instance, he completed the imperial palace and built two enormous and splendid halls which connected the throne room, the *chrysotriclinium*, with the palace of Daphne and the Hippodrome; one was called Justinian's *lausiacus* and the other his *triclinium*. Cf. D. Beljaev, *Byzantina* I (1891), 45 ff.; J. Ebersolt, *Le Grand Palais de Constantinople* (1910), 77 ff. and 93 ff.; J. B. Bury, 'The Great Palace', BZ 21 (1912), 219 ff.

[2] Georg. Mon. II, 731, 17 (ed. de Boor): στασιάσας Λεόντιος ὁ πατρίκιος ἀναγορεύεται νυκτὸς ὑπὸ τοῦ δήμου τῶν βενέτων βασιλεύς. M. Levčenko, 'Venety i prasiny v Vizantii v V–VII vv.' (Greens and Blues in Byzantium from the fifth to the seventh centuries), VV 26 (1947), 182, has pointed to this important passage, and has also made excellent use of the oriental sources on Justinian's struggle with the aristocracy. The passage cited from George the Monk shows that, like Heraclius himself, Justinian II supported the Greens and was an opponent of the Blues. It also shows, as Levčenko rightly emphasizes, the error of maintaining that the political activity of the demes ceased in the time of Heraclius, a view which until recently was generally accepted. This must now be rejected, particularly as the valuable evidence which Maricq ('Partis populaires' 63 ff.) has collected from the sources makes it plain that the political significance of the demes persisted until the beginning of the ninth century.

into Latin Africa and after a series of rapid successes they took Carthage. The Byzantine fleet, which the Emperor Leontius (695–8) had hurriedly dispatched to Africa, was able once more to take command of the situation. But in the next spring the Arabs brought up reinforcements by sea and land and the Byzantines had to yield to their superior strength and abandon the country. As a result of this defeat the Byzantine fleet rebelled against Leontius, and Apsimar the *drungarius* of the Cibyraeot theme was proclaimed Emperor. Thanks to the support of the city militia belonging to the faction of the Greens, he easily gained possession of the capital and ascended the imperial throne as Tiberius II (698–705). He owed as much to the help of the Greens as his predecessor had done to the Blues.[1] The deposed Leontius was shut up in a monastery after his nose had been cut off, the same penalty which he had inflicted on Justinian whom he had deposed three years before.

During his reign Tiberius II did not make any attempt to regain the lost exarchate of Carthage, or even to check the further advance of the Arabs in Africa. As they advanced the Arabs had therefore only to contend with the native Moorish tribes and by the beginning of the eighth century they had reached the shores of the Atlantic Ocean. The first real opposition which they met with was at Septem, the western outpost of the Byzantine Empire on the African coast (the modern Ceuta on the Straits of Gibraltar). With the fall of this fortress in 711, the Arabs were masters of the whole of the North African coast and they immediately turned to the conquest of Spain, where they soon overpowered the Visigoths. Thus the Arabs entered Europe by a devious route along the northern shores of Africa, after they had found their eastern entry through the Balkans barred by the strong walls of Constantinople.

However, the dynasty of Heraclius was destined to return to power in the person of Justinian II. Neither his cruel mutilation nor his banishment to distant Cherson could tame his restless spirit; he could not accept his fate with resignation, but he brooded over possibilities of return and revenge. He was particularly encouraged by the change of ruler in 698, and as his behaviour became daily more suspicious the local authorities of Cherson resolved to hand him over to the government of Constantinople. Warned in time,

---

[1] Cf. A. Maricq, 'Partis populaires' 66 ff., on the basis of the anonymous Brussels Chronicle ed. by F. Cumont, Chroniques byzantines du manuscrit 11376 (*Anecdota Bruxellensia* I), p. 30: Ἀψίμαρος ἀνηγορεύθη ὑπὸ τῶν πρασίνων, στεφθεὶς ὑπὸ τοῦ αὐτοῦ Καλλινίκου πατριάρχου.

Justinian managed to escape to the empire of the Khazars where he was received with honour by their Khan and even married his sister, who became a Christian and, significantly enough, took the name of Theodora, the wife of Justinian I. These escapades of Justinian roused great anxiety in Constantinople and Tiberius II sent an embassy to the court of the Khazars to demand the extradition of the deposed Heraclian. The Khan did not wish to endanger his good relations with Byzantium and he therefore agreed to comply with this demand. Once more Justinian was warned in time of the danger threatening him and he again escaped, and after countless adventures he reached the western shores of the Black Sea. Here he established relations with Tervel, the Khan of the Bulgars, and was assured of his assistance. Accompanied by Tervel, in the autumn of 705 he appeared before the walls of Constantinople at the head of a formidable army of Slavs and Bulgars. But even this force was powerless against the walls of the Byzantine capital. Three days passed without any result and Justinian's claims to the throne were rejected with scorn and derision. He then crawled through a pipe of the aqueduct into Constantinople at night with some bold followers and caused such panic in the astonished capital by this surprise attack that Tiberius fled and left the field to his daring rival. Justinian found supporters in the city and he was able to take possession of the Blachernae palace, and for a second time he ascended the throne of his ancestors after ten years of exile and adventure. For six years (705–11) the capital on the Bosphorus was ruled by the Emperor 'without a nose', the 'Rhinotmetus', who had disregarded the cruel mutilation and the disqualifications which normally went with it. Indeed, his strength of will showed the ineffectiveness of this form of penalty which had so often been used in the seventh century, and in future it was no longer practised on usurpers and deposed rulers. Justinian shared his throne with his wife Theodora. On the success of his *coup d'état* he had sent to the Khazars for her and she joined him, bringing with her the son who had been born during her husband's absence. The child was called Tiberius and made co-Emperor with his father.

The rewards which Justinian heaped upon his friends and the revenge which he took upon his enemies were certainly out of the ordinary. The Bulgars were to receive again the tribute which the Empire had had to pay them in Constantine IV's day,[1] and as a

[1] Cf. Dujčev, *Proučvanija vŭrchu bŭlgarskoto srednovekovie* (Studies in the Bulgarian Middle Ages), Sofia 1945, 5 ff.

special mark of honour the Bulgar Khan, Tervel, was given the title of Caesar, which even though it had lost its earlier significance (cf. above, p. 106) still ranked next to the imperial title. It was the first time that this distinction had been granted to a foreign prince; it did not confer imperial power, but it did carry with it a share in imperial honours. Before Tervel returned home again, laden with costly presents, he received the homage of the Byzantine people as Caesar, sitting enthroned beside the Emperor.[1] On the other hand, Tiberius-Apsimar, who was seized in flight, and Leontius, who had been deposed seven years earlier, were exposed to public ridicule and were then executed. A considerable number of the more important officers were hanged from the walls of Constantinople. The Patriarch Callinicus, who had crowned Leontius, was punished by having his eyes put out. These were only the first victims of a systematic reign of terror which aimed at exterminating all the Emperor's enemies. During his second period of government Justinian II more than earned the reputation of a blood-thirsty tyrant which was given him by his contemporaries and by posterity. Obsessed by an unquenchable lust for revenge, he was entirely blind to the most pressing needs of state, and neglecting the war against the enemies of the Empire, he concentrated all his strength on an exhausting conflict with his personal opponents.

It was the Arabs who profited by this. In 709 they besieged Tyana, one of the most important fortresses on the Cappadocian frontier. The Byzantine army which opposed them was inadequate and under poor leadership, since the best officers had fallen victims to the purge; it was badly defeated and Tyana, exhausted by a long siege and now without any hope of relief, surrendered to the enemy. In the course of 710 and 711 the Arabs made various inroads into Cilicia, apparently without meeting with any kind of opposition, and they occupied a number of fortresses. A small Arab detachment even got as far as Chrysopolis and did considerable damage there.

Meanwhile the Emperor's mass executions in Constantinople had not satisfied him and he sent a punitive expedition against Ravenna in revenge for the hostile attitude of the inhabitants towards him during his first reign. The city had to endure being sacked and pillaged and its most eminent citizens were brought in chains to Constantinople and executed there, while their Bishop had his eyes

---

[1] Nicephorus 42, 23. The information in Theophanes 376, that Justinian II broke the peace soon after and attacked the empire of the Bulgars is not reliable, especially as it is established that Tervel's troops helped Justinian in 711, as they had done in 705.

put out. But the dispute with Rome over the decrees of the Quini-sextum was settled in a peaceable manner, and towards the end of 710 Pope Constantine I visited Constantinople at the invitation of the Emperor and was received with the greatest honours.

Justinian's punitive expedition to Ravenna in 709 had been followed by an insurrection which broke out either late in 710 or early in 711, but failing to take warning, he took similar measures against Cherson, the place of his former exile. His vengeance here was even more ruthless than in Ravenna, and it was to cost him his life. The population of Cherson were the first to rebel and they were followed by the imperial army and navy whose leaders at each failure had laid themselves open to the revenge of the suspicious Emperor. The revolt was supported by the Khazars, who had expanded their authority to include the Crimean peninsula.[1] An Armenian, Bardanes, was proclaimed Emperor, and when he appeared with a fleet before Constantinople, the capital opened its gates to him. There was no one left within the city who would support Justinian and the deposed Emperor was killed by one of his own officers. His head was sent to Rome and Ravenna and publicly exposed. His small son and heir, Tiberius, was also murdered.[2] Thus the famous house of Heraclius came to an end in bloodshed and terror.

It was the first Byzantine dynasty in the real sense of the word, a dynasty whose representatives had ruled the Empire for five genera-tions during the course of a whole century. This gifted family pro-duced a series of men in whom a genuine capacity for statesmanship was combined with a peculiar instability: the great Heraclius brought new life to the Empire and at the head of his army led a holy crusade and celebrated fantastic victories over the mighty Persian Empire, and then, enervated and worn out, apathetically looked on while the Arabs advanced, and ended his life in brooding melancholia; Constans II, the son of a consumptive weakling, came to the throne as a child with living memories of a deadly family feud, showed himself to be a self-willed daredevil, and fell a victim to an impracticable ideal; Constantine IV, the heroic conqueror of the Arabs, who had most claim, after his grandfather, to be called the saviour of the Empire, great military commander and statesman, died at the early age of thirty-three; and, finally, Justinian II, an outstanding and gifted ruler, worked more than any other to build up the Heraclian

---

[1] Cf. A. Vasiliev, *The Goths in the Crimea* (1936), 83 ff.

[2] On the second reign of Justinian II and his downfall cf. Ch. Diehl, *Choses et gens de Byzance* (1926), 190 ff.

administrative system, but by his overweening despotism, by his lack of self-control and inhuman, almost morbidly perverse, cruelty, brought upon himself a tragic end and caused the downfall of his house.

The creative period of the Heraclian dynasty came to an end with the first reign of Justinian II. During the years between Heraclius' rise to power and the first downfall of Justinian, the Byzantine Empire had the hardest struggle for existence which it had ever known, and it underwent the most fundamental internal reorganization. Conqueror of the Persians and Avars, Byzantium had nevertheless to surrender extensive and wealthy territories to the Arabs. But after a bitter struggle it managed to retain its vital central lands and in so doing barred the Muslim's entry into Europe and effectively staked its claim to be a great power. The extent of the Empire had been drastically reduced, but within its new frontiers Byzantium stood more compact and united than before. Radical internal reforms and the infusion of young unexploited sources of energy from without brought a fresh lease of life to the worn-out Late Roman Empire. Its military system was tightened up and given a measure of uniformity and the army was reorganized by settling on the land small-holders with military obligations, and, finally, a strong free peasantry developed who brought the land under cultivation and as tax-payers formed the mainstay of the imperial exchequer. These fundamental principles were established in the seventh century and on them rested the future strength of the Byzantine polity. Thanks to the reforms of the Heraclian dynasty the Empire was able to defend itself against the Arab and the Bulgar and eventually to embark upon a victorious offensive in Asia and in the Balkan peninsula.

Though this age saw many heroic battles, it produced comparatively little in the way of cultural activity. For the decline of the old aristocratic class brought with it the dwindling of the ancient culture which it represented, and the splendour and riches of literature and art in the period of Justinian were followed in the seventh century by a period of cultural sterility. This deficiency gives the period a gloomy aspect, all the more so as a streak of real oriental cruelty appears in Byzantine life and customs. Little was produced in the field of the visual arts. Secular literature and learning had nothing to say. Their place was taken by theology spurred on by new doctrinal disputes. The power and prestige of the Church was on the increase. Byzantine life developed a strongly mystical and ascetic character. The Emperors themselves were mystics—Heraclius was the 'liberator of the Holy Land', Constantine was the 'torch of orthodoxy' and Justinian 'the servant of God'.

The universal Roman Empire now belonged to the past. While Germanic kingdoms were growing up in the West, Byzantium, however much it clung to Roman political conceptions and Roman traditions, became a medieval Greek Empire. Greek culture and the Greek language finally triumphed in the eastern reaches over the artificially cultivated Romanism of the early Byzantine transitional period, thus giving the Eastern Empire its own distinctive characteristics and guiding its development in a new direction.

III

The Age of the Iconoclast Crisis (711-843)

SOURCES

FOR the first part of this period the chronicles of the Patriarch Nicephorus (to 769) and of Theophanes (to 813) which have already been mentioned are fundamental. Both chroniclers describe the iconoclast controversies from the point of view of an iconodule, and the partiality of Theophanes is particularly noticeable.[1] The same iconodule outlook is also shown by the somewhat fuller historical writings which cover the second period of the iconoclast controversy. George the Monk wrote a world chronicle in Michael III's reign (842-67) which goes to 842 and is a typical product of monastic circles;[2] only the last part from 813 to 842 is of independent value, while the earlier years have been written up from Theophanes. The most valuable part of the very important world chronicle of Symeon Logothetes also begins where Theophanes left off. This chronicle was a tenth-century work which has survived in several versions: the chronicle of Theodosius Melitenus,[3] the Continuation of George the Monk and the chronicle of Leo Grammaticus, besides existing in many unedited manuscripts[4] and in an Old Slavonic transla-

---

[1] There is an extensive and critical examination of sources in the posthumous work of K. N. Uspenskij, 'Oćerki po istorii ikonoborćeskogo dviženija v vizantijskoj imperii v VIII–IX vv. Feofan i ego chronografija' (Studies in the history of the iconoclast movement in the Byzantine Empire in the eighth and ninth centuries: Theophanes and his chronicle), VV 3 (1950), 393–438 and 4 (1951), 211–62. He attempts to show that the source used by Theophanes and Nicephorus for this period comes from the iconoclast camp and is marked by a tendency to be pro-iconoclast which was twisted in the opposite direction by the two iconodule writers. A careful analysis of the sources does not, however, support this view. To take an example—both writers give the same reason for the lowering of the price of food under Constantine V, i.e. that the avaricious iconoclast had hoarded up gold, and they both therefore call him a new Midas (Theoph. 443, 19 and Niceph. 76, 5). It is quite obvious that this mocking comparison had been provided by their common source. For the same negative conclusion, based on the same arguments, but without knowledge of my observations, see Alexander, *Patr. Nicephorus* 158 ff.

[2] ed. C. de Boor, 2 vols., Leipzig 1904; the interpolated work and the continuation ed. E. Muralt, St. Petersburg 1859.

[3] ed. Th. Tafel, Munich 1859.

[4] Cf. S. P. Šestakov, VV 4 (1897), 167 ff. and 5 (1898), 19 ff.

tion.[1] For the second period of the iconoclast controversy there are also the first three books of Joseph Genesius who wrote under Constantine VII (945–59) and the first three books of a compilation likewise made at the instigation of Constantine, and known as the Continuation of Theophanes (Οἱ μετὰ Θεοφάνην, 'Theophanes continuatus').[2] On the Bulgarian campaign of Nicephorus I and the eventful battle of 26 July 811 there is now the source discovered by Dujčev, a detailed anonymous Διήγησις, based on a contemporary account written directly after the fight.[3] There is detailed work on the reign of Leo V (813–20) also by an anonymous hand,[4] and Grégoire[5] argues convincingly that this and the *Diegesis* on the Bulgarian campaign of 811 are by the same author and are fragments from a work which is now lost.[6] The important *Chronicle of Monemvasia* must be mentioned here for its information on the Slav occupation of the

[1] ed. V. I. Sreznevskij, St. Petersburg 1905. For the complicated problem of the compilation of this work and the relation between the different recensions cf. especially V. G. Vasiljevskij, 'Chronika Lagofeta na slavjanskom i greceskom' (The Chronicle of the Logothete in Slavonic and Greek), VV 2 (1895), 78–151; G. Ostrogorsky, 'Slavjanskij perevod chroniki Simeona Logofeta' (The Slavonic translation of the chronicle of Symeon the Logothete), SK 5 (1932), 17 ff.; A. Každan, 'Chronika Simeona Logofeta' (The Chronicle of Symeon the Logothete), VV 15 (1959), 125 ff. Cf. also the literature given in Moravcsik, *Byzantinoturcica*, I, 517 ff.

[2] For the question of the sources of Genesius and the 'Theophanes continuatus', see the recent study of F. Barišić, 'Les sources de Génésios et du continuateur de Théophane pour l'histoire du règne de Michel II', B 31 (1961), 257 ff., who demonstrates amongst other things that for the reign of Michael II (820–9) both authors use the contemporary work of Sergius Homologetes mentioned in the *Bibliotheca* of Photius. Cf. also idem, Dve verzije u izvorima o ustaniku Tomi (Two versions of the sources on Thomas' revolt), ZRVI 6 (1960), 145 ff., and see also p. 210 below under Ch. IV, Sources.

[3] There are at present three editions: Dujčev, *Spisanie na bŭlg. Akad. na naukite* (Publications of the Bulgarian Academy of Sciences), 54 (1936), 147 ff.; Beševliev, *Godišnik na Sofijskija Universitet* (Yearbook of the University of Sofia), 33, 2 (1936); Grégoire, B 11 (1936), 417 ff. In addition to the accounts of the Byzantine sources, the inscriptions in old Bulgarian are also important for the history of Bulgaria in the ninth century: V. Beševliev, 'Pŭrvobŭlgarski nadpisi' (The earliest Bulgarian inscriptions), *Godišnik na Sof. Univ.* 31, 1 (1934) and 'Dobavki i opravki', ibid. 32, 5 (1935); cf. H. Grégoire, 'Les sources épigraphiques de l'histoire bulgare', B 9 (1934), 745 ff.

[4] *Scriptor incertus de Leone Armenio*, in CB after Leo Grammaticus.

[5] H. Grégoire, 'Un nouveau fragment du "Scriptor incertus de Leone Armenio"', B 11 (1936), 417 ff., and 'Du nouveau sur la chronographie byzantine: le Scriptor incertus de Leone Armenio est le dernier continuateur de Malalas', *Bull. de l'Acad. de Belgique* 22 (1936), 420 ff.

[6] L. Tomić, 'Fragmenti jednog istoriskog spisa IX veka' (Fragments of a lost historical chronicle of the ninth century), ZRVI 1 (1952), 78 ff., shows that the lost work was written in the second half of the ninth century (after the Christianization of Bulgaria) and may be described, not as a continuation of the chronicle of Malalas as Grégoire thought, but rather as a contemporary history.

Peloponnese from the end of the sixth to the beginning of the ninth centuries.[1]

Accounts in Byzantine sources of Byzantino-Muslim relations are very considerably filled out by the information given by the Arab historians of whom Tabari (839–923) is one of the most important. He was an eminent scholar who compiled a world history from the creation to his own day, and he gives a good deal of detail on the wars between Byzantium and the Arabs; the older sources which he uses are usually quoted almost verbatim.[2] The descriptions of the Arab geographers are also of great value, in particular Ibn-Hordadbeh, Kudama and Ibn al Fakih, who give useful information on conditions in the Byzantine Empire with special reference to the military organization and the system of themes.[3] Recent research, especially the various pioneer investigations of Grégoire, has shown that the popular epic of Digenis Akritas contains rich historical material on the Byzantino-Muslim struggle.[4]

In their treatment of the iconoclast controversy the Byzantine chroniclers and historians mentioned above all adopt an iconophile point of view. The same is true to an even greater extent of the hagiographical writings of this period which are dedicated to the iconodule martyrs and are understandably in the nature of panegyric. In spite of this, several of these works have considerable value in supplementing the meagre accounts of the purely historical sources. Of the numerous saints' lives of the iconoclast period only those which are most important to the historian can be mentioned here.

[1] ed. N. Bees, Τὸ περὶ τῆς κτίσεως τῆς Μονεμβασίας χρονικόν, Βυζαντίς 1 (1909), 37 ff. On this cf. P. Charanis, 'The Chronicle of Monemvasia and the Question of the Slavonic Settlements in Greece', *Dumbarton Oaks Papers* 5 (1950), 141 ff., where details are given of the earlier works of this author and of existing literature on the problem. Charanis rightly stresses the reliability of the information given in the Chronicle of Monemvasia and makes the suggestion that it also lies behind the lost history mentioned above, as the *Diegesis* on the Bulgarian campaign of Nicephorus I and the history of Leo V can be identified as part of it.

[2] ed. M. J. de Goeje, 3 vols. (1879). Extracts from the most important accounts of Arab historians for the period of the Amorian dynasty are given in Vasiliev, *Byzance et les Arabes*, I, App. 267–394. For the period of the Macedonian dynasty see Vasiliev, *Byzance et les Arabes*, II, 2.

[3] M. J. de Goeje, *Bibl. geogr. Arab.* VI (1899), 77 ff. and 197 ff.; E. W. Brooks, 'Arabic Lists of the Byzantine Themes', JHS 21 (1901), 67 ff. Cf. Gelzer, 'Themenverfassung' 17 ff., 81 ff. See also the edition of an anonymous Persian geographical work of the year 982 by V. Minorsky, *Hudūd al-'Alam*, London 1937 (with English trans. and excellent notes).

[4] Cf. the survey by H. Grégoire, Ὁ Διγενὴς Ἀκρίτας. Ἡ βυζαντινὴ ἐποποιία στὴν ἱστορία καὶ στὴν ποίησι, New York 1942. There is an excellent new edition of the poem with an English translation and commentary by J. Mavrogordato, *Digenes Akrites*, Oxford 1956. There is a Russian translation by A. J. Syrkin, *Digenis Akrit*, Moscow 1960. See also his studies in VV 18 (1961), 124–49; 19 (1961), 97–119; 20 (1961). 129–55, as well as the detailed account of the research into the problem of Digenis, VV 17 (1960), 203–26.

The *Life of St. Stephen the Younger* († 767), written in 808 on the basis of earlier information by Stephen, deacon of Hagia Sophia, gives the oldest and fullest account of the persecutions under Constantine V, and the defects which characterize literary memorials of this kind are balanced by a wealth of historical detail.[1] Another source of primary importance is the *Life of Nicetas*, Abbot of the monastery of Medicium in Bithynia († 824), written by his pupil Theosterictus soon after the saint's death.[2] The *Life of Philaretus the Merciful* († 792), written in 821/22, is of significance, not however for the iconoclast controversy, but for the internal history of the Byzantine Empire.[3] The contemporary *Life of John*, Bishop of Gothia,[4] and the *Acta* of the forty-two martyrs of Amorium are also of great historical value.[5]

The most important writings on the question of icons in the first period of the iconoclast controversy are the letters of the Patriarch Germanus (715–30), which are of considerable significance,[6] and particularly the three orations of John of Damascus.[7] The Νουθεσία γέροντος περὶ τῶν ἁγίων εἰκόνων gives the teaching of George of Cyprus and the draft of the report of a debate between this saint and an iconoclast bishop, one of those disputations which were probably very frequent before the first iconoclast council was summoned.[8] The orations of John of Damascus and the *Nouthesia* formed the basis of John of Jerusalem's writings composed just before the Council of Nicaea was called,[9] and all of these three sources were used by the anonymous author who is known as the 'Adversus Constantinum Cabalinum'.[10] The most vital theological works of the second period of iconoclasm are the writings and letters of Theodore the Studite,[11] together with the numerous works of the Patriarch Nicephorus who has already been mentioned as an historian.[12] There is also the

---

[1] Migne, PG 100, 1069 ff.   [2] AASS, 1 April, App. 22-32.
[3] ed. A. Vasiliev, IRAI 5 (1900), 49–86. New edition with French trans. by M. H. Fourmy and M. Leroy, B 9 (1934), 112 ff.
[4] AASS, 25 June, 190 ff.
[5] ed. V. Vasiljevskij and P. Nikitin, *Mémoires de l'Acad. Imp. de St. Pétersburg*, VIII. Serie, VII, 2 (1905). Cf. A. Vasiliev, ibid. III, 3 (1898).
[6] Migne, PG 98, 156 ff.   [7] Migne, PG 94, 1232 ff.
[8] ed. and detailed commentary by Melioranskij, *Georgij Kiprjanin*, p. 1 ff. Cf. E. Kurtz, BZ 11 (1902), 538 ff.
[9] A στηλευτικὸς λόγος (Migne, PG 96, 1348 ff.) belongs to him and another unedited and apparently more important work. Cf. Melioranskij, *Georgij Kiprjanin*, 99 ff.
[10] Migne, PG 95, 309 ff.; cf. J. M. Hoeck, OCP 17 (1951), 26 and note 2.
[11] Migne, PG 99.
[12] Migne, PG 100, 169 ff.; Pitra, *Spicilegium Solesmense* I (1852), 302 ff., and IV, 233 ff. The main theological work of Nicephorus in MS. Coisl. 93, f. 1–158ᵛ and in Bibl. Nat. MS. gr. 250, f. 173–332 is unedited. A detailed account of its contents is now given by Alexander, *Patr. Nicephorus*, 242–62.

Figure 31: *St. Theodore the Studite.* Mosaic panel, Monastery of Nea Mone, Chios, Greece. Photo: Pericles Papahadjidakis.

Figure 32: (ABOVE) *Church of Hagia Sophia.* Trebizond, 10th century. Exterior view from the southeast. (BELOW) *City Walls of Nicaea.* Both views from engravings in Charles Texier, *Description de l'Asie Mineure*, Paris, 1839.

letter which the oriental Patriarchs addressed to the Emperor Theophilus (829–42) in order to encourage him in his iconoclast policy.[1]
Like the works of John of Damascus and Theodore the Studite, the
acta of the seventh oecumenical Council of Nicaea (787) are of first-
rate significance for the question of icons.[2] Not a single iconoclast
work has survived in its original form, because the general Council
of 787 ordered the destruction of writings of this kind and a similar
ruling must have been made by the Council of 843. A number of
fragments have been preserved in iconodule works where they were
cited for reasons of polemic. Thus the decisions of the first iconoclast synod of 754 can be reconstructed from the *acta* of the Nicene
Council, and similarly the writings of Patriarch Nicephorus provide
the substance of the decisions of the second iconoclast synod of
815 and of the Emperor Constantine V's two orations which are of
outstanding theological and historical significance.[3]

Among the biographies of contemporary Popes the *Life* of
Gregory III is particularly valuable, especially for the light which it
throws on relations between Rome and Byzantium.[4] The authenticity of the two letters of Gregory II to Leo III which have survived
in the Greek translation is debatable, but no one would now sweep
aside these two important documents as mere forgeries.[5] In addition

[1] ed. Duchesne, *Roma e l'Oriente* III (1912), 225 ff. A later version is found in the
Epist. ad Theophilum, Migne, PG 95, 345 ff.
[2] Mansi 12, 959 ff., and 13, 1 ff.
[3] Reconstructed with commentary by Ostrogorsky, *Bilderstreit* 46 ff. and 7 ff. For a
much better and fuller edition of the decrees of the iconoclast synod of 815 cf. P. J.
Alexander, 'The Iconoclastic Council of St. Sophia (815) and its Definition', DOP 7
(1953), 58 ff.
[4] Duchesne, *Liber Pontificalis* I, 415 ff.
[5] Jaffé 2180 and 2182; Mansi 12, 959 ff. Re-edited by E. Caspar, 'Papst Gregor II.
und der Bilderstreit', *Zeitschr. f. Kirchengesch.* 52 (1933), 72 ff. (This cannot be regarded
as a critical edition.) Against earlier research (Duchesne, *Liber Pontificalis* 413, note 45;
Schwarzlose, *Bilderstreit* 113 ff. and others) I have defended their authenticity, apart from
errors of translation and interpolations of later copyists (Ostrogorsky, 'Querelle des
Images', 224 ff.); for further detail cf. E. Caspar, op. cit. 29 ff., who considers that there
is extensive interpolation in the first letter. The authenticity of both letters is now also
supported by V. Grumel, EO 35 (1936), 234 ff.; H. Menges, *Die Bilderlehre des Johannes
von Damaskus* (1938), 167; Bréhier-Aigrain 452; Bréhier, *Vie et mort* 79; S. Der Nersessian, 'Une apologie des Images du VIIe siècle', B 17 (1944–5), 64, note 25. Cf. F. Dölger,
BZ 33 (1933), 451 f. On the other hand, H. Grégoire, B 8 (1933), 761 ff., wishes to
return to the position of Hartmann, *Byz. Verwaltung* 131 ff. (cf. also *Gesch. Italiens im
Mittelalter* II, 2, p. 118, note 22), who maintains that the second letter is genuine, but
the first a later forgery based on the second. J. Haller, *Das Papsttum* I (1936), 502,
considers both letters to be 'pure forgeries'. A. Faggiotto, 'Sulla discussa autenticità
delle due lettere di Gregorio II a Leone III Isaurico', *Studi biz. e neoell.* 5 (1939), 437 ff.,
tries to argue against their authenticity but does not make any new points and even
appears to ignore the paper of E. Caspar. J. Gouillard, 'Les Lettres de Grégoire
II à Léon III devant la critique du XIVe siècle', ZRVI 8, 1 (1961), 103 ff., presents an
interesting examination of the manuscript tradition of this exchange of letters as a
preliminary study to a critical edition on which he is engaged.

to these, there is another letter from Gregory II to the Patriarch Germanus the authenticity of which is uncontested.[1] Authoritative information on the attitude of the West to the question of icons is found in both the *Libri Carolini*[2] and the letters of Hadrian I to Charlemagne[3] and to the Byzantine rulers.[4]

The most important legal work of the period is the *Ecloga* of Leo III issued in 726.[5] For the laws attributed to Leo III by earlier scholars see above, pp. 90 f.

1. IMPERIAL RIVALRY

The grave crisis which befell Byzantium at the time of the icono-clast controversy had already been foreshadowed during the reign of Philippicus-Bardanes, and herein lay the historical significance of his brief and unfortunate reign. Philippicus revived the Christo-logical disputes, and he also provoked a peculiar conflict over icons, a conflict which was not concerned, it is true, with the cult of icons as such, yet used the symbolical nature of the icon as an instrument of controversy, and to this extent anticipated the great iconoclast struggle of the ensuing years.

An Armenian, more closely attached to his native land than the descendants of Heraclius, Bardanes-Philippicus seems to have had monophysite tendencies. Whilst not prepared to go so far as to risk a revival of monophysitism, he did in fact appear as a decisive

---

[1] Jaffé 2181; Migne, PG 98, 147 ff.

[2] MG Conc. II suppl.

[3] MG Ep. V, 1 p. 5 ff.

[4] Mansi 12, 1055 f.; this should be compared with the Greek translation which was used at the Council of Nicaea and contains very important deviations from the original (cf. my comments in *Sem. Kond.* 6 (1933), 73 ff.).

[5] ed. J. Leunclavius, *Jus graeco-romanum* II (1596), 79 ff. (apparently from a Vienna MS.); Zachariä von Lingenthal, *Collectio librorum iuris graeco-romani ineditorum* (1852) (from various MSS.); A. Monferratus, *Ecloga Leonis et Constantini* (1889) (from an Athens MS.); the text has been reprinted by Zepos, *Jus* II, 1 ff.; with French trans. and comment-ary by C. A. Spulber, *L'Éclogue des Isauriens* (1929); with Bulgarian trans. and commentary by N. P. Blagoev, *Ekloga* (1932). E. H. Freshfield, *A Manual of Roman Law, the Ecloga* (1926), gives an English trans. and commentary based on the text of Monferratus.

The date when the *Ecloga* was promulgated has been much disputed, but it seems certain that it was published in March 726. Cf. V. G. Vasiljevskij, 'Zakonodatelstvo ikonoborcev' (The legislation of the iconoclasts), *Trudy* IV (1930), 157 ff.; D. Ginis, BZ 24 (1924), 346 ff.; Ostrogorsky, 'Chronologie', 6 f.; Spulber, op. cit. 83. Blagoev, op. cit. 19 ff., supports the year 741, using the arguments which had been put forward by Biener for 739, and by G. E. Heimbach and Zachariä for 740 (and which had already been refuted by Vasiljevskij), but this position is untenable. V. Grumel, EO 34 (1935), 327 ff., also supports the same date, but this is based on his erroneous chronological calculations (cf. above, p. 88, note 1) and does not take account of the arguments of Vasiljevskij and Spulber.

advocate of monotheletism which had been condemned thirty years before at the sixth oecumenical Council. An imperial edict issued on his own authority rejected the decisions of this Council and declared monotheletism to be the only orthodox doctrine. This change found symbolical expression in the destruction of a representation of the sixth oecumenical Council in the imperial palace, and in the removal of an inscription commemorating the Council affixed to the Milion gate in front of the palace. In its place portraits of the Emperor and of the Patriarch Sergius were set up.[1] In the same way, the iconoclast Emperors in later years removed icons of a religious nature and gave the widest publicity to the imperial portrait. Though the monotheletism of Philippicus did not prevail and his ecclesiastical policy roused strong opposition and hastened his downfall, he found, all the same, many supporters, or at least sympathizers, amongst the higher Byzantine clergy, including the later Patriarch Germanus. Furthermore, monophysite tendencies were again discernible, thus showing that the monophysite-monothelete heresy had by no means been eradicated in Byzantium.

The Emperor's open profession of a heresy which had been rejected by the latest oecumenical Council naturally roused great antagonism in Rome, where this disapproval was shown in a somewhat peculiar way. When announcing his accession to the throne Philippicus had sent to Pope Constantine I, together with his portrait, a confession of faith imbued with the monothelete spirit. The picture of the heretical Emperor was rejected in Rome, permission to impress it on coins was refused and his name was omitted from prayers prescribed in the church services and from the dating of deeds and documents.[2] The Pope answered the removal of the representation of the sixth oecumencial Council from the imperial palace in Constantinople by ordering pictures of the entire six councils to be put up in St. Peter's.[3] Thus shortly before the outbreak of the great iconoclast controversy, this curious estrangement arose between the heretic Emperor and the Pope. The bone of contention in this dispute was the icon, and both parties demonstrated their convictions by their acceptance or refusal of certain pictorial representations.[4]

[1] Agathon Diac., Mansi 12, 192 DE.
[2] Cf. the excellent arguments of P. E. Schramm 'Die Anerkennung Karls des Grossen als Kaiser, Ein Kapitel aus der Geschichte der mittelalterlichen "Staatssymbolik"', HZ 172 (1951), 452 ff.
[3] Duchesne, *Liber Pontif.* 391. Cf. Kulakovskij, *Istorija* III, 309, note 2, contrary to Bury, BZ 5 (1896), 570 f.   [4] Cf. Grabar, *Iconoclasme*, 42 ff.

Serious convulsions in the sphere of foreign affairs served to increase existing confusion. The Arabs took advantage of the uncertainty created by the recent change of government in Byzantium to make renewed incursions into imperial territory. In particular, the Bulgar Khan Tervel lost no opportunity of avenging the murder of his former ally Justinian II by waging war against the new Byzantine Emperor. He advanced to the walls of Constantinople and laid waste the surrounding country. The rich villas and estates in the neighbourhood of the capital, where the leading families usually spent their summer, were plundered and devastated by the Bulgar hordes. The fact that Tervel was able to march through the whole of Thrace unmolested and advance as far as the walls of the capital showed how weak the Byzantine forces were in the European part of the Empire. In order to save the situation, soldiers had to be ferried across the Bosphorus from the Opsikion theme. But these troops revolted against Philippicus and on the 3 June 713 he was dethroned and blinded.

Although this revolt originated with the army, it was a civil servant, the *protoasecretis* Artemius, who was proclaimed Emperor. At his coronation he took the name Anastasius after his imperial predecessor Anastasius I at the turn of the fifth century, who had likewise been a civil servant before his accession and had distinguished himself as Emperor by his unusual capacity for financial administration. The first act of the new Emperor was to rescind the monothelete decrees of his predecessor, and solemnly to acknowledge the sixth oecumenical Council. The pictorial representation of this Council, which Philippicus had removed, was restored and the portraits of Philippicus and the Patriarch Sergius were destroyed.[1] The incursions of the Arabs, who seemed to be preparing an attack upon Constantinople, caused further concern. Anastasius II made every effort to remedy military inadequacies. He undertook the defence and provisioning of the capital, appointed his ablest generals as commanders and finally decided to anticipate the enemy by a surprise attack upon the Muslim fleet while it was still being fitted out. The island of Rhodes was selected as the base for the Byzantine forces, but scarcely had the Opsikians arrived here than they raised the standard of rebellion, sailed back to the mainland and proclaimed as Emperor a tax-gatherer of their own province, one Theodosius. In order to escape this unexpected and somewhat dangerous honour

---

[1] Agathon Diac., Mansi 12, 193 E–196 A.

Theodosius fled, but he was captured and compelled to accept the imperial crown. Instead of an attack on the Arabs, a civil war broke out which lasted a full six months until finally the Opsikians, with the support of the 'Gothogreeks' (Γοτθογραῖκοι),[1] i.e. the Hellenized Ostrogoths, who had inhabited the provinces of the present theme Opsikion since the days of the great migration, were able to install their candidate on the throne of Constantinople towards the end of the year 715. Anastasius became a monk and withdrew to Thessalonica.

Theodosius III, the 'reluctant' Emperor, reigned a still shorter time than his predecessor. He was not the central figure of subsequent developments, but Leo, the *strategus* of the Anatolikon theme. A *parvenu* of humble origin, Leo came from North Syria[2] and during the first reign of Justinian II was transferred with his parents to Thrace in accordance with the Emperor's policy of resettlement. Fortune had favoured him, for, when after a ten-years' exile the Emperor 'with the slit nose' advanced through Thrace in order to win back the throne of his fathers, the young peasant offered him his services and was rewarded with the office of *spartharius*. From this moment his rise to fame began, first in the service of Justinian II, and later, in that of his rapidly changing successors. A lengthy and hazardous expedition to the Caucasus gave him an opportunity of showing his military and diplomatic abilities. Anastasius II, whose aim was to put his ablest generals in positions of command, appointed him *strategus* of the Anatolikon theme and so placed him over one of the largest and most important Byzantine provinces. Leo used his position as a jumping-off ground for winning the imperial crown by revolting against the feeble Theodosius after the fall of Anastasius. He allied himself with Artabasdus, the *strategus* of the Armeniakon theme, promising him his daughter's hand in marriage and the high title of *curopalates*. The outcome of the struggle between the feeble Emperor and this powerful usurper was never in doubt, especially as Leo was in control of superior forces. The struggle was really a fight between the two eastern

---

[1] Theophanes 385 f. Cf. Kulakovskij, *Istorija* III, 414 ff.

[2] He originated in Germaniceia in North Syria. K. Schenk, BZ 5 (1896), 296 ff., shows that the words τῇ ἀληθείᾳ δὲ ἐκ τῆς Ἰσαυρίας in the chronicle of Theophanes (p. 391) are a later addition. I agree with this view, though some scholars support the Isaurian ancestry, e.g. Kulakovskij, *Istorija* III, 319, note 2, who relies on the tradition that at baptism Leo received the 'typically Isaurian' name of Conon. Pope Conon (686–7) was, however, certainly no Isaurian, but according to the *Liber Pontificalis* 'natione grecus, oriundus parte Tracesio, edocatus apud Siciliam'.

themes, the Anatolikon and the Armeniakon, and the Opsikion theme which supported Theodosius III. Leo marched through the Opsikion territory, captured the Emperor with his imperial household in Nicomedia and advanced to the gates of Chrysopolis. Negotiations were then opened, and once Theodosius had been given the necessary assurances for himself and his son, he abdicated and ended his life as a monk in Ephesus.

On 25 March 717 Leo entered Constantinople and was crowned Emperor in Hagia Sophia. Thus ended an era of struggles for the imperial throne. The Empire, which had seen seven violent changes of government in the course of twenty years, found in Leo III (717–41) a ruler who was not only to establish a firm and durable government but was also to found a new dynasty.

2. THE ICONOCLAST CONTROVERSY AND THE ARAB WARS: LEO III

General bibliography: K Schenk, *Kaiser Leo III,* Halle 1880; M. V. Anastos, 'Iconoclasm and imperial rule 717–842', CMH IV Pt. I (2nd. ed., 1966); F. Dvornik, 'Constantinople and Rome', ibid; M. Canard, 'Byzantium and the Muslim world to the middle of the eleventh century', ibid.,; H. J. Scheltema, 'Byzantine law', ibid., Pt. II (2nd. ed., 1967).; Schwarzlose, *Bilderstreit*; L. Bréhier, *La Querelle des Images,* Paris 1904; Martin, *Iconoclastic Controversy*; M. J. Sjuzjmov, 'Problemy ikionoborčeskogo dvizenija v Vizantii' (Problems of the iconoclast movement in Byzantium), *Učenye zapiski Sverdlovskogo gos. ped. inst.* 4, Sverdlovsk 1948, Lipšic, *Očerki,* 170 ff.; Andreev, *German i Tarasij*; Ostrogorsky, 'Querelle des Images'; idem, 'Über die vermeintliche Reformtätigkeit der Isaurier', BZ 30 (1929–30), 394–400; Diehl, *Exarchat*; Hartmann, *Byz. Verwaltung*; idem, *Geschichte Italiens im Mittelalter* II, 2, Gotha 1903.

The first and most urgent task of the new Emperor was the defence against the ever-growing menace of the Arabs, who again threatened the existence of the Empire. Since internal conflicts had foiled the Byzantine counter-attack under Anastasius II, the struggle was once more fought out beneath the walls of the Byzantine capital. Leo III hastily organized the city in preparation for the impending siege and perfected the defensive measures which Anastasius II had already begun in prudent anticipation. In August 717 the brother of the Caliph, Maslama, stood before Constantinople with an army and a fleet. As in the days of Constantine IV, there began once again a bitter struggle that was destined to determine the fate of the Byzantine Empire. And again, as forty years before, the decisive battle was won by Byzantium. With the help of Greek fire, the Byzantines managed to set alight the enemy's fleet, whilst Arab attempts to take Constantinople by storm failed before the strength of the city walls. In addition, the winter of 717–18 was particularly severe; Arabs perished in large numbers, and then the Arab camp was stricken by a terrible famine, which made even greater inroads upon them. In addition, the Arab army was attacked by the Bulgarians, who inflicted heavy losses on them. On 15 August 718, exactly a year after it had begun, the siege was lifted and the Muslim ships left Byzantine waters.[1] Thus for the second time the Arab onslaught upon the gates of Europe collapsed before the walls of the Byzantine capital.

But by land war was soon renewed and waged with extreme bitterness. Every year since 726 the Arabs had invaded Asia Minor; Caesarea was invested, Nicaea besieged and the Arab threat was only averted by the victory of Leo III at Acroinon, not far from Amorium, in the year 740. The Empire received strong support through its traditional friendship with the Khazars who felt themselves united with the Byzantines in common hostility to the Caliphate.[2] They created serious difficulties for the Arabs by incursions into the Caucasus and Armenia. The alliance with the Khazar kingdom was further strengthened by the marriage of Leo III's son and successor, Constantine, with the daughter of the Khazar Khan in 733.

The liberation of Constantinople and the expulsion of the Muslims from Asia Minor concluded an important phase in the Byzantino-Muslim struggle. Later attacks by the Arabs frequently caused considerable concern to the Empire, but they did not threaten its very existence. Never again did the Arabs lay siege to Constantinople, and Asia Minor, which, thanks to the organization of its themes, now rested on a sound and solid foundation, remained in spite of many reverses an integral part of the Empire.

In developing the new administrative system, Leo III partitioned the overlarge Anatolikon theme. The primary purpose of this measure was to forestall any usurpations of the throne such as had recently happened. None knew better than Leo the dangers to which the occupant of the throne would be exposed as long as a

[1] A detailed description of the siege, drawing on all the sources and relevant literature, is given by R. Guilland, 'L'expédition de Maslama contre Constantinople (717–18)', *Études byzantines*, Paris 1959, 109 ff.
[2] For the friendly relations between Byzantium and the Khazars in the eighth century see Vasiliev, *The Goths in the Crimea* (1936), 87.

single *strategus* controlled such a vast area. He therefore made the western part of the Anatolian district into an independent theme. This was called the Thracesion theme after the European regiments once settled there, who had originally formed a *turma* of the Anatolikon theme. This procedure throws considerable light on the genesis of the theme system.[1] The Opsikion theme, equally large if not larger, remained however unpartitioned. Leo seemed content to appoint his son-in-law Artabasdus as commander in the Opsikion theme. His son and successor was destined to discover the magnitude of his error; after a new and fateful warning his son halved the vast territory, and raised the eastern portion to the status of an independent theme, which was named Bucellarion after the ancient *bucellarii* who had settled there.[2] On the other hand, the maritime theme of the Carabisians, which originally included the entire naval strength of the imperial provinces, was divided into two between 710 and 732 under either Anastasius II or Leo III. Each subdivision previously governed by a *drungarius* under the *strategus* of the Carabisians now became an independent unit: the southern coast of Asia Minor with the neighbouring islands was from now onwards the Cibyraeot theme, while the Aegean islands formed the drungariate of the Aegean Sea (Aigaion Pelagos) which later attained the rank of a theme and was further divided.[3] Crete must have been raised to the status of a theme at about the same time.[4] The division of these enormous seventh-century themes was doubtless also significant from the point of view of administration; it lent elasticity to the administrative machinery and thus helped to perfect the entire system. In this way the Emperors of the eighth century continued the great work of the Heraclian dynasty, if only on a modest scale.

[1] See above, pp. 95 ff. and p. 100, note 3. A *strategus* of the Thracesion theme occurs for the first time in 741 (Theophanes 414). Cf. Diehl, 'Régime des thèmes' 282, and Gelzer, 'Themenverfassung' 77 f.

[2] A *strategus* of the Bucellarion theme occurs for the first time in 767 (Theophanes 440). Cf. Gelzer, 'Themenverfassung' 79.

[3] By 710 there is mention of a *patricius et stratigos caravisionorum* (*Liber Pont.* 390); in 732 the *strategus* of the Cibyraeots appears (Theophanes 410). Cf. Diehl, 'Régime des thèmes' 280 ff.; Gelzer, 'Themenverfassung' 34; R. Guilland, 'Études de titulature et de prosopographie byzantines. Les chefs de la marine byzantine', BZ 44 (1951) (*Dölger-Festschrift*) 212.

[4] A *strategus* of Crete is mentioned in the *Vita* of Stephen the Young († 767), Migne, PG 100, col. 1164. The credit for drawing attention to this passage belongs to G. Spyridakis, Τὸ θέμα Κρήτης πρὸ τῆς κατακτήσεως τῆς νήσου ὑπὸ τῶν Ἀράβων, ΕΕΒΣ 21 (1951), 59 ff., who would like to assume that Crete received the rank of theme under Leo III. Cf. also H. Glykatzi-Ahrweiler, 'L'administration militaire de la Crète byzantine,' B 31 (1961), 217 ff., who is probably right in supposing that Crete was previously subject to an *archon* and formed an archontate.

A more far-reaching development of the theme system was left to the following century.[1]

The legal manual which Leo III published in the year 726 in his own name and that of his son is a landmark in the history of the codification of Byzantine law.[2] The *Ecloga* of the Emperors Leo and Constantine offers a selection of the most important rulings of private and criminal law in existence at that time; particular attention was devoted to family law and the law of inheritance, whilst the law of property occupied a secondary place. The main purpose of publishing the *Ecloga* was to provide the judge with a legal manual which in scope and content was adapted to practical needs and would replace the cumbersome and rarely accessible legal manuals of Justinian I. The *Ecloga* was based on Roman law as laid down in the *Corpus Juris* of Justinian which continued to form the basis of Byzantine jurisprudence. The *Ecloga* was not meant, however, to be excerpts from the old laws, but it attempted a revision in the direction of 'greater humanity'. The *Ecloga* does in fact reveal considerable departures from the *Corpus* of Justinian, departures which are to be attributed on the one hand to the influence of canon law, on the other hand to the influence of oriental customary law. Thus the *patria potestas* was severely limited, while the rights of the wife and children were considerably extended and marriage enjoyed increased protection. Particularly noticeable were certain changes in criminal law which were scarcely dictated by a spirit of Christian philanthropy. Thus the *Ecloga* provided a whole system of penalties of life and limb such as was unknown to the law of Justinian, e.g. cutting off the nose, tearing out the tongue, chopping off the hands, blinding, shaving the head and burning off the hair and so on. These cruel punishments were indeed in some cases substitutes for the death sentence, in other cases they replaced the fines imposed by the law of Justinian. The truly oriental delight in mutilation and in horrible corporal punishments as revealed in the *Ecloga*, in contrast

[1] For a long time it was generally held by Byzantinists that Leo III was responsible for a fundamental reorganization of the themes as well as of other aspects of Byzantine administration, but this does not receive the slightest support from the sources. Cf. my arguments in 'Über die vermeintliche Reformtätigkeit der Isaurier', BZ 30 (1929–30), 394 ff. Ch. Diehl, *Le monde oriental de 395 à 1081* (1936), 255 f., attempts to revive the old theory, but in describing Leo III's 'work of reorganization' he relies on the νόμος στρατιωτικός and the νόμος γεωργικός, while admitting (p. 256) that they cannot be attributed to Leo with any certainty (on these laws cf. above, p. 90 f.).

[2] For the dates see above under Sources, p. 152, note 5, where bibliography is also given.

to Roman law, was not entirely unknown in Byzantium; the history of the seventh century provides ample evidence for this. In so far as the *Ecloga* departs from the law of Justinian, it provides a record of customary law as it had developed in the course of the seventh century.[1] It shows the changes which Byzantine law and legal consciousness had experienced since the days of Justinian, changes which were due partly to the deeper penetration of Christian ethics, partly to a coarsening of morals under oriental influence.

The publication of a new legal manual, easily accessible to all and generally comprehensible, was undoubtedly an advantage in the administration of law and justice. In the preface to the *Ecloga* there is a remarkable declaration wherein the Emperor voices his determination to put an end to bribery and corruption in legal appointments and to arrange for all judges, from the quaestor downwards, to have their salaries paid by the state.[2] In later years the *Ecloga* stood in low repute because it was the work of the iconoclasts Leo and Constantine; nevertheless, it was of considerable importance for future Byzantine legislation and exercised decisive influence upon the development of law in Slav countries beyond the frontiers of the Byzantine Empire.

The conflict over icons opened a new and unusual chapter in Byzantine history. Leo III's opposition to the cult of icons initiated the crisis which characterized this epoch and made the Empire the scene of severe internal struggles for more than a century. The storm gathered slowly. It took the form of a conflict over images because of the particular symbolical significance which attached to the icon according to the Byzantine conception. In the Greek Church the veneration of sacred icons had become increasingly widespread in the course of recent centuries, particularly in the period after Justinian, and it had become one of the chief expressions of Byzantine piety.[3] On the other hand, there were many within the Church itself who opposed this and maintained that Christianity, as

---

[1] R. S. Lopez, 'Byzantine Law in the Seventh Century and its Reception by the Germans and the Arabs', B 16 (1942–3), 445 ff., thinks that it is possible to assume that this customary law had been written down as early as Heraclius' day and that it would have influenced both Arab and Germanic law.

[2] Zepos, *Jus* II, 16.

[3] Cf. especially the important contribution by E. Kitzinger, 'The Cult of Images in the Age before Iconoclasm', DOP 8 (1954), 83–150.

a purely spiritual religion, must proscribe the cult of icons.[1] This opposition was particularly marked in the eastern districts of the Empire, for long the cradle of religious ferment, where considerable remnants of monophysitism persisted and where the Paulicians, a sect hostile to any ecclesiastical cult, were steadily gaining ground. But it was contact with the Muslim world which first fanned the smouldering distrust of icons into open flame.

The hostile attitude of Leo III was attributed by his opponents to Jewish and Muslim influences. It is true that Leo III persecuted the Jews and forced baptism upon them,[2] but this does not exclude the possibility that he was influenced by the Mosaic teaching with its strict repudiation of image-worship. In the same way, his struggle with Islam does not preclude a possible susceptibility to Muslim culture. The persecution of the Jews under Leo III, one of the relatively rare persecutions in Byzantine history, should be regarded rather as evidence of an increase in Jewish influence at the time. From the seventh century a good deal of Byzantine theological polemic was concerned with Jewish attacks upon Christianity. More significant still is the indication of Leo's friendly attitude towards the Muslims revealed by the nickname of 'Saracen-minded' (σαρακηνόφρων) which his contemporaries gave him. The Arabs, who for some years had ranged through Asia Minor, brought not only the sword, but also their own civilization and their peculiarly Muslim abhorrence of any pictorial representation of the human countenance. Thus the iconoclast controversy in the eastern districts of the Empire arose from the interaction of a Christian faith striving for pure spirituality, with the doctrines of iconoclast sectarians, the tenets of old Christological heresies and the influences of non-Christian religions, such as Judaism and especially Islam. The military challenge of the East had been met. Now the struggle began against the infiltration of oriental cultural influences, and this took the shape of a controversy over the use of icons. The pioneer

---

[1] Cf. the interesting comments on the whole problem by H. v. Campenhausen, 'Die Bilderfrage als theologisches Problem der alten Kirche', *Zeitschr. f. Theol. u. Kirche* 49 (1952), 33 ff., with full bibliography, and G. Ladner, 'The Concept of the Image in the Greek Fathers and the Byzantian Iconoclastic Controversy', DOP 7 (1953), 1 ff., and also S. Der Nersessian, 'Une apologie des images du septième siècle', B 17 (1944/5), 58 ff.; G. Florovsky, 'Origen, Eusebius and the Iconoclastic Controversy', *Church History* 19 (1950), 77 ff.. Cf. also N. H. Baynes, 'The Icons before Iconoclasm', *Harv. Theol. Rev.* 44 (1951), 93 ff. (reprinted in Baynes, *Byzantine Studies*).

[2] Theophanes 401. Details on this in J. Starr, *The Jews in the Byzantine Empire 641–1204*, Athens 1939.

in this battle was the very same Emperor who had driven back the Muslim onslaught from the gates of Constantinople.

Active measures against the veneration of icons were first taken by the Umayyid Empire several years before the outbreak of the iconoclast controversy in Byzantium.[1] At the same time a movement hostile to icons was growing stronger in Byzantine Asia Minor, where an influential iconoclast party had come into being. At its head stood the ecclesiastical dignitaries in Asia Minor, the Metropolitan Thomas of Claudiopolis and particularly Constantine of Nacolea, the real spiritual instigator of Byzantine iconoclasm, whom the orthodox Byzantines called 'the arch-heretic'. Leo III, himself an Asian, who had lived many years in the eastern districts of the Empire and as *strategus* of Anatolia had been in close contact with the Muslims, also associated himself with the iconoclast movement. Thus the latent iconophobia was transformed into open iconoclasm. In the year 726 Leo III publicly entered the lists against the iconodules for the first time.[2] He did so at the request of the iconoclast bishops of Asia Minor who had been staying in the capital shortly before;[3] he was strengthened in his resolution by a severe earthquake which, as a true son of his age, he regarded as a sign of divine wrath directed against the use of icons. The Emperor then delivered sermons in which he tried to convince his people of the folly of iconolatry.[4] This in itself showed that he regarded his imperial authority as being entrusted to him by God; as he later wrote to the Pope, he considered himself to be not only Emperor, but also High Priest.[5] But he soon resorted to active intervention. An icon of Christ over the Bronze Gate of the Imperial Palace was removed by an officer on the express orders of the Emperor. This first attempt at enforcing an iconoclast programme showed how fiercely the population in the capital resented the Emperor's policy, for the infuriated crowd slew the imperial agent on the spot. More significant than this street brawl was the insurrection which the

---

[1] Byzantine sources record that the Caliph Jezid II ordered the destruction of Christian icons of the saints in his kingdom in the year 723–4. In fact he ordered the destruction not only of Christian icons, but of all representations of living beings intended for religious purposes, and similar measures had already been taken by Jezid's predecessor, the Caliph Omar II (717–20). On all these problems see Grabar, *Iconoclasme*, 103 ff.

[2] Theophanes 404, 3. Τούτῳ τῷ ἔτει ἤρξατο ὁ δυσσεβὴς βασιλεὺς Λέων τῆς κατὰ τῶν ἁγίων καὶ σεπτῶν εἰκόνων καθαιρέσεως λόγον ποιεῖσθαι.

[3] On this and the following passage cf. Ostrogorsky, 'Querelle des Images', 235 ff.

[4] *Vita Stephani*, Migne PG 100, 1084 B; Nicephorus 57.

[5] Mansi 12, 975 (= Caspar, *Zeitschr. f. Kirchengesch.* 52, 85, l. 382), βασιλεὺς καὶ ἱερεύς εἰμι.

news of the Emperor's hostility to icons provoked in Greece. The theme Hellas set up a rival Emperor and sent its fleet to attack Constantinople. Thus, from the very first, the European parts of the Empire betrayed their iconodule sympathies, an attitude which was destined to reveal itself throughout the course of the controversy. The Emperor had no difficulty in supressing the rebellion, but the revolt of an entire province was a warning which could not be ignored.

Despite Leo's fanatical devotion to the cause of iconoclasm, he proceeded with the utmost caution. It was only in the tenth year of his reign that he had decided to come into the open against icons, and several more years were to pass before he took the final step.[1] These years were spent in negotiation with the chief ecclesiastical authorities; in order to strengthen his position he attempted to win over the Pope and the Patriarch of Constantinople. But his proposals were decisively rejected by the aged Patriarch Germanus, and his correspondence with Pope Gregory II only produced negative results.[2] Though Gregory II turned down the iconoclast overtures of the Emperor in an unusually caustic manner, he strove to avoid any breach with Byzantium. He went even further and tried to quell the disaffection against the Emperor which was continually manifesting itself in Italy. By dissociating the religious from the political question, he managed to preserve full loyalty towards the Byzantine Emperor whose protection against the Lombard danger was still essential to the Papacy.[3]

Next to the Patriarch Germanus and Pope Gregory II, the Emperor's principal opponent was John of Damascus. A Greek

[1] Leo III did not promulgate a 'first' edict against veneration of icons in 726, as has been argued from a misinterpretation of the passage from Theophanes 404 cited above (p. 162, note 2), but in this year he began to speak openly against icons (ἤρξατο λόγου ποιεῖσθαι), and his only (not his 'second') decree against them was first promulgated in 730. This view is based on the irrefutable evidence of the sources as I have shown, Ostrogorsky, 'Querelle des Images', 238 ff. E. Caspar's objection (*Zeitschr. f. Kirchengesch.* 52 (1933), 54 f.) is based on the erroneous assumption that the *Vita Gregori II* recognizes two edicts (*Liber Pontif.* pp. 404 and 409). In actual fact the passage which speaks of the '*iussiones*' of the Emperor is not referring to an edict, but to the famous (first) letter of Leo III to the Pope. It is known that in Rome this expression was often used when referring to imperial letters. Most scholars have accepted my interpretation: cf. F. Dölger, BZ 31 (1931), 458 ff.; H. Menges, *Die Bilderlehre des hl. Johannes von Damaskus* (1938), 33; L. Bréhier, EO 37 (1938), 21 f., and *Vie et mort* 79; Bréhier-Aigrain 448 ff.; J. Haller, *Das Papsttum* I (1936), 328 and 520; Alexander, *Patr. Nicephorus* 9; Beck, *Kirche* 299.

[2] On the authenticity of Gregory II's letters to Leo III see above under Sources, p. 151 f. Whatever conclusions are reached with regard to the texts in question, the fact remains that letters were exchanged and with negative results.

[3] In his useful book *Gesch. des Papsttums* II (1933), E. Caspar grossly distorts the figure of Gregory II whom he represents as a national revolutionary.

who had held high office at the court of the Caliph in Damascus and had later entered the monastery of St. Sabas near Jerusalem, John was the greatest theologian of the century. The three speeches which he wrote in defence of icons, although not among his best-known writings, are his finest and most original work.[1] In order to meet the accusation that the cult of icons was a revival of pagan idolatry, John developed his own views on icons in which he explained that the image was a symbol and a mediator in the neo-platonic sense, and he justified the use of the image of Christ by the doctrine of the incarnation, thus linking the whole question of icons with the doctrine of salvation.[2] This system worked out by John of Damascus determined the entire later development of iconodule teaching.

After all attempts at negotiation had failed, Leo III had to resort to force to carry through his plans. He took this course and issued an edict ordering the destruction of all holy icons. At the same time, he sought to maintain a pretence of legality. On 17 January 730 he convened an assembly of the highest secular and ecclesiastical dignitaries, the so-called *silentium*, and asked them to subscribe to the edict that was to be promulgated. The Patriarch Germanus refused and was immediately deposed. His former *syncellus* Anastasius, who was prepared to obey the Emperor's command without question, ascended the patriarchal throne on 22 January. By the promulgation of the iconoclast edict, the doctrine condemning the use of icons became legally valid. The icons were destroyed and the iconodules persecuted.

The Emperor was in no position to enforce iconoclasm in distant Italy. But the conflict over icons in Byzantium had serious repercussions upon the relationship between Constantinople and Rome. After the promulgation of the iconoclast edict establishing the iconoclast doctrine as the official teaching of Church and State, the long-delayed breach could no longer be avoided. Pope Gregory III, the successor to Gregory II, was compelled to condemn the Byzantine iconoclasm at a Council, while Leo III had the legates of Gregory III thrown into prison. The Emperor and Pope had both failed in their hopes of converting each other. Political estrangement

---

[1] Cf. H. Menges, *Die Bilderlehre des hl. Johannes von Damaskus*, Münster 1938.
[2] Cf. Schwarzlose, *Bilderstreit* 187 ff., and my study, 'Soedinenie voprosa o sv. ikonach s christologičeskoj dogmatikoj' (The holy icons and their connection with Christological doctrine), *Sem. Kond.* 1 (1927), 35 ff.

followed upon religious dissension. The first political effect was a widening of the gulf between Constantinople and Rome and a noticeable decline in the position of Byzantium in Italy.

3. ICONOCLASM AND THE WARS WITH BULGARIA: CONSTANTINE V

General bibliography: A. Lombard, *Constantin V, empereur des Romains*, Paris 1902; Melioranskij, *Georgij Kiprjanin*; Ostrogorsky, *Bilderstreit* (for the iconoclast controversy and relations with Italy see also the general bibliography cited above on p. 156); Zlatarski, *Istorija* I, 1; Mutafčiev, *Istorija* I; Runciman, *Bulgarian Empire*; D. Obolensky, 'The Empire and its northern neighbours 565-1018', CMH IV, Pt I (2nd ed., 1966).

Despite the high reputation which Leo III enjoyed as conqueror of the Arabs, the excesses of the iconoclasts had undermined his popularity. After Leo's decease the throne was occupied by his son, Constantine V (741-75). The young prince had been crowned co-Emperor by his father when he was only two years old (Easter 720) and his right to the imperial throne at Leo's death was unquestioned. Yet he had been barely in power for a year when a rival Emperor rose up against him and seized the throne for some months. This was Artabasdus, who as *strategus* of the Armeniakon theme had helped Leo III to gain the throne. In return for his services he had been given the Emperor's daughter in marriage, rewarded with the title of *curopalates* and then promoted to be count of the Opsikion theme. As supreme commander of the entire fighting forces of this vast and important military area, Artabasdus could risk insurrection against his young brother-in-law. Another powerful factor in winning him support was his opposition to iconoclasm. His struggle with the lawful Emperor, and indeed the whole epoch, was fundamentally affected by the iconoclast controversy. During a campaign which Constantine undertook in 742 against the Arabs, his army was suddenly attacked by Artabasdus as it marched through the Opsikion theme, and was defeated. Artabasdus then proclaimed himself Emperor and entered into negotiations with Theophanes Monutes, whom Constantine had left behind as regent in Constantinople. The latter, as well as several high officials, joined the rival Emperor—clear evidence that even the closest collaborators of the Emperor were not united in their support of the iconoclast policy. Artabasdus marched into Constantinople with his army and was crowned Emperor by the Patriarch Anastasius, who once more changed sides. Artabasdus made his elder son Nicephorus co-Emperor, while his younger son Nicetas was given supreme command of the army and despatched to the Armeniakon theme. The holy icons were again restored in Constantinople and it looked as though the iconoclast struggle had ended.

Meanwhile, Constantine V had fled and was enthusiastically received in Amorium which had once been the centre of his father's military command in the Anatolikon theme. Moreover, the Thracesion theme which had recently been split off from the vast original Anatolikon theme also supported the young iconoclast, whilst the iconodule Emperor found his strongest support in the European theme of Thrace, whose *strategus*, the son of the above-mentioned Theophanes Monutes, took over the defence of Constantinople. In Asia Minor Artabasdus was backed only by the two themes Opsikion and Armeniakon, which had formerly been under his command and had personal associations with him. His iconodule policy, however, apparently met with a cool reception even in these themes, and this was a factor which, together with the outstanding generalship of Constantine, materially affected the outcome of the struggle. The Opsikion troops of Artabasdus had only just appeared in the Thracesion theme and Nicetas had not had time to come to his father's assistance with the forces of the Armeniakon theme, when Constantine inflicted a heavy defeat on the rival Emperor at Sardes in May 743. He then advanced upon Nicetas, made contact with him at Modrina in August and routed his army. Thus his final victory was assured and in September 743 he stood before the walls of Constantinople. After a brief siege he celebrated his entry into the town on 2 November and took savage revenge upon his enemies. Artabasdus and his two sons suffered public ignominy and were blinded in the Hippodrome; some of his supporters were executed, others were mutilated by blinding or the cutting off of hands and feet. The faithless Patriarch Anastasius was led round the Hippodrome on a donkey, but was permitted to remain in office after this public disgrace; doubtless the punishment was deliberately aimed at discrediting the highest ecclesiastical office. Thus ended the rule of Artabasdus who had reigned a full sixteen months and had also been recognized as Emperor in Rome.[1]

---

[1] Cf. the two letters of Pope Zacharias (MG. Ep. III Nr. 57 and 58) which cite Artabasdus and his son Nicephorus as Emperors. On the chronology of Artabasdus' usurpation see Ostrogorsky, 'Chronologie' 18.

Constantine V was an even greater military commander and a more violent iconoclast than his father. Mentally and physically he was by no means the tough soldier that Leo III had been. Nervous, seriously impaired in health, a victim of unhealthy passions, he was a complex, divided personality. The excessive brutality with which he persecuted and tortured his religious opponents proceeded less from primitive cruelty than from abnormal hypersensitivity. He owed his brilliant victories over Arabs and Bulgars, which made him the idol of his soldiers, to the superior insight of a calculating strategist, allied to high personal courage.

The situation in the East had taken a favourable turn for Byzantium. The power of the Arabs was shattered by the wars of Leo III and a severe internal crisis. The illustrious Umayyad dynasty was drawing to its close, and after a lengthy civil war was replaced in 750 by the new Abbasid dynasty, thus entailing the transference of the central authority from Damascus to the more distant Baghdad and reducing Muslim pressure on Byzantium so that it could now undertake a forward policy. In 746 Constantine invaded northern Syria and occupied Germaniceia, the seat of his forefathers. In accordance with the traditional methods of Byzantine policy, he transplanted most of his prisoners to the remote territory of Thrace, where colonies of Syrian monophysites were still in existence in the ninth century.[1] At sea, too, Byzantium won a notable victory when the commander of the Byzantine navy, the *strategus* of the Cibyraeots, destroyed an Arab fleet despatched from Alexandria (747). The campaign which the Emperor undertook in Armenia and Mesopotamia was crowned with even greater success. Two important frontier fortresses, Theodosiopolis and Melitene, were captured and the prisoners were again settled in Thrace on the Bulgarian frontier which was fortified by the Emperor's orders.[2] These successes did not however bring any territorial gain to the Empire, for it was not long before the captured fortresses fell again into the hands of the Arabs. Even so, Constantine V's victories on the eastern frontier did symbolize the turn of the tide: Byzantium was no longer fighting for its very existence but could at last take the offensive. The conflict between Arab and Byzantine had now taken the form of a frontier war in which the initiative for a time lay in the hands of the Byzantine Emperor.

[1] Theophanes 422, ὧν οἱ πλείους εἰς τὴν Θρᾴκην οἰκοῦντες μέχρι τοῦ νῦν . . .
[2] Theophanes 429; Nicephorus 66.

Whilst the Arab danger grew less acute, the Bulgarian problem assumed alarming proportions. The measures undertaken by Constantine V for the protection of Thrace showed that the Byzantine government could no longer count on a continuation of the existing respite from hostilities on the Bulgarian frontier. The erection of fortifications on their frontier was interpreted by the Bulgars as a threat which they met by invading the imperial territories (756). This inaugurated a period of major wars between Byzantium and Bulgaria. Constantine V certainly felt that the Bulgars were the chief opponents of the Empire and he directed most of his military operations against them, fighting no less than nine campaigns on Bulgarian soil. The crisis was reached in 762 when Teletz, a representative of the aggressive anti-Byzantine party, gained control in Bulgaria after lengthy internal struggles. The Bulgarian principality was still rent by the conflict between the Slavs and the old Bulgar nobility intent upon the preservation of its privileges, particularly the intransigent boyar party which had come to power with Teletz.[1] After his accession a large proportion of Slavs emigrated from the Bulgarian frontier districts to Byzantium and were granted a refuge in Bithynia by the Byzantine Emperor, whose predecessors had already settled considerable numbers of Slavs in this district. Thus the Slav element in the themes of Asia Minor was powerfully reinforced.[2]

Constantine V met the invasion of the Bulgarian Khan in Thrace with a strongly equipped expedition. He despatched a fleet which brought large reinforcements of Byzantine cavalry to the estuary of the Danube and himself moved his army through Thrace into the enemy's territory. The cavalry proceeding southwards from the Danube linked up with the imperial army advancing northwards from Thrace at Anchialus on the shores of the Black Sea. On 30 June 763 a fierce battle raged lasting from dawn to dusk and

---

[1] Cf. Zlatarski, *Istorija* I, 1, 208 ff.

[2] Nicephorus 69, 1 puts the number of the Slav settlers at 208,000. This cannot simply be discarded as an exaggeration, as P. Charanis wishes to do ('The Slavic Element in Asia Minor', B 18 (1948), 77 f.). On the other hand, neither is it necessary to increase it, as Pančenko does, arguing that this figure stands only for warriors, and does not include the whole mass of the migrants with their women and children ('Pamjatnik slavjan v Vifinii' (Evidence of the Slavs in Bithynia), *Izv. Russk. Archeol. Inst. v Konstantinopole* 8 (1903), 35). Numerical exaggerations tend to be in round figures, but the closer exactness of Nicephorus' figure looks as though he most probably obtained it from official sources.

ending in the total defeat of the Bulgars.[1] Constantine V celebrated this greatest victory of his reign by a triumphant entry into Constantinople and festive games in the Hippodrome. Teletz subsequently fell victim to an insurrection, and for many years after this Bulgaria was the scene of constant revolts and changes of government. The pro-Byzantine and anti-Byzantine party alternately gained power, but the final word lay with the Byzantine Emperor who claimed the right to pronounce upon the internal affairs of Bulgaria; if events took an unfavourable turn he intervened by force. It was only when the efficient Telerig took over in 770 that Bulgaria recovered, and regained its former martial vigour. Constantine V then embarked on a vast campaign in the spring of 773; he repeated the tactics of his earlier double attack and compelled the Bulgars to sue for terms. Telerig's attempt to advance upon Thessaly in October of the same year was easily defeated by the imperial troops; but in spite of his superiority the Byzantine Emperor was unable to impose a lasting peace upon the Bulgars. To the end of his life Constantine had to wage war upon them, and it was during a campaign against these enemies that he died on 14 September 775. The wars against Byzantium had considerably weakened Bulgaria. Its military power was shattered and its administration paralysed. The courageous Telerig was himself compelled to seek refuge from the internal disorders in his country at the court of Constantine V's successor. The supremacy of the Byzantine Empire in the Balkan peninsula seemed firmly established, though in actual fact the future was fraught with danger because Bulgaria had now become the bitter enemy of Byzantium. This created a new situation in imperial foreign policy and meant that the Empire had to face prolonged and difficult warfare on its northern as well as its eastern frontier.

The great successes of Constantine against the Bulgars and Arabs were largely achieved at the expense of a foreign policy which concentrated upon the eastern sphere of influence. No ruler in Byzantium had ever shown so little concern for the maintenance of imperial authority in Italy. Whilst Constantine V was celebrating his victories

---

[1] A. Lombard, *Constantin V, empereur des Romains* 47, puts the battle of Anchialus in 762, Zlatarski, *Istorija* I, 1, 214, and Runciman, *Bulg. Empire* 38 in 763. This latter date is no doubt correct, not so much for the reasons put forward by Runciman (Zlatarski does not state the grounds for his view), as simply because Theophanes' information (433, 5) that the battle took place in indiction 1 and that 30 June was a Thursday is in complete accord; Lombard relies on the world year 6254 as given by Theophanes, but in this part of his chronicle there is the usual and, so to speak, normal discrepancy between the calculation of the year and the indiction.

in the East, Byzantine control in Italy was completely undermined. The tension between Rome and the iconoclast capital in the Bosphorus constantly increased. As long as the Papacy felt that it could count on the support of the Byzantine Empire in its resistance to Lombard pressure, and as long as there did not seem to be any other power to whom it could turn for help, it had seemed politic to ignore religious differences and to maintain complete loyalty to the Emperor. But in 751 Ravenna fell into the hands of the Lombards and the exarchate ceased to exist. This put an end to Byzantine rule in northern and central Italy and deprived the Pope of any hope of support from the Byzantine Emperor. At the same time the growing power of the Franks introduced a new factor into papal politics; Frankish protection promised more effective help against the Lombards and in many respects was more welcome to the Church of Rome than that of heretical Byzantium. Pope Stephen II crossed the Alps in person and met king Pepin at Ponthion on 6 January 754. This historic meeting was the beginning of the link between Rome and the Frankish kingdom and led to the foundation of the papal state. The Papacy turned its back upon the Byzantine Emperor and entered into an alliance with the Frankish king which less than half a century later was destined to give birth to the Western Empire.

But although Byzantium had suffered a severe setback in the West, its position was to be strengthened in the East and South. The strained relations with Rome gave the iconoclast Byzantine government the opportunity to adopt effective measures of the greatest significance for the future. The hellenized south Italian provinces of Sicily and Calabria, as well as Illyricum, had hitherto belonged to the Roman diocese; these were now separated from Rome and placed under the Patriarchate of Constantinople.[1] The repeated protests of Rome were ignored. The new boundaries between the two ecclesiastical centres now corresponded with the frontiers between the Greek East and the Latin West already defined by historical events. Thus the great champion of iconoclasm laid the foundation for the upsurge of the Byzantine Church by extending the ecclesias-

---

[1] V. Grumel, 'L'annexion de l'Illyricum oriental, de la Sicile et de la Calabre au patriarcat de Constantinople', *Recherches de science religieuse* 40 (1952), 191 ff., has shown that this step was not taken, as was previously thought, in the fourth decade of the eighth century under Leo III, but two decades later, after the collapse of Byzantine power in Italy under Constantine V. The earlier date is defended by M. V. Anastos, 'The Transfer of Illyricum, Calabria and Sicily to the Jurisdiction of the Patriarchate of Constantinople in 732–3', *Silloge bizantina in onore di S. G. Mercati*, Rome, 1957, 14 ff.

tical jurisdiction of Constantinople to the Balkan provinces of Illyricum and the hellenized region of south Italy. Once it had survived the iconoclast crisis, the Byzantine Church experienced a rapid revival which was followed by the powerful dissemination of its influence and civilization among the Slavs in the Balkans.

Thus Byzantine iconoclasm deepened the rift between the two world centres and ultimately had the effect of excluding Rome from the Greek East and Byzantium from the Latin West. This meant that the universalism of the Byzantine Empire and the universalism of the Roman Church had both lost ground.

It is no mere accident that these events coincided with the high tide of iconoclasm in Byzantium. The iconoclast struggle reached its zenith under Constantine V. To begin with, the reverberations of Artabasdus' insurrection within the European part of the Empire, and especially within the capital itself, invited caution. Constantine V, like his father, had learned how to wait, and it was not until the fifties that he proceeded to realize his plan. Under Leo an imperial decree had forbidden the use of icons; now a church council was called to sanction iconoclasm. In order to ensure a united front within the council, the Emperor attempted to appoint his own followers to episcopal sees, and in addition he set up new dioceses to which the adherents of the iconoclast doctrine were nominated. These practical measures were accompanied by vigorous literary and propagandist activity. Meetings were held in various places; leaders of the iconoclast party addressed the people, and lively debates took place between the two parties.[1] At the conclusion of such debates those who had had the courage to protest were arrested and were thus silenced for the duration of the council.

The Emperor himself played a leading part in the literary activity and composed no less than thirteen theological treatises. Only two, but apparently the most important two, have survived in fragmentary form.[2] The writings of Constantine were intended as a directive for the decisions of the impending council and they contributed materially towards a deeper understanding of iconoclast views. In contrast to the supporters of icons who drew a fundamental distinction between the icon and its prototype and regarded the icon as a symbol in the neoplatonic sense, Constantine V, influenced by occult and oriental conceptions, insisted on the complete identity,

---

[1] Cf. the *Nouthesia* of George of Cyprus, ed. Melioranskij, *Georgij Kiprjanin*, p. x ff.
[2] Collected together in Ostrogorsky, *Bilderstreit* 8 ff.

even the consubstantiality, of the picture with its prototype.[1] He introduced the Christological controversy into his arguments by his emphatic resistance to any representation of Christ, and in so doing went far beyond the arguments of the older iconoclasts who had rejected the cult of icons as a revival of idolatry. Constantine denied the possibility of any true representation of Christ by reason of His divine nature, while the iconodules such as the Patriarch Germanus, and particularly John of Damascus, justified the portrayal of Christ by virtue of His incarnation and regarded the representation of the Saviour in human form as confirmation of the reality and perfection of His incarnation. Thus both sides related the question of icons to Christological dogmatics, and the controversy continued the old Christological controversies in a new form. In its most radical forms iconoclasm encroached upon monophysitism, and even the writings of Constantine V, a representative of the extremists, revealed unmistakable monophysite tendencies.[2] This is not surprising when one remembers the strength of monophysitism on the Byzantine frontiers of Syria and Armenia, and its influence even on the teaching of Islam,[3] as well as its persistence within the Empire itself, as the monothelete reaction under Philippicus showed (cf. above, pp. 152f.).

The carefully packed council met on 10 February 754 in the imperial palace of Hieria on the Asian coast of the Bosphorus and its last session was held in the Church of the Blachernae in Constantinople on 8 August. The precautionary measures of the imperial government were successful and the assembly consisted of no less than 338 bishops, all of whom subscribed to iconoclasm, while Bishop Theodosius of Ephesus, a son of the former Emperor Tiberius-Apsimar, presided; for the Patriarch Anastasius had died towards the end of 753 and neither the Pope nor the oriental Patriarchs had sent their representatives. Their absence provoked the orthodox party into giving the assembly the nickname of 'the headless synod', but in spite of this the council demanded to be recognized as oecumenical. In drawing up its resolutions it took the imperial writings as its guide and therefore made the Christologica question the centre of its deliberations, at the same time avoiding all dangerous formulations and particularly the monophysite trends

---

[1] Ostrogorsky, *Bilderstreit* 8, fragment 2, καὶ εἰ καλῶς, ὁμοούσιον αὐτὴν (*sc.* τὴν εἰκόνα) εἶναι τοῦ εἰκονιζομένου.

[2] Cf. Ostrogorsky, *Bilderstreit* 24 ff.; Martin, *Iconoclastic Controversy* 42; Bréhier-Aigrain 467.

[3] Cf. H. Grégoire, 'Mahomet et le Monophysisme', *Mélanges Diehl* I (1930), 109 ff.

in the expositions of Constantine. The council maintained the contention that Christ could not be represented, but was careful to avoid any conflict with the findings of the earlier oecumenical councils. It explained with the greatest ingenuity that the supporters of icons were fatally committed to the monophysite or to the Nestorian heresy, since they either represented the human nature of Christ in the icon and thus separated, after the fashion of the Nestorians, the two indivisible natures of Christ, or they included in their representation His divine nature and so, like the monophysites, merged the two natures which were to be distinguished in one Person.[1] Endless passages from the Bible and patristic literature were cited in the discussions which ended in a sharp rejection of all icons of Christ, as well as of the Mother of God and the saints. During the final session the Emperor, who regarded himself as master of the Church, introduced Bishop Constantine of Sylaion, a former monk, as the new Patriarch; he had appointed him chief prelate on his own authority and had him acclaimed as such by the bishops who were present. Then on 29 August the decrees of the synod were promulgated in the forum of Constantinople, the total destruction of all icons of religious content was ordered and the leaders of the orthodox party, including the Patriarch Germanus and John of Damascus, were excommunicated. At the same time the Emperor was extolled as the equal of the Apostles.

It was now the Emperor's duty to put the recommendations of the council into action. Everywhere the holy icons were destroyed and replaced by secular paintings. Ornamental decoration, animal and plant motives, and especially portraits of the Emperor, battle and hunting scenes, theatrical scenes and chariot-racing which glorified him, were now to adorn churches and secular buildings alike. Side by side with ecclesiastical art, secular art had always played a greater part in Byzantium than is generally assumed.[2] Henceforth only this secular art lauding the Emperor and the Empire which he represented was to be cultivated. The hostility of Constantine V was not directed against art as such, but solely against religious art and the spirit which animated it, and his immediate aim was to destroy both. Supported by the findings of an ecclesiastical assembly which he regarded as having oecumenical authority, he proceeded to fulfil his mission by fire and sword.

[1] Mansi 13, 257 E–260 AB.
[2] Grabar, *Empereur*. Cf. idem, 'Les fresques des escaliers à Sainte-Sophie de Kiev et l'iconographie impériale byzantine', *Sem. Kond.* 7 (1935), 103 ff.

This fanatical lust for destruction encountered an opposition equally fanatical in its beliefs, and a bitter struggle followed which reached its climax in the sixties. Iconodule opposition rallied round Stephen, abbot of a monastery on Mt. Auxentius in Asia Minor, who found increasing support amongst all sections of the population. The Emperor failed in his attempt to compel Stephen to abandon his resistance and in November 765 he died a martyr's death in the streets of Constantinople where he was torn to pieces by the infuriated mob. There was, however, widespread discontent with the Emperor's régime as is shown by the fact that in August 766 he had to order the execution of nineteen high officials and officers, amongst them the *protostrator*, the logothete of the drome, the *domesticus* of the imperial guard, the count of the Opsikion theme and the *strategi* of Thrace and of Sicily.[1] The strongest opposition to the iconoclast policy came, however, from the monastic world and the punishment meted out to monks was particularly harsh. Persecution of the iconodules became more and more a crusade against monasticism, a policy which apparently found support in Asia Minor and amongst a section of the population of the capital. Monks were persecuted not only for their iconodule sympathies, but also simply because they were monks, and they were compelled to renounce their monastic way of life. Monasteries were closed or were converted into barracks, public baths and similar public buildings, and their vast properties confiscated by the Emperor. Thus iconoclasm in its heyday was closely associated with opposition to Byzantine monasticism and the powerful monastic houses.[2]

The uncompromising nature of Constantine's policy is shown by the action of the *strategus* of the Thracesion theme, Michael Lachanodracon, one of the most enthusiastic supporters of the Emperor, who offered the monks of his province the choice of breaking their vows and marrying or being blinded and banished.[3] A widespread

[1] Theophanes 438.

[2] This is not to imply that the struggle against monasticism was the real goal of the iconoclast movement and that 'iconomachy' was in reality 'monachomachy', as was maintained by Andreev, *German i Tarasij*, and has since been frequently repeated. The opposition to monasticism was a by-product of iconoclasm which first became noticeable in the sixties of the eighth century. Practically nothing is known about anti-monastic measures under Leo III, or even in the first half of Constantine V's reign, although it is obvious that the predominantly monastic and thoroughly iconodule sources on which we rely would certainly have made the most of any such measures had there been even the slightest hint of anything of this kind. Cf. also the criticisms of this theory by M. J. Sjuzjumov, 'Problemy ikonoborčeskogo dviženija v Vizantii' (Problems of the iconoclast movement in Byzantium), *Učenye zapiski Sverdlovskogo gos. ped. inst.* 4 (1948), 78 ff.

[3] Theophanes 445, 3.

emigration followed as refugee monks fled, particularly to South Italy where they founded monasteries and schools and so created new centres of Greek culture. In Byzantium the tide of iconoclasm rapidly mounted. In his radicalism the Emperor went far beyond the decrees of the council of 754 and even openly disagreed with them. He rejected the holy icons and relics and forbad the cult of saints and of the Mother of God. These were indeed radical innovations, and, if the work of Constantine V had not collapsed at his death, Byzantine religious life might have undergone a complete transformation.

The violent rule of Constantine V was regarded by posterity as a time of unmitigated terror; for centuries the name of Constantine Copronymus was associated with burning hatred, and after the restoration of orthodoxy his body was removed from the Church of the Holy Apostles. But the memory of his military successes and heroic deeds also lived on: when Byzantium was hard pressed by the Bulgars at the beginning of the ninth century, the despairing populace assembled at the tomb of Constantine V and besought the dead Emperor to come back and save them in their hour of need.

4. THE DECLINE OF THE ICONOCLAST MOVEMENT AND THE RESTORATION OF ICON VENERATION

The brief reign of Leo IV (775–80) is a transitional period between the peak of iconoclasm under Constantine V and the restoration of icon veneration under Irene. Leo IV, son of Constantine by his first marriage with a Khazar princess, was by nature a man of moderation. The attacks upon the cult of the Mother of God ceased, and even the anti-monastic policy which Constantine V had adopted in the second half of his reign was abandoned. The new Emperor did not hesitate to confer the most important bishoprics upon monks.[1] Nevertheless, he was not capable of a complete *volte-face* and he followed the traditional iconoclast policy and had several high officials who persisted in icon veneration publicly whipped and imprisoned (780). But this was a mild punishment compared with the treatment meted out by Constantine, and it was, moreover, the only recorded case of the persecution of iconodules in the time of Leo IV.[2] The

---

[1] Theophanes 449, 15.   [2] Theophanes 453, 10.

curbing of iconoclasm under Leo IV was a natural reaction against the excesses of Constantine V; the influence of the Empress Irene, Leo IV's resolute wife, who came from the iconodule town of Athens and was a devotee of icon veneration, must also be taken into account.

Nicephorus and Christopher, brothers of the Emperor, had received the title of Caesar in 769; Nicetas and Anthimus had been given the title of *nobilissimus* under Constantine V, whilst the youngest brother Eudocimus assumed this title under Leo IV. Yet none of these Caesars were crowned co-Emperor and successor to Leo IV, but his little son Constantine. It was significant that this was done at the request of the army which expressly demanded that the Emperor should crown his son. On 24 April 776 Leo IV, apparently in response to the popular will, crowned his son Emperor after demanding of the senators, the representatives of the metropolitan and provincial armies and the citizens,[1] a signed affirmation of loyalty to the newly-crowned Emperor as the sole heir to the throne. This tendency to rely upon popular support was characteristic of the reign and was probably a reaction against the despotic rule of Leo III and Constantine V. The participation of the people in the election of the new Emperor or co-Emperor in Byzantium was usually expressed in the acclamation of the Emperor by the people and the army immediately after his actual coronation; Leo, however, attempted to make the designation of his successor appear as an expression of the popular will. It is interesting to note that not only were the usual constituent bodies such as senate, people and army consulted, but also representatives of trade and industry in Constantinople. It must of course be assumed that when the army demanded the coronation of the Emperor's son, they were merely acting on a suggestion of the Emperor himself. Yet there is no denying the fact that since Constantine IV's day the ideas of the Byzantine army on the nature of imperial rule had undergone profound and important changes. It was this self-same army which had protested so energetically exactly a hundred years ago against the exclusion of the Emperor's brothers (cf. above, p. 128). The principle of single, undivided rule with restriction of the right of succession to the eldest son of the ruler had made great progress. But this system was not yet taken for granted by the Byzantines,

[1] Theophanes 449, Οἵ τε τῶν θεμάτων καὶ τῆς συγκλήτου καὶ τῶν ἔσω ταγμάτων καὶ τῶν πολιτῶν πάντων καὶ ἐργαστηριακῶν.

otherwise neither an army demonstration in favour of the natural heir nor written declarations of loyalty would have been necessary. A counter plot in favour of the Caesar Nicephorus threatened; the conspiracy was discovered in time and the offenders were banished to Cherson. On this occasion, too, Leo IV set out to frame his policy in accordance with public opinion. He summoned a *silentium* to the Magnaura palace, laid the accusation before the assembly and asked them to pass judgment on the conspirators.[1]

The premature death of Leo IV (8 September 780) brought his son Constantine VI to the throne at the age of ten. Empress Irene took over the regency for her son who was a minor, and officially she was also co-Emperor with him. Again there was an attempt to overthrow the régime in favour of the Caesar Nicephorus, but the resolute Empress rapidly suppressed the rebellion, which apparently had its origin in iconoclast elements and involved several high officials of the Empire. She also compelled the brothers of her late husband to enter the priesthood. By taking over affairs of state, Irene guaranteed the restoration of the icons, though she proceeded slowly and with caution. Any sudden change of ecclesiastical policy would have been impossible, for the iconoclast system had been in full force for half a century, the highest officers of Church and State were in the hands of its supporters, whether from conviction or expediency, and a large part of the army, faithful to the memory of the illustrious Emperor Constantine V, was devoted to its cause.

The government's plans were first made known at the end of 784 after Paul, whom Leo IV had made Patriarch, had been persuaded to resign (31 August 784). Irene assembled the 'entire people' in the Magnaura palace and thus lent to the appointment of the new Patriarch the appearance of a popular choice.[2] Tarasius, hitherto secretary to the Empress, a cultivated layman with sound theological training and clear political judgment, was elected. After Tarasius had been consecrated Patriarch, preparations were made for an oecumenical Council which should reject the decrees of the iconoclast synod of 754 and restore the orthodox use of icons. The Byzantine government entered into negotiations with Rome and the eastern

---

[1] Theophanes 450, 27.
[2] Theophanes 458, συναγοῦσα πάντα τὸν λαόν. The participation of the populace of Constantinople in the election of their spiritual pastor, even though purely formal, is also recorded for the period immediately preceding the iconoclast controversy. According to Theophanes 384, Germanus was called to the patriarchal throne ψήφῳ . . . παντὸς τοῦ εὐαγοῦς κλήρου, καὶ τῆς ἱερᾶς συγκλήτου, καὶ τοῦ φιλοχρίστου λαοῦ τῆς θεοφυλάκτου ταύτης καὶ βασιλίδος πόλεως.

Patriarchates, who all welcomed the change and despatched representatives to the Council.

The Council met in the Church of the Holy Apostles in Constantinople on 31 July 786.[1] Scarcely had the deliberations begun when an event occurred which showed that the preparations for the Council demanded even greater caution than Irene and Tarasius had shown. Mindful of the orders of Constantine V, soldiers of the regiments of the guard in the capital forced their way into the church with drawn swords and broke up the Council to the unconcealed delight of a section of the assembled bishops. The Empress remained undaunted by this failure. She had the iconoclast troops transferred to Asia Minor under the pretence of a campaign against the Arabs, whilst iconodule regiments were brought from Thrace and entrusted with the defence of the capital. In May 787 new invitations were sent to a Council to be held in Nicaea. Thus the seventh oecumenical Council, the last to be recognized by the Eastern Church, met in the very same city in which the first oecumenical Council had been convened under Constantine the Great.

In the presence of some 350 bishops and a large number of monks, seven sessions were held in rapid succession under the presidency of the Patriarch Tarasius between 24 September and 13 October, evidence of the careful preliminary work which had been done. The Council had first to deal with an important question of ecclesiastical policy and to decide upon the fate of the bishops who had participated in iconoclast activities, and who scarcely could have acted otherwise under the three preceding governments. As one of them declared, they were 'born, bred and trained in heresy'.[2] With real insight into the practical implications of the situation, the Council wisely received the former iconoclasts back into the Church after they had abjured their heresy before the assembly. This tolerant attitude did not, however, meet with the approval of the representatives of monasticism and heated exchanges took place. For the first time it became obvious that there was a cleavage within the Byzantine Church which was to affect the entire future history of Byzantium. This cleavage was between the so-called zealots on the one hand, who with their monastic radicalism religiously clung to the canonical rulings and were strictly opposed to any compromise, and the moderate party of the so-called politicians on the other hand, who from motives of expediency submitted to state interests

[1] On the date see Grumel, *Reg.* 355.   [2] Mansi 12, 1031.

and adapted themselves to political circumstances, a party which was not afraid of some compromise and was ready to co-operate with the secular power so long as it remained orthodox. At the Council of Nicaea the moderate party was victorious.

On questions of faith, however, the orthodox majority in the Council was completely unanimous. A series of passages from the Bible and patristic literature were cited in support of the cult of icons and the *acta* of the iconoclast synod of 754, together with a detailed refutation of these resolutions, probably from the pen of the Patriarch Tarasius, was read out.[1] The Council then condemned hostility to icons as heresy, ordered the destruction of iconoclast writings and restored the veneration of icons. Following St. John of Damascus, the Council linked the question of icons with the doctrine of salvation and emphasized that the veneration was directed, not to the icon, but to the holy person depicted on it, and was to be carefully distinguished from the worship due to God alone. A solemn final session on 23 October in the Magnaura palace in Constantinople confirmed the decisions of the Council and these were signed by the Empress and the young Emperor.

Iconoclast elements were not, however, entirely eradicated and their persistence was clearly revealed on the occasion of the struggle between the Empress and her son, a fact which gives greater historical interest to this unsavoury conflict. Though Constantine VI had already reached his majority, the ambitious Empress was unwilling to surrender her power. The young Emperor rebelled against the state of tutelage imposed on him and gradually found himself in increasing conflict with his mother and her adviser, the eunuch Stauracius. It was only natural that the opposition resisting Irene's iconodule policy should rally round him. One of the closest confidants of Constantine VI was the notorious iconoclast Michael Lachanodracon. The energetic Empress, however, was able to suppress an organized conspiracy in the spring of 790, and now felt herself strong enough to get official recognition of the undivided authority which had long been hers in actual fact. She required the army to take an oath recognizing her as senior ruler and placing her name before that of the co-Emperor Constantine VI. The troops of the capital, consisting for the most part of European contingents, unhesitatingly swore the oath demanded of them; but Irene met with strong resistance from the troops of the Armeniakon theme

---

[1] On the authorship of Tarasius cf. Andreev, *German i Tarasij*, 142 ff.

who were unfavourably disposed towards the iconodule Empress. An opposition movement arose which affected the remaining themes of Asia Minor. Finally, the army, defending the rights of the dynasty, rejected the demands of the ambitious Empress and proclaimed the legitimate Emperor Constantine VI as sole ruler (October 790).

Irene had lost the game and had to leave the imperial palace. But the partisans of the Empress did not rest until they had persuaded Constantine VI to ler her come back, and from January 792 the old formula—Constantine and Irene—was again being used. The weakness of the young Emperor caused great disappointment among his supporters, and there was considerable dissatisfaction over the unheroic behaviour of Constantine VI in the Bulgarian war of 792 (cf. below, p. 182). A movement developed in favour of the Caesar Nicephorus whom the opposition honoured as the oldest surviving descendant of Constantine V. But Constantine VI was now quick to act; he had his uncle's eyes put out and the tongues of his fathers' four other brothers cut off. At the same time he blinded Alexius, the *strategus* of the Armeniakon theme, who had led the attack upon Irene in his favour. Thereupon a powerful insurrection broke out in this theme and Constantine VI had to embark on a regular campaign against his former supporters in the spring of 793. The rebellion was crushed with extreme cruelty, but the sympathies which the Emperor once enjoyed here turned to bitter hostility. Soon afterwards he also incurred the displeasure of the orthodox party by divorcing his wife Maria, a beautiful Paphlagonian, whom he had married at the behest of his mother, and then taking as wife his mistress, a lady at court called Theodote. She was crowned Empress and the marriage festivities were celebrated with unusual splendour, a fact which could only serve to exacerbate public opinion. The behaviour of Constantine VI, which violated all ecclesiastical laws, caused the greatest indignation in orthodox circles. The adulterous Emperor was bitterly attacked by the radical monastic party of the zealots under the leadership of Plato, the well-known abbot of the monastery of Saccudium, and his still more famous nephew Theodore. The infuriated Emperor banished these courageous monks, but that was by no means the end of the affair. The so-called moechian controversy (from μοιχεία—adultery) occupied the Byzantines for a considerable period and created serious complications. It led to an intensification of the conflict between the radical party and the Patriarch Tarasius, for the zealots disapproved of the opportunist attitude of the Patriarch towards the adulterous Emperor, and they voiced their displeasure by severing communion with Tarasius. Thus it is strikingly clear that the Byzantine monks harboured a perpetual grievance after the restoration of orthodoxy and found themselves in strong opposition to the leaders of Church and State; the settlement adopted did not appease them and even the rule of Irene provided them with only temporary satisfaction.

By his recklessness, perfidy and cruelty Constantine had lost the support of both the ruling orthodox party and the iconoclast opposition, and he could now be removed without a finger being raised in his defence. On 15 August 797 by order of his mother he was blinded in the Purple Room where he had been born twenty-seven years before. Irene had achieved her aim; she was the sole ruler of the Byzantine Empire.

She was the first woman to control the Empire as an independent ruler in her own right and not as regent for an Emperor who was a minor or unfitted to rule. At a time when the office of Emperor according to Roman tradition was inseparably linked with the function of supreme military commander, the right of a woman to exercise this office was open to question, and it is significant that Irene described herself in the legal statutes not as Basilissa but as Basileus.[1]

Irene's methods of government had little success. At court an oppressive atmosphere of intrigue prevailed in which the chief counsellors of the Empress, the eunuchs Stauracius and Aetius, vied with each other. In order to maintain the dwindling sympathy of the population, the government, ignoring the demands of the budget, granted generous tax remissions. These reliefs were conceded to the monasteries, whose support was the corner-stone of Irene's popularity, and to the population of the capital on whose favour the fate of an unstable government to a large extent depended. The municipal tax, which was payable by the inhabitants of Constantinople, and appears to have been very heavy, was repealed. The import and export duties levied at the ports outside Constantinople, Abydus and Hierus, representing one of the most important sources of revenue of the Byzantine state, were considerably

---

[1] Zepos, *Jus* I, 45, Ἐν ὀνόματι τοῦ πατρὸς καὶ τοῦ υἱοῦ καὶ τοῦ ἁγίου πνεύματος Εἰρήνη πιστός βασιλεύς (see also ibid. 49). Cf. Bury, *Constitution* 23 f.

reduced.[1] These measures were enthusiastically received by the population of the capital and even Theodore of the Studite monastery warmly praised the generosity of the Empress. But unfortunately this generosity ruined the finances of the Byzantine state, the main source of Byzantine power, and they fell into the greatest confusion.

Imperial foreign policy had steadily deteriorated in the last two decades. This decline was partly due to the fact that the Abbasid Caliphate was in its prime. In 781 the Arabs had penetrated deep into imperial territory and had won a bloody, but decisive, battle in the Thracesion theme. Thereupon the Byzantine government concluded peace and pledged themselves to pay tribute to the Caliphate.[2] But even these humiliating terms could not ensure peace for any length of time. Soon Arab incursions began again in Asia Minor.[3] The operations on the Bulgarian frontier, which started in 789 under the direction of the Emperor Constantine VI, met with little success. In the summer of 792 the Byzantines suffered defeat at the frontier fortress Marcellae, a defeat made particularly humiliating through the flight of the Emperor and the capture of the leading Byzantine generals. The Byzantine government had once more to submit to the payment of tribute;[4] but again the peace was of short duration, for the Bulgars demanded increased payments. As Byzantium was inferior to its two most important enemies, it had no choice but to agree to pay the sums asked for, which was all the more distressing after its illustrious position under Constantine V.

5. BYZANTIUM AND CHARLES THE GREAT

General bibliography: K. Heldmann, *Das Kaisertum Karls des Grossen. Theorien und Wirklichkeit*, Weimar 1928; P. E. Schramm, *Kaiser, Rom und Renovatio I*, Leipzig-Berlin 1929; G. Ostrogorsky, 'Die byz. Staatenhierarchie', Sem. Kond. 8 (1936), 41 ff.; W. Ohnsorge, *Das Zweikaiserproblem im frühen Mittelalter. Die Bedeutung des byzantinischen Reiches für die Entwicklung der Staatsidee in Europa*, Hildesheim 1947; P. E. Schramm, 'Die Anerkennung Karls des Grossen als Kaiser. Ein Kapitel aus der Geschichte der mittelalterlichen 'Staatssymbolik', HZ 172 (1951), 449 ff.;

---

[1] Theophanes 475; Theodore Stud., *Ep.* I, 6: Migne, PG 99, 929 ff. Cf. Bury, *Eastern Rom. Empire* 3 and 212.

[2] Dölger, *Reg.* 340.

[3] In 798 the peace treaty was renewed and with it the imperial obligation to pay tribute, Dölger, *Reg.* 352.

[4] In spite of Runciman, *Bulgarian Empire* 49, it is clear from Theophanes A.M. 6288 (= 795/6) that Constantine VI paid tribute to the Bulgars as Bury, *Eastern Rom. Empire* 339, rightly states. To all appearances the obligation to pay tribute dated from the defeat of 792.

Figure 33: *Church of the Holy Cross*. Aght 'Amar, Armenia, 921. The small cruciform church stands on an island in Lake Van, facing the Caucasus Mountains. Photo: Josephine Powell, Rome.

Figure 34: *Textile Fragment.* Silk, in dark blue, green, yellow, and ivory, 8th to 9th centuries. This textile fragment illustrates the Byzantine adoption and treatment of Sassanian motifs. Cooper Union Collections, New York. Photo: Cooper Union Museum.

F. Dölger, *Byzanz und die Europäische Staatenwelt*, Ettal 1953, esp. 282 ff.; W. Ohnsorge, *Abendland und Byzanz. Gesammelte Aufsätze zur Geschichte der byzantinisch-abendländischen Beziehungen und des Kaisertums*, Darmstadt 1958, esp. 1 ff., 64 ff., 79 ff; see also general bibliography cited above, p. 156.

The loss of prestige which Byzantium suffered through developments in the West was of more importance historically than the military failures in Asia and the Balkans. It was the tragedy of the old Empire that, at a time when one of the greatest rulers stood at the head of the Frankish kingdom, its own history was determined by women and eunuchs. By incorporating Bavaria, Christianizing and absorbing Saxony, by expanding his territory at the expense of the Slavs in the East, destroying the kingdom of the Avars, and by overthrowing and annexing the Lombard kingdom, Charles the Great had made his realm the paramount power in the Christian world of his day. In suppressing the Lombards he had succeeded where Byzantium had failed, and this failure destroyed the authority of the Byzantine Empire in Rome. At the same time the Church of Rome strengthened its alliance with the kingdom of the Franks and decisively turned its back upon Byzantium. Even the fact that the ecclesiastical conflict between Rome and Constantinople had been resolved at the oecumenical Council of Nicaea, that Byzantium had returned to orthodoxy and was more zealous than ever in support of icon veneration, could not materially affect the situation. The Council of Nicaea had not fundamentally reconciled these two world powers. Rome anticipated the withdrawal of all measures taken against her during the iconoclast epoch, both in the sphere of religion and ecclesiastical politics, and she therefore expected complete restoration of the *status quo*, especially the return of the papal patrimonies and the restitution of Roman rights of jurisdiction in South Italy and Illyricum. Constantinople refused to listen to these demands and at the Council of Nicaea the question was not even raised. The relevant passage in the message of Pope Hadrian I to the Byzantine rulers was simply omitted from the Greek translation read before the Council. Those clauses in which the Pope claimed the right to censure the uncanonical consecration of the Patriarch Tarasius and to protest against the title of 'oecumenical' Patriarch were likewise deleted; and the many passages in the papal communication which raised the question of the rights of primacy of Rome,

or even only of the primacy of St. Peter, were carefully suppressed.[1]
The Papacy was virtually excluded from the East, just as the Byzantine Empire was excluded from the West. Although the Roman
Church seemed to be in agreement with Byzantium on the burning
religious issues of the day, there was no advantage to be derived
from an alliance with Constantinople. But an alliance with the
famous conqueror of the Lombards, on the other hand, promised
much, although any understanding with the Frankish king on the
question of icons appeared difficult and demanded considerable
concessions.

In a fierce controversy which found its ultimate formulation in the
famous *Libri Carolini*, Charles the Great rejected both the iconoclast
standpoint of the synod of Constantine V and the iconodule attitude
of the Council of Constantine VI and Irene. The *Libri Carolini* were
intended to emphasize the religious independence of the Frankish
kingdom in opposition to Byzantium and their purpose was above
all political. It is therefore immaterial that the real polemical issue
was avoided and that the Latin translation of the Nicene documents
laid before Charles the Great completely misrepresented the decisions
of the Council by gross linguistic errors and misunderstandings.
Furthermore, neither was the standpoint of Charles the Great at one
with the actual views of the Nicene Council; it coincided rather with
the old conception of Gregory the Great, who likewise had rejected
both the destruction and the veneration of icons. In the face of all
warnings and advice addressed to him by Pope Hadrian I, the
Frankish king persisted in his attitude and the Pope was finally
compelled to give way. The veneration of icons which the Council
of Nicaea of 787, in agreement with the two legates of Hadrian I,
had demanded of every pious Christian, was condemned in 794 at
the Frankfurt synod in the presence of two other representatives of
the same Pope.[2] Although the problem of icons was nothing like as
important for the West as it was for Byzantium, and although the
specific association of the use of icons with the doctrine of salvation

[1] On the differences between the original text of Hadrian's letter (Mansi 12, 1055–75) and the Greek translation read at the Council of Nicaea cf. my study, 'Rom und Byzanz im Kampfe um die Bilderverehrung', *Sem. Kond.* 6 (1933), 73 ff.

[2] W. von den Steinen, 'Entstehungsgeschichte der *Libri Carolini*', *Quellen und Forschungen aus italienischen Archiven und Bibl.* 21 (1929–30), 83 ff., attempts somewhat unsuccessfully to explain the decisions of the Frankfurt synod as an attempt to find a solution by compromising; apart from this, his important study deserves special consideration. Cf. idem, 'Karl der Grosse und die *Libri Carolini*', *N. Archiv d. Gesellschaft f. ältere deutsche Geschichtskunde* 49 (1932), 207 ff.

in Byzantine theology remained strange and even incomprehensible to the West, this step denoted considerable concessions and clearly showed that an alliance with the Frankish kingdom had become the corner-stone of papal policy. Hadrian I persisted in the undeniably successful policy inaugurated by Stephen II and unhesitatingly adhered to his alliance with the Frankish king. Carrying this still further, his successor Leo III then made a bold and fundamentally revolutionary decision which set the seal upon the admirably purposeful policy of the Roman Church in the eighth century: he crowned Charles as Emperor at Rome in the Church of St. Peter on 25 December 800.[1]

The foundation of the Empire of Charles the Great had the same revolutionary effect in the political sphere as the later schism in the religious sphere. At that time it was axiomatic that there could be only one Empire as there could be only one Church. The coronation of Charles the Great violated all traditional ideas and struck a hard blow at Byzantine interests, for hitherto Byzantium, the new Rome, had unquestionably been regarded as the sole Empire which had taken over the inheritance of the old Roman *imperium*. Conscious of its imperial rights, Byzantium could only consider the elevation of Charles the Great to be an act of usurpation. Rome, too, accepted the idea of a single Empire and never had any intention of establishing a second Empire, but meant to install the newly-created Empire in the place of the old Byzantine Empire. After the deposition of the legitimate Emperor Constantine VI, the imperial throne of Constantinople was held to have fallen vacant. To Rome, as to Byzantium, the sole conceivable world order was a hierarchy of states, embracing the entire Christian *oikoumene* and culminating in a single Empire. In actual fact, from the year 800 onwards two Empires, an Eastern and a Western Empire, stood face to face. The separation between East and West, anticipated by a century's development and already evident in the era of the iconoclast struggle, was now an accomplished fact in the political sphere. The *oikoumene* had split

---

[1] The coronation was modelled on the Byzantine ceremony; cf. E. Eichmann, *Die Kaiserkrönung im Abendland* I (1942), 23 ff. In the imperial election of Charles the Great, local Roman events played an important part, as is shown by E. Sackur, 'Ein römischer Majestätsprozess und die Kaiserkrönung Karls d. Gr.', HZ 87 (1901), 385 ff. This has since been increasingly and repeatedly stressed (cf. J. Haller, *Das Papsttum* II, 1 (1939), 18 ff.). But such events do not, however, provide the basic reason for the imperial coronation of Charles, and the historic act of 25 December 800 cannot be explained as the outcome of the situation of the moment without greatly oversimplifying the problem.

into two halves which in language, culture, politics and religion were poles apart.

Although the imperial coronation in St. Peter's had been the work of the Papacy and not of the Frankish king,[1] Charles had to face the momentous consequences of his step; he had to secure that recognition from Byzantium without which his imperial title was legally invalid. Obviously nothing could be achieved by using the empty claim that the imperial throne of Constantinople was vacant in so far as it was occupied by a woman, or by maintaining that Byzantium had succumbed to heresy as the *Libri Carolini* attempted to demonstrate. So in 802 the ambassadors of Charles the Great and the Pope were sent to Constantinople. They are alleged to have brought the Byzantine Empress an offer of marriage from Charles in the hope of 're-uniting East and West once more'.[2] Shortly after their arrival a palace revolution broke out which deposed Irene (31 October 802) and postponed the solution of the problem. The revolt originated with the higher officials and officers of the Empire and led to the proclamation of Nicephorus, the former logothete of the treasury (λογοθέτης γενικοῦ), as Emperor. Irene was exiled, first to the Princes' Islands, and then to Lesbos, where she died soon afterwards.

6. THE REFORMS OF NICEPHORUS AND COMPLICATIONS OF FOREIGN POLICY: BYZANTIUM AND KRUM

General bibliography: Bury, *Eastern Rom. Empire*; Zlatarski, *Istorija* I, 1; Mutafčiev, *Istorija* I; Runciman, *Bulgarian Empire*; Bratianu, *Études byz.* 183–216; see also general bibliography cited above, p. 165.

In Nicephorus I (802–11) the Empire had once more a competent ruler at its head. The claim of Theophanes that the Emperor's accession caused chagrin and dismay only reflected the views of certain elements in the extreme monastic party. The intense hatred which Theophanes bore towards the Emperor was not generally felt,

---

[1] Cf. the bibliography at the beginning of this chapter. A different view is taken by L. Halphen, *Charlemagne et l'Empire carolingien*, Paris, 1947, 120 ff.

[2] Theophanes 475, 27. On this much discussed passage cf. W. Ohnsorge, 'Orthodoxus imperator. Vom religiösen Motiv für das Kaisertum Karls des Grossen', *Jahrb. d. Gesellschaft f. niedersächs. Kirchengesch.* 48 (1950), 24 ff., whose stimulating, but oversubtle, arguments on Charles' position with regard to the question of icons I cannot however accept. Cf. my comments in BZ 46 (1953), 153 ff., especially p. 155.

even in orthodox Byzantine circles.[1] Nicephorus was no pillar of the Church; though himself orthodox and a supporter of the cult of icons, he demanded of the clergy submission to the imperial power. By marrying his son and heir Stauracius to the Athenian Theophano, a relative of Irene, he affirmed his resolve to preserve the iconodule policy of the previous régime. The relations of government and ecclesiastical authorities to the radical monastic party became strained again, particularly as the Emperor appointed the learned historian Nicephorus to the patriarchal throne on the death of Tarasius (25 February 806). Nicephorus, like Tarasius, was as well versed in secular learning as in theology, and excelled, not only as a historian, but also in later years as the author of a number of writings in defence of icons. And he too, like Tarasius, had been a higher government official before his appointment to the patriarchal throne and in matters of ecclesiastical policy followed the same course of moderation. The appointment of a layman to the patriarchal throne created great bitterness amongst the zealots as they had apparently counted on the election of their leader Theodore the Studite. To crown everything, the Emperor Nicephorus again revived the moechian controversy in order to demonstrate that the Emperor was not bound by the canons; a synod of lay and ecclesiastical representatives was ordered to recognize the marriage of Constantine VI with Theodote, and the priest Joseph who had solemnized the marriage was again received back into communion (January 809). This led to an open breach with the Studite monks, who broke away once more from the official ecclesiastical authorities and laid themselves open to persecution by the state.

The first efforts of the Emperor were directed to stabilizing the country's economy and remedying the penury of the exchequer caused by the irresponsibility of the previous government. As a former high official in the financial administration he was admirably suited to this function and adopted many important and astute measures. Theophanes, his embittered opponent, describes these measures with mingled abuse and protest as the 'ten misdeeds' of the Emperor Nicephorus.[2] To begin with Nicephorus cancelled the tax remissions granted by Irene. Then he ordered a general reassessment of his subjects; in comparison with the former level, taxes were increased and a charge of two *keratia* (apparently per *nomisma*, i.e.

---

[1] The monk Theosterictus praises him as εὐσεβέστατος καὶ φιλόπτωχος καὶ φιλομόναχος, *Vita Nicetae*, AASS, 1 April, p. xxix.

[2] Theophanes 486–7.

8⅓ per cent) was made for being entered on the tax-roll. The *paroikoi* (peasant tenants) of monasteries and churches, as well as of the numerous charitable institutions in Byzantium, were subjected to a hearth tax. This is the first mention in a Byzantine document of the hearth tax (καπνικόν), in reality a poll tax levied according to families. Together with the land tax, it was the most important source of revenue in the middle Byzantine period. Nicephorus was not the first to introduce it, for in his day it appears to have been already a recognized form of taxation, but it is of interest at this point since it was now applied to a category of peasants who had hitherto been exempt from payment. This exemption probably dated only from the time of Irene, as the properties of churches and monasteries in Byzantium were in principle normally liable to taxation. Thus Nicephorus was no innovator in this respect; he simply revived the old regulations. In the twenties of the ninth century the hearth tax, as other sources reveal, amounted to two *milesaria* and was payable by the whole rural population who were liable to taxation.[1] In order to secure the treasury against loss, Nicephorus made the taxpayers collectively responsible for the tax receipts, i.e. a total tax liability was fixed for a specific area for which all inhabitants of the area were answerable; any failure to pay had to be made good by the neighbours of the defaulters. Even this regulation was not new; it was the application of the ἀλληλέγγυον system, already met with in the *Farmer's Law* (cf. above, p. 137), although the technical term appears here for the first time.[2]

---

[1] Theoph. cont. 54. Dölger, *Finanzverwaltung* 62 ff., and N. A. Constantinescu, *Bulletin de l'Acad. Roumaine*, Section hist. 11 (1924) and *Deutsche Literaturzeitung* 1928, Heft 31, col. 161 ff., think that only serfs paid the *kapnikon*, although this is contradicted in Theoph. cont. 54 and also in Scylitzes—Cedrenus II, 413 and Ibn Hordadbeh (ed. de Goeje), 84. Cf. my comments in B 6 (1931), 234 f., and 'Steuergemeinde', 49 ff., and also Stein, 'Vom Altertum' 160. Dölger, BZ 34 (1934), 371 ff., still maintains his view.

[2] Theophanes 486, 26, ἀλληλεγγύως τὰ ∂ημόσια. Dölger, *Finanzverwaltung* 130 and BZ 36 (1936), 158 with note 1, denies that the expression had a technical significance, though he would be inclined to make an exception in the case of the *allelengyon* of Basil II. He is now followed by Lemerle, 'Histoire Agraire', 261 ff. But the *Ashburner Treatise* §14 (= Dölger, *Finanzverwaltung*, 119, 24) shows that it did have a technical significance: ἔποικοι ἀλληλέγγυα ἀπαιτούμενοι. This is also recognized by K. A. Osipova, 'Allilengij v Vizantii v X veke' (The *allelengyon* in Byzantium in the tenth century), VV 17 (1960), 28 ff. This study is devoted in the first place to the *allelengyon* in the *Ashburner Treatise*, but the author wrongly follows Každan, 'K voprosu ob osobennostjach feodal'noj sobstvennosti v Vizantii VIII–X vv.' (On the question of the characteristics of feudal holdings in Byzantium from the eighth to the tenth centuries), VV 10 (1956), 63 ff. and 'Ešče raz ob agrarnych otnošenijach v Vizantii IV–XI vv.' (Further thoughts on the agrarian situation in Byzantium from the fourth to the eleventh centuries), VV 16 (1959), 107 ff., in supposing that the reassessment system was interrupted in the early middle ages and reintroduced in the ninth century.

Nicephorus brought certain ecclesiastical possessions under the control of the imperial demesne, though he did not lower the tax assessment of the properties thus curtailed. It is fairly safe to assume that this measure was only concerned with reclaiming the overlavish gifts made by the Empress Irene. The recovery of taxes on inheritance and on treasure trove was to be more rigorously enforced, and such taxes were even to be exacted from those whose sudden rise from poverty to riches excited suspicion. Slaves purchased beyond the customs barrier of Abydus, and particularly in the area of the Dodecanese, were taxed at the rate of two *nomismata*.[1] Furthermore, by issuing a decree prohibiting his subjects from accepting interest and thereby authorizing the state alone to draw interest, the Emperor compelled the rich shipbuilders of Constantinople to take up state loans of twelve pounds in gold and to pay interest on them at the rate of four *keratia* for each *nomisma*, i.e. at 16.66 per cent.[2] Although the acceptance of interest infringed the theoretical moral standards of the middle ages, decrees prohibiting interest, such as were promulgated by Nicephorus and later by Basil I for instance, were seldom met with in Byzantium. The demands of the complex Byzantine monetary economy ignored ethical norms and the granting of loans was at all times widespread in Byzantium. In any case, the prohibition of interest by Nicephorus,

---

[1] That was on an average an addition of about 10 per cent to the cost price as the slaves in question here were probably unskilled imported labour. Under Justinian (*Cod. Just.* VI 43, 3 of the year 531) ordinary adult slaves cost up to 20 *nomismata*, artisans up to 30, slaves with professional qualifications, as notaries or doctors, up to 50 or 60. In the first half of the seventh century educated slaves were bought in Jerusalem for 30 *nomismata* (cf. *Life of St. John the Merciful*, ed. H. Gelzer, p. 44). The Russo-Byzantine treaty of 911 fixes the price of slaves to be imported from Russia at 20 *nomismata* and the treaty of 944, which was less favourable to Russia, gives 10 *nomismata* as the price for young prisoners of either sex (*Polnoe sobr. russk. letop.* I², 36 and 50, trans. R. Trautmann, *Die Nestorchronik* 22 and 32). For the position of slaves in Byzantium in general cf. A. J. Hadjinicolaou-Marava, *Recherches sur la vie des esclaves dans le monde byzantin*, Athens 1950, 89 ff. who attempts a comprehensive study of this subject. But cf. the criticism of A. P. Každan, *Vestnik drevnej istorii*, 1952, 4, p. 121 ff. Cf. also the important articles by A. P. Každan, 'Raby i mistii v Vizantii IX–XI vv.' (Slaves and hired labour in Byzantium from the ninth to the eleventh centuries), *Učenye zapiski Tul'skogo gos. ped. inst.* 1951, 63 ff., M. J. Sjuzjumov, 'O pravovom položenii rabov v Vizantii' (On the legal status of slaves in Byzantium, *Učenye zapiskii Sverdlovskogo gos. ped. inst.* 1955; R. Browning, 'Rabstvo v Vizantijskoj imperii (600–1200 gg.)' (Slavery in the Byzantine Empire 600–1200), VV 14 (1958), 38 ff.

[2] The interpretation of this measure which is given by Cassimatis, B 7 (1932), 149 ff., as also by Bury, *Eastern Rom. Empire* 216 f., seems to me to be untenable. On the whole I prefer the views of Monnier, 'Épibole' 19, p. 87 ff., Stein, *Studien* 156 f., Dölger, *Reg.* 378, and Bratianu, *Études byz.* 208 ff. Cf. my criticisms of Cassimatis and Bury in 'Löhne und Preise in Byzanz', BZ 32 (1932), 308, note 4. For further information on interest and usury in Byzantium, ibid. 308 ff.; for more detail cf. Cassimatis, *Les intérêts dans la législation de Justinien et dans le droit byzantin* (1931).

himself a stern realist, did not spring from disinterested motives; by throttling private initiative, by making the granting of loans a state monopoly and fixing a high rate of interest, he found a new source of revenue for the treasury.[1]

The Emperor Nicephorus took important steps to improve the system of defence which since the seventh century had depended upon a system of small-holders with military obligations. According to reports of the tenth century, the property which would form the basis of the economic existence of a soldier had to be of the value of at least four pounds of gold, as he was expected to report with a horse and full equipment when he was called upon to perform military service. Since there was apparently an insufficient number of peasant soldiers who possessed this amount of property, Nicephorus made even the poorer peasants liable for military service by arranging that the village community should cover the cost of their equipment by an annual contribution of $18\frac{1}{2}$ *nomismata*.[2] According to this decree the holding of the prescribed value need not necessarily consist of the private property of a single individual, but could be made up of the combined property of several peasants, one of whom would perform the military service, while the others would be collectively responsible for financing his equipment. And in the event of a soldier becoming impoverished and being unable himself to meet the cost of his equipment, the same method of making the village community responsible for the financial burden could be applied in his case, thus guaranteeing the state against any reduction in its military manpower. This system ensured the recruitment of the army as effectively as the ἀλληλέγγυον ensured the regular payment of the taxes.

According to tenth-century evidence, sailors, like the soldiers, owned property which provided them with a livelihood. The

---

[1] Justinianian law (*Cod. Just.* IV, 32, 26) limited the rates of interest as follows: persons of high rank were allowed 4 per cent (*trientes usurae*), merchants 8 per cent (*besses usurae*), all others 6 per cent (*semisses usurae*), while the state was also limited to 6 per cent (*Cod. Just.* X, 8, 3). The official rate of interest was however later raised, and this was managed without an open breach with the Justinianian law by adjusting the rate to the value of the current coinage under Leo VI (Nov. 83): *trientes usurae* amounted to 1 *keration* for each *nomisma* so that the rate was actually $4\frac{1}{2}$ per cent instead of 4 per cent. In the eleventh century (*Peira* XIX, 1) *trientes usurae*, *semisses usurae* and *besses usurae* amounted respectively to 4, 6 and 8 *nomismata* per 1 gold pound, thus amounting in practice to 5.55 per cent, 8.33 per cent and 11.71 per cent. Each gold pound equalled 72 gold *nomismata*, 1 gold *nomisma* equalled 12 silver *miliaresia* or 24 *keratia*, and 1 *miliaresion* equalled 24 copper *folleis*.

[2] Theophanes 486, 24: προσέταξε στρατεύεσθαι πτωχοὺς καὶ ἐξοπλίζεσθαι παρὰ τῶν ὁμοχώρων, παρέχοντας καὶ ἀνὰ ὀκτωκαίδεκα ἡμίσους νομισμάτων τῷ Δημοσίῳ. Cf. Glykatzi-Ahrweiler, *Recherches*, 19 f.

purpose of these measures of Nicephorus, which Theophanes cites as his ninth misdeed, was no doubt to create holdings of this kind. He declared that the Emperor had compelled mariners of the coastal area, particularly in Asia Minor, who had never practised agriculture, to purchase small-holdings from areas no longer in cultivation at a price fixed by himself.[1] This seems to be the first example of sailors' properties,[2] a highly significant measure for the Byzantine navy; to begin with it referred primarily to the mariners of the Cibyraeot theme.

In addition, Nicephorus undertook colonization with the avowed political intention of protecting particularly vulnerable territories. The inhabitants of the themes of Asia Minor were compelled to sell their possessions and were transplanted to 'Sclavinia', i.e. to the Slav districts of the Balkan peninsula, where the colonists doubtless were granted new lands and, as *stratiotai*, had to undertake military service. This measure, which Theophanes cordially disliked, is linked with the policy of colonization found in the two previous centuries. There was certainly no revolutionary intention behind Nicephorus' policy. In fact, by remedying the defects and neglect of his predecessors, he performed a necessary work of reform and in all new measures he adhered strictly to traditional Byzantine policy. First he directed his attention to the twin pillars of the Byzantine state—the revenue and the army. He considerably increased the financial power of the Empire, albeit by violent means. His extensive activity in this sphere gives an insight into the methods of Byzantine financial administration and reveals the extremely highly developed state of Byzantine economy during the early period of the middle ages. Equally he very much strengthened the military forces of the Empire: the most novel and decisive measures of the former finance minister were directed to this end.

The colonizing methods of Nicephorus were of especial importance as they affected the Slav area of the Balkan peninsula, above all

---

[1] Theophanes 487, τοὺς τὰς παραθαλασσίας οἰκοῦντας, μάλιστα τῆς μικρᾶς Ἀσίας ναυκλήρους μηδέποτε γηπονικῶς ζήσαντας ἄκοντας ὠνεῖσθαι ἐκ τῶν καθαρπαγέντων αὐτῷ κτημάτων, ὡς ἂν ἐκτιμηθῶσι παρ' αὐτῷ.

[2] Uspenskij, *Istorija* II, 239 ff., gives the correct interpretation of this long misunderstood passage. Following on his theory of the late introduction of soldiers' properties, Lemerle 'Histoire Agraire' 219, 73 n. 2 disputes this interpretation, though without offering any other conclusive alternative. In support of the same theory, he also doubts (loc. cit.) whether the above measures respecting the soldier-farmers who were not 'poor' (i.e. who were not included amongst the πτωχοί and who were not armed by the other inhabitants of their village but provided their own arms) assume the existence of soldiers' properties.

the districts of Thrace and eastern Macedonia adjoining Bulgaria.[1] The great Slav invasion of the sixth and seventh centuries compelled the Byzantine Empire to withdraw from the majority of its positions in the area of the Balkan peninsula and from that time onwards the Slav influx continuously increased. According to Constantine Porphyrogenitus, the Peloponnese was still predominantly a Slav and barbarian country in the middle of the eighth century.[2] But at the end of the eighth and in the opening years of the ninth centuries the Byzantines slowly strengthened their position. During the reign of Irene Byzantium launched an offensive on the grand scale against the Slavs in Greece; in the year 783 the Logothete Stauracius invaded the region of Thessalonica with a powerful army, then advanced on central Greece and the Peloponnese and compelled the Slav tribes there to recognize Byzantine sovereignty and to pay tribute. So great was the importance which Byzantium attached to Stauracius' victory over the Slav tribes in Greece that, on his return from this successful campaign, he was allowed to celebrate his victory in the Hippodrome.[3] But in the last years of the eighth century the Slavs in Greece under the leadership of the archon of the Velziti tribe conspired against the Empress Irene in favour of the sons of Constantine V held captive in Athens,[4] and at the beginning of the ninth century the Slavs in the Peloponnese broke into open rebellion. They plundered the possessions of their Greek neighbours and then made a strong attack upon Patras in 805.[5] The city was closely invested, but ultimately the Slavs were defeated. The citizens ascribed their salvation to the miraculous intervention of the Apostle Andrew, just as the salvation of Thessalonica was ascribed in its day to the aid of St. Demetrius. Together with the entire booty, the defeated Slavs and their families were delivered in bondage by the Emperor to the Church of St. Andrew, whereby they lost their independence and also their personal freedom. The Slavs in the

---

[1] Hopf, *Geschichte Griechenlands* I, 98 f., and Vasiliev, *Slavjane v Grecii* (The Slavs in Greece), VV 5 (1898), 422, suspected that the *stratiotai* of Asia Minor had also been settled in Greece, overrun as it was by Slavs. This view has been advanced in greater detail and in a more positive form by P. Charanis, 'Nicephorus I, the Saviour of Greece from the Slavs', *Byzantina-Metabyzantina* 1 (1946), 76 ff. But compare the telling objections raised by Kyriakides, Βυζ. Μελέται VI, 7 ff. Cf. also *Viz. Izvori* I, 235, n. 67.

[2] *De thematibus* 6, 33 (ed. Pertusi), ἐσθλαβώθη δὲ πᾶσα ἡ χώρα καὶ γέγονε βάρβαρος. Cf. *Vita S. Willibaldi*, MGH SS XV 93, which tells how St. Willibald, Bishop of Eichstätt (*c.* 723–8), travelling to Palestine, stopped at Monemvasia, a city 'in Slawinia terrae'. Cf. below, p. 193, note 2.

[3] Theophanes 456 f.   [4] Theophanes 473.

[5] *De adm. imp.*, c. 49, p. 228 ff. (ed. Moravcsik-Jenkins).

Peloponnese did, in effect, create further difficulties for the Byzantine government; the tribes of the Melingi and Ezeritae on the Taygetus, against whom the Franks waged bitter war in the thirteenth century, preserved their nationality until the Turkish era.[1] All the same, the defeat of the Slavs at Patras marked an important stage in the re-Hellenization of southern Greece. For the Byzantines, this event was the moment of the restoration of Byzantine power in the Peloponnese after more than two centuries of Slav domination.[2]

The gradual consolidation of Byzantine rule in certain districts of the Balkan peninsula is most clearly reflected in the extension of the organization of themes and in the establishment of new themes. In order to understand which areas were in fact under the control of the Byzantine Empire, i.e. areas which not merely nominally, but actually, recognized Byzantine sovereignty, it is necessary to ascertain how far the Byzantine organization of themes extended. That is the only true measure of actual conditions. For only where themes

[1] There is no need to discuss in greater detail here the disputed question of the etymology of the names of these Slav tribes. D. J. Georgacas, 'The Mediaeval Names Melingi and Ezeritae of Slavic Groups in the Peloponnesus', BZ 43 (1950), 301 ff., does not doubt that these tribes came from the Slav world, but assigns to both names, even to that of the Ezeritae, a Greek origin which is certainly incorrect. Cf. the excellent criticism of H. Grégoire, B 21 (1951), 247 ff., 280, and 'L'étymologie slav du nom des Melingi et des Ezerites', *Nouv. Clio* 4 (1952), 293 ff. See also H. Glykatzi-Ahrweiler, 'Une inscription méconnue sur les Mélingues du Taygète', *Bull. de corr. hell.* 86 (1962), 1 ff., who demonstrates that the Slav tribes of the Melingi still existed in the fourteenth century.

[2] According to the Chronicle of Monemvasia the Peloponnese was under Slav rule for 218 years, i.e. from the sixth year of Maurice's reign (587) until the fourth year of Nicephorus I (805), when Byzantine control was finally restored; cf. N. Bees, Τὸ περὶ τῆς κτίσεως τῆς Μονεμβασίας χρονικόν, Βυζαντίς 1 (1909), 73ff. See also the gloss of Arethas for the year 932 (S. Kougeas, *Neos Hellenomn.* 9, 1912, 473 ff.) and the synodal letter of the Patriarch Nicholas III (1084–1111) to the Emperor Alexius I Comnenus (Le Quien, *Oriens Christianus* II, 179). On the reliability of this source cf. P. Charanis, BS 10 (1948), 92 ff. and 254 ff.; he rightly opposes the view widely held today among Greek historians that the Slavs did not take possession of the Peloponnese at the end of the sixth century, as the sources state, but only settled there in any number after the epidemic of 746. On the problem of the sources of the Chronicle of Monemvasia cf. P. Charanis, 'The Chronicle of Monemvasia and the Question of the Slavonic Settlements in Greece', *Dumbarton Oaks Papers* 5 (1950), 141 ff., where the text of the relevant passages is reprinted and translated into English and the relevant literature considered. The information given in the literary sources, including the Chronicle of Monemvasia, is confirmed by the archaeological and especially the numismatic evidence; cf. the informative comments of A. Bon, 'Le problème slave dans le Péloponnèse à la lumière de l'archéologie', B 20 (1950), 13 ff., and also the important survey, *Le Péloponnèse byzantin jusqu'en 1204*, Paris 1951. K. M. Setton, 'The Bulgars in the Balkans and the Occupation of Corinth in the Seventh Century', *Speculum* 25 (1950), 502 ff., concludes that the account in the Chronicle of Monemvasia of a Slav-Avar attack at the end of the sixth century really refers to the capture of Corinth by the Onogur Bulgars in 641–2 and that Byzantine rule here was restored by Constans II on the occasion of his campaign against 'Sclavinia' in 658. Charanis, *Speculum* 27 (1952), 343 ff., rejects this on good grounds. Cf. also Dölger, BZ 45 (1952), 218. Setton, *Speculum* 27 (1952), 351 ff., has attempted to save his theory, but unsuccessfully.

existed was a more or less organized Byzantine administration to be found. Thrace and Hellas were the only themes which Byzantium possessed in the Balkan peninsula at the end of the seventh century, and for a long time this situation continued. But from the end of the eighth century there existed, apart from Thrace, the independent theme of Macedonia, which did not cover purely Macedonian territory but in effect included the territory of western Thrace.[1] The theme of the Peloponnese was also established around this time,[2] and in the early years of the ninth century there also arose the theme of Cephalonia which embraced the Ionian islands.[3] In the first half of the ninth century Thessalonica and Dyrrachium, the most important bases of Byzantine sea-power on the Aegean and Adriatic coasts, were organized with their hinterland into special themes.[4] Somewhat later the theme system was extended into the region of Epirus by the foundation of the theme of Nicopolis, while the theme of Thessalonica was linked with the Thracian themes of Thrace and Macedonia by the organization of the Strymon theme. Finally in the second half of the ninth century, the theme of Dalmatia which included the Dalmatian cities and islands came into

[1] Macedonia is referred to as a separate theme for the first time in 802 (Theophanes 475). Lemerle, *Philippes* 122 f., shows that it was established between 789 and 802. According to the information given by the Arab geographers, Constantinople and its environs also formed a separate theme (cf. Gelzer, 'Themenverfassung', 86 ff.; Bury, *Eastern Rom. Empire*, 224), but this is based on a misunderstanding; cf. H. Grégoire, 'Le thème byzantin de Tafla-Tablan', *Nouv. Clio* 4 (1952), 388 ff.

[2] A *strategus* of the Peloponnese was first specifically mentioned in 812, *Scriptor incertus de Leone* 336. The theme of the Peloponnese did not, however, originate after the Slav attack on Patras in 805, as scholars used to think, but as can be seen from the *De adm. imp.*, c. 49, 13 (ed. Moravcsik-Jenkins), already existed at the time of the Slav attack on Patras. It is possible that its foundation took place soon after the Greek campaign of the Logothete Staurachius: cf. G. Ostrogorsky, 'Postanak teme Hellada i Peloponez' (The setting up of the themes Hellas and Peloponnese), ZRVI (1952), 64 ff.

[3] A *strategus* of Cephalonia is first mentioned in 809, *Einh. Annal.*, MGH SS I, 196 f. Dvornik, *Légendes* 12, considers that the theme of Cephalonia was set up in the eighth century, relying on a lead seal published by B. Pančenko, 'Katalog Molevdovulov' (Catalogue of lead seals), *Izv. Russk. Archeol. Inst. v Kiple* 13 (1908), 117, which Pančenko dated to the seventh-eighth centuries. Pančenko's reading στρ[ατ]ηγῷ Κε[φα]λ[ην(ίας)] is, however, quite unreliable and his comments, op. cit. 118, not very convincing.

[4] The theme of Thessalonica is first met with in the *Life of Gregory Decapolites* (ed. Dvornik 36 and 62 f.), the theme of Dyrrachium in the *Tacticon* dating from the period 845–56 (Uspenskij, p. 115). Dvornik's suggestion (*Légendes* 9) that the theme of Thessalonica originated under Nicephorus I is possible; he puts the creation of the theme of Dyrrachium in the time of Theophilus (*Légendes* 12). It is more likely that both themes were set up at the same time. J. Ferluga, 'Sur la création du thème de Dyrrachium', XII *Congrès Intern. des études byz. Résumés des communications*, Belgrade-Ochrida, 1961, 32, briefly mentions a letter of Theodore the Studite (Migne PG 99, Epist. II, No. 157), which seems to show that the theme Dyrrachium existed even during the lifetime of Theodore, that is, before 826 at the latest. Ferluga would actually like to place its organization in the period of Nicephorus I.

existence (cf. below, p. 235 f.). The extension of the theme system to the Balkan peninsula is a sign of the gradual restoration of Byzantine authority there after its severe limitation by the Slav migrations. It indicates the progress and the limits of the Byzantine re-occupation and of the re-hellenization which went with this. Byzantium gradually managed to extend its system of themes to the whole coastal area, fitting in now a wider area, now a narrower strip of territory. In the coastal regions, accessible to its maritime power and rich in ancient cities and harbours, the Empire restored its rule and its administrative system. But the success of the Byzantine reoccupation went no further: the interior of the Balkan peninsula remained for the most part outside the confines of the Empire.

The settlement of the *stratiotai* of Asia Minor in the territory of the Sclavinias is one aspect of the process of consolidating the Byzantine position in the Balkans. But is was also due to the impending struggle with Bulgaria. Though not a born soldier, Nicephorus waged the war with great vigour and often led the army in person. Immediately after his imperial accession, he ended the tributary payments to the Caliphate which Irene had been compelled to furnish. But the forces of the Empire in the East were exhausted by a civil war caused by the usurpation of Bardanes Turcus, promoted to be supreme head of all themes of Asia Minor in the summer of 803. The Muslims again began to invade the imperial territory, and in 806 Harun al Rashid advanced with a powerful army, captured several frontier fortresses, occupied Tyana and despatched a larger force to the region of Ancyra. The Emperor was obliged to sue for peace, submit to payment of tribute and in addition accede to the still more humiliating obligation of paying the Caliph on behalf of himself and his son three gold pieces annually as poll-tax.[1] Meanwhile the death of Harun (809) and the ensuing unrest in the Caliphate brought a respite. The main direction of Byzantine foreign policy shifted increasingly towards the Balkans.

The destruction of the Avar might by Charles the Great enabled the Bulgars in Pannonia to shake off the Avar yoke. In consequence, the Bulgar kingdom experienced a vast extension of power and territory, and on the river Theiss it abutted on the Empire of Charles the Great. Krum, a chieftain of the Pannonian Bulgars, ascended the Bulgarian throne; he was a rugged fighter, pugnacious and aggressive, and soon destined to become the scourge of the Byzantines.

---

[1] Theophanes 482; Dölger, *Reg.* 366.

Byzantium had erected a strong line of fortifications as a barrier against the Bulgar kingdom; Develtus, Adrianople, Philippopolis and Sardica acted as key points. In the spring of 809 Sardica was overrun by Krum, the fortress destroyed and the powerful garrison massacred. The Byzantine Emperor immediately intervened, advanced on Pliska, and after this impressive demonstration made for Sardica with the object of restoring the fortifications. His decisive counter-offensive followed two years later after careful preparation which included the re-settlement of the *stratiotai* of Asia Minor in the Slav areas of the Balkans. In the spring of 811 Nicephorus crossed the frontier with a powerful army and ignoring the peace overtures of Krum, advanced on Pliska, destroyed the Bulgar capital and burned down the palace of the Khan. The victorious Emperor rejected renewed supplications for peace; he was determined finally to make an end of the Bulgar kingdom and pursued the Khan who had fled with his followers into the mountains. Here fate overtook him. The Byzantine army was surrounded by Krum in the mountain passes and cut to pieces (26 July 811). The Emperor himself was slain and the victorious Khan fashioned from his skull a goblet, out of which he toasted his boyars at banquets.

The consequences of this terrible and totally unexpected catastrophe were incalculable, for the blow to Byzantine prestige was far more serious than the military defeat. No Byzantine Emperor had been slain by barbarians since the days of the great migrations when Valens perished in the year 378 in the battle against the Visigoths at Adrianople. Byzantium, whose superiority had been clearly demonstrated at the opening of hostilities, lay prostrate, whilst Krum, who shortly before had sued for peace, emerged as triumphant victor. His presumption knew no bounds and his lust for conquest found unexpected opportunities. Troubled and anxious years for the Empire lay ahead.

In the battle which cost the Emperor Nicephorus his life, his son and successor, Stauracius, was severely wounded, but managed to escape with some followers to Adrianople. Here in strict conformity with the principle of legitimacy he was proclaimed Emperor. This act had only a formal and provisional character as there was little hope of Stauracius' recovery. The final settlement of the succession was to take place in Constantinople whither the Emperor, mortally wounded, was transported in order to crown his successor. The natural candidate for the throne was the nearest relative of the childless Emperor, his brother-in-law, the *curopalates* Michael Rangabe. His candidature was supported by the Emperor's comrades in arms and by the Patriarch Nicephorus. The wife of the dying Emperor, the Athenian Theophano, opposed this solution for, following the example of Irene, she hoped to take over the reins herself. Whilst Stauracius, fearing severe repercussions,[1] delayed his decision, passions flared up in the capital. At a time of impending danger in the field of foreign politics an interregnum seemed particularly undesirable; a return to normal conditions was imperative. A *coup d'état* brought the solution which could not be achieved by constitutional means. On 2 October Michael Rangabe was proclaimed Emperor in the Hippodrome by the army and senate and was crowned a few hours later by the Patriarch Nicephorus in Hagia Sophia. Stauracius resigned in face of a *fait accompli* and withdrew to a monastery where he lingered for another three months.

Michael I Rangabe[2] (811–13) was a feeble ruler. He was easily influenced by stronger personalities and lacked the courage to introduce unpopular measures for which the Emperor Nicephorus had been famous. He ended the policy of economy and at every opportunity distributed gratuities to the army, the court and especially the clergy. Michael I fervently venerated icons and was a faithful servant of the Church; orthodoxy prospered under his régime, though an outbreak of iconoclasm was imminent. The Studites were recalled from exile and made their peace with the ecclesiastical authorities after the moechian question had been decided in their favour by the repeal of the synodal decree of 809 and by the renewed

---

[1] Theophanes 492, ὁ δὲ Σταυράκιος ἀνιάτως ὁρῶν ἑαυτὸν διακείμενον τῇ γαμετῇ τὴν βασιλείαν ἐσπούδαζε περιποιήσασθαι, ἢ Δημοκρατίαν ἐγεῖραι Χριστιανοῖς ἐπὶ τοῖς προλαβοῦσι κακοῖς. Until recently this passage was generally interpreted to mean that Stauracius had contemplated founding a democracy after the Athenian model (cf. Bury, *Eastern Rom. Empire* 18; Bratianu, *Privilèges*, 50 ff.). It really only implies that the dying Emperor feared that his ambitious wife might add civil war or a rising of the demes to all the other troubles. F. Dölger was the first to interpret this passage correctly, and his suggestion was developed on the right lines by Bratianu, 'Empire et "Démocratie" à Byzance', BZ 37 (1937), 88, note 3 = *Études byzantines* (1938), 97, note 4. Maricq, 'Partis populaires', 70 ff., has recently used a hitherto unnoticed passage in the *Origines* of the Pseudo-Codinus to show that a political move on the part of the demes was still within the bounds of possibility.

[2] Michael Rangabe is the first Byzantine ruler to have a family name. The appearance of surnames reflects the rise of the families of great magnates, such as the Melisseni, which appear in Byzantium from the middle of the eighth century onwards. The name of Rangabe is first met with at the end of the eighth century (cf. Theoph. 454, Θεοφύλακτος, ὁ τοῦ 'Ραγγαβέ, δρουγγάριος τῆς Δωδεκανήσου, apparently Michael I's father) and it has been suggested that the name is of Slav origin and a Hellenized form of 'rǫkavŭ' which—and this does not seem to me entirely convincing—must be construed by analogy with similar forms to have the meaning of 'the great (strong) hand', cf. H. Grégoire, B 9 (1934), 793 f.

excommunication of the priest Joseph. The influence of Theodore the Studite was unprecedented; his extraordinary vigour and inexhaustible energy fascinated the Emperor and the famous Studite abbot had the last word even on matters of peace or war.

The attitude of the Byzantine government towards the Western Empire was revised completely. Nicephorus I chose to ignore the claim of Charles the Great to the imperial title; he even went so far as to refuse the Patriarch Nicephorus permission to despatch the customary *synodica* to the Pope.[1] Towards his real rival, the Carolingian ruler, and the Papacy which supported him he showed uncompromising hostility. Meanwhile, the power of Charles the Great steadily increased and extended to Byzantine domains. After Charles had subdued Istria and several Dalmatian towns during the reign of Irene, the young king Pepin brought Venice also under his sway (810). Charles now had a means of bringing pressure to bear which could not fail in its effect upon an already enfeebled Byzantium. In return for the restoration of part of the captured territory Michael I's government was ready to acknowledge the imperial dignity of Charles the Great, and in 812 the Byzantine legates in Aachen recognized him as Basileus. From now on there were two Empires in actual fact as well as in theory.[2] It is true that as yet the Frankish ruler was recognized only as Emperor and not as Emperor of the Romans. Indeed, Charles himself always avoided the designation

[1] According to Theophanes 494 it was in 812 that the Patriarch Nicephorus with the consent of the Emperor Michael I sent his synodal letter to Pope Leo III, πρὸ τούτου γὰρ ἐκωλύετο ὑπὸ Νικηφόρου τοῦτο ποιῆσαι.

[2] Bury, *Eastern Rom. Empire* 325, holds the view that the act of 812 implied that Charles the Great had been made a colleague of the Byzantine Emperor, so that while maintaining the conception of imperial unity there was a return to the position in the fourth and fifth centuries when two Emperors, one in the East and one in the West, normally exercised joint rule over the Roman Empire. The authority of Bury ensured the acceptance of this interpretation. But conditions at this time were entirely different from those of the late Roman period, and Bury's view is not tenable because the collegiate rule of the fourth and fifth centuries was based on the assumption that the senior Emperor had the right of confirmation. Neither the successors of Charles the Great nor the Byzantine Emperors ever obtained the confirmation of the other party. The sanction which Louis the Pious received from Leo V in 814 in the name of Charles the Great, and in his own name in 815, had an entirely different significance, for it was not concerned with the accession of Louis the Pious, but was simply a documentary confirmation of the recognition of the Western Empire pronounced in 812. Bury himself describes this fresh document issued for the same purpose in Louis the Pious' name as nothing more than 'punctiliousness of the diplomatic forms'. On the other hand, by crowning Louis in 813 Charles acquired his own co-Emperor after the Byzantine manner, a significant fact which is in itself sufficient to refute Bury's view. Cf. the excellent criticisms of F. Dölger, 'Europas Gestaltung im Spiegel der fränkisch-byzantinischen Auseinandersetzung des 9. Jahrhunderts', *Der Vertrag von Verdun*, ed. Th. Mayer (1943), 221 (reprinted in Dölger, *Byzanz*).

'Emperor of the Romans'.[1] The Byzantines maintained that they alone had the right to this title and stressed the difference between the western Emperor and the sole Emperor of the Romans in Constantinople. But the connection with Rome was an essential part of the medieval conception of Empire. Byzantium had always considered itself to be a Roman Empire for all time, though before the ninth century this is rarely expressed in the imperial title;[2] in the same way the Western Empire was closely linked to Rome through the Papacy, although it was not until the age of the Ottos that the link with Rome was finally expressed in a similar title.[3] The founding and recognition of a second Empire was also a challenge to the sole right of the Byzantine Empire to the Roman heritage. The disintegration of the Carolingian Empire and the renewed vigour of Byzantium did, however, make it possible for later rulers of Constantinople to ignore the recognition given to the Western Empire in 812.

Nicephorus I's refusal to acknowledge Charles the Great and the reversal of this policy by Michael I was due not only to the different personalities of these two rulers, but to a great extent to the change in circumstances brought about by the disaster of 811. The impending threat from the Balkans made it difficult for the Byzantines to carry on the struggle against the West. In the spring of 812 Krum captured the town of Develtus on the Black Sea, destroyed the fortress and after the Byzantine manner carried off the inhabitants to his own territory. Not only was Byzantine resistance weak, but the inhabitants of several other towns on the frontier took to flight.

---

[1] Cf. the bibliography to Ch. III. 5.

[2] E. Stein, *Forschungen und Fortschritte* 1930, p. 182 f., maintained that the title βασιλεὺς 'Ρωμαίων in Byzantium first came into use with Michael I as a result of recognizing Charles the Great's assumption of the bare title of Basileus. This must, however, be modified in the light of the examples of earlier usage of which we now have knowledge. Cf. especially the imperial seal published by N. Lichačev, 'Sceaux de l'empereur Léon III l'Isaurien', B 11 (1936), 469 ff. (with the additional note by H. Grégoire, ib. 482) and V. Laurent, 'Note de titulature byzantine', EO 38 (1939), 355 ff. (idem 'Βασιλεὺς 'Ρωμαίων, l'histoire d'un titre et le témoignage de la numismatique', *Cronica numismatiă si archeologică* 15, 1940, 198 ff., is inaccessible to me). All the same, it remains true that before 812 the title of Basileus seldom appeared with the addition 'Ρωμαίων, and after 812 seldom appeared without this, so that the simple designation of Basileus was gradually superseded by the title βασιλεὺς 'Ρωμαίων. This was not a mere accident, and Dölger (BZ 37 (1937) 579) rightly asserts that the Byzantines 'den Titel in der Form βασιλεὺς 'Ρωμαίων zwar auch vor 812 gelegentlich gebraucht haben, dass sie ihn jedoch mit grösserer Konsequenz und demonstrativer Bewusstheit erst nach 812 stärker betont und bis zum Ende des Reiches beibehalten haben'. Cf. also Dölger, BZ 36 (1936), 132 f., and especially 40 (1940), 518 f., also 'Rom in der Gedankenwelt der Byzantiner', *Zeitschr. f. Kirchengesch.* 56 (1937), 7 ff. (reprinted in Dölger, *Byzanz*).

[3] P. E. Schramm, *Kaiser, Rom und Renovatio* I (1929), 12 ff. and 83 f.

Krum offered the imperial government peace terms which took the form of an ultimatum, and when Byzantium hesitated to accept, he occupied the important port of Mesembria in the early November of 812. Here a considerable amount of gold and silver fell into his hands as well as supplies of the famous Greek fire. Some of the Emperor's counsellors, led by the Patriarch Nicephorus, shared his views and they urged acceptance of the terms offered, but others, of whom the most prominent member was Theodore, abbot of the Studite monastery, agitated for the vigorous prosecution of the war. Theodore's counsel prevailed and in June 813 a large Byzantine army met the advancing hordes of Krum at Versinicia near Adrianople. The two armies faced each other for some time in indecision and then the *strategus* of Thrace and Macedonia attacked on 22 June. But the troops from Asia Minor, commanded by Leo the Armenian, *strategus* of the Anatolikon theme, refused to follow the European army, and they suddenly took to flight. Two years earlier fate had decided against Byzantium; now poor military leadership, and particularly the internal dissensions of the Byzantines, gave another victory to Krum. The severe defeat of the orthodox Emperor Michael Rangabe shook his prestige and prepared the way for a change of policy and a revival of iconoclasm. On 11 July 813 Michael I was deposed and Leo the Armenian came to the throne.

7. THE ICONOCLAST REACTION

General bibliography: Bury, *Eastern Rom. Empire*; Vasiliev, *Byzance et les Arabes* I; Schwarzlose, *Bilderstreit*; Ostrogorsky, *Bilderstreit*; Martin, *Iconoclastic Controversy*; A. Dobroklonskij, *Prepodobnyj Fedor, ispovednik i igumen studijskij* (St. Theodore the Studite, confessor and abbot), 2 vols., Odessa 1913–14; Alexander, *Patr. Nicephorus*; Grabar, *Iconoclasme*. See also general bibliography cited above, p. 156.

Leo V the Armenian (813–20) came from those circles in Asia Minor which were distinguished for their military ability and their iconoclast outlook. Like Leo III, his origins were in the East, and like him he also was *strategus* of the Anatolikon theme before he came to the throne. He modelled himself on the great generals and iconoclasts, such as Leo III and Constantine V, and he planned to restore the military power of the Empire and to revive the iconoclast movement. Neither he nor his followers had any doubt whatsoever that the military disasters of the last reign were the result of its iconodule policy.

He was faced with pressing military problems. After his victory at Versinikia, Krum had taken the offensive swiftly and in great strength by besieging Adrianople, and only a few days after Leo V's accession he appeared with the greater part of his army at the gates of the Byzantine capital. But Krum was powerless against the walls of Constantinople which had withstood even the Muslim attack, and he asked the Emperor for a personal interview in order to discuss peace terms. Krum trusted the word of the Byzantine Emperor and came to the conference unarmed, but a treacherous attack was made on him and he was only saved by his presence of mind and the rapidity of his flight. The furious leader of the Bulgars now laid waste the whole countryside surrounding the capital, entered Adrianople which had been starved into surrender, and carried off its inhabitants, as well as those of the neighbouring villages, to the districts beyond the Danube. The Emperor, however, did succeed in winning a notable victory in the region of Mesembria in the autumn of 813, but in the following spring Krum again marched on Constantinople. Providence saved Byzantium from the threatening danger for, like Attila, Krum suddenly died of cerebral haemorrhage on 13 April 814.

After an interval of two short reigns,[1] the Bulgars found another outstanding leader in the person of Omurtag. His main aims were, however, the development of Bulgarian power in the north-west and the internal consolidation of his kingdom, and he therefore concluded a thirty years' peace with Byzantium. This was naturally advantageous to the Bulgars and virtually restored the territorial position of Tervel's day: Thrace was divided between the two powers, the boundaries running along the so-called Great Wall from Develtus to Makrolivada, i.e. between Adrianople and Philippopolis, and thence northwards to the Balkan Mountains.[2] After the dramatic events of the last few years Byzantium's Balkan frontier was now to enjoy a long period of undisturbed peace. In the East the Empire was also freed from anxiety because after the death of Harun al Rashid the Caliphate was rent by internal dissension.

During this period of peace Leo V attempted to carry out his iconoclast plans. The situation had scarcely begun to improve after Krum's death when he commissioned the learned John Grammaticus, the moving spirit of the new iconoclast movement, to get together

---

[1] Dukum and Dicevg who both only reigned for a short time; cf. Beševliev, *Godišnik na Sofijskija Univ.* (Yearbook of the University of Sofia), 32, 9, p. 1 ff.
[2] Cf. Runciman, *Bulgarian Empire* 72 f.

theological ammunition for the impending council against the iconodules. This iconoclast policy had the effect of uniting the various discordant elements within the ranks of the orthodox party. The Patriarch Nicephorus now found himself involved in a struggle against the newly revived opposition to icons side by side with his former opponent, Theodore the Studite. In a number of writings they both supported the traditional use of icons with unabating zeal and protested against the imperial interference in matters of belief. Still more clearly than in the eighth century, ecclesiastical and political threads were interwoven in this second phase of the iconoclast movement: the imperial authority sought to control religious life and had to face the obstinate opposition of the Church, especially of its more radical wing. The Emperor had his way to begin with, because he had ready means of enforcing his authority. Theodore and a number of his followers had to go into exile and were subjected to much ill-treatment. Nicephorus was deposed and the courtier Theodotus Melissenus, thanks to his distinguished ancestry and his relationship with the third wife of Constantine V, ascended the patriarchal throne on Easter Day, 1 April 815.

Soon after Easter a synod was held in Hagia Sophia under the presidency of the newly appointed Patriarch; it repudiated the oecumenical second Council of Nicaea of 787 and recognized the *acta* of the iconoclast council of 754. It stated that it did not regard the icons as idols,[1] but all the same it ordered their destruction. This was characteristic of Leo V's synod: it was in fact entirely committed to the fundamentals of the old iconoclasm, but it made some concessions in formulating its doctrinal position. The *acta* of the council of 754 provided its only source of inspiration and it repeated these old views, but at the same time watered them down and glided over the essentials in vague, meaningless phrases.[2] Like the whole iconoclast revival of the ninth century, the synod of 815 was marked

---

[1] Ostrogorsky, *Bilderstreit*, p. 51, fragment 17, εἴδωλα δὲ ταύτας εἰπεῖν φεισάμενοι.

[2] The *acta* of the Council of 754 attempted to establish the iconoclast point of view by a detailed discussion on a Christological basis; the iconodules throughout the controversy, but especially during the latter period, also emphasized the extent to which the teaching about icons was bound up with Christological doctrine. The whole problem is summed up by a single sentence of the synod of 815 when the iconodules are reproached because they ἢ συμπεριγράφοντες τῇ εἰκόνι τὸν ἀπερίγραφον, ἢ τὴν σάρκα ἐκ τῆς θεότητος κατατέμνοντες, κακῷ τὸ κακὸν διορθούμενοι (Ostrogorsky, *Bilderstreit*, p. 50, fragment 14). Only those sufficiently familiar with the *acta* of 754 will appreciate the significance of this sentence upholding the provocative and ingenious thesis then expounded by which the iconodules were accused of falling into the heresies either of monophysism or of Nestorianism.

with the stamp of impotence. The iconoclasm of Leo III and Constantine V was a movement of great and dynamic vigour, while the movement of the following century showed all the signs of a reaction which was essentially imitative in character.[1] Its inherent weakness, however, could not disguise the fact that the Emperor commanded resources enabling him to enforce his will and that he cruelly persecuted those who defied him. Leo V had but little of the support which had been given the iconoclast Emperors of the eighth century, and he was continually fearing for his throne. His terror of deposition became a positive mania during the last years of his life. In spite of all precautions he could not elude his fate and on Christmas Day 820, while he was at a service in Hagia Sophia, he was murdered in front of the high altar by the followers of his old comrade in arms, Michael the Amorian.

Michael II (820–29), the founder of the Amorian dynasty, was a rough soldier whose lack of education was a source of derision to the cultured Byzantines. But he had common sense and energy and a sense of moderation. During his reign religious dissension died down, the persecution of the iconodules ceased and the exiles were recalled with the Patriarch Nicephorus and Theodore the Studite at their head. But to the great disappointment of the orthodox, and in spite of their repeated representations, the restoration of the veneration of icons did not follow. Michael II took up a reserved attitude: he recognized neither the oecumenical second Council of Nicaea nor the iconoclast synod and he forthwith forbad all discussion on the question of icons. The Emperor himself came from Phrygia, the former stronghold of iconoclasm, and there is no doubt that his personal convictions were opposed to the use of icons. This is clearly shown in his letter to Louis the Pious in which he complains of certain abuses of the cult of icons.[2] It is also shown by the fact that he entrusted the education of his son and heir Theophilus to the iconoclast John Grammaticus, and after the death of Theodotus Melissenus he did not recall the orthodox Nicephorus to the patriarchal throne but nominated Antony, Bishop of Sylaion, who, together with John Grammaticus, had been largely responsible for drawing

[1] I must maintain this view, in spite of the different opinion of P. J. Alexander. 'The Iconoclast Council of St. Sophia and its Definition', *Dumbarton Oaks Papers* 7 (1953), 35 ff., and all the more so since the conceptions which he puts forward as representing the new teaching of the synod of 815 are not their own ideas but only a citation from Basil the Great, so that it is clear that the views which Alexander would like to attribute to the ninth-century iconoclasts are really taken from Basil.

[2] Mansi 14, 417 ff.

up the synodal *acta* of 815. The reserved attitude of the Emperor was due not so much to indifference as to the realization that the iconoclast movement had spent its force. The only iconodule against whom Michael II took action was the Sicilian Methodius who brought him a papal admonition in support of icons. Methodius was ill-treated and thrown into prison, not because he venerated icons, but because the Emperor thought that the understanding between the Byzantine iconodules and Rome was open to suspicion on political grounds.

The central event of home politics during Michael's reign was the severe civil war provoked by Thomas, a Slav from Asia Minor and an old fellow soldier of the Emperor.[1] Actively supported by the Arabs, Thomas had got together a large and heterogeneous following on the eastern frontier districts during the reign of Leo V. Arabs, Persians, Armenians, Iberians and other Caucasian peoples placed themselves under his standard. Asia Minor, racially so mixed and including many Slavs among its population, was an admirable breeding ground for such a movement. It was greatly strengthened by those elements which felt themselves banned from Constantinople for religious reasons, for Thomas proclaimed himself the champion of the iconodules and even asserted that he was the illegally deposed Emperor, Constantine VI. It is particularly significant that the revolt offered something in the nature of a social revolution: Thomas appeared as the protector of the poor whose burdens he promised to lighten. In this way he drew into the movement the masses who were embittered by economic want, crushing taxation and the arbitrary

[1] In Vasiliev, *Byzance et les Arabes* I, 22 ff., it is maintained that Thomas was an Armenian. This is not, however, Vasiliev's own view (in the original text he openly declares for the Slav origin of Thomas, cf. *Vizantija i Araby* I, 24, and see also *History* 275, n. 131), but it is the opinion of the editors of the French translation who revised Vasiliev's work. It is not quite clear why the editors decide so firmly and unreservedly in favour of the Armenian reading in the two contradictory passages in Genesius (p. 8 and p. 32, where Thomas is described as being of Armenian and Scythian ancestry respectively), and disregard the clear statement of Theophanes cont., p. 50, on the Slav ancestry of Thomas. Vasiliev, and before him Bury, 'The Identity of Thomas the Slavonian', BZ 1 (1892), 55 ff. (cf. also *Eastern Rom. Empire* 85 *et passim*), thought that it was possible to regard Thomas as a Slav from Asia Minor on the evidence of the information in Theophanes cont. which agrees with that of Genesius, p. 32. Most scholars now support this view. Cf. M. Rajković, 'O poreklu Tome, vodje ustanka 821–3 g.', *Zbornik radova Viz. Inst.* 2 (1953), 33 ff. (French résumé), which in my view has finally decided the question. See the important examination of the sources by F. Barišić, 'Dve verzije u izvorima o ustaniku Tomi' (Two versions of the sources for the revolt of Thomas), ZRVI 6 (1959) 145 ff. E. Lipšic, 'Vosstanie Fomy Slavjanina i vizantijskoe krestjanstvo na grani VIII–IX vv.' (The rising of Thomas the Slav and the Byzantine peasantry at the turn of the eighth and ninth centuries), *Vestnik drevnej istorii* 1939 Nr. 1, and *Očerki*, 212 ff., provides a much fuller description of this revolt.

Figure 35: *Chronicle of John Scylitzes.* Miniature paintings on parchment, 14th century. Above, the dead body of Leo V is carried from the palace. Below, Michael II is proclaimed emperor. Biblioteca Nacional, Madrid. Photo: Biblioteca Nacional.

Figure 36: *Chronicle of John Scylitzes.* Miniature paintings on parchment, 14th century. Above, the rebel Thomas parleys with the Saracens. Below, Thomas defeats the imperial army. Biblioteca Nacional, Madrid. Photo: Biblioteca Nacional.

exactions of government officials. And so, as a Byzantine chronicler wrote, 'the slave raised his hand against his master and the soldier against his officer'.[1] The rebellion, relying on racial, religious and social antagonisms, soon spread over most of Asia Minor, and of the six Asian themes then in existence, only the Opsikion and the Armeniakon remained true to Michael II. Thomas was crowned Emperor by the Patriarch of Antioch, which could not have happened without the consent of the Caliph. The support of the Cibyraeot theme secured him command of the fleet and gave him the means of crossing to Europe and rallying the iconodule population there to his banner. The siege of Constantinople, which began in December 821, lasted more than a year and it finally broke the power of the usurper. The superior military leadership of the Emperor of Constantinople prevailed over the badly organized mass movement. Above all Michael II owed his salvation to the help of the Khan of the Bulgars. Just as Tervel had once come to the rescue of Leo III against the Arabs, so Omurtag, the son of Byzantium's bitterest foe, now supported Michael II against Thomas and scattered the rebel's forces. In the spring of 823 Thomas had to raise the siege and the movement collapsed. It was not until October that Thomas, who had entrenched himself in Arcadiopolis with a small following, fell into the hands of the Emperor and was put to death after terrible tortures.

Thus Michael II remained master of the situation, but Byzantium had been considerably weakened by a civil war that had lasted for nearly three years. It was also evident that there was a good deal of social unrest in a State already rent by religious controversy. Meanwhile, although the Caliph, who had supported Thomas' rebellion with all the means in his power, was not in a position to launch a vigorous attack against Byzantium by reason of the internal troubles of the Caliphate, other parts of the Arab world seriously threatened the Byzantine Empire. Muslim adventurers from Spain, who had occupied Egypt in 816 and temporarily gained control of it, captured Crete about ten years later.[2] This meant that one of the most

[1] Theophanes cont. 53.

[2] Vasiliev, *Byzance et les Arabes* I, 49 ff. It is not possible to determine the precise date when Crete was captured. Statements in the relevant literature vary and put it between 823 and 828; the investigation of J. Papadopulos, Ἡ Κρήτη ὑπὸ τοὺς Σαρακηνούς (824–961), (*Texte und Forschungen zur byz.-neugr. Philol.* 43), Athens 1948, 58 ff., does not seem to me to have yielded any more definite result. The latest study of the history of the Arab rule in Crete, N. Tomadakes, 'Προβλήματα τῆς ἐν Κρήτη ἀραβοκρατίας (826–961)', EEBS 30 (1960), 1 ff., does not discuss the question of the year in which it was captured.

strategic bases in the eastern Mediterranean was lost to Byzantium. All attempts by Michael II and his successors to regain the lost possession failed and for nearly a century and a half the Muslims held this important island, using it as a centre from which they conducted ceaseless acts of piracy against the whole surrounding area. At the same time Byzantium suffered a heavy setback in the West. Taking advantage of the quarrels of the local Byzantine commanders, the African Muslims appeared in Sicily in 827. Arab raids on Sicily had been of frequent occurrence from the middle of the seventh century onward, but now a planned occupation of the island began. Thus Byzantine predominance in the Mediterranean and particularly in the Adriatic was completely undermined. Constantine VII Porphyrogenitus regarded the reign of Michael II as the period which saw the most severe setback to Byzantine influence on the Adriatic coast and in the Slav territories in the western Balkans.[1] The Byzantines had paid little attention to the fleet since the downfall of the naval-minded Umayyad Caliphs, and this neglect was now having disastrous consequences.

The upstart Michael II could scarcely read or write, but his son and heir Theophilus (829–42) had a liberal education and showed real interest in art and learning. This was not unusual in Byzantium— Justinian I, though the nephew of the uneducated soldier Justin I, was one of the most erudite men of his day. Instances of this kind show the cultural influence of the Byzantine capital and the high level of its court life. Theophilus was not only alive to the civilization of Constantinople, but to the cultural influences which emanated from the court of the Caliph of Baghdad. His enthusiasm for Muslim art was probably derived from his tutor John Grammaticus, as well as the zeal for iconoclasm which made him a vigorous opponent of the iconodules. His reign saw the last wave of iconoclasm; it was also the period when Muslim culture exercised its strongest influence on the Byzantine world.

Theophilus was not a remarkable ruler, but all the same he had a most interesting personality. He was a romantic as he showed by his attachment to the iconoclasm which was now on its death-bed and by his enthusiasm for the art and culture of the Arab world whose great days already belonged to the past. Although he indulged in real cruelty by reason of his religious fanaticism, there was something attractive about him and it is understandable that legends grew

---

[1] *De adm. imp.*, c. 29, 60 (ed. Moravcsik-Jenkins).

up round his name.[1] He wanted to be an ideal ruler and he was moved by a strong sense of justice which he displayed in a somewhat theatrical manner. In imitation of the upright Caliph Harun al Rashid, he used to prowl about the city, talking to the poorest and meanest of his subjects and hearing their grievances, so that he might punish offenders without any consideration of rank or office.

The organization of themes in the Balkan peninsula at the end of the eighth century and beginning of the ninth century (cf. above, p. 193) was further extended in the east and in the distant north by Theophilus. The new themes of Paphlagonia and Chaldia were created to strengthen the Byzantine position on the Black Sea. Paphlagonia consisted of the north-east corner of the earlier Bucellarion theme and Chaldia was the north-east part of the Armeniakon theme. In addition, three new military and administrative units in the mountainous region of the Arab frontier were created out of part of the Armeniakon theme on the one side and the Anatolikon on the other. These were called *kleisurai* (κλεισοῦραι = mountain passes) and were the little military frontier zones of Charsianon, Cappadocia and Seleucia, which were later to become themes.[2]

Still more significant was the organization of the so-called *klimata*, i.e. the Byzantine possessions on the north coast of the Black Sea with Cherson as their centre, as a theme under the command of a *strategus*, which took place during Theophilus' reign. The disturbances in the great north-eastern plains of Europe forced not only Byzantium, but its ally the Khazar empire, to take defence measures, and at the same time that the theme system was introduced into the Cherson district, Byzantine architects at the request of the Khan of the Khazars were constructing the fortress of Sarkel at the mouth of

[1] Cf. Ch. Diehl, 'La Légende de l'empereur Théophile', *Sem. Kond.* 4 (1931), 33 ff.
[2] Apart from the maritime Cibyraeot theme, five themes (Opsikion, Bucellarion, Armeniakon, Anatolikon and Thracesion) are found in Asia Minor in 803 (Theoph. cont. 6) and also in 819 (Theodore Stud. *Epistolae* II, 64 = Migne, PG 99, 1284). In 838 seven themes are mentioned in the Acts of the 42 martyrs of Amorium (ed. Vasiljevskij and Nikitin, *Zapiski Imp. Akad. Nauk*, VIII Ser., VII 2, p. 65), and in 834 eight (apparently including the Cibyraeot theme) are spoken of in the Life of the Empress Theodora (ed. Regel, *Analecta byzantino-russica*, p. 9). Nikitin, op. cit., 244 ff., unnecessarily finds an error in one of the two texts. It was in the time of Theophilus that there was increased Byzantine political activity in the Black Sea area (see below on the establishment of a theme in the Cherson region), so that it is probable, as Bury assumed, *Eastern Rom. Empire* 221 ff., that the creation of the two themes of Paphlagonia and Chaldia took place under Theophilus and not under Michael II. I should, however, differ from Bury in that I should also place the establishment of the *kleisurai* on the Arab frontier in the time of Theophilus under whom the Byzantino-Arab war in Asia Minor broke out again after a long period of peace. On the *kleisurai* in general cf. J. Ferluga, Niže vojno-administrativne jedinice tematskog uredjenja (Smaller units of military administration in the theme system), ZRVI 2 (1953), 76 ff.

the Don, thus setting up a monument to Byzantine skill in the distant steppes.[1]

The Emperor Theophilus, despite his enthusiasm for their art and culture, was compelled to war with the Muslims throughout his whole reign. The Caliph Mamun (813–33) had at first been fully occupied with internal struggles, and in particular the movement of the Khurramite sect led by the Persian Babek, but in the last part of his reign from 830 onwards he was sufficiently master of the situation to be able to resume the struggle with Byzantium which had for some years been lying dormant. He was quick to take advantage of the difficulties of the Byzantine Empire which was not in a position to concentrate all its forces in the theatre of war in Asia Minor, since it had at the same time to fight in Sicily where the Muslims were increasing their hold on the island in spite of every defence measure and had already taken Palermo by 831. On the eastern frontier war was continued with varying success. Sometimes the Byzantines would advance into enemy territory and Theophilus would then celebrate a splendid triumph in Constantinople, some-times—and only too often—the Arabs would press into Byzantine lands and then the Emperor's festive mood would quickly change and he would despatch embassies to the Caliph with costly presents and proposals for peace. The situation grew really serious when the Caliph Mutasim, Mamun's brother, having settled the internal dis-turbances which usually accompanied a change of ruler in the Caliphate, undertook a great expedition in 838. This was not directed against the border fortresses as in previous attacks, but against the most important centres of Asia Minor. Part of Mutasim's powerful army advanced to the north-west, defeated the Byzantine army com-manded by the Emperor himself in a bloody battle at Dazimon (Dazmana) on 22 July and occupied Ancyra. Meanwhile, Mutasim with the main part of his forces stormed Amorium on 12 August.[2] This event made an overwhelming impression in Byzantium. Amorium was the largest and most important fortress of the Anatoli-kon theme, and indeed the city from which the reigning dynasty

[1] *De admin. imp.*, c. 42, 24 (ed. Moravcsik-Jenkins); Theoph. cont. 122 f. The identity of the people menacing the Khazar empire and the Byzantine possessions in the region of the Crimea at that time is a disputed question. Cf. Vasiliev, *The Goths in the Crimea* (1936), 108 ff., who discusses the opinions of earlier scholars and thinks that the measures taken by the Byzantines and Khazars were the result of dangers threatening from the Russian Northmen.

[2] Vasiliev, *Byzance et les Arabes* I, 144 ff.; Grégoire, 'Michel III', 328 ff.; Bury, 'Muta-sim's March through Cappadocia in A.D. 838', JHS 29 (1909), 120 ff.

came. The Emperor even sought help against the Muslims in western lands, from the Franks and from Venice.[1]

Under Theophilus iconoclasm made its last move. In 837 the leader of the iconoclasts, John Grammaticus, ascended the patriarchal throne and once more instituted sharp persecution of the iconodules.[2] As in Constantine V's day the attack was directed against the monastic world. A particular kind of martyrdom was reserved for the brothers Theodore and Theophanes from Palestine: iconoclast verses were written on their foreheads with red hot irons and for this reason they were given the nickname of 'graptoi'. Theophanes was a poet, well known for his verses written in praise of the holy icons, and after the restoration of orthodoxy he became Metropolitan of Nicaea.

Although the Emperor and Patriarch used every possible means to revive the iconoclast movement, their failure to do so became daily more apparent. Its sphere of influence was now largely confined to the capital and it was only the will of the Emperor and his few faithful followers which upheld its authority.[3] On 20 January 842, Theophilus died and iconoclasm did not survive him. The movement collapsed and the great crisis which it had brought also passed away.

[1] The well-known imperial letter of St. Denis may well be related to an embassy sent at that time to the Emperor Lothair. Cf. F. Dölger, 'Der Pariser Papyrus von St. Denis als ältestes Kreuzzugsdokument', *Byzantinische Diplomatik* (Ettal 1956), 204 ff. W. Ohnsorge, 'Das Kaiserbündnis von 842–4 gegen die Sarazenen. Datum, Inhalt und politische Bedeutung des "Kaiserbriefes aus St. Denis" ', *Abendland und Byzanz* (Darmstadt 1958), 131 ff.

[2] V. Grumel, 'Recherches récentes sur l'iconoclasme', EO 29 (1930), 99, refers to an account of the summoning of an iconoclast synod under Theophilus. But Grumel himself admits (*Reg.* 413) that this late evidence is open to suspicion as this supposed synod is not mentioned in contemporary sources.

[3] Cf. Bury, *Eastern Rom. Empire* 141. But cf. also Alexander, *Patr. Nicephorus* 142 ff.

The Golden Age of the Byzantine Empire
(843–1025)

SOURCES

THE chronicle of Symeon Logothetes mentioned above (p. 147) appears to have extended as far as the death of Romanus Lecapenus (948) and shows a sympathetic attitude towards this Emperor. This chronicle was very frequently copied and worked over, and in some versions of it the central core of the work was added to and brought down to the second half of the eleventh century or beyond, though these additions are of little value. The fourth and last book of Joseph Genesius deals with the age of Michael III and Basil I; this work is the official account of the Macedonian dynasty and is of considerable historical value in spite of a markedly tendentious outlook in its attempt to glorify the founder of the Macedonian house and to blacken his murdered victim, Michael III. The same is true of Book IV of Theophanes Continuatus, which is concerned with the age of Michael III and is closely related to Genesius, and indeed the two works appear to be drawing on a common source. Book V in the compilation known as Theophanes Continuatus comes from the Emperor Constantine VII himself; it is a full biography of his grandfather Basil I and is exceedingly laudatory in character. Book VI consists of two heterogeneous sections. The first part covers the reigns of Leo VI and Alexander, the minority of Constantine VII, the rule of Romanus I Lecapenus and Constantine VII as sole Emperor up to 948, and it is of little value for it slavishly reproduces the chronicle of Symeon Logothetes. The important concluding section consists of the main part of Constantine VII's rule alone and an unfinished history of Romanus II and appears to be the work of a well informed contemporary, perhaps Theodore Daphnopates whom Scylitzes mentions in his preface as having written a history.[1]

---

[1] Cf. the recent very detailed discussions by A. P. Každan, 'Iz istorii vizantijskoj chronografii X v.' (From the history of Byzantine chronography of the tenth century), VV 19 (1961), 76 ff. and 21 (1962), 35 ff. For the deliberately classical features of the work compare the interesting observations of R. J. H. Jenkins, 'The Classical Background of the *Scriptores post Theophanem*', DOP 8 (1954), 11 ff.

There is an eye-witness account of the sack of Thessalonica by the Arabs in 904 by the priest John Cameniates.[1] Towards the end of the tenth century (some time after 992), Leo the Deacon wrote a history divided into ten books in which he deals with the period 959–76 and gives a picture of the military achievements of Nicephorus Phocas and John Tzimisces. His work was modelled on the history of Agathias which gives a somewhat artificial flavour to his descriptions. Michael Psellus touches on the age of Basil II in the first book of his famous *Chronographia*, but only by way of introduction (cf. below, p. 316). At the end of the eleventh century John Scylitzes, a high Byzantine official, produced a chronicle from 811 to 1057. For the period down to the fall of Romanus Lecapenus he used above all Theophanes Continuatus, but the rest of his history relies for the most part on sources no longer extant and is therefore of great value. For the period down to towards the end of Nicephorus Phocas Scylitzes drew on a kind of chronicle of the Phocas family which Leo the Deacon used, as well as an additional source of ecclesiastical origin.[2] The part of Scylitzes which covers the age of Basil II is particularly important. The original text of this remarkable work is still unedited; and CB, like the older editions, only gives George Cedrenus' copy of the main part of Scylitzes,[3] and under the name of Scylitzes it prints the continuation for the years 1057 to 1079 not given by Cedrenus, which is found in some manuscripts of Scylitzes' work. Modern research has shown, however, that this is not by Scylitzes and is merely the compilation of an unknown author.[4] John Zonaras, also an important official, retired to a monastery and about the middle of the twelfth century wrote a comprehensive world chronicle going to the year 1118. Zonaras has little fresh to add to the earlier sources for this period, but his

[1] In CB after Theoph. Cont. See R. A. Nasledova, *Dve vizantijskie chroniki X veka*, Moscow 1959, for a Russian translation with introduction and commentary.

[2] Cf. M. Sjuzjumov, 'Ob istočnikach Ljva Djakona i Skilicy' (On the sources of Leo the Deacon and Scylitzes), *Viz. Obozrenie* 2 (1916), 106 ff., whose detailed discussions have made the relations between Leo Deacon and Scylitzes very much clearer. Further important notes on this problem are given by A. P. Každan, 'Iz istorii vizantijskoj chronografii' VV 20 (1961) 106 ff.

[3] Important additions from a MS. of Scylitzes, which deal with the history of Samuel and his kingdom, are given by B. Prokić, *Die Zusätze in der Hs. des J. Skylitzes cod. Vindob. hist. gr. LXXIV*, Munich 1906. On the MSS. of Scylitzes cf. C. de Boor, BZ 13 (1904), 356 ff., and 14 (1905), 409 ff., 757 ff., and on the MSS. of Cedrenus, K. Schweinburg, BZ 30 (1929–30), 68 ff.

[4] Moravcsik, *Byzantinoturcica* I, 340, rightly cites this as 'Ioannes Scylitzes continuatus'.

work is of value because of the independent way in which he handles his material.

Arab sources make important contributions towards filling in the gaps in Byzantine historical works, and in particular the chronicle of Jahja of Antioch († 1066) is exceedingly useful for the Macedonian dynasty.[1] An outstanding Latin source for Byzantine history in the mid-tenth century is Liutprand of Cremona's *Antapodosis*, while his account of his embassy from Otto I to Nicephorus Phocas is a masterly pamphlet of inestimable value for the cultural history of this time. The *Russian Primary Chronicle* offers much important information on the relations between Russia and Byzantium and contains the Old Slavonic translation of the trade agreements between the Russians and Constantinople of which the originals have not survived.[2]

With the restoration of the use of icons in 843, a *Synodicon* was read out in the Greek Orthodox Church each year on the first Sunday of Lent. The oldest part of this document deals with the final rulings on the question of icons and is to some extent a compensation for the lost *acta* of the Council of 843. As other religious disputes arose in later centuries, further definitions of orthodoxy were added to the *Synodicon* from time to time, and it is therefore an important document for the history of Byzantine spiritual life from the ninth to the fourteenth centuries.[3] The work of Peter of Sicily

---

[1] All the passages referring to Byzantine history in Basil II's time, as well as a number of fragments from other parts of this chronicle were published and translated into Russian by Rosen, *Bolgarobojca*. The part up to the death of John Tzimisces is given in the original text with a French translation in the edition of J. Kratschkovskij and A. Vasiliev, *Patrologia orientalis* XVIII (1924), 705 ff. Some extracts for the period 940–60 are given in Russian translation in Vasiliev, *Vizantija i Araby* II, Pril. p. 61 ff., and in French translation in Vasiliev, *Byzance et les Arabes* II, 2, pp. 91 ff. Other Arabic sources for Byzantine history are also found in this work (there are considerably fuller extracts in the French translation).

[2] *Polnoe Sobranie Russkich Letopisej* (A complete collection of Russian chronicles) I (1926–8) and II (1908). German trans. by R. Trautmann, *Die altrussische Nestor-Chronik*, Leipzig 1931; English trans. by S. H. Cross and O. P. Sherbowitz-Wetzor, *The Russian Primary Chronicle: Laurentian Text*, Cambridge, Mass. 1953.

[3] ed. F. I. Uspenskij, *Sinodik v nedelju pravoslavija* (*Synodicon for Orthodoxy Sunday*), Odessa 1893. Also Uspenskij, *Očerki* I ff. Cf. Michel, *Kerullarios* II, I ff., and *Oriens Christianus* N.S. 12 (1925), 151 ff. Cf. also V. A. Mošin, 'Serbskaja redakcija Sinodika v nedelju pravoslavija' (A Serbian redaction of the *Synodicon* for Orthodoxy Sunday), VV 16 (1959), 317–94; 17 (1960), 278–353 and 18 (1961), 359 f. This comprehensive article studies in detail not only the Greek but also the Slavonic (Bulgarian, Russian and Serbian) redactions of the *Synodicon*, and gives an edition of the text of the Serbian recension with a parallel text in Greek.

is fundamental for the history and teaching of the Paulician sects.[1] The main authorities for the beginnings of the Bogomil heresy are a letter from the Patriarch Theophylact (933–56) to the Bulgarian tzar Peter[2] and above all the oration of the Bulgarian priest Cosmas.[3] On the Bulgarian ecclesiastical question and the dispute between the Churches of Rome and Constantinople the *acta* of the Councils of 869–70 and 879[4] should be consulted, and especially the letters of the Patriarch Photius[5] and of the contemporary Popes.[6] The important documents of 1020 in which Basil II regulated the affairs of the Archbishopric of Ochrida after the conquest of Samuel's empire have survived in a chrysobull of Michael VIII of 1272.[7] The Lives of the two apostles to the Slavs, Constantine-Cyril and Methodius, throw much light on the great mission to the Slavs in Moravia and their

[1] Stimulated by H. Grégoire, 'Les sources de l'histoire des Pauliciens', *Bulletin de l'Acad. de Belgique* 22 (1936), 95 ff. and 'Précision sgéographiques et chronologiques sur les Pauliciens' ibid. 33 (1947), 289 ff., several recent studies have gone much more deeply into the question of these sources for the history of the Paulicians. Grégoire's thesis that all other sources go back to Peter of Sicily and have no independent value has been considerably modified by these later studies. Thus F. Scheidweiler, 'Paulikianerprobleme', BZ 43 (1950), 10 ff., 366 ff., also defends the importance of the account of the Paulician sect given in the chronicle of George the Monk. Of the three different versions of this account Scheidweiler (like J. Friedrich, S.B. d. Bayr. Akad. d. Wiss., 1896, 70 ff.) considers that the 'short account 3' is the original, probably also deriving from Peter of Sicily. A similar conclusion has been reached by M. Loos, 'Deux contributions à l'histoire des Pauliciens', BS 17 (1956), 90 ff. Furthermore, J. Scharf, 'Zur Echtheitsfrage der Manichäerbuch des Photios', BZ 44 (1951), 487 ff. regards the second and third books of Photius, writings amongst the Paulicians as also genuine, and not merely, like Grégoire, only the fourth and last, and is of the opinion that even in the first book 'there are at least traces of the great Patriarch's hand'. Cf. also E. E. Lipšic, "Pavlikianskoe dviženie v Vizantii v VIII i pervoj polovine IX vv.' (The Paulician Movement in Byzantium in the eighth century and the first half of the ninth century) VV 5 (1952), 49 ff. and *Očerki*, 133 ff.

[2] Grumel, *Reg.* 789. Text in N. Petrovskij, 'Pis'mo patriarcha Konstant. Feofilakta Carju Bolgarii Petru' (The letter of Theophylact, Patriarch of Constantinople, to the Bulgarian czar Peter), *Izvest. otd. russ. jaz. i slov. Imp. Akad. Nauk*, St. Petersburg 1913, XVIII, III, 365 ff. English in Sharenkoff, A Study of Manichaeism in Bulgaria, 1927, 63–5, Bulgarian in Zlatarski, *Istorija* I, 2, pp. 840–5.

[3] ed. Popruženko, *Kozma Presviter, bolgarskij pisatel'* X v. (The priest Cosmas, a Bulgarian writer of the tenth century), Sofia 1936. French trans. with excellent commentary in H. Ch. Puech and A. Vaillant, *Le traité contre les Bogomiles de Cosmas le Prêtre*, Paris 1945.

[4] Mansi 16, 1 ff., and 17, 372 ff. The collection of documents appended to the *acta* of the Council of 869/70 (Mansi 16, 409–57) until recently were regarded as the chief source for the history of the relations between Rome and Constantinople during Photius' second patriarchate. It has now been shown that these are a tendentious, specially adapted anti-Photian compilation dating from the time of Pope Formosus (891–6). Cf. Dvornik, *Photian Schism* 216 ff., 271 ff., and also below p. 239, note 1.

[5] Migne, PG 102, 585 ff.

[6] MGH Ep. VI, II, 1, ed. E. Perels (Nicholas I); Ep. VI, II, 2, ed. E. Perels (Hadrian II); Ep. VII, 1, ed. E. Caspar (John VIII).

[7] Critical ed. by V. N. Beneševič, *Catalogus cod. manuscr. gr. in mon. St. Catharinae n Monte Sina* I (1911), p. 542 ff. Cf. also B. Granić, 'Kirchenrechtliche Glossen zu den von Kaiser Basileios II. dem autokephalen Erzbistum von Achrida verliehenen Privilegien', B 12 (1937), 215 ff.

value as historical sources has been well established.[1] The most valuable Greek hagiographical works for this period are the *Vita* of the Empress Theodora,[2] the *Vita* of the Empress Theophano the first wife of Leo VI,[3] the *Vita* of Patriarch Ignatius by David Nicetas,[4] and particularly the *Vita* of the Patriarch Euthymius, one of the most informative historical sources of this period.[5] The many letters of the Patriarch Nicholas Mysticus[6] are of first-rate importance, as also the two letters of Romanus Lecapenus to Symeon of Bulgaria[7] which illuminate Byzantino-Bulgarian relations during the critical years 913 to 925. The letters of the ambassador Leo Choerosphactes to Symeon are of particular interest for Byzantium's relations with Bulgaria during the reign of Leo VI.[8]

The writings of Constantine VII are among the most significant Byzantine sources of any period: the treatise on the themes (*De thematibus*) is a historical and geographical description of the Byzantine provinces, which admittedly is drawn in the main from older writings, especially from Hierocles,[9] the treatise on the countries and peoples with whom the Byzantine Empire came into contact (*De administrando imperio*) is a handbook for diplomats and is of unique importance;[10] and the all-embracing book of ceremonies (*De cerimoniis*

---

[1] Cf. Dvornik, *Légendes*, who also gives a French trans. of the two Lives; for the many editions of the text see ibid. 342 f.

[2] ed. Regel, *Analecta Byzantinorossica*, St. Petersburg 1891, 1–19, with commentary, pp. iii–xix.

[3] ed. E. Kurtz, *Mém. de l'Acad. Imp. de St. Pétersbourg*, VIII Série III, 2 (1898).

[4] Migne, PG 105, 488 ff.

[5] ed. with detailed historical commentary by C. de Boor, Berlin 1888. A new edition (based on De Boor's edition) with an English translation has been made by P. Karlin-Hayter, 'Vita S. Euthymii', B 25/27 (1955/57), 1–172. There is a Russian translation with a detailed introduction and extensive commentary by A. P. Každan in *Dve vizantijskie chroniki X veka* (Two Byzantine chronicles of the tenth century), Moscow, 1959, 7–139.

[6] Migne, PG 111, 40 ff. Bulgarian trans. with detailed commentary by V. Zlatarski, *Sbornik na nar. unmotv. i knižn.* (Collection of national folklore and literature) 10 (1894), 372–428, 11 (1894), 5–54, 12 (1895), 121–211. Cf. also J. Dujčev, *Sbornik Nikov* (1940), 212 ff.

[7] ed. Sakkelion, Δελτίον 1 (1884), 658 ff., and 2 (1885), 40 ff.; Dölger, *Reg.* 606 and 607.

[8] ed. with French trans. by G. Kolias, *Léon Choerosphactès*, Athens 1939, 76 ff.

[9] New edition with detailed commentary by A. Pertusi, *Costantino Porfirogenito De thematibus* (Studi e Testi 160), Vatican 1952. The view of the editor that the second part of this work was not written until the last years of the tenth century is untenable. The statements about Romanus I Lecapenus in Book II (6, 42) as well as Book I (13,12) leave no doubt that both parts were written in this Emperor's reign. Cf. my discussion in 'Sur la date de la composition du Livre des Thèmes et sur l'époque de la constitution des premiers thèmes d'Asie Mineure', B 23 (1954), 31 ff.

[10] Definitive edition with English trans. by Gy. Moravcsik-R. J. H. Jenkins, *Constantine Porphyrogenitus. De Administrando Imperio*, Budapest 1949. Cf. also the full commentary in *Constantine Porphyrogenitus: De Administrando Imperio*, II, *Commentary*, London, 1962, ed. by R. J. H. Jenkins. Individual sections are by F. Dvornik, R. J. H. Jenkins, B. Lewis, G. Moravcsik, D. Obolensky and S. Runciman.

aulae byzantinae) is a real mine of information on historical and archaeological subjects.[1] These works contain material from different periods, and are also of value for the preceding periods. The *Cletorologion* of Philotheus, which describes the Byzantine machinery of government about the year 900, is included in the *De cerimoniis*.[2] The various ranks of Byzantine officials are given in the *Tacticon* of the time of Michael III and Theodora (845–56) edited by Uspenskij[3] and in that compiled between 921 and 943 edited by Beneševič[4] The *Tactica* of Leo VI, concerned with the art of war, are derived from the so-called *Strategicon* of Maurice and embody material from later legislation, as well as the military experience gained during the first period of Leo VI's government.[5] The so-called *Sylloge Tacticorum* is a similar work which probably dates from the middle of the tenth century.[6] The *Book of the Eparch*, a collection of government regulations for the control of trade and industry, gives considerable

[1] New ed. of Book I, c. 1–83, with French trans. and detailed commentary by A. Vogt, *Constantin VII Porphyrogénète. Le Livre des Cérémonies*, Paris 1935, 1939–40. Textual emendations to the edition of J. J. Reiske in CB, and more especially to A. Vogt, are given by Ph. Kukules, Διορθωτικὰ καὶ ἑρμηνευτικὰ εἰς τὴν Ἐκθεσιν τῆς βασιλείας τάξεως Κωνσταντίνου τοῦ Πορφυρογεννήτου καὶ τὸ Κλητορολόγιον τοῦ Φιλοθέου, EEBS 19 (1949), 75 ff. Until recently the text of the *De cerimoniis* was only known from the Leipzig manuscript (Lipsiensis bibl. urb. Rep. I 17). C. Mango and I. Ševčenko, 'A New Manuscript of the *De cerimoniis*', DOP 14 (1960), 247 ff., report the surprising news that the Cod. Chalcensis S. Trinitatis (125) 133 contains considerable portions of the work with some very important variants from the Leipzig MS.

[2] ed. with excellent commentary by Bury, *Admin. System*. In the inscription the *Cleterologion* is dated September 899. The view of P. Maas, BZ 34 (1934), 257 ff., that it contains interpolations dating from about 910 has proved incorrect; cf. Grumel, 'Chronologie', 13 ff. and 19 ff. See also R. Guilland, 'Études sur l'histoire administrative de Byzance: Observations sur le Clètorologe de Philothée', REB 20 (1962), 156 ff.

[3] F. Uspenskij, 'Vizant. tabel o rangach' (The Byzantine list of ranks), *Izv. Russk. Archeol. Inst. v K/le* 3 (1898), 98 ff. On the date of its origin cf. my paper, 'Taktikon Uspenskog i Taktikon Beneševiča', *Zbornik radova Viz. Inst.* 2 (1953), 39 ff., where I define more precisely the chronology suggested by Bury, *Admin. System* 12 ff., and oppose that of Kyriakides, Buз. Μελέται, 235 ff., who considers that the work must be dated to the period 809–28.

[4] Beneševič, 'Ranglisten', 97 ff. The lists of ranks in Philotheus and in the *Tacticon Uspenskij* are reprinted here so that the lists of the ninth and tenth centuries in this edition can be easily studied and compared. On the chronology cf. my paper cited in the preceding note. At the XIIth International Byzantine Congress at Ochrida, N. Oikonomides described a *tacticon* from the seventies of the tenth century, discovered in a MS. in the Escurial, which may be a rich source of information on the history of Byzantine administration. See *Actes du XII Congrès int. d'Études Byz.*, II, Belgrade 1964, 177 ff.

[5] New ed. (containing Const. I to Const. XIV. §§ 1–38) by R. Vári, *Leonis imp. Tactica*, 2 vols., Budapest 1917 and 1922. J. Kulakovskij, VV 5 (1898), 398 ff., and M. Mitard, BZ 12 (1903), 585 ff., had already made it clear that this work belonged to the period of Leo VI, and not Leo III as older scholars used to think.

[6] ed. A. Dain, *Sylloge Tacticorum quae olim 'inedita Leonis Tactica' dicebatur*, Paris 1938. The view of R. Vári, BZ 27 (1927), 241 ff., that this work is not by Leo VI but dates from his reign and came from the co-Emperor Alexander has rightly been disproved by Dain.

information about the economic life, and particularly the guilds, of Constantinople under the Macedonians.[1] It is very probable that the main body of the collection dates from the time of Leo VI, though there were doubtless later additions made up to the time of Nicephorus II Phocas, or even John I Tzimisces.[2] An anonymous treatise on the imposition of taxes greatly adds to our knowledge of the system of taxation and agrarian conditions in the Byzantine Empire in the tenth century.[3] Like the *Farmer's Law*, this most important treatise had in mind village settlements inhabited by free peasants. Finally, attention should also be paid to the *Geoponica*, a handbook of Byzantian rural economy compiled under Constantine VII.[4] Relevant legal sources for this section are the codifications of the two first Macedonian Emperors—the *Procheiron* and the *Epanagoge* of Basil I

---

[1] ed. by J. Nicole, Λέοντος τοῦ Σοφοῦ τὸ Ἐπαρχικὸν βιβλίον, Geneva 1893 (from a Geneva MS.); reprinted by Zepos, *Jus* II, 371-92; French trans. with commentary by Nicole, *Le Livre du Préfet ou l'édit de l'empereur Léon la Sage sur les corporations de Constantinople*, Geneva 1894; English trans. by E. H. Freshfield, *Roman Law in the Later Roman Empire*, Cambridge 1938. Russian translation with a detailed commentary by M. J. Sjuzjumov, *Kniga Eparcha* (The Book of the Eparch), Sverdlovsk 1949, and new edition with Russian translation, introduction and commentary, Moscow 1962. Following Papadopulos-Kerameus, Ἱεροσαλυμιτικὴ βιβλιοθήκη IV (1899), 37 f., it was generally thought that a Constantinople MS. contained the *Book of the Eparch* of Leo VI, but this has proved an error; cf. the communication of D. Ginis, Τὸ ἐπαρχικὸν βιβλίον καὶ οἱ νόμοι Ἰουλιανοῦ τοῦ Ἀσκαλωνίτου, EEBS 13 (1937), 183 ff.

[2] Cf. the regulations in which the *tetarteron* is mentioned, which caused Stöckle, *Zünfte*, to place the redaction of the *Book of the Eparch* in the time of Nicephorus II Phocas; cf. also Kubitschek, *Num. Zeitschr.* 44 (1911), 185 ff. Christophilopulos, Ἐπαρχικὸν βιβλίον 22, dismisses these passages too lightly. Mickwitz, *Zünfte* 205 and BNJ 12 (1936), 368 ff., rightly considers they were supplementary rulings. R. S. Lopez, 'La crise du besant au Xᵉ siècle et la date du Livre du Préfet', *Mélanges Grégoire* II (1950), 403 ff., considers there were even additions from the time of John I Tzimisces, since as well as references to the νόμισμα τεταρτηρόν, whose introduction Scylitzes attributes to Nicephorus Phocas, the δύο τετάρτων νόμισμα is found, a type of coin belonging to John Tzimisces' period. Cf. below, p. 293, note 1, for further bibliography on the question of the *tetarteron*.

[3] First ed. by W. Ashburner, JHS 35 (1915), 76 ff.; a later and revised ed. by Dölger, in *Finanzverwaltung*, with detailed study; German trans. and study in Ostrogorsky, 'Steuergemeinde'. Dölger, *Finanzverwaltung* 8, places the treatise in the period between 913 and 1139. As against this I attempt to show, op. cit. 3 ff., and *Recueil Kondakov* (1926), 109 ff., that it probably appeared under Constantine VII, and in any case before 1002; this view is shared by most scholars. Cf. for example Stein, 'Vom Altertum', 158 ff.; Andreades, BZ 28 (1928), 292 ff.; Constantinescu, 'La communauté de village byzantin et ses rapports avec le petit Traité fiscal byzantin', *Bulletin de la Section hist. de l'Acad. Roumaine* 13 (1927), 160 ff., and *Deutsche Literaturzeitung* 1928, col. 1619 ff.; Lemerle, 'Histoire Agraire', 257 ff.; Každan, *Derevnja i gorod*, 85.

[4] ed. H. Beckh, Leipzig (Teubner), 1895. Russian translation with commentary by E. E. Lipšic, *Geoponiki, viz jantijskaja sel'skochozajstvennaja enciklopedija X veka* (Geoponica, a Byzantine agricultural encyclopaedia of the tenth century), Moscow-Leningrad 1960; she shows that although this writing is for the most part a compilation of material from older sources, it nevertheless is of greater importance for the tenth century than has usually been supposed.

and the *Basilica* and the novels of Leo VI—as well as the novels protecting the small-holders which reveal the main internal problem of Byzantium in the tenth century.[1]

1. THE DAWN OF THE NEW AGE

General bibliography: Bury, *Eastern Rom. Empire*; Grégoire, 'Inscriptions'; 'Michel III'; 'Neuvième Siècle'; 'L'épopée byzantine'; 'The Amorians and Macedonians 842-1025', CMH IV, Pt. I (2nd ed., 1966); Uspenskij, *Očerki*; Fuchs, *Höhere Schulen*; Dvornik, *Légendes*; *Les Slaves*; A. Vasiliev, *The Russian Attack on Constantinople*, Cambridge, Mass. 1946; Dvornik, *Photian Schism*; 'Constantinople and Rome', CMH IV, Part I (2nd ed., 1966); Vasiliev, *Byzance et les Arabes* I; M. Canard, 'Byzantium and the Muslim world to the eleventh century', CMH IV, Pt. I (2nd ed., 1966).

The iconoclast crisis was a period as decisive for the spiritual development of the Byzantine Empire as the struggle against the Persian and Arab invasions had been for its political existence. The military invasion from the East was followed up by a spiritual onslaught, which rolled over the Empire in the form of the iconoclast controversy. Its defeat was as significant for the cultural life of the Byzantine Empire as military success had been for its political growth. The downfall of the campaign against icons signified the victory of the Greek religious and cultural outlook over the Asian characteristics embodied in iconoclasm. Henceforth Byzantium, as a Graeco-Christian Empire, also occupied a unique cultural position, set midway between the East and the West.

A new era was opening for Byzantium, an age of a great cultural resurgence, which was soon to be followed by a marked political advance. Its initiation took place not under the Macedonian dynasty but during the time of the last of the Amorians, the much-harassed Michael III, and Bardas, Photius and Constantine are the three great figures who proclaim the advent of this new epoch.

[1] Reprinted by Zepos, *Jus* I, 198 ff., from Zachariä von Lingenthal, *Jus graeco-romanum* III: the *Procheiron* = Zepos, II, 114-228; the *Epanagoge*, ibid. II, 236-368; the Novels of Leo VI, ibid I, 54-191; the *Basilica*, ed. G. E. and C.G.E. Heimbach, *Basilicorum libri LX*, Leipzig 1833-70, and Ferrini e Mercati, *Editionis Basilicorum Heimbachianae supplementum alterum*, Leipzig 1897. New ed. of the novels with French trans. by P. Noaille and A. Dain, *Les Novelles de Léon VI le Sage*, Paris 1944; French trans. also by H. Monnier, *Les Novelles de Léon le Sage*, Bordeaux 1923, and A. Spulber, *Les Novelles de Léon le Sage*, Cernautsi 1934. A new edition of the *Basilica* and the *scholia* is being prepared by H. J. Scheltema and others, of which Books I-XXXIV and the *Scholia* on Books I-XIII, 1 have so far appeared.

The period of the iconoclast crisis brought with it a perceptible narrowing of the political field of vision, characterized by a marked recession of the concept of a universal Empire and a collapse of the powerful position Byzantium had held in the West. The ecclesiastical policy of the iconoclast Emperors, together with their lack of interest in the western portion of the Empire, had accelerated the separation of Byzantium from the West and had thus set in motion the train of events which led from the foundation of the Papal State to the imperial coronation of Charlemagne. But if the universalism of the Byzantine state had suffered shipwreck, the universalism of the Roman Church was also being undermined in the East, and it was Leo III who had already taken the first step by placing the major part of the Balkan peninsula and southern Italy under the jurisdiction of the Patriarch of Constantinople. But it was only after the over-throw of iconoclasm that the Patriarchate of Constantinople was in a position to enter the lists as a rival to the Papacy on an equal footing and engage in a contest with Rome. Just as the Western Empire had risen at the expense of the universalism of the Byzantine State, so did the Patriarchate of Constantinople now gain the ascendancy at the expense of the universalism of the Roman Church. This entire process thus had two stages: the first, during which Byzantium lagged behind, belongs to the period of the crisis; the second, which restored an equilibrium favourable to Byzantium but on a new foundation, began with the opening of the new era and was ushered in by the great Photian conflict.

But much more important still is the fact that within the eastern orbit, to which the course of history had reduced the direct sphere of influence exerted by Byzantium, both Church and State found new and weighty tasks awaiting them. The work of converting to Christianity the southern and eastern Slavs opened up a new world for Byzantium, whose outlook was now unexpectedly enlarged. From the time of Photius, Constantine and Methodius the Byzantine world became as vast as it had once, during the period of the icono-clast crisis, been narrow.

Political and military expansion followed on the heels of cultural development. The Empire, which by the end of the iconoclast period had been forced into a precarious defensive position against both the Caliphate and the Bulgars, now advanced its frontiers well forward in the East, though only after bitter and protracted fighting, and once more subordinated to itself the whole Balkan peninsula.

The powerful position of Byzantium in the Mediterranean, which had been lost during the period of crisis, was also regained.

The final restoration of the icons after the death of Theophilus was achieved, as had been the earlier temporary restoration at the end of the eighth century, under the leadership of a woman. For at the time of Theophilus' death, his son and heir Michael III (842–67) was in his third year,[1] and his mother Theodora acted as regent. It appears that officially his eldest surviving sister, Thecla, was also entitled to share in the regency, since she was portrayed on the coins together with Michael and Theodora and was named with them in government pronouncements; but she seems to have completely withheld herself from affairs of state.[2] The most important members of the council formed to assist Theodora which, with the co-operation of the new Patriarch, carried out the restoration of veneration of the icons, were her brothers Bardas and Petronas, the *magister* Sergius Nicetiates, who seems to have been her uncle, and, above all, her favourite, the Logothete of the Drome, Theoctistus.[3] It is significant that the new rulers, despite their largely eastern origin— Theodora's family came from Paphlagonia and was of Armenian descent—saw the restoration of the cult of the icons as their first and most pressing task. Once the deposition of John Grammaticus had been achieved and Methodius installed as Patriarch, a synod proclaimed the solemn rehabilitation of the veneration of icons (March 843).[4]

In remembrance of this action, the Greek Orthodox Church celebrates every year on the first Sunday in Lent the 'Festival of Ortho-

[1] According to *Theophanes Cont.* 148, 8. E. Stein, *Annuaire de l'Inst. de phil. et d'Hist. Orientales* 2 (1934), 899 ff., n. 2, puts the birth of Michael III at about 836, but cf. the critical comments of A. P. Každan 'Iz istorii vizantijskoj chronografii', VV 21 (1962) 96 f., who refers to a marginal note on Genesius which agrees in substance with the date given by the *Theoph. Cont.* In addition to Michael, Theophilus and Theodora had a son Constantine, who died as a child apparently soon after 830 (cf. Ostrogorsky and Stein, B 7 (1932), 226 ff.), and five daughters—Mary, Thecla, Anna, Anastasia and Pulcheria (cf. Bury, *Eastern Rom. Empire*, 465 ff.). Because of the length of time without a male heir, the daughters of Theophilus enjoyed a position not usually accorded to princesses. A coin shows the portraits of Thecla, Anna and Anastasia, as well as Theophilus and Theodora (Woth, *Byz. Coins* II, 418).
[2] Cf. the coins in Woth, *Byz. Coins* II, 431, and the *Acta* of the forty-two martyrs of Amorium, ed. Vasiljevskij-Nitikin, p. 52, βασιλεύοντος τῆς Ῥωμαίων ἀρχῆς Μιχαὴλ καὶ Θεοδώρας καὶ Θέκλης. Cf. Vasiliev, *Byzance et les Arabes* I, 191.
[3] On the composition of the council cf. Vasiliev, *Byzance et les Arabes* I, 191 f., note 2; instead of Sergius Nicetiates some sources cite Manuel who had died by 838, cf. Grégoire, 'Neuvième siècle', 515 ff., and F. Dvornik, 'The Patriarch Photius and Iconoclasm', *Dumbarton Oaks Papers* 7 (1953), 69 ff.
[4] On the chronology see Grumel, *Reg.* 416, 425.

doxy', which commemorates the victory over iconoclasm and over the older heresies. In fact, the suppression of iconoclasm brought to a close the period of the great doctrinal conflicts within Byzantium. But the defeat of iconoclasm was also of importance for the relationship of Church and State, since it meant the frustration of an attempt to bring about a total subordination of the Church to the power of the State. However, neither then, nor at any later time, did the Church attain the freedom which the zealots, with Theodore the Studite at their head, had claimed for it. A close co-operation of Church and State remained a characteristic feature of the Byzantine policy, and this co-operation normally took the form of a closely protective tutelage of the Church by the power of the State.

The entire direction of policy soon fell within the grasp of the Logothete Theoctistus, who had ousted Bardas, his chief rival, and had become the sole adviser of the Empress. Highly cultured himself, Theoctistus furthered the cause of education within Byzantium and helped to prepare for the nascent cultural revival. His skilful financial policy secured abundant gold reserves for the state. In contrast to what had happened in the time of Irene, the reversal of ecclesiastical policy was carried through without friction, since the iconoclast movement had collapsed and there was no longer any strong party of opposition.[1] Nevertheless, Theodora and Theoctistus, with the support of the Patriarch Methodius, were circumspect in their liquidation of the régime which had so recently been in the ascendant, and showed considerable moderation towards the former adherents of iconoclasm.[2] This policy, however, found little favour with the zealot party, and the Orthodox Byzantine Church, which had been temporarily united by the struggle against iconoclasm, once again found itself rent by the old schism. The Studite monks fought the Patriarch Methodius with all the fervour they had once shown against the Patriarchs Tarasius and Nicephorus. The quarrel waxed intense and led to the excommunication of the Studites. But on 14 June 847 Methodius died. The next Patriarch was Ignatius,

---

[1] One does indeed still find traces of the iconoclast teaching long after 843. Cf. F. Dvornik, 'The Patriarch Photius and Iconoclasm', *Dumbarton Oaks Papers* 7 (1953), 69 ff., though he tends to over-emphasize the significance of this when he speaks of iconoclasm as a danger in the time of Photius. Cf. also Dvornik's earlier discussion in B 10 (1935), 5 ff. On the problem of the persistence of iconoclast teaching cf. the interesting paper by J. Gouillard, 'Deux figures mal connues du second Iconoclasme', B 31 (1961), 371 ff., esp. 387 ff.

[2] Cf. Dvornik, *Légendes*, 39 ff.

a son of the former Emperor Michael Rangabe, who had been castrated after the deposition of his father and had taken the monastic
habit. His elevation meant a concession to the Studites, for, although
Ignatius had taken no part in the opposition directed against the
leaders of the Church, as a strict monk he stood close to the ideals
of the zealot persuasion. However, as the adversary of Photius,
Ignatius, who should have been the means of reconciling the
conflicting parties, himself became immersed in an even more
furious conflict.

Once the icons had been restored, there was an immediate resumption of the war with the Arabs. The logothete Theoctistus led a
powerful naval force against Crete and Byzantine rule was once
again restored there, though only for a very short time (843/44).[1]
This temporary success was even less effective, in that the Byzantines
sustained a severe defeat as early as 844 on land, on the Mauropo-
tamus, which enters the Bosphorus.[2] It was the victorious campaigns of Caliph Mutasim (cf. above, p. 208) which had made it
possible for the Arabs to venture so far inside Byzantine territory.
But internal dissensions forced his successor to make peace with
Byzantium, and an exchange of prisoners took place (845–6) at the
river Lamus, on the frontier between Arab and Byzantine territory.
The strength of the Caliphate was being paralysed by the intrusion
of a Turkish element and by the operation of centrifugal feudal
tendencies, which led to the formation of a number of separate
kingdoms. But there was still in store for Byzantium a bitter struggle
with the Paulician sect. This sect, which had been supported by the
iconoclast Emperors of the eighth century and which had also found
favour with Nicephorus I, had become so widespread in the eastern
part of Asia Minor that action had to be taken against them, not
only by the orthodox Michael Rangabe, but even by his iconoclast
successors.[3] It appears that as a result of these persecutions a large
number of them had already migrated into the territory of the emir
of Melitene and were fighting in the ranks of the Arabs against
Byzantium. The renewed persecution under Theodora was particularly savage and cost thousands of Paulicians their lives. It was

---

[1] See I. B. Papadopulos, Ἡ Κρήτη ὑπὸ τοὺς Σαρακηνούς, Athens, 1948, 71 f. H.
Glykatzi-Ahrweiler, 'L'administration militaire de la Crète byzantine', B 31 (1961), 220 f.
[2] For the identification of the district cf. Vasiliev, *Byzance et les Arabes* I, 196 f., note 2.
[3] Vasiliev, *Byzance et les Arabes* I, 227 ff. Cf. also E. Lipšic, 'Pavlikianskoe diviženie v
Vizantii v VIII i pervoj polovine IX vv.' (The Paulician movement in Byzantium in the
eighth and first half of the ninth centuries), VV 5 (1952), 49 ff., 235 ff. and *Očerki*, 132 ff.

accompanied by the mass resettlement of Paulicians in Thrace. In addition, Theodore's government was forced to undertake a new campaign against the refractory Slav tribes in southern Greece. It was only with the assistance of the military forces of the themes of Thrace and Macedonia and 'the other western themes' that the *strategus* of the Peloponnese, Theoctistus Byrennius, succeeded after a long struggle in compelling the Slav tribes in the Peloponnese to recognize Byzantine supremacy and in forcing them to pay tribute.[1]

Byzantine generalship in the wars against the Arabs was remarkable for a new and growing spirit of daring and enterprise. In 853 a large Byzantine fleet suddenly made its appearance off the coast of Egypt, which was then, as formerly, providing support for the rulers of Crete. Damietta, a stronghold situated close to the mouth of the Nile, was sacked and burnt to the ground.[2] This was the first time, since the beginning of the Arab invasions, that the Byzantines had dared to venture so far into hostile waters. However, the immediate result of this impressive demonstration was that the Egyptian Arabs energetically began to build up their fleet and thus to construct the foundations of the maritime power which was to reach such formidable proportions in the tenth century under the Fatimid Caliphate.

But the period of really intense political and cultural activity in the Byzantine Empire only began after the *coup d'état* of 856, by which the exercise of the prerogatives of government was transferred to the young Emperor Michael III in person and the direction of affairs to Bardas, his uncle. Both victims of the régime established by Theodora and Theoctistus, Bardas and Michael were natural allies. For if Bardas felt aggrieved at his supersession by the now all-powerful Theoctistus, the young Emperor, now growing to manhood, felt himself equally injured by his mother's tutelage, since she not only debarred him from the government but also interfered in his private life, parting him from his mistress, Eudocia Ingerina, and compelling him to marry Eudocia Decapolita (855). Unknown to the Empress, Bardas returned to court, acting in secret agreement with the young Emperor. The conspirators surprised Theoctistus in the imperial palace and in the presence of Michael III murdered

---

[1] *De adm. imp.* 50, 9-25, ed. Moravcsik-Jenkins. Nevertheless, the Melingi and Jezerites rose again against Byzantine rule in the time of Romanus I Lecapenus, which led to a renewed outbreak of war (ibid. 50, 25-70). Cf. *Viz. izvori* II, 69 ff.

[2] Grégoire, 'Neuvième siècle', 515 ff. Cf. G. Levi della Vida, 'A Papyrus reference to the Damietta Raid of 853 A.D.', B 17 (1944-5), 212 ff.

him. Michael was then proclaimed by the senate as independent ruler.[1] Theodora was forced to surrender control of the government, while her daughters were shut up in a nunnery; two years later, after an abortive attack on her brother Bardas, she shared the same fate.

Today our picture of Michael III is very different from that portrayed in older historical works where, following the biased historiography of the Macedonian period, he is depicted as a mere drunken sot.[2] It is certainly true that his life was not exactly a model of exemplary conduct, but he was not ungifted, nor indeed lacking in courage. It would, however, be wrong to go from one extreme to the other and to regard him as one of the great rulers. He did, indeed, sincerely devote himself to the defence of the Empire and repeatedly led his army into the field in person. But most Byzantine rulers did as much. He lacked a strong and well-defined will of his own. In large matters as in small, in well and evil doing, he allowed himself to be led by others, constantly adapting himself to the changeable influences and insinuations current at court, and was capricious and fickle to the point of complete unreliability. He can himself claim no credit for initiating the great deeds in which his reign was so unusually prolific. He was not great, but there was greatness in his time, the time of Bardas and Photius.

Bardas was now the real ruler of the Byzantine state, as Theoctistus had been under Theodora. Formal recognition of his outstanding position was expressed by the conferment on him of the highest honours and by his final designation as Caesar. In energy and political sagacity he surpassed his predecessors and former rivals. The signs of the nascent great political advance of the Byzantine Empire are clearly visible during this period. The high-flying cultural aspirations which had already made an appearance during the regency now reached their fulfilment, and the irradiating power and activity of Byzantine culture was revealed in all its greatness.

[1] Pseudo-Symeon Magister 658, καὶ ὑπὸ τῆς συγκλήτου πάσης ἀναγορεύεται καὶ αὐτοκράτορεῖ. Cf. Sym. Log., Georg. Mon. cont. 823.

[2] The rehabilitation of Michael III is due above all to H. Grégoire (cf. 'Inscriptions', 437 ff.; 'Michel III', 327 ff.; 'Neuvième siècle', 515 ff.; 'L'épopée byzantine', 29 ff.). His brilliant work on the subject has rightly received approbation; I indicate below where he seems to me to press his point too far. Cf. the fine paper by R. J. H. Jenkins, 'Constantine VII's portrait of Michael III', *Bull. de l'Acad. de Belgique* 34 (1948), 71 ff., and A. Vasiliev, 'The Emperor Michael III in Apocryphal Literature', *Byzantina-Metabyzantina* 1 (1946), 237 ff.; F. Dvornik, B 10 (1935), 5 ff.; R. J. H. Jenkins-C. Mango, 'The Date and Significance of the Xth Homily of Photius', DOP 9–10 (1956), 128 ff.; C. Mango, *The Homilies of Photius Patriarch of Constantinople*, Cambridge, Mass. 1958, 181 ff.

The university at the Magnaura palace, organized by Caesar Bardas, became an important centre of Byzantine learning and education, and in it were cultivated all branches of secular learning known to the period.[1] Bardas, enlightened statesman that he was, summoned to it the strongest possible contingent of scholars and set at their head Leo the Mathematician, a scholar of encyclopaedic attainments, although he was a nephew of the iconoclast John Grammaticus and had during the time of Theophilus shown himself to be of the same persuasion.[2] Photius, at once the greatest teacher and the greatest student of his century, also worked in the university.

The change in the government of the state brought in its train a change in the government of the Church. There was no possibility of harmonious co-operation between the new regent and Ignatius, who was so closely connected with the former régime and with the zealot party. Ignatius was compelled to resign, and on 25 December 858 the scholar Photius succeeded to the patriarchal throne. For the Church this marked the opening of a time of upheaval, probably the most disturbed period which the Byzantine Church had known. Photius was the most distinguished thinker, the most outstanding politician and the most skilful diplomat ever to hold office as Patriarch of Constantinople. In ecclesiastical policy he followed the same direction as Tarasius, Nicephorus and Methodius. Like them, he was on that account opposed by the zealots, who, with the Studite abbot Nicholas at their head, objected to his uncanonical appointment and remained faithful to Ignatius. Two parties arose, of which

[1] In spite of various noteworthy attempts the history of higher education in Byzantium has not yet been sufficiently elucidated. Fuchs, *Höhere Schulen*, points to a constantly fluctuating development: Theodosius II's university vanished under Phocas and a new foundation was made under Heraclius; under Leo III this was closed (not burnt, as later sources wrongly affirm) and higher education came to a standstill until the mid-ninth century. On the other hand, Bréhier maintains that there was no break in the life of the university from Constantine the Great to the fifteenth century, and that there was always a theological school attached to the Church of St. Sophia, as the state university was exclusively concerned with secular learning and the provision of suitably educated civil servants. Cf. L. Bréhier, 'Notes sur l'histoire de l'enseignement supérieur à Constantinople', B 3 (1926), 73 ff., 4 (1927-8), 13 ff.; idem, 'L'enseignement classique et l'enseignement religieux à Byzance', *Revue d'histoire et de philosophie religieuse* 21 (1941), 34 ff.; idem, *Civilisation* 456 ff. Bréhier's view tends to oversimplify, but in spite of various gaps in the evidence it seems nearer the truth. Cf. H. Grégoire, B 4 (1927-8), 771 ff.; F. Dvornik, 'Photius et la réorganisation de l'Académie patriarcale', *Mélanges Peeters* II (1950), 108 ff.; G. Buckler, 'Byzantine Education', in Baynes-Moss, *Byzantium* 216 ff. For the history of Byzantine education, see also R. Browning, 'The Patriarchal School at Constantinople in the Twelfth Century', B 32 (1962) 167 ff.; he gives valuable material concerning the Patriarchal School in the twelfth century, its teachers and their writings, largely drawn from unpublished manuscripts.

[2] Cf. E. E. Lipšic, 'Vizantijskij učenyj Lev Matematik' (The Byzantine scholar Leo the Mathematician), VV 27 (1949), 106 ff. Cf. also the observations of C. Mango, 'The Legend of Leo The Wise', ZRVI 6 (1960), 91 ff.

one favoured Photius, while the other remained true to the dis-possessed Ignatius.

But much more important than this internal conflict was the struggle with Rome which the new Patriarch had to face. Following the events of the iconoclast epoch, and even more directly as a consequence of the establishment of the Western Empire, the relationship between the two focal points of the Church had entered on a new phase. The zealots, blind as they were to the signs of the times, continued to appeal to Rome on every occasion, their narrow dogmatism alone remaining proof against the realities of the new situation. The facts were clear not only to the Emperor Nicephorus, who had forbidden his Patriarch to send the customary *synodica* to the Pope (cf. above, p. 198), but also to the pious Empress Theodora, and the Patriarch Methodius who could hardly be described as an enemy of Rome (cf. above, p. 204). Theodora and Methodius did not consider it necessary to apply for Rome's consent to the restora-tion of the cult of the icons, as Irene had done before summoning her Council. Historical necessity demanded that Byzantium should deprive Rome of her ecclesiastical universalism, just as the West had destroyed the universalism of the Byzantine state. The decisive step in this process was taken by Photius.

Immersed as he was in the controversy with the Ignatian faction, Photius, to begin with at least, neither desired nor expected the con-flict with Rome. He despatched his *synodica* to Rome in the hope that Papal recognition would provide him with a weapon against his Byzantine opponents. But it was only a few months before his own elevation to the patriarchal throne that the chair of St. Peter had received Nicholas I, a politician of much audacity and energy, whose life's ambition was to establish Roman universalism on a firm founda-tion.[1] Nicholas intruded himself into the quarrel within the Byzan-tine Church, setting himself up as the final judge, and decided in favour of Ignatius, withholding recognition from Photius by reason of the uncanonical manner of his appointment. Photius' appoint-ment was in fact uncanonical, but it in no way differed from that of Tarasius, who had received from Rome recognition and support, and who had also been translated straight from the ranks of the laity to the patriarchal throne, after his predecessor's resignation had been extracted from him by force. But Nicholas I was intent on

[1] J. Haller, *Das Papsttum* II, 1 (1939), 65 ff., attempts to limit the part played by Nicholas I's personality.

establishing the principle that as head of Christendom he was entitled to the last word in disputes over ecclesiastical matters as much in the East as in the West. Therefore, he did not waver from this purpose even when his legates in Constantinople capitulated in the face of Photius' superior diplomatic cunning and acquiesced in the decision of a Council which confirmed the election of Photius and the deposition of Ignatius (861). Disavowing his representatives, Nicholas caused a synod held in the Lateran to pronounce a contrary judgment and declare Photius deposed (863).

But the Pope had underestimated the strength of his opponent. Photius took up the challenge. If Rome had set itself the task of validating its claims to universal dominion, it was equally the task of the Patriarchate of Constantinople to assert its independence. The ideal of fivefold leadership of the Church which had been the dream of Theodore the Studite[1] was long a thing of the past. Gone was the time when orthodox Byzantium, languishing under the despotism of heretical emperors, awaited salvation from Rome; the other three heads of the Church, the leaders of the oriental Patriarchates, were condemned to impotence under the foreign yoke of the Arabs. The Byzantine Church had only one leader, the Patriarch of Constantinople. The Patriarchate of Constantinople had established its power and prestige in the course of centuries of development. It had emerged victorious from the internal struggle against heresy; it now enjoyed the support of an orthodox and strong temporal power fully conscious of its aims, and its sway extended over the entire territory of the Byzantine Empire and was soon to reach out far beyond it. The Byzantine Church, like the Empire, was about to experience its best period: a period which would witness a powerful extension of its sphere of influence into the Slav world. The greatness of Photius lies in his appreciation, clearer than that of anyone else at the time, of the near approach of this era of new tasks and possibilities, for which he, more than anybody, helped to prepare the way.

Michael III, ably supported by his generals, pursued the war with the Arabs with great energy. Nevertheless, the Byzantines lost one position after another in Sicily and despite all their exertions could prevent neither the conquest of the island nor the advance of the Arabs into southern Italy, so that at the end of the reign of Michael III Syracuse and Taormina were the only important Sicilian cities

---

[1] Theod. Stud., *Ep.* II, 129; Migne, PG 99, 1416 ff.

still within the Empire. In Asia Minor, however, Byzantium went over to the attack. As early as 856, Petronas, brother of Bardas Caesar, who was *strategus* of the Thracesion theme, launched a campaign in the neighbourhood of Samosata and thrust forward as far as Amida. Thence he drove against Tephrice, and returned home with many prisoners.[1] A campaign which took place three years later, also in the Samosata district, under the leadership of Bardas and the young Emperor himself, seems also to have been fruitful.[2] About the same time, the Byzantine fleet appeared once more off Damietta. Particular attention was devoted to the building of fortifications in Asia Minor: the Emperor caused Ancyra, which had been destroyed under Mutasim, to be rebuilt and Nicaea to be refortified.[3] These recent successes and bold advances on sea and land certainly raised the battle spirit of the Byzantines, but brought little concrete advantage to the Empire, especially as there was no lack of Arab counter-attacks, and the war was frequently interrupted by temporary peace treaties accompanied by the usual exchange of prisoners. But in 863, in warding off an attack by Omar, the emir of Melitene, the Byzantines achieved a great and decisive victory. Omar had crossed the Armeniakon theme and occupied the important port of Amisus on the coast of the Black Sea. On the frontier between the themes of Armeniakon and Paphlagonia, however, he was met by the able general Petronas with a large army. Here, on 3 September, a fierce battle developed, in which the Arab army was annihilated and in which Omar himself perished.[4] This great victory was a turning point in this struggle between Byzantine and the Arabs. From the time of the first inroads made by the Arabs up to the victory of Leo III at Constantinople, Byzantium had had to struggle for mere survival; then for more than a century it had been occupied with an arduous defensive war; but now, after the victory of 863, the tide turned and there began the era of Byzantine attack in Asia, an offensive which opened slowly but which for the second half of the tenth century moved forwards with ever increasing celerity.

It would be impossible to overestimate the important contribution made by the establishment of this powerful position in the East

---

[1] Tabari III, 1434 (= Vasiliev, *Byzance et les Arabes* I, App. 318 f.). Cf. Grégoire, 'L'épopée byzantine', 36 f.

[2] Tabari III, 1447 (= Vasiliev I, App. 319). Cf. Grégoire, 'Inscriptions' 437 ff. and 'L'épopée byzantine' 37 f.

[3] Grégoire, 'Inscriptions' 441 ff. and 'Michel III' 327 ff.

[4] For details and closer identification of the battlefield cf. Vasiliev, *Byzance et les Arabes* I, 251 ff.; Grégoire, 'Michel III' 331 ff. and 'Neuvième siècle' 534 ff.; Bury, JHS 29 (1909), 124 ff.

towards the discharge of the serious tasks awaiting the Empire in the Slav world. These tasks crowded in on the Empire from several directions, from Russia, Moravia and the lands of the southern Slavs. The Russians first appeared before Constantinople as early as 860.[1] They made a landing, surrounded the city and laid waste the whole neighbourhood. The Emperor, who had just set out against the Arabs, turned back with the utmost despatch and forced his way into the beleaguered city to undertake the task of defence and, with the help of the Patriarch, to bring encouragement to the trembling population. The memory of this powerful onslaught impressed itself deeply on the Byzantines, who ascribed their salvation to nothing less than the intervention of the Virgin.[2] From this time dates the beginning of relations between Byzantium and the Russian kingdom, which had only just come into being, and of the missionary work among this people, hitherto almost completely unknown to the Byzantines, which was to have such important consequences in the future. The great Patriarch had realized that to convert the young nation to Christianity and to bring it within the Byzantine sphere of influence was the most effective method of averting the danger threatening the Empire from this direction. A few years later, with justifiable pride, he was able to point to the first results of his missionary undertaking.[3]

[1] The chronology is established by the *Anecdota Bruxellensia* I, *Chroniques byzantines du Manuscrit 11376*, ed. F. Cumont (1894), 33. Cf. C. de Boor, 'Der Angriff der Rhos auf Byzanz', BZ 4 (1895), 445 ff. The correct year had been determined from Venetian sources by Fr. Kruse, *Chronicon Nortmannorum* (1851), 261 f. A vivid account of the impression made by the Russian attack is found in Photius' two homilies, Müller, FHG V, 162 ff. C. Mango, *The Homilies of Photius Patr. of Constantinople* (1958), 74 ff. gives an English translation with a good commentary. The other Greek sources are well correlated by G. Laehr, *Die Anfänge des russischen Reiches* (1930), 91 ff. Cf. also Vasiliev, *Byzance et les Arabes* I, 241 ff. All the sources and relevant literature are now to be found in the detailed study by A. Vasiliev, *The Russian Attack on Constantinople*, Cambridge, Mass. 1946.

[2] According to the legendary and embroidered account of Symeon Logothetes (and the Old Russian chronicle which follows Sym. Log., George. Mon. cont. here) the Russian ships were destroyed by a storm and only a few escaped total wreckage. But Photius and Theophanes cont. know nothing about any destruction of the Russian fleet and, according to J. Diacon., MGH SS VII, 18, the Russians returned home 'cum triumpho'.

[3] *Photii Epistolae*, Migne, PG 102, 736 f. It is a much discussed question as to whether the Russians who attacked Constantinople in 860 came from Kiev or from the Tmutorakan district; cf. full bibliography in the detailed and exhaustive survey by V. Mošin, 'Varjagorusskij vopros' (The Varango-Russian question), *Slavia* 10 (1931), 109–36, 343–79, 501–37, and 'Načalo Rusi, Normany v vostočnoj Evrope' (The origins of Russia: the Normans in eastern Europe), BS 3 (1931), 38–58, 285–307. A. Vasiliev, *The Russian Attack on Constantinople* 169 ff., has now decided in favour of Kiev.

The Russian attack caused the Empire to renew its relations with the Khazars, an embassy being sent to them for this purpose. It is significant of the new spirit prevailing in Byzantium that this embassy was linked with a missionary enterprise and that its leader was Constantine of Thessalonica, a young man who, more than anyone else, was eminently fitted by his brilliant grasp of philology and comprehensive knowledge to champion the cause of the Christian religion and civilization in the face of Jewish and Islamic influences.

But a far more important task still was laid on Constantine and his brother Methodius when the Moravian prince Rastislav sent an embassy to Constantinople requesting the despatch of missionaries to his people. The fact that Rastislav turned to Byzantium is probably explained by his apprehensions of the influence of the Frankish clergy and by his desire to find in Byzantium a counterpoise to the danger of Frankish-Bulgarian encirclement. Byzantium, on the other hand, was presented with the possibility of extending its influence into a new and remote territory and of applying pressure on the Bulgars, conveniently placed in between. Proof of the discernment of the Byzantine government, both of Church and State, is afforded by the fact that they entrusted this important mission to the brothers from Thessalonica and allowed them to preach the new faith in Slav lands in the Slavonic tongue. Constantine and Methodius share with the Patriarch Photius and Bardas Caesar the credit for converting the Slavs to the Christian faith. The Byzantines had embarked on the conversion of the Slavs living within the Empire some time before.[1] But there now began a period of intensive missionary activity in the wider Slav world beyond the frontiers of the Empire. Constantine's first step was to invent a Slavonic script (the so-called glagolithic alphabet); he then proceeded to translate the Bible into Slavonic (using the Macedonian Slavonic dialect). The liturgy was also imported into Moravia by the two brothers in the Slavonic tongue. The success of the mission was thus assured. It is true that Methodius was later worsted in his struggle with the Frankish clergy (after the premature death of Constantine, which took place on 14 February 869, in a Greek monastery at Rome, where he had taken the name of Cyril), for Byzantine protection was too remote to carry the necessary weight in such an obscure outpost, while Rome after initial support ended by abandoning him. His disciples were expelled from the country,

---

[1] Cf. Dvornik, *Les Slaves* 60 ff.

but nevertheless his work, and that of his distinguished brother, had rooted Byzantine culture so deeply in Slav soil that the fruits it bore were all the richer for it. For the southern and eastern Slavs this achievement was of undying significance. These peoples are, indeed, indebted to the brothers from Thessalonica, 'the Apostles of the Slavs', for their alphabet and for the very beginnings of their national literature and culture.[1]

Once the Moravians had become Christian, the Bulgars could no longer shrink from the necessary step of setting their own political and cultural existence on a firmer foundation by the adoption of Christianity. But since the Moravians were allied with Byzantium, Boris, the Bulgarian prince, sent his embassy to the Franks. Byzantium swiftly intervened, for there could be no question of allowing a spiritual alliance between the neighbouring Bulgars and the Franks and through them with Rome. The recent victory over the Arabs, which had strengthened the position of the Empire and heightened its prestige, had also increased the determination of the government and the effectiveness of its actions. The arrival of the Byzantine army on his frontiers, together with an impressive appearance of the imperial navy off the Bulgarian coast, persuaded Boris to comply with Byzantine demands. In 864 he received baptism from Byzantium, taking the name of Michael, after the Byzantine Emperor who stood as sponsor for him.[2] Acting under instructions from the Patriarch, the Greek clergy proceeded at once to the organization of the Bulgarian Church.

Conversion to Christianity marked for the Bulgars not only a great step forward in their cultural development but also the completion of the movement towards Slavism and with it the fulfilment of the political and racial unification of the young state. Boris-Michael overthrew the Bulgarian boyars, who had risen in opposition to the Christianization of the country and its trend towards Slavism, and had fifty-two of them beheaded. But great as were the advantages bestowed by the conversion on the cultural progress and

---

[1] The very extensive literature on the Apostles to the Slavs has been compiled by G. A. Iljinskij, *Opyt sistematičeskoj kirillo-mefodievskoj bibliografii* (An attempt at a systematic Cyrillo-Methodian bibliography), Sofia 1934. This has been continued by M. Popru-ženko–S. Romanski, *Kirilometodievska bibliografija za 1934–40 g.* (Cyrillo-Methodian bibliography 1934–40), Sofia 1942.

[2] A. Vaillant and M. Lascaris, 'La date de la conversion des Bulgares', *Revue des études slaves* 13 (1933), 5 ff. (and see also D. Anastasijević, *Archiv za arbanasku starinu* (Archives for early Albanian history), 2 (1924), 137 ff.) show that the date of the baptism of Boris-Michael was in all probability in 864 and not 865 (as in Zlatarski, *Istorija* I, 2, p. 27 ff., and Runciman, *Bulgarian Empire* 104).

internal harmony of the Bulgar kingdom, the newly converted prince was soon to suffer disillusionment. The intention on the side of the Empire had been that the Bulgarian Church, under the direction of a Greek bishop, should be annexed to the Patriarchate of Constantinople. But Boris-Michael aspired to complete independence for his young Church under its own Patriarch, and when his claims remained unsatisfied turned his back on Byzantium and made overtures to Rome. Nothing could have pleased Pope Nicholas I more than this chance of drawing the Bulgars away from the Byzantine Church and subjecting them to the jurisdiction of Rome. He sent his legates to the Bulgars, who set to work with such great energy that the Bulgars seemed about to be drawn completely into the Roman wake. In fact, this state of affairs was not to last for long, for bitter disillusionment here also lay in store, but for the present Rome seemed to have won the day. Byzantium was forced to watch its Slavonic neighbour sliding away and the extension of the Roman sphere of influence almost to the heart of the Empire.

It was now that the conflict between Rome and Constantinople reached its climax. In making his stand against Rome, Photius was the champion not only of the independence of the Byzantine Church but also of the most vital interests of the Byzantine Empire. The imperial government of the day ranged itself without reserve behind the great Patriarch. Bardas Caesar and the Emperor Michael III afforded him full support. The Emperor sent the Pope a letter which expressed the Byzantine belief in their own independence and supremacy with unparalleled arrogance. The letter demanded, in the form of an ultimatum, that the Papal decision against Photius be withdrawn, and rejected with cutting acrimony the Roman claim to supremacy.[1] The Patriarch even went one stage further; he in effect set himself up as judge over the Western Church, by accusing her of errors in the liturgy and church discipline, and above all by his attack on Western teaching on the procession of the Holy Ghost from the Father and the Son (*ex patre filioque*). Photius, whom the Pope had thought to summon to stand accused before his chair of judgment, himself in the name of orthodoxy accused Rome of heresy. In 867 a synod, held in Constantinople and presided over by the Emperor, excommunicated Pope Nicholas, rejected the Roman doctrine of the

---

[1] This can be reconstructed from *Epist. Nicolai* 86 and 98 *ad Michaelem imp.*, MGH Ep. VI, II, 1, pp. 454 ff., 488 ff. (ed. Perels), Dölger, *Reg.* 464.

procession of the Holy Ghost as heretical and pronounced Roman interference in the affairs of the Byzantine Church as unlawful. A circular letter from the Patriarch, which discussed at length the doctrines and usages of the Roman Church, above all the *filioque*, strongly condemning them, was despatched to the oriental Patriarchates.[1]

But at this moment of extreme tension in the conflict a palace revolution took place in Constantinople which reshuffled all the cards in the game. To his own ruin Michael III had befriended Basil 'the Macedonian'. Basil came of a family settled in the theme of Macedonia[2] and he had grown up in circumstances of the utmost poverty. He came to Constantinople to seek his fortune, and, thanks to his unusual physical strength, secured a position as groom at the imperial court. With this began his fabulous ascent, for which his own outstanding abilities and the caprice of the Emperor were equally responsible. This clever and crafty peasant's son became the most intimate friend of Michael III, whose former mistress, Eudocia Ingerina, became his wife. With iron determination which stopped at nothing he strove to gain for himself complete power. In doing so he came into conflict with the Caesar Bardas, but Michael III had fallen so deeply under the spell of his favourite that he sacrificed his uncle without hesitation. Heaping one treachery on another, Basil and Michael III trapped the great statesman in their snare: in the course of a campaign against Crete, whilst the Caesar was enthroned side by side with his nephew at an intermediate station, Basil slew him with his own hand (21 April 865). His reward was the crown of co-Emperor which was offered to him by Michael III after their return to Constantinople on 26 May 866. Basil had now won from his patron everything he had to offer. The last act of the bloody tragedy was hastened by the fact that Michael III, capricious and unpredictable as he was, began to change his attitude towards the co-Emperor. On the night of 23–4 September 867, after a banquet, Basil had the drunken Emperor murdered in his bed-chamber.

---

[1] Grumel, *Reg.* 481.

[2] That is, from north-western Thrace (see above, p. 194). Although he is usually described as Macedonian, and the dynasty he founded is referred to as the Macedonian dynasty, he had nothing to do with Macedonia proper, but rather was born in Thrace, in the region of Adrianople. It is also far from certain that he was of Armenian extraction, as is usually assumed, and as is asserted with great conviction by Adontz, 'Basile I'.

Figure 37: *An Emperor Kneeling before Christ Enthroned.* Mosaic lunette over the Imperial Door, narthex of Hagia Sophia, Constantinople, 886–912. The emperor (Basil I or Leo VI) kneels before Christ, with the Virgin (left) as intercessor and the Angel Gabriel (right) as protector. Below is a detail of the emperor. Photos: Byzantine Institute, Inc., Washington, D.C.

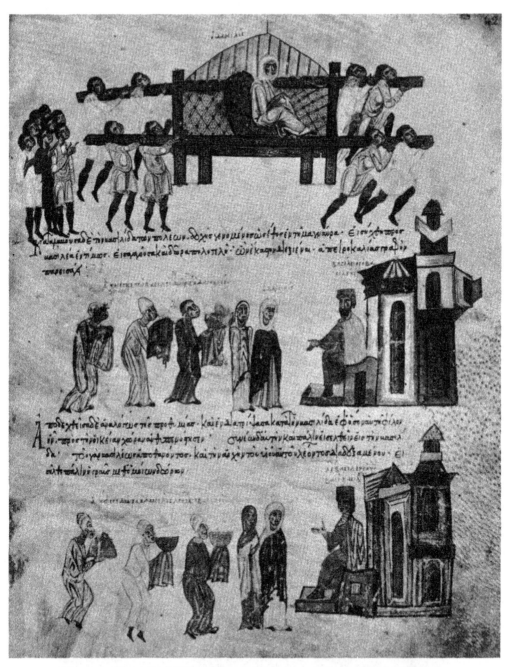

Figure 38: *Chronicle of John Scylitzes.* Miniature paintings on parchment, 14th century. Above, Danielis is carried in a litter to the imperial court. Center, Danielis presents gifts to Basil I. Below, Danielis, on a subsequent visit, offers gifts to Leo VI. Biblioteca Nacional, Madrid. Photo: Biblioteca Nacional.

2. THE PERIOD OF THE CODIFICATION OF THE LAW: BASIL I AND LEO VI

General bibliography: Vogt, *Basile I*; idem, 'La jeunesse de Leon VI le Sage', *Revue Hist.* 174 (1934), 389 ff.; G. Moravcsik, 'Sagen und Legenden über Kaiser Basileos I', DOP 15 (1961), 59–126; N. A. Popov, *Imperator Lev VI i ego pravlenie v cerkovnom otnošenii* (The Emperor Leo VI and his administration in relation to the Church), Moscow 1892; M. Mitard, 'Le pouvoir impérial au temps de Léon VI', *Mélanges Diehl* I (1930), 215 ff.; G. Kolias, *Léon Choerosphactès*, Athens 1939; Grumel, 'Chronologie'; M. Benemanskij, Ὁ πρόχειρος νόμος, Sergiev Posad 1906; Monnier, *Les Novelles de Léon le Sage*, Bordeaux 1923; Spulber, *Les Novelles de Léon le Sage*, Cernautsi 1934; P. Noaille and A. Dain, *Les Novelles de Léon VI le Sage*, Paris 1944; Bury, *Admin. System*; Dölger, *Finanzverwaltung*; Stöckle, *Zünfte* (for further bibliography on the *Book of the Eparch* see below, p. 253, note 1); Dvornik, *Photian Schism*; Vasiliev, *Vizantija i Araby* II; idem, 'The Struggle with the Saracens II (867–1057)', CMH IV (1923), 139–50; Glykatzi-Ahrweiler, *Recherches*; Gay, *Italie*. H. Scheltema, 'Byzantine Law', CMH IV Pt II (2nd ed., 1967); see also general bibliography cited above, p. 217.

The path by which Basil I (867–86), the founder of the Macedonian dynasty, reached the imperial throne was murky indeed. At his side was his wife, Eudocia Ingerina, the former mistress of the murdered Michael. To safeguard the succession to the throne he crowned his eldest son Constantine as co-Emperor as early as 6 January 869; exactly a year after, Leo, his second son, was also crowned, and then later on his third son, Alexander (about 879, after the premature death of Constantine), while his youngest son, Stephen, entered on an ecclesiastical career and was to hold the office of Patriarch during the reign of his brother, Leo VI. Constantine, the Emperor's first-born and his favourite, was the issue of a youthful marriage with Maria, a Macedonian. Leo, Alexander and Stephen were the sons of Eudocia Ingerina,[1] the two younger boys being born only after Basil had become Emperor.[2]

---

[1] The question as to whether Leo VI was the legitimate son of Basil I or the illegitimate son of Michael III has been frequently and hotly disputed, but it cannot now be taken as proved that he was the son of Basil I; cf. N. Adontz, 'Basile I', 501 ff. A. Vogt, *Oraison funèbre de Basile I par son fils Leon VI le Sage* (1932), 10 ff., no longer maintains his earlier view that Leo was illegitimate (*Basile I*, 60 ff., and CMH IV, 51 and 54). Vogt's new chronology is, however, open to question and it seems preferable to hold with Adontz that Constantine was the son of Basil's first marriage and that he did not marry Eudocia Ingerina until about 865, and also with Grumel, 'Notes de chronologie byzantine', EO 35 (1936), 331 ff., that Leo was born on 19 September 866 (cf. also Vogt, *Revue hist.* 174 (1934), 389, note 1, where Leo VI's birth is no longer put in 864, but on 1 September 866).

[2] The sources give conflicting information on the ages of Alexander and Stephen, and Adontz, 'Basile I', 503 ff., sets out to prove that Alexander, born in 870, was Basil I's

Like every other Byzantine ruler, Basil concerned himself very closely with the affairs of the Church, and at first he pursued a course contrary to the direction followed by the ecclesiastical policy of Bardas and Michael III. Immediately after his accession he had Photius confined in a monastery, thus stabbing the great Patriarch in the back at the most critical moment of his historic struggle. He then reinstated Ignatius on the patriarchal throne (23 November 867) and resumed relations with Rome. In 869–70 a Council was held at Constantinople in the presence of the legates of Hadrian II, which pronounced excommunication on Photius; this Council is counted by the Roman Church as the eighth oecumenical Council. Yet no unanimity prevailed between Basil I and the legates on a material point of principle, for the two parties held diametrically opposed views on the rights of jurisdiction of the Roman See, and whereas for the legates the affair of Photius had fundamentally been already decided by the Pope's judgment, the Emperor was concerned that the question should be reopened in the synod meeting under his direction, and that the decision should come from him. Moreover, the synod had a sequel wholly unexpected by Rome. Three days after the session had ended, a Bulgarian embassy appeared in Constantinople, and the Council reassembled to consider the question of whether the Bulgarian Church belonged to the diocese of Rome or of Constantinople. For the expectations which Boris, the Bulgar prince, had entertained of his alliance with Rome had not in fact been fulfilled; his connection with Rome had brought Boris not a step nearer to his real aim, the establishment of an

youngest son. The clear account in the *Vita Euthymii*, ed. P. Karlin-Hayter, B 25/27 (1955/7), 10, 20 and in Constantine Porphyrogenitus himself seems to me to be preferable to the information in the Logothete's chronicle which is not always reliable on the family history of Basil I. It is highly improbable that Constantine VII did not know the respective ages of his uncles and therefore had to puzzle them out from the acrostic ΒΕΚΛΑΣ, as Adontz suggests. The acrostic, which is attributed to Photius, consists of the initial letters of the names Basil, Eudocia, Constantine, Leo, Alexander and Stephen, and in any case it also shows that Stephen was the youngest son of Basil I, and as such he was destined for an ecclesiastical career. In a similar manner Romanus I had dedicated his fourth and youngest son to the Church. Both of them ascended the patriarchal throne at the age of sixteen, for Stephen according to the above account was born about 871 and became Patriarch in December 886 (cf. below, p. 214, note 1). G. Kolias, 'Βιογραφικὰ Στεφάνου Α΄ Οἰκουμενικοῦ Πατριάρχου (886–93)', Προσφορὰ εἰς Στ. Κυριακίδην (1953), 361, refers to an iambic poem by Leo Choerosphactes, according to which Stephen lived 'πενταπλῆν πεντάδα χρόνων'. It is, however, very doubtful whether one can take this poetic turn of phrase as literally as Kolias does, for he supposes that Stephen, who died on the 17th or 18th May 893, was born, by this reckoning, a little before or after the 17th or 18th May 868', that is exactly twenty-five years previously, and is thereby also forced to alter the date of birth of Leo VI and Alexander accordingly.

independent Church in the Bulgar kingdom: both his candidates for the archbishopric to be founded in Bulgaria had been rejected by Rome, and he therefore turned once again to Constantinople. This was the background of the Bulgarian embassy and of the question posed to the Council, which, despite the vehement protests of the Roman legates, was decided in favour of Byzantium by the arbitration of the representatives of the three eastern Patriarchates. Byzantium had learned something from the events of recent years and now showed itself more indulgent: the Emperor permitted the Patriarch Ignatius to consecrate an archbishop and several bishops for the Bulgars. The Bulgarian Church did indeed recognize the supremacy of the Patriarchate of Constantinople, but retained a measure of autonomy.[1]

Thus the Bulgar prince had attained his objective by making adroit use of the rivalry between Rome and Byzantium, but Byzantium had won back the Bulgars. Henceforth the Bulgar kingdom, notwithstanding repeated remonstrances from Rome, remained in the bosom of the Byzantine Church and within the orbit of Byzantine civilization.[2] But this was achieved at the cost of undermining the friendship with Rome so greatly valued by Basil and for which Photius had been sacrificed. In fact, Basil's conception of the role Byzantium had to play in the Slav world was identical with that of Photius, whom he had deposed, and of Bardas, whom he had murdered. His prosecution of the struggle for the Bulgars, which he conducted to a victorious conclusion, was wholly in accordance with their attitude. He also further extended the missionary work undertaken in Russia, and moreover won for Christendom the Slavs in the western portion of the Balkan peninsula, and in doing so subjected them to the influence of Byzantium.

In the period of the iconoclast crisis the western part of the Balkans had become increasingly withdrawn from the influence of the Byzantine Empire. In the first half of the ninth century, the Dalmatian cities and the Slav tribes of both the coastal and the

---

[1] Evidence of the special position of the Bulgarian Archbishopric within the Byzantine Church is the high rank accorded the head of the Bulgarian Church: cf. the *Cletorologion* of Philotheus (Bury, *Admin. System,* p. 146) and the *Tacticon Beneševič* ('Ranglisten' 114 ff.) where of all the office-holders both lay and ecclesiastical the Bulgarian Archbishop is given the sixteenth place coming immediately after the *syncellus* of the Patriarch, while the Byzantine metropolitans and archbishops occupy the fifty-eighth and fifty-ninth places, and the bishops the sixtieth.

[2] There is no foundation for Zlatarski's theory (*Istorija* I, 2, pp. 133 ff.) that the Roman legates had agreed to the Council's decision; cf. my criticisms in *Jugoslov. Istor. Casopis* 1 (1935), 512 ff.

inland districts seem to have severed their connection with Byzantium.[1] There also arose during this period an independent Serbian kingdom under prince Vlastimir. Meanwhile, the Adriatic coast was threatened by a new danger, this time from the Arabs of South Italy, in which the help of Byzantine naval power was vital. When the Arab fleet, after attacks on Budva and Kotor (Cottaro), laid siege to Dubrovnik (Ragusa) in 867 a call for help went out from the beleaguered city to Constantinople. The arrival of a powerful Byzantine squadron forced the Arabs to abandon the siege, which had lasted for fifteen months, and retire to South Italy. The authority of the Byzantine Empire was thus reaffirmed and Byzantine sovereignty over the eastern Adriatic coast re-established. The creation of the theme of Dalmatia, which embraced the Byzantine cities and islands of Dalmatia, dates from this time.[2] It is true that in fact the Dalmatian cities and islands were more dependent on the Slav hinterland than on Constantinople: they paid their tribute to the Slav tribes, and the trivial payments they made to the imperial *strategi* had only a symbolic character.[3] On the other hand, not only the Dalmatian cities, but also the Slav tribes both of the coast and the interior acknowledged the prerogatives of Byzantium and were obliged to give military support to the Empire. Byzantine influence in the Balkans was considerably strengthened, and in consequence there followed a rapid spread of Christianity. It was at this time that the Serbs and the Slav tribes of the southern coastal districts were converted to Christianity from Byzantium,[4] and Byzantine influence even won a temporary victory over the ascendancy of the Frankish kingdom and the Roman Church in Croatia. Moreover, Byzantine missionary efforts in the Balkans, particularly in Macedonia and Bulgaria, received a further powerful stimulus from the arrival there of disciples of Methodius († 885) who had been expelled from Moravia and were now spreading the Christian faith and Byzantine civilization among the Slav peoples by their preaching and evangelistic work, carried out in a Slavonic tongue. The historically natural situation was thus restored: Moravia fell to the Roman sphere of influence, while Bulgaria, Macedonia and Serbia came within the orbit of Byzantium.

[1] *De adm. imp.*, c. 29, 58 f.
[2] Cf. J. Ferluga, *Vizantiska uprava u Dalmacijia* (Byzantine administration in Dalmatia), Belgrade, 1958.
[3] *De adm. imp.*, c. 30, 127 f.
[4] Cf. G. Sp. Radojičić, 'La date de la conversion des Serbes', B 22 (1952), 255 ff., who puts the baptism of the Serbs in the period 867–74.

Once the imperial fleet had deflected the attacks of the Arabs on the Dalmatian coast and raised the siege of Dubrovnik, the Byzantines intervened in South Italy. Basil I was planning a combined action by himself, the Emperor Louis II and Rome against the Arab advance, and it was this intention which lay at the bottom of the policy of friendship towards Rome which he had initiated. Nothing, however, was achieved in Sicily: on the contrary, in 870 the Arabs occupied Malta, thus gaining fresh support for their position in the Mediterranean. It is true that Louis II took Bari in 871, but for the Byzantines, who came back empty-handed, this meant only a fresh disillusionment. Relations between the two rulers became very ruffled and Basil, who had a short while before consented to the marriage of his eldest son with Louis' daughter, now loaded his former ally with reproaches and denied his right to the title of Roman Emperor.[1]

Byzantium devoted the next few years to the war in the East, where the Paulicians were all too prevalent and were spreading over the whole of Asia Minor. In 872 Christopher, the Emperor's brother-in-law, who in his capacity as *domesticus* of the *scholae* was commander-in-chief, gained a decisive victory over the Paulicians, destroying their stronghold of Tephrice as well as many other fortifications and scattering their forces in a bloody battle in which Chrysocheirus, the leader of the Paulicians, lost his life. This victory enabled the Byzantines to make further advances in the east. In 873 Basil thrust forwards in the region of the Euphrates and seized Zapetra and Samosata. Even so, the Emperor did not achieve his principal aim, for in attempting to take the important fortress of Melitene, he suffered an irksome defeat. But although on this occasion, as also on his later expeditions in the Euphrates region and on the fringes of the Taurus, Basil had to be content with partial success, this nevertheless marks the beginning of a period of the systematic advance of the Byzantine Empire on its eastern frontiers.[2] Furthermore, the weakening of the Arab kingdom facilitated the development of Armenia. The recognition of Ashot I as King by both the Caliph (885) and the Byzantine Emperor (887), meant for Armenia the beginning of a period of expansion under the national royal dynasty of the Bagratuni.[3]

[1] This can be reconstructed from *Epist. Ludovici imp. ad Basilium*, MGH SS III, 521 ff. Dölger, *Reg.* 487.
[2] Honigmann, *Ostgrenze* 64.
[3] Cf. J. Laurent, *L'Arménie entre Byzance et l'Islam depuis la conquête arabe jusqu'en* 886, Paris 1919; R. Grousset, *Histoire de l'Arménie*, Paris 1947.

The Byzantine position in Italy was also consolidated. The prince of Benevento, who had rebelled against Louis II, placed himself under the Byzantine protectorate (873) and after the death of Louis II (875) Bari also opened its doors to the Byzantine *strategus* at the end of 876. Byzantium was able to beat back new Arab attacks on the coastal regions of Dalmatia, Greece and the Peloponnese, and even managed to occupy Cyprus for seven years.[1] This in no way altered the fact that the Arabs were still masters of the Mediterranean, and Byzantium soon suffered a particularly hard blow on the most vulnerable point, Sicily: Syracuse, which had long defied the enemy, in 878 fell into the hands of the Arabs. Yet it was a considerable gain that Byzantium had at least recovered a footing on the South Italian mainland, and after the arrival there of the outstanding general Nicephorus Phocas in the last years of Basil's reign, a strong and successful Byzantine offensive began. South Italy again came under Byzantine rule.[2] Byzantium stood in the midst of the mutually hostile small Italian states as the one stable and powerful factor, and even Rome, who saw herself threatened by the continual attacks of the Arabs on the Italian coasts, had to seek help from the Byzantine Emperor. This state of affairs explains the indulgent attitude in ecclesiastical matters which the Papacy now adopted towards Byzantium.

The Emperor Basil was forced to recognize that in his reversal of Church policy after his accession he had been beating the air. His attempt to settle the clerical conflict in Byzantium by removing Photius was frustrated, since the adherents of Photius were not so easily subdued and the party strife continued. A conflict with Rome was inevitable, with or without Photius, on account of the Bulgarian issue, and after the disillusionments which attended his alliance with the western powers in southern Italy, the Emperor realized that he was also being cheated of the political reward of his ecclesiastical change of front. Thus, about 875, he allowed Photius to return to Constantinople and entrusted him with the education of his sons.

[1] R. H. Dolley, 'A forgotten byzantine conquest of Kypros', *Bull. de l'Acad. de Belgique* 34 (1948), 209 ff., puts forward the theory that the Byzantines were not in possession of Cyprus in Basil I's reign, as is expressly stated in Constantine Porphyrogenitus, *De them.* 40, but regained it under Leo VI, and were in occupation from 906 to 915. This is untenable, as is shown by the sources in Vasiliev, *Vizantija i Araby* II, 50 ff. and 164 ff. Cf. the comments of R. J. H. Jenkins, 'Cyprus between Byzantium and Islam', *Studies Presented to D. M. Robinson*, II (1953), 1008, n. 15. On the naval operations of Himerius under Leo VI see below, p. 258 f.
[2] Cf. Gay, *Italie* 132 ff.

Three days after the death of the aged Ignatius on 23 October 877, Photius ascended the patriarchal throne for the second time and was now also accorded recognition by Rome. The conditions which Pope John VIII attached to his recognition had little practical significance. In November 879, in the presence of the Papal legates, Photius held a Council of 383 bishops, handsome compensation indeed for his condemnation by the Synod of 869–70 and a veritable triumph for the restored Patriarch.[1]

Although himself an upstart of the meanest ancestry, the Emperor Basil I had a fervent admiration for both Greek civilization and the Roman imperial idea and Roman law. During his time, the cultural upsurge which had begun under Theoctistus and Bardas continued. As legislator he deliberately initated a revival of Roman law. He planned a comprehensive collection of laws, a revision of the law-books of Justinian which would also contain supplements from more recent laws. This great work, to which the Emperor gave the descriptive title 'Purification of the old law' (ἀνακάθαρσις τῶν παλαιῶν νόμων) was never published, and apparently never completed, but it forms the basis on which Leo VI built and is the foundation-stone of his *Basilica*. Two smaller books of law which Basil I made as an introduction to his major work have come down to us. The first to appear was the *Procheiron* (ὁ πρόχειρος νόμος) published in the names of the Emperors Basil, Constantine and Leo, and thus belonging to the period between 870 and 879. As the title suggests, the *Procheiron* was a text-book for practical use. It contained a selection, drawn from the overwhelming mass of laws, of the most important and most frequently applicable precepts of both the civil and the public law, and arranged them systematically under forty titles. In view of its aim of providing a general popular law-book, it was natural that the *Procheiron* should make the most use of the material in the *Institutes*, and pay very much less attention to the other parts of Justinian's codification; in fact, it only rarely makes reference to the original source itself,

[1] The Council of 879 did not lead to a fresh break between Rome and Constantinople and the 'second schism' of Photius never occurred. This was first made clear by F. Dvornik, 'Le second schisme de Photius', B 8 (1933), 425 ff., and V. Grumel, 'Y-eut-il un second schisme de Photius?' *Revue des Sciences philos. et théol.* 32 (1933), 432 ff., and 'La liquidation de la querelle Photienne', EO 33 (1934), 257 ff. Their important conclusions have been confirmed by further investigations; cf. the comprehensive work of Dvornik, *Photian Schism*, especially pp. 202 ff., and Grumel, *Reg.* 445–589.

preferring to use later Greek translations and commentaries. At bottom, the aim of the *Procheiron* was similar to that of the *Ecloga* of Leo III, which was also a practical law-book meeting the day-to-day needs of the judges. It is true that Basil I, who was attempting to bring about a revival of Roman law, tried with the utmost asperity to dissociate himself from the work of the iconoclastic Emperor, which he described as the 'destruction of the good laws'.[1] In fact, however, the *Procheiron* was greatly indebted to the law-book of Leo III which had proved useful and popular. Despite the aspersions cast on the *Ecloga*, the *Procheiron* draws on it freely, particularly in its second part, which covers the law of inheritance and public law. The *Procheiron* had a wide circulation within Byzantium and retained its value until the dissolution of the Empire. It was, moreover, like the *Ecloga* before it, translated into Slavonic at an early date and acquired great authority in the eyes of the Bulgars, Serbs and Russians.

The *Epanagoge*, compiled in the names of the Emperors Basil, Leo and Alexander, which was planned as an introduction to the projected great collection of the laws, belongs to the period after 879.[2] To a large extent the *Epanagoge* simply reproduces the *Procheiron*, but with a new arrangement and some important alterations. The *Epanagoge* relies even more heavily than the *Procheiron* on the *Ecloga*, since it starts its dependence on the banned law-book of the iconoclasts with the law of marriage, while the *Procheiron* still adheres to the law of Justinian on this point, only beginning to depend on the *Ecloga* in the later sections. But in addition the *Epanagoge* has some quite original portions, highly deserving of attention, concerning the rights and obligations of the Emperor, the Patriarch and other lay and ecclesiastical dignitaries. The polity of State and Church is expounded as a unity composed of many parts and members,

---

[1] *Procheiron*, in Zepos, *Jus* II, 116.

[2] Zachariä, *Geschichte* 22, takes the view that the *Epanagoge* was never officially published, and he is followed by Vogt, *Basile I*, 135, and P. Collinet, CMH IV (1924), 712; the official character of the *Epanagoge* is defended with arguments well worth considering by V. Sokoljskij, 'O charaktere i značenii Epanagogi' (On the character and significance of the Epanagoge), VV I (1894), 18 ff., and likewise G. Vernadskij, 'Vizantijskije učenija o vlasti carja i patriarcha' (Byzantine teaching on the authority of the Emperor and the Patriarch), *Recueil Kondakov* (1926), 152; idem, 'Die kirchlich-politische Lehre der Epanagoge', BNJ 6 (1928), 121; and idem, 'The Tactics of Leo the Wise and the Epanagoge', B 6 (1931), 333 ff. In any case, the *Epanagoge* never enjoyed the position and widespread usage of the *Procheiron*, and in contrast to the *Ecloga* and *Procheiron* it was never completely translated into Slavonic. Its pronouncements on the respective positions of Emperor and Patriarch (cf. below) were, however, known in the Slav world through the *Syntagma* of Matthew Blastares which was translated into Slavonic in 1335 by order of Stephen Dušan.

presided over by the Emperor and the Patriarch as the two heads of the universe, whose task is to work together in close and peaceful harmony for the good of mankind. The functions of the two powers are set forth as completely parallel: the lay head is to foster the material well-being of the subject, the spiritual head is charged with his spiritual welfare. The author of this theory of dual control was undoubtedly none other than Photius, who by this time had again become Patriarch. This circumstance explains the fact that the *Epanagoge* assumes an ideal relation between the lay and ecclesiastical power in accord with the ideas prevalent in orthodox Church circles.

Photius knew only too well, and was shortly to have this knowledge reinforced by personal experience, that practice was sharply at variance with this theory. For the next change of ruler once again brought about his fall. After the early death of Constantine (879) the right of succession was vested in Leo, despite the antipathy and deep mistrust which his father felt towards him. Basil was never able to reconcile himself to the premature death of his favourite and passed the last years of his life in a state of deep mental depression. On 29 August 886 he met with a fatal accident while hunting. After his accession, Leo VI deposed Photius and entrusted the office of Patriarch to his youthful brother Stephen.[1] Photius now finally disappeared from the historical scene: he died in exile in Armenia.

As a matter of form, Leo VI shared the throne with his brother Alexander, but the latter lived only for his pleasures and did not

---

[1] According to Grégoire, 'Neuvième siècle' 549 (cf. also B 8 (1933), 503, note 2), and A. Vogt, 'Note sur la chronologie des patriarches de Constantinople au IX⁰ et au X⁰ siècles', EO 32 (1933), 276, Stephen was raised to the patriarchate in December 887. The chronology usually followed by earlier scholars, i.e. that Stephen became Patriarch in December 886, a few months after Leo VI ascended the throne, is supported with fresh arguments by Grumel, 'Chronologie' 10 ff. Cf. Grumel, *Reg.* II, p. 130 (18 December 866). Cf. also G. Kolias, 'Βιογραφικὰ Στεφάνου Α' Οἰκουμενικοῦ Πατριάρχου (886–93)', Προσφορὰ εἰς Στ. Κυριακίδην (1953), 358 ff. The main reason why Leo VI banished the powerful and self-willed Photius was probably to enable him to confer the office of Patriarch on his barely sixteen-year-old brother and thus secure for himself unlimited control over ecclesiastical affairs. In any case, this seems to me to be a more satisfactory explanation than Dvornik's suggestion, *Photian Schism* 241 ff., that Leo VI was moved to depose Photius because he opposed his father's policy in the struggle between the Byzantine ecclesiastical parties and wanted, therefore, to support the more extreme party in the Church. But it was only after the difficulties raised by his fourth marriage nearly twenty years later that Leo VI allied with the monastic party, and it is making something of nothing to suggest that his personal antagonism towards his father provoked a change of policy. The reverse is more true, as is plainly evidenced by the legal work of codification. As Dvornik, op. cit., rightly says, the second fall of Photius has nothing to do with the question of an approach to Rome.

trouble himself with affairs of state.¹ The Emperor's most important counsellor during the first and most fruitful period of his reign
was the Armenian Stylianus Zautzes († 896). He was the father of
Zoe, Leo's mistress first and later his wife, and he held the high
office of *basileopator*, expressly created for him.

As the pupil of Photius, to whom he had shown himself so ungrateful, he had a first-class education and his learning was many-sided.²
He was a prolific writer and was above all an inspired rhetorician.
The worship of the past showed itself even more strongly in him
than in his father, whom he naturally far surpassed in educational
attainment; but, unlike Basil, this archaistic tendency expressed itself
not in political action but chiefly in literary form, with a strong
emphasis on theology. Leo was a devout ruler with marked ecclesiastical and theological interests. There have survived from his pen a
number of liturgical poems, and numerous sermons and addresses
which he would deliver in person at church festivals, mingling
widely-ranging dogmatic utterances with classical reminiscences.
He also composed a long funeral oration on his father and a number
of very affected secular verses. It appears that it was these writings
which earned for him, even during his lifetime, the venerable
cognomen of 'sophos', 'the Wise'.³ Later on, legends seized hold of
the person of Leo the Wise and turned the rather colourless ruler
into a prophet, magician and astrologer. He was regarded as the
author of a collection of oracles on the destiny of the Empire which
was really of much later origin. These became extraordinarily
popular and were widely read in Byzantium, as also in the Latin and
Slav world, both in the Byzantine period and later.⁴

Without question Leo the Wise was, however, the most prolific
law-giver since Justinian. The legislative work which falls within
his reign is of great importance and extremely comprehensive.

¹ Relations between the two brothers were extremely tense and on occasion even
hostile, but it cannot be shown that Leo VI temporarily deprived his brother of the
office of co-Emperor (as in Lambros BZ 4 (1895), 92, and Runciman, *Romanus Lecapenus*
45). Cf. my remarks in *Sem. Kond.* 5 (1932), 253, note 10. Spulber, *Les Novelles de Léon
le Sage* (1934), 47, considers that Alexander ceased to be co-Emperor on the coronation
of Constantine (VII) which is equally erroneous; there is evidence to the contrary in
the Byzantino-Russian treaty of 911 which mentions the Emperors Leo, Alexander and
Constantine, Trautmann, *Die Nestorchronik*, p. 19 (the date of the treaty is wrongly given
as 912); see also Cross, *Russian Primary Chronicle*, p. 65.
² Cf. A. Vogt, 'La jeunesse de Léon VI le Sage', *Revue Hist.* 174 (1934), 403 ff.
³ Cf. H. Grégoire, B 5 (1929), 399 f.; V. Laurent, *ÉO* 34 (1935), 461; C. A. Spulber,
Les Novelles de Léon le Sage, 1934, 42.
⁴ Cf. the detailed study by C. Mango, 'The Legend of Leo the Wise', ZRVI 6 (1950),
59 ff.

Nevertheless, it would be wrong to overestimate the extent of Leo's personal contribution to this work, even though there can be no doubt that his learning and assiduity as an author were assets to the undertaking. As already mentioned, extensive preparatory work already existed dating from the time of his father, and it must also be observed that the great period of legislative activity falls in the first decade of his reign, i.e. in the period during which Stylianus Zautzes was still at his side. Compared with this first period, the later part of Leo's reign, the time of his own maturity, seems less fruitful.

Despite the deep and mutual antipathy which subsisted between father and son, and despite the great disparity of their natures the aims of Leo VI were very similar to those of Basil. The revision of the law of Justinian taken in hand by Basil I had its completion in the *Basilica* of Leo VI. The Imperial Laws of Leo the Wise (τὰ Βασιλικά) which were divided into sixty books and occupied six volumes (and are hence called Ἑξηκοντάβιβλος as well as Ἑξάβιβλος) form the greatest collection of laws of the medieval Byzantine Empire. They were prepared by a commission of lawyers under the presidency of the *protospatharius* Symbatius and published in the early years of the reign of Leo VI, in itself one more proof that the preparatory work for the 'purification' of Basil had been well advanced and was put to good account in the work of Leo VI. The *Basilica* were as much a collection of canon law as of civil and public law. The *Basilica* drew above all on the *Codex Justinianus* and the *Digest*, to a lesser extent on the *Institutes*, and also on the novels of Justinian, as well as those of Justin II and Tiberius, which had been appended to those of Justinian in the later collection of the so-called CLXVIII Novels; finally, there was also considerable reliance on the *Procheiron*. Leo VI's legal scholars, like those of Basil I, referred little to the Latin sources, using instead Greek versions and commentaries of the sixth and seventh centuries. In contrast with the *Corpus Juris* of Justinian, the *Basilica* had the great advantage for Byzantine users of being written in Greek, and on the other hand it was more practical to handle. For in the *Basilica* the whole body of the material was collected in one work and systematically arranged, while the *Corpus Juris* treats of the same subject in a number of different places; the Prooimion to the *Basilica* singles this out as the greatest defect of the *Corpus Juris*. It is thus not surprising that the *Basilica* drove Justinian's legal work almost completely out of use and that it became the foundation of the juristic scholarship of medieval Byzantium. The text was soon embellished by numerous commentaries; the most important of these, the so-called 'old commentaries', go back to the time of Constantine VII, but the 'newer commentaries' date from the eleventh, twelfth and thirteenth centuries. In the twelfth century an index was made of the *Basilica*, known as the *Tipoukeitos* (from τί ποῦ κεῖται;) whose chief value for us lies in the information it gives concerning the contents of the books which no longer survive.[1]

But however important the *Basilica* may be for the development of Byzantine law, its value as an historical source is very limited. The great legal compilation reflects little, if anything, of the historical reality of the age in which it was drawn up. For the most part it only repeats the old, and for the most part already revised, legal enactments of earlier centuries.[2] It is in Leo's 'novels' that contemporary conditions are reflected. Leo VI in fact published a collection of 113 decrees for which the title Collection of Novels—following the example of the novels of Justinian—has become general. But the original title of the collection was 'Rectification and purification of the laws' (αἱ τῶν νόμων ἐπανορθωτικαὶ ἀνακαθάρσεις), which again calls attention to the close connection between the legislative work of Leo VI and that of his father. The novels of Leo VI deal with a wide variety of topics, which seem to follow each other without any fixed system, and set out, with the appropriate reasons, changes in the old laws or their revocation, together with precepts endowing customary usages with the force of law. The purely ecclesiastical enactments (*Nov.* 2-17 and 75) are addressed to the Patriarch Stephen, all the others, with the exception of a few which have no ascription at all, to

---

[1] M. Κριτοῦ τοῦ Πατзῆ Τιποῦκειτος, lib. I-XII ed. C. Ferrini and J. Mercati, *Studi e Testi* 25 (1914); lib. XIII-XXIII ed. F. Dölger, ibid. 51 (1929), lib. XXIV-XXXVII ed. St. Hoermann and E. Seidl, ibid. 107 (1943). Cf. F. Dölger and E. Seidl, 'Beiträge und Berichtigungen zum Tipukeitos', BZ 39 (1939), 146 ff.; E. Seidl, 'Die Basilikenscholien im Tipukeitos', BZ 44 (1951) (*Dölger-Festschrift*), 534 ff.

[2] Insufficient account is often taken of this fact, and the *Basilica* are often accepted as a source for the ninth century without the necessary caution. Cf. A. P. Každan, 'Vasiliki kak istoričeskij istočnik' (The *Basilica* as an historical source), VV 14 (1958), 56 f., who rightly emphasizes that the *Basilica* reflect the political and social situation of the sixth century, not of the ninth. This view is not substantially repudiated by the objections of M. J. Sjuzjumov, 'Vasiliki kak istočnik dlja vnutrennej istorii Vizantii' (The *Basilica* as a source for the internal history of Byzantium), ibid. 67 ff., and E. E. Lipšic, 'Neskol'ko zamečanij o Vasilikach kak istočnike' (Some observations on the *Basilica* as a source), ibid. 76 ff.

Stylianus Zautzes.[1] As was the case with Justinian and John of Cappadocia, his praetorian prefect, the person addressed was probably in fact the real author, which would explain why Leo's legislation was so extensive while Stylianus was alive and relatively slight after his death.

Particularly worthy of attention are those novels of Leo VI in which the ancient rights of the curia and the senate are revoked.[2] In any case, the order of the *curiales* had long fallen into decay, and the administrative and legislative authority of the senate existed only on paper. Yet their final abrogation by legal decree is important, particularly since it is expressly justified in each of the three novels on the grounds that complete power now rested with the ruler. The legislation of Leo VI marks the culmination of an important historical process which had united the total power of the state in the hands of the ruler and placed all affairs of state in the care of the imperial bureaucracy. The omnipotence of the Emperor and the transformation of the state into a bureaucracy realized their full development under the Macedonian dynasty. The senate, composed of higher imperial officials, now led a shadowy existence having completely lost not only its former legislative and administrative functions but also the importance it had acquired in the seventh and eighth centuries (cf. above, p. 114). The state was completely identified with the Emperor and with his military and bureaucratic machine. The Emperor is chosen of God, and under the protection of Divine Providence. He is entire master of the government of the Empire, commander-in-chief of the army, supreme judge and sole law-giver, protector of the Church and guardian of the true faith. With him rest decisions of war and peace, his judicial sentence is final and irrevocable, his laws are considered to be inspired by God. It is true that he has to observe the existing law, but it is in his power to promulgate new laws and revoke old ones. As master of

[1] In spite of Spulber, *Les Novelles de Léon le Sage* (1934), 81 f., the widely-held view that the novels were published before Leo VI concluded his second marriage still stands, for Novel 90 expressly condemns second marriages. It must however be remembered that Leo VI did not contract his second marriage until the spring of 898, as Grumel, 'Chronologie' 5 ff., has shown. An earlier date than this is indicated by the fact that the only Patriarch mentioned in the novels of Leo is Stephen who died on 17 May 893. Cf. C. Kržišnik, BZ 37 (1937), 486 ff.

[2] *Nov.* 46, 47 and 78: Zepos, *Jus* I, pp. 116, 116 f. and 147; Noaille-Dain, *Les Novelles de Léon VI le Sage* (1944), pp. 182, 184, 270.

the state the Emperor has in practice unrestricted power, qualified only by moral precept and tradition.[1]

Only in religious affairs does the absolutism of the Emperor find itself genuinely limited. However strongly the influence of the Emperor might exert itself on the form of ecclesiastical organization, he is still only a layman, and as such can merely be protector and not the head of the Church. The Church has its own leader, the Patriarch of Constantinople, whose power and prestige are continuously in the ascendant. However, in fact it is the Emperor who decides who should be appointed to the patriarchal office, and in his capacity as law-giver he also has a part in the government of the Church. But in contrast to the appointment and retirement of holders of secular office, a privilege which belongs to the Emperor alone, the appointment, and even more definitely, the dismissal, of princes of the Church requires the consent of the clergy; and although he can alter the laws made by his predecessors, the Emperor can neither revoke nor alter the decisions of Church Councils. The Church Council is the highest court of appeal in the Church, and to it also belongs the right of decision in matters of faith. The task of the Emperor is merely to safeguard the existing creed. While the lay elements which once acted as a check on absolute power have now lost all their former importance, the power of the Church is advancing side by side with that of the Emperor.[2]

The epoch of the Macedonian dynasty also marked a definite stage in the development of the administrative and bureaucratic

---

[1] It is true that Leo's laws frequently expatiate on the general good of his subjects, equal justice for all, and so on, but these pious didactic maxims do not justify the conclusions which many modern scholars would like to deduce. Cf. G. Michaélidès-Nouraos, 'Les idées philosophiques de Léon le Sage sur les limites du pouvoir législatif et son attitude envers les coutûmes', *Mnemosynon Bizoukidès* (1960), 27 ff., who describes the legislation of Leo VI as being inspired by the spirit of humanity and liberalism, having its roots in public opinion.

[2] The word 'caesaropapism' so frequently used in connection with Byzantium gives a false impression of the actual relations between Church and State in the medieval Byzantine Empire. Cf. my arguments in 'Otnošenie cerkvi i gosudarstva v Vizantii' (Relations between Church and State in Byzantium), *Sem. Kond.* 4 (1931), 121 ff. Although I do not entirely hold to all my previous views, I am still of the opinion that there was an essential difference between relations between Church and State in the half Roman Empire of the early centuries and in the medieval Byzantine Empire. On the other hand, Dölger, BZ 31 (1931), 449 f., considers that relations between Church and State at any given period were determined by the personalities of individual leaders, lay or ecclesiastic. A typical example of the view that the Church was continually subjected to the 'caesaropapist' Byzantine State is to be found in the well-known essay of H. Gelzer, 'Das Verhältnis von Staat und Kirche in Byzanz' HZ 86 (1901), 193 ff. My own views on the development of relations between Church and State in Byzantium are fully confirmed by the evidence of representative art; cf. the excellent comments of A. Grabar, *Empereur* 175 ff. and elsewhere.

system of the Byzantine Empire.[1] The direction which had been taken since the seventh century was pursued still further and the final result presented a picture which sharply contrasted with the original Roman political system, which had been the point of departure.

The organization of the theme system had been brought to a conclusion by the end of the ninth and the beginning of the tenth centuries. As a result of the gradual division of the original large themes into smaller ones and the introduction of the theme system in other regions, the number of themes had considerably increased. At the same time a significant simplification of the civil administration of the provinces took place. Since the themes of the ninth century were scarcely any larger than the old provinces, the theme proconsulate became merged with the provincial governorship. During the second half of the ninth century the office of theme proconsul was also abolished, and with it disappeared the last remnant of the organization of Diocletian and Constantine. The πρωτονοτάριοι of the themes, the former directors of the proconsular chancery, now replaced the ἀνθύπατοι as the heads of the civil administration.[2] As a result, the superiority of the military power, the *strategus*, became all the more apparent. In place of the many variations which were to be found in the organization of the themes in the previous centuries there now emerged a highly unified system. The different military zones of lesser rank, the clisurarchies, archontates, duchies, catepanates, and drungariates, which had existed side by side with the theme unit properly speaking, were increasingly given the rank of theme.[3] Thus the picture presented by the theme divisions at the beginning of the tenth century was as follows: in Asia there were the themes of Opsikion, Bucellarion, Optimaton, Paphlagonia, Armeniakon, Chaldia, Colonea, Charsianon, Anatolikon, Thracesion, Cappadocia, Mesopotamia, Sebastea, Lycandus, Leontocomis, Seleucia,[4] and the maritime theme

---

[1] Cf. Bury, *Admin. System*; Bréhier, *Institutions* 121 ff.; W. Ensslin, 'The Emperor and the Imperial Administration', Baynes–Moss, *Byzantium* (1949), 268 ff.

[2] Cf. the important comments of Stein, 'Ein Kapitel' 70 ff.

[3] On the military zones of lesser rank and their significance in the earlier theme organization cf. the excellent treatment by J. Ferluga, 'Niže vojno-administrativne jedinice tematskog uredjenja' (The military and administrative theme units of lesser rank), *Zbornik radova Viz. Inst.* 2 (1953), 61 ff. (English résumé).

[4] The themes of Mesopotamia, Lycandus, Sebastea, Leontocomis, and Seleucia are still not mentioned in the *Cletorologion* of Philotheus, but they do appear as themes in both the *Tacticon Benešivič* and the *De Thematibus* of Constantine VII (where however Leontocomis is missing, as are also Charsianon, Cappadocia and Dalmatia, for no apparent reason). Mesopotamia is found with the rank of theme in a list of the salaries

of the Cibyraeots; in the archipelago, the themes of Samos and the Aegean Sea (Aigaion Pelagos); in Europe, Thrace, Macedonia, Strymon, Thessalonica, Hellas, Peloponnese, Cephalonia, Nicopolis, Dyrrachium, Dalmatia, Sicily, Longobardia and Cherson.[1] The theme organization was to undergo further changes, particularly as the result of the creation of fresh themes in districts newly annexed to the Empire by conquest, although the foundation of new themes in older territory was by now a very rare event. It was only the decay of the Byzantine political order that brought about, from the end of the eleventh century, a further fragmentation of the theme units.[2]

In considering the Byzantine bureaucratic machinery, the information given by Philotheus and the closely related lists of officials of the ninth and tenth centuries[3] are our sources for this period, and a sharp distinction must be made between genuine offices and honorary titles. The distinction is outwardly expressed by the fact that offices are conferred by drawing a deed of appointment (διὰ λόγου) whilst titles are bestowed by investiture with insignia (διὰ βραβείων). For the most part, the titles are nothing but former offices which have lost their earlier significance with the course of time and retain only their titular character. In this connection it must always be borne in mind that the lists of officials of the ninth and tenth centuries show us the Byzantine bureaucratic structure as it was at one definite period, and that it is only for this period that they can be used without reservation as contemporary sources, though this period, admittedly, happened to coincide with the great age of Byzantium's existence as a state. For, in contrast with the idea once widely held concerning its alleged rigidity, the Byzantine state, and with it the Byzantine governmental machine, underwent a continuous process of reconstruction.

According to the *Cletorologion* of Philotheus, Byzantine titles were graded into eighteen ranks, of which the three highest honours (Caesar, *nobilissimus* and *curopalates*) were in fact relatively seldom

payable to *strategi* of themes, drawn up about 908–10, which appears in the *De cerimoniis* (697, 3), while the four other zones still appear as *kleisurai*. For this salary list and the date of its compilation cf. J. Ferluga, 'Prilog datiranju Platnog spiska stratega iz De caerimoniis' (Further comments on the dating of the salary list of *strategi* from the *De cerimoniis*), ZRVI 4 (1956), 63 ff.

[1] The theme of Cyprus mentioned in the *De thematibus* in reality only existed for a short time under Basil I and then fell once again into the hands of the Arabs (cf. p. 238 above).

[2] Cf. Stein, 'Untersuchungen' 19 ff.

[3] See above, p. 215, under Sources.

bestowed, and then normally only on members of the imperial family.[1] These were followed by the *ʒoste patricia*, the highest court dignity for women,[2] and then by the *magistri, anthypati, patricii, protospatharii, dishypati, spatharocandidati, spatharii, hypati* and so on. Eight honorary titles, which begin with the *patricius*, but which for the most part have names of their own, are reserved for the eunuchs, and the patrician eunuchs in fact occupied a position superior to that of the other patricians and *anthypati*. The eunuchs played an important part at the Byzantine court. No office, however high, in Church and State (with the single exception of the imperial dignity itself) was withheld from the eunuchs on principle, and many of the patriarchs, statesmen and generals who distinguished themselves in Byzantine history were eunuchs. There were, however, a number of court offices which were normally, though not without exception, held by eunuchs. The most important of these were the office of the *paracoemomenus*, who slept near the imperial bed-chamber and who was usually one of the Emperor's most trusted confidants (under Michael III, however, this office had been held for a time by Basil the Macedonian), and the office of the *protovestarius*, the head of the imperial wardrobe.[3] Other officers with very important functions at court were the *rector*, one of the highest of the court officials, who first makes his appearance under the Macedonian dynasty,[4] the *proto-praepositus* or the Master of Ceremonies (ὁ ἐπὶ τῆς καταστάσεως), the imperial *protostrator*[5] or the chief Master of the Horse (κόμης τοῦ στάβλου) and many others.

Of particular eminence among the officials of the central government was the eparch of Constantinople whose task was to watch over all the life of the capital city, 'the father of the city', as he is

---

[1] On the title of Caesar cf. the careful investigations of R. Guilland, 'Études sur l'histoire administrative de l'Empire byzantin: le césarat', OCP 13 (1947), 168 ff.; see also R. Guilland, 'Et. sur l'hist. admin. de Byzance: Observation sur le Clétorologe de Philothée', REB 20 (1962), 159 ff.

[2] Cf. A. Vogt, 'La patricienne à ceinture', EO 37 (1938), 352 ff.; cf. H. E. Del Medico, 'Byzance avant Byzance: la Patricienne à ceinture', *Actes du VIᵉ Congrès International d'Études byzantines* I (1950), 73 ff.

[3] Cf. R. Guilland, 'Les eunuques dans l'Empire byzantin; EB 1 (1943) 196 ff.; idem, 2 (1944) 185 ff.; 3 (1945), 179 ff.; idem, 'Études de titulature byzantine: les titres auliques reservés aux eunuques', REB 13 (1955), 50 ff.; 14 (1956) 122 ff.; idem 'Études sur l'histoire administrative de l'Empire byzantin: les titres auliques des eunuques' B 25/27 (1955/57), 649 ff.

[4] R. Guilland, 'Études de titulature byzantine: le rectorat', *Mémorial L. Pétit* (1948), 185 ff.

[5] R. Guilland, 'Études de titulature et de prosopographie byzantines: le protostrator', REB 7 (1950), 156 ff.

described in the *Book of Ceremonies* of Constantine VII.[1] The office of logothete τοῦ Δρόμου, held under Theodora by Theoctistus and under Leo VI by Stylianus Zautzes, was of great and growing importance.[2] During this period the Logothete of the Drome was the real director of imperial policy; although the status of principal minister does not seem to have been linked automatically to a particular function. Quite apart from the office he held, the leading statesman, the chief adviser and counsellor of the Emperor, was the παραδυναστεύων, as he was often called in this period or even earlier. In the later period he was usually termed as the μεσάζων, or μεσιτεύων.[3] In view of the important place occupied by finance in the Byzantine state, it is scarcely surprising that the financial administration had a particularly large part in the bureaucratic organization. In the mid-Byzantine period there appeared the *sacellarius*, who controlled the whole corps of financial officials and who was supplanted in the twelfth century by the *megas logariastes*; the state treasury was managed by the *chartularius* τοῦ σακελλίου and the state store of provisions in kind by the *chartularius* τοῦ βεσταρίου.[4] From the seventh century, the logothetes τοῦ γενικοῦ, τοῦ στρατιωτικοῦ and τοῦ ἰδικοῦ acted as directors of the separate financial departments. The head of the imperial chancery (πρωτοασήκρητις),[5] the receiver of petitions (ὁ ἐπὶ τῶν Δεήσεων) and the imperial secretary (ὁ ἐπὶ τοῦ κανικλείου) all enjoyed great importance on account of their close proximity to the Emperor; the last of these offices was often united with that of the Logothete of the Drome, as it had already been in the case of Theoctistus.[6]

In the military organization there is a cardinal distinction to be made between the *themata* of the provinces and the *tagmata* (regiments) stationed in Constantinople. The soldiers of the *themata*, settled on the land, did in fact represent a peasant militia. The *tagmata* of the capital consisted of professional soldiers.[7] At the heads of the *themata* were the *strategi*, at once the commanders of the local

---

[1] De cerim. 264 and 528, πατὴρ πόλεως. Cf. F. Uspenskij, 'Konstantinopoljskij eparch', *Izv. Russk. Archeol. Inst. v K/le* 4 (1899), 90 ff.

[2] Bury, *Admin. System* 91 f.; Dölger, 'Kodikellos' 53 f. and *Finanzverwaltung* 22 f.

[3] Cf. H. G. Beck, 'Der byzantinische "Ministerpräsident",' BZ 48 (1955), 309 ff.; J. Verpeaux, 'Contribution a l'étude de l'administration byzantine: ὁ μεσάζων, BS 16 (1955), 270 ff.

[4] Cf. Dölger, *Finanzverwaltung* 24 f.   [5] Cf. Dölger, *Byz. Diplomatik*, 62 f.

[6] Cf. Dölger, *Byz. Diplomatik*, 50 ff.

[7] This has already been emphasized by Uspenskij, 'Voennoe ustrojstvo, 154 ff. Recently Glykatzi-Ahrweiler, *Recherches*, 2 ff., 24 ff., has clearly demonstrated this distinction in a detailed study.

forces and the governors of the local administration (the commander of the Opsikion, however, bore the title κόμης, while that of the Optimaton was usually called δομέστικος and was even classified by Philotheus with the *domestici* of the *tagmata*). At the head of the *tagmata* were the *domestici*. The most important were the four *tagmata* of the *scholae*, the *excubitores*, the *arithmus* (whose commander was called *drungarius* instead of *domesticus*) and the *hikanatai* (first created under Nicephorus I). The *domesticus* of the *scholae* often appears as the commander-in-chief of the whole army. As the military tasks of the Empire increased in complexity, the office was divided, and from the second half of the tenth century at latest, there was normally one *domesticus* for the East and another for the West.[1] As regards the navy, a distinction must be made between the imperial fleet, commanded by the δρουγγάριος τῶν πλοΐμων, and the levy from the maritime themes, which were under the local *strategi*.[2] It is striking that in the ninth century and even in the twenties of the tenth century the *drungarius* of the imperial fleet occupied a lower rank than all the *strategi* of the themes. But by the middle of the tenth century he had already become, next to the *domesticus* of the *scholae*, the most important military official of the Empire, a clear indication of the growing importance of the navy.[3] Other imperial officials, though relatively low-ranking, were the demarchs of the two parties, the Greens and the Blues: the once so mighty demes had now lost their political importance and now played a purely decorative role at the imperial court, assisting on ceremonial occasions and acclaiming the ruler.

The list of offices of Philotheus gives altogether sixty leading officials of the military, civil and court administration who were directly responsible to the Emperor and apart from the Emperor had no superior (there were in addition eight 'eunuch offices' which Philotheus classifies separately). The majority of these dignitaries were in charge of numerous offices which were provided with staffs of varying size. The whole rigidly centralized machine was directed by the Emperor, who personally appointed all the leading officials

[1] Cf. R. Guilland, 'Etudes sur l'histoire administrative de Byzance: le Domestique des Scholes', REB 8 (1950), 5 ff.; Glykatzi-Ahrweiler, *Recherches*, 26 and 55 ff.

[2] Cf. R. Guilland, 'Études de titulature et de prosopographie byzantines. Les chefs de la marine byzantine', BZ 44 (1951) (*Dölger-Festschrift*), 212 ff.

[3] Cf. on the one hand the *Taticon Uspenskij*, the *Cletorologion* of Philotheus and the *Taticon Beneševič*, (Beneševič, 'Ranglisten' 124–5), and on the other hand Liutprand, *Antapodosis* VI 10.

and also their chief underlings, and who could dismiss any of them at will.

In later times the Byzantine bureaucratic hierarchy became still more complicated: new institutions and offices were created, whilst the older ones fell into decay or altered in importance. A pronounced feature of the administrative organization of the middle Byzantine period is the strong preponderance of military offices and the outstanding position of the theme *strategi*. The exceedingly important office of city eparch is placed eighteenth in the list of Philotheus, and ranks after twelve theme *strategi* and the *domestici* of the *scholae* and the *excubitores*.[1] Moreover, all the twenty-five theme *strategi* of that period rank above the *sacellarius* and the logothetes, only the *domesticus* of the Optimaton having a lower degree. Among the *strategi* themselves, it is significant that the commanders of the themes of Asia Minor, the backbone of the military power of the Empire, have the highest place: almost all the theme *strategi* of Asia Minor have a higher rank than the *strategi* of Macedonia and Thrace, the two most important European commanders. This is to some extent also shown in the salaries drawn by the theme *strategi*. Thus, under Leo VI the *strategi* of the Anatolikon, Armeniakon and Thracesion themes each received forty gold pounds (measured by the value of the metal, 4438.40 gold francs), those of Opsikion, Bucellarion and Macedonia thirty pounds each, those of Cappadocia, Charsianon, Paphlagonia, Thrace and Colonea twenty pounds each and the others ten or five pounds each.[2] But there was no very rigid distinction between the different categories of officials and their functions, with the result that it was not unusual for an individual serving in a civilian office to change over to a military one, or for an army command to be given to a civilian or even to a court official. The deciding factor was always the will of the Emperor and the confidence he felt in the individual concerned.

[1] The *strategus* of the Anatolikon theme was followed by the *domesticus* of the *scholae*, the *strategus* of the Armeniakon theme and then the rest of the *strategi*, and according to Philotheus only three officials took precedence of him, and they were, in ascending order, the *syncellus* of the Patriarch of Constantinople, the rector, and the *basileopator* (a title created by Leo VI for his father-in-law Stylianus which should really not have been included in the list of offices).

[2] *De cerim.* 696 f. In comparison it should be noted that according to Liutprand (*Antip.* VI, 10) in the mid-tenth century officials holding the title of patrician each received 12 pounds of gold and a ceremonial robe, the *magistri* 24 pounds of gold and 2 robes, the rector, the *domesticus* of the *scholae* and the *drungarius* of the imperial fleet each 48 pounds and 4 robes (on the honorarium of the last three cf. Stein, BZ 24 (1924), 385 and note 1).

The autocratic centralization of the Byzantine state also conferred its distinctive stamp on urban life and economy. All the economic activity of the Byzantine capital was controlled by the eparch of Constantinople and, as is shown by the so-called *Book of the Eparch*, in the tenth century, when the executive power of the State was at its height, this control was far-reaching in the extreme.[1] The traders and merchants of Constantinople, and probably also of the other cities, were organized into guilds. Particular importance was attached to the guilds who were engaged in supplying provisions in the capital: the cattle traders, butchers, fishmongers, bakers and innkeepers. The flourishing trade in wax, ointments and spices was carried on by the guilds of ointment merchants, soap merchants and soap-makers, candle-makers and spice merchants. As a result of the outstanding importance of the silk trade in Byzantium, a particularly large number of guilds were concerned with the manufacture and trading of silken goods, whose activities were more markedly specialized than those of other industries, showing a clear distinction between producers and traders: the silk twisters, the silk weavers and dyers in purple, the dealers in raw silk, the dealers in Syrian silks and finally the dealers in silken clothing, all had their own guilds. The linen-drapers and leather workers also formed special corporations. But there can be no doubt that the *Book of the Eparch*, of which there is no final systematically arranged version, deals with only some of the guilds which actually existed at Constantinople. The fact that even notaries, money-changers and goldsmiths were

[1] On the origin of the *Book of the Eparch* cf. above, p. 215f., under Sources. Valuable research on this has been done by Stöckle, *Zünfte*; and Christophilopulos, Ἐπαρχικὸν βιβλίον, and Mickwitz, *Zünfte* 205 ff. are important, as well as the comments of Černousov, ZMNP 1914 Sept., 154 ff., and Kubitschek, *Num. Zeitschr.* 44 (1911), 185 ff. In particular cf. also the important discussions by M. J. Sjuzjumov, *Kniga Eparcha* (The Book of the Eparch), Sverdlovsk 1949 and Moscow 1962, and 'Remeslo i torgovlja v Konstantinopole v načale X v.' (Crafts and trade in Constantinople at the beginning of the tenth century), VV 4 (1951), 11 ff. and A. P. Každan, 'Cechi i gosudarstvennye masterskie v Konstantinopole v. IX–X vv.' (Guilds and state stores in Constantinople in the ninth and tenth centuries), VV 6 (1953), 132 ff., and *Derevnja i gorod* 301 ff. Cf. also Nicole's commentary on the text (1893) and the French trans. (1894); Freshfield's brief commentary to the English trans. (1938); Zachariä, BZ 2 (1893), 132 ff. and 177; L. M. Hartmann, *Zeitschr. f. Sozial- u. Wirtschaftsgesch.* 3 (1894) and *Analekten zur Wirtschaftsgesch. Italiens im frühen Mittelalter* (1904), 16 ff.; F. Uspenskij, 'Konstantinopolskij eparch', *Izv. Russk. Archeol. Inst. v K/le* 4 (1899), 90 ff.; Gehrig, *Jahrb. f. Nationalökonomie u. Statistik* 38 (1909), 577 ff.; Waltzing, *Études hist. sur les corporations* II (1896), 347 ff.; Kornemann, PW IV (1901), 478 f.; Vogt, *Basile I*, 139 ff. and 389 ff.; G. Marzemini, *Atti del R. Istit. Veneto di scienze, lettere ed arti* 94 (1934–5), 381 ff.; Mickwitz, BZ 36 (1936). The books of Christo Macri, *L'organisation de l'économie urbaine dans Byzance* (1925), and G. Zoras, *Le corporazioni bizantini* (1931), seem to me to be unsatisfactory.

organized in special corporations shows how far-reaching the Byzantine guild system really was.

The Byzantine corporations are genetically related to the Roman *collegia*,[1] but differ from these in many respects and resemble typical medieval guild organizations.[2] Thus in the Byzantine period the individual was not so strictly bound to his calling as had been the case in Roman times. Membership of a guild was no longer hereditary, it was no longer compulsory for citizens to belong to a guild, and entry into a guild was linked rather to certain conditions and depended on ability to prove an aptitude for the craft. This, however, meant that the state had stronger control. For if, as a result of the changed conditions of the Byzantine period, individuals were no longer so closely tied to their calling, their connection with the state, by contrast, had become all the stronger. Not only were the guilds required by the state to perform services, as they had been in Roman times, but also their whole activity was carefully supervised and scrupulously regulated through the channel of the city eparch. Particular attention was devoted to the actions of those guilds on which the capital was dependent for provisions. To ensure that the capital city had adequate supplies, the government regulated the amount of goods to be bought, supervised their quality and fixed a buying and market price. Imports to Constantinople both from the provinces and from foreign countries were vigorously encouraged, while exports, on the other hand, were strictly limited.[3] The principal object of the guild organization was not indeed to serve the interests of the producers and dealers, but rather to facilitate control of economic life by the government in the interests of the state and the consumer.[4] The state appointed the heads of the guilds and employed officials who were especially concerned with their affairs; the government, in fact, in this way controlled the entire economy of the city and the economic processes which took place within it.

The legislation of Leo VI reflects not only the establishment of imperial omnipotence, but also the growing strength of the Byzantine aristocracy, a process which in its later stages was to shake the

---

[1] This is particularly stressed by Stöckle, *Zünfte*, 135 ff., L. M. Hartmann, *Analekten* 16 ff., S. P. Waltzing, op. cit. 347 f., and E. Kornemann, PW IV, 478.

[2] See H. Gehrig, op. cit. 592 ff.; A. P. Každan, VV 6 (1953), 143 ff. and *Derevnja i gorod*, 305 ff.

[3] Cf. M. J. Sjuzjumov, VV 4 (1951), 33 ff.; A. P. Každan *Derevnja i gorod*, 291 ff.

[4] Mickwitz, *Zünfte* 206 ff., who stresses the economic advantages of the guild organization for its own members, disagrees with this.

absolutism of the Emperor and undermine the whole edifice of the state. The beginnings of this development reach back into the eighth century, for by that time a number of dynasties of magnates had already made their appearance. But by the time of Leo VI, the aristocracy already possessed such power, and had already advanced so far towards becoming a class apart, having enforced acceptance of their privileges, that the *Tactica* of Leo VI expressly recommend that the office of *strategus* and the higher commissions should be given only to persons of rank and wealth.[1] An increasingly marked social differentiation thus made itself felt, so much so that even the imperial government had to take it into account. The danger this represented to the life of the state went unrecognized by Leo's administration, which even gave assistance to aristocratic ambitions in the economic sphere. The old restriction which prohibited officials during their term of office from purchasing goods or receiving legacies and gifts without the especial permission of the Emperor,[2] was raised by Leo VI in respect of the officials of Constantinople, although it was merely relaxed in the case of provincial officials, and was retained for the theme *strategi*.[3] A later novel of Leo VI also revoked the right of pre-emption (προτίμησις) of neighbours, which was hindering the alienation of peasant lands to the landlord: the neighbours were to have a right of eviction against payment of the purchase price for only six months.[4] As a result of these dispositions, it became much easier for the aristocracy to acquire peasant land, which in its turn meant a further strengthening of the landed aristocracy and an acceleration of the trend towards feudalism, against which the successors of Leo VI were to face so desperate a struggle.

Unlike Basil I, Leo VI had no clear programme of foreign policy. His reign is also distinguished from that of his father by the fact that it was no longer possible to limit action to the war against the Arabs, a difference which was to be to the disadvantage of the Empire. Following a long period of peace, there was a crisis in the relations

---

[1] *Tactica Leonis* II, 21 (Vari I, p. 29), προχειριζέσθω μὲν στρατηγὸς, ἀγαθός, εὐγενής, πλούσιος . . . IV, 3 (Vari I, p. 50), καὶ εὐπορωτάτους αὐτοὺς εἶναι καὶ εὐγενεῖς κατά τε τὸ γένος . . . Cf. the important comments on this by M. Mitard, 'Le pouvoir impérial au temps de Léon VI le Sage', *Mélanges Diehl* I (1930), 215 ff.

[2] *Cod. Just.* I, 53, 1, of the year 158.

[3] *Nov.* 84 (Zepos, *Jus* I, pp. 152 f.).

[4] *Nov.* 114 (Zepos, *Jus* I, pp. 186 f.). Dölger, *Reg.* 558. Zachariä's doubts (*Geschichte* 239) about the validity of this novel are unfounded.

between Byzantium and the Bulgars. After the abdication of the
first Christian Bulgar ruler, Boris-Michael (889), and after his elder
son Vladimir had been the victim of an attempted return to paganism
(893), power fell into the hands of Boris' younger son, Symeon
(893–927), who was to become the greatest ruler of the medieval
Bulgar kingdom. Soon after his accession a quarrel broke out
between Bulgaria and Byzantium; the background of this quarrel,
significantly enough, was provided by commercial policy.[1] Two
Byzantine merchants had been given the monopoly of the Bulgar
trade. With the consent of Stylianus Zautzes, they had removed the
Bulgarian market from Constantinople to Thessalonica and very
much increased the duty. This seemed prejudicial to Bulgarian
commercial interests, and since Bulgarian protests remained without
effect, Symeon invaded imperial territory and attacked the Byzantine
army (894).[2] Byzantium, whose fighting resources in the Balkans
were inadequate, tried to meet the danger by a diplomatic chess
move: a call for help was sent to the Magyars, who then occupied
the region between the Dnieper and the Danube.

This Byzantine appeal allowed the Magyars for the first time to
make an active intervention in the politics of the European states.
Obeying the call from Byzantium, the Magyars attacked Symeon in
the rear, inflicted on him a number of defeats and laid waste the
northern Bulgarian territories. Meanwhile, Nicephorus Phocas, the
Byzantine general, occupied the southern borders of Bulgaria and
Eustathius, the *drungarius* of the imperial fleet, blockaded the mouth
of the Danube. Symeon concluded an armistice with Byzantium.
He thereby gained time, and, since the Byzantine Emperor had
turned to the Magyars, Symeon himself now turned to a warlike
nomadic people, the Patzinaks, from the plains of southern Russia.
With their help he was able to overcome the Magyars and then to
fall again on the Byzantines, over whom he gained a decisive victory
at Bulgarophygon (896). Peace was then made and Byzantium was
obliged to pay annual tribute to the Bulgar kingdom. Under Patzinak
pressure the Magyars moved westwards and settled in their present-
day home in the Danube plain, thus driving a wedge through the

[1] Cf. G. J. Bratianu, 'Le commerce bulgare dans l'Empire byzantin et le monopole de
l'empereur Léon VI à Thessalonique', *Sbornik Nikov* (1940), 30 ff.
[2] The chronology of this war is based on the convincing account of Zlatarski, *Izvestijata* 88 ff. Cf. also G. Kolias, *Léon Choerosphactès* (1939), 23 ff.

middle of Slav territory, separating the southern Slavs from their tribal fellows in the north and east.[1]

Byzantine strength *vis-à-vis* the Arabs was also enfeebled, both in the East and the West, as a result of the war with Symeon. Nicephorus Phocas had to interrupt his successful campaigns in South Italy to take over the Balkan command.[2] In the East, Armenia was delivered up to Arab plunderers, and the Arabs began an advance into Cilicia, accompanied by widely ranging naval operations off the south coasts of Asia Minor. On the mainland of Asia Minor, however, the Byzantine position was strengthened about 900, after Nicephorus Phocas the Elder, as *strategus* of the Thracesion theme, had led an expeditition into the Cilician passes and won a victory over the Arabs near Adana. But in the West and at sea the Empire met with one catastrophe after another. Taormina, the last Byzantine stronghold in Sicily, fell on 1 August 902, and with it Sicily was also effectually lost, after seventy-five years of bitter fighting in which so much had been sacrificed. But in the East the Arabs controlled not only the Mediterranean but also the Aegean, surrounded by Byzantine territories. Both the archipelago and the coast of the Peloponnese and Thessaly were intermittently laid waste, and in 902 the wealthy town of Demetrias on the coast of Thessaly was destroyed.[3] But particularly momentous was the great expedition of 904, led by the Greek renegade, Leo of Tripoli. At first Leo of Tripoli turned towards Constantinople. After the capture of Abydus, however, which opened up the way to the Byzantine capital, he suddenly changed his plans and descended on Thessalonica. This great centre of cultural and commercial activity, after Constantinople the most important and wealthiest city of the

[1] On the origin, early history and migration of the Magyars from the mouth of the Volga to their new home cf. Gy. Moravcsik, 'Zur Geschichte der Onoguren', *Ungar. Jahrb.* 10 (1930), 53 ff.; C. A. Macartney, *The Magyars in the Ninth Century*, Cambridge 1930. Cf. also H. Grégoire, 'Le nom et l'origine des Hongrois', *Zeitschr. d. Deutschen Morgenl. Ges.* 91 (1937), 630 ff. See also the bibliography, complete as always, in Moravcsik, *Byzantinoturcica*, I, 134 ff.

[2] Vasiliev, *Vizantija Araby* II (1902), 114, and CMH IV, 140 ff., take the view that Nicephorus Phocas was only recalled from Italy about 900. This is incorrect since all the sources agree that during the Bulgarian war of 894 Nicephorus Phocas commanded the Byzantine army as *domesticus* of the *scholae* (cf. Zlatarski, *Izvestijata*). At the instigation of Stylianus Zautzes he was shortly afterwards relieved of this office and replaced by Leo Catacalon who was in command of the Bulgarian war in 896; cf. Grumel, 'Chronologie' 24 ff., and H. Grégoire, 'La carrière du premier Nicéphore Phocas', Προσφορὰ εἰς Στ. Π. Κυριακίδην (1953), 237 ff., where the biography of the great general is reconstructed and the accounts previously given are corrected on several points.

[3] On the chronology cf. Grumel, 'Chronologie' 34 ff., as against H. Grégoire, B 5 (1930), 394 ff., who supports the year 897.

Empire, fell into Arab hands on 31 July 904, after a three-day siege.[1] The victors staged a horrible blood-bath, and then withdrew, taking with them many prisoners and a vast quantity of booty. Symeon made good use of the Byzantine defeat: Byzantium was forced to agree to a readjustment of the frontiers, as a result of which the Bulgarian boundary reached almost up to Thessalonica.[2]

Made wiser by such heavy blows of fate, the Byzantine government now caused stronger fortifications to be erected at Thessalonica and Attaleia, and took energetic measures to reinforce the fleet. The result soon showed itself: in October 905 Himerius, the Logothete of the Drome, won a brilliant victory over the Arab fleet in the Aegean Sea.[3] Some years later he made a landing in Cyprus, and from here he turned against the Syrian coast and stormed Laodicea. But the greatest naval expedition took place in 911.[4] An exceptionally strong fleet was fitted out and was led by this same Himerius against Crete. Here he met with a serious disaster. After a long and unsuccessful fight the imperial fleet had to withdraw. On its way back it was attacked in the spring of 912 off Chios by an Arab squadron led by Leo of Tripoli and Damian, another Greek renegade, and suffered a crushing defeat. Thus the grand expedition foundered: the extraordinary military and financial exertions of the Empire had a wholly negative result.

The detailed description of this expedition given in the *Book of Ceremonies* of Constantine VII mentions that the Byzantine forces included seven hundred Russian sailors, who had to be rewarded with a *kentenarion* of gold. The participation of Russians in a Byzantine campaign was a consequence of the new relationship between

---

[1] Until recently on the evidence of Tabari it was generally accepted that the Arab expedition of 904 began with the siege of Attaleia. But H. Grégoire, 'Le communiqué arabe sur la prise de Thessalonique', B 22 (1952), 375 ff., shows that the account of Tabari really refers to the attack on Thessalonica and not to an attack on Attaleia of which the Byzantine sources make no mention.

[2] This is shown by an inscription on boundary stones of the year 6412 (= 904) which have been found near the village of Narysch-Kaj about 20 km. from Thessalonica; cf. F. Uspenskij, *Izv. Russk. Archeol. Inst. v Konstantinopole* 3 (1898), 184 ff. There is not the slightest doubt about the authenticity of this inscription, as is admirably shown by M. Lascaris, 'Les sources épigraphiques de la légende d'Oleg', *Mélanges Grégoire* III (1951) 213 ff. (as the author himself emphasizes, this inscription has nothing to do with the Russian prince Oleg); reprinted in M. Lascaris, *Deux notes sur le règne de Syméon de Bulgarie*, Wetteren 1952, 5 ff.

[3] R. J. H. Jenkins, 'Leo Choerosphactes and the Saracen Vizier', ZRVI 8 1 (1963) 167 ff. shows that the victory of the Logothete Himerius over the Arab fleet took place on 6 October 905 and not in 908 as previously thought.

[4] On what follows cf. R. J. H. Jenkins, 'The Date of Leo VI's Cretan Expedition', Προσφρὰ εἰς Στ. Κυριακίδην (1953), 277 ff.

Byzantium and Russia.[1] The Russian prince Oleg, who had established himself in Kiev and had secured for himself 'the route which led from the Varangians to the Greeks', appeared in 907 before Constantinople with a large fleet and extracted from the Byzantine government a treaty, which guaranteed the legal position of merchants coming from Russia to Byzantium. This treaty, officially ratified in September 911, marked the beginning of regular trading relations between Byzantium and the young Russian kingdom. Amongst other things, it also afforded the Russians the right to take part in imperial campaigns.[2]

In addition to these failures of foreign policy, there were internal complications, arising from Leo VI's four marriages. His youthful marriage with Theophano, into which he had entered at the wish of Basil I, was not a happy one. After the death of the pious Empress (10 November 897)—she is venerated as a saint by the Greek Church —Leo married early in 898 Zoe, his mistress, the daughter of Stylianus Zautzes.[3] Zoe, however, died at the end of 899 without leaving any male issue, and in the summer of 900 the Emperor took a third wife, Eudocia Baiana, a Phrygian. This was an open breach of the rules of both Church and State, and the situation was made all the worse by the fact that a few years previously Leo VI had himself strengthened the prohibition against third marriages by a special law and had even disapproved of the conclusion of a second marriage.[4] But misfortune dogged the Emperor: Eudocia Baiana soon died, on 12 April 901, and Leo, once again a widower, soon began to occupy himself with plans for a fourth marriage, for which purpose his eye had fallen on the beautiful Zoe Carbonopsina. Since his third marriage had already provoked a conflict with the Church, and his new plans now encountered stiff general opposition, the Emperor would probably have decided against a further and even

---

[1] Cf. the judicious comments of Vasiliev, *Vizantija i Araby* II, 167 ff.

[2] *Polnoe Sobranie Russk. Letopisej* I, 2 (1926), 30 ff. German trans. by Trautmann, *Die Nestor-Chronik* (1931), 19 ff.; English trans. by Cross, *The Russian Primary Chronicle* (1953), 65 ff. Doubts concerning the historicity of Oleg's expedition to Constantinople have frequently been expressed; cf. especially H. Grégoire, 'La légende d'Oleg et l'expédition d'Igor', *Bull. de l'Acad. de Belg.* 23 (1937), 80 ff., R. H. Dolley, 'Oleg's mythical campaign against Constantinople', ibid. 35 (1949), 106 ff., and again Grégoire, 'L'histoire et la légende d'Oleg, prince de Kiev', *Nouv. Clio* 4 (1952), 281 ff. I had already shown ('L'expédition du prince Oleg contre Constantinople en 907', *Annales de l'Inst. Kond.* 11 (1939), 47 ff., 296 ff.) that these doubts are entirely without foundation. This has recently been demonstrated again in a detailed study by A. A. Vasiliev, 'The Second Russian Attack on Constantinople', *Dumbarton Oaks Papers* 6 (1951), 161–225. Cf. also R. J. H. Jenkins, 'The supposed Russian attack on Constantinople in 907: Evidence of the Pseudo-Symeon', *Speculum* 24 (1949), 403 ff.

[3] Cf. Grumel, 'Chronologie' 5 ff.   [4] *Nov.* 90 (Zepos, *Jus* I, 156 f.).

more serious violation of the canons of the Church and of the laws. But in 905 Zoe Carbonopsina bore him a son, and it was now important to legalize the birth of the heir to the throne. On 6 January 906 the baby was baptized in Hagia Sophia by the Patriarch Nicholas Mysticus and given the name Constantine, but on condition that the Emperor separated from Zoe. Notwithstanding, three days later Leo married the mother of his only son and raised her to the dignity of Augusta. This action raised a storm of angry indignation on all sides. The tension between the Emperor and the Church leaders increased steadily. The Patriarch forbade the Emperor to enter a church: at Christmas 906 and on the Feast of the Epiphany 907 the Byzantine Basileus was forced to turn back from the very doors of Hagia Sophia. But the path which had always been taken by Byzantine Emperors who needed support against their own Church still remained open: Leo turned to Rome and received a dispensation from Pope Sergius III. One reason for this was that the Roman marriage regulations were less strict than the Byzantine; another, and all-important, reason was that the Pope could scarcely repulse an Emperor who appealed to him over the head of his own Patriarch and thereby acknowledged papal supremacy. With the papal vote in his favour, Leo was able to compel the resignation of Nicholas Mysticus and put in his place the both devout and simple-minded Euthymius (February 907).[1] But this only provoked fresh dissensions within the Byzantine Church, which gave nourishment to the older quarrels.[2] Leo VI had realized his intentions, his son was crowned Emperor on 15 May 908,[3] and thus, with toil and trouble, the continuance of the dynasty was ensured. Meanwhile, the strife aroused by the temporary deposition of the Patriarch was by no means composed, but was in fact to outlast the reign of Leo VI and be finally decided in favour of the Patriarch.

3. BYZANTIUM AND SYMEON OF BULGARIA

General bibliography: Zlatarski, *Istorija* I, 2; Runciman, *Bulgarian Empire*; D. Obolensky, 'Byzantium and its northern neighbours 565–1018', CMH IV, Pt I (2nd ed. 1966); Mutafčiev, *Istorija* I; F. Dölger, 'Bulgarisches Zartum und byzantinisches Kaisertum', *Bulletin de l'Inst. archéol. bulgare* 9

[1] Grumel, 'Chronologie' 8 ff.   [2] Cf. Dvornik, *Photian Schism* 275 ff.
[3] P. Grierson and R. J. H. Jenkins, 'The Date of Constantine VII's Coronation', B 32 (1962), 133 ff., show that Constantine Porphyrogenitus was probably crowned on 15 May 908 (and not on 9 June 911 as previously supposed).

(1935), 57 ff. (reprinted in Dölger, *Byzanz* 140 ff.); G. Ostrogorsky, 'Die Krönung Symeons von Bulgarien durch den Patriarchen Nikolaos Mystikos', ibid. 275 ff.

Leo VI died on 12 May 912. The government passed into the hands of the frivolous and pleasure-seeking Alexander, the uncle of the six year old Constantine.[1] His main desire was to disembarrass himself of the inheritance of his dead brother. He had the Empress Zoe enclosed in a nunnery and also deprived of their offices the most important of Leo's advisers, replacing them by his own men. But this policy also entailed the recall of Nicholas Mysticus, in whose favour Euthymius had to vacate the patriarchal throne.[2] The behaviour of the new ruler had a particularly momentous effect on external affairs. Irresponsible as he was, he withheld from the Bulgars the annual payments Byzantium was obliged to make under the peace treaty of 896. By this means he gave Symeon, whose power was steadily increasing, the pretext he desired for re-opening the war. No greater misfortune could have befallen the Empire. Soon after the outbreak of the war he had provoked, Alexander died on 6 June 913.[3] The only surviving representative of the Macedonian dynasty, Constantine, was now seven years old and the conduct of affairs fell to a council of regency, with the Patriarch Nicholas Mysticus at its head.

The situation was both complicated and precarious. Faced with a strong opposition, composed of the elements most loyal to the dynasty and centring in the person of Zoe, the widow of the Emperor, and regarded with hostility by a section of the clergy who remained faithful to the deposed Euthymius, Nicholas Mysticus had to act as regent for a child whom he could regard as neither legitimate nor

[1] To express his satisfaction at finally becoming senior Emperor after being co-Emperor for thirty-three years Alexander even styled himself in his coins as αὐτοκράτωρ πιστὸς εὐσεβὴς βασιλεὺς ʻΡωμαίων; cf. Mušmov, B 6 (1931), 99 f. Both this informative legend on the coinage—the oldest known use of the title 'autocrator' on coins—and all the literary evidence serve to refute Spulber, *Les Novelles de Léon le Sage* (1934), 47, note 1, who maintains that Alexander was never senior Emperor but only ruled in the name of Constantine VII.

[2] Runciman, *Romanus Lecapenus* 45, is rightly suspicious of the assertion of Nicholas Mysticus (Migne, PG 111, 217) that Leo VI had penitently recalled him to the patriarchal throne. This is not supported by Byzantine chroniclers who on the contrary refer to his reinstatement as the first act of Alexander; cf. Sym. Log., Georg. Mon. cont. 871.

[3] According to A. P. Každan, 'K voprosu o načale vtoroj bolgaro-vizantijskoj vojny pri Simeone' (On the question of the beginning of the second war between the Bulgars and Byzantium under Symeon), *Slavjanskij Arhiv*, Moscow 1959, 23 ff., the war with Symeon did not begin after the death of Alexander, as was argued by Zlatarski, *Istorija* I 2, 358 ff., and 'Pervyj pochod bolgarskogo carja Simeona na Konstantinopol' (The first campaign of the Bulgarian tzar Symeon against Constantinople), *Recueil Kondakov*, Prague 1926, 19 ff., but, apparently, while he was still alive.

legally entitled to the crown. The confusion was further increased by an attempt at usurpation on the part of the supreme commander, Constantine Ducas, *domesticus* of the *scholae*. It was in this situation that the disastrous war with the powerful Bulgar ruler, provoked by Alexander, was begun. Without encountering any opposition, Symeon drove through Byzantine territory and soon, in August 913, appeared beneath the walls of the Byzantine capital. Moreover, this was no mere plundering expedition nor even simply a campaign for the sake of conquests: Symeon's real objective was the imperial crown. As the tutelary of Byzantium, Symeon was deeply impressed by the grandeur of the imperial office, and knew fully as well as the Byzantines did themselves that there could be only one temporal Empire. His ambition was not the foundation of a national Bulgarian empire, confined within territorial limits and existing side by side with the Byzantine Empire, but the creation of a new universal Empire which would take the place of Byzantium.[1] It was this ambition which gave to the conflict between Symeon and Byzantium its particular character, raising it above the perpetual state of flux which always marked the warlike relations of the Byzantine state with its unruly neighbours and which made the struggle one of the severest tests which the Byzantine Empire ever had to face. The struggle for the imperial dignity is the medieval equivalent of the struggle for the hegemony. Symeon imposed on Byzantium the necessity of defending the position of the Empire as first in the hierarchy of the Christian states.

But if Symeon differed radically in his intentions from the former enemies of the Empire who had appeared before the gates of Constantinople, he nevertheless shared their fate at least in this, that he had soon to acknowledge the impregnability of the strongest fortification of his time. He entered into negotiations with the Byzantine government and was admitted with great ceremony into the imperial city, to be received by the Patriarch Nicholas Mysticus in the presence of the young Emperor Constantine VII. The parley between Symeon and the intimidated regency government resulted in unprecedented concessions. In fact, the regency completely capitulated before the powerful Bulgar ruler. One of his daughters was to become the wife of the youthful Emperor Constantine VII whilst

[1] Cf. Dölger, 'Bulgarisches Zartum und byzantisches Kaisertum', *Bull. de l'Inst. archéol. bulgare* 9 (1935), 57 ff. (reprinted in Dölger, *Byzanz* 140 ff.); Ostrogorsky, 'Avtokrator' 121 ff., and 'Die byzantinische Staatenhierarchie', *Sem. Kond.* 8 (1936), 45. Cf. also Dölger, 'Der Bulgarenherrscher als geistlicher Sohn des byzantinischen Kaisers' *Sbornik Nikov* 1940, 219 ff. (reprinted in Dölger, *Byzanz* 183 ff.).

he himself was crowned Emperor at the hands of the Patriarch.[1] Although this meant that Symeon was recognized only as Basileus of Bulgaria and not as the co-Emperor of Constantine VII, his goal, nevertheless, must have seemed not far distant: dignified by the title of Basileus and as the father-in-law of the Emperor, who was still in his minority, the mastery of the Byzantine Empire would lie within his grasp. Thus, having vowed lasting peace to Byzantium, he could forthwith return home.

Soon after his departure, however, a palace revolution took place in Byzantium which sounded the knell of all his high hopes. To all appearances, it was in fact these extravagant concessions to Symeon which brought about the collapse of the regency of Patriarch Nicholas. Zoe, the dowager Empress, returned to the palace and assumed power. The projected Bulgar-Byzantine marriage alliance went by the board and the validity of Symeon's coronation as Emperor was disallowed. The result was a fresh outbreak of hostilities between Byzantium and the Bulgars. The Bulgars overran the region of Thrace and Symeon claimed that the Byzantine population should recognize him as Emperor.[2] In September 914 Adrianople surrendered to him and in the next few years he laid waste the district surrounding Dyrrachium and Thessalonica. The government of the Empress was confronted with the necessity of making a counter-attack. The supreme command rested with the *domesticus* of the *scholae*, Leo Phocas, son of the famous Nicephorus, who had not, however, inherited his father's gifts as a general. His colleagues included his brother Bardas, father of the future Emperor Nicephorus II Phocas, and a number of other representatives of the most important Byzantine families. The leadership of the army had already to a very large extent become aristocratic, as enjoined in the *Tactica* of Leo VI (cf. above, p. 255). But the fleet was commanded by Romanus Lecapenus, the son of an Armenian peasant, who was to get the better of his aristocratic rivals. After extensive preparations, the Byzantine army invaded enemy territory all along the Black Sea coast. But on 20 August 917, at Achelous, near Anchialus, they were attacked by Symeon and annihilated. This catastrophe was soon followed by a disaster near Catasyrtae, not far from the Byzantine capital. Symeon was master of the Balkan

---

[1] On the coronation of Symeon as Emperor cf. Ostrogorsky, 'Avtokrator' 121 ff., and 'Die Krönung Symeons von Bulgarien', *Bull. de l'Inst. archéol. bulgare* 9 (1935), 275 ff.

[2] Leo the Deacon 123, αὐτοκράτορα ἑαυτὸν ἀνακηρύττειν Ῥωμαίοις ἐκέλευεν.

peninsula. In 918 he invaded northern Greece and thrust forward as far as the Gulf of Corinth.[1]

If the regency of the Patriarch Nicholas was shipwrecked on his over-great compliance with the demands of Symeon, the rule of Zoe was doomed to failure because her unyielding attitude was entirely out of touch with the forces and abilities at her disposal. The desperate situation in which the Empire was plunged demanded a strong military régime, confident of its aims. The only person who appeared equal to this task was the *drungarius* Romanus Lecapenus. He succeeded in stealing a march on Leo Phocas, the candidate favoured by the Empress, and seized the reins of government. With great cunning, he had gradually removed Zoe and her advisers from their influential positions and step by step established his own control. In May 919[2] the young Emperor Constantine VII married Helena, the daughter of the new regent. Romanus Lecapenus now took the title *basileopator* formerly held by Stylianus Zautzes under Leo VI. But he soon rose even higher: on 24 September 920, his son-in-law raised him to the rank of Caesar, and on 17 December of the same year created him co-Emperor.[3] Romanus, the Armenian peasant's son, had succeeded where Symeon had failed: he was father-in-law and co-ruler with the young legitimate Emperor and as such the master of the Byzantine Empire.

The rise of Romanus Lecapenus was a tremendous blow to Symeon. The attempts of the Patriarch Nicholas Mysticus to act as mediator, and his numerous letters seeking to appease the Bulgarian ruler were all in vain. Symeon demanded nothing less than the

[1] According to the *Life of St. Luke the Younger* (Migne, PG 111, 449 ff.) the Bulgarian invasion forced the saint to leave his abode on Mt. Joannitza in Phocis for the neighbourhood of Patras where he spent ten years, only returning home after Symeon's death († 927). Diehl, *Choses et gens de Byzance* 3 f., therefore puts the Bulgarian invasion of northern Greece in 917. But this is impossible as Symeon fought at Achelous in August 917 and at Catasyrtae at the end of 917 or beginning of 918. This has been noted by Runciman, *Romanus Lecapenus* 84 and *Bulgarian Empire* 159, but he is wrong in suggesting 916 as the date. He rightly remarks, however, that the phrase 'ten years' should not be taken too literally, and I would suggest that a round figure of this kind stands for a shorter, rather than a longer, period than the specified ten. As Diehl has already emphasized, Symeon's strong drive into northern Greece was undoubtedly the result of the victory at Achelous. Everything therefore points to 918 as the date for the Greek campaign. There seems to be no reason for putting it in the period after the accession of Romanus Lecapenus as Zlatarski does, giving the date as 920 (*Istorija* I, 2, pp. 405 ff.; cf. Mutafčiev, *Istorija* I, 232).

[2] Cf. V. Grumel, EO 36 (1937) 52 ff., and F. Dölger, BZ 37 (1937), 532.

[3] For the year 920 (not 919) cf. V. Grumel, 'Notes de chronologie byzantine', EO 35 (1936), 333 ff. Romanus appeared at the council of union of July 920 as *basileopator*, which indicates (as Grumel notes) that his coronation as Emperor did not take place in 919, and also that he had not yet been given the title of Caesar.

deposition of his successful rival. For if Romanus Lecapenus were to remain both protector and father-in-law of the young legitimate Emperor, the paths which led to the fulfilment of Symeon's life's ambition would be closed to him. But only the capture of the imperial city could have enforced Symeon's bold demands. His repeated devastations of imperial territory and his recapture of Adrianople (923) in no way altered the existing situation. Romanus remained inviolate behind the fortified walls of his capital and quietly bided his time. He who held Constantinople was master of the situation: Symeon knew this full well, but lacked the fleet which was so necessary for the storming of this unrivalled fortress. He therefore concluded an alliance with the Arabs of Egypt, with a view to employing their seafaring talents in a common assault on Constantinople. This plan, however, was thwarted by vigilant Byzantine diplomacy. It was no difficult task for the Byzantine Emperor to outbid the offers of the Bulgar ruler and win over the Arabs by gifts and the prospect of regular payments. When, in 924, Symeon once more appeared before Constantinople, he had to recognize, as on that other occasion in 913, that his power stopped short at the walls of the imperial city: and so, once again, he requested an interview with the leader of the Byzantine state. In the autumn of 924[1] there took place between the two rulers a meeting which was long to remain in the memory of contemporaries and of posterity, and which has become embroidered by legend. But if the reception of Symeon by the Patriarch Nicholas Mysticus in 913 marked the auspicious beginning of his great project, his meeting with the Emperor Romanus eleven years later sounded the knell of his hopes.

Romanus I, unlike his predecessors during the period of the rule of the Empress Zoe, never attempted to deal slightingly with his powerful adversary. It is true that in a letter to Symeon in 925 he protested vigorously against Symeon's description of himself as Basileus of the Bulgars and Romans (*Romaioi*); but this letter was followed by another in which he explained that his protest was directed more against Symeon's claim to the Roman imperial office

[1] On the chronology cf. Dölger, *Reg.* 604, where it is rightly emphasized that it is not possible to define the date more closely in view of the conflicting and unreliable statements of the sources. The date 9 September 924, recently defended by Runciman, *Romanus Lecapenus* 246 ff., appears to be as doubtful as the other suggestions.

than his possession of the imperial title.[1] Although reluctantly, Byzantium thus accepted the compromise of recognizing that the Bulgar ruler possessed the title of Emperor, with the reservation that its validity remained restricted to Bulgar territory. In the same spirit, Symeon had already in 920 been offered through the Patriarch Nicholas Mysticus the possibility of a marriage alliance with the new ruling house of the Lecapeni, which would bring him honour but exclude him from any influence on the destinies of the Byzantine Empire. But Romanus would have no truck with further concessions, and would not even consider making territorial adjustments. In fact, the lesson to be learnt from the experiences of recent years was that, despite his military superiority, Symeon was in no position to realize his plans by force of arms, and that the Byzantines could corner him increasingly narrowly by the exercise of their diplomatic cunning.

The war between the Byzantines and Bulgars, which governed the whole course of events in the Balkan peninsula, involved the other Balkan lands in its toils. In Serbia, lines of influence extended both from Byzantium and from Bulgaria, crossing and conflicting with each other. Members of the Serbian princely house turned for support to the two great powers, and were played off by them one against the other. Now Symeon, now Romanus Lecapenus, succeeded in gaining control in Serbia for one of their protégées, ousting the favourite of the other side. When, after a long struggle, and repeated changes, Byzantine influence gained the upper hand and Zacharias, who had been raised to the Serbian throne with the help of the Bulgars, turned towards Byzantium, Symeon decided to suppress this focus of discontent which threatened him from the rear. The Bulgarian army sent against the Serbs was, however, defeated, and a stronger contingent had to be sent, which, after wreaking terrible devastation, subdued the whole country to the power of Symeon (*c.* 924). The subjugation of the Serbs brought the Bulgar ruler to the borders of Croatia, which at that time possessed considerable power under the rule of its first king, Tomislav (910–28; king from about 925); and he was soon again faced with the necessity of a warlike action and thus also with the necessity of again turning aside from the main Byzantine theatre of war. The

---

[1] According to the letter of Romanus I, Symeon styled himself βασιλεὺς Βουλγάρων καὶ Ῥωμαίων (Δελτίον I, 659). He seemed more concerned with the Ῥωμαίων than with the Βουλγάρων. A lead seal has been discovered on which Symeon simply calls himself Emperor of the Romans, Συμεὼν ἐν χρισ[τῷ] βασιλε[ὺς] Ῥωμέων (T. Gerasimov, *Bull. de l'Inst. archéol. bulgare* 8 (1934), 350).

invasion of Croatia cost Symeon his greatest defeat: his army was badly beaten (*c.* 926), and Symeon, with the Pope as intermediary, had to make peace with the Croats.[1] After that he seems to have been planning a further campaign against Byzantium, but was suddenly overtaken by death on 27 May 927.

After the death of Symeon, the whole situation changed, as though at a single stroke. The proud ambitions and restless bellicosity of Symeon were completely alien to the nature of his successor, his son Peter. Further conflict seemed hopeless. Peter hastened to make peace with Byzantium, was recognized tzar of the Bulgars, and received in marriage the Princess Maria Lecapena, a grand-daughter of the Emperor Romanus, the daughter of his eldest son Christopher. Recognition was also accorded to the Bulgarian Patriarchate, which Symeon appears to have established during his later years. Symeon's great successes in wars were not without after-effects. If his own ambitious programme had proved impossible to realize, the policy of completely rejecting all Bulgar claims, chosen by Zoe, was shown to be equally impracticable. Victory lay with the middle course adopted by the perspicacious Romanus. The Bulgar ruler could take the title of Basileus, but it was to be expressly restricted to the Bulgar kingdom; he might also conclude a marriage alliance with the Byzantine ruling house, but only with the Lecapeni, not with the legitimate ruling house, born in the purple. There had also been an exchange of roles: the father-in-law and protector of the Emperor of Byzantium was not, as Symeon had envisaged, the ruler of the Bulgars; rather, the Byzantine Emperors Romanus and Christopher found in the Bulgar tzar Peter their obedient son-in-law. The very considerable concessions which Romanus I—from now on without external pressure—made to the Bulgars brought about an extremely favourable position in the relationship between the Bulgars and Byzantium. The quietness of the Bulgar-Byzantine frontier was never so untroubled, and the influence of Byzantium in Bulgaria was never so powerful, as in the decades which followed the peace treaty of 927.

The Byzantine position was also strengthened in the other southern Slav territories. Serbia, subdued and devastated by Symeon, awoke to a new independent existence under the Prince Časlav, who soon after the death of Symeon had escaped from Preslav and on returning

---

[1] Cf. Šišić, *Povijest* 407 ff.; Jireček, *Geschichte* I, 199 ff.

to his native land had taken over the government, while acknowledging Byzantine supremacy.[1] Michael of Zachlumia, an ally of Symeon, also accepted an alliance with Byzantium and received from Constantinople the title of *anthypatus* and *patricius*.[2] Thus Byzantine influence everywhere increased and Bulgar influence everywhere receded. Bulgaria itself fell completely under the spell of Byzantium. The work of introducing Bulgaria to Byzantine civilization, which had been going swiftly forward since the time of the conversion to Christianity, now reached its highest point.[3] Politically and economically, however, the country was in a decaying condition, exhausted by the continuous wars of the time of Symeon. A period of crisis followed the rapid advances of recent decades. Strong social antagonisms made themselves felt in Bulgaria, as in Byzantium itself. Large estates, ecclesiastical as well as lay, were everywhere on the increase, for since the coming of Christianity the foundation of churches, and even more so of monasteries, was much in vogue, both in Bulgaria itself and in the annexed territory of Macedonia. In addition to the monastic life encouraged by the official Church, a number of sects hostile to the Church also blossomed out, which particularly in times of crisis had an especially strong appeal for dissatisfied souls and discontented spirits.

There thus appeared in the Bulgarian kingdom during the reign of Peter the sect of the Bogomils, radically opposed to the Church. The teaching of the priest (*pop*) Bogomil, the founder of the heresy, had as its starting point the doctrine of the Massalians and in particular of the Paulicians who had long lived side by side with the Slavonic population of Bulgaria and Macedonia, having been transported to Thrace in large numbers by the Byzantine government. Like Paulicianism, which in its turn derived from the old Manichaeism, Bogomilism was a dualistic doctrine, according to which the world is governed by two principles, Good (God) and Evil (Satanael), and the conflict between the two opposing powers determines all that happens on earth and in the lives of men. The whole visible world is the work of Satan and as such is given over to Evil. Like their

---

[1] Časlav took control in 927 or 928 and not in the thirties as was thought; cf. my arguments in 'Porfirogenitova hronika srpskih vladara i njeni hronološki podaci' (Constantine Porphyrogenitus' chronicle of the Serbian rulers and its chronological data), *Istor. časopis* 1 (1948), 24 ff.

[2] *De adm. imp.* c. 33, 16 (ed. Moravcsik-Jenkins). In spite of Šišić, *Povijest* 412, I should support Jireček's suggestion (*Geschichte* I, 202) that Michael's understanding with Byzantium dates from after the death of Symeon.

[3] Cf. P. Mutafčiev, 'Der Byzantinismus im mittelalterlichen Bulgarien', BZ 30 (1929–30), 387 ff.

eastern predecessors, the Bogomils strove after a purely spiritual religiousness and a strongly ascetic way of life. They vehemently rejected any outward worship, any ecclesiastical ritual, and indeed the whole Christian church order. The rebellion of the Bogomils against the ruling Church entailed also rebellion against the existing temporal order, whose most powerful spiritual support lay in the Church. The Bogomil movement was an expression of protest against the rulers, the powerful and the wealthy.

Bogomilism struck deep roots in Bulgaria and particularly in Macedonia, and was also most favourably received far beyond the borders of the Bulgarian kingdom and showed itself under a variety of designations in Byzantium itself, in Serbia and above all in Bosnia, Italy and southern France. The sects of the Bogomils, the Babuni, the Patarenes, the Cathars, the Albigenses, as also their predecessors in Asia Minor, are all so many outward expressions of the great movement which spread from the hills of Armenia to the south of France and flared up sporadically in different places. The heresy gained ground most rapidly in times of crisis and oppression, for it was in such periods that its basically pessimistic outlook, which rejected not only one definite order, but the terrestial world as such, found richest nourishment, and in which its protest made its most effective impression.[1]

4. THE STRUGGLE OF THE CENTRAL GOVERNMENT AGAINST THE FEUDAL MAGNATES AND CULTURAL ACTIVITIES AT THE IMPERIAL COURT: ROMANUS LECAPENUS AND CONSTANTINE PORPHYROGENITUS

General bibliography: A. Rambaud, *L'empire grec au Xe siècle : Constantin Porphyrogénète*, Paris 1870; Runciman, *Romanus Lecapenus*; H. Grégoire, 'The Amorians and Macedonians 842–1025', CMH IV, Pt. I (2nd. ed.,

---

[1] There is a considerable literature, which has much increased in recent years, on the history of the Bogomils of which the following should be specially noted: D. Angelov, *Bogomilstvoto v Bŭlgarija*, Sofia 1947 (2nd ed., much enlarged, Sofia 1961), and *Der Bogomilismus auf dem Gebiet des byzantinischen Reiches* I, Sofia 1948; H. Ch. Puech and A. Vaillant, *Le traité contre les Bogomiles de Cosmas le Prêtre*, Paris 1945; S. Runciman, *The Medieval Manichee: A Study of the Christian Dualist Heresy*, Cambridge 1946; D. Obolensky, *The Bogomils: A Study in Balkan Neo-Manichaeism*, Cambridge 1948; A. Soloviev, 'La doctrine de l'Église de Bosnie', *Bull. de l'Acad. de Belgique* 34 (1948), 481–534; H. Grégoire, 'Cathares d'Asie Mineure, d'Italie et de France', *Mémorial L. Petit* (1948), 142–51. Cf. also the valuable report by A. Schmaus, 'Der Neumanichäismus auf dem Balkan', *Saeculum* 2 (1951), 271 ff.

1966); Vasiliev, *Vizantija i Araby* II; M. Canard, 'Byzantium and the Muslim world to the middle of the eleventh century', CMH IV, Pt. I (2nd. ed., 1966); Vasiljevskil, *Materialy*; Ostrogorsky, 'Agrarian Conditions'; idem, *Paysannerie*; Lemerle, 'Histoire agraire'; Každan, *Gorod i Derevnja*.

Romanus Lecapenus had created for himself a strong position within the Empire, which explains the great assurance of his handling of external affairs. He was not long content to be co-Emperor with his son-in-law. Even the official order of precedence of the two rulers was soon changed: Romanus became the senior Emperor, while the young Constantine VII became co-Emperor with his father-in-law. The sons of Romanus Lecapenus were also raised to the dignity of co-Emperors: Christopher on 20 May 921, Stephen and Constantine on 25 December 924, Christopher even taking precedence over the legitimate Emperor, Constantine VII. Christopher became second Emperor, directly after his father, and heir presumptive to the throne, while the representative of the Macedonian dynasty had to content himself with the decorative role of a third Emperor.[1] Thus Romanus I set up his own dynasty side by side with the legitimate Macedonian house and gave his own the precedence. Three of his sons were crowned Emperors, the fourth, Theophylact, was destined for an ecclesiastical career; while he was still a child he was invested with the dignity of being the *syncellus* of Nicholas Mysticus and was marked out as a future Patriarch. The system of government created by Romanus I was strongly reminiscent of that set up by Basil I. But unlike Basil I, Romanus had not got rid of the representative of the legitimate dynasty by violent methods, but preferred instead to bind him to his own house by ties of kinship and then gradually and almost imperceptibly to push him into the background.

A talented statesman and diplomat, Romanus I was the embodiment of prudent moderation. Energetic and strong-willed in charac-

[1] Romanus Lecapenus took precedence over Constantine VII some time between 20 May 921 and April 922. For Christopher Lecapenus was crowned on 20 May 921 not by Romanus but by Constantine VII (Theoph. cont. 398), while later on the younger Lecapeni were crowned by Romanus himself (ibid. 409); on the other hand, the novel of April 922 (the *protimesis* novel which is probably to be dated in this year, cf. p. 273, n. 1 below) is already in the name of the Emperors Romanus, Constantine and Christopher. Christopher took precedence of Constantine some time after April 922 and before 25 December 924 when the younger Lecapeni were crowned because we have the evidence of two chrysobulls issued in the name of the Emperors Romanus, Christopher and Constantine (Zepos, *Jus* I, 204; Dölger, *Reg.* 593 and 594; consequently both these documents should be dated to the period between April 922 and 25 December 924). Christopher's precedence over Constantine was not connected with the marriage of his daughter to the Bulgarian tzar Peter in 927 as Theoph. cont. 414 says (followed by Runciman, *Romanus Lecapenus* 67).

ter, though entirely averse from any form of radicalism, he pursued his plans with cold-blooded perseverance, without undue haste but also without any lowering of his aim. In addition, he possessed one of the most important qualities in a ruler, the ability to choose his colleagues wisely. He discovered an outstanding minister in Theophanes, *protovestarius* and later *paracoemomenus*, and a brilliant general in John Curcuas, whom he appointed *domesticus* of the *scholae* in 923. As a parvenu of lowly origin he was of course hardly acceptable to the Byzantine aristocracy. But his younger daughters were now the sisters-in-law of Constantine VII, the Emperor born in the purple, and by marrying them to members of high-born families, he acquired ties of kinship with such as the Argyri and the Musele.

The Church was loyal to him: the Patriarch Nicholas Mysticus was attached to him by bonds of friendship and common interest, the dwindling party of the adherents of Euthymius, who was now dead (he died in 917), was no longer of importance, and the Roman Church, which was passing through one of the darkest periods of its history, was always obedient to the wishes of the powerful Emperor. Even before the formal elevation of Romanus, a council of July 920, held in the presence of the papal legates, had decided the question of Leo VI's four marriages in favour of the Patriarch Nicholas Mysticus, by pronouncing the fourth illicit and the third as admissible only in certain circumstances. This decision gave the Patriarch a feeling of intense moral satisfaction, and was for Romanus doubly advantageous, since it detracted from the prestige of the Macedonian house but surrounded him with a halo as one who had restored unity to the Church. After protracted and unprofitable quarrels, the Byzantine Church was at last united, and Nicholas Mysticus could proclaim his triumph in a τόμος ἐνώσεως.[1] There followed years of peaceful co-operation between the temporal and spiritual powers, which call to mind the ideal picture outlined in the *Epanagoge* (cf. above, p. 240 f.). Since the ruler of the state had assisted the Patriarch to recover his rights, the Patriarch in his turn stood by the Emperor during his great struggle with Symeon as his staunchest helper and adviser.

But the situation of the Byzantine Church nevertheless lacked stability, principally because it depended so much on the personality of the Church's leader and because the will of the Emperor was decisive in the appointment of the Patriarch. After the death of Nicholas Mysticus (925), the relationship between Church and State

[1] Grumel, *Reg.* 669.

underwent a fundamental alteration as a result of which nothing remained of the great authority once held by the Byzantine Church. After two insignificant Patriarchs had come and gone, Romanus allowed a long vacancy to intervene and then raised his sixteen-year-old son Theophylact to the patriarchal throne. The youth was consecrated on 2 February 933 by papal legates, whom the Emperor had caused to come to Constantinople expressly for this purpose. The young Patriarch blindly did as his father willed. For the rest, he was more at home in the stables than in the Church, and this discreditable state of affairs lasted until his death in 956, without the intervention of any change in his tastes and inclinations.

The greatness of Romanus Lecapenus as a statesman showed itself most clearly in his legislation for the protection of small-holders. The Byzantine state was confronted with a very serious problem: the 'powerful' (οἱ δυνατοί) were rapidly buying up the property of the 'poor' (οἱ πτωχοί, οἱ πένητες) and making them their dependants (πάροικοι). This process, a phenomenon associated with the strengthening of the Byzantine aristocracy, constituted a great danger for the Byzantine state, whose financial, economic and military strength had rested since the time of Heraclius on the small-holdings of the peasants and on the soldiers' holdings. Romanus Lecapenus was the first ruler to recognize this danger, to which his predecessors had been completely blind. 'The small-holding is of great benefit by reason of the payment of state taxes and the duty of military service; this advantage would be completely lost if the number of small-holders were to be diminished.'[1] These words of the Emperor Romanus show how clearly he saw the essence and gravity of the problem. If the system tested by centuries of struggle was to be maintained, and with it the financial and military strength of the Byzantine state, it was essential that the government should oppose the absorption of the small-holders by the 'powerful'. Thus began a bitter struggle between the central government and the landowning aristocracy which was to determine the whole future development of the Byzantine state.

His first step, by a novel probably of April 922, was to reinstate the right of pre-emption of the neighbours which had been restricted by Leo VI (cf. above, p. 255) and to devise a new and pregnant

---

[1] Zepos, *Jus* I, 209

formulation of the προτίμησις order.[1] In alienations of peasant land, whether by sale or lease, five categories, in a fixed order of precedence, were to enjoy the rights of pre-emption: (1) any relatives holding the land conjointly, (2) other conjoint holders, (3) holders of property intermingled with the plot to be alienated, (4) holders of adjoining land paying taxes in common, (5) other holders of adjoining land. The land could only be alienated to an outsider if all five categories refused to purchase. This carefully thought-out system,[2] in which every detail had been thoroughly considered, had as its object the protection of small-holdings both from speculative buying by the 'powerful' and from excessive sub-division. Indeed, the magnates were no longer to be allowed to buy or lease peasant land, except when they already had property in the village concerned—that is to say, when they fell into one of the five categories—neither might they even receive gifts or legacies from the 'poor', unless they were related to them.[3] Anyone violating these regulations, unless he was

[1] Zepos, *Jus* I, 198 ff.; Dölger, *Reg.* 595. Lemerle, 'Histoire Agraire' 219, 1, 265 ff., has recently raised the question of the textual tradition of this and other novels designed to protect small property owners, and puts forward the view that these novels —their text, their dating, and their authorship—demand serious reconsideration. In a note which (as Lemerle correctly remarks) has not been sufficiently taken into account by scholars, Zachariä had already observed that the text as we possess it shows signs of having been compiled from extracts of several novels (Zachariä, *Jus* III, 234, n. 1). In fact on closer examination I am forced to the conclusion that c. 2 is not entirely in agreement with c. 1, the main part of the novel, but represents a further stage in the legislation (gifts and legacies in favour of the 'powerful' which are not dealt with as such by the *protimesis* order are expressly forbidden in c. 2). Thus Lemerle is right in emphasizing the need for a critical examination of the extant text of this novel—and likewise of the other novels aimed at the protection of the small property-owner—and in insisting that a fresh study of this entire group of novels is an urgent *desideratum*. But it would be taking scepticism too far to doubt that this novel, with its basic provisions concerning the law of *protimesis*, comes from Romanus I. Zachariä, *Geschichte*, 238 ff., 265 ff., etc., was certainly right in regarding this 'berühmte und für alle Folgezeit massgebende Novelle' as without question—in spite of his note mentioned above—the law of Romanus I from the year 922. The date — April of the tenth indiction in the year 6430 (922)—is indeed first given in later law books. Thus although it is not completely certain that it is correct, there is on the other hand no good reason for rejecting it, since its indiction number and year correspond exactly.

A critical edition and textual study of this group of novels should shortly be published by N. Svoronos, as announced in his communication to the XIIth Byzantine Congress at Ochrida (1961).

[2] Cf. Ostrogorsky, 'Steuergemeinde' 32 ff.

[3] As is implied by note 1 above, this provision was probably added later to the *protimesis* novel, which, however, does not necessarily mean that it was not introduced by Romanus I, especially since the novel of Romanus I promulgated after the famine of 927/28 seems to refer to this very provision (Zepos, *Jus* I, 210, 27–29). The same is true of the provision concerning soldiers' properties which supplements it. The lack of any mention of this provision in the novel of Constantine VII concerning the properties of the *stratiotai* is of course no proof that it was enacted later. The novel of Romanus II, likewise issued by Theodore Decapolites, not only omits all reference to Romanus Lecapenus, but even asserts that the restitution without compensation of the illegally acquired land was first provided for by Constantine VII (Zepos, *Jus.* 1, 240).

protected by a ten-year limitation, was obliged to restore the property acquired, without compensation, and to pay a money fine to the exchequer. In the case of soldiers' holdings, reinstatement without compensation was made to apply retrospectively to properties alienated during the last thirty years, if as a result of that alienation the value of the holding had fallen below that which was necessary for the equipment of a soldier.

The ordinance did not however have the desired effect. In consequence of an unusually long and hard winter in 927–8, there was a serious failure in the harvest which brought with it a grave famine and devastating epidemics. The 'powerful', however, took advantage of the emergency, purchasing land from the hungry population at cut prices or taking it as payment for the advance of provisions. Such was the situation which preceded and provoked a new novel from Romanus I.[1] The Emperor censured the selfishness of the 'powerful' who had 'shown themselves more merciless than hunger or pestilence' with the greatest severity and bitterness. Nevertheless, he did not ordain a general confiscation of the peasant lands they had acquired, as might have been expected from a close adherence to the law of 922. Certainly, all gifts, legacies and similar agreements were again declared illicit. Also, all property for which the sum paid was less than half that which was to be considered as the just price, was to be restored without compensation. But where a purchase had been regular, the return of the property was linked with the condition of repayment of the purchase price within three years. For the future, any acquisition of peasant land by the 'powerful' was again prohibited and the restoration of properties so acquired to their former owners without compensation, together with the payment of a fine to the exchequer, again ordained. In conclusion, the Emperor expressed his conviction that by the power of this law he would conquer the internal enemies of the Empire as surely as he had overcome its external foes.

Despite the Emperor's sharpness of tone, this novel nevertheless clearly shows that governmental measures could not be applied with the force which was to be expected. It must be taken as certain that a large part of the peasant property sold during the emergency

---

[1] Zepos, *Jus* I, 205 ff.; Dölger, *Reg.* 628. The date of this novel is likewise only given in later law books, and some give September of the second indiction (928), while others give September of the eighth indiction (934). Zachariä decided in favour of the latter date and was followed by all later scholars. There is no need here to discuss whether he was right. In any case the uncertainty of this date seems to me to be greater than that of the *protimesis* novel.

of the famine remained in the hands of the magnates. For it is scarcely conceivable that a peasant who was forced by necessity to alienate his property would find the means of repaying the purchase price within three years. Even in cases of irregular sale, which should have resulted in a free restitution of the property gained thereby, it is probable that the right of possession was not in fact everywhere restored to the peasantry, since in the majority of cases the guilty purchasers were one and the same as the local officials, or their relatives or friends. The landed proprietors and the officials together formed a caste. Just as it was the natural ambition of a favourably placed official to acquire property in his province, so it was the constant ambition of a wealthy land-owner to break into the official class, and thus to create for himself the necessary social importance and useful connections either by accepting an official position or through the acquisition of an official title. As a rule, the 'powerful' was both a landed proprietor and an official.[1] The will of the central government was opposed by the solid determination of the economically most powerful and socially most respected sections of the community. Those who were responsible for executing the orders of the Emperor were largely interested in frustrating them.[2]

Moreover the small landowners themselves whom the imperial government was trying to protect from the greed of the 'powerful' often resisted its intentions. The excessive burden of taxation provoked a wave of movements in favour of patronage. The peasantry, economically ruined, renounced the anxieties of freedom, preferring the patronage of a powerful lord, which held out the promise of a relief from pressing burdens and obligations. This explains why, as we have seen from the imperial legislation, peasants not only sold, but even on occasion gave, their property to the magnates; this signified nothing less than that they entered into dependence on the landlords of their own freewill in order to escape misery and insecurity and to find protection against the oppressive tax demands of the state, and above all against the extortions of the tax-collectors. In actual fact the state was not defending the rights and the independence of small property-holders as the imperial novels try to claim. It was defending its own rights over the alienation and direction of the small-holders—rights which were being challenged by the great

---

[1] Cf. the weighty arguments of Vasiljevskij, 'Materialy' (*Trudy* IV), 254 ff.

[2] The various means whereby imperial officials and judges evaded the law are indicated in my article 'The Peasant's Pre-emption Right', JRS 37 (1947), 117 ff.

land-owning aristocracy. The severe crisis that was taking place was due to the fact that the strengthened feudal magnates tried to deprive the state of its peasants and soldiers by increasing their own lands and the numbers of their dependent tenants (*paroikoi*). The struggle between the central government and the feudal aristocracy was increasingly concerned not only with land owned by peasants and *stratiotai* but with the small land-owners themselves who were in actual fact the real bone of contention between the two sides.[1]

Externally, until 927 the Empire was fully occupied with the struggle with Symeon. But during this period a certain consolidation of Byzantine military power becomes evident. In particular, Byzantine naval power was strengthened under the rule of the former Drungarius of the fleet Romanus Lecapenus. As early as 924, the imperial navy annihilated off Lemnos the fleet of Leo of Tripoli, the conqueror of Thessalonica, and restored its control over the Ægean Sea. But once the Bulgarian danger had been suppressed, the Byzantine offensive on land began under the leadership of the outstanding general John Curcuas.[2] As formerly, the area surrounding the Taurus remained stable, and the theatre of military operations was Armenia and, above all, northern Mesopotamia.[3] The first great success was the capture of Melitene: this important city, which had repeatedly been the object of Byzantine endeavours, was first occupied by John Curcuas in 931, but fell again into Arab hands, only to surrender once more to the Byzantine general on 19 May 934, after which it remained for a long period under Byzantine rule. However, John Curcuas met with a worthy adversary in the person of the emir of Mosul and Aleppo, Saif-ad-Daulah, a member of the Hamdanid dynasty. While the power of the Abbasid Caliphate was continuously on the decline, that of the Hamdanid was on the increase, with the result that the conduct of the war against Byzantium devolved on Saif-ad-Daulah. To defend themselves against this new enemy, the Byzantines were obliged to enter into friendly relations with the Caliphate of Baghdad and with the Ikhshidids of Egypt. In September 938 the Hamdanid gained a significant victory over John Curcuas in the region of the Upper Euphrates, and then

---

[1] Cf. Ostrogorsky, *Paysannerie*, 11 ff.

[2] There is an excellent survey of the foreign policy of this period in Runciman, *Romanus Lecapenus*.

[3] On the stability of the Taurus frontier from the seventh to the mid-tenth century see the excellent comments of Honigmann, *Ostgrenze* 39 ff.

invaded Armenia, forcing many of the Armenian and Iberian princes to recognize his overlordship and, after marching through the subjected territory, appeared on Byzantine soil, to devastate the region around Colonea (940). Meanwhile, however, internal struggles broke out in the Caliphate, and Saif-ad-Daulah, who did not wish to let slip the opportunity of intervening in affairs in Baghdad, retraced his steps.

This was all the more fortunate for Byzantium since, in June 941, there was a surprise attack by the Russians, who made a landing on the Bithynian coast and laid waste the entire Asiatic shore of the Bosphorus. The breathing-space in the East provided an opportunity for taking effective counter-action against the enemy. John Curcuas himself went to the theatre of war, the Russians suffered severe defeat and, while they were preparing to retreat, their ships were destroyed by Greek fire in a sea battle led by the *paracoemomenus* Theophanes.[1] The contrast between the outcome of the two Russian attacks of 907 and 941 shows how much the military might of the Byzantine state had increased during the intervening period. However, when in the autumn of 943 the Russian Prince Igor appeared on the Danube with a large battle force of Russians and Patzinaks, the Byzantine government thought it advisable to come to an agreement and renew their commercial treaty with Kiev.[2] This treaty, which was signed in 944, corresponds in essentials with that made after Oleg's attack on Constantinople in 911, but was in several respects more favourable to Byzantium.[3]

After the defeat of the Russians on the Bosphorus, John Curcuas could again depart to the East to resume his operations in Mesopotamia. In a swift and victorious campaign he took Martyropolis, Amida, Dara and Nisibis (943), and then turned against Edessa, where one of the most important Christian relics, the miracle-working picture of Christ, known to us from the Abgar legend, was preserved. After a hard siege, the town was forced to surrender the sacred Mandylion 'not made by the hands of men'. With the utmost

---

[1] Levčenko, *Očerki* 128 ff., gives a very detailed description of the Russian attack of 941.

[2] N. J. Polovoj, 'O date vtorogo pochoda Igorja na Grekov i pochoda russkich na Berdaa' (On the date of the second campaign of Igor against the Greeks and the Russian campaign against Berda), VV 14, 1958, 138 ff.; Igor's second campaign against Byzantium apparently did not take place in 944, as had been universally accepted, but in 943.

[3] *Polnoe Sobr. Russk. Letopisej* I (1926–28), 46 ff.; German trans. Trautmann, *Die Nestor-Chronik* (1931), 29 ff., English trans. by Cross, *Russian Primary Chronicle* (1953), 73 ff.; Dölger, *Reg.* 647.

ceremony, the relic which had been liberated from the power of the infidel by the strength of Byzantine arms was conveyed to Constantinople; its reception in the Byzantine capital on 15 August 944 took the form of a unique religious festival.

By the brilliant victories of John Curcuas, the Byzantine frontier in the East was considerably advanced, Byzantine prestige in Asia materially enhanced and the way prepared for the decisive offensive under the Emperors Nicephorus Phocas and John Tzimisces. Impressed by the display of Byzantine power, whole Arab tribes went over to the Empire to be settled in Byzantine provinces after accepting the Christian religion. The further advances of the Byzantines were perceptibly made easier by this depopulation of the Arab frontier territories.

The recovery of the sacred Mandylion was the last triumph of the Emperor Romanus I. A strangely tragic end was in store for the great ruler, proving the truth of the biblical saying that a man's worst enemies are those who are closest to him. Romanus, whose position seemed unassailable, was sacrificed to the lust for power of his own sons. The eldest, Christopher, whom he had designated as his heir, died in 931. Rightly assessing his younger offspring, Romanus had not given them precedence before the legitimate Emperor.[1] Anxious lest on the death of their ageing father the rule should fall to Constantine Porphyrogenitus, Stephen and Constantine Lecapeni (sons of Romanus) resolved on a *coup d'état*. On 16 December 944 the old Emperor was seized on the orders of his sons and deported to the Island of Prote. Here, on 15 June 948, he who was one of the most important rulers in Byzantine history ended his life in lonely exile and as a monk.

It was soon evident that the young Lecapeni had very badly miscalculated. It is possible that their actions were prompted by the whispered suggestions of the adherents of Constantine VII.[2] In any case, the advantage was reaped entirely by Porphyrogenitus, since he found support in the growing sentiment in favour of legitimism among the Byzantine populace, whilst the two authors of the *coup d'état* had no one behind them: by the exile of their aged father they had themselves removed their only sure support. The second part of their plan, the removal of the legitimate Emperor, was never to be put into action. On 27 January 945 they were arrested by order

[1] The statement of Scylitzes-Cedrenus II, 321, that Constantine VII ranked last of the co-Emperors of Romanus Lecapenus is incorrect; cf. Theoph. cont. 435.
[2] Cf. Scylitzes-Cedrenus II, 322 ff.

Figure 39: *Christ Crowning Emperor Constantine VII Porphyrogenitus.* Ivory plaque, circa 945. Ht. 7⁵⁄16″, w. 3¹¹⁄16″. Pushkin Museum of Fine Arts, Moscow. Photo: Victoria & Albert Museum, London.

Figure 40: *Chronicle of John Scylitzes.* Miniature paintings on parchment, 14th century. Above, Nicephorus Phocas storms the city of Berrhoea in Syria. Below, the death of Romanus II. Biblioteca Nacional, Madrid. Photo: Biblioteca Nacional.

of Constantine VII and sent into exile, where both were later to die a violent death.

Thus Constantine VII Porphyrogenitus, now nearly forty years old, succeeded at last to his rights as ruler, after having worn the imperial crown since his earliest childhood, a period of thirty-three years. On Easter Sunday (6 April 945) his son, who bore the name Romanus after his grandfather, was also raised to the imperial dignity.[1] The fact that Constantine VII remained so long excluded from the government and that he acquiesced in his relegation, although it deeply wounded his self-esteem, is to be explained less by external circumstances than by the personal disposition of the legitimate Emperor himself. Even more strongly than in his father Leo VI, the scholarly littérateur in Constantine VII outweighed the politician. A bibliophile eager for knowledge, a diligent researcher with strong historical interests, whose only passions were study and writing, Constantine lived more in the past than in the present. He certainly had some interest in political matters and even in the art of war, but this was only theoretical and similar to the interest he felt for any intellectual subject. Thus, even during the period of his sole rule, he was always ready to follow the lead of others, in particular that of his wife Helena in whose veins flowed the blood of the power-seeking Lecapeni.

The historical importance of Constantine VII is not in his ineffective political influence but in his exceptionally stimulating and fruitful activities in the realms of education and scholarship. He compiled, under the title of the *Book of Ceremonies*, an encyclopaedia of unequalled value as a source, and his other writings included a geographical and historical survey of the provinces of the Empire, a very important treatise on foreign lands and peoples, and also a biography of his grandfather, Basil I. A series of important historical works and a number of writings on a great variety of learned subjects and on practical matters owed their origin to his orders or suggestion, and the older authors, particularly the ancient historians, were summarized with great assiduity. The crowned littérateur and Maecenas also gave a great stimulus to the cultural forces of the Empire and kindled intellectual activity to an unprecedented degree of fervour. The period of his shadow-rule was no less glorious and no less momentous in its effects on the total development of the

---

[1] On the chronology cf. G. Ostrogorsky-E. Stein, 'Die Krönungsordnungen des Zeremonienbuches', B 7 (1932), 197, note 3; cf. also G. de Jerphanion, 'La date du couronnement de Romain II', OCP 1 (1935), 490 ff.

Empire than were the periods of the greatest Byzantine statesmen and military leaders. It is true that the scholarly contribution of the Emperor and his entourage took chiefly the form of compilation. His creative capacity was insufficient to evoke new cultural values. What mattered was the collection together of worth-while knowledge, and indeed of all knowledge which should be preserved and handed down as the raw material of civilization and education. The literary activity of Constantine VII had a practical and didactic object: the works he composed and inspired were to provide guidance and instruction for his contemporaries and descendants, above all for his son and successor, Romanus. They were, in fact, works of reference. The encyclopaedia, the treatise, the historical narrative—such were the literary forms affected by Constantine VII and his circle.

After the downfall of the Lecapeni, far-reaching changes took place in the personnel of the Byzantine court, as was only to be expected. Constantine threw himself into the arms of the powerful Phocas family. Bardas Phocas, the brother of the former rival of Romanus Lecapenus, took over the high command as *domesticus* of the *scholae* of the East; at his side in the most important posts in the army were his three sons. Despite these changes, and although Constantine VII was to nurse feelings of bitterness against his father-in-law all his life,[1] the political course adopted by that great ruler was maintained without alteration in both internal and external affairs. The government of Constantine VII even remained true to the agrarian policy marked out by Romanus Lecapenus and promulgated further laws to protect small property-owners, though without referring explicitly to the originator of this legislation.

A law of March 947,[2] drawn up by the *patricius* and *quaestor* Theophilus and designed in the first instance for the Anatolikon and Thracesion themes, ordered the immediate restitution without compensation of all peasant lands which had been acquired by the 'powerful' since the beginning of Constantine's sole rule or should be acquired in the future. Even where alienations of property were made by the 'powerful', the peasants were henceforth to have the right of pre-emption, other things being equal. For the older sales,

---

[1] Cf. *De admin. imp.* c. 13, 149 (ed. Moravcsik-Jenkins), where Constantine VII says: 'The lord Romanus the Emperor was a common illiterate fellow, and not from among those who have been bred up in the palace and have followed the Roman national customs from the beginning; nor was he of imperial and noble stock. . . .'

[2] Zepos, *Jus* I, 214 ff.; Dölger, *Reg.* 656.

however, the earlier regulations were valid and this meant that the obligation to repay the purchase price—undoubtedly an important concession to the magnates—was extended to the whole period up to 945. However, by the law of Constantine VII the poorer vendors, those whose means amounted to less than fifty gold pieces, were exempted from repayment of the purchase price. But we also know, from a novel of his son's, no longer extant, that Constantine VII, at the instigation of the magnates, was forced to revoke this qualification by a later law and merely extended the period of grace for the repayment of the purchase price from three to five years.[1]

A further law of Constantine VII, from the pen of the *patricius* and *quaestor* Theodore Decapolites,[2] concerned soldiers' holdings. It laid down that properties from which soldiers derived their livelihood and means of equipping themselves should not be alienated, and indeed, in accordance with custom, that the plots of cavalry soldiers and of the marines of the themes (those of the Cibyraeot, the Ægean Sea and the island of Samos) should each have a value of at least four pounds of gold, and that those of the paid sailors serving in the imperial navy should each have a value of not less than two pounds of gold.[3] Partition of soldiers' holdings by inheritance was allowed, on condition that the heirs combined forces to fulfil the obligations of service. If the value of a soldier's holding exceeded the statutory minimum, the portion in excess could only be alienated if it was not entered in the roll of the *stratiotai*. Forty years were to elapse before possession of what was formerly a soldier's holding became incontrovertible. The old regulations that soldiers' holdings illicitly surrendered should be taken away from the purchasers without any compensation were to be more strictly observed. Moreover, the right to claim for reinstatement in a soldier's holding was not to rest only with the former owner, but, in conformity with the right of pre-emption, was to extend to kindred up to the sixth degree; then to those who had been under a common obligation with the former holder to provide for the military service due or who had together with him performed the service themselves; and also to the poorer *stratiotai* who had paid taxes in common with him, and finally to the peasants who belonged to the same taxation unit.

[1] Zepos, *Jus* I, 240 f.
[2] Zepos, *Jus* I, 222 ff.; Dölger, *Reg.* 673.
[3] These important rulings are repeated by Constantine VII, *De cerim.* 695, where it is, however, laid down that the holdings of mounted troops shall be worth five, or at least four, pounds of gold, while those of the imperial marines are to be worth three pounds.

This same Theodore Decapolites was also the author of a novel promulgated during the reign of Constantine's son, Romanus II, which elucidated the earlier regulations and once again grappled with the question, still not completely settled, of the properties sold during the famine since 927; but for the rest this novel reiterated that peasant and soldiers' properties alienated after the beginning of the sole rule of Constantine VII should be restored without any compensation.[1] A novel of the same Emperor of March 962 for the Thracesion theme elaborated the old ordinances concerning alienated military holdings and decreed that purchasers in good faith were only under an obligation to restore the property without compensation, but that ill-intentioned purchasers must also suffer a further penalty.[2]

In external affairs, the centre of the stage continued to be held by the war with the eastern Arabs. The tedious struggle continued in South Italy without having any marked effect on the evolution as a whole. An untroubled peace prevailed on the Bulgarian frontiers, and it was found possible to repel the attacks of the Magyars (in 934 and 943, and also in 959 and 961). Thus Byzantine forces were concentrated on the struggle in Asia and in the eastern end of the Mediterranean. In 949 the government of Constantine VII carried out an offensive against the nest of corsairs off Crete, an enterprise which in scope and display recalled the great expeditions of the time of Leo VI.[3] Yet on this occasion too all this military exertion and financial sacrifice were in vain. The undertaking was lamentably wrecked on the incompetence of the commander, Constantine Gongylas. Better, though very varying, success attended the continuation of the struggle begun by John Curcuas in northern Syria and Mesopotamia, where the Byzantines were opposed by their old enemy Saif-ad-Daulah. In 949 they captured Germaniceia and inflicted several defeats on the enemy, and in 952 they crossed the Euphrates. But then their luck changed, Saif-ad-Daulah reconquered Germaniceia, invaded imperial territory and took prisoner Constantine Phocas, the son of the *domesticus* (953). Saif-ad-Daulah continued victorious for the next few years, and it was only in 957 (after Nicephorus Phocas had replaced his father Bardas Phocas as commander of the army at the end of 954) that Byzantium regained the initiative. The town of Hadath in northern Syria surrendered

[1] Zepos, *Jus* I, 240 ff.
[2] Zepos, *Jus* I, 243 f.; Dölger, *Reg.* 690.
[3] Cf. *De cerim.* 664 ff. for a detailed description.

(June 957) and in 958 John Tzimisces, after a heated battle, took Samosata in northern Mesopotamia.

A characteristic trait of the reign of Constantine VII was the extremely lively diplomatic relations maintained with foreign courts. Apart from the numerous embassies which conducted negotiations with the warring Arab states and their neighbours, ostentatious embassies were exchanged with the Umayyad Caliph Abd-ar-Rahman III of Cordova and with Otto the Great. Of greater historical importance, however, was the ceremonious reception accorded to the Russian Princess Olga, who spent some time at the imperial court in the autumn of 957. The personal visit of the regent of the young Kievan state who had a short time previously been converted to Christianity, taking at baptism the name of the Byzantine Empress, Helena, initiated a new era in Byzantino-Russian relations and gave a fresh stimulus to the promising missionary work of the Byzantine Church in Russia.[1]

5. THE PERIOD OF CONQUESTS: NICEPHORUS PHOCAS AND JOHN TZIMISCES

General bibliography: Schlumberger, *Nicéphore Phocas*; idem, *Épopée byzantine* I; D. Obolensky, 'Byzantium and its northern neighbours 565–1018', CMH IV, Pt. I (2nd. ed., 1966); Ferradou, *Des biens des monastères à Byzance*, Bordeaux 1896; Charanis, 'Monastic Properties'. Cf. also the bibliography to Section 4 above, pp. 269 f.

After the death of Constantine VII (9 November 959) his son, Romanus II, ascended the throne, a handsome and charming youth, but weak-willed and frivolous, who had indeed inherited his father's political incapacity without his devotion to scholarship. As a child, at the wish of Romanus Lecapenus, he had been married to an illegitimate daughter of Hugh of Provence, but the early death of the little princess dissolved the bonds of this alliance, so unworthy of an imperial son born in the purple, before it had become a real marriage. About 956, suiting his own inclinations, Romanus married the

---

[1] A detailed account of the reception of the Princess Olga in the Imperial Palace can be found in the *De cerimoniis*, 594 ff. A thorough analysis of the subject has recently been made by Levčenko, *Očerki*, 217 ff., who also discusses the divergent views of scholars on the date and place of Olga's baptism. Levčenko himself favours the view that Olga was baptized on the occasion of her visit to Constantinople. This is however contradicted by Constantine's complete silence on the matter, as well as by the fact that Olga's retinue already included a priest. The Russian chronicles place Olga's baptism in the year 954 or 955 and this also supports the view that in reality she had adopted Christianity in Kiev before her journey to Constantinople.

daughter of a publican, Anastaso, who as Empress took the name Theophano. This extraordinarily beautiful, but entirely immoral and immeasurably ambitious woman was destined to play an unusual role in the history of the Byzantine Empire.[1] Romanus II was completely under her spell. To please her, the Emperor's mother, Helena, had to withdraw from the scene and the Emperor's five sisters were forcibly placed in convents. Romanus II never troubled himself with the conduct of state affairs but preferred to leave them in the hands of the capable eunuch Joseph Bringas, who ultimately held the office of *paracoemomenus* and acted as *paradynasteuon*. But above all, the Emperor fed on the fame of the *domesticus* Nicephorus Phocas, and his brief rule is worthy of attention only because it leads up to the great reign of this commander of genius.

In the summer of 960 Nicephorus Phocas, at the head of a large squadron, moved against Crete.[2] After a very hard and protracted siege, which lasted the whole winter, in March 961 his troops stormed Chandax (Candia), the capital of the island. Crete again fell under Byzantine rule, after belonging to the Arabs for nearly a century and a half and providing the most important foothold for their sea power in the eastern Mediterranean basin. Byzantium could record no victory of greater moment for centuries past.

After a triumphant welcome in Constantinople, Nicephorus Phocas took up the struggle with Saif-ad-Daulah in Asia. There, too, his measures were crowned with great success. With stroke after stroke he took Cilician Anazarbus, the much fought over Germaniceia, Raban and Duluk (Doliche, Teluch), and in December 962 even Aleppo, the capital of Saif-ad-Daulah, surrendered to him after a heavy siege. Although the capture of these towns still did not guarantee their possession, the victorious advance of the Byzantine general nevertheless demonstrated his great superiority. The struggle with the Hamdanids, which had been in the forefront of Byzantine foreign policy for thirty years, was now decided in favour of the Byzantines. This victory over Saif-ad-Daulah eradicated the most dangerous centre of Arab power in Asia, just as the conquest of Crete had removed their base in the eastern Mediterranean, and the way lay open for a further advance in the East.

The reward for the famous general was the imperial crown. On the early death of Romanus II on 15 March 963, immediate power

---

[1] Cf. Diehl's brilliant essay in *Figures* I, 217 ff.

[2] Schlumberger, *Nicéphore Phocas* 25–79, gives a detailed description of the campaign; cf. I. B. Papadopulos, Ἡ Κρήτη ὑπὸ τοὺς Σαρακηνούς (824–961), Athens 1948, 90 ff.

fell into the hands of the Empress Theophano, who assumed the regency for her small sons, Basil II and Constantine VIII. The shrewd Empress knew well that this arrangement could not be of long duration. Thwarting the designs of Joseph Bringas, she came to an understanding with Nicephorus Phocas. The latter was acclaimed as Emperor by his troops at Caesarea; and on 14 August he marched on Constantinople, and having broken the resistance of Bringas in bloody street fighting, was crowned in St. Sophia on 16 August. The young Empress then offered herself in marriage to this hoary veteran, grown grey in service. Thus the usurper became allied with the legitimate Macedonian dynasty, and as their stepfather became the protector of both the young princes born in the purple, whose imperial rights remained unaffected. Bringas was replaced as head of the civil government by the eunuch Basil, an illegitimate son of Romanus Lecapenus, a man of truly Byzantine cunning and unrestrained greed, but who was also endowed with extraordinary gifts of statesmanship. He had already occupied an important role in the reign of Constantine VII, and as *paracoemomenus*, honoured with the newly created high-ranking title of *proedrus*,[1] he now became the right hand of the new Emperor. The supreme command in the East was entrusted to the brilliant general John Tzimisces, who was made *domesticus* of the East; John Tzimisces was a member of an eminent Armenian family and, next to the Emperor, the most outstanding general of his time. The brother and former companion in arms of the Emperor, Leo Phocas, as *domesticus* of the West held the title of *curopalates*, whilst distinction was accorded the aged father of the Emperor, Bardas Phocas, by conferring on him the dignity of Caesar.[2]

With Nicephorus Phocas (963–9) there came to power one of the most important of the great families of Asia Minor. It must be admitted that neither the appearance nor the demeanour of the new Emperor betrayed his aristocratic descent. His exterior was unattractive, his nature rough and sullen, his way of life ascetically simple. Fighting on the battlefield was his only passion, prayer and intercourse with holy men his only spiritual need. At once warrior and monk, he was a friend and fervent admirer of St. Athanasius, the founder of the great monastery of the Lavra on Mount Athos. It was under Nicephorus that this famous centre of Greek monasticism

[1] On this title cf. Ch. Diehl, 'De la signification du titre de "proèdre" à Byzance', *Mélanges Schlumberger* I (1924), 105 ff.
[2] Leo Diac. 49; Scylitzes-Cedren. II, 379.

first began to flourish, and all his life Nicephorus, 'the white death of the Saracens', is supposed to have cherished the intention of withdrawing from the world and becoming a monk.[1]

But despite his unaristocratic habits, Nicephorus was and remained a true representative of the 'powerful' and his rise to supreme power signified a triumph for the Byzantine aristocracy. If hitherto the Byzantine government had fought against the expansion of landed estates, the magnates now counter-attacked. A law of Nicephorus Phocas, which can probably be dated to the year 967,[2] opens with the statement that his predecessors had shown themselves partisans of the peasants and had thus offended against the principle of providing equal justice for all their subjects. The poor are now deprived of their right of pre-emption in the alienation of the property of the 'powerful': poor men are to acquire property only from the poor, the rich only from the rich. For the rest, the old law remains in force, but any right of claim in respect of properties acquired in the period before the famine of 927 is no longer valid, since the forty years' period of grace has now lapsed. These regulations in themselves do not seem over-harsh, since it is at least questionable whether the peasants in fact were often in a position to exercise their right of pre-emption against the magnates. But the psychological effect of the new law must nevertheless have been enormous, since in the name of justice the rich were now protected against the attacks made on them in former legislation. Nicephorus Phocas had turned his back on the markedly favourable policy towards the peasants adopted by his predecessors.

On the other hand, the soldiers' Emperor took steps to consolidate and increase the military holdings. According to the old rule, in the case of reclamation of soldiers' property alienated at an earlier date, the minimum value of four gold pounds was to be observed, and any property up to this minimum value had to be restored without compensation; anything above this had to be restored on repayment of the purchase price. Henceforth, in view of the increased cost of the new and stronger equipment required for soldiers, the inalienable minimum value for military holdings was to be twelve gold pounds, which meant that a *stratiotes* was to alienate no part of his property if its total value fell below this limit, and any alienation which brought his property below this minimum was to be cancelled by

---

[1] Cf. Schlumberger, *Nicéphore Phocas* 249 ff.
[2] Zepos, *Jus* I, 253 ff.; Dölger, *Reg.* 712.

the unrequited return of the alienated plot; the purchase price could only be recovered in cases of alienation above this minimum.[1] This attempt by Nicephorus to treble the value of soldiers' holdings doubtless produced a change in the social composition of the army. To this extent, this arrangement entailed a fundamental deviation from the policy adopted hitherto, which was based on the small-holding of the 'poor'. The heavily armed *stratiotes* of Nicephorus, for whom he tried to guarantee a property worth twelve gold pounds, would not be 'poor'.[2] He could probably only be recruited from the rising class of newly developing lesser nobility, the class from which the later pronoiars were drawn.

At the same time, Nicephorus attempted to curb the growth of large ecclesiastical and monastic estates, and in 964 he issued a special edict against the increase of church property, an edict which is one of the most audacious specimens of Byzantine legislation.[3] The growth of ecclesiastical property was almost as rapid as that of lay estates, and was continually being nourished by gifts and legacies from pious persons from all classes of the population. There was also a constant flow of new monastic foundations, endowed with the corresponding landed resources. Although in principle amortized land was liable to taxation, it could hardly be regarded as liable to the same obligations as other classes of property, and in any case, the principle of liability to taxation was often infringed by grants of privilege. At a time when land hunger was making itself felt in the Empire—and the bitter struggle over the holdings of the peasants and the soldiers showed that such a condition already existed in the tenth century—the increase of ecclesiastical property was unprofitable for the state, in so far as this increase was achieved at the cost of more productive land-ownership. Other considerations, of a religious and moral nature, weighed just as strongly with this devout believer among Emperors in bringing him to his decision. He was unsparing in his castigation of the greed which led the monks to think only of heaping up possessions and to forget their sworn vows, making the monastic life an 'empty theatrical performance, bringing dishonour on the name of Christ'. The alienation of land to monasteries, to ecclesiastical institutions and to individuals of clerical status was to cease. The foundation of new monasteries and

[1] Zepos, *Jus* I, 255 f.; Dölger, *Reg.* 721.
[2] Cf. Neumann, *Weltstellung* 56.
[3] Zepos, *Jus* I, 249 ff.; Dölger, *Reg.* 699; cf. Charanis, 'Monastic Properties' 56 ff., where an English translation of the law is given.

ecclesiastical institutions was also prohibited, since the motive was usually a vain desire for fame. Anyone wishing to give proof of his generosity in a pious cause should succour older foundations which had fallen into decay; even so they should not give land to such an institution but should sell the property they had in mind for the purpose and make over to it the sum thus acquired; the purchaser might be any lay land-owner, and thus could quite well be one of the 'powerful'. On the other hand, the establishment of cells and hermitages in desolate regions, for which no other land was sought, is not only permitted but also represented as a laudable action. This bold decree did not long remain in force, but is very clearly indicative of both the political principle and the puritanical piety of the Emperor Nicephorus.

The fact that the expansion of the economically strongest class in the Empire was directed towards agriculture and was effected by buying up peasant property is explained not least by the situation in the Byzantine urban economy. Government restraint on the free play of economic forces was applied even more stringently in the town than in the country. The strongly constricted urban economy, with its draconian control, left no place for the deployment of private initiative to any great extent (cf. above, p. 253 f.), and the acquisition of land remained the only practicable method of investing surplus capital.

The movement to acquire more land worked itself out in two ways. One form it took was the absorption of small-holdings in the Byzantine provinces, undermining the existing social structure of the Byzantine state, the other reached out beyond the frontiers of the Empire, contriving to win over land from the enemies of the Empire.[1] The acquisition of territory by the state in the East in the tenth century was above all the work of the aristocracy of Asia Minor. At the same time, however, these great conquests must be regarded as evidence of the powerful religious enthusiasm which inspired the Byzantines in their struggle against the infidel.

Nicephorus Phocas was entirely possessed by this enthusiasm. For him, the war with Islam was a kind of sacred mission. He even claimed that all those who fell in fighting the infidel should be declared martyrs. This claim expressed with curious intensity the Byzantine feeling that the war with the Muslims was a Holy War,

---

[1] This has already been pointed out by Neumann, *Weltstellung*, 24.

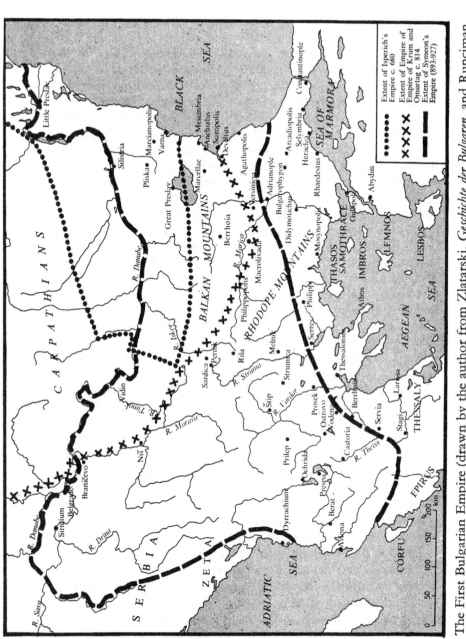

The First Bulgarian Empire (drawn by the author from Zlatarski, *Geschichte der Bulgaren*, and Runciman, *Bulgarian Empire*)

Map labels:

BLACK SEA

SEA OF MARMORA

AEGEAN SEA

ADRIATIC SEA

CARPATHIANS

BALKÁN MOUNTAINS

RHODOPE MOUNTAINS

SERBIA

ZETA

THESSALY

EPIRUS

Constantinople
Little Preslav
Pliska
Marcianopolis
Varna
Mesembria
Anchialus
Sozopolis
Develtus
Silistria
Great Preslav
Marcellae
Agathopolis
Arcadiopolis
Selymbria
Heraclea
Versinicia
Adrianople
Bulgarophygon
Didymotichus
Mesynopolis
Rhaedestus
Abydus
Berrhoia
Macrolivada
R. Marica
Philippopolis
R. Isker
R. Danube
Sardica
Pernik
Rila
Philippi
Strumica
Melnik
R. Struma
Štip
R. Vardar
Prosek
Ostrovo Vodena
Serres
Thessalonica
Berrhoea
Larissa
Servia
Stagi
LEMNOS
LESBOS
IMBROS
SAMOTHRACE
THASOS
Athos
Gallipoli
Niš
Braničevo
Belgrade
Sirmium
R. Morava
R. Theiss
Vidin
R. Timok
Prilep
Ohrida
Castoria
Prespa
Berat
Avlona
Dyrrachium
CORFU
R. Drina
R. Save
R. Danube

Legend:
- Extent of Isperich's Empire c. 680
- Extent of Empire of Empire of Krum and Omurtag c. 814
- Extent of Symeon's Empire (893-927)

0   50   100   150   200
Km

an emotion which provided a strong motive force for the Byzantine state's urge to expand.

Nicephorus as Emperor extended the conquests which he had begun as *domesticus* of Romanus II. His reign and that of his two successors form together the epoch of greatest military splendour reached by medieval Byzantium. The powerful advance of the Emperor Nicephorus broke through the Taurus frontier which had remained fast for centuries. The first two years of his reign were devoted to warfare in the Cilician Mountains, which was warfare at its most exhausting and laborious; the highlights of the campaign were the sieges of Tarsus and Mopsuestia. These citadels fell only in 965, having been finally starved out. In the same year, Cyprus was occupied by the Byzantine fleet. This signified a new and very important reinforcement to the maritime power of the Byzantine state. But the chief importance of the conquest of Cilicia and Cyprus lay in the fact that the way was prepared for Nicephorus' long-planned master stroke, the campaign against Syria. In October 966 the Emperor was already able to stand below the walls of Antioch, but was forced to return empty-handed. He did not reappear in Syria until 968, when he advanced along the coast far into the south, taking one town after another, and then turned again against Antioch. Despite his great show of strength, the siege dragged on and the Emperor returned to Constantinople; it was only on 28 October 969, in the absence of the Emperor, that the generals Peter Phocas and Michael Burtzes at last succeeded in capturing the Syrian capital. A few months later Aleppo also fell and its emir, the next successor but one to Saif-ad-Daulah († 697) was forced to conclude a humiliating peace with Byzantium. Part of Syria, including Antioch, was annexed to the Empire, and a further part, that containing Aleppo, recognized Byzantine suzerainty.

By the annexation of Cilicia and a large part of Syria, the territorial extent of the Byzantine Empire was greatly enlarged; furthermore, one of the most important centres of the East was now within the boundaries of the Empire, the patriarchal city of Antioch, which had been under Muslim rule for more than three centuries and had seemed permanently lost to the Empire. This metropolis, so rich in historical associations and religious traditions, was once again Byzantine. Nor was the authority of the Byzantine Emperor confined to this area of direct occupation, but extended, in the form of a protectorate, into the region of the capital of the once formidable

Hamdanids; the emir of Aleppo was a Byzantine vassal and his non-Christian subjects paid taxes to the Empire.

But this period of powerful expansion by the Byzantine Empire saw also the revival of the Western Empire. The rivalry between the two Empires was reawakened, a rivalry which had two aspects, one theoretical and the other political; theoretically speaking, the imperial idea was based on the uniqueness of the Empire, yet there were two Empires which claimed to be the heirs of Rome; politically speaking, both powers had conflicting interests in South Italy. Otto the Great, who was crowned Emperor in Rome a year before the accession of Nicephorus Phocas, and who had subjected to himself almost the whole of Italy, in 968 sent an embassy to Constantinople in the hope of reaching a friendly agreement on the possession of those parts of Italy which had not yet fallen to him. His ambassador, Bishop Liutprand of Cremona, who had already visited the Byzantine capital in 949 in the time of Constantine VII, as the emissary of Berengar II, unfolded to the Byzantine government a plan for a marriage alliance between the son of Otto I and one of the sisters of the young imperial princes, whose dowry was to be provided by the South Italian possessions of the Byzantine Empire. This offer was regarded in Byzantium as derisive and was derisively rejected. The Byzantine ruler felt keenly that the interests and prestige of this Empire were injured by recent events in the West in a large variety of ways. That Otto should have taken the imperial crown, made himself master of Rome and of the Roman Church, that he had a firm grip on almost the whole of Italy, that he had allied himself with the Princes of Capua and Benevento, vassals of the Byzantine Empire, and had even dared to attack (admittedly without success) the Byzantine possession of Bari—all these deeds were galling to the Byzantine Emperor, who, after the unique success of his recent undertakings in the East, was more than ever conscious of his power and importance. Otto's valiant envoy, who was treated almost like a prisoner in Constantinople, was made to listen to tales to the effect that his master was neither an Emperor nor a Roman, but merely a barbarian king, and that there could be no question of a marriage between the son of a barbarian ruler and an imperial princess born in the purple.

Nor did Byzantium's Bulgar neighbours immediately appreciate the significance of the great increase of power which had come to

Byzantine state. In the autumn of 965, after the conquest of Cilicia and Cyprus had already been completed, Bulgarian envoys appeared in Constantinople to demand the tribute paid by earlier Byzantine governments.[1] Enraged by this presumption, the Emperor had the envoys scourged and sent them home heaped with invective and threats. However, after demolishing a few Bulgar frontier forts, he abstained from entering on openly bellicose relations with the Bulgars, as he did not wish to be diverted from his eastern enterprises, and called in the Russian Prince Svjatoslav to subdue the Bulgars for him, in return for good payment. This appeal from the Emperor was very welcome to the warlike son of Olga, the Christian friend of Byzantium, who had destroyed the kingdom of the Khazars and made himself a considerable power. In 968 he appeared on the Danube, and with ease defeated the Bulgars, who were politically disintegrated:[2] in doing so, however, he was seeking not to perform a service for the Emperor but to establish his own authority on the Danube. In 969 an attack of the Patzinaks on Kiev forced him to return home, but in the summer of the same year he appeared again in the Balkans and this time made himself master of Bulgaria by deposing the tzar Boris II, the son of Peter, who had meanwhile died. Nicephorus was forced to recognize that as a result of his own actions his former weak adversary had been replaced by a new, far stronger and more dangerous enemy. He now tried to ally himself with the Bulgars against Svjatoslav, and went so far as to plan a marriage between the young imperial princes with two Bulgar princesses.[3] But his serious miscalculation was not to be so easily rectified: Nicephorus bequeathed a very troublesome legacy in the Balkans to his successor.

Six weeks after the capture of Antioch, Nicephorus Phocas fell victim to an attack on his life. Despite his imposing successes, he could never be a popular prince. His militaristic rule, in which the whole life of the state was subordinated to the interests of the army, and the screw relentlessly tightened to produce taxes to defray the cost of his great campaigns, pressed heavily on the population. We hear during this period of great dearth and debasement of the

---

[1] This chronology follows Runciman, *Bulgarian Empire* 303 ff.

[2] On the chronology cf. P. O. Karyškovskij, 'O chronologii russko-vizantijskoj vojny pri Svjatoslave' (The chronology of the Russo-Byzantine war in the time of Svjatoslav), VV 5 (1952), 136 ff.

[3] On the date (969, not 968) and the circumstances of this alliance cf. D. Anastasijević, *Glasnik Skopskog Naučnog Društva* 11 (1932), 51 ff.

coinage.[1] It was not, however, the resentment of the people which brought Nicephorus to his doom, but a quarrel with his former friend, John Tzimisces, and the treachery of his wife, Theophano. She became the mistress and abettor of the brilliant young general, who, although small in stature, was very handsome and of a distinguished and engaging personality, in contrast to the Emperor Nicephorus. Theophano prepared the way for the attack on her husband, Tzimisces and his friends carried it out; Nicephorus Phocas was murdered in his bed-chamber on the night of 10–11 December 969.

John Tzimisces (969–76) became Emperor. Theophano, however, was bitterly disappointed of her hope of being able to offer him her hand. The murdered Emperor found his avenger in the Patriarch Polyeuctes, who was firmly resolved that the atrocity should not go unpunished. He demanded that Tzimisces should do penance, that he should expel his mistress, the Empress Theophano, from the palace, and that he should punish his own coadjutors in the murder of the Emperor Nicephorus. The Emperor had to yield to all the Patriarch's demands. Only when he had done so did the Patriarch permit him to enter a church and proceed to his coronation.

It could hardly be expected that this Byzantine Canossa would have no effect on shaping relations between Church and State. The moral triumph of the Church was completed by forcing Tzimisces to revoke the law of his predecessor against monastic and ecclesiastical possessions.[2] A saying of Tzimisces, one of the greatest and

---

[1] Scylitzes-Cedren. II, 369; Zonaras III, 507. Considerable work has been done on the question of the *tetarteron*, a coin of inferior quality issued by Nicephorus Phocas. Cf. especially W. Kubitschek, 'Zum 'Επαρχικòν βιβλίον', *Numism. Zeitschr.* 44 (1911), 194 ff.; G. Mickwitz, 'Die Organisationsformen zweier byzantinischer Gewerbe im 10. Jahrhundert', BZ 36 (1936), 66 ff.; F. Dworschak, 'Studien zum byzantinischen Münzwesen', *Numism. Zeitschr.* N. F. 29 (1936), 77 ff.; R. S. Lopez, 'La crise du besant au Xe siècle et la date du Livre du Préfet', *Mélanges Grégoire* II (1950), 403 ff.; A. Christophilopulos, 'Ζητήματά τινα ἐκ τοῦ 'Επαρχικοῦ βιβλίου', 'Ελληνικά (1939), 125 ff.; A. Frolow, 'Les noms des monnaies dans le Typicon du Pantocrator', BS 10 (1949), 251 f.; V. Laurent, 'Bulletin de Numismatique byzantine', REB 9 (1951), 204 f., who rightly concludes 'A mon sens, rien n'est tranché dans cette question de tetarteron'. But see now the interesting, and in my opinion convincing, attempt at an interpretation of this difficult problem by Hélène Ahrweiler-Glykatzi, 'Nouvelle hypothèse sur le tétartèron d'or et la politique monétaire de Nicéphore Phocas', ZRVI 8, 1 (1963), 1 ff. According to her, the tetarteron of Nicephorus Phocas contained only one-twelfth less gold than the *nomisma* of normal weight, and was therefore of 22 carat gold.

[2] Cf. the note in Cod. Vindob. suppl. 47 and 48 (Zepos, *Jus* I, 249, n. 1) on Nicephorus Phocas' novel against the monasteries, ὅρα αὕτη ἡ νεαρὰ κατηργήθη παρὰ τοῦ τζυμισχῆ· κακῶς 2ἑ. Charanis, 'Monastic Properties' 61, again puts forward the view that the law of Nicephorus Phocas was not revoked until Basil II's novel of 4 April 988, but he overlooks the fact that the authenticity of this novel is highly doubtful. Cf. Dölger, *Reg.* 772, and below p. 307, note 1. Charanis' suggestion that the note in Cod. Vindob. confuses Tzimisces with Basil II is not very convincing.

most powerful of the Emperors, has been handed down which has the ring of being an avowal of the Photian doctrine of the *Epanagoge*: 'I acknowledge two powers in this life: the priesthood and the Empire; the Creator of the world has entrusted to the former the cure of souls, to the latter the care of bodies; if neither part is damaged, the well-being of the world is secure'.[1] Theophano went into exile, from which she returned only after the accession of her sons; this put an end to the historic role played by this woman in Byzantine history, in which she occupies a special place as the wife and murderess of Nicephorus Phocas, mistress of John Tzimisces and mother of Basil II. Tzimisces made a politic marriage, which took the fullest possible account of legitimist sentiment: he married Theodora, the no longer young daughter of Constantine VII and aunt of the young Emperors Basil and Constantine. Tzimisces, like Nicephorus Phocas before him, assumed the role of protector of the two princes born in the purple. The conduct of civil affairs remained in the hands of Basil, the *paracoemomenus*, who had gone over to Tzimisces in good time and who was henceforth to enjoy even greater influence than in the time of Nicephorus Phocas. The relatives of the murdered Emperor tried in vain to contest the throne with Tzimisces. Bardas Phocas, a nephew of the Emperor Nicephorus and son of Leo the *curopalates*, had himself proclaimed as Emperor in Caesarea, the stronghold of the Phocas family, but was overpowered by Bardas Sclerus, a brother-in-law of John Tzimisces, and was incarcerated with his family in a monastery on the island of Chios. Leo, the *curopalates*, was himself blinded after an abortive rising.

Tzimisces, like his predecessor, belonged to the first rank of the aristocracy. On his father's side he was related to the Curcuas, on his mother's with the Phocas themselves, and his first wife was a Sclerina. Nevertheless, unlike his predecessor, he did not give way to the aristocracy in his agrarian policy. There exist two documents which show that Tzimisces ordered the officials in the themes to investigate the estates of the monasteries and the secular magnates. If they found on them *stratiotai* or peasants formerly under obligation to the state, they were to bring them under state authority again. This shows very clearly that in its struggle against the growth of large estates, the Byzantine government was defending its own vital interests and rights. In order not to lose control over its peasants

---

[1] Leo the Deacon 101.

and soldiers, the imperial government made use of severe police measures, instigated raids on the estates of the magnates, forcing the *stratiotai* and state farmers who had settled there to return to their previous dwelling places. As a result, the formerly independent small land owners became *paroikoi* of the state, in that the state deprived them not only of the right to dispose freely of their own land, but also of their freedom of movement.[1]

Like Nicephorus Phocas, John Tzimisces was a general of great genius; as a statesman he surpassed his all too impulsive predecessor. The very complicated situation which had been created in the Balkans by the employment of Svjatoslav demanded a speedy solution for the attitude of the powerful Russian prince was becoming increasingly threatening and it seemed that the Bulgars were allying themselves with him in preparation for a common struggle with Byzantium.[2] The endeavours of the Emperor to achieve a peaceful settlement with Svjatoslav were fruitless. Since the new master of Bulgaria demanded nothing less than that the Byzantines should withdraw to Asia and leave the European portion of the Empire, including Constantinople, to him, the Emperor had no choice but to appeal to force. His campaign against Svjatoslav ranks among the most splendid achievements in the annals of Byzantine military history. In April 971[3] he moved against Great Preslav and stormed the Bulgarian capital after a brief but furious battle. Among his captives was the dethroned tzar, whom he hailed as ruler of the Bulgars. This cleverly calculated attitude, together with the victorious advance of the Byzantine army, did not fail to make an impression on the Bulgars, who began to desert from Svjatoslav. From Preslav Tzimisces marched in haste against the Danube town of Silistria (Dorostolon) where Svjatoslav had shut himself up. Silistria was surrounded and at the same moment the Byzantine fleet appeared on the Danube, armed with the

---

[1] Cf. G. Ostrogorsky, 'O visantiskim državnim seljacima i vojnicima—dve povelje iz doba Jovana Cimiska' (On Byzantine state peasants and soldiers—two ordinances from the reign of John Tzimisces), *Glas Srpske Akad. Nauka* 214 (1954), 23 ff. and *Paysannerie*, 11 ff.

[2] Cf. P. Mutafčiev, 'Russko-bolgarskie otnošenija pri Svjatoslave' (Russo-Bulgarian relations in the time of Svjatoslav), *Sem. Kond.* 4 (1931), 77 ff.

[3] This chronology follows F. Dölger, 'Die Chronologie des grossen Feldzuges des Kaisers Johannes Tzimiskes gegen die Russen', BZ 32 (1932), 275 ff. For different views cf. D. Anastasijević *Sem. Kond.* 3 (1929), 1 ff.; BZ 30 (1929–30), 400 ff., and 31 (1931), 328 ff.; *Mélanges Diehl* I (1930), 1 ff.; B 6 (1931), 337 ff., who tries to defend the thesis that the war against Svjatoslav did not last three months, but three years (up to 974); but cf. H. Grégoire, B 12 (1937), 267 ff., who, like Dölger, places the campaign in the period April–July 971 (cf. F. Dölger, BZ 38 (1938), 232 ff.); cf. also P. Karyškovskij, 'O chronologii russko-vizantijskoj vojny pri Svjatoslave' (The chronology of the Russo-Byzantine war in the time of Svjatoslav), VV 5 (1952), 136 ff.

fearsome Greek fire. The Russians put up a desperate resistance, but the imperial army repelled all their attempts at breaking out and the famine in the beleaguered town became increasingly hard to bear. At the end of July, after a last attempt to break the bonds of the siege had failed, and the Russians had been forced back behind the city walls after a battle contested with unprecedented severity, which had even strained the Byzantines to the limit of their resources, Svjatoslav surrendered to the victor. He bound himself to withdraw from Bulgaria at once and never to appear in the Balkans again; furthermore, he undertook to make no attacks on the Byzantine territory of Cherson, and to assist the Byzantines in defence against any adversary.[1] The Emperor thereupon released supplies to Svjatoslav's famished warriors, and renewed the old trading privileges of the Russians. After a personal interview with his conqueror, Svjatoslav returned home, but died on the way in a battle with the Patzinaks on the rapids of the Dnieper. The great victory of John Tzimisces carried with it two advantages for the Byzantines: the Empire was rid of a dangerous enemy, who had demonstrated his power by his conquest of the Khazar kingdom and the subjection of the Bulgars, and secondly, Bulgaria was brought under Byzantine domination. For although during the struggle with Svjatoslav Tzimisces had posed as the liberator of the Bulgars, he had no intention of resurrecting the old régime. He annexed the country which now lay at his feet, the tzar Boris was taken to Constantinople as a prisoner and the Bulgarian Patriarchate was abolished.

John Tzimisces managed to handle the other unsolved problem bequeathed to him by his predecessor by diplomatic means. He despatched to the heir of Otto the Great, not the princess born in the purple, as had been requested, but his own kinswoman Theophano,[2]

---

[1] The terms of the capitulation are preserved in the Old Russian Chronicle, *Poln. Sobr. Russk. Letop.* I, 72 f. (German trans. by Trautmann, *Die Nestor-Chronik* 49 ff.; English trans. by Cross, *Russian Primary Chronicle* (1953), 89 ff.). It is dated July of the 14th indiction of the year 6479, which is July 971. This fact itself, though it has been ignored in the dispute between Dölger and Anastasijević (cf. the previous note), decisively settles the question of the duration of the war with Svjatoslav.

[2] P. E. Schramm, 'Kaiser, Basileus und Papst in der Zeit der Ottonen', HZ 129 (1924), 424 ff., had adduced strong arguments in support of the view that Theophano was a relation of John Tzimisces (cf. J. Moltmann, *Theophano, die Gemahlin Ottos II*, Diss. Göttingen 1878) and not the daughter of Romanus II, as K. Uhlirz, BZ 4 (1895), 466 ff., tried to show. Attempts to identify her as the daughter of Constantine VII (H. Moritz, 'Die Herkunft der Theophano, der Gemahlin des Kaisers Otto II', BZ 39 (1939), 387 ff.) or the daughter of Stephen Lecapenus (M. Uhlirz, 'Studien über Theophano', *Deutsch. Archiv. f. Gesch. d. Mittelalt.* 6 (1943), 442 ff.) have been refuted by F. Dölger, 'Wer war Theophano?' *Hist. Jahrb.* 62-9 (1949), 546 ff., who reconsiders the question and shows that the supposition of Moltmann and Schramm is undoubtedly

who was married to Otto II in Rome on 14 April 972. The conflict with the Western Empire, which as a result of the arrogance of Nicephorus Phocas had been considerably inflamed, had now at least temporarily died down, and the territorial *status quo* was apparently restored.

The war in the East was renewed in 972 and as a prelude, the Emperor advanced into the Mesopotamian region of Nisibis and Majafarkin (Martyropolis).[1] The main struggle, however, took place in Syria, where the work of Nicephorus Phocas was consolidated and continued. The Fatimids, who had a short time previously established their rule in Egypt, started to extend their power into Asia, and as early as 971 made a strong attack on Antioch. This was powerfully countered by the campaign of John Tzimisces of 974 and, even more so, by that of 975, which breathed the veritable crusading spirit. From Antioch the Emperor marched at the beginning of April against Emesa, going from thence to Baalbek, which fell after a brief resistance. Damascus also surrendered to the victorious Emperor, recognized his authority and the obligation to pay tribute. Tzimisces then invaded the Holy Land, took Tiberias, Nazareth, the coast town of Akkon and finally Caesarea, the chief stronghold of the African Arabs. Jerusalem, the Holy City, was now not far distant, but the Emperor recognized the dangers of a precipitate advance yet further afield. He moved northwards, taking as he went a number of important coastal towns, including Beyrut and Sidon. Imperial commanders were appointed in all the captured towns. Tzimisces sent to his ally, the Armenian king Ashot III, a victory message which began 'Hear and receive the wonderful tale' and which culminated with the declaration: 'All Phoenicia, Palestine and Syria are freed from the yoke of the Saracen and recognize the rule of the Romans'.[2] These words are obviously much exaggerated, for they do not describe what had in fact been achieved, but only the goal towards which the Emperor directed the crusade. But even what had actually been gained in his rapid campaign of conquest amounted to an overwhelming success: the conquests of Nicephorus

correct (cf. also Addenda in BZ 43 (1950), 338 f.). A. A. Vasiliev, 'Hugh Capet of France and Byzantium', *Dumbarton Oaks Papers* 6 (1951), 227–51, mistakenly reverts to the old theory that Theophano was a daughter of Romanus II; cf. my comments in BZ 46 (1953), 156.

[1] Tzimisces' campaign in Mesopotamia as early as 972 has been established by M. Canard, 'La date des expéditions mésopotamiennes de Jean Tzimiscès', *Mélanges Grégoire* II (1950), 99 ff.

[2] E. Dulaurier, *Chronique de Matthieu d'Edesse* (1858), 22; C. Kučuk-Ioannesov, VV 10 (1903), 100.

Phocas were not only consolidated but also considerably enlarged, and as a result the predominance of the Byzantine Empire in the Near East was firmly established. John Tzimisces returned to Constantinople fatally ill, apparently with typhoid. He died on 10 January 976; his glorious reign came to an abrupt and unexpected end after lasting six short years.

6. THE APOGEE OF BYZANTINE POWER: BASIL II

General bibliography: Schlumberger, *Épopée byzantine* I and II; Rosen, *Bolgarobojca*; Zlatarski, *Istorija* I, 2; Mutafčiev, *Istorija* I; Runciman, *Bulgarian Empire*; Litavrin, *Bolgarija i Vizantija*; C. Toumanoff, 'Armenia and Georgia', CMH IV, Pt I (2nd ed., 1966); Neumann, *Weltstellung*; Gay, *Italie*. See also the general bibliography for Sections 4 and 5, p. 269 and p. 283 above.

Although the imperial rights of the legitimate representatives of the Macedonian dynasty remained formally intact under Nicephorus Phocas and John Tzimisces, the idea that the throne belonged rightly to those born in the purple was becoming less and less real in the minds of the Byzantine magnates. It had become a habit for power to be concentrated in the hands of one of the generals belonging to the great families, and on the death of John Tzimisces, his brother-in-law, Bardas Sclerus, therefore came forward in the expectation of filling the vacant position of co-Emperor. It appeared as if the Macedonian imperial house was destined, like the Merovingian, to become the victim of a more vigorous mayoralty of the palace, or to be condemned, like the Caliphs of Baghdad, to live out a shadowy and merely decorative existence under the wing of an over-powerful military Sultanate.[1] The unique vitality of the young Emperor Basil II is responsible for their escape from this fate.

The sons of Romanus II had reached an age at which they were competent to rule: Basil was eighteen, Constantine sixteen.[2] Effectively supported by their great-uncle, the eunuch Basil, they assumed power. But it was to be exercised in practice only by the elder brother. For Constantine VIII was a true son of his father: of frivolous disposition, he desired nothing more than to pass his life

[1] Cf. Neumann, *Weltstellung* 49.
[2] On the year of Basil II's birth (958) cf. G. Ostrogorsky and E. Stein, B 7 (1932), 198, note 1.

wallowing in extravagant pleasures. It was quite otherwise with Basil II, who soon emerged to show himself as a man of iron strength of purpose and unique ability: among all the descendants of Basil I, he alone was a natural ruler and a truly great statesman. Yet he was totally unprepared for the exercise of his vocation as ruler. Having from childhood been regarded as a mere puppet in the ceremonies of the court, and treated as a decorative but basically inessential appendage of the powerful usurpers, even he was at first helpless when faced with the activities of the world outside. It was the searching tasks that devolved on him after his accession to power which steeled his character and brought him to maturity. The rudder of the ship of state was in the experienced hands of Basil, the *paracoemomenus*. The rebellious movement unleashed by Bardas Sclerus was directed more against him than against his great-nephews, who in themselves seemed innocuous. Bardas, who represented one of the oldest and most wealthy Byzantine families and who was an outstanding general, having held under Tzimisces, his brother-in-law, the highest military office, that of *domesticus* of the East, had himself acclaimed as Emperor by his troops in the summer of 976. He gained repeated victories over the loyalist generals who were sent against him, and gradually brought the whole of Asia Minor under his domination, until, at the beginning of 978, after the capture of Nicaea, he was able to approach the capital itself. At this moment of extreme peril, the eunuch Basil turned to Bardas Phocas, a nephew of the Emperor Nicephorus and a bold warrior of gigantic stature, who had himself attempted a usurpation under John Tzimisces. He was now to crush Sclerus in the name of the new rulers just as he himself had been crushed by Sclerus in the name of John Tzimisces. Bardas Phocas did indeed overcome his former rival, but his action was performed not so much in his capacity as the servant of the legitimate Emperors but as the champion of the powerful house of Phocas. In order not to enter into an engagement near Constantinople, he marched to Caesarea, the stronghold of the Phocas, and by so doing he forced the usurper to turn back. Sclerus won the first battle, but on 24 May 979, in the plains of Pankaleia, not far from Amorium, Phocas defeated first his rival in single combat and then his army, with a decisive stroke. Sclerus fled to the court of the Caliph, and with his flight came to an end the three years of the first civil war, though it was to be followed soon after by serious complications.

A few years later a discord developed between the young Emperor Basil and his all-powerful great-uncle. Basil was no longer the inexperienced stripling who needed support and for whom external guidance was not only necessary but also beneficial. His strength and his will to rule had now emerged to view: the tutelage which he had at first willingly accepted became increasingly burdensome, until finally his unsatisfied thirst for power and his mortification at his continued relegation were concentrated in a feeling of irreconcilable hatred against the man to whom he was indebted for his political education and even, perhaps, for the throne itself. And so it came to pass that the great statesman who had known how to handle the powerful soldier-emperors, was now a victim of the youthful urge to power of his great-nephew. It appears that he had foreseen his disgrace, and was plotting, in association with Bardas Phocas and other generals, against his ungrateful protégé. But the Emperor forestalled him; he was arrested like a common rebel and, after the confiscation of all his vast wealth, sent into exile, where he soon died, broken by the harshness of fate.

Although the sole rule of Basil II is officially reckoned from 976 his independence only really began after the deportation of the great eunuch in 985.[1] One fact shows clearly how omnipotent the *paracoemomenus* had been and how strong and enduring was the Emperor's resentment of his own relegation to the background: Basil II took it on himself to declare invalid all edicts promulgated before the removal of his great-uncle, unless they bore retrospective confirmation in the form of a note in his own hand that he had viewed them: 'for at the beginning of our own reign, until the deposition of Basil the *paracoemomenus*, ... many things happened which were not according to our wish, for he decided and appointed everything according to his own will'.[2]

The first independent undertaking of Basil II was his Balkan campaign of 986. The death of the great Tzimisces had brought deliverance to the enemies of the Empire as though from a nightmare. The civil war and the other embroilments which followed in Byzantium left them free to indulge in their own activities for several years. And even though it was possible to beat off the frontier attacks of the

[1] This chronology follows Rosen, *Bolgarobojca* and Schlumberger, *Épopée byzantine* I (1925), 510, based on Jahja who is in general agreement with Scylitzes. Psellus wrongly places the deposition of the *paracoemomenus* Basil in the period after the death of Bardas Phocas, i.e. some time in 989.

[2] Basil's novel of 996, Zepos, *Jus* I, 270; cf. also Psellus' statement, *Chronographia* I, 12 f. (ed. Renauld; Eng. trans. Sewter, 19 f.).

distant Fatimid Caliphate of Egypt, the only remaining serious danger to the Empire in the East, the weakening of the central authority of the Empire had far-reaching consequences for the development of the Balkan situation. After the death of John Tzimisces, a revolt broke out in the Macedonian region, led by the four Cometopuli, the sons of the *comes* Nicholas, a provincial governor in Macedonia.[1] The rising took on serious proportions and became a war of liberation, which spread over the whole of Macedonia and sought to remove the greater part of the Balkans from Byzantine rule. On hearing the news of the rising, Boris II, the tzar of the Bulgars, together with his brother, Romanus, fled from Constantinople, but was killed crossing the border; Romanus reached home, but could lay no claim to the crown because he had been castrated by the Byzantines.[2] The leadership, and later the crown itself, fell to the heroic Samuel, the youngest of the Cometopuli; for his two elder brothers had perished and the third later met his death at Samuel's own hands.

Samuel became the founder of a powerful Empire, which had its centre first at Prespa and later at Ochrida. Little by little he gathered under his sway the whole Macedonian region except Thessalonica, the old Bulgar territory between the Danube and the Balkan range, Thessaly, Epirus, part of Albania including Dyrrachium, and finally Rascia and Dioclea. The Bulgarian Patriarchate, abolished by Tzimisces, was also able to celebrate its revival under Samuel. After various peregrinations, it finally found a home in Ochrida, Samuel's capital city, which as an ecclesiastical centre was to survive Samuel's empire by several centuries. Politically and ecclesiastically, the new empire was the direct descendant of the empire of Symeon and

---

[1] Nothing definite is known about the early history of the Cometopuli. The contemporary Armenian historian Stephen of Taron (Asolik), trans. Gelzer and Burckhardt (1907), 185 f., says that they were of Armenian descent. In spite of N. Adontz, 'Samuel l'Arménien' 3 ff., it remains doubtful how much weight can be given to the statement of this Armenian historian whose information on Samuel is full of obvious errors. N. P. Blagoev, 'Bratjata David, Moisej, Aaron i Samuil' (The brothers David, Moses, Aaron and Samuel), *Godišnik na Sofijsk. Univ.*, Jurid. Fak. 37, 14 (1941–2), 28 ff., considers that Count Nicholas was a descendant of the proto-Bulgar Asparuch, and his wife Ripsimia, the mother of the Cometopuli, a daughter of the czar Symeon, which is entirely without foundation. His 'Teorijata za Zapadno bŭlgarsko carstvo' (Theories on the West Bulgarian Empire), ibid. 16 ff., contains equally fantastic views.

[2] Cf. Runciman, *Bulgarian Empire* 221, who is certainly right. Zlatarski, *Istorija* I, 2, 647 ff., and Adontz, 'Samuel l'Arménien' 9 ff., following the fabulous story of Jahja (ed. Rosen, 20 f.) and the Armenian Asolik, consider that Romanus was recognized as tzar. The would-be tzar turns up later as commander of Skŏplje and in 1004 he surrendered the city to the Byzantines, received the title of patrician from Basil II and became the Byzantine *strategus* in Abydus; cf. Scylitzes-Cedren. II, 455.

Peter, and was regarded by Samuel and the Byzantines alike as being simply the Bulgarian Empire. For apart from Byzantium, only Bulgaria at that time possessed a tradition of empire with a patriarchate of its own. Samuel was entirely committed to these traditions. But in reality his Macedonian kingdom was essentially different from the former kingdom of the Bulgars. In composition and character, it represented a new and distinctive phenomenon. The balance had shifted towards the west and south, and Macedonia, a peripheral region in the old Bulgarian kingdom, was its real centre.[1]

Samuel first began a movement of expansion in a southerly direction. Attacks on Serres and Thessalonica were followed up by repeated descents into Thessaly, which finally led to an important success: after a long siege Larissa fell into Samuel's hands at the end

---

[1] The history of the origin of Samuel's empire is a much debated question. Scholars no longer support Drinov's theory of a West Bulgarian empire of the Šišmanids founded in 963, and today two different and conflicting views are current. One view holds that by 969 a West Bulgarian (Macedonian) kingdom under the Cometopuli had split off from the empire of the tzar Peter and that this existed independently side by side with the East Bulgarian empire (on the Danube); further, they consider that it was only the eastern part which was conquered by Tzimisces, while the western part continued and formed the nucleus of Samuel's empire. The second view, worked out in detail by D. Anastasijević, 'L'hypothèse de la Bulgaric Occidentale', *Recueil Uspenskij* I (1930), 20 ff., insists that there was no separation between an eastern and western Bulgaria, and that Tzimisces conquered the whole of Bulgaria which only regained its independence with the Cometopuli's revolt in 976 and the foundation of a new empire in Macedonia. This latter interpretation seems to me to be in the main correct, though both theories appear to go astray in so far as they imply that the subjection of the country took the form of a regular occupation of the whole countryside. Anastasijević rightly emphasizes that the sources give practically no ground for the assumption that an independent West Bulgaria ever existed side by side with an East Bulgaria, and they afford equally slight evidence for the statement that there was a revolt of the Cometopuli before 976. The frequently quoted statement in Scylitzes-Cedren. II, 347, dated rather arbitrarily to the year 969 and equally arbitrarily regarded as an account of a revolt of the Cometopuli said to have broken out in this year, is in reality only a casual comment, by way of an aside, which anticipates the events it refers to (cf. the doubts of Runciman, *Bulgarian Empire* 218, and Adontz, 'Samuel l'Arménien', 5 ff.). On the other hand, the sources make it quite clear that Tzimisces—like Svjatoslav—never set foot in Macedonia (the entirely unsupported statement of the later Priest of Dioclea who says that Tzimisces took possession of Serbia, and consequently Macedonia as well, is of no importance). The capture of the capital and the deposition of the ruler signified the subjection of the country without any need to conquer its territory inch by inch. It is, however, true that control which was limited to occupying the centre could in certain circumstances easily be overthrown from the periphery, and this was in fact what happened after the death of John Tzimisces and the outbreak of internal conflicts in Byzantium. This problem has been recently discussed by Litavrin, *Bolgarija i Vizantija* 261 ff., who does not, however, advance any new or compelling arguments for the view he adopts, i.e. that 'Bulgaria continued its existence in the West'. He concludes: 'The period from 969 to 976 was in Western Bulgaria a time when its forces were consolidated under the rule of the Cometopuli. . . .' But, as our observations above make clear, this assertion has not the slightest foundation in the sources.

of 985 or the beginning of 986.[1] This provoked a counter-offensive from the Emperor Basil II, but his first encounter with Samuel was not a happy one. He invaded the region of Sardica by the so-called 'Trajan's Gates' but his attempt at capturing the town was unsuccessful and his army was attacked and beaten whilst making its retreat (August 986).[2] Samuel was then able to build up his power undisturbed and extend the frontiers of his empire up to the Black Sea on one side and to the Adriatic on the other. For a new, and much more serious, civil war had broken out in Byzantium.

Encouraged by the Emperor's lack of success, the Byzantine aristocracy had risen against him. The beginning of 987 saw the reappearance of Bardas Sclerus on Byzantine soil and his resumption of the purple. Bardas Phocas, who had been disgraced on account of his association with Basil the *paracoemomenus*, resumed the supreme command in Asia and was to have once again entered the lists against his namesake. Instead, however, he himself rebelled against the Emperor, the author of his neglect during the past few years, which he bitterly resented, and, with the example of his great-uncle before his eyes, had himself proclaimed Emperor on 15 August 987. His revolt was made particularly dangerous by the fact that it had been preceded by an assembly of high-ranking army officers and of many members of the landed aristocracy of Asia Minor. Behind the usurper were ranged the senior officers of the army, who were nettled by the self-will of the young Emperor, and by the landed nobility, who saw in him a hindrance to their ambitions. Bardas Phocas now entered on an agreement with his former rival and namesake; the Empire was to be divided, Phocas taking the European portion, including Constantinople, and Sclerus the Asiatic portion. After a short period of co-operation, however, Bardas Phocas, who realized his superiority, caused the other aspirant to the throne to be arrested and was henceforth the only pretender. The whole of Asia Minor succumbed to him, and at the beginning of 988 he approached Constantinople. A two-headed attack from sea and land was prepared against the capital, part of his army being stationed at Chrysopolis and the rest at Abydus.

[1] For the chronology, cf. the recent study by P. Lemerle, *Prolégomènes à une édition critique et commentée des 'Conseils et Récits' de Kékauménos, Mémoires de l'Acad. royale de Belgique* LIV, 1 (1960), 26 f.
[2] Cf. the detailed account of this campaign by P. Mutafčiev, 'Starijat drum prez "Trajanova vrata"' (The ancient road through the 'Trajan gates'), *Spisanie na Bŭlg. Akad.* 55 (1937), 101 ff.

The situation of the legitimate Emperor was desperate. Only external aid could save him from ruin. Basil II had recognized this in good time and had directed an appeal for help to the Russian prince Vladimir. In the spring of 988, a Russian battle contingent of six thousand entered Byzantine territory, and thus the famous Varangian Družina saved the situation at the eleventh hour. Led by the Emperor in person, the valiant Varangians inflicted a crushing defeat on the rebels at Chrysopolis. The battle of Abydus, on 13 April 989, in the course of which Bardas Phocas died, apparently as a result of a heart attack, was decisive. The rebellion had collapsed. A fresh revolt on the part of Bardas Sclerus ended in a peaceful settlement and the submission of the usurper. The Varangian Družina remained in the service of Byzantium and, reinforced by frequent additions of Varangians and other Northmen, played an important role in the Byzantine army.[1]

As a reward for his act of deliverance, the prince of Kiev was promised as his bride Anna, the purple-born sister of the Emperor, on condition that he and his people received baptism. This was a very great concession: no Byzantine princess born in the purple had ever before been married to a foreigner. Peter, the tzar of the Bulgars, had had to content himself with a Lecapena, Otto II with a kinswoman of the usurper Tzimisces; it was only the ruler of the youthful Russian kingdom who was accorded the unique honour of becoming related by marriage to the legitimate imperial house. Such an alliance was so contrary to Byzantine self-esteem that once the danger was past there was some feeling in Constantinople that the promise given during so critical a moment should not be honoured. In order to enforce his claims to the princess, Vladimir felt constrained to invade Byzantine possessions on the far side of the Black Sea and occupy Cherson (in the summer of 989).

The conversion of the state of Kiev to Christianity marked not only the beginning of a new era in the development of Russia but also an impressive triumph for Byzantium. The Byzantine sphere of influence was enlarged to an extent undreamed of, and the largest and most promising of the Slav states came under the spiritual guidance of Constantinople. The new Russian Church was subordinate to the Patriarchate of Constantinople and was, to begin

---

[1] On the Russian Normans (Varangians) in Byzantine service cf. the exhaustive account of Vasiljevskij, *Družina* 176 ff. On the English Normans in Byzantium cf. also Vasiliev, *Annales de l'Inst.Kondakov* 9 (1937), 39 ff., and R. M. Dawkins, 'The later history of the Varangian Guard: some notes', JRS 37 (1947), 39 ff.

with, directed by Oreek metropolitans sent out from Byzantium.[1] The cultural development of Russia was to be under the aegis of Byzantium for some time to come.

Basil II emerged victorious from his conflict with the aristocracy of Asia Minor. After desperate struggles and terrible civil wars all his enemies and opponents were vanquished. But the struggle had lasted a full thirteen years, and the Emperor's character had undergone a powerful transformation in the course of the bitter experience of these years. He had lost all joy in the pleasures of life to which he had surrendered himself with unrestrained passion in his youth. He became sombre and suspicious, trusting none and knowing neither friendship nor love. He remained unmarried all his life. He lived alone withdrawn into himself, just as he governed the Empire alone, shunning all advice, an autocratic ruler in the fullest sense of the term. His way of life was that of an ascetic or a campaigner. He had no use for the ceremonial of the court, and, grandson of the scholarly Constantine VII though he was, he had no time for art and learning. The art of rhetoric, so highly prized in Byzantium, was completely abhorrent to him. His mode of expression was simple and abrupt, appearing coarse and unpolished to the sensibilities of the cultivated Byzantines. Although he was the enemy of the aristocracy, he made no attempt to win the favour of the people. He required from his subjects not love but obedience. His whole ambition was directed towards increasing the power of the state and to overpowering the external and internal enemies of the Empire.[2]

Once the political aspirations of the Byzantine aristocracy had been broken in cruel civil strife, it was possible to set about restraining their economic ambitions. Romanus Lecapenus had already realized how great a burden the expansion of landed estates in the provinces laid upon the social and economic structure of the Byzantine state. The political consequences only Basil II could gauge, from the experience of his childhood and youth. He resumed the anti-aristocratic agrarian policy begun by Romanus Lecapenus, with the

---

[1] E. Honigmann, 'Studies in Slavic Church History', B 17 (1944–5), 128 ff., shows that Theophylact, Metropolitan of Sebastea, was the first Metropolitan appointed to Russia. Honigmann's detailed and successful investigations entirely refute the theories of N. Baumgarten, 'Saint Vladimir et la conversion de la Russie', OCP 27 (1932), and M. Jugie, 'Les origines de l'Eglise russe', EO 36 (1937), 257 ff., and *Le schisme byzantin* (1941), 172 ff., who attempt to show that Russia was Christianized from Rome, and his strong criticism of the methods of these two scholars is certainly justified.

[2] Cf. the excellent character sketch by Psellus, *Chronographia* I, 18 ff. (ed. Renauld; English trans. Sewter, 24 ff.), and also Zonaras III, 561.

intention not only of extending it along the same lines but also of making it considerably more stringent. Added to the political insight which caused him to pledge himself to maintaining peasant and military holdings, was his personal hatred of the dynastic families which had disputed his claim to the throne of his fathers. His radicalism had the further consequence of leading him to disregard the demands of right and justice. This is illustrated by the case of Eustathius Maleinus, a former comrade in arms of Bardas Phocas, whose hospitality Basil had claimed on his return from the Syrian campaign. The remarkable wealth of this Cappodocian magnate, his enormous estates and, above all, the number of his slaves and other dependants who were capable of forming a military contingent of several thousand men, all impressed themselves so much on the Emperor that he invited his host to Constantinople and held him there in honourable captivity. His property was confiscated by the state.

Basil II, in his novel of 996,[1] expressly mentions the houses of the Phocas and the Maleini as being the most outstanding representatives of the now over-mighty landed aristocracy. The most important addition which this novel makes to the provisions of the older legislation is the abolition of the forty years' period of grace, after which, according to the old rules, any right to the restitution of property illegally acquired was extinguished. The novel of Basil II stresses the fact that the magnates, thanks to their influential position, could easily and with impunity circumvent the period of grace and make their ill-gotten possessions secure. The Emperor therefore decreed that all property acquired by the 'powerful' from the 'poor' since the time of the first relevant edict, that of Romanus Lecapenus, should be restored to their previous owners without any regard for a period of grace and without any compensation. The fisc, however, was according to Basil II exempt from the observance of any period of grace: the state's right of eviction reached back to the time of Augustus.

In this novel Basil II also tried to restrict the extension of ecclesiastical property at the expense of peasant land. Monasteries which were peasant foundations and stood on peasant land and which had only a small number of monks, were to be regarded not as monasteries but as chapels of ease, subordinate to the village community and exempt from paying tribute to the bishop. Larger establish-

---

[1] Zepos, *Jus* I, 262 ff.; Dölger, *Reg.* 783.

ments, however, with eight or more monks, did indeed remain subordinate to the bishop, but they were to make no new acquisitions. This provision made a further link between Basil and the edict of his great-grandfather, Romanus Lecapenus. On the other hand, he avoided any allusion to the still more radical edict of his stepfather, Nicephorus Phocas, which had been revoked by John Tzimisces.[1]

Basil II's measures against the magnates became increasingly stringent. A few years after his abolition of the period of grace, he saddled them with the obligation of paying the *allelengyon* on behalf of the poor; that is to say, he made them responsible for the outstanding tax payments of the peasantry.[2] Thus the burden of the *allelengyon* which had hitherto—in accordance with the principle of collective payment of taxes by the village community—fallen on the neighbours of the insolvent tax-payer (cf. above, p. 136 f. and p. 110), was now shifted on to the shoulders of the great landowners alone. This incisive measure had a twofold effect: a new and heavy blow was struck at the magnates and the fisc had greater security for the payment of the *allelengyon*. For the payment of taxes on behalf of the decayed property of a neighbour was often beyond the resources of the peasants and drove them to migrate, which only inflicted fresh damage on the state.[3] Basil II did not allow himself to be moved by the protests of the magnates, even though they were supported by the Patriarch Sergius himself. His fixed resolve was to break the overweening power of the aristocracy, against which his ancestors had striven in vain.

Immediately after the conclusion of the civil war he took up with equal energy the struggle against his external enemies. By far the most dangerous of all his foes was the tzar Samuel. For Basil II, the struggle with Samuel became his chief task and the annihilation of Samuel's empire his life's ambition. He seems to have sought the support of other Balkan rulers against the powerful Macedonian Empire, and to have made an alliance with the prince John Vladimir of Dioclea. A Serbian embassy, apparently from Dioclea, arrived by the sea route in Byzantium in 992, after encountering many

---

[1] The chrysobull dated 4 April 988 and attributed to Basil II which again repeals that decree of Nicephorus Phocas and which, unlike the novel of 996, shows a distinctly pro-monastic emphasis, can hardly be genuine; cf. Dölger, *Reg.* 772.

[2] Scylitzes-Cedren. II, 456; cf. also Zonaras III, 561.

[3] This comes out particularly clearly in the Ashburner treatise §§ 12 and 14 (ed. Dölger, *Finanzverwaltung*, p. 119).

adventures.[1] They found that the Emperor had already gone into battle. For early in the spring of 991 Basil II had invaded Macedonia, where he was to pursue the struggle against Samuel for several years.

However, he was forced to interrupt his successful campaign to betake himself to the East. For the Fatimids had in 994 inflicted a serious defeat on the imperial commander of Antioch on the Orontes, with the result that Aleppo was besieged and Antioch itself seriously endangered. The Byzantine Empire was always doomed to fight on two fronts. Heavy punishment always followed any attempt at evading this fate. The Balkan question was as prominent in the eyes of Basil II as the Syrian had been once for Nicephorus Phocas. But Basil did not fall into the error of his great stepfather, who in his preoccupation with Syria had lost sight of his obligations in the Balkans. In 995 Basil appeared in person under the walls of Aleppo, repulsed the enemy, whom he took by surprise, and occupied Raphanea and Emesa. Several years later he returned to Syria, once more saving the situation after the *dux* of Antioch had again been defeated by the Fatimids. But his efforts to take Tripolis were once more frustrated. After restoring the *status quo* in Syria he went to the Caucasus region to supervise affairs in Armenia and Iberia.

Samuel took advantage of the Emperor's absence and embarked on a campaign against Greece, advancing as far as the Peloponnese. On the return home, however, he was surprised and beaten by the able Byzantine general Nicephorus Uranus; Samuel was himself wounded in the fight and only narrowly escaped death (997). The ambitions of Samuel were unappeased despite this disaster, and the capture of Dyrrachium and the annexation of Rascia and Dioclea probably took place in the years which immediately followed.[2] The alliance with Byzantium brought little practical advantage to prince Vladimir. His country was annexed to Samuel's empire whilst he

---

[1] This information is found in a document of September 993 in the monastery of the Laura, Rouillard-Collomp, *Actes de Lavra* I (1937), Nr. 12. On this cf. G. Ostrogorsky, 'Serbskoe posol'stvo k imperatoru Vasiliju II' (A Serbian embassy to the Emperor Basil II), *Glas Srpske Akad. Nauka* 193 (1949), 15 ff., and 'Une ambassade serbe auprès de l'empereur Basile II', B 19 (1949) 187 ff. (abbreviated version). Cf. also Dujčev, 'Proučvanija vŭrchu bŭlgarskoto srednovekovie' (Studies in the Bulgarian middle ages), Sofia 1945, 27 ff. D. S. Radojičić, 'Srpsko Zagorje, das spätere Raszien', *Südost-Forschung* 17 (1957), 276 ff., puts forward the suggestion that this embassy came from Rascia, since the Lavra documents describe the ambassadors as Serbians. But the Byzantines also referred to Dioclea (Zeta) as Serbian and its inhabitants as Serbs. For this period cf. especially Scylitzes-Cedren. II, 515, 8; 526, 14, 15; 543, 13; 544, 5, 8.

[2] On the disputed chronology cf. my comments in the paper cited in the previous note.

himself was first taken captive and later married to a daughter of the powerful tzar and reinstated as his vassal on the throne of Dioclea.

It was only after Basil II's return from Asia in 1001 and his reappearance in the Balkans that the great Byzantine counter-offensive opened, a carefully considered campaign led by the Emperor in person which aimed with relentless logic at cutting the enemy's life-line. The Emperor first advanced in the region of Sardica and captured the surrounding fortifications. By this means Samuel was cut off from the old Bulgarian territories on the Danube, and the former Bulgarian capital Pliska and both Great and Little Preslav were occupied by imperial generals. Basil II then turned back into Macedonia. Berrhoia surrendered, Servia was taken by storm and the way to northern Greece lay open. Byzantine rule was soon re-established in Thessaly, Basil appeared again in Macedonia and after a hard struggle took the strongly fortified town of Vodena. His next stroke brought him Vidin, the important stronghold on the Danube which he subdued after a siege lasting eight months, without allowing himself to be distracted by an audacious counter-manœuvre on the part of Samuel, the capture and plundering of Adrianople. From Vidin the Emperor pressed on by rapid marches to the south. On the river Vardar, not far from Skoplje, he gained a decisive victory over Samuel's army, and Skoplje thereupon opened its doors to him (1004).[1] The capture of Skoplje on the one side and of Vodena on the other meant that the kernel of Samuel's territory was held in a pincer. After four years of unceasing strife, in which Byzantium had advanced from one victory to another, the adversary had lost more than half his territory. For the first time Basil decided to allow himself an interval and returned, by way of Philippopolis, to Constantinople for the winter. In the words of a contemporary: 'Basil II did not conduct his wars like most other Emperors, who set out in spring and returned home late in summer; for Basil, the time of return was decided by the achievement of the objective which he had in mind when he had started out'.[2]

In fact, no one could be in any further doubt as to the outcome of the war. The Byzantine state, backed by centuries-old-tradition, had once again shown its superiority. The valiant tzar could not match the skilful military leadership, organization and technical

---

[1] Adontz, 'Samuel l'Arménien' 24 ff., doubts the campaign against Vidin as well as the battle on the Vardar without sufficient reason. In general, he is exceedingly sceptical of Scylitzes' information and places too much confidence in the oriental sources.

[2] Psellus, *Chronographia* I, 20 (ed. Renauld; Sewter, 25).

resources of the old Empire. His generals and governors began to desert him; in 1005 Dyrrachium fell to the Byzantine Emperor as a result of an act of treachery. But the final annihilation came only in July 1014, after protracted struggles about which little is known. Samuel's army was surrounded in a narrow pass of the Belasica mountains, the so-called Kleidion, in the region of the upper Struma; it is true that the tzar managed to escape to Prilep, but a large number of his army were killed and still more were taken prisoner. Basil the Bulgaroctonus celebrated his victory in a terrible fashion. The captives—allegedly numbering fourteen thousand[1]—were blinded, and were then despatched in batches of a hundred men, each group having a one-eyed man as guide, to their tzar at Prilep. When Samuel beheld the approach of this gruesome cavalcade, he fell senseless to the ground. Two days later the gallant tzar was dead (6 October 1014).

His empire survived him by only a few years. His conqueror was assisted by internal dissensions. Samuel's son and successor, Gabriel Radomir, was in 1015 murdered by his cousin, John Vladislav. Gabriel's wife and his brother-in-law, John Vladimir of Dioclea, shared his fate. The subjugation of the country went steadily forward, until the death of John Vladislav, which took place in an attack on Dyrrachium in February 1018, brought the struggle to an end. Basil made a ceremonious entry into Ochrida and received homage from the tzar's widow and from the other surviving members of the royal family. He had reached his goal: this rebellious country, against which he had begun the struggle more than thirty years before, lay at the feet of the Emperor, now sixty years old, and was annexed to his Empire. The whole Balkan peninsula once again belonged to the Byzantine Empire, for the first time since the Slav occupation. After Basil had traversed the subjugated country, everywhere establishing his rule, he paid a visit to the venerable city of Athens. The feelings of exaltation released by the revival of the Empire found striking expression in the victorious Emperor's solemn thanksgiving in the Parthenon, at that time a church dedicated to the Mother of God.

The policy of Basil the Bulgar-Slayer (Bulgaroctonus) towards the subjugated country was as moderate and sensible as his conduct on the field of battle had been inhuman and ruthless. Having

---

[1] Cecaumenus (ed. Vasiljevsky-Jernstedt) 18; Scylitzes-Cedren. 458 puts it at 15,000. In spite of the close agreement between these two independent sources, the figure seems exaggerated, cf. J. Ivanov, 'Belasickata bitka 29 Juli 1014' (The battle of Belasica 29 July 1014), *Izvestija na Istor. Druž.* 3 (1911), 12, note 1.

Figure 41: (ABOVE) *Czar Samuel's Fortress*. Ochrida, Yugoslavia (Macedonia), 10th century. (BELOW) *Church of St. Sophia*. Ochrida, Yugoslavia (Macedonia), 9th century, with later additions. West façade, showing exonarthex and flanking towers. Photos: Bildarchiv Foto Marburg.

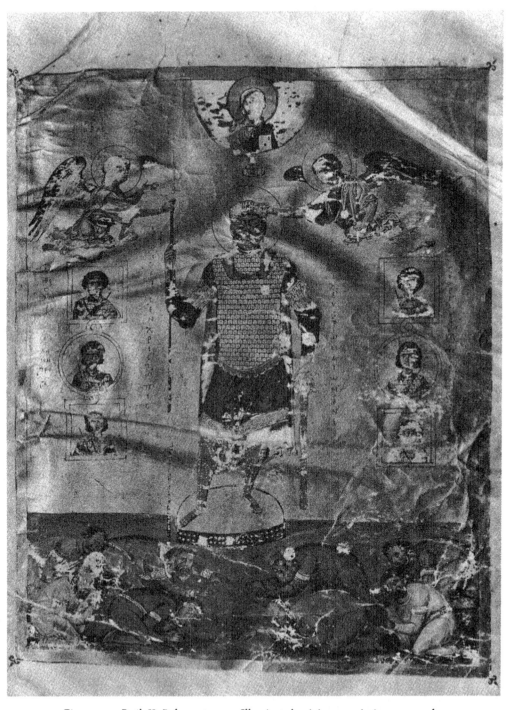

Figure 42: *Basil II Bulgaroctonus.* Illuminated miniature painting on parchment, Psalter of Basil II, circa 1021. Ht. 15⅝″, w. 11⅞″. Marcian Library, Venice; *Cod. gr. 17.* Photo: Hirmer Fotoarchiv, Munich.

regard to the situation of the country and its existing customs, he excused his new subjects from the obligation of paying taxes in gold which was imposed on the economically further developed parts of the Empire, accepting instead payment in kind. The Patriarchate of Ochrida was degraded to an archbishopric; but the new archbishopric ranked as autocephalous, had many important privileges and was given control of all the bishoprics which had earlier belonged to the empire of Samuel and of the tzar Peter. In practice, what was meant by the autocephalous nature of the archbishopric of Ochrida was that it was subject not to the Patriarch of Constantinople but to the will of the Emperor, who reserved to himself the right of appointment to the see.[1] This arrangement—a real master-stroke of imperial policy—secured for Byzantium control over the churches of the southern Slavs, but avoided any further extension of the already vast sphere of jurisdiction of the Patriarch of Constantinople, and at the same time properly emphasized the special claims as an ecclesiastical centre of Ochrida, whose autocephalous archbishops occupied in the hierarchy of the Greek Church a significantly higher place than the other princes of the Church who were subordinate to the Patriarchate of Constantinople.

As a component of the Byzantine Empire, the newly-conquered region was divided into themes,[2] like any other Byzantine territory. The lands which had been the kernel of Samuel's empire now formed the theme of Bulgaria and, out of respect to the great importance

[1] The Archbishop of Ochrida was not elected by the local bishops but appointed by the Emperor, as I have shown in *Jugosl. Istor. Casopis* I (1935), 516 f., against Zlatarski, *Istorija* II, 17 ff. Cf. the excellent comments of B. Granić, 'Kirchenrechtliche Glossen zu den vom Kaiser Basileios II. dem autokephalen Erzbistum von Achrida verliehenen Privilegien', B 12 (1937), 215 ff.

[2] Zlatarski, *Istorija* II, 1 ff., and *Sem. Kond.* 4 (1931), 49 ff., maintains that the former empire of Samuel was not split up under Byzantine rule, but remained a single administrative unit, a view which cannot be accepted; cf. F. Dölger, BZ 31 (1931), 443 f. There is no doubt that the former empire of Samuel was divided into several themes, but the precise nature of this division is a complicated problem which requires further investigation. Cf. Skabalanovič, *Viz. gosudarstvo* 226 ff. (still important, though needing correction in points of detail), P. Mutafčiev, 'Sudbinite na srednevekovnija Drŭstŭr' (The fate of the medieval Durostorum), *Sbornik Silistra i Dobrudža* I (1927), 158 ff. Particular attention has been paid to this question by N.Banescu, in numerous studies on individual problems, and finally in a monograph in which he sums up and expands the results of his investigations: *Les duchés byzantins de Paristrion (Paradounavon) et de Bulgare,* Bucharest 1946 (this work, which was inaccessible to me during the preparation of the first two editions and the French and English translations of this book, has now reached me through the kindness of the author). Cf. Kyriakides, Βυζ. Μελέται 144 ff., who overlooks however, the fact that the mention of a *strategus* in any particular town by no means implies that this town was the centre of a theme; his map of the Balkans in the time of Basil II shows a swarm of minute themes which either belong to a later period or else never existed. This problem has now been examined in detail by Litavrin, *Bolgarija i Vizantija,* 250 ff.

of this new theme, it was governed first by a catepan, and later, indeed, by a *dux*. Its centre was at Skoplje.[1] Along the lower reaches of the Danube lay the theme of Paristrion or Paradunavon, with its centre at the Danube town of Silistria, which was also later raised to a catepanate, and then to a duchy (*ducatus*). The region of Sirmium seems to have formed a further theme on the northern boundary of the Empire.[2] The region on the Adriatic coast, including Zadar (Zara) in the north and Dubrovnik (Ragusa) in the south, formed the theme of Dalmatia as before. The territory of Dioclea, however, and the regions of Zachlumia, Rascia and Bosnia were not organized as themes but on the contrary continued, as did Croatia, to be under the rule of their native princes, thus forming vassal principalities of the Byzantine Empire rather than provinces proper.[3]

---

[1] A widespread but erroneous view puts the seat of the *strategus* of the theme first in Ochrida, then in Skoplje, in Sardica and finally back again to Skoplje; cf. Mutafčiev, BZ 26 (1926), 251, and Zlatarski, *Istorija* II, 14 ff., following Skabalanovič. When Basil II was subduing the empire of Samuel he appointed the patrician Eustathius Daphnomeles in Ochrida as ἄρχων τῆς πόλεως (Scylitzes II, 468, 14), but this only indicates that he had been made commander of the city of Ochrida, and not that he had been raised to the position of *strategus* of the theme of Bulgaria, and indeed shortly afterwards Eustathius was made *strategus* of the theme of Dyrrachium (ibid. 474, 3). On the other hand, the patrician David Areianites was appointed στρατηγὸς αὐτοκράτωρ in Skoplje and simultaneously as κατεπάνω Βουλγαρίας (expressly stated, Prokić, Zusätze Nr. 41 to Scylitzes II, 468, 1). Later on Romanus Diogenes appears as *dux* of Sardica about 1067 (Attaleiates 97, 16; Scylitzes II, 663, 12; Zonaras III, 684, 8) which does not imply that the seat of the *strategus* of the theme of Bulgaria had been moved from Skoplje to Sardica, but that the region of Sardica had become a separate theme and that the process of splitting up the original theme in order to create new themes had already begun. The seat of the *strategus* of Bulgaria still remained as before in Skoplje as a number of sources show. This is also rightly emphasized by Banescu, *Duchés byzantins*, 121 ff.

[2] This was long ago accepted by Skabalanovič, *Viz. gosudarstvo* 228 ff., and following him by Mutafčiev, *Sbornik Silistra i Dobrudža* I (1927) and *Istorija* II, 1. Litravin, *Bolgarija i Vizantija* 273 ff., also inclines to this view. On the other hand, Banescu, *Duchés byzantins* 24 ff., decisively rejects it. He is quite right in pointing out that Skabalanovič quoted several sources as referring to this theme which in reality refer to the theme Paristrion. But there is still the statement of Scylitzes-Cedren. (II, 476, 24) that after the murder of Sermon, Samuel's commander in Sirmium, Constantine Diogenes, was 'entrusted with the government of the newly-conquered region' (ἄρχειν ἐτάχθη τῆς νεοκτήτου χώρας), which means at least that he was appointed not only as commander of the city of Sirmium, but also as governor of the surrounding district. It is difficult to imagine that the theme of Bulgaria stretched, as Banescu believes, from southern Macedonia right to the Sava and the Danube. In the twelfth century, according to Nicetas Choniates (p. 133, 9), the region of Belgrade and Braničevo, or according to Cinnamus, the region of Braničevo and Niš, formed a separate theme. Its *dux* was the later Emperor Andronicus Comnenus.

[3] This is clearly evidenced by the Priest of Dioclea (ed. Šišić, 346 f.). Besides the prince Stephen Voislav (Dobroslav) of Dioclea who fought against the Byzantines in the thirties and forties of the eleventh century, he cites the Župan of Rascia, the Ban of Bosnia and the prince of Zachlumia whom the Byzantine Emperor lured with costly gifts into an alliance against the rebellious prince of Dioclea. These clear and unambiguous statements seem difficult to reconcile with the two recently published seals. One seal mentions Anthypatus Patricius Constantinus, *dux* Θεσσαλονίκης, Βουλγαρίας

The region south of Lake Scadar (Scodra) belonged now as formerly to the duchy of Dyrrachium, which formed the most important strategic stronghold of the Byzantine Empire on the Adriatic, just as the theme Thessalonica, created a duchy at the same time, was its most important bastion on the Ægean. The recovery of the entire Balkan peninsula was also of the utmost importance in internal politics. It was certainly not by chance that the conquests of Nicephorus, a grandee of Asia Minor, were made in Asian territory, nor that Basil II, the great antagonist of the landed aristocracy of Asia Minor, chiefly devoted his attention to the European portion of the Empire. Once imperial territory again extended as far as the Danube and the Adriatic, the position of outstanding importance held in the Empire by Asia Minor during recent centuries was a thing of the past.[1]

However, Basil II did not shut his eyes to the tasks which awaited the Empire in Asia. During the last years of his reign he was active at the other end of the Byzantine world, in the Caucasus region. After the death of Gagik I (990–1020), whose reign had seen the

καὶ Σέρβας (ed. I. Swiencickyj, 'Byzantinische Bleisiegel in der Sammlung von Lwow', *Sbornik Nikov* (1940), 439 f.) and the other refers to Constantine Diogenes, *strategus* Σερβίας (ed. V. Laurent, 'Le thème byzantin de Serbie au XIᵉ siecle', REB 15 (1957), 190). The enigma posed by these seals is not easy to solve, and I do not believe it has been resolved by the learned editor of the second seal. Laurent, op. cit. 185 ff. (cf. also the earlier article, 'Le thème byzantin de Serbie', *Balcania* 6 (1943), 35 ff.), firmly advances the view, on the basis of this seal, that after the overthrow of Samuel's kingdom, a theme of Serbia existed, if only for a short while. He was, however, unable to give any satisfactory definition either of the territory of this theme or of the period at which Constantine Diogenes is supposed to have governed it. Against the statement of the priest of Dioclea, which he is too ready to sweep aside, Laurent seems to wish to include Rascia and Zachlumia in this theme. Whether he would also include Dioclea is not clear to me; and indeed his ideas on the history and geography of the South Slav lands, at this period, do lack clarity. He cites in support of his view the unauthentic document of Lutovid, allegedly a *strategus Servie et Zachulmie*, on the strength of which Skabalanovič, *Viz. gosudarstvo* 219 ff., accepted the existence of a theme of Serbia or Zachlumia (unfortunately I followed this view in the first edition of this book, but admitted that it was untenable in the second edition). Constantine Diogenes, to whom Laurent attributes both seals, is a person familiar from the sources (the principal dates in his career are given by Banescu, *Duchés byzantins*). We know that he was appointed *strategus* of Thessalonica in 1015 (Scylitz.-Cedr. II, 461, 16; he still held this post in 1017: ibid., 466, 7); after the murder of Sermon in 1019 he took over the government of the district of Sirmium (ibid. 476, 24; see the previous note); about 1026 he was at the same time appointed *dux* of Bulgaria (ibid. 483, 21); and about 1030 was recalled from Sirmium and appointed *dux* of Thessalonica (ibid. 487, 18). On the other hand we hear nothing of his ever being *strategus* of Serbia. But by 1031 he had become a monk (ibid. 497, 8; in the year 6539, indiction 14). Laurent seems to hold that he took over the government of the 'theme of Serbia' during the time when he was *dux* of Bulgaria and of Thessalonica (and thus governed only during the short period from 1030–31?), but he fails to give any explanation as to why the seals which he publishes fail to mention the two duchies.

[1] Cf. the stimulating arguments of Neumann, *Weltstellung* 62.

greatest period of the kingdom of the Bagratids, disorder broke out in Armenia. This gave the Emperor the opportunity for a successful intervention; the region of Vaspurkan, together with a part of Iberia, was annexed to Byzantium, while the Armenian kingdom of Ani was to remain under King John Smbat (the son and successor of Gagik) during his lifetime, but was thereafter to fall to the Byzantine Emperor. As testimony to the glorious conquests of the last three reigns, the new themes in Asia spread out in a wide arc to east and south beyond the former territory of the Empire: Antioch, Teluch, the so-called 'Euphrates cities' (παρευφρατίδιαι πόλεις, later 'Edessa'), Melitene, and next to it the older theme territory of Mesopotamia, the theme Taron, and then the newly-conquered provinces once more, Vaspurkan, Iberia and Theodosiopolis.[1] While the old themes of Asia Minor declined in prestige, the new provinces acquired great importance as frontier districts and were designated either duchies (e.g. Antioch and later Mesopotamia) or catepanates (Edessa and the Armenian-Iberian provinces).[2]

Before his death the restless Emperor turned his attention to the West. The Byzantine position in South Italy, which from the time of Otto the Great had seemed threatened by the advances of the German Empire, had been stabilized as a result of Otto II's war with the Arabs which had ended so unfortunately for him. The idea of a *renovatio romana* which took root under the youthful Emperor Otto III, the son of the Byzantine princess Theophano, meant that Byzantine influence had a chance to gain ground within the Western Empire. The Byzantine position was also administratively strengthened by the grouping together of all Byzantine possessions in Italy under one catepanate.[3] The able catepan Basil Boioannes had achieved several victories over the enemies of the Empire. It was Basil's intention to build further on these successes, and he started preparations for a great campaign against the Arabs in Sicily. But on 15 December 1025 he died. He left behind him an Empire which reached from the mountains of Armenia to the Adriatic and from the Euphrates to the Danube. Annexed to this *imperium* was one great Slav kingdom, and another, still greater, lay under its spiritual influence.

---

[1] The general position of the various themes of this period is indicated on the appended map.

[2] Cf. Skabalanovič, *Viz. gosudarstvo* 193 ff.

[3] Gay, *Italie* 343 ff.

As late as the thirteenth century, a writer could still name Heraclius and Basil II as the greatest Emperors of Byzantium.[1] These names, which are indeed the greatest in all the history of Byzantium, together symbolize the heroic age of Byzantium, which had its beginning with the one and its conclusion with the other.

[1] Mich. Choniates II, 354 (ed. Lambros).

Figure 43: *Ring of Michael Attaleiates.* Gold, with cloisonné enamel in pink, green, and blue, Constantinople, late 11th century. On the bezel, a bust of the Virgin, with Her monogram; around the hoop, an engraved inscription, "Mother of God, help thy servant, Michael Attaleiates." Diam. 1⅛". Dumbarton Oaks Collections, Washington, D.C. Photo: Dumbarton Oaks Collections.

Government by the Civil Aristocracy of the Capital (1025–81)

SOURCES

A SOURCE of primary importance is the *Chronographia* of Michael (Constantine) Psellus (b. 1018).[1] He was the greatest scholar and clearest thinker of his day, and he was also a master of his art. His *Chronographia* is the outstanding memoirs of the middle ages, unparalleled in its intellectual vigour, its lively descriptions, its discriminating psychological insight and its clear-cut and brilliant characterization. As a statesman of considerable eminence Psellus had not only had intimate first-hand knowledge of the history of his own times, but he had helped to make it. This is also the explanation of the bias of his presentation in which much is omitted and much is distorted. His work falls into two parts. The first section was written about 1059–63 at the instigation of a friend, probably Constantine Leichudes, and it covers the period from Basil II to the abdication of Isaac Comnenus; his treatment of Basil II is brief, but with each succeeding reign becomes increasingly detailed, particularly for Michael V (1041–2) when Psellus came to court as imperial secretary. The second section, dealing with the time of the Ducas (1059–78), was written at the imperial request during Michael VII's lifetime, which explains the exceedingly tendentious character of this part of the work. Psellus' numerous letters, speeches and other writings are also of great historical value.[2] Particularly important for the intellectual and religious life of the eleventh century are the

---

[1] New edition with French translation by E. Renauld, Michel Psellos, *Chronographie*, 2 vols., Paris 1926, 1928. Cf. H. Grégoire's emendations in B 2, 550 ff., and B 4, 716 ff. J. Sykutris, BZ 27, 99 ff., and BZ 29, 40 ff. English trans. by E. R. A. Sewter, London 1953.

[2] E. Kurt-F. Drexl, *Michaelis Pselli scripta minora*, I–II, Milan 1936, 1941. Vol. I contains a collection of speeches and occasional pieces, many of which were previously unknown; vol. II gives 273 letters of Psellus of which all but sixty are published here for the first time. Cf. also F. Drexl, 'Nachträge zur Ausgabe der Psellosbriefen von Kurtz-Drexl', BZ 41 (1941), 309 f.; idem, '*Index nominum* zu den von Sathas, Boissonade, Hase, Ruelle und Tafel edierten Psellosbriefen', ibid. 299 ff.; and J. Darrouzès, 'Notes d'épistolographie et d'histoire de textes', REB 12 (1954) 176 ff.

letters, sermons and poems of the scholar John Mauropous, Arch-bishop of Euchaita.[1]

Another important source is the history of Michael Attaleiates, who also held a high position at court and wrote as an eye-witness on the period 1034-79.[2] Psellus had belonged to the civil party, but Attaleiates supported the feudal military aristocracy and he dedicated his work to Nicephorus Botaneiates (1078-81). He first rose to importance under Romanus Diogenes (1068-71) and from the time of this Emperor's accession to power his account becomes much fuller, though more subjective. The last part of the chronicle of John Scylitzes covers this period to the accession of Isaac Comnenus and is very important. This is supplemented by a continuation, by an unknown author, dealing with the period 1057-79 (cf. p. 211 above). This is largely based on Attaleiates and also makes occasional use of Psellus, but in parts—as in the description of the Slav revolt of 1072—is independent of these sources. The chronicle of John Zonaras draws on Scylitzes and Psellus for the periods covered by them, and to a lesser extent on Attaleiates. Zonaras also makes use of a source which is otherwise unknown to us, and this, together with the independent manner in which he handles his material, makes his work of considerable value.[3]

A very interesting source for both Byzantine and Balkan history is the so-called *Strategicon* of Cecaumenus, written between 1075 and 1078. The author, a general belonging to the Byzantine aristocracy, writes with great vivacity about his experiences and imparts good advice from the conclusions which he draws. His spontaneous and lively notes are based on his direct contact with the events and situations described and they provide a highly individual and important source for both the political and cultural history of his day. This work appears to have survived only in a Moscow manu-script of the fourteenth or fifteenth century, and it is followed by a

---

[1] ed. P. de Lagarde, Göttingen 1882. Further references in J. M. Hussey, 'The Writings of John Mauropous: A Bibliographical Note', BZ 44 (1951), 278 ff. On the significance of this scholar cf. idem, *Church and Learning*, 39 ff., 52 ff.; 'The Canons of John Mauropous', JRS 37 (1947), 70 ff.; 'The Byzantine Empire in the Eleventh Century', *Trans. Roy. Hist. Soc.* 32 (1950), 84 ff.

[2] French translation (to 1056), H. Grégoire, B 28 (1958), 325-62.

[3] Skabalanović, *Viz. gosudarstvo* pp. XIII and XVIII, shows the individual use which Scylitzes and Zonaras both made of their material for this period. On the relation of Zonaras to Psellus cf. the paper of O. Lampsides, Ὁ Μιχαήλ Ψελλός ὡς πηγὴ τῆς ' Ἐπιτομῆς' τοῦ Ἰωάννου Ζωναρᾶ, EEBS 19 (1949), 170 ff.

smaller work which contains good counsel for an Emperor, doubt-less from the pen of the same author.[1]

Rich material for the study of legal conditions, administrative practice, the system of taxation, agrarian conditions and the like is found in the so-called *Peira*, a number of legal rulings by Magister Eustathius Romaius which were apparently collected together some time after 1034 by one of the subordinates of this eminent Byzantine judge.[2] The recently discovered land-register of Thebes from the second half of the eleventh century, describes, like the *Ashburner Treatise*, the Byzantine tax system, and in particular illuminates the changes that took place in the Byzantine village at this time.[3] Another document that is most valuable from the point of view of social history is the will of the Protospatharius of the Chrysotri-clinium, Eustathius Boilas.[4]

Documentary evidence, which was sparse for the earlier period, becomes more plentiful from the second half of the eleventh century

---

[1] edd. B. Wassiliewsky-V. Jernstedt, *Cecaumeni strategicon et incerti scriptoris de officiis regiis libellus*, St. Petersburg 1896. Part is edited with a Russian translation and very valuable commentary by V. Vasiljevskij, 'Sovety i rasskazy vizantijskogo bojarina XI v'. (The advice and admonitions of a Byzantine nobleman of the eleventh century), ZMNP 215 (1881), 242–99, 216 (1881), 102–71, 316–57. German translation with a good introduction, H. Beck, *Vademecum des byzantinischen Aristokraten. Das sogenannte Strategikon des Kekaumenos*, in *Byzantinische Geschichtsschreiber* V, Graz.-Vienna-Cologne, 1956. The assumption of G. Buckler, 'Authorship of the Strategikon of Cecaumenus', BZ 36 (1936), 7 ff., and 'Can Cecaumenus be the author of the Strategikon?', B 13 (1938), 139 ff., that the famous Byzantine general Cecaumenus was the author of both works has met with a certain amount of scepticism. Cf. N. Banescu, 'A propos de Kekaumenos', B 13 (1938), 129 ff. (cf. also 'Autour de Kekaumenos', REB 6 (1948), 191 ff.); P. Orgels, 'Kekaumenos et la guerre pétchénègue', ibid. 402 ff.; M. Gyoni, 'L'œuvre de Kékauménos, source de l'histoire roumaine', *Revue d'histoire comparée* 23 (1945), 96–180. But H. G. Beck, op. cit. argues for the identification proposed by Buckler, as does Moravcsik, who at first was sceptical (*Byzantinoturcica* I (1st ed.), 112, 201 f.), but now agrees with her (*Byzantinoturcica* I (2nd ed.) 350 f.). In his latest work P. Lemerle remains, however, sceptical: 'Prolégomènes à une edition critique et commentée des 'Conseils et Récits' de Kekaumenos' *Mémoires de l'Acad. Royale de Belgique LIV* (1960), 37 ff, and in my opinion he is right. J. Karayannopulos is also sceptical in an article in which he reflects in the main the view of previous studies: 'Zur Frage der Autorschaft am Strategikon des Kekaumenos, BZ 54 (1961), 257 ff. For the date of composition of the work, cf. Lemerle, op. cit. 20. Cf. also G. G. Litavrin, Byl li Kekavmen, avtor 'Strategikona', feodalom?' (Was Cecaumenus, the author of the *Strategicon*, a feudal lord?), *Vizantijskie očerki*, Moscow, 1961, 217 ff.

[2] Zepos, *Jus* IV, 1–260.

[3] ed. N. Svoronos, *Recherches sur le cadastre byzantin et la fiscalité aux XIe et XIIe siècles: le cadastre de Thèbes*, Paris-Athens, 1959.

[4] ed. V. N. Beneševič, Zaveščanie vizantijskogo bojarina XI v. (The will of a Byzantine nobleman of the eleventh century), ZMNP, n.s. 9 (1907), 219 ff. English translation, S. Vryonis, 'The Will of a Provincial Magnate, Eustathius Boilas', DOP 11 (1957), 263 ff. Abbreviated Russian translation by M. Levčenko, in *Sbornik dokumentov po social'-no-ekonomiceskoj istorii Vizantii*, Moscow, 1961, 169 ff. Textual emendations by R. M. Bartikjan, VV 19 (1961), 26 ff.

onwards and throws much light on the internal history of the Empire. This is particularly true of documents from monastic archives.[1]

The central ecclesiastical event of this century, the schism of 1054 between the two Churches, is completely ignored by contemporary Byzantine historians. The most important Western account, which provides the material for later Latin writings on the subject, is the *Commemoratio brevis*,[2] apparently drawn up by Cardinal Humbert. Fuller details are found in the correspondence of contemporary Greek and Latin Church leaders, especially the two letters of Michael Cerularius to Peter of Antioch and the latter's reply,[3] the letters of Pope Leo IX to the Emperor Constantine IX, to Michael Cerularius and Leo of Ochrida and to Peter of Antioch.[4] As A. Michel has shown, the letters under the Pope's name, and in particular the great polemical letter addressed to Cerularius, were written by Cardinal Humbert.[5] The same scholar has also published a treatise by Humbert on the procession of the Holy Ghost, as well as a number of other theological works of the period, including the Michael Cerularius' comprehensive *Panoplia*.[6]

[1] The most important publications for this and the succeeding centuries are: Miklosich-Müller; 'Actes de l'Athos'; Zachariae, *Jus* III = Zepos, *Jus* I; 'Akty Russkogo na sv. Afone monastyrja sv. velikomučenika Panteleimona' (Documents of the Russian monastery of the holy martyr Panteleimon on Mt. Athos), Kiev 1873; T. Florinskij, *Afonskie akty*, St. Petersburg 1880; Ph. Meyer, *Haupturkunden zur Geschichte der Athosklöster*, Leipzig 1894; W. Regel, Χρυσόβουλλα καὶ γράμματα τῆς ἐν τῷ Ἁγίῳ Ὄρει Ἄθῳ ἱερᾶς καὶ σεβασμίας μονῆς τοῦ Βατοπεδίου, St. Petersburg 1898; M. Gudas, Βυζαντιακὰ ἔγγραφα τῆς ἐν Ἄθῳ ἱερᾶς μονῆς τοῦ Βατοπεδίου, EEBS 4 (1927), 211–48; Ch. Ktenas, Χρυσόβουλλοι λόγοι τῆς ἐν Ἄθῳ ἱερᾶς μονῆς τοῦ Δοχειαρίου, ibid. 285–311; N. Bees, Σερβικὰ καὶ βυζαντιακὰ γράμματα Μετεώρου, Βυζαντίς 2 (1911–12), 1–100 Th. Ouspensky et V. Bénéchévitch, *Actes de Vazélon*, Leningrad 1927; A. Solovjev-V. Mošin, *Grčke povelje srpskih vladara* (Greek documents of the Serbian rulers), Belgrade 1936; V. Mošin, 'Akti iz svetogorskih arhiva' (Documents from the archives of the Holy Mountain), *Spomenik* 91 (1939); V. Mošin-A. Sovre, *Supplementa ad acta graeca Chilandarii*, Ljubljana 1948; G. Rouillard et P. Collomp, *Actes de Lavra* I (897–1178), Paris 1937; P. Lemerle, *Actes de Kutlumus*, Paris 1945; F. Dölger, *Aus den Schatzkammern des Heiligen Berges*, Munich 1948; F. Dölger, *Sechs byzantinische Praktika des 14. Jahrhunderts für das Athoskloster Iberon*, *Abh. d. Bayer. Akad. d. Wiss.*, N.F. 28, Munich 1949; A. Guillou, *Les archives de Saint-Jean-Prodrome sur le mont Ménécée*, Paris, 1955. The publications of Rouillard-Collomp, Lemerle, and Dölger's great collection, provide facsimiles of the documents and seals.
[2] C. Will, *Acta et scripta quae de controversiis ecclesiae graecae et latinae saec. XI composita extant*, Leipzig and Marburg 1861, pp. 150–2.
[3] Ibid. 172–204. [4] Ibid. 85–9; 65–85; 89–92; 168–71.
[5] Michel, *Kerullarios* I, 44 ff.
[6] Michel, *Kerullarios* I, 76 ff., and II, 41 ff. The authorship of the *Panoplia* is disputed: V. Laurent, EO 31 (1932), 105 ff., and M. Jugie, B 8 (1933), 323 ff., regard it as the work of a contemporary of the Council of Lyons. Cf., however, Michel's reply, 'Von Photios zu Kerullarios', *Röm. Quartalschr.* 41 (1933), 125 ff., and especially 'Die Echtheit der Panoplia des Michael Kerullarios', *Oriens Christ.* 36 (1941), 168 ff.

1. THE DISINTEGRATION OF THE POLITICAL SYSTEM OF THE MIDDLE BYZANTINE PERIOD

General bibliography: Bury, 'Roman Emperors from Basil II to Isaac Komnenos', EHR 4 (1889), 41–64, 251–85 (= *Selected Essays* [1930], 126–214); Schlumberger, *Épopée byzantine* III; Skabalanovič, *Viz. gosudarstvo*; Neumann, *Weltstellung*: J. M. Hussey, 'The Later Macedonians, the Comneni and the Angeli 1025–1204', CMH IV, Pt I (2nd. ed., 1966); W. Fischer, *Studien zur byzantinischen Geschichte des 11. Jahrhunderts*, Progr. Plauen 1883; H. Mädler, *Theodora, Michael Strätiotikos, Isaak Komnenos*, Progr. Plauen 1894; Vasiljevskij, *Pečenegi*; M. Dinić, 'The Balkans 1018–1499', CMH IV, Pt I (2nd. ed., 1966); Fuchs, *Höhere Schulen*; Hussey, *Church and Learning*; P. Bezobrazov, *Michail Psell*, Moscow 1890; Chr. Zervos, *Michel Psellos*, Paris 1920 (for further bibliography on Psellus cf. below, p. 327, note 2); Ostrogorsky, *Féodalité*, Glykatzi-Ahrweiler, *Recherches*; Bréhier, *Schisme*; idem, 'The Greek Church: its Relations with the West up to 1054', CMH IV (1923), 246–73; Norden, *Papsttum und Byznaz*; Michel, *Kerullarios*; M. Jugie, *Le schisme byzantin*, Paris 1941; N. Suvorov, *Vizantijskij papa* (A Byzantine Pope), Moscow 1902; S. Runciman, *The Eastern Schism. A study of the Papacy and the Eastern Churches during the XIth and XIIth Centuries*, Oxford, 1955.

The death of Basil II marked a turning point in Byzantine history. It was followed by a period of decline during which in its foreign policy Byzantium lived on the prestige won in the previous age and at home gave free play to all the forces making for disintegration. After the heroic achievements of the last three reigns Byzantium seemed invincible and there began a time of comparative peace such as the Empire had hardly ever known. Unfortunately, this breathing space was not spent in conservation and consolidation, but was a time of internal relaxation which resulted in the break-up of the system inaugurated by Heraclius and maintained up to the end of Basil II's reign. The ineffective successors of Basil II were not capable of carrying on the struggle against the feudal magnates; and the collapse of the military small-holdings proceeded at a break-neck pace, thus undermining the imperial defences and the state's system of taxation. The economic and social structure of the Empire underwent a radical change. Byzantine imperial authority not only ceased its struggle to keep the feudal nobility in check, but became itself the tool of this powerful class. The landed aristocracy had won the game and the only question which remained was which particular section of them should take control—the civil or the military aristocracy. At first sight Byzantine history during the following years appears to be merely a confused chaos of court intrigue, but in reality its course was determined by the clash between the rival forces of the civil nobility of the capital and the military aristocracy of the provinces. The latter was the stronger party, but it lost ground to begin with, owing to the way in which it had been crushed by Basil II, and the civil aristocracy in Constantinople therefore gained control. Their supremacy set the tone for the coming years: unending court intrigues were merely an external manifestation of their régime, and characteristic developments of the period were the intellectual renaissance in the capital and the collapse of the military power of the Empire.

Basil II's successor, his brother Constantine VIII (1025–8), was the first of the *epigoni*. Co-Emperor for half a century, he had stood a negligible figure at the side of his forceful brother, and now as an old man he was an Emperor in name rather than in fact. He was not entirely ungifted, but he lacked character and a sense of responsibility. He left the affairs of state to others, and he spent his time at banquets or enjoying the entertainments of the Hippodrome on which he heedlessly lavished the imperial funds which Basil II had accumulated.

The most pressing problem was the settlement of the succession, for the aged Emperor had no sons. Of his three daughters, the eldest, Eudocia, whose face was disfigured by smallpox, had become a nun. The two younger princesses, Zoe and Theodora, were by now long past their prime, and as the last members of the Macedonian house were destined to play important roles in Byzantine history during the following years. It was an extraordinary fact that it was only when he lay on his death-bed that Constantine VIII tried to arrange a marriage for one of these aged princesses and cast about for a suitable husband. At the last moment his choice fell on the eparch of the city, Romanus Argyrus.

The office of eparch of Constantinople had always been a distinguished one and by the eleventh century its importance had grown still greater. In the tenth century the *Book of Ceremonies* had described the eparch as 'the father of the city', and an eleventh-century writer went still further and said that the office of eparch was an imperial dignity, except that it fell short of the purple.[1] As holder of this high office, and as member of one of the most eminent Byzantine families, Romanus Argyrus was a distinguished repre-

---

[1] *De cerim.* 264 and 528. Psellus I, 30 (ed. Renauld), βασίλειος ʒὲ αὔτη ἀρχή, εἰ μὴ ὅσον ἀπόρφυρος.

sentative of the civil aristocracy of the capital. On 12 November 1028 he married the fifty-year-old Zoe, and three days later—after the death of Constantine VIII—he ascended the throne as Romanus III Argyrus.[1] He was a typical aristocrat, and although he was past sixty he had preserved his good looks, and he possessed a measure of culture. As a ruler he had no ability whatsoever, and in the weakness and boundless vanity of a true decadent he tried to model himself on certain outstanding figures of the past, visions of whom were always swimming before his eyes. At one moment Marcus Aurelius was his ideal and he would embark on philosophical discourses, the next moment it was Justinian and he would launch a magnificent building programme. Then it was Trajan or Hadrian who inspired him and he visualized himself as a great general devoted to war, until a serious defeat in Syria brought him to his senses. On this occasion the situation was saved by the brilliant general, George Maniaces, who made his first appearance, and once more emphasized the superiority of Byzantine arms by a series of victorious campaigns culminating in the capture of Edessa (1032).

The most important feature of Romanus Argyrus' short reign was the complete abandonment of Basil II's policy. Basil II had made the 'powerful' responsible for the additional tax for peasant holdings which had gone to waste, but Romanus III yielded to the pressure of the wealthy landlords and took a different attitude.[2] Thus the old system of extra payment, which had been a basic element in Byzantine taxation, first as the *epibole*, and then as the *allelengyon*, disappeared for good.[3] The peasants were no longer in a position to pay the tax,[4] and the 'powerful' were not willing to do so, while the Emperor Romanus III, who was himself a member of the aristocracy, never

[1] On Zoe's age and the date of the accession of Romanus III (15 November 1028) cf. Skabalanovič, *Viz. gosudarstvo* 11, note 2, and 14, note 1. For further chronological data cf. also Skabalanovič's careful statements.

[2] Scylitzes-Cedren. II, 486, 7, ἐξέκοψε δὲ καὶ τέλεον ἀπερρίζωσε τὸ ἀλληλέγγυον. Scylitzes' statement (II, 486, 8) that Constantine VIII had already resolved to abolish the *allelengyon* is also significant.

[3] Dölger, 'Das Fortbestehen der Epibole in mittel- und spätbyz. Zeit', *Studi Albertoni* II (1934), 3 ff., und BZ 35 (1935), 14, maintains, in opposition to my statements in 'Steuergemeinde' 1 ff. and B 6 (1931), 227 ff., that the *epibole* survived into the later period. This is in contradiction to the plain statements of the sources and is further disproved by the new material brought forward by G. Rouillard, 'L'épibolé au temps d'Alexis Comnéne', B 10 (1935), 81 ff., in spite of Dölger's arguments, BZ 36 (1936), 157 ff. Cf. also the texts since published by G. Rouillard-P. Collomp, *Actes de Lavra* I (1937), Nos. 43, 48, 53, where the word *epibole* is frequently met with in the sources of the later period, but is always used in the general sense of a tax levied or a distribution of land (as rightly indicated by Bréhier, *Institutions* 260).

[4] This is clearly shown by the Ashburner Treatise §§ 12 and 14 (ed. Dölger, *Finanzverwaltung* 119). Cf. Ostrogorsky, 'Steuergemeinde' 31.

entertained any thought of braving the opposition of the wealthy landed nobility. The older laws forbidding the powerful to acquire the lands of the peasants or military small-holdings were not, however, officially repealed and conscientious judges at this time still regarded them as legally valid.[1] But it was sufficient that the long series of decrees protecting the small-holder came to an abrupt end with the death of Basil II. Even the government regulations of the tenth century with all their severity had not been entirely able to prevent the acquisition of land from peasant or military holdings, but now the negative attitude of the state meant that it was possible for the wealthy landlords to expand at will. Both in political and economic issues the 'powerful' had won all along the line. From Romanus I to Basil II the central authority had tried to erect a barrier against the great magnates' urge to acquire land, and this had now been broken down. The free small-holdings rapidly disappeared without a protest, and the wealthy landlords absorbed the property of peasant and soldier, turning the former owners into dependents. Thus the very foundations on which Byzantium had built ever since its revival in the seventh century were swept away, with the result that the strength of the armed forces and of the revenue declined, and the consequent impoverishment weakened the military power of the state still further.

There is not, however, any justification for regarding the rulers of this period as responsible for initiating this process. The change of policy which appeared to originate with them was in reality due to a development which it was no longer possible to control. They were merely the exponents of vigorous and irresistible social and economic forces. And so the situation remained practically unchanged by the removal of Romanus Argyrus, even though this was the work of a party drawn from a very different social stratum. For some years there had been a deep rift between the Emperor Romanus and the Empress Zoe, for, once he had ascended the throne, Romanus' interest in the elderly Empress petered out, and he began to neglect her, and even kept her short of money. But this ageing woman had considerable zest for life; for the first time she was experiencing the taste of worldly pleasures and she refused to allow her style to be cramped. Her eye fell on a young man called Michael, a peasant's son from Paphlagonia, who had been brought into the women's

[1] Cf. the legal rulings of Magister Eustathius in the *Peira*, Zepos, *Jus* IV, 32 (VIII, 1) and 38 (IX, 1); cf. also 51 ff. (XV, 10); 167 (XL, 12); 228 (LVII, 1).

quarters of the imperial palace by his brother John the Orphanotrophus, an influential eunuch. The whole intrigue was really due to the manipulations of this same John, an unusually capable, but entirely unscrupulous, man who was determined to win for his brother the throne from which he himself was debarred on account of being a eunuch. Zoe fell in love with the handsome youth with all the passion of an elderly lover, and so it came about that Romanus III died in his bath on 11 April 1034. That same evening the Empress married her young lover who ascended the throne as Michael IV (1034–41).

Once again Zoe had miscalculated, for Michael also lost interest in her as soon as he had secured the throne. Even her freedom of movement was limited since John the Orphanotrophus had her very carefully watched in order to avoid any repetition of the fate which had befallen Romanus Argyrus. As Emperor, Michael proved to be a capable ruler and a brave general, but he suffered from epileptic fits which increased in severity as time went on. It was the cunning eunuch who gained most from the change of régime, for the entire administration of the Empire fell into his hands.[1] He steered the ship of State with great skill, though he ruthlessly increased financial demands and exacted taxes with the utmost callousness.[2] As a man who had risen from the lower classes by his own efforts, John the Orphanotrophus stood for the old centralized bureaucracy without special allegiance to a particular social class, and to this extent his administration may be said to have had an anti-aristocratic bias. The feudal and military aristocracy of Asia Minor were the chief sufferers, and therefore the civil nobility of the capital now gave their support to the government. Psellus, who was a characteristic representative of the civil party, mentions with satisfaction that during Michael IV's reign the government did not alter the *status quo* and did nothing to the detriment of the members of the senate.[3] The Paphlagonians made no attempt to revive the policy of the Macedonian rulers. Nevertheless, the ruthless methods of the Orphanotrophus were a sore trial to the people, while he himself never forgot his own interests and made sure that all his own family lived off the fat of the land.

[1] Cf. R. Janin, 'Un ministre byzantin: Jean l'Orphanotrophe', EO 30 (1929), 431 ff.
[2] Scylitzes-Cedren. II, 521, says that there were then so many different kinds of tax that he was ashamed to enumerate them.
[3] Psellus I, 57 (ed. Renauld; trans. Sewter, 60).

The merciless fiscal policy of the government provoked the Slav population of the Balkans to rebellion. Basil II's wise policy of allowing them to pay their taxes in kind was revoked and they now had to find them in money. In addition, when the Slav John, Archbishop of Ochrida, died in 1037, a Greek, Leo, the chartophylax of Hagia Sophia, was appointed in his place. The rebellion assumed dangerous proportions. Peter Deljan, who claimed to be a grandson of Samuel,[1] was proclaimed tzar in Belgrade in 1040. Shortly afterwards he was joined by Alusianus, a son of John Vladislav, who had escaped from Constantinople, though this move created great difficulties for the rebels. The revolt spread over the greater part of the Slav Balkans and even penetrated into the districts of northern Greece. Owing to lack of unity among the leaders of the rebels, the rising was suppressed by 1041, sooner than its dangerous appearance had led one to expect. It left, however, a serious weakness in the structure which Basil II had built up.

After the revolt of Peter Deljan had been put down Byzantium attempted to exact recognition from the insubordinate prince of Zeta, Stephen Voislav. Zeta was the name now usually given to the old Dioclea, and since about 1035 its ruler had refused to acknowedge Byzantine overlordship.[2] His first attempt at independence misfired, but after enduring defeat and imprisonment he once more made a bid for freedom, and even before the outbreak of the general revolt in the Balkans he had emerged the victor in repeated combat against the expeditions sent against him by the Byzantines. Byzantium then launched a fresh large-scale punitive expedition in 1042, but this also proved a complete failure, even though the Byzantines called in the vassal rulers of Rascia, Bosnia and Zachlumia against the refractory prince of Zeta.[3] Stephen Voislav, operating in his own mountainous countryside, inflicted a crushing defeat upon the powerful forces of the *strategus* of Dyrrachium. This finally secured the independence of his principality. His authority now extended over the adjacent Trebunia, as well as over Zachlumia.[4] Thus Zeta

---

[1] Cf. Zlatarski, 'Wer war Peter Deljan?' *Annales Acad. Scient. Fennicae* 27 (1932), 354 ff., and *Istorija* II, 41 ff., who argues that he was in fact a grandson of Samuel (the son of Gabriel Radomir by his marriage to a Hungarian princess). But cf. Litavrin, *Bolgarija i Vizantija* 379 ff., who is rightly cautious.

[2] Cf. Jireček, *Geschichte* I, 231 ff.   [3] *Letopis Popa Dukljanina*, ed. Šišić, 34 f.

[4] This certainly took place after the victory of 1042, but not immediately after Voislav's return from Byzantine captivity, as Jireček, *Geschichte* I, 231, seems to suppose, and also *Istorija naroda Jugoslavije* I (1953), 239. It is clear from the account of the Priest of Dioclea referred to above that Zachlumia was not under the control of Voislav at the time of the Byzantine attack on Zeta in 1042.

became the first of the Slav countries of the Balkans to break away from Byzantine rule.

After suppressing Deljan's revolt, Michael IV had returned from the Balkans fatally ill. Realizing that the Emperor could not live long, John had taken the necessary step to insure that the imperial throne remained in his family. The Empress Zoe was induced to adopt Michael, the nephew of the two rulers, who was given the name of Calaphates after the craft which his father had formerly practised. As heir presumptive to the throne, he was given the title of Caesar. Worn out by increased sufferings, on 10 December 1041 Michael IV retired to the monastery of the holy Anargyri, where he died the same day.

The rule of Michael Calaphates brought the régime of the Paphlagonian family to an abrupt conclusion. John the Orphanotrophus fell a victim to the tool whom he had raised up; Michael repaid the help which his uncle had given him by sending him into exile. No one raised a finger in support of the eunuch who was detested by all. Encouraged by this, the Calaphates was then rash enough to banish the Empress Zoe to a nunnery, a step which cost him his throne. Relying on the dynastic loyalty of the city population, aristocracy and Church united against the presumptuous upstart, and, indeed, during the age of the Macedonians popular feeling for the principle of legitimacy was so strong that the people clamoured even for Zoe and Theodora. The Calaphates, who had raised his hand against one born in the purple, was deposed and blinded on 20 April 1042. Zoe and Theodora were now to rule jointly. Theodora, who had taken the veil at Zoe's request, was supported by an influential party, particularly the Church. The claim of women to rule in their own right was no longer questioned, but the incompetence of the two Empresses, and their hatred of each other, very soon made it clear that it was essential to have a man at the head of the government. Theodora had no desire to wed, but Zoe, though now sixty-four years old, eagerly embarked on her third marriage, and on 11 June 1042 she took as her husband the eminent senator Constantine Monomachus who received the imperial crown on the following day.

By his second marriage to a Sclerina, Constantine IX Monomachus (1042-55) was related to Romanus III Argyrus, and like him he was a member of the Byzantine civil aristocracy. He too was an insignificant and weak-willed ruler. He took life and his imperial duties

Figure 44: *The Empress Zoë*. Detail of a mosaic panel, south gallery of Hagia Sophia, Constantinople, 1028–1042. The entire panel depicts Christ enthroned, with Zoë at right and her third husband, Constantine IX Monomachus (see Figure 45), at left. Photo: Byzantine Institute, Inc., Washington, D.C.

Figure 45: *Constantine IX Monomachus.* Detail of a mosaic panel, south gallery of Hagia Sophia, Constantinople, 1028–1042. The third husband of Empress Zoë (see Figure 44), he survived her for 5 years as emperor. Photo: Byzantine Institute, Inc., Washington, D.C.

lightly and made no attempt to check the unfortunate developments of his day.[1] He placed no restraint upon the two old Empresses with whom he officially shared the throne. Together with the pleasure-loving Emperor, they could enjoy dissipating the public treasury. Zoe for her part had become more tolerant with advancing age, and the love affair which Constantine quite openly carried on with the fascinating and clever Sclerina, a niece of his second wife, scandalized the people but left the Empress unmoved. Adorned with the newly-created title of Sebaste, the mistress of the Emperor took her place beside the two Empresses at all court ceremonies, and when she died both her title and function were passed on to a beautiful Alan princess.

The light-hearted and elegant life of Constantinople certainly possessed considerable attractions, and there was at this time a new blossoming of intellectual activity after the desiccating influence of Basil II's military régime. The civil aristocracy of the capital who set the tone were undoubtedly the most cultured class of the Empire. The throne was surrounded by men of genuine learning, such as Constantine Leichudes who as first minister (μεσάζων) directed affairs of state, the distinguished jurist John Xiphilinus, and the famous philosopher Michael Psellus. In his particularly stimulating influence on cultural developments, as well as his most unfortunate political activities and his abysmal moral depravity, Psellus was the most outstanding figure of his age.[2] He was not altogether devoid of piety and was at times deeply moved, if only aesthetically, by the religion of his forefathers. When Leichudes' circle temporarily lost power towards the end of Constantine IX's reign, Psellus even took the monk's habit in a fit of disappointment and resignation, and entered a monastery together with his friend Xiphilinus. But his whole existence was, and remained, bound up with the things of this world;

[1] Neumann, *Weltstellung* 64 ff. makes an unsuccessful attempt to whitewash him.

[2] On Psellus cf. P. Bezobrazov, *Michail Psell*, Moscow 1890; Chr. Zervos, *Michel Psellos*, Paris 1920; A. Rambaud, 'Michel Psellos', *Études sur l'histoire byzantine* (1912), 111–71; Diehl, *Figures* I, 291–317; Neumann, *Weltstellung* 81–93 (the best and most stimulating discussion of Psellus); E. Renauld, *Études de la langue et du style de Michel Psellos*, Paris 1920; J. Hussey, 'Michael Psellus, the Byzantine Historian', *Speculum* 10 (1935), 81–90 and *Church and Learning* 73 ff.; B. Tatakis, *La philosophie byzantine*, Paris 1949, 161 ff.; J. Dräseke, 'Aus dem Byzanz des XI. Jahrhunderts', *Neue Jahrb. f. d. klass. Altertum* 27 (1911), 561–76; V. Valdenberg, 'Filosofskie vzgljady Michaila Psella' (The philosophical views of Michael Psellus), VS (1945), 249–55; P. Joannou, *Christliche Metaphysik in Byzanz*, I. *Die Illuminationslehre des Michael Psellos und Joannes Italos*, Ettal 1956; cf. also the bibliography in Moravcsik, *Byzantinoturcica* I, 2nd ed., 439 ff. On Xiphilinus cf. K. G. Bonis, Ἰωάννης ὁ Ξιφιλῖνος, *Texte und Forsch. zur byz.-neugr. Philol.* 24 (1938).

he thirsted after secular learning with an unquenchable craving and he observed and analysed the motives of his fellow-beings with unerring accuracy and exploited his knowledge for his own political ends. As a writer and an orator he was unequalled, and in the Byzantine world, where the art of rhetoric was so highly prized, his skill in this direction was a weapon of quite irresistible persuasion. As a politician he made full use of these gifts and indeed often misused them in a way which invites strong condemnation. At the same time, the intellectual capacity of this remarkable man deserves full praise. His knowledge covered all fields and simply astounded his contemporaries. He was passionately devoted to the wisdom and literature of the ancient world. The classical tradition had never completely died out in Byzantium, but Psellus' relationship to the culture of ancient Greece was something different, based on a direct and intimate knowledge. He was not satisfied with studying the neoplatonists, he went direct to the source and learned to know Plato, and to make him known, and in so doing conferred incalculable benefits on both his own contemporaries and posterity. He was the greatest Byzantine philosopher and the first great humanist.

The learned circle of imperial counsellors included Psellus, Xiphilinus and Leichudes, as well as Psellus' teacher, the distinguished poet and scholar John Mauropous, and it was these men who urged the revival of facilities for higher education. In 1045 a university was established in Constantinople with faculties of philosophy and law. The curriculum of philosophy was based on the system of the *trivium* and the *quadrivium* and the syllabus opened with grammar, rhetoric and dialectic, to be followed by arithmetic, geometry, music and astronomy, while the course culminated in philosophy, the ultimate synthesis of all knowledge. This faculty was presided over by Psellus, who was given the high-sounding title of 'consul (*hypatus*) of philosophers'. The head of the law school was John Xiphilinus, who was called 'the guardian of law' (*nomophylax*). In this way a new centre was built up for the promotion of Greek learning and Roman law, both of which were indebted to Byzantium for their preservation and development. The newly-found university also served an important practical purpose in providing the state with qualified judges and civil servants.[1]

[1] Cf. Fuchs, *Höhere Schulen* 24 ff.; Zervos, *Michel Psellos* (1920), 76 ff.; Hussey, *Church and Learning* 51 ff. Cf. also J. M. Hussey, 'The Byzantine Empire in the Eleventh Century: Some Different Interpretations', *Transact. of the Royal Hist. Society* 32 (1950), 71 ff., where the author disagrees with some of my views on the development of the

During the last two centuries imperial prestige had stood high and consequently the senate had only played a decorative role, but now the ruling class consisted of the higher officials of the capital who usually bore the title of senator and the position of the senate was no longer merely an honorary one. The more firmly the bureaucracy of the capital dug themselves in as the mainstay of the government, the more numerous became the wearers of the senatorial dignity. Entry into the senatorial ranks was also thrown open to a wider section of the population of Constantinople, and in this way the basis of the administrative system was broadened and fresh elements became interested in the maintenance of senatorial control.

The preponderance of the high administrative officials of the capital did not necessarily imply any strengthening of the central authority against the feudal magnates. While small property ownership declined more and more, the ownership of large estates constantly increased.[1] Furthermore, the great estates were constantly granted fresh privileges. The privilege most sought after by large landowners was that of exemption from taxes, immunity, or as it was termed in Byzantium, *exkousseia*. In the eleventh century the central government paid more and more attention to the wishes of the feudal lords and granted this privilege with great munificence. The great secular and ecclesiastical estates were exempted from certain taxes, and the most powerful and influential among them from all taxes, enjoying full immunity. Therefore the taxes and the other dues of the serfs on these estates no longer went into the imperial treasury, but came to the land owners. In addition to fiscal immunity, this period also saw the beginning of legal immunity: the magnates acted as judges over their own tenants. Thus to an ever increasing degree they escaped from the control of the state. The great estates, which enjoyed full fiscal and legal immunity,

Byzantine Empire in the eleventh century and would pass a more favourable verdict on this period by reason of its achievements in the fields of intellectual and religious life. I would not underestimate such achievements, but here I can only refer very briefly to their effect on the political development of Byzantium; this book is primarily concerned with the Byzantine State and in the political sphere the eleventh century proved to be the fatal turning-point when its decline began.

[1] How great a change had taken place in the social structure of the Byzantine village is shown by the recently published land-register of Thebes, dating from the second half of the eleventh century: N. Svoronos, *Recherches sur le cadastre byzantin et la fiscalité aux XIe et XIIe siècles: le cadastre de Thèbes*, Paris 1959. While according to the Ashburner *Treatise* the Byzantine village was a community of farmers, in the land register of Thebes we find a village which has gone over to the feudal system, and this is why this new source is so important. Cf. my article: 'Vizantijska seoska opština' *Glas srpske akad. nauka iumetnosti* 210 (1961), 141 ff. A translation of the article, 'La commune rurale byzantine', appeared in B 22 (1962) 139 ff.

slipped out of the net of the central administration and imperial officials were even forbidden to enter the territory of these estates.[1]

However willing the central government may seem to have been to meet the demands of the large land-owning aristocracy, there was nevertheless a point at which its generosity came to an end. Now, as previously, it sought to set certain limits on the numbers of peasants settled on large estates. The imperial charters which granted these privileges defined the number of *paroikoi* who were permitted to settle on the estate, and invariably emphasized that these *paroikoi* should not be drawn from amongst the state farmers and *stratiotai*. In actual fact the government could not avoid raising the previous allocation of *paroikoi* by granting new privileges, especially when influential magnates were involved; but it did not abandon control. Although the dramatic struggle between the central government and the feudal magnates had come to an end, a silent conflict over *paroikoi* still continued for many years. This shows once again that the setting up of new rent-paying tenant farmers was a more important problem than the acquisition of new landed properties.[2]

The obstinacy displayed by the central government in this question is all the more notable, in that in every other field its power was allowed to decline. A new break was made in the imperial administrative system by the rise of the *pronoia* system. As a reward for certain specified services, property was handed over to eminent Byzantines to administer (εἰς πρόνοιαν), together with the entire revenue from the estate thus granted. A grant of *pronoia* differed from an ordinary gift of land in that it was held, at least originally, by the recipient for a defined period, usually until his death, and was therefore not transferable either by alienation or by inheritance. In

---

[1] Until comparatively recently only two specialist studies of immunity in Byzantium were available: P. J. Jakovenko, *K istorii immuniteta v Vizantii* (On the history of immunity in Byzantium), Jurjev 1908, and K. N. Uspenskij, 'Ekskussija-immunitet v Vizantijskoj imperii' (Exkousseia—immunity in the Byzantine Empire), VV 23 (1917/22), 74-117. It is only in the last few years that more attention has been paid to this problem. Cf. B. T. Gorjanov, 'Pozdnevizantijskij immunitet' (Late Byzantine immunity), VV 11 (1956), 177-99, 12 (1957), 97-116; G. A. Ostrogorskij, 'K istorii immuniteta v Vizantii', VV 13 (1958), 35-106 (French translation: 'Pour l'histoire de l'immunité à Byzance', B 28 (1958), 165-254); M. M. Frejdenberg, 'Ekskussija v Vizantii XI–XII vv.' (Exkousseia in Byzantium in the eleventh and twelfth centuries), *Uč. zap. Velikolukskogo gos. ped. inst.* 3 (1958), 339-65; A. P. Každan, 'Ekskussija i ekskussaty v Vizantii X–XII vv.' (Exkousseia and those who enjoyed immunity in Byzantium from the tenth to the twelfth centuries), *Viz. očerki* (1961), 186 ff., and *Gorod i Derevnja*, 178 ff.

[2] Cf. Ostrogorsky, *Paysannerie*, 25 ff.

the development of Byzantium the *pronoia* system which appeared for the first time in the middle of the eleventh century had a long future before it.[1]

Limitations were increasingly imposed on the supreme power and ubiquity of the imperial civil service. The central government did in fact even curtail itself in one of its most vital functions, the collection of taxes, by farming this out in certain districts.[2] By this device the treasury made sure of a more or less fixed revenue, for the tax-farmers had to guarantee to collect a definite sum to be turned over to the state. But apart from this they were free to manage the districts leased to them in their own interests, and the inhabitants were squeezed dry, though not to the government's profit. What all this really meant was that the owners of large estates (pronoiars) and private contractors (tax farmers) had their own administrative system modelled on that of the state and existing side by side with it. It also meant that the population had to bear an increasing burden only part of which ever found its way to the treasury.

One most obvious and ominous effect of this financial disorder was the debasement of the coinage. In minting coins, the state found itself obliged to include a portion of base metal in its gold coins. This began the devaluation of the *nomisma* which had maintained its value virtually unchanged for centuries.[3] The Byzantine currency lost its unique fixed valuation and the high international prestige which it had previously enjoyed.

The principal characteristic of this period is however the decay of the Byzantine army. The civil government so hated the military aristocracy that it had systematically reduced the strength of the armed forces and in its attempt to discover fresh sources of revenue

[1] The first-known pronoiar was Constantine Leichudes. Cf. Scylitzes-Cedren. II, 645, and Zonaras III, 670, ᾧπερ ὁ Μονομάχος καὶ τὴν τῶν Μαγγάνων ἀνέθετο πρόνοιαν καὶ τὰ περὶ τῆς ἐλευθερείας αὐτῶν ἐνεπίστευσεν ἔγγραφα. The rights of the central authority were considerably restricted by the grants in *pronoia*, as is shown by the fact that the Emperor Isaac Comnenus later made every attempt to deprive Leichudes of the estates granted him in *pronoia*. By the seventies, grants in *pronoia* were already being made in large numbers; cf. Attaleïates 200. For further details cf. Ostrogorsky, *La féodalité*, 20 ff.

[2] From Cecaumenus 39 ff. (edd. Vasiljevskij and Jernstedt) it can be deduced with certainty that the system of farming out the taxes was already being used under the *epigoni* of the Macedonian dynasty. Cf. Ostrogorsky, 'Steuergemeinde' 66 f.

[3] P. Grierson, 'The Debasement of the Bezant in the Eleventh Century', BZ 47 (1954), has shown that the debasement of the Byzantine *nomisma* did not begin, as was previously supposed, under Nicephorus III Botaneiates, but as early as the reign of Constantine IX Monomachus.

had converted the peasant-soldiers into taxpayers. As though it was not sufficient that a considerable number of the military holdings should have fallen a prey to the acquisitiveness of the great magnates, many of the surviving *stratiotai* were induced to buy exemption from military service by paying an agreed sum.[1] The army of the themes ceased to exist, and even the word 'theme', for troops of the provincial army of *stratiotai*, fell out of use in the eleventh century.[2] At the same time the *strategus* of the theme lost his power as provincial governor, while the magistrate of the theme (κριτής or πραίτωρ) came to be of increasing importance and controlled the provincial administration to an ever greater extent.[3] This undermining of the organization of the themes meant nothing less than the disintegration of the system of government on which Byzantine greatness had been built during the preceding centuries.

The steady reduction of native troops once more brought mercenaries into prominence. This was a reversion to pre-Heraclian days, only, instead of the Goths, it was now the Normans who made so valuable a contribution to the Byzantine armed forces. The magnificent Varangian Russian Družina and the Scandinavian warrior and hero of legend, Harold, fought under the banner of George Maniaces in Sicily. The Varangians now formed the actual imperial bodyguard, although they were no longer recruited from Russia as in Basil II's day, but, from the seventies of the eleventh century, largely from England, so that the Russian Varangian guard was being replaced by an English Varangian corps.[4] The Norman guard more or less took the place of the old Byzantine guard regiments which gradually disappeared altogether.[5]

The military exploits of George Maniaces in Sicily provided a last ray of light on the darkening Byzantine horizon. He attempted to carry out the task which Basil II had left unfulfilled, and to continue the successful Macedonian policy of expansion by the

---

[1] Scylitzes-Cedren. II, 608; cf. Neumann, *Weltstellung* 69.

[2] Cf. Glykatzi-Ahrweiler, *Recherches*, 23 f.

[3] Cf. G. Stadtmüller, 'Landverteidigung und Siedlungspolitik im oströmischen Reich', *Bulletin de l'Inst. Archéol. Bulgare* 9 (1935), 396 ff. and especially Glykatzi-Ahrweiler, *Recherches*, 67 ff.

[4] Cf. Vasiljevskij, *Družina* 176 ff., and Vasiliev, 'The Opening Stages of the Anglo-Saxon Immigration to Byzantium in the Eleventh Century', *Annales de l'Inst. Kondakov* 9 (1937), 39 ff. Cf. the important supplementary notes to Vasiliev's paper by F. Dölger, BZ 38 (1938), 235 f.

[5] The *scholae*, the most distinguished guards regiment of the middle Byzantine period, is last met with in 1068; cf. Attaleiates 112, Scylitzes-Cedren. II, 674, and also Stein's important remarks on this ('Untersuchungen' 47 ff.). The new *tagmata* formed in the eleventh century soon disappeared. Cf. Glykatzi-Ahrweiler, *Recherches*, 28 f.

reconquest of Sicily. The weakened power of the Sicilian Muslims promised success to the undertaking, and in a rapid series of victories George Maniaces seized the eastern part of the island, including Messina and Syracuse. Every success was, however, neutralized by the suspicions of those in power at Constantinople, and at a decisive moment Constantine IX deprived the victorious general of his post. Maniaces took up the challenge. He allowed his troops to proclaim him Emperor, crossed to Dyrrachium and marched on Thessalonica. Victory seemed within his grasp and with it a complete reversal of Byzantine policy, but in 1043, during a battle which was as good as won, he was suddenly killed by an arrow. A few years later there was another attempt to seize the throne, this time characterized by its Macedonian (Thracian) origin. In addition to the resentment against the anti-militarist bureaucracy felt by the army, there was also the opposition of the provinces to the centralization of government in Constantinople. The revolt was headed by the leader of the 'Macedonian party', Leo Tornices, who, although of Armenian stock, lived in Adrianople and had strong ties with this region.[1] The rising under Tornices assumed an even more dangerous aspect than that of Maniaces; in 1047 Constantinople was besieged and came near to falling. Chance had intervened in 1043, and this time the government of Constantine IX was saved by the indecisiveness of the rival claimant who missed an obvious opportunity to enter the capital.

The Byzantine government's systematic reduction of the armed forces can to some extent be explained by the fact that the frontiers had been strengthened by the great victories of the preceding period. George Maniaces' successful campaigns in the East, as well as in Sicily, demonstrated the superiority of the Byzantine Empire over the Muslims. Constantine IX was able to continue Basil II's policy towards Armenia, and to bring his work to its conclusion by annexing the kingdom of Ani.

Meanwhile, this period of peace and good fortune was drawing to an end. While the power of the old enemies of the Empire was broken, new and warlike foes were soon to appear on the Byzantine frontiers. The arrival of these not only affected the general position of the Empire, but its whole foreign policy had to be changed to meet the altered circumstances. In the east the place of the Arabs was taken by the Seljuq Turks, in the north instead of the Bulgars

[1] Psellus II, 14 (ed. Renauld), said that he Μακεδονικὴν ἐρυγγάνων μεγαλαυχίαν and that ἡ Μακεδονικὴ μερὶς καθάπαξ αὐτῷ προσετέθη.

and Russians there were the peoples of the steppes, the Patzinaks, the Uzes and the Cumans, while from the west came the Normans. The last Russian attack on Constantinople took place in 1043; then from the middle of the eleventh century and for many years to come Russia ceased to be an immediate factor in Byzantine policy by reason of the advance of the steppe tribes and the north-eastward orientation of the Russian Empire. About 1047 the Patzinaks crossed the Danube, an event which had the gravest consequences for Byzantium.[1] In his treatise on foreign policy, Constantine Porphyrogenitus had already laid great emphasis on the importance of the Patzinaks.[2] The Byzantines used them as allies against their northern enemies, and in the tenth century it was a fundamental principle of Byzantine foreign policy to co-operate with these warlike nomads, who could attack the Bulgarians or Hungarians in the rear when required, and could also prevent the Russians from advancing southwards. With the conquest of Bulgaria the situation was, however, completely changed; the barrier between Byzantium and the hordes of nomads no longer existed and imperial territory now reached to the Danube, while the plundering inroads of the Patzinaks were now directed, not against the enemies of Byzantium, but against the Empire itself. Byzantium was not in a position to drive back the invading bands which crossed the Danube. They were allowed to settle on imperial soil, and by making a virtue of necessity the newcomers were employed to garrison the frontier and used for military service. But it was not long before the Byzantine government had to take up arms against its new subjects whose addiction to banditry was making the whole countryside unsafe. After several defeats Byzantium was finally forced to buy a modicum of peace with gifts, further grants of land and the bestowal of court titles on the Patzinak chiefs.[3]

Towards the end of Constantine IX's ineffective rule, the schism between the two Churches, an event of world-wide significance,

---

[1] A. P. Každan, 'Ioann Mavropod, pečenegi i russkie v seredine XI v.' (John Mauropous, Patzinaks and Russians in the mid-eleventh century), ZRVI 8, 1 (1963) 177 ff., uses a speech by John Mauropous, to show that the first Patzinak settlement in the Balkans seems to have occurred not in 1048, but in 1047 or even 1046.

[2] *De adm. imp.*, pp. 49 ff. (ed. Moravcsik-Jenkins).

[3] Vasiljevskij, *Pečenegi* 1 ff. is still fundamental. On the Patzinaks cf. also J. Marquart, *Osteurop. und ostasiat. Streifzüge* (1903), 63 ff.; D. Rasovskij, 'Pečenegi, Torki i Berendei na Rusi i v Ugrii' (Patzinaks, Torks and Berendei in Russia and Hungary), *Sem. Kond.* 6 (1933), 1 ff., and further bibliography in Moravcsik, *Byzantinoturcica* I, 2nd ed., 89 ff. Cf. also the observations of G. Moravcsik in *Constantine Porphyrogenitus, De Administrando Imperio*, II, *Commentary*, London 1962, 12 ff.

occurred. After the past centuries, the final break between the Churches of Rome and Constantinople was merely a question of time. East and west had developed along very different lines, and the deep estrangement between the two world centres and the increasing contrasts in their outlooks, made it quite impossible to maintain the fiction of a common intellectual and religious life. For centuries Christendom had been torn by political and cultural rifts, and everything seemed against the preservation of a single universal Church. It was not Byzantine caesaropapism which caused the breach, as has so often been maintained; on the contrary, in Byzantium there was indeed no stronger supporter of ecclesiastical union than the imperial rulers. The Byzantine Emperors—for instance, Basil I and his successors—backed the conception of the universality of the Roman Church against their own Church, because they for their part wished to preserve the universality of the Byzantine state and to maintain their claim to Italy. In actual fact, the growth of independent states in the West had upset the Byzantine idea of a universal state, and the allegiance of the Slav world to the Church of Constantinople had cut the ground in the East from beneath the Roman conception of a universal Church. The southern Slavs had been won over to the Orthodox Church, and this was followed by Russia's recognition of the Patriarch of Constantinople; it was, indeed, no mere accident that soon after the latter event anti-Roman feeling in Byzantium grew more marked. Supported by the powerful Slav hinterland, the Byzantine Church no longer needed to acknowledge Roman supremacy. By Basil II's day, the friendly relations with Rome which were traditional in the Macedonian house were no longer being maintained, for under the Patriarch Sergius (999–1019) the Pope's name disappeared from the diptychs.[1] An attempt at a peaceful division of authority was put forward in a compromise which the weak Papacy agreed to in 1024; this provided that the Church of Constantinople was to be recognized as 'universal in her sphere'.[2] This effort to come to terms was, however, swept aside

[1] The significance of this circumstance has been specially emphasized by Michel, *Kerullarios* I, 20 ff. and II, 22 ff. He goes too far, however, in maintaining that there was a schism between the two Churches as early as this period. Criticisms of this view are therefore justified; cf. especially V. Laurent, EO 35 (1935), 97 ff. But it remains true that the rift of 1054 was only the culmination of earlier developments. On the background of the schism cf. also V. Grumel, 'Les préliminaires du schisme de Michel Cérulaire ou la Question Romaine avant 1054', RÉB 10 (1952), 5 ff.

[2] R. Glaber IV, 1: MGH SS VII, 66. Cf. Bréhier, *Schisme* 8 ff. and CMH IV (1923), 262. Grumel, *Reg.* 828. Many scholars have questioned the reliability of this information (cf. Michel, *Kerullarios* I, 37 ff. and especially *Hist. Jahrb.* 70 (1951), 53 ff.), but on insufficient grounds.

by the new spirit of the pre-Gregorian reform movement in the West. The limitation of spheres of influence towards which historical developments were already pointing did actually come about, but only as the result of a violent schism.

The matter was brought to a head by a particular combination of factors—a strong and uncompromising Papacy, an equally powerful Patriarchate keenly aware of its own dignity and a weak Emperor no longer capable of controlling the course of events. This situation arose towards the middle of the eleventh century. The Pope was Leo IX, a true representative of the pre-Gregorian reformers; and Michael Cerularius, the most strong-willed and ambitious prelate of Byzantine history, sat on the patriarchal throne of Constantinople, while imperial authority was controlled by the ineffective Constantine IX Monomachus. Michael Cerularius had had a life of change and upheaval. As the instigator of a conspiracy of the Byzantine aristocracy against the Paphlagonian Michael IV, he had spent some years in exile. After the fall of the Paphlagonian family he returned to Constantinople, but as he had become a monk during his exile he had to confine his aspirations to an ecclesiastical career. In 1043 he became Patriarch, and his restless and bellicose nature thus found a new outlet. He was as conscious of the dignity of his office as was his rival in Rome, and this awareness was bound up with a ruthlessness which did not hesitate to go to any lengths. The Pope had the support of Cardinal Humbert, who was the leader of the party which was uncompromisingly hostile to the Byzantine point of view. The personalities of Michael Cerularius and Humbert inevitably came into conflict, for both were reckless and unrestrained, and bent on the swift achievement of their respective goals; nor did they hesitate to tear down the veil concealing the age-long latent differences, forcing the world to choose one way or the other. The controversy flared up against the will of the Emperor and in complete disregard of the urgent needs of the political situation. It broke out in South Italy where the claims of the two ecclesiastical centres had always clashed, but precisely where a political understanding between Rome and Constantinople was now most desirable in view of the inroads of the Normans. But once dogmatic and liturgical questions came under discussion the danger point was reached and any hope of agreement was doomed at the outset, for here one doctrine was opposed to another, and one custom to another. It was again the old problems which had troubled men's minds since the days of

Photius, the western teaching of the double procession of the Holy
Ghost, the Roman fasting on the Sabbath and prohibition of
married clergy, and the use of leavened bread for the Communion
Service in the Byzantine Church and unleavened bread in the
Roman Church. It was significant that this last point was most
bitterly debated. For tactical reasons Cerularius brought liturgical
differences into the foreground, as these were easier for the general
public to understand than the far more complicated, and incompar-
ably more important, differences of dogmatic interpretation. Behind
the Byzantine Patriarch stood the Orthodox Churches of the East
and of the Slav countries. The evenly-balanced Patriarch Peter of
Antioch was in the end convinced by Cerularius, and Leo, the Greek
Archbishop of Ochrida, was one of the first to open the polemic
against Rome.

The controversy was brought to a dramatic end by the arrival of
the Roman legates, who were sent to Constantinople under
the leadership of Cardinal Humbert. Encouraged by the attitude of the
Emperor, who appeared to be ready to sacrifice his Patriarch for the
sake of friendship with Rome, the papal legates laid down a bull of
excommunication against Cerularius and his chief supporters on the
altar of Hagia Sophia on 16 July 1054. Meanwhile, the Patriarch,
who had the Church and the people behind him, managed to persuade
the vacillating Emperor to change his policy and fall into line. With
the consent of the Emperor, he summoned a synod which returned
blow for blow by excommunicating the Roman legates. The significance of this event was not realized until later, and at the time little
notice was taken of it, a fact which throws considerable light on the
relations between Rome and Byzantium during the previous years.
Misunderstandings between the two ecclesiastical centres were all
too common and no one was to guess that the quarrel of 1054 was
of greater significance than earlier disputes, or that it marked a
schism which was never again to be healed.[1]

Constantine IX Monomachus died on 11 January 1055, and once
more Theodora exercised the imperial power in her own name. She
was the last surviving member of the Macedonian house, and with

---

[1] The events of 1054 are of special importance in the history of the relations between
Constantinople and Rome, because this schism—in contrast to all earlier disputes—
was never healed and the numerous attempts at reunion failed. This must be emphasized, in spite of the frequently stimulating arguments of S. Runciman, *The Eastern
Schism*, Oxford, 1955, who would link the final break with the developments during the
crusading period. The long series of reunion discussions which begins in the second
half of the eleventh century shows in itself that a rift existed.

her death in early September of 1056 the famous dynasty became extinct. Strange indeed was the fate of this greatest of Byzantine imperial dynasties. It had great difficulty in establishing itself to begin with, and at the end it clung tenaciously to life, leading a strange shadow-existence for its last thirty years. And for all the far-famed greatness of its deeds, it passed away unsung.

The dying Empress nominated as her successor the man whom the dominating party wanted as Emperor, a retired official 'less fitted to rule than to be ruled and directed'.[1] This was Michael, who appears to have held the office of λογοθέτης στρατιωτικοῦ, for he was called either 'the old' or 'the *stratioticus*'. His accession was a real triumph for the civil party. There seemed to be no end to the promotion of civil servants: the senators in particular were loaded with titles and gifts. In contrast, the Emperor curtly dismissed a deputation of generals led by Isaac Comnenus and Catacalon Cecaumenus. This brought matters to a head, and the infuriated military commanders revolted against the government of Constantinople. In Paphlagonia, Isaac Comnenus was proclaimed Emperor on 8 June 1057; supporters flocked to him from all parts of Asia Minor and within a short time he appeared in Nicaea with his army. The imperial forces sent against him were defeated and Michael VI was forced to open negotiations with his rival. An embassy consisting of Constantine Leichudes, Leo Alopus and Michael Psellus was sent to offer Isaac the title of Caesar and recognition as heir to the throne. Such concessions only served to encourage the Emperor's enemies and to disappoint his supporters, and at this point the opposition party in Constantinople rose up against Michael and made overtures to Isaac Comnenus. But the balance between the two rival aristocratic factions was held by a third power and it was the Church which was to be the deciding factor. The forceful Patriarch Michael Cerularius placed himself at the head of the opposition and Hagia Sophia became the centre of the hostile agitation against the government.[2] It was here that Michael VI took the monk's habit after he had been forced to abdicate, and on 1 September 1057 Isaac Comnenus entered Constantinople and was crowned Emperor by the Patriarch.

[1] Psellus II, 82 (ed. Renauld; trans. Sewter, 205).
[2] In spite of Skabalanovič, *Viz. gosudarstvo* 77 ff. and 384, the leading role of Michael Cerularius is clearly emphasized in Attaleiates 56, Scylitzes-Cedren. II, 635 ff., Psellus II 89 and 106 (who expressly emphasizes that the inability of the Emperor to come to an understanding with the Patriarch hastened his downfall and that the insurgents in Constantinople made the latter the κορυφαῖον τοῦ χοροῦ).

Figure 46: *Upper Arm of a Cross.* Silver, with gilding and niello, Constantinople, 1057–1058. The decoration purportedly represents Constantine the Great inclining his head before the icons of SS. Peter and Paul held by Pope Sylvester, standing at right; however, the scene has a contemporary reference to the introduction of the Emperor Isaac I Comnenus into Constantinople (September 1, 1057) by the Patriarch Michael I Cerularius. The Patriarch Michael was arrested and exiled by the same emperor on November 8, 1058. (See pp. 338–341, and Jenkins and Kitzinger, *D.O.P.*, 21 [1967].) Height of detail shown approx. 4″. Dumbarton Oaks Collections, Washington, D.C. Photo: Dumbarton Oaks Collections.

Figure 47: *Christ Crowning Romanus IV Diogenes and Eudocia.* Ivory plaque, circa 1068. Ht. 9½″, w. 6″. Cabinet des Médailles, Bibliothèque Nationale, Paris. Photo: Bibliothèque Nationale.

During the past decades each successive reign had seen an increase in the power of the bureaucratic aristocracy, but with the accession of Isaac Comnenus a marked reaction set in. The reign of the first ruler of the Comnenian dynasty was indeed brief, but even so a real attempt was made to strengthen the military defences of the Empire. The eastern frontiers were successfully defended, a Hungarian attack was beaten off and even the Patzinaks, against whom his predecessors had been powerless, were kept within bounds. Isaac belonged to the military aristocracy of Asia Minor and he worked to build up a strong military rule. On the coinage he had himself portrayed with a drawn sword.[1] After his accession the reception which he gave the senators was as cold as that which he himself and his military deputation had received at the hands of his predecessor. All the same, he did not go to extremes as his rivals had done under Michael VI. The members of the civil party who had acted as intermediaries between him and Michael VI had apparently perceived the lie of the land and changed sides at the right moment, and they were now to receive fresh honours. Psellus was invested with the exalted title of *proedrus*, Leichudes became head of the imperial administration, as he had been under Constantine IX, and later ascended the patriarchal throne. Isaac was, however, more radical in the methods which he employed in trying to make good the material damage caused by the previous system of government. The vast financial reserves which Basil II had left in the treasury had been squandered and the estates of the crown had melted away as the result of endless gifts. Isaac seized on the dangerous expedient of confiscating property and he even laid hands on the possessions of the Church. This brought him into sharp conflict with the powerful Patriarch Michael Cerularius.

The growing strength of the Byzantine Church in the eleventh century was reflected in the policy and personality of Michael Cerularius. The achievement of complete independence of Rome was only part of his programme and equally important in his eyes was a modification in the relations between Church and State in Constantinople itself. He had helped Isaac to the throne and he expected something in return. Nor was he disappointed. The administration of Hagia Sophia, which had hitherto been an imperial privilege, was handed over to the Patriarch, and the Emperor had to pledge himself not to interfere in the affairs of the Church. The Emperor was to be

[1] Scylitzes-Cedren. II, 641; Zonaras III, 666 (cf. also Attaleiates 60); Wroth, *Byz. Coins* II, 512 and pl. LX, 12.

responsible for ruling the State, and the Church was to be the concern of the Patriarch alone, which, if judged by Byzantine standards, denoted an enormous increase in ecclesiastical authority. This attempt to arrive at a division of authority by defining the two respective spheres of influence fell to the ground because neither party would keep to the arrangement. The Emperor confiscated church property and the Patriarch carried on with his plans for exalting the spiritual power at the expense of the secular. Michael Cerularius characteristically based his high claims on the Donation of Constantine, which now for the first time played a decisive part in influencing Byzantine development. He is said to have put on the purple imperial boots and to have threatened the Emperor with deposition.[1] But the Emperor, however, was equally filled with strong self-confidence and a firm belief in the dignity of his office, and the result was a struggle which eventually brought about the downfall of both partners. To begin with, mere superiority of strength gave the Emperor the upper hand. But the popularity of the Patriarch was so great that no one dared take up arms against him in Constantinople, and it was not until he left the capital in order to visit a monastery outside the walls that he was seized by the imperial guards on 8 November 1058 and carried into exile. Nothing could persuade him to renounce his rights by resigning and the Emperor was therefore compelled to summon a synod in order to pass sentence of deposition on him. Again, it was too risky to hold this council in Constantinople, and it was forced to sit in a provincial town. The case for the prosecution (*The Accusation*) was drawn up by Psellus who had no qualms about accusing his former friend of the most improbable heresies and blasphemies. Nor did this prevent him from eulogizing him in a commemorative oration shortly afterwards as the foremost champion of orthodoxy and the epitome of all the virtues. For Michael Cerularius had died while the synod was still sitting. Constantine Leichudes was raised to the Patriarchate, while Psellus took over the office of first minister.

It looked as though the Emperor had emerged victorious, but he soon found that the dead Patriarch was more dangerous to him as a martyr than he had been as a living rival. The seething resentment of the populace at the abduction of their pastoral head rose to boiling point after his death, and so the animosity of the people, as

---

[1] Scylitzes-Cedren. II, 643; Zonaras III, 668. Cf. also Balsamon in Rhalles and Potles I, 147.

well as the enmity of the Church, was added to the opposition of the bureaucratic aristocracy. The position continually grew more precarious, and in the end proved too much for the Emperor. Two years earlier the Church in alliance with the military magnates had brought about the downfall of Michael VI, and now the Church combined with the hostile leaders of the civil aristocracy to overthrow Isaac Comnenus. In a moment of despondency during a period of illness in December 1059 he resigned his throne on the urgent advice of Psellus and retired to the Studite monastery as a monk.

2. POLITICAL COLLAPSE
AT HOME AND ABROAD

General bibliography: Jorga, *Geschichte* I; F. Taeschner, 'The Turks and the Byzantine Empire to the end of the thirteenth century', CMH IV, Pt I (2nd ed., 1966); P. Wittek, 'Deux chapitres de l'histoire des Turcs de Roum', B 11 (1936), 285–319; C. Cahen, 'La première pénétration turque en Asie Mineure', B 18 (1948), 5–67; V. Gordlevskij, *Gosudarstvo Sel'džukidov Maloj Azii* (The Seljuq State in Asia Minor), Moscow-Leningrad 1941; Gay, *Italie*; F. Chalandon, *Domination normande* I; B. Leib, *Rome, Kiev et Byzance à la fin du XIᵉ siècle*, Paris 1924; see also general bibliography above, p. 320.

Constantine X Ducas (1059–67) came to the throne as a result of the alliance of the Church with the civil party which had brought about the downfall of Comnenus. He was an intimate friend of Psellus and of the Patriarch Constantine Leichudes, and he was married to Eudocia Macrembolitissa, the niece of Michael Cerularius. The abdication of Isaac Comnenus and the accession of Constantine Ducas were both the work of Psellus, and with his own hands he had placed the purple buskins on the new Emperor's feet in the presence of the most distinguished representatives of the senatorial party. Psellus had now achieved his goal: as the chief adviser of the Emperor and the tutor of his son and heir he had control over all aspects of imperial policy. The Emperor was filled with admiration for the learned philosopher and practised orator. As Psellus himself said, 'He was fonder of me than of anyone else so that he hung on my lips and completely depended on me for advice. If he did not see me several times a day, he complained and was annoyed. . . . He lapped up my words as though they were nectar.'[1]

[1] Psellus II, 135 and 150 (ed. Renauld; trans. Sewter, 249 and 261).

Just as the Comneni had stood for the military aristocracy of Asia Minor, so the Ducas family at this time represented the civil nobility of the capital. For the time being the military reaction under Isaac was merely an interlude and the civil party was destined to regain and to consolidate its influence. Following the policy of Constantine IX's day, it tried to strengthen its position by extending widely amongst the citizens of Constantinople the privilege of admission to the senatorial class, with the result that, as a contemporary remarked, the number of the senators was legion.[1] The administration continued more and more to lose its strong centralized character. Constantine Ducas made full use of the practice of farming out the taxes, and he went even further in introducing the sale of offices in the central departments of finance, so that not only the actual collection of revenue, but the highest departments in control of financial administration, could be bought.[2] The army was completely neglected and its effective strength reduced to an extent that was most unfortunate, as even Psellus himself had to admit when he looked back on the reign.[3] This was partly because fear of the military party had greatly increased after Isaac Comnenus had gained the throne, and partly because financial straits had suggested the policy of economizing on the army in order to make good deficits in revenue from taxation and greatly increased expenditure in other fields. The cost of the civil service rose with the growth in its numbers and the continual increase in the demands of what was now the ruling element in the government; the expenses of the court mounted with its extravagant expenditure, while the impoverished State approached collapse; gifts to the Church increased, for it was dangerous to risk her disfavour, and presents to foreign rulers were also multiplied in an attempt to placate them. Thus the political ambitions of the ruling class combined with the financial troubles to undermine the defences of the Empire. The attitude of the government was similar to that of the Macedonian *epigoni*; but now the foreign situation had become much more menacing. The anti-military policy of the Ducas was doubly disastrous because it occurred at a time when the Empire was threatened by external dangers of considerable magnitude.

In South Italy the Normans, since 1059 under the leadership of the redoubtable Robert Guiscard, were achieving success after success.

---

[1] Attaleiates 275. [2] Zonaras III, 676 f.
[3] Psellus II, 146 f. (ed. Renauld; trans. Sewter, 259 f.).

The Hungarians had made a vigorous attack and occupied the important Danubian fortress of Belgrade in 1064. In addition to the Patzinaks, the kindred tribes of the Uzes now appeared, and these proved a new and formidable menace. Earlier on the Patzinaks had had to yield before the pressure of the Uzes, and now in turn the latter fled before the advancing Cumans, and leaving the steppes of South Russia their countless hordes poured into the Balkans in the autumn of 1064.[1] Bulgarian territory, Macedonia, Thrace and even Greece were ravaged by these savage invaders. Their plundering raids were so terrible that, as a contemporary wrote, 'the entire population of Europe thought of emigrating'.[2] However, a devastating plague rid the Empire of the Uzes. Many perished on the spot, others retreated over the Danube, while the rest settled on imperial territory and entered the Emperor's service.

Far more fatal to the Empire than this onslaught of Turkish tribesmen from the north was the advance of the Seljuq Turks in the east. The remnants of Arab power in Asia had been swept away by the Seljuqs with a rapidity which put the glory of former Byzantine conquests in the shade. They subdued the Persian lands, drove through Mesopotamia and captured Baghdad, the capital of the Caliph. The Caliphate, by now little more than a symbol of religious unity, came under the protectorate of the powerful military Sultanate which was to have political control over the Muslim world in Asia. The Seljuqs soon gained possession of the whole of the Near East up to the borders of the Byzantine Empire and the Fatimid Caliphate of Egypt. Then they turned their attention to Byzantium. Just as the subjugation of Bulgaria had removed the buffer state between the Empire and the nomads of the north, so the annexation of Armenia under Constantine IX had facilitated the Seljuq attack. The internal weakness of the Empire and the collapse of its system of defence meant that the way was open into the heart of the vital Byzantine provinces. Led by Alp Arslan, the second Seljuq Sultan, the Turks broke into Armenia and took possession of Ani (1065), laid waste Cilicia, forced their way into Asia Minor and stormed Caesarea (1067).[3] The policy of the Byzantine rulers of the day thus stood self-condemned.

[1] The chronology has been correctly worked out by Zlatarski, *Istorija* II, (following Attaleiates 83 and Scylitzes II, 657). On the Uzes (the Torks of the Russian chronicles) cf. the comprehensive treatment of D. Rasovskij, 'Pečenegi, Torki i Berendei na Rusi i v Ugrii' (Patzinaks, Torks and Berendei in Russia and Hungary), *Sem. Kond.* 6 (1933), 1–65.　　　　　　　　　　　　　　　[2] Attaleiates 84.

[3] Cf. C. Cahen, 'La première pénétration turque en Asie Mineure', B 18 (1948), 23 ff.

With the death of Constantine X Ducas in May 1067, control passed to the hands of his wife Eudocia, who was to act as regent for her young sons Michael, Andronicus and Constantine. In actual fact the government was directed by Psellus and the Caesar John Ducas, a brother of the late Emperor.[1] Meanwhile, the series of disasters on the frontiers had strengthened the hand of the opposition. These catastrophes so reinforced their imperative demand for the establishment of a strong military government that the Patriarch John Xiphilinus, although he was a friend of Psellus, had to come to terms with them, and in the end the Empress herself was forced to give in. In spite of the opposition of Psellus and the Caesar John, she agreed to marry the general Romanus Diogenes, a Cappadocian magnate, who was recognized as Emperor on 1 January 1068.

Romanus IV Diogenes (1068–71) was an experienced and brave commander who had distinguished himself in the wars against the Patzinaks and well deserved the high reputation which he enjoyed in the military party. He at once took up the struggle against the Seljuqs, but disintegration had gone too far, while the imperial attempt to save the situation was undermined by the insidious scheming of Psellus' faction. With a great effort Romanus got together an army consisting mainly of foreign mercenaries—Patzinaks, Uzes, Normans and Franks. In spite of all difficulties his first two campaigns in 1068 and 1069 met with some success, but the third ended in a crushing defeat, largely due to the treachery of Andronicus Ducas, a son of the Caesar John. At the Armenian town of Mantzikert in the neighbourhood of Lake Van, the numerically superior, but heterogeneous and undisciplined, Byzantine army was annihilated by the forces of Alp Arslan on 19 August 1071 and the Emperor himself was taken prisoner.

While he was still in captivity, Romanus Diogenes concluded a treaty with the Seljuqs which allowed him his liberty on condition that he promised payment of an annual tribute and a ransom for his own person, and in addition pledged himself to release the Turkish prisoners and provide military help.[2] Meanwhile, in Constantinople

---

[1] Cf. B. Leib, 'Jean Doukas, César et moine. Son jeu politique à Byzance de 1067 à 1081', *Mélanges Peeters* II (1950), 163 ff.

[2] Dölger, *Reg.* 972. C. Cahen, 'La campagne de Mantzikert d'après les sources musulmanes', B 9 (1934), 613 ff.; R. Grousset, *Histoire de l'Arménie*, Paris 1947, 624 ff. Cf. also M. Mathieu, 'Une source négligée de la bataille de Mantzikert: les "Gesta Roberti Wiscardi" de Guillaume d'Apulie', B 20 (1950), 89 ff. Cf. Matthieu's excellent edition with translation and full commentary: *Guillaume de Pouille, La geste de Robert Guiscard*, Palermo 1961, 164 ff., 293 ff.

the opposition, urged on by the Caesar John, had deposed him. At first the joint rule of the Empress Eudocia and her eldest son Michael Ducas was established, but after a short time the Empress was immured in a nunnery and on 24 October 1071 Psellus' pupil, Michael VII, was proclaimed sole Emperor. When the Emperor Romanus returned from Turkish captivity he was met by the faction in power in Constantinople as an enemy, and civil war flared up. Romanus finally surrendered himself, trusting in the guarantee promising him complete immunity of person which was signed by three metropolitans on behalf of Michael VII. But before he had even set foot in Constantinople his eyes were put out with red-hot irons. Psellus surpassed himself on this occasion by sending the blinded Emperor a letter in which he addressed him—his own victim—as a fortunate martyr whom God had deprived of his eyes because He had found him worthy of a higher light.[1] As the result of his terrible injuries Romanus Diogenes died soon afterwards in the summer of 1072.

It was really this appalling epilogue which turned the defeat at Mantzikert into a disastrous tragedy, for now the treaty which Alp Arslan had made with the Emperor Romanus fell to the ground and the Turks made this the excuse for the invasion and conquest of Byzantium. The Empire was once more in danger of foreign conquest as it had been earlier on in the days of the Arab attacks. But then the onslaught of the enemy had been stemmed by the heroic spirit of resistance of Heraclius' successors and the internal condition of the Empire was sound, while now everything was in complete chaos. The effective system of defence based on military holdings had collapsed, and as counterpart to the powerful Turkish Sultan there sat on the imperial throne in Constantinople Psellus' pitiful puppet, a cloistered bookworm, prematurely worn out intellectually and physically, surrounded by court intriguers and long-winded pedants. There was no hope for Asia Minor. The way lay open to the Seljuqs and there was neither the will nor the strength to resist their advance.

The collapse occurred simultaneously at both extremes of the Byzantine world. Fate willed that the same year (1071) which brought the catastrophe of Mantzikert should see Bari fall into the hands of Robert Guiscard. The Norman conquest of the Byzantine possessions in Italy was thus completed and great danger threatened

---

[1] Sathas, Μεσαιωνικὴ βιβλ. V, 316 ff.

from this quarter.[1] In their distress the government of Michael VII appealed to Gregory VII for help, and in so doing furthered the great Pope's efforts to bring about ecclesiastical union on the basis of the universal supremacy of Rome.

At the same time Byzantine authority in the Balkans was shaken. In 1072 a fresh revolt broke out in the territory which had once been part of the empire of the tzar Samuel, and it received strong support from the independent principality of Zeta. Constantine Bodin, the son of prince Michael of Zeta, was crowned tzar in Prizren, and it was only with the greatest difficulty that the imperial generals succeeded in quelling the insurrection.[2] On the Adriatic coast Byzantium continued to lose ground. The recognition of Byzantine suzerainty which the Croats had had to pledge Basil II did not last long, and after Peter Cresimir (1058–74) had greatly extended the frontiers of his realm, his successor Demetrius Zvonimir as a papal vassal was crowned king by the legates of Gregory VII in 1075.[3] It was a still more bitter blow to Byzantium when in 1077 Michael of Zeta also received his royal crown from Rome.[4] The plundering expeditions of the Patzinaks and the increasing inroads of the Hungarians only added to the general confusion in the Balkans.

In addition to the troubles abroad, a serious economic crisis now developed. This was very largely brought about by the government's own measures, a fact which Michael VII had to thank for his nickname of Parapinaces. Prices had risen so high that a gold piece (a *nomisma*) would no longer purchase a whole *medimnus* of wheat, but only a *medimnus* minus a quarter (i.e. minus a *pinakion*, παρὰ πινάκιον)[5]. It was not without its tragic side that Psellus, who up to the present had passed unscathed through every vicissitude and seen his influence grow from reign to reign, and to whom the house of Ducas were indebted for much, and Michael VII for everything, had now to see his career shipwrecked during the rule of his own pupil. The timid Emperor had completely fallen under the spell of the

---

[1] Gay, *Italie* 520 ff.; Chalandon, *Domination normande* I, 189 ff.

[2] Jireček, *Geschichte* I, 234 ff.; Zlatarski, *Istorija* II, 140 ff. Litavrin, *Bolgarija i Vizantija*, 397 ff.

[3] Cf. Šišić, *Geschichte* I, 284 ff.

[4] Cf. St. Stanojević, *Borba za samostalnost katoličke crkve u Nemanjićskoj državi* (The struggle for independence of the Catholic Church under the Nemanići dynasty), Belgrade 1912, 31 ff.

[5] Zonaras III, 712, 13. Cf. F. Dölger, *Deutsche Literaturzeitung* 74 (1953), 598. On the prices of grain in Byzantium and their relatively high stability cf. Ostrogorsky, 'Löhne und Preise in Byzanz', BZ 32 (1932), 319 ff.

dominating Logothete Nicephoritzes who thrust aside Psellus, as
well as the Caesar John. He seized the helm of government and held
it with the same energy and ruthlessness as the Orphanotrophus
John had once done. Like him, he was of humble birth and owed
his rise to power to his own skill and cunning. He planned to combat
the centrifugal feudal elements by means of a centralized bureaucracy; and he went as far as to make the corn trade a state monopoly
and to build a government depot in Rhaedestus for corn shipped to
Constantinople, while free trade in corn was forbidden under
penalty.[1] As we know from the *Book of the Eparch* (cf. p. 253 f.), in
the tenth century the Byzantine state had rigorously controlled the
food supply of the capital and in addition had special reserves of
grain which it sold to the people in time of famine. But what had
been feasible in the tenth century was no longer possible at a time
when the central authority was in decline. The state control of
trade had lapsed, just as in the countryside the embargo on the sale
of peasant holdings was ignored. The measures of Nicephoritzes
provoked most bitter resentment. The landed proprietors, as the
chief purveyors of grain, were involved in considerable losses, and
the urban population, as consumers, were also penalized, for the
monopoly did not aim at ensuring supplies but merely attempted to
meet fiscal needs by screwing up the price of bread. This increase in
the cost of bread meant a general rise in prices and finally a rise in the
cost of labour.[2] Nicephoritzes fell a victim to his own experiment;
after the fall of Michael Parapinaces he was tortured to a death and
the storehouse in Rhaedestus was razed to the ground by the mob
in a revolt which preceded the Emperor's fall.

Under the rule of Michael VII Ducas there could not fail to be
military revolts. It was significant of the times that the hero of one
of these rebellions was Roussel of Bailleul, the commander of the
Norman mercenaries; his candidate for the throne was the Caesar
John Ducas whom he proclaimed as rival Emperor.[3] And it is
equally significant that the Byzantine government called upon the

---

[1] Cf. the very informative description of M. Attaleiates 201–4, who himself owned
property in Rhaedestus, and cf. the excellent comments of G. I. Bratianu, 'Une expéri-
ence d'économie dirigée, le monopole de blé à Byzance au XIe siècle', B 9 (1934),
643 ff. (= *Études byz.* 141 ff.).

[2] On the relationship between the price of grain and the price of goods and the level
of wages Attaleiates 204 expounds views well worth consideration from the point of
view of the history of economic theory.

[3] Cf. G. Schlumberger, 'Deux chefs normands des armées byzantines', *Revue hist.* 16
(1881), 296 ff.

Turks for help against him. They captured the adventurous condottiere and in return for an appropriate ransom they handed him over to the imperial general, Alexius Comnenus. But the government, however, soon found itself in need of the services of this experienced soldier and after a short term of imprisonment he was released to fight together with Alexius Comnenus against new rival claimants to Michael VII's throne. Almost simultaneously two pretenders had arisen from among the Byzantine military aristocracy, one in Asia Minor and the other in the Balkans. The *dux* of Dyrrachium, Nicephorus Bryennius, who had put down the Slav revolt of 1072, was the most outstanding member of the Byzantine military party in the European territories of the Empire. Early in November 1077 he entered his native town of Adrianople as rival Emperor, and from here he despatched an army which advanced to the walls of Constantinople. In Asia Minor the lead was taken by the *strategus* of the Anatolikon theme, Nicephorus Botaneiates, a typical representative of the Asiatic military nobility, who significantly could claim descent from the family of the Phocas. On 7 January 1078 he had himself proclaimed Emperor, and he also marched on Constantinople after he had first made sure of the support of Suleiman, the son of Kutalmish and the cousin of the Sultan Alp Arslan. Even in these chaotic times the advantage was with Asia Minor: Nicephorus Botaneiates forestalled his European rival and namesake.[1] After the unpopular measures of Nicephoritzes the opposition in Constantinople had steadily won ground and they pinned all their hopes on the movement in Asia Minor. Botaneiates had scarcely entered Nicaea with his forces in March 1078, when a revolt broke out in the capital in which the Church also played an important part. Michael Parapinaces was forced to abdicate and go into the Studite monastery, and Nicephorus Botaneiates was proclaimed Emperor. On 24 March he entered Constantinople and on the very same day he was crowned by the Patriarch. Although his predecessor was still living, he married his wife, the Empress Maria, thus strengthening his alliance with the Ducas family and placating the Byzantine sentiment for legitimacy.[2]

---

[1] Michael Attaleiates 288, a supporter of Botaneiates, contemptuously says of Bryennius that he was less distinguished and merely originated in the western provinces, αὐτὸς δ' ἑσπέριος καὶ δυσγενής ἐστι; cf. Neumann, *Weltstellung* 62.

[2] Cf. B. Leib, 'Nicéphore III Botaniatès (1078–81) et Marie d'Alanie', *Actes du VIe Congrès Intern. d'Études byz.* I (1950), 129 ff.

The Empire was in chaos, and the aged Botaneiates could not save the situation. His brief reign was nothing more than the final scene in this tragic period of disintegration, and was marked by a series of revolts and civil wars. With the collapse of senatorial rule, a bitter struggle for the supreme control began among the military commanders. In the end this fell to the most able of them—the young Alexius Comnenus. Alexius had begun by supporting the new Emperor: he had dealt with the pretender Nicephorus Bryennius, and had overthrown Nicephorus Basilacius who had taken Bryennius' place as *dux* of Dyrrachium and then as claimant to the throne. But Alexius held aloof when Nicephorus Melissenus appeared as rival Emperor in Nicaea towards the end of 1080 and appealed to Suleiman for help as Botaneiates had done. He was now feeling his way towards his own elevation.

Meanwhile, the Turks had been considerably assisted in their conquest of Asia Minor by their alliance first with Botaneiates, and then with Melissenus. By about 1080 the Sultan was already in control of the entire territory of Asia Minor from Cilicia to the Hellespont and had founded the Sultanate of Rum, i.e. the 'Roman' Sultanate, on what was the most hallowed soil of Byzantium.[1] With the break up of the effective defences and administration of the Asiatic provinces and with the widespread collapse of the system of military smallholdings, Asia Minor itself was rapidly lost to the Empire.

Alexius Comnenus was not only the most distinguished general of all the members of the military aristocracy who were casting their eyes towards the imperial throne, but he was also the only real politician, and in this respect superior to his uncle Isaac Comnenus and to the unfortunate Romanus Diogenes. Both in the army and in the capital he prepared his ground with cunning foresight and great diplomatic skill, and took great care to win over the opposite party.[2] He married Irene Ducas, the grand-daughter of the Caesar John and the daughter of Andronicus, the traitor of Mantzikert. The Empress Maria regarded him as the guardian angel of her little boy, Constantine Ducas, whom she still hoped might one day become Emperor. After his elder brother, Isaac Comnenus, Alexius'

---

[1] Cf. J. Laurent, 'Byzance et les origines du Soultanat Roum', *Mélanges Diehl* I (1930), 177 ff.; P. Wittek, 'Deux chapitres de l'histoire des Turcs de Roum', B 11 (1936), 285 ff., and 'Le Sultan de Rûm', *Annuaire de l'Inst. de philol. et d'hist. orientales et slaves* 6 (1938), 361 ff.; C. Cahen, 'La première pénétration turque en Asie Mineure', B 18 (1948), 5 ff.

[2] Cf. Chalandon, *Alexis I*, 28 ff., 41 ff.

most ardent supporter was the Caesar John Ducas. The meeting at Tzurullum in Thrace, when the plans were laid for his elevation to the throne, had been in the nature of a family conference of the Comneni and the Ducas. Alexius also came to terms with the rival claimant Nicephorus Melissenus, who was his brother-in-law. Nicephorus offered him the European part of the Empire, keeping for himself the territory in Asia Minor. Thus once again, as in the rebellion of the two Bardas against Basil II, a feudal magnate conceived the plan of dividing up the Empire, but Alexius Comnenus refused to consider this and pacified his brother-in-law with the promise of the title of Caesar. In the capital, the garrison was largely made up of foreign mercenaries, including German soldiers, and it was with the connivance of the commander of the German troops that Alexius gained his entrance. Alexius' own army, like the forces in Constantinople, also consisted of a motley collection of foreigners, and for three days long the capital was the scene of unrestrained plundering and violence. Botaneiates, realizing that there was no point in struggling on, was persuaded by the Patriarch to abdicate, and on Easter Day, 4 April 1081, Alexius Comnenus was crowned Byzantine Emperor.

Figure 48: *Pectoral Cross.* Gold, with cloisonné enamel, 10th to 11th centuries. A bust of Christ adorns the central beaded medallion; the 4 trefoil arms each bear incised crosses and 3 gold beads. Ht. 2⁹/₁₆″. Walters Art Gallery, Baltimore. Photo: Walters Art Gallery.

VI

The Rule of the Military Aristocracy (1081–1204)

SOURCES

THE epoch of the Comneni is one of the most flourishing periods of Byzantine historiography largely thanks to the works of Anna Comnena, John Cinnamus and Nicetas Choniates.[1] Anna Comnena, the intellectual and highly cultured eldest daughter of Alexius I (1081–1118) portrayed the history of her father from his earliest beginnings to his death in her *Alexiad* which covers the years 1069 to 1118.[2] This work was written in a deliberately archaic style by a princess who had been brought up on the classical models and was steeped in the historical writings, poetry and philosophy of ancient Greece, and it is an outstanding witness to Byzantine humanism as well as being an historical source of first importance. Anna's detailed account is the chief basis of our knowledge of the important period which saw the restoration of Byzantine power, the meeting of Byzantium and the West in the First Crusade, and the struggles with the Normans and the steppe tribes from the north and east. The laudatory tendencies in the *Alexiad* and certain other shortcomings, particularly its confused chronology, are more than balanced by the comprehensive mine of information which the authoress was able to provide, due partly to the special facilities afforded by her high position and partly to her own thirst for knowledge. Her husband, the Caesar Nicephorus Bryennius, who was the grandson[3] of the Nicephorus Bryennius who had proclaimed himself rival Emperor during the reigns of both Michael Ducas and Nicephorus Botaneiates, was also an historian. His work was unfinished and it bears no

---

[1] Cf. C. Neumann, *Griechische Geschichtsschreiber und Geschichtsquellen im 12. Jahrhundert*, Leipzig 1888.

[2] ed. A. Reifferscheid, 2 vols., Leipzig 1884; new ed. with French trans. and detailed commentary by B. Leib, *Anne Comnène. Alexiade*, I–III, Paris 1937–45; English trans. by E. Dawes, *The Alexias of the Princess Anna Comnena*, London 1928. Cf. the detailed study of G. Buckler, *Anna Comnena*, London 1929.

[3] Not his son, as was previously supposed; cf. S. Wittek—De Jongh 'Le César Nicéphore Bryennios, l'historien, et ses ascendants', B 23 (1953), 463 ff.

comparison to that of his wife: it deals briefly with the history of the
Comnenian house from the days of Isaac Comnenus, becomes more
detailed from the time of Romanus IV and then breaks off in the
middle of Nicephorus Botaneiates' reign.[1] The period of Alexius I
Comnenus is included in the last part of John Zonaras' world
chronicle (already referred to above, cf. p. 317) and although he
gives a brief account largely based on the *Alexiad*, he does contribute
valuable addenda to Anna Comnena's work. On the other hand,
there is little of independent historical value in Constantine Manasses'
world chronicle in verse which ends with Alexius' accession to the
throne, and this is also true of the world chronicle of Michael Glycas
which goes up to the same ruler's death. And the barren world
chronicle of Joel, which extends to the Latin conquest of 1204, is
on an even lower level.

Like the *Alexiad* for the time of Alexius I, a vital source for
Manuel I (1143–80) is provided by the work of John Cinnamus,
while the writings of Nicetas Choniates cover both this period and
that of the last Comneni and the Angeli. Although both Cinnamus
and Nicetas Choniates begin with the death of Alexius I, they treat
the reign of John II (1118–43) with marked brevity, as being merely
introductory to their period, and we therefore have far less information about this remarkable ruler than about his predecessor or his
successor. John Cinnamus, born some time after 1143 of distinguished parents, was secretary (βασιλικὸς γραμματικός) to the
Emperor Manuel. His work was written shortly after Manuel's
death and has only survived in a single manuscript of the thirteenth
century (with sixteenth- and seventeenth-century copies), mutilated
towards the end.[2] The younger Nicetas[3] came from Chonae in
Phrygia, and he too began his career as imperial secretary; he
attained high office under the Angeli, ending as Grand Logothete.
His work extends to 1206 and was finished in Nicaea after the fall
of Constantinople.[4] The two works are very different in character
and each has its own particular merits: Cinnamus is distinguished by
his straightforward approach and his economy of presentation;

[1] H. Grégoire, B 23 (1953), 469–530 and 25/27 (1955/57), 881–926, gives a French
translation of Bryennius.

[2] This manuscript (Vatic gr. 163) has been collated with the unsatisfactory CB
edition by F. Babos, *Symbolae ad historiam textus Cinnami*, Budapest 1944.

[3] He (and his brother Michael) have been given the name of Acominatus incorrectly,
as is shown by Stadtmüller, *Michael Choniates* 274 ff. The origin of this error is wittily
explained by V. Grumel, 'De l'origine du nom 'Ακομινᾶτος', EEBS 23 (1953), 165 ff.

[4] There is now a German translation of this work by F. Grabler, *Byz. Geschichtsschreiber*
VII–IX, Graz-Vienna-Cologne, 1958.

Nicetas Choniates has a wider outlook, and a rare power of vivid description which singles him out as the most brilliant historian of medieval Byzantium after Psellus. Both were fervent Greek patriots and in writing about the Emperor Manuel I with his Western sympathies they showed their disapproval of the Latins and thus reflected the rising Byzantine nationalism. Nevertheless, the objectivity and reliability of the two works and the personal scrupulousness of their authors was most remarkable for those days.[1] A short supplement to the history of Nicetas Choniates deals with the statues in Constantinople which were destroyed by the Latins in 1204.[2] The capture of Thessalonica by the Normans in 1185 is vividly described in great detail by Eustathius, the learned Metropolitan of Thessalonica,[3] and Nicetas Choniates made use of this treatise in his history.

There are very numerous Latin sources which throw light on relations between Byzantium and the West at this time and give accounts of the crusades from the *Gesta Francorum* to Villehardouin and Robert of Clari.[4] These cannot be enumerated here in detail,[5] but special mention must be made of Alexius I's letter to Count Robert of Flanders because of its significance for the question of the crusading movement. It has survived in its Latin version and is apparently a summons to a crusade.[6] It is, however, most probable that the document in this form is a forgery based on a genuine imperial letter whose purpose was the recruitment of Western

---

[1] On the disputed question as to whether Nicetas Choniates was acquainted with the history of Cinnamus or not, cf. V. Grecu, 'Nicétas Choniatès a-t-il connu l'histoire de Jean Cinnamos?' REB 7 (1950), 194 ff., who concludes in the affirmative. On the historical work of Cinnamus and Nicetas Choniates and the question of their mutual relationship, see the important discussion by A. P. Každan, 'Ešče raz o Kinname i Nikite Choniate' (Further thoughts on Cinnamus and Nicetas Choniates), BS 24 (1963), 4–31.

[2] F. Uspenskij, *Vizantijskij pisatel' Nikita Akominat iz Chon* (The Byzantine writer Nicetas Acominatus from Chonae) (1874), 140 ff., questions the authorship of Nicetas Choniates, but on insufficient grounds. Cf. V. Grecu, 'Autour du *De signis* de Nicétas Choniate', REB 6 (1948), 58 ff., who considers the work was written by Nicetas Choniates and was a part of his history.

[3] New edition with introduction and commentary by S. Kyriakides, *Eustazio di Tessalonica, La espugnazione di Tessalonica* (with an Italian translation by V. Rotolo), Palemo 1961. German translation with introduction and commentary by H. Hunger, in *Byz. Geschichtsschreiber* III, Graz-Vienna-Cologne 1955. On Eustathius' life and the significance of his work cf. K. Bonis, Εὐστάθιος ἀρχιεπίσκοπος Θεσσαλονίκης, Thessalonica 1950.

[4] Recent editions are—Geoffrey de Villehardouin, *La conquête de Constantinople*, ed. and trans. E. Faral, I–II, Paris 1938, 1939; Robert de Clari, *La conquête de Constantinople*, trans. P. Charlot, Paris 1939.

[5] Cf. for instance, the summary in Bréhier, *L'Église et l'Orient au Moyen Age. Les croisades* (1921), p. 1 ff.

[6] The text may be found conveniently appended to Anna Comnena II, 573–6, CB (= Migne, PG 131, 564–8, and PL 155, 466–70).

mercenaries.[1] On the relations between Byzantium and the southern Slav lands, in addition to the Byzantine sources, information is also found in the chronicle of the Priest of Dioclea, dating from the middle or second half of the twelfth century which has survived in Latin[2] as well as in the two lives of Stephen Nemanja in Old Slavonic by his sons, St. Sava and Stephen the First-Crowned,[3] and two Slav lives of St. Sava by Domentijan and Theodosius.[4]

The occasional writings and letters of Byzantine authors of this period form an important supplement to historical works. The correspondence of Archbishop Theophylact of Ochrida is of the greatest value in throwing light on the conditions in Macedonia under Byzantine rule in Alexius I's reign.[5] Much historical material for the period of John II and the first half of Manuel I's reign is to be found in the poems of the exceedingly prolific poet Theodore Prodromus; his numerous literary remains have presented a considerable problem to those writing the history of Byzantine literature, and have even caused some scholars to conclude that there were two, or even more, poets of the same name.[6] Then there are the orations which Michael of Thessalonica (condemned as a heretic in 1156) dedicated to the Emperor Manuel during the years 1150–5,[7] a

---

[1] Cf. Chalandon, *Alexis I*, 325 ff.; Dölger, *Reg.* 1152; Vasiliev, *History* 386 ff. Grousset, *Histoire des croisades et du royaume franc de Jérusalem* I (1934), 1 f. C. Erdmann, *Die Entstehung des Kreuzzugsgedankens* (1935), 365, note 7, makes out a very good case for considering that the forgery was first made in the years 1105–6 and was used as part of Bohemund of Antioch's propaganda to stir up a crusade against Byzantium. A similar view is found in E. Joranson, 'The Problem of the Spurious Letter of Emperor Alexius to the Count of Flanders', *Am. Hist. Rev.* 55 (1950), 811 ff. who gives an English trans. of the letter and a detailed survey of the older literature on the subject.

[2] ed. F. Šišić, *Letopis popa Dukljanina* (The chronicle of the Priest of Doclea), Belgrade 1928, with an old Italian and a Croat trans. and a most valuable historical commentary. Cf. also the ed. (based on Šišić) with good commentary and modern Serbo-Croat trans. by V. Mošin, *Ljetopis popa Dukljanina*, Zagreb 1950.

[3] ed. V. Ćorović, *Spisi sv. Save* (The writings of St. Sava) (1928), 151 ff.; P. J. Šafařík, *Pamatky dřevniho pisemnictvi Jihosl.* (Memorials of ancient South Slav literature) (1873), 1 ff.; German translation and commentary by S. Hafner, *Stefan Nemanja nach den Viten des hl. Sava und Stefans des Erstgekrönten*, Graz-Vienna-Cologne 1962.

[4] ed. Daničić, 1860 and 1865.

[5] Migne, PG 126; cf. Uspenskij, *Obrazovanie* 1–58 and Appendix 10–20, 25–9; Vasiljevskij, *Pečenegi* 134–49 and ŽMNP 204 (1879), 144–217, 318–48; Zlatarski, *Istorija* II, 262–350; Xanalatos, *Beiträge*. Bulgarian trans. of the letters by Mitrop. Simeon, 'Prevod na pismata na Teofilakta Ochridski, archiepiskop bŭlgarski' (Translation of the letters of Theophylact of Ochrida, Archbishop in Bulgaria), *Sbornik na Bŭlg. Akad. na Naukite* 27 (1931), 1–279. Cf. the important preliminary notes on the pressing need for a new critical edition by A. Leroy-Molinghen, 'Prolégomènes à une édition critique des Lettres de Théophylacte de Bulgarie', B 13 (1938), 253 ff.

[6] Migne, PG 133, 1003–1424. On the other editions, the manuscript tradition and bibliography on the problem of Prodromus cf. the comprehensive survey by Moravcsik, *Byzantinoturcica* I, (2nd ed.), 522 ff.

[7] W. Regel, *Fontes rerum byzantinarum* I, 1 (1892), 131–82; I, 2 (1917), 183–228 (fasc. 2 is inaccessible to me).

speech by the *hypatus* of the philosophers and later Patriarch of Constantinople, Michael of Anchialus, which contains interesting information about Manuel's battles with the Hungarians and Serbs,[1] the funeral oration dedicated by Basil of Ochrida, Archbishop of Thessalonica, to the Empress Irene, the first wife of Manuel,[2] and Constantine Manasses' *Hodoiporicon*, a lengthy poem in iambics describing the preliminary negotiations for Manuel's second marriage.[3] Eustathius of Thessalonica (already mentioned above) left a number of literary works of considerable historical significance, particularly various pamphlets, speeches and letters covering the period from the sixties to the nineties of the twelfth century.[4] John Syropulus' speech addressed to Isaac II in 1192 contains important evidence.[5] Nicetas Choniates also left speeches and writings from the years 1180–1210, which give useful information on the contemporary events, such as the rise of the second Bulgarian Empire and conditions after the Latin conquest.[6] The letters and writings of the Metropolitan of Athens, Michael Choniates, the elder brother of Nicetas, are of inestimable value;[7] they present a vivid picture of the hopeless condition of the Byzantine Empire before the collapse and of the position after the capture of Constantinople. The material on the internal condition of the Empire offered by the letters of both Theophylact of Ochrida and Michael Choniates is considerably supplemented by the evidence found in contemporary documents.

Among the documents of the period (cf. above, p. 318, note 1, for bibliographical details) the *memoranda* submitted to Alexius I

[1] Edited with a commentary by R. Browning, 'A New Source on Byzantine-Hungarian Relations in the Twelfth Century', *Balkan Studies* 2 (1961), 173 ff. Cf. also P. Wirth, 'Das bislang erste literarische Zeugnis für die Stephanskrone', *BZ* 52 (1960), 79 ff.

[2] ed. V. Vasiljevskij, VV I (1892), 55–132, with Russian trans. and a valuable introduction.

[3] ed. K. Korna, 'Das Hodoiporikon des Konstantin Manasses', *BZ* 13 (1904), 313–55.

[4] Tafel, *Eustathii opuscula*, 1832 (where several letters of M. Psellus are attributed to him; cf. K. Sathas, Μεσαιωνικὴ βιβλ. IV, 30, 67; V, 75); idem, *De Thessalonica eiusque agro* (1839), 401–39, reprinted in Migne, PG 135 and 136. Seven political orations of Eustathius, two already edited by Tafel, and five hitherto unknown, are published by Regel, *Fontes rerum byz.* I, 1 (1892), 1–131.

[5] ed. with full discussion by M. Bachmann, *Die Rede des Johannes Syropulos an den Kaiser Isaak II. Angelos*, Diss. Munich 1935. He also considers in detail the orations made in 1193 by Sergius Colybas and George Tornices (ed. Regel, *Fontes rerum byz.* I, 2). Cf. also J. Dujčev, *Proučvanija vůrchu bůlgarskoto srednovekovie* (Studies in the Bulgarian middle ages), Sofia 1945, 52 ff.

[6] K. Sathas, Μεσαιωνικὴ βιβλ. I (1872), 73–136; Uspenskij, *Obrazovanie*, Appendix 39 f.; Miller, *Recueil des hist. grecs des croisades* II (1881), 496–502, 615–19, 737–41.

[7] Sp. Lampros, Μιχαὴλ Ἀκομινάτου τοῦ Χωνιάτου τὰ σωζομένα, 2 vols., Athens 1879–80. Cf. also the excellent work of Stadtmüller, *Michael Choniates*, where there is a new edition of the important memorandum (ὑπομνηστικόν) to Alexius III (pp. 283–6).

by financial officials should be specially noted, and the decisions (λύσεις) of the Emperor, which are particularly informative on Byzantine methods of tax administration and on the state of the currency and exchange at the beginning of the twelfth century.[1] Equally important for both the political and the economic development of the Byzantine Empire are the treaties with Venice.[2]

1. THE REVIVAL OF THE BYZANTINE EMPIRE: ALEXIUS I COMNENUS

General bibliography: Chalandon, *Alexis I*; idem, *Domination normande* I; idem, *Histoire de la Première Croisade*, Paris 1925; G. Buckler, *Anna Comnena*, Oxford 1929; Ch. Diehl, *La société byzantine à l'époque des Comnènes*, Paris 1919; Hussey, *Church and Learning*; idem, The Later Macedonians, the Comneni and the Angeli 1025–1204', CMH IV, Pt I (2nd. ed., 1966); H. v. Sybel, *Geschichte des ersten Kreuzzuges*, Leipzig 1841; H. Hagenmayer, *Geschichte des ersten Kreuzzuges*, Innsbruck 1901; L. Bréhier, *L'Église et l'Orient au Moyen Âge. Les Croisades*, Paris 1928; R. Grousset, *Histoire des Croisades et du royaume franc de Jerusalem* I, Paris 1934; C. Erdmann, *Die Entstehung des Kreuzzugsgedankens*, Stuttgart 1935; Runcimann, *Crusades* I–II, Cambridge 1951–2; Setton, Crusades I; H. Kretschmayr, *Venedig* I; Diehl, *Venise*; R. Cessi, 'Venice to the eve of the Fourth Crusade', CMH IV, Pt I (2nd. ed., 1966); Heyd, *Commerce du Levant* I; F. Taeschner, 'The Turks and the Byzantine Empire to the end of the thirteenth century', CMH IV, Pt I (2nd. ed., 1966); C. Toumanoff, 'Armenia and Georgia', ibid.; Jireček *Geschichte* I; M. Dinić, 'The Balkans 1018–1499', CMH IV Pt I, (2nd. ed., 1966); Vasiljevskij, 'Materialy'; Stein 'Untersuchungen'; Ostrogorshy, *Féodalité*.

In the distressing period between the death of Basil II and the accession of Alexius Comnenus the foreign political situation was marked by the complete collapse of Byzantine power in Asia, by the final loss of the Italian possessions and by a serious weakening of Byzantine authority in the Balkans. In internal affairs, the balance sheet showed a central government greatly impaired, serious economic difficulties, the devaluation of the currency and the disintegration of the social and economic structure of the preceding period. Alexius I (1081–1118) was forced to rebuild on new foundations, and new elements provided the pillars of the edifice of state which he constructed.

His work of restoration could, however, only have a superficial and temporary success. In the early middle ages Byzantium had faced a similar situation in the days of Heraclius and Leo III and had

---

[1] Zepos, *Jus.* I, 326 ff.; on the chronology cf. Dölger, *Reg.* 1245.
[2] Tafel and Thomas I [814–1205].

Figure 49: *Church of the Virgin Kamariotissa.* Thessalonica, 1028. Exterior view of the south flank and the apse. Photo: Cyril Mango.

ΕΥ ΑΓΓΕΛΙΟΝ Κ ΤΑ ΜΡ

ρχὴ τοῦ εὐαγγελίου Ἰῦ χῦ ϊοῦ τοῦ θῦ ὡς γέ
γραπται ἐν τοῖς προφήταις. Ἰδοὺ ἐγὼ ἀπο
στέλλω τὸν ἄγγελόν μου πρὸ προσώπου σου
ὃς κατασκευάσει τὴν ὁδόν σου. ἐμπροσθέν
σου φωνὴ βοῶντος ἐν τῇ ἐρήμῳ. ἑτοιμά
σατε τὴν ὁδὸν κῦ εὐθείας ποιεῖτε τὰς τρί
βους αὐτοῦ. ἐγένετο Ἰωάννης βαπτίζων
ἐν τῇ ἐρήμῳ. καὶ κηρύσσων βάπτισμα με
τανοίας, εἰς ἄφεσιν ἁμαρτιῶν. καὶ ἐξεπο
ρεύετο πρὸς αὐτὸν πᾶσα ἡ ἰουδαία χώρα
καὶ οἱ ἱεροσολυμῖται καὶ ἐβαπτίζοντο πάντες
ἐν τῷ ἰορδάνῃ ποταμῷ, ὑπ' αὐτοῦ ἐξομολο
γούμενοι τὰς ἁμαρτίας αὐτῶν·

Figure 50: *Headpiece from the Four Gospels*. Illuminated manuscript on parchment, Byzantine, 11th century. Ht. 11¼", w. 9¼". Cleveland Museum of Art, J. H. Wade Collection. Photo: Cleveland Museum of Art.

seemed to be on the verge of collapse, but at that time the Empire still had unexploited internal resources which made possible a long-term policy of reconstruction, and throughout all its trials it had managed to keep Asia Minor, the very heart of the Empire. It had therefore been able not merely to reinstate itself, but gradually to regain both territorial and maritime predominance in the whole area of the East Mediterranean basin. Now on the contrary the Empire was internally played out: the system wherein its strength had lain during the previous centuries had broken down, and, for precisely this reason, the real source of its strength—Asia Minor—had been abandoned almost without a blow. The Comnenian recovery here was virtually limited to the coastal territory, and it was indeed in this very period that Byzantium lost her maritime supremacy for good. Both from the point of view of strategy and trade the lead passed to the Italian maritime republics; this is the outstanding development of the period, an event of international significance which emphasized the superiority of the rising forces of the West and was to culminate in the Byzantine disaster of 1204. The position of the Byzantine Empire as a great power under the Comneni was not based on a sound internal position, and for this reason, however imposing the results of their skilful policy might be, the Comnenian rulers achieved no lasting success.

From the very beginning Alexius had shown himself to be an unusually clever politician. His task was certainly difficult enough: he had to set on its feet an Empire which was internally exhausted, an Empire deprived of its means of defence, while on all sides it was being attacked by enemies—Normans, Patzinaks, Seljuqs. He had to resign himself to the fact that the whole of Asia Minor was as good as lost to the Turks. He had no option but to concede the lost territory to Suleiman in retrospect as a grant for purposes of colonization, so that Byzantine rights of overlordship might be formally maintained and the fiction established that the rulers of Asia Minor were not a sovereign power, but *foederati* of the Empire, occupying land by imperial concession, like the Patzinaks in the Balkans. In the struggle with the Normans Alexius I had to draw on all his resources. After he had liquidated the Byzantine possessions in South Italy, Robert Guiscard turned to the east coast of the Adriatic. The final goal of the Norman was nothing less than the imperial throne of Byzantium, while his immediate objective was the capture of Dyrrachium which would open the way to Constantinople. Hard upon his accession, without sufficient forces or money, Alexius I had then to take up a struggle in which the very existence of the Empire was at stake. The ecclesiastical vessels had to be pawned and by such means the Emperor managed to get together an army which could only consist largely of foreign mercenaries, a great number of whom were Anglo-Normans. Yet to consider putting up a fight with his own forces was out of the question. Alexius spared no effort to find allies against this formidable enemy, and he opened negotiations with both Gregory VII and Henry IV, and secured the help of Venice.

The motive force which was to prove the determining factor in Venetian foreign policy was thus already clearly apparent: the maritime republic had to be sure of freedom of action in the Adriatic whatever the price, and it was therefore equally anxious to prevent the establishment of any power on either coast of the Adriatic. Thus Venice was on this occasion hostile towards Robert Guiscard and regarded Byzantium as its natural ally. It was particularly important for Byzantium to have the assistance of the seafaring republic, because her fleet had deteriorated even more hopelessly than her army, and the Empire was completely defenceless at sea.

Venice did in actual fact inflict a severe defeat on the Norman fleet, thus forcing them to raise the blockade of Dyrrachium from the sea. On land the siege continued until Robert Guiscard's victory over the imperial army in October 1081 delivered the city into his hands. Thus he had forced open the gateway to Byzantium and the Norman hordes advanced deep into imperial territory, passing through Epirus, Macedonia and Thessaly and even besieging Larissa. Meanwhile, early in 1082 Robert Guiscard was recalled to Italy to deal with a rising stirred up there by imperial partizans, and he had to hand over the command to his son Bohemund. Byzantine resistance gradually increased and under pressure from the imperial army the Normans began to withdraw. In the meantime the Venetians, as allies of the Empire, retook Dyrrachium. Robert Guiscard managed to quell the revolt and again took up the fight against Byzantium, but at the beginning of 1085 he was carried off by the plague. His death was followed by a period of confusion in Italy and Byzantium was freed from the Norman peril for some years to come.[1]

---

[1] The relationship between Robert Guiscard's campaign against Byzantium and certain parts of the Chanson de Roland has been admirably brought out by H. Grégoire, 'La Chanson de Roland de l'an 1085', *Bull. de l'Acad. de Belgique* 25 (1939), 211 ff., and H. Grégoire et R. de Keyser, 'La Chanson de Roland et Byzance, ou de l'utilité du grec pour les romanistes', B 14 (1939), 265 ff., 689 ff.

Venice exacted heavy payment for her timely aid. By the treaty of May 1082 the Doge of Venice and his successors were granted the title of *protosebastus* with the appropriate annual honorarium, the Patriarch of Grado received the title of *hypertimus* and the Church of Venice an annual gift of twenty pounds of gold as a mark of respect. Particularly significant were the enormous trading privileges granted to Venice. In future the Venetians were allowed unrestricted trade in any kind of merchandise with exemption from all customs dues throughout the Empire, including even Constantinople itself, so that they were in a far more favoured position than the native Byzantine merchants. In addition, Venice was given several warehouses in Constantinople and three quays on the shore opposite Galata.[1] This laid the foundation stone of Venice's colonial power in the East, and it made a wide breach in the commercial system of the Byzantine State. The situation was in no way altered by the fact that Venice continued to recognize the sovereign rights of the Byzantine Empire. From now onwards the Italian maritime republic was a determining factor in Byzantine development.

During the war between the Byzantines and Normans a significant role was played by the neighbouring Slav lands which were directly concerned in the struggle of the great powers for supremacy in the Balkans. Dubrovnik and other Dalmatian cities, and probably Croatia itself, decided for the Normans.[2] On the contrary, Constantine Bodin of Zeta, the former leader of the Slav rebellion of 1072, began by supporting the Byzantine Emperor, but during the decisive battle for Dyrrachium he withdrew his troops and thus contributed to the defeat of the Byzantines. He then took advantage of the fact that the Byzantine Empire was involved in further warfare with the Normans, and also with the Patzinaks, to extend his own power to Rascia and Bosnia. It was from Rascia that the offensive against Byzantium began, thus already pointing the way to later Serbian expansion and to the reorientation within Serbian lands which was to displace Zeta by Rascia.[3]

Scarcely had the Byzantine Emperor warded off the Norman danger than he was involved in war with the Patzinaks. During the last decades the threat from the Patzinaks had hung over the Empire

[1] Tafel and Thomas I, 51 ff.; Dölger, *Reg.* 1081. Cf. Heyd, *Commerce du Levant* I, 118 ff.; Kretschmayr, *Venedig* I, 161 ff.

[2] Cf. Jireček, *Die Bedeutung von Ragusa in der Handelsgeschichte des Mittelalters* (1899), 9 and 50; Šišić, *Geschichte* 308 ff; Ferluga, *Viz uprava u Dalmaciji*, 123.

[3] Cf. Jireček, *Geschichte* I, 237 f.; Stanojević, *Istorija Srpskoga Naroda*[3] (History of the Serbian people) (1926), 75 ff.; *Istorija naroda Jugoslavije* I (1953), 248 ff.

like the sword of Damocles, and latterly it had been increased by the support which the Bogomils in the eastern Balkans gave to the invading hordes. The crisis came to a head in 1090 when the Patzinaks reached the walls of the Byzantine capital after a series of hotly-contested struggles with the imperial troops. As though this was not sufficient, Constantinople was at the same time attacked by sea. The emir of Smyrna, Tzachas, one of the emirs who had shared in the heritage of Suleiman († 1085), allied with the Patzinaks and threatened Constantinople with his fleet. He had once been a prisoner at the court of Nicephorus Botaneiates, and being familiar with the tactics of Byzantine warfare he rightly recognized that the decisive blow against the imperial city must come from the sea.

During the winter of 1090–91 Constantinople, besieged by land and by sea, experienced a time of distress and terror. Once again, help could only be found in the outside world, and in his dire need Alexius I resorted to the well-tried, though somewhat dangerous, methods of Byzantine foreign policy towards the barbarian tribes by calling in the Cumans to help him against the Patzinaks. The Cumans, who had arrived in the steppes of South Russia after the Patzinaks and Uzes, were, like them, genuine nomads and were Turkic in language if not by ethnical descent.[1] The leaders of this warlike people were now to decide the fate of the Empire owing to the Emperor Alexius' appeal for help. On 29 April 1091 at the foot of Mt. Levunion[2] a devastatingly fierce battle was fought between the Byzantines with their Cuman allies and the Patzinaks in which the latter were completely wiped out. This wholesale slaughter made a deep impression on contemporaries which is reflected in the *Alexiad* where Anna Comnena wrote: 'An entire people, numbering myriads, was exterminated on a single day'.[3] The cordon which had been drawn round Constantinople was broken. Tzachas' plans had been shattered by the battle of Mt. Levunion, and he was defeated. He was then checkmated by a clever diplomatic move on the part of the Emperor. In the same way in which he had spurred on the Cumans against the Patzinaks, so Alexius now incited Tzachas' son--in-law, the emir of Nicaea, Abul Kasim, against his father-in-law

---

[1] There is an important series of articles on the Cumans by D. Rasovskij, *Sem. Kond.* 7 (1935), 245 ff.; 8 (1936), 161 ff.; 9 (1937), 71 ff.; 10 (1938), 155 ff.; for further bibliography cf. Moravcsik, *Byzantinoturcica* I, 2nd ed., 92 ff.

[2] Cf. B. Leib, *Alexiade* II, 141, n. 3; M. Gyoni, 'Le nom de Βλάχοι dans l'Alexiade d'Anne Comnène', BZ 44 (1951) (*Dölger-Festschrift*), 243, note 1.

[3] *Alexias* II, 16, 15 (ed. Reifferscheid); II, 144, 2 (ed. Leib).

and concluded a treaty with him, and afterwards with his successor, Kilij Arslan, the son of Suleiman.

The relief of Constantinople made it possible to take steps against the Serbs, in particular against Vukan, the Župan of Rascia, whose constant raids made the frontier lands unsafe. But in 1094 the Emperor was forced to break off the struggle and make content with the apparent submission of Vukan. His former allies, the Cumans, had broken into imperial territory and had advanced as far as Adrianople, plundering the countryside as they went. Their leader was a Byzantine pretender who claimed to be Constantine Diogenes, a son of the Emperor Romanus IV.[1] This added to the gravity of the situation, but it also proved to be the weak spot in the enterprise. The pretender was removed by a cunning ruse, and after this the leaderless Cuman hordes were scattered by the imperial troops.

Thus in the European lands of the Empire the worst dangers seemed to have been overcome. In the East the situation also appeared to be easing, for the partition of the Sultanate of Rum and the continual mutual hostility of the emirs seemed to bring Byzantine reconquest of Asia Minor within the bounds of possibility. But at the very moment when Alexius was able to turn to this problem an event occurred which upset all the Emperor's plans and confronted the Empire with countless fresh difficulties: the crusaders were approaching. The Papacy was now growing in strength, and had seen in the conception of the crusade a new means whereby it could extend its authority in the Christian East. Pope Urban II's appeal to the Council of Clermont found a great response in the religious zeal which had been growing in the Western world side by side with the reform movement in the Church. It awoke a longing for the Holy Land whose attractions and whose plight—Jerusalem had been captured by the Seljuqs in 1077—had been made known to Latin Christendom by the countless returning pilgrims; and it drew the feudal lords of the West in search of fresh lands and adventure, as well as the humble folk crushed by economic needs and fired by religious enthusiasm. Yet the crusading movement as the West conceived it was something entirely foreign to the Byzantine Empire. There was nothing new in a war with the infidel, but to the Byzantines this was the outcome of hard political necessity, and they regarded the liberation of the Holy Land, which had in any case

[1] M. Mathieu, 'Les Faux Diogènes', B 22 (1952), 133 ff.

once been Byzantine territory, as the duty of their state, and not an obligation on Christendom in general. The rift between the two Churches made it more unlikely than ever that there would be any basis for combined action with the West. What Byzantium wanted from the West was mercenaries, not crusaders.

When pressed by the Patzinaks and Cumans, as also on other occasions, the Byzantine Emperor had in actual fact tried to recruit mercenaries from the West. Among others, he seems to have written at this time to Count Robert of Flanders, who had visited him while on pilgrimage towards the end of 1089 or at the beginning of 1090, had sworn an oath of homage to him and had promised to send him five hundred Flemish knights.[1] And he had the same thing in mind when he asked Rome for assistance and was discussing the question of ecclesiastical union in his correspondence with Urban II.[2] The turn which events took was both undesired and unexpected.[3] He saw the crusaders approach at the very time when the condition of the Empire had taken a turn for the better and he himself was preparing for a campaign in Asia Minor. His position as guardian of eastern Christendom was usurped by the crusaders, and his Empire, which after fifteen years of long and exhausting defensive warfare he had freed from pressing dangers, was plunged into new

[1] Cf. above, p. 353, under Sources. On the relations between Alexius I and Robert of Flanders cf. the interesting article by F. L. Ganshof, 'Robert le Frison et Alexis Comnène', B 31 (1961), 57 ff. The excellent troops which Count Robert did in fact send fought in the service of Byzantium at Nicomedia and also seem to have taken part in the battle at Mt. Levunion.

[2] Cf. W. Holtzmann, 'Studien zur Orientpolitik des Reformpapsttums und zur Entstehung des ersten Kreuzzuges', *Hist. Vierteljahrsschr.* 22 (1924), 167 ff., and 'Die Unionsverhandlungen zwischen Kaiser Alexios I. und Papst Urban II. im Jahre 1089', BZ 28 (1928), 38 ff.

[3] It was Chalandon, *Alexis I*, who pointed out that, contrary to older opinion, the Byzantine Emperor never invited the West to embark on a crusade, and that this was not only a complete surprise to him but exceedingly inopportune. This view has been accepted by most scholars, including a recent historian of the first crusade, Runciman, *Crusades* I, 116 ff. On the other hand P. Charanis, 'Byzantium, the West, and the Origin of the First Crusade', B 19 (1949), 17 ff., and 'Aims of the Medieval Crusades and how they were viewed by Byzantium', *Church History* 21, 2 (1952), 3 ff., uses the evidence of the *Synopsis Sathas* (Theodore Scutariotes) which seems to indicate that the Byzantine Emperor launched the crusade by an appeal to Urban II. It is, however, a question here of something which is in fact a later and pro-Latin source. But cf. the note by D. C. Munro, 'Did the Emperor Alexius I ask for aid at the Council of Piacenza 1095?' *Am. Hist. Rev.* 27 (1922), 731 ff. For criticism of Charanis, cf. also P. Lemerle, 'Byzance et la Croisade', *Relazioni di X Congresso Intern. di Scienze Storiche*, Rome, 1955, III, 600 f., n. 3. In any case, the point is not whether Alexius I did, or did not, ask the West for help, for there is no doubt that he had done so time and again. The real problem is the kind of help which he had in mind: did he want auxiliary troops for his Empire, or did he wish to kindle a crusade? To attribute this latter plan to the Byzantine Emperor would be to credit him with an intention he could never have had, and, moreover, to ignore the fact that the crusading movement was the outcome of Western development and feeling.

and unforeseen difficulties. At that time no one could have guessed that the Holy War of the West against the infidel would eventually turn into a fight to the death against the schismatic Greeks, but from the outset the western brethren were received with the deepest distrust. The thought of a fresh foreign invasion was already in men's minds at that time, and the behaviour of the crusaders certainly gave support to this fear.

Their arrival was heralded by the so-called Hermit, Peter of Amiens. A motley crowd came with him, and in their passage through Hungary and the Balkans this undisciplined and neglected horde had already indulged in the wildest excesses of plunder and had had to be repeatedly restrained by armed force. On 1 August 1096 this rabble reached Constantinople and continued its looting, where-upon the Emperor arranged for speedy transport across the Bosphorus. In Asia Minor the inadequately armed crowds were mown down by the Turks and only a very few of them escaped to Constantinople in the shipping which the Emperor had put at their disposal.

From the close of 1096 onwards the great feudal lords and their followers gradually assembled, and Constantinople received the flower of West European chivalry, including Godfrey of Bouillon, the Duke of Lorraine, Count Raymond of Toulouse, Hugh of Vermandois, the brother of the French king, Robert of Normandy, the brother of the English king and the son of William the Conqueror, Robert, the son of Count Robert of Flanders, and not least the Norman prince Bohemund, the son of Robert Guiscard. Although the undertaking upset his plans and was a positive menace to the Byzantine Empire, the Emperor tried to make it serve his own interests and those of his state as far as he could, by demanding that the crusaders should take an oath of allegiance to him and pledge themselves to restore to him all captured towns which had formerly belonged to the Byzantine Empire. For his part, the Emperor promised to supply the crusaders with victuals and materials of war, and held out the prospect of taking the cross himself and joining the crusading army as its leader, together with all his forces. With the exception of Raymond of Toulouse, all the crusaders finally accepted the Emperor's demands—even Godfrey of Bouillon gave in after lengthy negotiations. On this basis, agreements were made early in 1097 with individual leaders,[1] including Bohemund, who not only gave his full consent at once, but tried to win over Raymond of Toulouse to agree to the Emperor's terms, and offered his own services for the post of imperial *domesticus* of the East. Meanwhile, the Norman troops had already reached Asia Minor under the leadership of Bohemund's nephew Tancred, who had thus managed to evade taking the oath. In actual fact the crusade was an opportunity for Bohemund to resume his father's plans of conquest.

The first success of the crusade was the capture of Nicaea in June 1097, and in accordance with the terms of the agreement the city was handed over to the Byzantine Emperor and occupied by an imperial garrison. Alexius hastened to make use of this success and his troops occupied Smyrna, Ephesus and Sardes, as well as a number of other towns in what used to be Lydia, thus restoring Byzantine sovereignty in the western part of Asia Minor. After they had taken Nicaea, the crusaders had met the Emperor again at Pelecanum and had renewed their oaths to him, and then, accompanied by a Byzantine corps, they had taken the old military road towards Antioch by way of Dorylaeum, Iconium, Caesarea and Germaniceia. The good understanding between the crusaders and Alexius was maintained up to the time when Antioch was reached, although Godfrey of Bouillon's brother Baldwin and Bohemund's nephew Tancred turned aside towards Cilicia and were engaged in a dispute over Tarsus which the terms of their agreement pledged them to hand over to the Byzantine Emperor and Baldwin subsequently struck into northern Mesopotamia and carved out for himself a principality centred in Edessa. The capture of Antioch on 3 June 1098 was an outstanding triumph for the crusaders, but it put an end to their harmonious relations with Byzantium and brought out the underlying rivalry between the crusading leaders themselves. A bitter quarrel arose between Raymond of Toulouse and Bohemund for the possession of the Syrian capital. The crafty Norman won the game and established himself firmly in Antioch as an independent ruler. All the Emperor's protests were ignored: Bohemund sat tight in Antioch while the other crusading leaders moved on to Jerusalem without waiting for the Emperor, even though Alexius had sent a message to say that if Antioch was handed over to him he would join the crusade as he had promised, and his point of view

---

[1] Dölger, *Reg.* 1196, 1200, 1202, 1203. On the purely western character of the feudal relationship between the crusaders and the Emperor Alexius, cf. J. Ferluga, 'La ligesse dans l'Empire byzantin', ZRVI 7 (1961), 104 ff.

was now supported by Raymond of Toulouse who urged the surrender of the city. There was something of a *rapprochement* between the defrauded Count of Toulouse and the Byzantine Emperor,[1] and in contrast to those who, in spite of their oath of allegiance to Byzantium, were busy founding their own principalities, Raymond, who had refused to swear this, handed over several captured Syrian ports to the Emperor. After Jerusalem was taken on 15 July 1099, a still closer understanding developed between the two. For Raymond, the real leader of the crusade since the fall of Antioch, was again outwitted, and not he, but Godfrey of Bouillon became the head of the new kingdom as 'Defender (*advocatus*) of the Holy Sepulchre'.

Byzantium could afford to countenance the founding of the kingdom of Jerusalem in distant Palestine, but the establishment of Bohemund in Antioch was another matter. The Norman principality in Syria impinged directly upon vital interests of the Byzantine Empire, and all the more so since Bohemund no longer made any secret of his enmity towards Byzantium and had been in open hostility since 1099. The situation was, however, somewhat mitigated for the Byzantine Emperor by the fact that Bohemund also had to fight the Turks at the same time, for his principality was equally a thorn in their flesh. In 1101 he was captured by the emir Malik Ghazi of the Danishmend house, but he was ransomed by the crusaders and he returned to Antioch. In 1104 the Turks inflicted a crushing defeat on the Latins at Harran, and this gave the imperial army an opportunity of taking possession of the important fortresses of Tarsus, Adana and Mamistra, while the Byzantine fleet captured Laodicea and other coastal towns as far as Tripolis.

At this point Bohemund was forced to realize that a simultaneous war against the Turks and Byzantines was beyond his resources. Leaving Tancred in Antioch he returned to the West to launch a full-scale expedition against Byzantium. As he journeyed through Italy and France recruiting help he was responsible more than anyone else for spreading the story that the Byzantine Emperor had betrayed the crusaders.[2] He adopted his father's programme and

---

[1] Cf. Runciman, *Crusades* I, 301 ff.; J. H. Hill, 'Raymond of Saint Gilles in Urban's Plan of Greek and Latin Friendship', *Speculum* 26 (1951), 265 ff.; J. H. Hill—L. L. Hill, 'The Convention of Alexius Comnenus and Raymond of Saint Gilles', *Am. Hist. Rev.* 58 (1953), 322 ff.

[2] Cf. C. Erdmann, *Die Entstehung des Kreuzzugsgedankens* (1935); E. Joranson, 'The Problem of the Spurious Letter of Emperor Alexius to the Count of Flanders', *Am. Hist. Rev.* 55 (1950), 820 ff. Cf. also p. 354, note 1.

plan of campaign and in October 1107 he landed at Avlona with a large force and from there moved against Dyrrachium. After a quarter of a century the Normans and Byzantines once more met before the walls of Dyrrachium. But the Byzantine Emperor was in a very different position this time, and the struggle ended with a Byzantine victory and the complete defeat of Bohemund. In the treaty of 1108 the latter penitently promised to be faithful to the Emperor as his liege-man (λίζιος ἄνθρωπος), and to give him assistance against all the enemies of the Empire, as was his duty as vassal. In recognition of this the principality of Antioch was granted him as an imperial fief.[1] Meanwhile Tancred, as was only to be expected, refused to recognize this treaty, and after Bohemund's death (1111?) he remained the sole master of Antioch. Alexius tried to get the rest of the crusading rulers to ally with him against Tancred, but he was unsuccessful. He had not the energy to renew the war against the refractory Norman principality, but he spent his last years fighting against the Turks in Asia Minor.

Thus the treaty of 1108 had no immediate results, but it was significant as foreshadowing the policy of future governments. The defeat of Bohemund on the Adriatic did, however, help to strengthen the Byzantine position in the Balkans. But a new and powerful factor was making itself felt in the affairs of the Balkans: this was Hungary, which had brought Croatia and Dalmatia under its control at the beginning of the twelfth century. The growing influence of Hungary in Byzantine politics was reflected in the marriage alliance which the Emperor Alexius arranged when his heir John wed a Hungarian princess. But, as both powers had strong interests in the Balkans and the Adriatic, a clash over their respective spheres of influence was inevitable, and during the following years Hungary was to be one of the chief opponents of the Byzantine Empire.

Alexius Comnenus had maintained his struggle unceasingly for nearly forty years and he had done a considerable amount to restore the power of the Byzantine Empire. At every stage of this struggle his statesmanship and his unrivalled skill as a diplomat had been in evidence. He played off Venice against Robert Guiscard, the rival emirs against Tzachas, he overcame the Patzinaks with the help of

---

[1] The text of this document, which is of great constitutional importance, is given in Anna Comnena, *Alexiad*, II, 209 ff. (ed. Reifferscheid); III, 125 ff. (ed. Leib); Dölger, *Reg.* 1243. A detailed analysis of the treaty is given by J. Ferluga, 'La ligesse dans l'Empire byzantin', ZRVI 7 (1961), 99 ff.

the Cumans, and he used the crusaders against the Turks and the Turks against the crusaders. Side by side with this brilliant exploitation of foreign elements, he was able steadily to increase his own resources. The military strength of Byzantium grew from war to war and from year to year. When the struggle with Robert Guiscard was going on Byzantine sea power was non-existent, but in the war against Tzachas, and particularly against Bohemund, an active part was taken by the fleet and with marked success. The early defeats were redeemed by the victorious campaigns against the Cumans and the Seljuqs, while the notable strengthening of the Byzantine army is obvious if the two encounters with the Normans on the east coast of the Adriatic are compared. Alexius I was responsible for more than the extension of the Empire's frontiers: he achieved a measure of internal consolidation and re-established its means of defence. It is true that the political system which he inaugurated differed from the stern régime of the middle Byzantine period. The undesirable developments of the eleventh century, such as the farming out of taxes, the granting of rights of immunity to private landowners, the depreciation of the coinage, persisted, and even increased. A new factor was the increasingly predominant part which the Italian maritime republics took in Byzantine trade: from 1082 onwards Venice was all powerful in Byzantine waters, and by a treaty of October 1111 Alexius granted important trading privileges to Pisa.[1]

The changes which Alexius introduced into the system of court titles were exceedingly characteristic of the disintegration of the Byzantine administrative system.[2] The extravagant distribution of honours under the régime of the civil aristocracy had meant that the old titles had lost their value, and therefore fresh dignities had to be created for those in high positions. The titles of patrician, *protospatharius* and *spatharocandidatus* had denoted important office in the tenth century, but by the middle of the eleventh century they meant very little, and by the turn of the century had fallen out of use. Only the three highest honours of the middle Byzantine period— Caesar, *nobilissimus* and *curopalates*—survived this curious titular inflation, and even they had depreciated somewhat in value. Alexius created for his brother Isaac the new title of Sebastocrator (a combination of *sebastus* and *autocrator*) which he gave him in preference to that of Caesar. This meant that he need have no hesitation in keeping his promise to the former pretender Nicephorus Melissenus (cf.

[1] Miklosich-Müller III, 9 ff.; Dölger, *Reg.* 1254 and 1255.
[2] Cf. Stein, 'Untersuchungen' 29 ff.; Bréhier, *Institutions* 138 ff.

above, p. 350) who was granted the title of Caesar, still a very high honour but now no longer the highest. The old official titles disappeared and the more important functionaries were given titles which used to be imperial attributes, or reserved for use among the younger members of the reigning house. By combining individual titles and attributes it was possible to obtain endless variety—*sebastus, protosebastus, panhypersebastus*; or *sebastohypertatus, pansebastohypertatus, protopansebastohypertatus*; or *entimohypertatus, panentimohypertatus, protopanentimohypertatus*; or *nobilissimus, protonobilissimus, protonobilissimohypertatus*, and so on. Such changes in the system of titles reflect the developments which had come about in Byzantine administration since the eleventh century; the more rigid centralized bureaucracy had gone and with it the carefully observed hierarchy of rank which had characterized the middle Byzantine period.

A similar depreciation is also to be observed in the titles of the commanders of the themes. Towards the end of the tenth century there were three different designations in use, *strategus*, catepan and *dux*; but now only the highest of these was retained. By the eleventh century the oldest title of *strategus* had almost completely disappeared, and in the Comnenian period the title of *dux* was applied to all the governors of the themes, and their subordinates were called catepans. This change was particularly characteristic in that it went hand in hand with the diminution in the importance and extent of the individual themes.[1] From the time of Alexius down to the fall of the Empire, the title of *megas dux* was borne by the High Admiral who commanded the entire naval forces.[2] From the second half of the tenth century, the supreme military command had been shared by the two *domestici* of the East and West, and from the mid-eleventh century onwards they were usually given the title of *megas domesticus*.[3] From Alexius I's day, the control of the whole civil service was entrusted to the λογοθέτης τῶν σεκρέτων, designated from the end

[1] The statements of Stein on the use of the title of *dux* ('Untersuchungen' 21 ff.) should be corrected in the light of what has been said, for he overlooks the fact that by the end of the tenth century the governor-generals of the most important Byzantine themes had regularly had this title and that since then there was a distinct difference of rank between the *dux*, the catepan and the *strategus*, as Skabalanovič, *Viz. gosudarstvo* 187 ff. had already pointed out. Cf. above, p. 311 f. Cf. also the well-documented study by Glykatzi-Ahrweiler, *Recherches* 52 ff.

[2] Cf. Stein, 'Untersuchungen' 57. R. Guilland, 'Études de titulature et de prosopographie byzantines. Les chefs de la marine byzantine: Drongaire de la flotte, Grand Drongaire de la Flotte, Mégaduc', BZ 44 (1951) (*Dölger-Festschrift*), 222 ff., gives a very thorough account of all the holders of this office known from the sources.

[3] Stein, 'Untersuchungen' 50 f. and 56 f.; R. Guilland, 'Le grand domesticat à Byzance', EO 37 (1938), 53–64; V. Laurent, 'Le grand domesticat. Notes complémentaires', ibid. 65–72.

of the twelfth century as the Grand Logothete.[1] From now onwards the functions of the chief minister, the μεσάζων, were frequently (though by no means invariably) linked with this office, as they had been with that of the Logothete of the Drome in the middle Byzantine period.[2]

The disintegration of the army and the pressing financial needs had been the two outstanding characteristics of the internal life of the Byzantine Empire from the mid-eleventh century onwards, and Alexius I's efforts at home were particularly concerned with these problems. The debasement of the coinage, which had begun in the middle of the eleventh century, was continued to a much greater extent under Alexius Comnenus, so that side by side with the standard gold *nomisma* new coins of inferior metals, and varying in value, were being put into circulation.[3] This naturally caused great confusion in economic life, but at the same time the exchequer profited because it demanded that payments should be made to it in gold of full weight, although it was issuing a debased coinage. Such a state of affairs could not last long, and the government was soon compelled to accept coins of the lesser value. At first the rate of exchange was subject to great fluctuation, and the tax collectors calculated it to suit their own ends and brazenly pocketed the difference until the Emperor ruled that the *nomisma* should have the value of four *miliaresia* (silver coins), thus stabilizing the current value of the Byzantine gold coin at exactly one-third of what it had originally been.[4] In addition to the principal taxes, a number of supplements were added, called the Διπέρατον, the ἐξάφολλον, the συνήθεια and the ἐλατικόν, which together made up about 23 per cent. of the principal taxes. In assessing the principal tax, the value of the gold coin was reckoned at a third, but to begin with the subsidiary taxes were calculated at the old rate. When the taxpayers protested, the Emperor compromised by fixing the rate of the *nomisma* at one-half of its original value for purposes of calculating the additional taxes. This meant an increase of 50 per cent. from the

---

[1] Cf. Ch. Diehl, 'Un haut fonctionnaire byzantin, le logothète τῶν σεκρέτων', *Mélanges Jorga* (1933), 217 ff.; cf. the review of this by G. Stadtmüller, BZ 34 (1934), 373 ff.

[2] Cf. H. G. Beck, 'Der byzantinische "Ministerpräsident"', BZ 48 (1955), 321 ff.

[3] From the period of Alexius I, in addition to the sterling gold *nomisma*, six different types of *nomismata* minted in various kinds of metal have been preserved, cf. Wroth, *Byz. Coins* I, pl. LXI and II, 540 ff.

[4] In actual fact the Byzantine *nomisma* sank still lower in value. The important imperial rulings (λύσεις) on the questions raised by the tax collectors on this matter are given in Zepos, *Jus* I, 319 ff. Cf. Vasiljevskij, 'Materialy', vol. 210, 385 ff.; Chalandon, *Alexis I*, 320 ff.; Ostrogorsky, 'Steuergemeinde' 63 ff.; Dölger, *Reg.* 1230, 1234, 1245, 1246, 1247.

supplementary taxes, and in actual fact the exchequer gained even more, because these taxes were calculated on a fixed amount of the principal tax, but, with the devaluation of the *nomisma*, the face value of the taxes had correspondingly increased, thus penalizing even the very poorest classes who had never before been liable to be called upon to pay the supplementary taxes. In this way the Emperor very cleverly contrived to derive considerable advantage from the debasement of the currency.

The brunt of this was borne by the taxpayer, whose lot became daily worse. Even more oppressive than the burden of taxation was the tyranny of the revenue officials and the tax-farmers, whose arbitrary exactions raised more bitter protests than the actual raising of the taxes. At the beginning of the twelfth century the farming out of the taxes became the regular procedure, and even entire provinces were turned over to individual tax-farmers. It was taken as a matter of course that these pledged themselves to exact twice as much tax as was formerly due.[1] In addition to the payment of taxation, there were many charges to be paid in kind, as well as obligatory labour services, all of which were particularly heavy at this time. The population had to provide both materials and labour for constructing ships, fortifications, bridges and roads. They were also bound to furnish board and lodging for imperial officials and for the army, to provide transport, and to supply troops passing through with all kinds of provisions either free of cost or at a very low price.[2] This meant that the upkeep of the imperial defences and the maintenance of the army were only partly met by the state, while the rest of the cost fell directly on the shoulders of the people who appear at this time to have borne a particularly heavy burden. In this way the government was afforded a measure of relief in a period of great financial straits when one of its immediate problems was the reconstruction of its defences, a task which necessitated the recruitment of large numbers of foreign mercenaries. For at this period the Byzantine army consisted of a variety of foreign peoples—Varangians, Russians, Patzinaks, Cumans, Turks, French, Germans, English, Bulgars, Abasgi and Alans.[3]

[1] Zepos, *Jus* I, 334. Cf. Dölger, *Finanzverwaltung* 75.
[2] Cf. also the lengthy lists of different kinds of tax and of payments in kind in Alexius I's charters, Miklosich-Müller VI, 27 f., 47 f.
[3] Cf. the enumerations in the documents of Alexius I of May 1086 and April 1088, Rouillard-Collomp, *Actes de Lavra* I, 111, and Miklosich-Müller VI, 47. Cf. also the interesting information about the racial composition of the Byzantine army in the seventies and eighties of the eleventh century given by A. A. Vasiliev, 'The Anglo-Saxon Immigration to Byzantium', *Annales de l'Inst. Kondakov* 9 (1937), 58 f.

Side by side with the mercenaries the native troops began to gain in importance. The small-holder could of course no longer be the mainstay of the Byzantine forces for the old military holdings had nearly all fallen victim to the process of feudalization, and although the soldier-farmer had not entirely disappeared, he played only a very minor role. The Byzantine military system was now based on a purely feudal device of conditional grants and its real strength was the great estate of the *pronoia*. The use of the *pronoia* for military ends was indeed the main reason why the Byzantine Empire strengthened its defences under the rule of the military aristocracy personified in the Comnenian dynasty. In contrast, the granting out of *pronoiai* which is found under the *epigoni* of the Macedonian house and the dynasty of the Ducas (cf. above, p. 330 f.) was not yet concerned with military obligations. It was under Alexius I Comnenus[1] that this system received the military character which it retained until the downfall of the Empire. The pronoiar now had the obligation of military service and for this reason was generally called 'soldier' (στρατιώτης). He was an equipped and mounted knight and, in accordance with the value of his *pronoia* grant, he was accompanied by a varying number of troops.[2] As well as this, other estates, and even those of the Church, were also liable to compulsory recruitment, though it was the lightly-armed infantry which they provided.[3]

The *pronoia* estate was not the private property of the pronoiar, but was unalienable, and to begin with it was also not heritable. Ownership and unlimited rights of disposition remained with the state, who granted it out and withheld it at discretion. But as long as it was in his possession, the pronoiar was, however, the absolute lord and master of the estate granted him and of the peasants settled on it, and as a rule he would keep it until the end of his life. The pronoiar and the *stratiotes* of the middle Byzantine period each came from an entirely different social milieu. The old *stratiotai* were a militia of small farmers, while although the pronoiars were also called *stratiotai*, they were drawn from the ranks of the feudal aristocracy

[1] Cf. Ostrogorsky, *Féodalité*, 26 ff.

[2] Byzantine sources do not provide direct evidence on this, but the numerous and precise references in the Chronicle of the Morea, and in the Venetian documents for the district of Scadar, point to this conclusion. Cf. Ostrogorsky, *La féodalité* 57 ff. and 237 ff.

[3] In Theophylact of Ochrida, Migne, P.G. 126, 532 f., it is significant that the recruits are called πεζοί; for further information cf. Mutafčiev, *Vojniški zemi* 53 ff., and Xanalatos, *Beiträge* 44 ff.

and especially from the lesser nobility. They were greater or lesser feudal lords, whose estates were farmed by the peasants on them. The grant of a *pronoia* not only involved transference of the land itself, but the transaction just as often included the peasants settled on the estate, who then became the *paroikoi* of the pronoiar,[1] and had to pay all their dues and taxes to him. It was this right to the taxes and income of the *pronoia* that constituted its value and attraction in the eyes of the recipient.

The significant role of the system of the *pronoia* in the attempts of the government to solve its pressing problems naturally resulted in a constant increase from now on in the number of estates granted out in this way. Thus the process of feudalization was hastened and strengthened: the *pronoia* is the most marked characteristic of the form which Byzantine feudalism took. It was later to spread beyond the Byzantine Empire and take firm root in the lands of the southern Slavs and it played a vital part in the development of feudalism in those countries.[2]

Under Alexius I there was also a change in the use of the *charisticium*, or handing over the administration of monasteries and monastic property to laymen. This practice, which had greatly increased in the eleventh century, aimed at promoting the economic development of monastic property, but it was open to serious abuse and thus roused the resentment of a section of the clergy and was frequently condemned in church councils.[3] It did, however, persist, and was even defended by several ecclesiastics of repute and standing, largely because it afforded an outlet for monastic economic activity, which was otherwise closely restricted by the inalienability of church property. In the early period such grants had mostly been made by the ecclesiastical authorities, but now the Emperor himself bestowed

---

[1] Charanis, 'Monastic Properties' 90, makes many excellent observations on the question of the *pronoia*, but he is in error when he believes that the peasant population could keep their independence on a *pronoia* estate; cf. also Charanis, 'On the Social Structure and Economic Organization of the Byzantine Empire in the Thirteenth Century and later', BS 12 (1951), 142, 152 f. On this, however, cf. Dölger, BZ 45 (1952), 476; Ostrogorsky, *La féodalité*, 71 ff. *et passim*.

[2] Cf. Ostrogorsky, *La féodalité, La* 187 ff.

[3] F. Uspenskij, 'Mnenija i postanovlenija konstantinop. pomestnych soborov XI i XII v. o razdače cerkovnych imuščestv' (Opinions and rulings of the local synods of Constantinople of the eleventh and twelfth centuries on the granting of ecclesiastical property), *Izv. Russk. Archeol. Inst. v K/pole* 5 (1900), 1 ff. Cf. also Vasiljevskij, 'Materialy', vol. 202, 400 ff.; Ferradou, *Des biens des monastères à Byzance* (1896), 233 ff.; W. Nissen, *Die Diataxis des Michael Attaleiates von 1077* (1894), 52 ff.; Chalandon, *Alexis I*, XXVIII ff., 233 ff.; Xanalatos, *Beiträge* 32 ff.; Charanis, 'Monastic Properties', 72 ff.

monastic property in this way as a kind of benefice.[1] A grant of *charisticium*, unlike that of a *pronoia*, did not compel the recipient to perform any service, but it did provide the state with an easy means of remuneration. It is also possible that the Emperor wished to restrict the enormous growth of monastic property: in any case, it is not surprising that his use of monasteries in this way caused much bad blood in ecclesiastical circles.[2]

Similarly, Alexius I met with strong opposition from the Church when he was compelled to lay his hands on church treasure after the outbreak of war with the Normans, and under pressure from this opposition he had to promise restitution of the confiscated wealth and in the year 1082 he even promulgated a decree in which he repudiated his own action and forbade for the future all alienation of church property.[3] This did not, however, prevent him from again seizing church treasure a few years later when he had to find ways and means of dealing with a new threat.[4] But estrangement of this kind was only temporary, and between the secular and spiritual powers there was, as a rule, understanding and co-operation based on their strong common interests. Emperor and Church fought together against the heretical movements which threatened to undermine the organization of both parties, and it was the Emperor who took the lead in such proceedings. The teaching of the Bogomils, which had developed on Slav territory in the Balkans under the strong influence of various eastern heresies, was at this time so widespread, and had so many followers, in the Byzantine Empire, and even in the capital itself, that the Emperor regarded the extermination of this dangerous heresy as the solemn duty of the state. Basil, the leader of the Bogomils, and those of his disciples who refused to recant were burnt at the stake.[5]

[1] This was rightly pointed out by Chalandon, *Alexis I*, 283. It is often maintained by scholars, including Chalandon, that the *charisticium* system was associated with the anti-monastic measures of the iconoclasts. This is not, however, the case, for the system was not in itself characterized by hostility to monasticism.

[2] Cf. the homily against the practice of granting *charisticia* by John, the Patriarch of Antioch, a contemporary of Alexius I—his allusion to the iconoclasts here is naturally only polemic; Migne, PG 132, 1117 ff. (cf. Chalandon, *Alexis I*, p. XXVIII f.). Balsamon, however, disapproved of this homily, and Eustathius of Thessalonica also supported the system of *charisticia*.

[3] Zepos, *Jus* I, 302 ff.; Dölger, *Reg.* 1085. For an analysis of this decree and its disputed chronology cf. V. Grumel, 'L'affaire de Léon de Chalcédoine. Le chrysobulle d'Alexis Ier sur les objets sacrés', EB 2 (1944), 126 ff.

[4] Cf. Grumel, p. cit. 131 ff.

[5] Cf. D. Angelov, *Der Bogomilismus auf dem Gebiet des byzantinischen Reiches* (1948), 12 ff. and passim; S. Runciman, *The Medieval Manichee* (1946), 69 ff.; D. Obolensky, *The Bogomils* (1948), 197 ff.

As the protector of orthodoxy, the Emperor Alexius also took an active part in the proceedings against John Italus, 'the *hypatus* of the philosophers', who like his great predecessor Psellus was an ardent supporter of Plato and neoplatonism, and was also well versed in Aristotelian teaching. Ancient philosophy, which since Psellus had taken pride of place in the highest philosophical school in the Empire, now in the person of John Italus came into conflict with Christian doctrine. Psellus had been clever enough to keep within the bounds prescribed by Christian dogma, but John Italus, on the contrary, could not manage this, and he paid for his partiality for the 'foolish and empty wisdom of the pagans' by being excommunicated.[1] Alexius I was not only anxious to preserve the orthodox faith but he did what he could to promote a high standard of discipline and conduct in the Christian life; he supported the strictly ascetic monasteries of Mt. Athos, and he gave special encouragement to the monk Christodoulus who had established himself in the island of Patmos as a monastic reformer. Patmos and the neighbouring islands were granted to him in perpetuity and, like Athos, they formed a monastic republic with far-reaching rights of immunity.[2]

Not only the Empire itself, but the authority of the Emperor was strengthened under Alexius Comnenus. But in structure the Empire now differed considerably from the rigid centralized state of the middle Byzantine period. The age of the Comneni saw an intensification of the feudalizing process and those very feudal elements in the provinces, against which the tenth-century Emperors had battled with such insistence, were to become the mainstay of the new state. Alexius gave the preference to those powerful social factors which had persisted in spite of the opposition of the middle Byzantine state, and it was on these that he built his political and military organization. Therein lies the secret of his success as well as its limitations. Byzantium had finally thrown over its once solid foundations and its defences, and its economic and financial strength

---

[1] Cf. F. Uspenskij, 'Deloproizvodstvo po obvineniju Ioanna Itala v eresi' (The proceedings against John Italus for heresy), *Izv. Russk. Archeol. Inst. v K/pole* 2 (1897), 38 ff., and *Očerki* 146 ff.; Hussey, *Church and Learning* 89 ff.; S. Salaville, 'Philosophie et Théologie ou épisodes scolastiques à Byzance de 1059 à 1117', EO 29 (1930), 141 ff.; P. E. Stephanou, *Jean Italos*, ibid. 32 (1933), 413 ff., and particularly *Jean Italos, philosophe et humaniste* (*Orient. Christ. Anal.* 134, 1949); J. Dujčev, 'L'umanesimo di Giovani Italo', *Studi biz. e neoell.* 5 (1939), 432 ff.; B. Tatakis, *La philosophie byzantine*, Paris 1949, 210 ff.; P. Joannou, *Christliche Metaphysik in Byzanz I. Die Illuminationslehre des Michael Psellos und Joannes Italos*, Ettal 1956.

[2] Cf. the numerous documents in which Alexius I bestowed privileges and gifts on Christodoulus and his monastery of St. John Baptist on Patmos, Dölger, *Reg.* 1123, 1139, 1141, 1147, 1150, 1153, 1170, 1214.

were greatly diminished. This is the explanation why the successes of the Comnenian epoch were not enduring and were followed by the collapse of the Byzantine state.

For the rest, contact with the West had also contributed to the acceleration of the feudal process. Fate had willed that Byzantium should come into close relationship with the Western world soon after the fellowship of the Churches (which at this period included intellectual contacts) had been disrupted. Hatred and contempt were the feelings which the Byzantine and Western lands felt for each other, and closer acquaintance only strengthened this antagonism. Nevertheless, from this time onwards the influence of the West began to make itself felt in Byzantium in many ways, both culturally and politically. The feudalization of the Byzantine state was the result of its own internal development,[1] but it was understandable that it could not remain unaffected by the establishment in the Near East of a number of Latin principalities in which Western feudalism took root in its purest form. The bond between the crusading princes and the Emperor Alexius I, modelled as it was on Western lines, introduced a new principle into the political world of Byzantium. This relationship of vassalage was soon applied to other princes in the Byzantine sphere and thus became a permanent feature of the late Byzantine state.[2]

2. THE FURTHER EXPANSION OF BYZANTINE POWER AND THE FIRST SET-BACKS: JOHN II AND MANUEL I

General bibliography: Chalandon, *Les Comnènes* II; *Domination normande* I and II; Kap-Herr, *Kaiser Manuel*; E. Caspar, *Roger II und die Gründung der normannisch-sizilischen Monarchie*, Innsbruck 1904; B. Kugler, *Studien zur Geschichte des zweiten Kreuzzuges*, Stuttgart 1866; idem, *Analekten zur Gesch. des zweiten Kreuzzuges*, Tübingen 1878; idem, *Neue Analekten zur Gesch. des zweiten Kreuzzuges*, Tübingen 1883; R. Grousset, *Histoire des croisades* I and II, Paris 1934, 1935; Runciman, *Crusades* II; Setton, *Crusades*

---

[1] To explain Byzantine feudalism in terms of borrowing from the West is completely untenable, even though scholars have often advanced this view and still do so. For the opposite view cf. D. Angelov, 'Feodalizmŭt vŭv Vizantija' (Feudalism in Byzantium), *Istor. Pregled* 2 (1946/47), 217 ff.; M. J. Sjuzjumov, 'K voprosu ob osobennostjach genezisa i razvitija feodalizma v Vizantii' (On the question of the genesis and development of feudalism in Byzantium), VV 17 (1960), 3 ff.

[2] Yet the two-way contract between lord and man which was characteristic of Western feudalism would have been inconceivable between Emperor and subject in Byzantium. Cf., however, N. Svoronos, 'Le serment de fidélité à l'empereur byzantin et sa signification constitutionelle', REB 9 (1951), 106 ff.; J. Ferluga, 'La ligesse dans l'Empire byzantin', ZRVI 7 (1961).

I; P. Lamma, *Comneni e Staufer. Ricerche sui rapporti fra Bisanzio e l'Occidente nel secolo XII*, 2 vols., Rome, 1955, 1957; Gy. Moravcsik, 'Hungary and Byzantium in the middle ages', CMH IV, Pt. I (2nd ed., 1966). See also bibliography cited on p. 356.

One result of the strengthening of imperial authority was the firm rooting of the new dynasty of the Comneni. In spite of the dissension which was rampant within the imperial family itself and in spite of the persistent struggles for the succession which poisoned the last days and hours of the Emperor Alexius, his eldest son John succeeded him on the throne. Alexius, who had come to supreme power in alliance with the Ducas, had at first recognized the young Constantine Ducas, the son of Michael VII, as his heir and had arranged that he should marry his elder daughter Anna.[1] When his first son John was born the right of succession was, however, transferred to him (1092).[2] Thus the decisive step towards the founding of the Comnenian dynasty was taken and the death of Constantine Ducas soon afterwards seemed to remove any possible difficulties. But the ambitions of the Princess Anna had been roused and proved an obstacle to the new arrangement. After the premature death of Constantine, she had married Nicephorus Bryennius (1097) and she wanted the imperial crown for him. Alexius, the great statesman and brilliant general, had always been very susceptible to feminine influence. At first he had been under the spell of the widowed Empress Maria, the wife of his two predecessors and mother of the heir Constantine, and he was so passionately attached to this beautiful and clever woman that he was ready to sacrifice his own wife Irene for her; he was only saved from this false step, which might have had grave political consequences, by the energetic protests of the Patriarch Cosmas who insisted on the crowning of Irene. Then the Emperor's mother, Anna Dalassena, exercised great influence over him, and she acted as regent during his absence from Constantinople at the time of the war against Robert Guiscard. Finally, the once disdained Empress Irene had him in her power, and in the question of the succession she sided with her favourite Anna and her husband, the Caesar Nicephorus Bryennius, against her son John. Mother and daughter combined in the attempt to induce the

---

[1] In the acclamations at court ceremonies Anna Comnena and her betrothed were named together with the Emperor and the Empress, *Alexias* I, 204, 8 (ed. Reifferscheid); II, 62, 13 (ed. Leib).
[2] Chalandon, *Alexis I*, 371 ff., has shown the connection between Alexius I's recognition of John Comnenus as heir and his dissension with the Ducas family.

Figure 51: *John II Comnenus.* Detail of a mosaic panel, south gallery of Hagia Sophia, Constantinople, circa 1118. In the complete panel, the Virgin stands holding the Child, with John at left and his wife, the Empress Irene (see Figure 52) at right. Photo: Byzantine Institute, Inc., Washington, D.C.

Figure 52: *The Empress Irene*. Detail of a mosaic panel, south gallery of Hagia Sophia, Constantinople, circa 1118. Irene, a princess of the Hungarian royal family, was the wife of John II Comnenus (see Figure 51) and the mother of Manuel I Comnenus. Photo: Byzantine Institute, Inc., Washington, D.C.

Emperor to transfer the sovereign rights to Bryennius, and even on his deathbed Alexius had to endure the importunate entreaties of the two women. Without committing himself to an outright decision, Alexius contrived to pass the crown to his son who was clever and energetic enough to seize it. But thanks to the intrigues of his mother and sister, the succession of the legal heir to the throne had the appearance of a *coup d'état*. And Anna refused to accept her fate. She plotted against her brother, and only when this extreme measure failed did she throw in her hand and seek consolation in learning. It was in her enforced retirement that she wrote the history of her father, the *Alexiad* which has made her name immortal.[1]

The verdict of both contemporaries and posterity has acclaimed John (1118–43) as the greatest of the Comneni.[2] As a ruler he combined clever prudence with purposeful energy, while at the same time he was a man of upright, steadfast character and high principled far beyond his day. Moderate, yet firm and forceful in pursuing his goal, he carried on his father's policy with iron determination, never losing sight of the bounds of possibility.

In the foreground was the struggle with the Norman principality of Antioch, and there were also pressing problems in the West which demanded constant vigilance. From Antioch the threads led to Sicily, and the Norman question in Sicily, as well as that of the Serbs in the Balkans, brought the Empire up against a number of other Western powers. John tried without success to sever the link which bound the Empire to Venice and strangled Byzantine trade. The republic refused to be elbowed out of the position which it had gained by the treaty of 1082; its fleet attacked the Byzantine islands in the Aegean and the Emperor was forced to ratify all the Venetian privileges in a fresh treaty (1126).[3]

On the other hand, John was able to gain important successes in the Balkans. After the defeat of the Patzinaks in Alexius' day, the Empire had enjoyed thirty years' respite from their marauding inroads. But in 1122 a fresh horde of Patzinaks crossed the Danube and plundered as far south as Thrace and Macedonia.[4] This proved to be the last attack which Byzantium had to suffer from them, for the crushing defeat which John II inflicted on them put an end to

[1] Cf. the brilliant essays by Ch. Diehl on Anna Comnena, *Figures* II, 26–52; on Irene Ducas, ibid. 53–85; and on Anna Dalassena, ibid. I, 317–42.

[2] Nic. Choniates 63 f.

[3] Tafel and Thomas I, 96; Dölger, *Reg.* 1304.

[4] On the chronology cf. E. Kurtz, 'Unedierte Texte aus der Zeit des Kaisers Johannes Komnenos', BZ 16 (1907), 86.

this once and for all. Countless prisoners were settled in the Empire and new Patzinak contingents drafted into the Byzantine army. As a factor in Byzantine foreign policy, the Patzinaks now ceased to exist. The Emperor instituted a special 'Patzinak holiday' to commemorate the victory, and at the end of the twelfth century this was still observed.[1]

After his defeat of the Patzinaks, John turned to the Serbian lands which were a permanent centre of unrest. While Alexius had had to content himself with partial success, John won a decisive victory over the Župan of Rascia, and returned with valuable booty and a number of prisoners whom he settled in Asia Minor. Serbia had to acknowledge the overlordship of Byzantium, but her anxiety to regain her independence led to frequent revolts which caused the Empire considerable trouble, particularly as the Serbs were supported by the Hungarians. The consolidation of Hungary's position as a new power in the Balkans and Adriatic and her close relations with Serbia, were to determine events in the Balkans for many years to come. The Byzantine Emperor was related to the Hungarian royal family and that gave him an excuse to intervene in the frequent disputes over the succession to the Hungarian throne and to support Hungarian claimants. Such a policy made it possible for Byzantium to exercise some influence over Hungarian affairs, but it also led to considerable tension in relations between the two powers. Stephen II (1114–31), whose blinded brother Almus had found refuge in Constantinople, declared war against Byzantium about 1128. The Hungarians destroyed Braničevo and Belgrade,[2] but the superiority of the Byzantine Emperor forced them to retreat and make peace.

About 1130 John was at last able to turn his attention to the East and take up once more the struggle which had engaged him on his accession to the throne, but had been temporarily broken off by the complications in the Balkans. His chief opponent in Asia Minor was not the sultanate of Iconium which was at that time weakened by internal dissension, but the emirate of the Danishmends of Melitene. After its defeat in 1135, the Emperor was faced with a further problem before he could turn to his real objective, the subjugation of Antioch. The way to Syria was barred by the kingdom

---

[1] Nic. Choniates 23.

[2] For the uncertain chronology of these events cf. B. Radojčić, 'O hronologiji ugarsko-vizantijskih borbi i ustanku Srba za vreme Jovana II Komnina' (On the chronology of the conflict between the Hungarians and Byzantium and the revolt of Serbia during the time of John II Comnenus), ZRVI 7 (1961), 177 ff. But see also A. P. Každan, *Voprosy istorii* 1962, no. 2, p. 202.

of Lesser Armenia in Cilicia which had been founded by the Armenian prince Ruben who had established himself as ruler in the Taurus mountains about 1071.[1] Prince Leo of Lesser Armenia, a successor of Ruben, had since 1129 seized the most important fortresses of Cilicia in co-operation with the crusading principalities, and had thus driven a wedge between the Byzantine lands in Asia Minor and the principality of Antioch. John II's expedition to Cilicia against Lesser Armenia in the spring of 1137 turned into a triumphal progress. Tarsus, Adana, Mamistra fell in rapid succession and the prince of Little Armenia fled, only to fall into Byzantine hands a year later when he was taken prisoner to Constantinople together with his two sons. With the overthrow of Cilicia the way to Syria was open, and by August 1137 John II stood before the walls of Antioch. After a short siege, the city surrendered, its ruler Raymond of Poitiers, Bohemund's son-in-law, swore allegiance to the Emperor, and the imperial standard was flown on the city walls. A year later John came back to Syria and made his victorious entry into Antioch.[2]

While he was subduing the principality of Antioch by force of arms, John was employing diplomatic weapons against the Norman kingdom in South Italy. After a period of eclipse this was now coming to the fore again, and Roger II, after uniting Sicily and Apulia under his rule, had been crowned as king in Palermo at Christmas 1130.[3] Both Byzantium and Germany regarded the growth of Norman power in South Italy as a menace and the two empires drew together. John II allied with Lothair, and after his death with Conrad III. Pisa was also drawn into this anti-Norman alliance and in 1136 John confirmed the trading privileges which his father had once granted it.[4] By means of these political alliances John obtained the necessary backing for his active policy in the East, where the problem of Antioch had not yet been finally solved. Relations with the crusading states grew steadily worse, and in 1142 the prince of Antioch, supported by the Latin clergy, repudiated the agreement he had made. The Emperor decided on another expedition against Antioch which he visualized as the prelude to a larger undertaking. He seems to have played with the idea of

[1] Cf. N. Adontz, 'L'aieul des Roubéniens', B 10 (1935), 185 ff.
[2] Chalandon, *Les Commènes* II, 110 ff., 119 ff.
[3] Chalandon, *Domination normande* II, 1 ff.; Caspar, *Roger II. und die Gründung der normannisch-sizilianischen Monarchie* (1904).
[4] Dölger, *Reg.* 1312.

restoring Byzantine rule in Palestine as well, but his death put an end to these plans. He was wounded by a poisoned arrow while out hunting and he died on 8 April 1143.[1] As a result of his vigorous and tenacious policy, the power and influence of the Byzantine state were greatly enhanced, its military defences strengthened and its authority revived and extended once more in the East and in the Balkans.

The two elder sons of John II, Alexius and Andronicus, had both died in 1142. According to the Emperor's last wish, his fourth and youngest son Manuel succeeded to the throne. Manuel I (1143-80) was a brilliant, versatile and gifted ruler. He was a born commander and a brave soldier who shrank from no personal danger, but above all he was a skilled diplomat, and a statesman with bold and far-reaching ideas. He was a true Byzantine, convinced of the validity of the conception of universal imperial sovereignty and possessed of the characteristic Byzantine passion for theological discussion. At the same time his whole way of life bore the stamp of Western chivalry and in this respect he represented a new type among Byzantine rulers. He shows clearly how deeply contact with the crusaders had influenced the Byzantine world. He liked Western customs and introduced them at his court. His two marriages with Western princesses also contributed to the fact that his residence took on a new appearance. A spirit of gaiety and *joie de vivre* reigned supreme in the Comnenian palace of the Blachernae, and the majestic Eastern splendour which used to surround the Byzantine Emperors in the Great Palace on the Golden Horn gave way to the more informal elegant chivalry of the Western kind. Knightly tournaments were held in which the Emperor himself took part—a new and unusual spectacle for the Byzantines. Foreigners from the West became increasingly predominant and were given high office in the state, to the lasting annoyance of the Greeks.[2]

Manuel's personal inclinations undoubtedly influenced his policy, and his fiery temperament urged him to take risks which his father's clever prudence would have avoided. But it is a mistake to see a fundamental contrast between Manuel's aims with their Western emphasis and the eastward orientation of his father's policy. At this time it was more than ever impossible to separate the problems of

[1] According to R. Browning, 'The Death of John II Comnenus', B 31 (1961), 229 ff., his death was probably no accident but assassination.

[2] Chalandon, *Les Comnènes* II, 200 ff., 226 ff.; Ch. Diehl, *La société byzantine à l'époque des Comnènes* (1919), 13 ff., 23 ff.

East and West, as developments in John's day had already clearly shown. Manuel continued the policy of his father, as the latter had continued that of Alexius I. The Byzantine conflict with the Normans was in the foreground in Manuel's reign, as it had been under John, and it was due to changes in the political situation, and recent shifts in the balance of power, that John had approached the problem from the side of Antioch, whereas Manuel now attacked it from the Italian angle. Manuel's Western emphasis was not mere caprice, but fate itself had determined that his policy should be intimately concerned with the West. At this time the period began when the policies of European rulers were closely linked, and it was in the Mediterranean that the various threads met. As a Mediterranean power, it was impossible for Byzantium to stand aloof. She was compelled to take an active part because her position as a great power was based on the Mediterranean, and her claims were bound up with her conception of imperial authority, precisely because her whole tradition pointed in this direction. Manuel's desire to establish his universal authority was the age-long desire of Byzantium, which John had also shared. Manuel's whole programme had already been sketched out by the balanced and careful John. The political aims of the two rulers were identical, but Manuel's fatal mistake lay in his impatience to turn the will into deed without reckoning sufficiently with the inadequacy of his resources.

Manuel tried to strengthen the alliance with Germany which had been a cornerstone of John's policy, and as his father had arranged he married Conrad III's sister-in-law, Bertha of Sulzbach. The main reason for the alliance had been the co-operation of the two rulers against the Norman king, but this was frustrated by the outbreak of the second crusade which was joined not only by the French, but also by the German king, spurred on by the fiery preaching of Bernard of Clairvaux. This was certainly as awkward for the western-minded Manuel as the first crusade had been for his grandfather. A successful crusade would assist the Latin principalities in the East, and particularly the principality of Antioch, the old enemy of Byzantium. Moreover Conrad's move towards the Holy Land meant that Manuel was isolated in the West and his freedom of action against the Norman king was still more hampered by his disputes with the crusaders.

The passage of the crusaders through the Empire was accompanied by the usual excesses which greatly embittered the relations between the Germans and the Byzantines. There appears to have been no personal encounter between Manuel and his brother-in-law.[1] Still more strained was the relationship between Byzantium and the French king Louis VII, the friend of Roger II; in his circle the possibility of the capture of Constantinople by the crusaders was already being discussed. Like Alexius before him, Manuel made every effort to transport the crusaders to Asia Minor at the earliest opportunity, and like Alexius he also demanded an oath of allegiance from the crusaders and the surrender of any lands they conquered.[2] It was the approach of the French, rather than any pressing demands from Manuel, that decided Conrad III to cross over to Asia Minor. There, however, his army hurried towards its doom and in its first engagement with the forces of the Sultan of Iconium it was cut to pieces. After lengthy unprofitable negotiations, Louis VII also moved into Asia Minor where he joined up with the remnants of the German troops. Abandoning the plan of a campaign against Iconium, the crusaders advanced in the direction of Attaleia. The passage through difficult country was accompanied by acts of violence towards the native population, quarrels between the French and Germans, and clashes of the Latins with the Greeks, all of which contributed to the complete exhaustion of the crusading forces. Conrad III was taken ill *en route* and he left the crusade at Ephesus. At Attaleia, Louis VII and his barons took ship for Syria and left their wretched men to their fate.[3]

Except for the Turks, the only one to gain anything from this inglorious crusade was the Norman king Roger II. While Manuel was held up in the East by his transactions with the crusaders, Roger launched a direct attack on the Byzantine Empire in the autumn of 1147 and he seized Corfu and took Corinth and Thebes, then the

[1] Cinnamus, 77, states that there had actually been an armed clash between Germans and Byzantines before Constantinople, thus showing how ticklish the situation had become. In opposition to Kugler, *Studien zur Gesch. d. zweiten Kreuzzuges* (1866), 36 ff., and *Analekten zur Gesch. d. zweiten Kreuzzuges* (1878), 60 ff., Giesebrecht, *Gesch. d. deutschen Kaiserzeit* IV (1877), 479 ff., and Kap-Herr, *Kaiser Manuel* 16 ff. deny any importance to Cinnamus' information and in particular to his account of the exchange of letters between Manuel and Conrad III. This scepticism is rightly repudiated by Chalandon, *Les Comnènes* II, 279. Cf. also Dölger, *Reg.* 1360.

[2] Manuel's letters to Pope Eugenius III of August 1146 and March 1147 were characteristic on this. Cf. W. Ohnsorge, 'Ein Beitrag zur Geschichte Manuels I. von Byzanz', *Brackmann-Festschrift* (1931), 371 ff., and V. Grumel, 'Au seuil de la deuxième croisade: deux lettres de Manuel Comnène au pape', EB 3 (1945), 142 ff. In the second letter Manuel was, however, silent on the question of exacting an oath of allegiance from the kings of France and Germany.

[3] The most recent detailed accounts of the second crusade are given by Runciman, *Crusades* II, 264 ff. and in Setton, *Crusades* I, 463 ff. Cf. also P. Lamma, *Comneni e Staufer* I (1955), 56 ff.

wealthiest cities of Greece and important centres of the Byzantine silk industry. He plundered both cities and carried off the expert Byzantine silk weavers to Palermo where they were employed in the recently established Norman silk industry.[1] It is true that the failure of the crusade facilitated a fresh understanding between Byzantium and Germany. When he returned from Asia, Conrad was received in Constantinople with every honour and he pledged himself to lead an expedition against Roger II. Venice also joined the anti-Norman coalition and helped the Byzantine Emperor to retake Corfu (1149). But in spite of this the after-effects of the unfortunate crusade persisted to the advantage of the Norman king and the lasting detriment of the Byzantine Emperor and his German ally.

The plan for a joint Byzantine and German campaign in Italy was wrecked by the successful counter-moves of Roger II's diplomacy. He concluded an alliance with Duke Welf and supported him in his resistance to the Hohenstaufen, so that Conrad had to hurry back to Germany and was kept busy there for some time dealing with internal disputes. Against the Byzantine Emperor, Roger stirred up the Hungarians and Serbs. Manuel had to suppress a revolt by the Župan of Rascia in 1149, and this was followed by a war with Hungary which opened a long series of hostilities between Byzantium and the Magyars. Moreover, the French king Louis VII, who was antagonistic to the Byzantine Emperor and thus the natural ally of Roger II, had fresh crusading plans which had the approval of Bernard of Clairvaux, as well as of Pope Eugenius III who was trying to win the German king from his alliance with schismatic Byzantium. Thus a strong anti-Byzantine coalition came into being under the leadership of Roger II. The crusade as planned would virtually have meant a Franco-Norman attack on the Byzantine Empire, but it was, however, wrecked by the opposition of the French knights, while Conrad III remained true to his ally. The European states were divided into two great camps: Byzantium, Germany and Venice stood on one side, and opposed to them were the Normans, the Guelfs, France, Hungary and Serbia, with the Papacy in the background. Thus began the far-reaching system of alliances among the European states which in the course of time was to undergo frequent regrouping and to draw new powers into its circle. The hostility between Byzantium and Hungary was even felt in distant Russia: the two powers took a hand in the disputes of

---

[1] Chalandon, *Les Comnènes* II, 317 ff., and *Domination normande* II, 136 f.

the Russian princes, and while Hungary allied with Izjaslav of Kiev, Byzantium supported the princes Jurij Dolgorukij of Suzdal and Vladimirko of Galicia.[1] In the opposite direction, Manuel stretched out feelers to England and carried on a lively correspondence with Henry II during the seventies of the century.[2]

After subduing Duke Welf, Conrad III began to prepare for his Italian campaign, but at the very moment when the Byzantino-German war against the Normans was finally about to break out, he died (1152). In spite of repeated attempts, Manuel never came to any really satisfactory arrangement with Conrad's successor, Frederick I Barbarossa. As in the case of Manuel, the conception of imperial sovereignty was the cornerstone of Frederick's political aspirations. At this time Western knowledge of the Roman law of Justinian was growing and it strengthened the view that universality was inherent in imperial sovereignty. Frederick contested the Byzantine claims to Italy and was suspicious of the universal claims of Manuel whom he regarded as nothing more than a Greek king. And so in place of the alliance between Germany and Byzantium, there appeared the rivalry of the two Empires, each claiming for itself alone the imperial sovereignty and the Roman heritage. Instead of co-operating against the Normans, each partner was doing his best to outwit the other in Italy.

Manuel had restored the situation in the Balkans, hostilities with Hungary had ceased and the Byzantine ally, Jurij Dolgorukij, was installed on the throne of Kiev. In addition, the enemy of Byzantium, Roger II, had died (1154). The time had come to reopen the offensive in Italy, either with or without the German Emperor, or, if need be, against him. In 1155 Manuel sent a fleet to Ancona and from here the great advance began. With the assistance of the renegade Norman vassals the emissaries of the Byzantine Emperor were able to subdue the most important cities of Apulia with a small force in a very short time, and the whole district from Ancona to Tarento recognized his sovereignty.[3]

This success surpassed the most optimistic expectations, and turned Manuel's policy into new channels. It looked as though the restoration of the *romanum imperium*, the last and highest goal of

---

[1] V. Vasiljevskij, 'Sojuz dvuch imperij' (The alliance of the two Empires), *Trudy* IV, 45 ff. Cf. also G. Vernadskij, 'Relations byzantino-russes au XIIe siècle', B 4 (1927–8), 269 ff.

[2] Cf. A. Vasiliev, 'Manuel Comnenus and Henry Plantagenet', BZ 29 (1929–30), 233 ff.

[3] Cf. Chalandon, *Les Comnènes* II, 349 ff., and 'The Later Comneni', CMH IV, 369.

Byzantine policy, was within the bounds of possibility. In 1141 John II had written to Pope Innocent II saying that there were two swords, the secular which he himself would wield, and the spiritual which he would leave to the Pope, and together they would restore the unity of the Christian Church and establish the world supremacy of the one Roman Empire.[1] This was the programme which was now to be carried out. Its aim was the realization of the old unquenchable longing of Byzantium and the re-establishment, with papal help and at the price of the union of the Churches, of the Empire of Justinian and of Constantine.[2]

And yet, if Justinian's work of reviving the Empire had not lasted long, Manuel's efforts were frustrated when the first step had scarcely been taken. The gulf between the Emperor's goal and the means at his disposal was now far greater than in the sixth century, and the hostility of the surrounding world was also far stronger. There was no place for a world Empire in the complicated system of European states which had grown up. All the powers which had interests in Italy united against Manuel. Frederick I was not the only one who had been turned into an open enemy by the attack on Ancona and the overwhelming success of the Byzantine offensive. Venice, the old ally of Byzantium against the Normans and Hungarians, felt herself endangered by the Byzantine occupation in Italy and severed relations with the Emperor. The Norman king, William I, swiftly prepared a counter-attack; in 1156 he inflicted a heavy defeat upon the Byzantines at Brindisi and the whole of the conquered territory soon fell into his hands. This demonstrated the weakness of the Byzantine position in Italy, based as it was on money and diplomacy rather than on military strength. Through the mediation of the Pope, Manuel signed a treaty with William I in 1158, for he recognized that the real enemy of his imperial plans was Frederick Barbarossa rather than the Normans. The conception of

---

[1] Sp. Lampros, ʽΑὐτοκρατόρων τοῦ Βυζαντίου χρυσόβουλλα καὶ χρυσᾶ γράμματα ἀναφερόμενα εἰς τὴν ἕνωσιν τῶν ἐκκλησιῶνʼ, Νέος Ἑλληνομνήμων 11 (1914), 109–11 = Theiner-Miklosich, *Monumenta spectant a ad unionem ecclesiarum graecae et romanae* (1872), 4–6; Dölger, *Reg.* 1303. On the determination of the date (1141, not 1126) cf. J. Haller, *Das Papsttum* II, 2 (1939), 555. What the Emperor John is expounding here is not indeed mere 'généralités sur les bienfaits de la réunion', as Chalandon says (*Les Comnènes* II, 163), but rather an extensive political programme for establishing universal Roman sovereignty under the Byzantine sceptre.

[2] When J. Haller, loc. cit., thinks that Manuel 'originally attempted no more than the recovery of Apulia and Calabria and a base in Ancona against the Venetians who were troubling him', he fails to recognize the real goal of Manuel's policy and the traditional imperial struggle for universal rule which he personified. But admittedly he qualifies his statement by his use of the word 'originally'.

world supremacy still held him under its spell and continued to determine his policy, though in actual fact the conclusion of peace with the Normans, and the evacuation of Byzantine troops from Italy, denoted the end of this Byzantine dream.

On the other hand, as regards the weakened Latin states in the East, Manuel continued his father's policy and brought it to a successful conclusion. The Armenian Prince Thoros, who had established himself in Cilicia and had allied with Renauld of Antioch, was overthrown in 1158, and the Emperor counted him 'among the vassals of the Romans'.[1] The final overthrow of the principality of Antioch was of even greater importance. Its ruler had to recognize the sovereign rights of the Byzantine Emperor and pledged himself to provide military aid. In addition, the Emperor reserved to himself the right to appoint the Patriarch of Antioch. As a sign of submission, Renauld appeared in the Byzantine Emperor's camp with head uncovered, unshod, his arms bared to the elbows, a rope round his neck and bearing his sword in his left hand.[2] King Baldwin III of Jerusalem also presented himself before the Emperor and placed himself under his protection; in the words of a Byzantine contemporary, 'he hastened from Jerusalem to come to us, overpowered by the fame and great exploits of the Emperor, and he acknowledged his sovereignty'.[3] The supreme position of Byzantium in the Latin East was impressively displayed in the ceremonial entrance which Manuel made into Antioch in 1159. The Emperor rode on a charger decorated with all the imperial insignia, the king of Jerusalem followed on horseback at a considerable distance and without any insignia, while the prince of Antioch walked beside the Emperor's horse and 'was busied with the stirrup-leather of the imperial saddle'.[4] It was an extraordinary spectacle and a vivid illustration of the hierarchical ordering of the powers.[5] The catastrophe which awaited Manuel at the hand of the Turks at the end of his reign should not be allowed to obscure the great success of his policy in the Latin orient. The establishment of the crusading states had created difficult problems for Byzantium, problems with which Alexius I

---

[1] Cinnamus 186, 16.   [2] Cinnamus 182, 13.

[3] Eustathius of Thessalonica, ed. Regel, *Fontes rerum byzantinarum* I (1892), 39. Even in the time of Baldwin's successor there was an inscription dating from 1169 in the Church of the Nativity at Bethlehem giving first 'the great Emperor Manuel Comnenus the Porphyrogenitus', and then after him 'the great king of Jerusalem Amalric'. Cf. Vincent and Abel, *Bethléem: Le sanctuaire de la Nativité* (1914), 157 ff.; G. de Jerphanion, OCP 1 (1935), 239 ff.; Chalandon, *Les Comnènes* II, 449; Vasiliev, *History* 427.

[4] Cinnamus 187 f.

[5] Cf. G. Ostrogorsky, 'Die byzantinische Staatenhierarchie', *Sem. Kond.* 8 (1936), 56.

and John II had wrestled for many years, and now a solution had been found in the establishment of Byzantine hegemony. The Byzantine Emperor controlled the whole Christian East and the Latin states, harried by the Turks, looked up to him as their protector.

In Hungary Manuel followed the lines laid down by his father and used the same methods and, like John, he interfered in the disputes over the succession to the Hungarian throne. But his political activity was on a far larger scale, and the final goal which he had in mind was the complete subjugation of the country and its incorporation into the Byzantine Empire.[1] The death of Geisa II in 1161 provided an opportunity to interfere once more in the affairs of Hungary. He supported Geisa's brothers Stephen IV and Ladislaus with money and weapons against Stephen III, Geisa's son and successor. This led to a long struggle. Manuel succeeded in gaining considerable support in Hungary, especially among the clergy, and the opposition turned to the German Emperor and won the support of the Bohemian king Vladislav. Meanwhile, as he had fought at Conrad's side at the time of the second crusade, the Bohemian king was counted as a vassal of the Byzantine Emperor;[2] he was induced to suspend hostilities and he even acted as mediator between Stephen III and the Emperor Manuel. In 1164 a treaty with Hungary was drawn up which promised the Byzantine Emperor great advantages. Bela, the brother of Stephen III, who was recognized as heir to the Hungarian throne and given the Croatian and Dalmatian territory, was sent to Constantinople.[3] But as it turned out, the advantages of the treaty could only be realized by fresh conflict. Considerable military and diplomatic preparations preceded the actual outbreak of war. A special imperial ambassador was sent to Russia and secured for Byzantium the support of the princes of Kiev and Galicia. All this outlay was fully repaid with success: Dalmatia, Croatia and Bosnia, as well as the district of Sirmium, came under the sceptre of the Byzantine Emperor (1167).[4]

The importance of the Hungarian problem in Manuel's eyes is shown by his decision to marry prince Bela, who had been given

---

[1] Cf. Gy. Moravcsik, 'Pour une alliance byzantino-hongroise', B 8 (1933), 555 ff.; F. Dölger, 'Ungarn in der byzantinischen Reichspolitik', *Archivum Europae Centro-orient.* 8 (1942), pt. 3–4, 5 ff.

[2] As Cinnamus 223 says, Vladislav was Manuel's λίζιος (cf. also Vincent of Prague, M.G.H. SS. XVII, 681). In the view of the Byzantine historian this feudal expression was the same as a voluntary servant, δοῦλος ἐθελόδουλος.

[3] Dölger, *Reg.* 1455. Cf. Šišić, *Povijest* II, 80 ff.

[4] Cf. Šišić, *Povijest* II, 91.

the name of Alexius in Constantinople, to his daughter and to make him his heir, thus securing the union of Hungary with the Empire.[1] As heir-presumptive to the throne Bela-Alexius received the title of Despot which had previously been applied only to the Emperor himself, but from now on was used as a special title which came immediately after the Emperor in the hierarchy of dignities and took precedence of the Sebastocrator and Caesar.[2] However, the birth of a son compelled the Emperor to abandon this plan which had roused great opposition in Constantinople, but he succeeded in placing his favourite Bela-Alexius on the Hungarian throne after the death of Stephen II, and in this way secured his influence in Hungary.

At the same time as the wars with Hungary, a struggle with the Serbs was in process. In trying to gain their independence from Byzantine control, the Serbs found support in Hungary. In Rascia one revolt succeeded another, and although Manuel was able to crush these outbreaks, he could not put an end to them, however often he changed the disloyal Župans. In 1166 or 1167 Stephen Nemanja was made Grand Župan of Rascia,[3] but he too rebelled against the Byzantine Emperor and gained a notable victory over the Byzantines. But Manuel's success in Hungary influenced the situation here, because it deprived the Serbs of Hungarian support. The alliance with Venice did not prove very effective, and when in 1172 the Emperor led a large army into Serbia, Nemanja gave up the pointless struggle. He had to show his submission in the same theatrical way as Renauld of Antioch, and he took part in the Emperor's triumphal entry into Constantinople as a conquered rebel.[4] Court orators celebrated the submission of the unruly Slavs in eloquent speeches[5] and the wall-paintings in the imperial palace glorified the victory of the Byzantine Emperor over the refractory Serbian Grand Župan.[6] And so the forefather of the famous Nemanjid dynasty and the future founder of the independent

---

[1] Cf. Gy. Moravcsik, 'Pour une alliance byzantino-hongroise', B 8 (1933), 555 ff.; F. Dölger, 'Ungarn in der byzantinischen Reichspolitik', *Archivum Europae centro-orientalis* 8 (1942), pt. 3–4, 5 ff.

[2] Cf. G. Ostrogorsky, 'Urum-Despotes. Die Anfänge der Despoteswürde in Byzanz', BZ 44 (1951) (*Dölger-Festschrift*), 448 ff. R. Guilland, 'Études sur l'histoire administrative de l'Empire byzantine. Le despote', REB 17 (1959), 52 ff.; Ferjančić, *Despoti*, 27 ff.

[3] On the chronology cf. V. Ćorović, 'Pitanje o hronologiji u delima sv. Save' (Problems of chronology in the writings of St. Sava), Godišnjica N. Čupića 49 (1940), 1 ff., and 43 ff., and esp. R. Novaković, *Istor. glasnik* 3/4 (1958), 165ff.

[4] Cinnamus 287.

[5] Eustathius of Thessalonica, ed. Regel, *Fontes rerum byz.* I, 43 ff.; Const. Manasses, ed. Kurtz, VV 12 (1906), 89, 44 ff.

[6] Cf. Grabar, *Empereur* 40 ff., 84, with information on the sources.

Serbian state, isolated as he was, had for a time to refrain from further action against the Byzantine Empire, and remained Emperor Manuel's true vassal until the end of his life.

Venetian co-operation in Italy had been lost by the Byzantine attack on Ancona, and the common interests of Venice and Byzantium in allying against Hungary were brought to an end by the annexation of the Dalmatian coast. On the other hand, the privileged position of the Venetian merchants in the Empire was a heavy burden on the Byzantine population. Manuel tried to strengthen his connections with other Italian maritime cities and he concluded alliances with Genoa in 1169 and with Pisa in 1170.[1] Relations between Constantinople and Venice grew more and more strained, and in 1171 a sharp conflict broke out. On 12 March every Venetian throughout the Empire was arrested and his goods, ships and wares were confiscated—and this on one and the same day, thanks to careful organization and the splendid running of the Byzantine administrative machine. Venice was not slow to retaliate. A strong fleet attacked the Byzantine coast and sacked the islands of Chios and Lesbos. Negotiations dragged on for some time but without any appreciable result. For fully ten years relations between Byzantium and Venice were broken off.[2]

In spite of brilliant successes in the Latin East and in Hungary, the isolation of the Byzantine Empire was increasingly marked, and towards the end of the seventies Manuel's position was exceedingly insecure. Any hope of co-operation with Rome had vanished: on either side there was no real basis for ecclesiastical union, and everywhere—in Venice, Dalmatia, Hungary—papal influence was

[1] Dölger, *Reg.* 1488, 1497, 1498 (Genoa), 1499 (Pisa).

[2] Nic. Choniates 225 certainly maintains that the conclusion of an alliance between Venice and the Norman king William II compelled Manuel to give in and induced him to restore their privileges to the Venetians and to compensate them for any loss. But the Chronicle of Andreas Dandolo (Muratori XII, 309) and the anonymous history of the doges from the beginning of the thirteenth century (MGH. SS. XIV, 92) say that relations between Venice and Byzantium were not restored until Andronicus I. Most scholars, including Chalandon, *Les Commènes* II, 592, Heyd, *Commerce du Levant* I, 220, Kretschmayr, *Venedig* I, 261, and others, have given preference to Nic. Choniates (as I myself did). The case for believing the Venetian sources to be more reliable was put by F. Cognasso, *Partiti politici e lotte dinastiche in Bizanzio alla morte di Manuele Comneno*, Turin 1912, 294 ff. Without knowing Cognasso's work, N. P. Sokolov has now put this point of view most convincingly in 'K voprosu o vzaimootnošenijach Vizantii i Venecii v poslednie gody pravlenija Komninov' (On the question of the relations between Byzantium and Venice in the last years of the Comneni), VV 5 (1952), 139 ff., on the basis of the *Documenti del commercio veneziano*, ed. della Rocca e Lombardo, I–II, Turin 1940.

directed against the Byzantine Emperor.[1] Suspicion of the schismatic Greeks persisted in the West, and there was intense dislike of the Latins in Byzantium. Nicetas Choniates expressed the normal Byzantine attitude when he wrote: 'The accursed Latins . . . lust after our possessions and would like to destroy our race . . . between them and us there is a wide gulf of hatred, our outlooks are completely different, and our paths go in opposite directions'.[2] Manuel was undaunted in his attempt to find new ways and means, and he supported the league of the Lombard cities in their struggle against Frederick Barbarossa with substantial subsidies. He was deprived even of this weapon by the treaty of Venice 1177, which concluded the war of the Lombard league and led to a reconciliation between the Pope and Frederick I. He had most cleverly utilized the Western schism, but when this was brought to an end the last hope of an understanding between the Pope and Byzantium vanished.[3]

Manuel tended to regard Barbarossa's enemies as his friends and it was not surprising that Frederick I for his part attempted to establish good relations with the opponents of the Byzantine Emperor. He had been in touch with the Sultan Kilij Arslan of Iconium since 1173. The authoritative position which Manuel had succeeded in establishing for himself in the Latin East had for some time strengthened Byzantium against possible attacks from the Sultanate of Iconium, and Manuel had safeguarded this measure of superiority still further by cleverly exploiting the disputes between the various Seljuq rulers as well as by certain military successes in Asia Minor. In 1162 Kilij Arslan had spent three months in Constantinople and had signed a treaty in which he agreed to give military aid and to hand over several cities to Byzantium.[4] He did not, however, keep his promise, and, while Manuel was occupied in Hungary and in the West, he was able to strengthen his own position in Asia Minor. The support of the German Emperor encouraged him to resist, and the break between Byzantium and Iconium came in 1175. The next year the Byzantine Emperor moved against Iconium with a strong force. He pushed on into the Phrygian mountain passes and here he was overwhelmingly defeated at Myriocephalon on 17 September 1176: the Byzantine army was

[1] This has been well dealt with by Kap-Herr, *Kaiser Manuel* 90 ff., though in other respects his account must be treated with caution.

[2] Nic. Choniates 391 f.

[3] Cf. W. Ohnsorge, 'Ein Beitrag zur Geschichte Manuels I. von Byzanz', *Brackmann-Festschrift* (1931), 371 ff.

[4] Dölger, *Reg.* 1446.

surrounded by the Turks and was almost annihilated.[1] Manuel himself compared this catastrophe with that which had befallen Romanus IV Diogenes at Mantzikert a century earlier.[2] This reversal was doubly severe in that it coincided with the setbacks which the imperial policy was experiencing in the West. The prestige of the Byzantine Empire was severely shaken, how severely is shown by a letter which Manuel received at the time from Frederick I.[3] In his capacity as Roman Emperor, Frederick demanded that the Greek king should show him the obedience which he owed him. It was an open secret that Manuel's policy had finally suffered shipwreck. The countless projects into which he had been drawn, and had gaily undertaken in the heat of the moment, had in the end completely overwhelmed him. It was useless for him to triumph over the Latin states in the East, to achieve brilliant successes in Hungary, and for a time even to occupy extensive territory in Italy; to maintain his position in all these fields and to pursue an active and indeed an aggressive policy in European and Near Eastern spheres of influence was clearly impossible. Heavy counterblows came from all sides. The Byzantine position in the East was undermined, once and for all Byzantium was driven out of Italy, and it stood exhausted and completely isolated before a hostile coalition of Western powers.

The superhuman effort had even worse effects on the internal condition of the Empire than on its prestige abroad. Campaigns on a grand scale and perpetual warfare demanded sacrifices beyond the strength and means of the Byzantine Empire of that day, and it was drained dry of its economic and military resources. John II had indeed attempted to set up again on a new basis the old military holdings which had once been the mainstay of the Empire. After defeating the Patzinaks, he had settled the prisoners in the Empire, making them liable for military service, and after his victory over Serbia the captive Serbs were established in the region of Nicomedia,

[1] Cf. A. Vasiliev, 'Das genaue Datum der Schlacht von Myriokephalon', BZ 27 (1927), 288 ff.
[2] Nic. Choniates 248; cf. also Manuel's letter to the English king Henry II, Roger of Hovedene (ed. W. Stubbs), II, 102-4 (English trans. in A. Vasiliev, 'Manuel Comnenus and Henry Plantagenet', BZ 29 (1929-30), 237-40). P. Wirth, 'Kaiser Manuel Komnenos und die Ostgrenze, Rückeroberung und Wiederaufbau der Festung Dorylaion', BZ 55 (1962), 22 ff., assumes that after the battle of Myriocephalon, Manuel I had to undertake to evacuate Dorylaeum. If so, then towards the end of the reign of Manuel the eastern frontier of the Byzantine Empire must have been considerably further west than was previously supposed, and than is shown in our map of the Empire under the Comneni
[3] Printed in Kap-Herr, *Kaiser Manuel* 156 f.

some as *stratiotai*, others as taxpayers.[1] Manuel continued this policy and he too settled Serbian soldiers on imperial territory at Sardica and elsewhere.[2] According to the treaty which he made with the Hungarian king Geisa II, Manuel was to retain 10,000 Hungarian prisoners, no doubt also with a view to using these as Byzantine *stratiotai*.[3] The creation of new military holdings and the influx of new, usually foreign, soldier-farmers indicated a return to the effective military organization of the middle Byzantine period. But even this was not adequate to meet the increased military needs of the time and grants of *pronoia* property in return for the recipient's undertaking to do military service were greatly extended under Manuel. Westerners were also more frequently endowed in this way, and the native peasantry on the estate would be assigned to them as *paroikoi*.[4]

The rule of the military aristocracy promoted and favoured the great estates, particularly those of the laity. A chrysobull of March 1158 issued by Manuel forbad monasteries in Constantinople and the environs from any further extension of their lands.[5] At the same time, it was laid down that grants of property could only be alienated to those of senatorial rank or members of the *stratiotes* class, i.e. to pronoiars, a significant ruling which was repeated in a later decree.[6] The Emperor Manuel was in no way hostile to monasticism as such; not only did he most carefully guarantee existing monastic possessions, but granted them far-reaching privileges and immunities.[7] But in the competition between spiritual and secular landownership, he supported the latter, and openly helped the lay magnates and more

[1] On the Patzinaks cf. Cinnamus 8; on the Serbs, Nic. Choniates 23, καὶ κατὰ τὴν Νικομήδους ἐπαρχίαν ἀποτάξας αὐτῷ κατοίκησιν καὶ γῆν Διαρκεστάτην ἀποΔιασάμενος, τὸ μὲν τοῦ Δορυκτήτου λεὼ τοῖς στρατεύμασιν ἐγκατέμιξε, τὸ Δὲ παρῆκεν εἰς Δασμοφόρησιν.

[2] Cinnamus 103.   [3] Cinnamus 120.

[4] Nic. Choniates 273; on this cf. Ostrogorsky, *La féodalité* 28 ff.

[5] Zepos, *Jus* I, 381 ff.; Dölger, *Reg.* 1418 and 1419. Nic. Choniates 270 f. and Cinnamus 276 also mention these measures; cf. Charanis, 'Monastic Properties' 82 ff.

[6] Dölger, *Reg.* 1333 and 1398. The two decrees are only mentioned in Balsamon (Rhalles-Potles II, 653). On the basis of the indictions given Dölger puts the first decree in either September 1143 or 1158 or 1173, and its re-issue in the February of either 1156 or 1170. Obviously 1173 can be eliminated for the first decree, and in all probability this was issued in September 1158, soon after the order of March 1158 forbidding any further increase in monastic property, and the second decree would then fall in February 1170.

[7] Cf. the characteristic formula of immunity in the chrysobull of May 1158 issued to monasteries in Constantinople and its environs, 'Thus my imperial majesty desires that all real estate of the aforementioned monasteries is to be regarded as outside the control and authority of the practors, and as the practors have no right to exact dues or anything else in themes not subordinated to them, similarly the practors of the theme in which the real estate lies shall not be regarded as practors in so far as this real estate is concerned' (Zepos, *Jus* I, 384).

particularly the pronoiars whose possessions had been granted in return for service.

As well as the pronoiars, there were a substantial number of mercenaries in the Byzantine army. The burden of supporting these fell even more heavily than ever upon the population, who were oppressed on all sides by obligations of provisioning and compulsory labour services. The resources of the state were inadequate and it was left to the troops to help themselves to what they wanted from the people. 'The inhabitants of the provinces suffered the most grievous depredations through the unquenchable greed of the troops who took not only their money but even the very shirt off their backs.'[1]

The military were the ruling class in the state and they lived off the rest of the population. The whole situation differed radically from that of the pre-Comnenian period. In those days, when the civil aristocracy under the Ducas was in power, everyone avoided military service: 'Soldiers laid aside their arms and became lawyers and jurists'.[2] Now everyone thronged to enlist: 'all wished to be soldiers; some laid aside their needles which had provided them with the bare necessities of life at the cost of much toil, others left the stables, others shook off brick dust or the soot of the smithy, and they all hastened to the recruiting officers, presented them with a Persian horse, or some gold pieces, and without further ado were enrolled in the armed forces'.[3] Military service had become the only lucrative profession. The army swallowed up the resources of the Empire. The people were crushed by intolerable burdens. The state increased its demands for taxation, and the last straw was provided by the usual extortions of the tax-collectors, who now included a number of foreigners to the great resentment of the taxpayers.[4] On the cities a great many sold their freedom in order to find protection in the service of some powerful lord, a practice by no means unusual in Byzantium. Manuel tried to stem this development by a law by which any freeborn man who had sold himself into slavery was allowed to get back his freedom, and the Emperor even seems to have provided the ransom from the state treasury, at least in the capital.[5] But the whole trend of the times,

---

[1] Nic. Choniates 272 f.   [2] Scylitzes-Cedren. II, 652.
[3] Nic. Choniates 273.   [4] Nic. Choniates 265 f.
[5] Cinnamus 275; Dölger, *Reg.* 1476; Chalandon, *Les Comnènes* II, 611 f.; A. Hadjinico-laou-Marava, *Recherches sur la vie des esclaves dans le Monde Byzantin*, Athens 1950, 54 ff., 94 ff.

with the growth of the great estates, and the overburdening and impoverishment of the lower classes, made it inevitable that ever wider strata of the population were bartering their freedom to become, if not slaves, then at least serfs. In the end, the triumphant advance of feudal processes weakened the authority of the state and undermined the Byzantine polity's power of resistance. By manning all its resources Byzantium was still capable on occasion of winning great victories abroad, but it was unable to sustain reversal and defeat. The apparent brilliance of Manuel's day was rapidly followed by the internal collapse of the Byzantine state.

3. THE CHANGE OF POLICY UNDER ANDRONICUS COMNENUS

General bibliography: F. Uspenskij, 'Imperatory Aleksej II i Andronik Komneny', ZMNP 212 (1880), 95–130 and 214 (1881), 52–85; idem, 'Poslednie Komneny: Načalo reakcii (The last Comneni: the beginning of the reaction)', VV 25 (1927–8), 1–23; N. Radojčić, *Dva posljednja Komnena na carigradskom prijestolu* (The two last Comneni on the throne of Constantinople), Zagreb 1907; F. Cognasso, *Partiti politici e lotte dinastiche in Bizanzio alla morte di Manuele Comneno*, Turin 1912; Diehl, *Figures II*, 68 ff.; M. J. Sjuzjumov, 'Vnutrennjaja politika Andronika Komnina i razgrom prigorodov Konstantinopolja v 1187 godu' (The internal policy of Andronicus Comnenus and the destruction of the suburbs of Constantinople in the year 1187), VV 12 (1957), 58–74.; O. Jurewicz, *Andronik I Komnenos*, Warsaw 1962; see also general bibliography cited on pp. 356 and 375 f.

The weaknesses in the Byzantine state became very evident after the death of Manuel, when his twelve-year-old son Alexius II came to the throne and his widow the Empress Mary of Antioch took over the regency. The favour of the Empress fell on the *protosebastus* Alexius Comnenus, a nephew of the late Emperor, and he gained virtual control over the government. It was an unfortunate choice and the preference shown to this vain and insignificant man roused very great bitterness among others of the Comnenian family. The Western Mary and her favourite were equally detested by the people. As was only to be expected, under such a régime the Latins received still more partial treatment, while the ordinary Byzantine citizen blamed this policy for the rapid deterioration of the situation both at home and abroad. Resentment against the Latins grew: the Italian merchants who made their fortunes in Byzantium and the Western

Figure 53: *Relief of a Byzantine Emperor*. Marble roundel, carved in low relief, late 12th century. An emperor, crowned and in full regalia, holds a scepter in his right hand and an orb with a triform cross in his left. The roundel has an overall pattern of radiating quatrefoils. Diam. 35″. Dumbarton Oaks Collections, Washington, D.C. Photo: Dumbarton Oaks Collections.

Figure 54: *Sculptured Panel Icon.* Steatite, carved in low relief, 12th to 13th centuries. This fragment of a small devotional icon is carved in grey-green steatite, a frequent substitute for the more costly ivory. The icon appears originally to have been 5 zones wide and either 4 or 5 zones high. The fragment reveals 4 standing female saints in the bottom zone, part of an oddly clothed praying figure (possibly St. John the Baptist) and 2 stylite male saints (busts on columns) in the second zone, 2 standing male saints (one fragmented) in the third zone, and the feet of a robed saint in the fourth zone. Ht. 3⁹⁄₁₆″, w. 2⅞″. Malcove Collection, New York. Photo: Geoffrey Clements.

mercenaries who formed the mainstay of the regency were increasingly hated. Members of the Comnenian family, supported by the people and the Church, made attempts to overthrow the régime, but all such efforts failed, for the opposition lacked any effective leader in Constantinople. The decisive role was to be played by Andronicus Comnenus, a cousin of Manuel, who was then living as a governor in the district of Pontus.

Andronicus Comnenus is one of the most interesting figures of Byzantine history.[1] At this point he was in his sixties and had already lived a life crowded with varied experience. His bold escapades and adventurous love affairs had been the talk of the day in Byzantium. He had great charm of manner, was highly educated, witty and eloquent, brave in the field and outspoken at court; he was the only man who dared to oppose the Emperor Manuel to his face. Andronicus and Manuel had long been rivals and the latter suspected his ambitious cousin of having designs upon the throne, and not without reason. Andronicus was ready for anything, his desire for power and fame was insatiable, he shrank from nothing and was completely ruthless. Each attempt at reconciliation was followed by further quarrels. Taking refuge in flight to avoid his cousin's suspicions, for many years Andronicus led a wandering life of adventure and was a welcome guest at the court of the Russian prince of Gallicia, as well as at those of the Muslim rulers in the Near East. These two outstanding members of the Comneni family were divided by differences of policy, as well as by personal rivalry. Andronicus was the enemy of the feudal aristocracy and a bitter opponent of any Western orientation. He was, therefore, an obvious person to turn to when it was a question of overthrowing the pro-Latin regency in Constantinople.

Passing through Asia Minor, Andronicus met with practically no opposition, and as he went his modest forces were increased by the addition of malcontents. In the spring of 1182 he reached Chalcedon and pitched his camp here. The *protosebastus* Alexius attempted to block the Bosphorus, relying on the fleet which was largely manned by Westerners, but the Admiral of the navy, the *megas dux* Andronicus Contostephanus, went over to the side of the usurper, and this decided the fate of the regency. A revolt broke out in the capital and the *protosebastus* Alexius was thrown into prison and blinded.

[1] Diehl, *Figures* II, 68 ff., gives a lively biography and a vivid character study of Andronicus.

Byzantine fury against the Latins was now unleashed in a terrible massacre (May 1182). In its blind rage the mob attacked the houses of foreigners living in Constantinople, plundered their goods and chattels and brutally murdered all who had not managed to escape in time.

Such was the prelude to the reign of Andronicus Comnenus. Amid the general rejoicing of the populace, he celebrated his entry into Constantinople, where he began by playing the role of saviour and protector of the young Emperor Alexius II. His opponents were found guilty of treason to the state and the legitimate Emperor and were executed, including amongst many others the Dowager Empress Mary, whose death warrant the young Alexius was forced to sign with his own hand. When the ground had been thus cleared, Andronicus, apparently yielding to the entreaties of the court and clergy, decided to adopt the purple and was crowned as the co-Emperor of his young protégé in September 1183. Two months later the unhappy boy was strangled by Andronicus' minions and his body thrown into the sea. As a concession to the principle of legitimacy, the sixty-five-year-old Andronicus married the thirteen-year-old widow of his murdered nephew, Agnes-Anna, the daughter of Louis VII.

The statesmanship of Andronicus, like his character, was full of astounding contrasts.[1] He attempted to put new life into the Empire; he took a firm stand against the evils which his predecessors had let loose; he desired to uproot the over-powerful aristocracy. Since, however, he knew no other method of government but brute force, his reign was therefore a series of acts of violence, conspiracies and fearful cruelty. But even his enemies had to admit that the measures which he employed in the imperial provinces produced a speedy and marked improvement. With an iron hand he rooted out many an evil in the ageing state which his contemporaries had regarded as being inevitable. The sale of offices ceased; the best men were selected; and officials were paid an adequate salary so that they were less open to bribery. Every form of corruption was fiercely combated and the Emperor impressed upon his servants

[1] Eustathius of Thessalonica, *Opuscula*, ed. Tafel, 270 ff., observes that Andronicus was by nature so full of contradictions that he could be given the highest praise or the most severe blame according to which side of his character was being looked at. This is borne out by the account given by the oustanding historian of the day, Nicetas Choniates, where the greatest admiration is found side by side with horror and revulsion. In any case, his somewhat naive descriptions are probably nearer the historical truth than the representations of most modern historians who either regard Andronicus as a tyrant or else try to whitewash his misdeeds.

that they must 'cease either from ill-doing or from living'.[1] Insisting on these principles he even succeeded in overcoming the greatest evil of all, the abuses of the tax-collectors. It was this fact above all which accounted for the improvement in the condition of the provinces under Andronicus, for it had been the oppression of the officials, rather than the demands of the state, which had made the people's lot so insupportable. The energetic attack upon apparently ineradicable abuses was sufficient to alleviate the condition of the populace, and it gave the sorely-tried Byzantine peasantry a feeling of security which had been quite unknown to them. 'He who rendered unto Caesar the things which were Caesar's was left unmolested; he was no longer deprived, as he had previously been, of the last shirt from his body, nor was he tortured to death. For the name of Andronicus acted like a magic spell in driving away the greedy tax-collectors.'[2] A great impression was also made on contemporaries by the abolition of the widely-spread custom of plundering wrecked ships. Andronicus put an end to this evil practice, which his predecessors had failed to root out, by ordering the culprits to be hung from the yard-arms of the plundered vessels.[3] It was his unshakable conviction that 'there was nothing which the Emperors could not set right, nor any injustice which it was not within their power to destroy'.[4]

There was, however, considerable danger in this mounting consciousness of power. The rule of Andronicus became a reign of terror, and the struggle against the nobles turned into a wholesale slaughter. The ruthless means which he employed in the fight were always violent and frequently infamous, and they only defeated his ends which were often admirable. Violence was answered with violence, while risings and conspiracies were an almost daily occurrence. Maddened by such opposition, the Emperor, whose blind rages and suspicion had become by now almost a disease, resorted to still sharper measures which only gained him new enemies. The Empire was in a state of underground civil war and it was clear that there were still things which the Emperor was powerless to control. Andronicus had failed in his attempt to reverse the historical process.

[1] Nic. Choniates 430.
[2] Nic. Choniates 422. These general statements of Nicetas Choniates should be compared with the similar information given by his brother Michael Choniates, the Metropolitan of Athens, whose letters and speeches throw light on local conditions in the see of Athens (Mich. Chon. ed. Lampros I, 142 ff., 157 ff.; II, 54).
[3] Nic. Choniates 423 ff.   [4] Nic. Choniates 424.

The landed aristocracy had long become the vital element in the state and in its defences. It could not be dispensed with and its destruction by mass execution shook the foundations of Byzantine military power.[1]

Andronicus' work in vigorously rooting out corruption had been most salutary, as even his opponents, such as Nicetas Choniates and Eustathius of Thessalonica, freely admit; but his programme with its radical change of emphasis was a complete failure. The anti-Latin policy increased the hostility of the Western powers towards Byzantium, and the bias against the aristocracy weakened the already debilitated Byzantine state. When the inevitable reckoning came, Byzantium's military strength was found entirely wanting, and this in itself pronounces the verdict of failure upon Andronicus' attempt to revive the Empire.

The dazzling brilliance of the position achieved by Manuel soon paled and the first threatening clouds came from Serbia and Hungary where his policy had seemed to be most successful. It had been Manuel's personal authority which had been largely responsible for keeping the Hungarian king Bela III at peace with Byzantium and compelling the Serbian Grand Župan Stephen Nemanja to keep his promises. With Manuel's death these personal ties were loosened, and the obvious weakness of the Empire, involved as it was in internal dissension owing to the ineffective regency of the Dowager Empress Mary and the brutal rule of Andronicus, seemed to promise an easy victory. By 1181 Bela III had seized Dalmatia, part of Croatia and the district of Sirmium,[2] which meant the loss of all that had been won by Manuel's long and costly wars with Hungary. The fruits of the weary and exhausting struggle with Serbia vanished with equal rapidity, for it was now an easy matter for Stephen Nemanja to break away from Byzantium. By his murder of the Empress Mary, Andronicus had himself placed a weapon in the hand of the Hungarian king, and Bela III now came forward as the

[1] M. J. Sjuzjumov, 'Vnutrennjaja politika Andronika Komnina i razgrom prigorodov Konstantinopolja v 1187 godu' (The internal policy of Andronicus Comnenus and the destruction of the suburbs of Constantinople in the year 1187), VV 12 (1957), 64 f., believes, on the basis of insufficient evidence, that it is possible to speak of the abandonment of the *pronoia* system under Andronicus. On the other hand, he does not agree that Andronicus' reign of terror was directed against the aristocracy as such. Neither is he convincing in his thesis that the policy of Andronicus served the interests of the business classes of Constantinople.

[2] The sources have been collected by N. Radojčić, *Dva posljednja Komnena na carigradskom prijestolu* (The last two Comneni on the throne of Constantinople), 1907, 25, note 3.

avenger of Manuel's widow.[1] In 1183 the Hungarians and Serbians in alliance invaded the Empire, and Belgrade, Braničevo, Niš and Sofia were sacked. Six years later the crusaders passing these cities found them deserted and partly in ruins. In the struggle against Byzantium Stephen Nemanja was now able to secure the independence of his country and to expand his territory to the east and south at the Empire's expense. At the same time he extended his authority to include Zeta which now joined with Rascia to form a single principality under his leadership.[2]

Meanwhile in Asia the internal tension invited one revolt after another. The great landowners, led by the Comneni family itself, offered desperate resistance to the régime of Andronicus. Things even got to such a point that Isaac Comnenus, a great-nephew of Manuel, established himself in Cyprus, making the island independent of the Empire. Although he assumed the imperial title and minted his own coinage,[3] his presumption went unpunished, and all that could be done was to execute with great cruelty those of his friends who were caught in Constantinople. This strategically vital island was lost to Byzantium. The disintegration of the Byzantine Empire had begun.

The hardest blow to the Empire was struck by the Sicilian Normans who once again launched a vigorous attack against Byzantium. It was useless for Andronicus to conclude an alliance with the powerful Saladin who had been in control of Egypt since 1171, when the Fatimids were overthrown, and had conquered Syria after the death of his former master, the great Syrian ruler Nuredin († 1174).[4] It was equally useless for him to attempt to strengthen the Byzantine position in the West by ignoring his Latin animosity and resuming relations with Venice which had been broken off since 1171 and pledging himself to pay compensation to

---

[1] Gy. Moravcsik, 'Pour une alliance byzantino-hongroise', B 8 (1933), 555 ff., makes some interesting observations on the policy of Bela III, but he seems to go too far when he attributes to the Hungarian king the intention of gaining the Byzantine imperial throne and putting into practice Manuel's plan for a political union of Byzantium and Hungary by action from the Hungarian side.

[2] Cf. Jireček, *Geschichte* I, 264 ff.

[3] Wroth, *Byz. Coins* II, 597 f.

[4] There seems no reason to doubt the fact of the treaty with Saladin mentioned in the *Annales Reichersperg.*, M.G.H. SS. XXVII, 511 (Dölger, *Reg.* 1563). Cf. C. M. Brand, 'The Byzantines and Saladin, 1185–92. Opponents of the Third Crusade', *Speculum* 37 (1962), 167 ff., 181.

the Venetians.[1] Following the example of Robert Guiscard the Normans began by attacking Dyrrachium in June 1185. The city was quickly stormed and the Norman army then advanced by land towards Thessalonica, while the fleet approached it by sea, occupying the islands of Corfu, Cephalonia and Zacynthus on the way. Although it was only a few years after the close of Manuel's glorious reign, it was evident that the Empire was now far weaker than in the memorable days when, after a period of hopeless decline, Alexius I Comnenus began his struggle against Robert Guiscard. Alexius had been able to put up keen resistance to the enemy both at Dyrrachium and, after its fall, in the interior, so that the enemy never got to Thessalonica. Now they did not meet with the slightest opposition on their march and they reached their objective on 6 August. On 15 August the Norman fleet sailed into the harbour of Thessalonica, and the siege by land and sea began. The defences of the city were poor, the provisions inadequate, the commander David Comnenus proved incapable and the relief forces sent from Constantinople arrived too late: on 24 August the second city of the Empire fell to the Normans. The greed and hatred of the victors knew no bounds and terrible scenes of violence were enacted in the conquered city.[2] Just as three years before the Greeks had illtreated the Latins in Constantinople, so now the Normans inflicted on the inhabitants of Thessalonica insults, tortures and deaths of the cruellest kind.

From Thessalonica a detachment of the Norman army advanced on Serres, while the greater part of it set out for Constantinople. In the Byzantine capital the atmosphere was steadily becoming more oppressive; an unrestrained régime of terror was established and fear grew apace that the city would be captured by the enemy approaching fresh from its conquest of Thessalonica. The storm broke on 12 September 1185. The last of the Comnenian rulers met a terrible fate: the Emperor who had been idolized as the saviour of the Empire only a few years before was now torn to pieces in the streets of Constantinople by the bestial fury of the enraged mob.

---

[1] Cf. above, p. 389, note 2. The return to normal trading relations with Venice does not justify the conclusion that Andronicus had completely abandoned his anti-Latin policy—as is asserted by F. Cognasso, *Partiti politici e lotte dinastiche in Bizanzio alla morte di Manuele Comneno* (1912) 294 ff. and 'Un imperatore bizantino della decadenza: Isacco II Angelo', *Bessarione* 19 (1915), 44 ff. This is rightly pointed out by M. J. Sjuzjumov, 'Vnutrennjaja politika Andronika Komnina', VV 12 (1957) 66, against the view of M. Frejdenberg, K istorii klassovoj bor'by v Vizantii v XII veke' (On the history of the class struggle in Byzantium in the twelfth century), *Uč. zap. Velikolukskogo gos. ped. inst.* 1954, 37.

[2] Eustathius of Thessalonica 365 ff. gives an eye-witness account.

4. THE COLLAPSE

General bibliography: F. Cognasso, 'Un imperatore bizantino della decadenza: Isacco II Angelo', *Bessarione* 19 (1915), 29–60; M. Bachmann, *Die Rede des Johannes Syropulos an den Kaiser Isaak II Angelos*, Diss. Munich 1935; Stadtmüller, *Michael Choniates*; Norden, *Papsttum und Byzanz*; idem, *Der vierte Kreuzzug im Rahmen der Beziehungen des Abendlandes zu Byzanz*, Berlin 1898; A. Frolow, *Recherches sur la déviation de la IVe croisade vers Constantinople*, Paris 1955; Diehl, *Venise*; Kretschmayr, *Venedig* I; Heyd, *Commerce du Levant* I; Uspenskij, *Obrazovanie*; Zlatarski, *Istorija* II and III; Mutafčiev, *Istorija* II; Jireček, *Geschichte* I; Runciman, *Crusades* III; Setton, *Crusades* II; see also general bibliography cited on p. 394.

The tragic downfall of Andronicus meant the end of his attempts to retrieve the situation for the Empire. The feudal aristocracy had won the day and they not only maintained, but increased, their authority under the dynasty of the Angeli. After the desperate struggle against the intransigent absolutism of the last Comnenus, the conflicting forces in the state took their course unrestrained.

The Angeli did not come from one of the old noble families of the Empire, but from an obscure Philadelphian family who owed their rise to the fact that Alexius I's youngest daughter Theodora fell in love with Constantine Angelus and married him. As kinsmen of the imperial house, the Angeli from then on enjoyed high honours; they were particularly prominent in Manuel I's reign and they took the lead in the opposition of the aristocracy to Andronicus. Fate willed that the victory of the nobles should raise one of their own kind to the imperial throne. Isaac II (1185–95), the grandson of Constantine Angelus and the born-in-the-purple Theodora, was an entire contrast to the autocratic Andronicus and he allowed free play to those developments which his predecessor had so energetically opposed. The old administrative abuses which had been concealed by the outward brilliance of power, now appeared in all their nakedness, and the rottenness of the whole organism of government was revealed with terrifying clarity. There was no longer any attempt to curb mismanagement in the central and provincial administration: the sale of offices, the venality of officials and the extortion of the tax-collectors assumed the most blatant forms. It was said of the Emperor Isaac II that he sold government posts like vegetables in a market.[1] A special tax was extracted from the provinces for his wedding which was celebrated with great splendour. He regarded the Empire which fate had bestowed on him as

---

[1] Nic. Choniates 584; cf. also Mich. Choniates II, 99 (ed. Lampros).

though it was his own private property and he governed it as though he was the head of a family estate. Under his brother Alexius III (1195–1203) conditions became infinitely worse. The provincial population were driven to starvation by the excessive burden of taxation, due to the abuses of the tax-collectors and the swollen demands of the government.[1] Vast sums were swallowed up by the ostentatious pomp of the feckless court and by the payments to foreign countries which the ineffective government considered the easiest way of warding off its powerful opponents. At the same time the provinces were continually exposed to enemy attacks and the coastal districts to raids from pirates, nor did it improve matters that the taxes for the building and equipment of ships was extorted three times in a single year in some districts.[2] While the burden of taxes on the population continually grew more oppressive, influential owners of large estates maintained and increased their privileges. Unfortunately all efforts of the state to limit the constant growth of privileges failed because the weak imperial government had no means of defending itself against the harassing demands of the magnates, who invariably emerged victorious.[3] Practically nothing was left of the theme system which had once been the backbone of Byzantine administration and defences. Although the extent of the Empire had considerably shrunk, at the end of the twelfth century Byzantium possessed nearly twice the number of themes as in the days of the Macedonian dynasty.[4] The Byzantine administrative machine was broken up into little units which resembled the old themes in name only. With the steady growth of private estates, the administrative system of the dwarf provinces became unavoidably dependent upon the local landed proprietors. The weakness of the central government was such that it was only a step to the replacement of the provincial governor by the landowner and to the development of independent principalities.[5]

[1] In this respect the ὑπομνηστικόν of Michael Choniates to the Emperor Alexius III in 1198 is most instructive, ed. Lampros I, 307–11; new ed. in Stadtmüller, *Michael Choniates* 283–6.

[2] e.g. in the region of Attica in 1197–8. Cf. the *hypomnestikon* of Mich. Choniates: Lampros I, 308; Stadtmüller, *Michael Choniates* 283 f., and also the comments on this by Stadtmüller 174 and 289.

[3] Cf. the valuable article by P. Lemerle, 'Notes sur l'administration byzantine à la veille de la IVe croisade d'après deux documents inédits des archives de Lavra', REB 19 (1961), 258 ff.

[4] Cf. the list of Byzantine themes in Alexius III's chrysobull of November 1198 for Venice, Zepos, *Jus.* I, 469–80 (= Tafel and Thomas I, 248–78); Dölger, *Reg.* 1647.

[5] Stein, 'Untersuchungen' 19 ff., has noted this development. Cf. also Stadtmüller, *Michael Choniates* 145 f.

Fortunately, the fear of the Norman danger which cost Androni-cus his throne proved to be exaggerated. The Norman forces were demoralized by greed and self-indulgence and their ranks thinned by epidemics. The skilful general Alexius Branas was therefore able to beat them decisively at Mosynopolis and later on 7 November 1185 at Dimitrica, and they retreated, evacuating first Thessalonica and later Dyrrachium and Corfu. Only Cephalonia and Zacynthus remained in Western hands and were finally lost to Byzantium. The other enemy who had threatened the Empire under Andronicus, the Hungarian king Bela III, was persuaded to conclude a treaty with Isaac Comnenus, who married his ten-year-old daughter Margaret.

The double safeguard against Norman and Hungarian aggression was all the more important since a revolt broke out in Bulgaria at the end of 1185.[1] The appearance of the brothers Peter (Theodore) and Asen at first only indicated that the immediate ties of imperial authority were being loosened in Bulgarian territory as elsewhere in the Empire. Here the symptoms appeared which were already apparent throughout the Empire and which were embodied in the territorial claims of the local magnates. Peter and Asen began by claiming certain lands as grants of *pronoiai*.[2] Events were precipitated by the arrogance of the Byzantine government in harshly sweeping aside this claim, which was put forward somewhat disrespectfully. The rejected claimants unleashed a revolt among the tax-ridden and exasperated people which led eventually to the complete liberation of Bulgaria from Byzantine control and the foundation of the Second Bulgarian Empire.

Two centuries of Byzantine rule had weakened the Slav element in Bulgaria as well as in Macedonia, and in these areas there was noticeable Hellenization, as well as the strengthening of other foreign elements at the expense of the Slav.[3] There were many Jews and Armenians around Thessalonica, the Danube basin har-boured a number of Cumans, and the Wallachians, the ancestors of the present-day Rumanians, were living in the Danube area as well as in Macedonia and Thessaly, which was known as Great Wallachia.

---

[1] For the chronology cf. J. Dujčev, 'La date de la révolte des Asênides', BS 13 (1953), 227 ff.

[2] Nic. Choniates 482, 15–17, and on the correct interpretation cf. Uspenskij, 'Pronija' 32, and Zlatarski, *Istorija* II, 435 f. Ostrogorsky, *Féodalité*, 53 f.

[3] Cf. Uspenskij, *Obrazovanie* 66 ff.

In the revolt stirred up by Peter and Asen, the Cumans and Wallachians took a prominent part.[1]

The difficulties of the situation were complicated by internal
developments. Alexius Branas, the conqueror of the Normans, was
sent to deal with the revolt, but he assumed the imperial purple and

[1] The ethnical composition of the Second Bulgarian Empire is a difficult and much
disputed question. In the relevant passages of Nicetas Choniates the reference is not to
the Bulgarians as one would expect, but to the Wallachians, and contemporary Western
sources (Ansbert, Robert of Clari, Villehardouin) also stress these. On the other hand,
contemporary Slav sources and the later Byzantine historians, from George Acropolites
onwards, do not mention the Wallachians. But in the correspondence between Innocent
III and Kalojan, the Pope describes the Bulgarian ruler as lord of the Bulgarians and the
Wallachians, and in four letters Kalojan speaks of himself as *imperator totius Bulgarie et
Vlachie*, and in one letter as *imperator Bulgarorum* (new ed. by I. Dujčev, *Innocentii PP. III
epistolae ad Bulgariae historiam spectantes, Godsišnik. na Sofijsk. Univ.*, Ist.-filol. Fak. 37, 3
(1942), Nr. II, XV, XVIII, XXX and IX). Kalojan not only describes himself but
Symeon, Peter and Samuel as *imperatores Bulgarorum et Blachorum* (ib. Nr. XV), and
Nicetas Choniates 482, 3, expressly says that the barbarians of the Haemus region who
used to be called Moesians, were now called Wallachians (τοὺς κατὰ τὸν Αἶμον τὸ ὄρος
βαρβάρους, οἱ Μυσοὶ πρότερον ὠνομάζοντο, νυνὶ Δὲ Βλάχοι κικλήσκονται), and Th. Scutariotes (Sathas VII, 370, 19) later gives the explanation, Βλάχοι Δὲ νῦν καὶ Βούλγαροι.
It is clear that the term Wallachian was used not only racially but as a collective expression for the nomad tribes, and everything points to the conclusion that it was applied
at that time to the population of the old Moesia, i.e. the later Paristrion theme, while
the Bulgarians were those who lived in the Bulgarian theme, i.e. in Macedonia (cf.
Mutafčiev, 'Proizchodût na Asenevci' (The origins of the Asens), *Maked. Pregled* IV, 4
(1928), 1 ff., and *Istorija* II, 36 ff.; Dujčev, op. cit. 85 ff., and *Proučvanija vŭrchu bŭlgarskoto
srednoevekovie* (Studies in the Bulgarian middle ages) (1945), 45 f.; Zlatarski, *Istorija* II,
416 ff.). N. Banescu, *Un problème d'histoire médiévale. Création et caractère du second empire
bulgare*, Bucharest 1942, rejects this explanation, which in my view is the only possible
one, while he attacks certain untenable views of Uspenskij and Zlatarski. He believes he can thus show that the second Bulgarian empire was created by the Wallachians. On the other hand he can find no satisfactory interpretation of the statements of
Nicetas Choniates already mentioned nor does he pay any attention to the gloss of
Scutariotes or to the correspondence of Kalojan with Innocent III. Cf. also R. L. Wolff,
'The "Second Bulgarian Empire". Its Origin and History to 1204', *Speculum* 24 (1949),
167 ff. There can be no doubt that the Asenid empire was a Bulgarian empire. It is true
that there is no need to deny the part played by the Wallachians and the Cumans in the
formative stages of this empire, nor to agree with Mutafčiev that at this period there
were no Wallachian elements in the population of the Bulgar region. The fact
that it was usual at that time to refer to the population of Bulgaria as Wallachian
is sufficient to prove the contrary. See the carefully considered article by V. G. Vasiljevskij, ZMNP 204 (1879), 173 ff. (review of Uspenskij, *Obrazovanie*). Finally cf. Litavrin,
Bolgarija i Vizantija, 431 ff. As for the brothers Peter and Asen, according to Vasilievskij,
loc. cit., they were of Bulgar-Wallachian descent. Zlatarski, 'Potekloto na Petra i
Asenja' (The ancestry of Peter and Asen), *Spisanie na Bŭlg. Akad.* 45 (1933), 7 ff., considers
them to have come of distinguished Bulgar-Cuman stock (as Uspenskij had done,
Obrazovanie 105 ff.). Mutafčiev, op. cit. 3 ff., supports a Russian ancestry, pointing out
that Russian settlements on the Lower Danube were frequent at that time, that the
Cuman name Asen is often found in Old Russian chronicles, that the Russian prince
Jurij Dolgorukij married the grand-daughter of the Cuman prince Asen in 1107 and
that the son of this marriage, Vasilko, received four cities on the Danube from the
Emperor Manuel I. V. Nikolaev, *Potekloto na Asenevci i etničeskijat charakter na osnovanata
ot tjach dŭržava* (The ancestry of the Asens and the racial character of the state founded
by them), Sofia 1940, rejects all earlier suggestions and supports the notoriously inconsis-
tent explanation that Peter and Asen were descended from the family of the old Bulgarian
czars. Cf. the criticism of this by D. Angelov, BS 9 (1948), 358.

turned against Isaac II. He was, however, killed in the fighting before Constantinople, and in the summer of 1186 the Emperor himself marched into Bulgaria at the head of his troops. No one could accuse Isaac II of lack of vigour in his action against the Bulgarian rebels. He was indeed no statesman, but he was not the cowardly weakling that he has generally been depicted. His reign was certainly unfortunate, but the Norman and Bulgarian wars do at least show that under his government the military position of the Empire was not as ineffective as it had been under the despotic rule of Andronicus.[1]

The rebels were dispersed and Peter and Asen fled across the Danube. They soon returned with strong reinforcements of Cuman troops and the fighting flared up again.[2] In October 1186 Isaac hurried to meet them, but this time he met with stronger opposition and it was only with great difficulty that he managed to put the Bulgarian and Cuman hordes to flight. In the spring of 1187 he undertook a fresh expedition and by way of Sardica tried to outflank the rebels who were hiding in the mountains. The result was not decisive and Byzantium was in no position to face a protracted war. Difficulties increased on all sides. The Serbian Grand Župan Stephen Nemanja supported the Bulgarian rebels and took the opportunity of the Byzantino-Bulgarian war to increase his own authority at the expense of the Byzantine Empire. A rebellion broke out in Asia Minor. Isaac II therefore brought the fighting in Bulgaria to a close and came to an understanding with the rebels who handed over Kalojan, the younger brother of Peter and Asen, as hostage.

The peace treaty signified a tacit acceptance of the new situation: Byzantium had released its hold on the territory between the Balkan mountains and the Danube and an independent Bulgarian Empire had once more arisen. The Archbishopric of Trnovo was founded at the same time and Asen received the crown of the tzars at the hand of the new Bulgarian Archbishop in the Church of St. Demetrius in Trnovo.[3] It was said that after the capture of Thessalonica by the

[1] M. Bachmann, *Die Rede des Joh. Syropulos an den Kaiser Isaak II. Angelos* (1935), also takes a more favourable view of Isaac II.

[2] D. Rasovskij, 'Rol' Polovcev v vojnach Asenij s vizantijskoj i latinskoj imperijami v 1186–1207 g.' (The role of the Cumans in the wars of the Asens with the Bulgarian and Latin Empires), *Spisanie na Bŭlg. Akad.* 1939, 203 ff., has admirably demonstrated that the participation of the Cumans had a decisive effect in the Byzantine-Bulgarian and later in the Latin-Bulgarian struggle, but that the Cumans took no part in the Bulgarian campaigns in summer for climatic reasons.

[3] Cf. Zlatarski, *Istorija* II, 472 ff.

Normans, St. Demetrius had left the Greek city and gone to Trnovo, the capital of the Second Bulgarian Empire. The era of Byzantine domination in the Balkans had gone for ever. The Bulgarians, like the Serbs, had finally emancipated themselves from the control of an Empire now rent by internal conflicts. The dangers inherent in the new situation became only too clear when Byzantium had the misfortune to be involved in a fresh crusade.

The Holy Sepulchre had once more fallen into the hands of the infidel. Saladin had extended his sovereignty from Egypt to Syria and in 1187 was advancing on Palestine. On 4 July he badly defeated the Latin forces at Hattin, took king Guy of Lusignan prisoner and entered Jerusalem on 2 October. Frederick I Barbarossa, Philip II Augustus and Richard Lionheart, the most prominent rulers in the West, took the cross. Frederick I chose the land route through Hungary and by the summer of 1189 he had reached the Balkans. He had made an attempt to come to an understanding with the Byzantines and as early as the autumn of 1188 a treaty had been signed in Nuremberg concerning the passage of the crusaders.[1] But this by no means allayed the suspicions of the Byzantines, for in actual fact Barbarossa had also negotiated with the enemies of the Byzantine Empire, the Serbs and the Sultan of Iconium, through whose territory the road to the Holy Land passed. Frederick's arrival, unpalatable as it was to the Byzantines, was all the more welcome to the southern Slavs, and the inevitable tension between Byzantium and the German Emperor was something that could be turned to the advantage of the Slav kingdoms. For decades alliance with Hungary had been the cornerstone of Serbian policy, but now that Hungary was on friendly terms with Byzantium, whose power was no longer to be feared, a change of policy was necessitated. Stephen Nemanja therefore turned for support to the powerful German Emperor, and Bulgaria followed his example. Barbarossa was received by Nemanja with great ceremony in Niš, and he entered into negotiations with the Serbian Grand Župan, as well as with the Bulgarian ambassadors. Serbia and Bulgaria offered to take an oath of allegiance and to conclude an alliance against Byzantium.[2]

These negotiations naturally roused the greatest uneasiness in Constantinople. The Byzantine government threw itself into the arms of Saladin, the most bitter foe of the crusaders, and renewed

[1] Dölger, *Reg.* 1581.
[2] Cf. M. Paulová, BS 5 (1933–4), 235 ff.

the treaty of alliance made by Andronicus, with the proviso that the passage of the German crusading army must be held up.[1] This brought matters to a head as far as the relations between Byzantium and the German Emperor were concerned. Frederick occupied Philippopolis as though it were a city in enemy territory. This led to a lively exchange of letters charged with insults and bitter recriminations. Matters even went so far that Frederick determined if necessary to subdue Byzantium by force of arms and occupy Constantinople. After taking Adrianople the German Emperor once again met the Serbian and Bulgarian envoys there, and then he marched on Constantinople, while his son Henry was ordered to sail with a fleet up to the walls of the capital. At this Isaac gave in: in February 1190 a treaty was concluded in Adrianople whereby the German Emperor was to receive transport ships, hostages of high rank were to be handed over and he was to secure provisions at low prices.[2] All Barbarossa's demands were fulfilled and Byzantium thus had to bow to the superiority of the German Emperor. In the spring Frederick I crossed over to Asia Minor with his army and pushed on towards the Holy Land, which he was destined never to reach.

The expeditions of the kings of England and France went by the sea route to Palestine, and they hardly affected Byzantium at all, since its sphere of influence no longer extended to Palestine. Their efforts also proved a failure, for by the peace of 1192 Saladin kept Jerusalem and the Latins were limited to a narrow strip of land between Jaffa and Tyre. Byzantium was more directly concerned with a by-product of the crusade when Richard Lionheart took Cyprus, imprisoned its ruler Isaac Comnenus and handed over the island first to the Templars, and then (1192) to Guy of Lusignan, the former king of Jerusalem. After this Cyprus remained in Western hands.

After the departure and tragic death of Barbarossa, Byzantium regained her freedom of action in the Balkans. Without delay Isaac II marched against the Bulgarians, who had invaded Thrace, and against the Serbs, who had profited by the hostility between the two Empires to make fresh conquests and had destroyed the most important cities from Sofia to Skoplje and Prizren. In the autumn of 1190

[1] Dölger, *Reg.* 1591. Cf. C. M. Brand, 'The Byzantines and Saladin, 1185–92: Opponents of the Third Crusade', *Speculum* 37 (1962), 170 ff.

[2] Dölger, *Reg.* 1603; K. Zimmert, 'Der Friede zu Adrianopel', BZ 11 (1902), 303 ff.; also cf. idem, 'Der deutsch-byz. Konflikt vom Juli 1189 bis Februar 1190', BZ 12 (1903), 42 ff.

Stephen Nemanja was defeated on the Morava and had to agree to a peace treaty whereby he surrendered his recent acquisitions but kept his earlier conquests.[1] But the apparent triumph of the Emperor was not as complete as Byzantine sources would make out. The signing of a formal peace treaty implied the express recognition of Serbia's existence as an independent state and this act was sealed by a marriage alliance between the two dynasties. Stephen, Nemanja's second son, married the Emperor's niece Eudocia and was given the high rank of Sebastocrator.[2] The marriage with an imperial princess and the granting of the title of Sebastocrator was signal recognition, while at the same time the incorporation of the heir to the Serbian throne into the Byzantine hierarchy of nobility emphasized the conception of the supreme position of the Byzantine Emperor, the Basileus and Autocrator.[3]

Byzantium was less fortunate in its renewed struggle with Bulgaria. The great campaign of 1190 ended in a severe defeat. After reaching the walls of Trnovo the Byzantines failed to take the Bulgarian capital, and during their retreat the Byzantine forces were surprised in the passes of the Balkan range and the Emperor himself only just escaped destruction. Further attempts to relieve Bulgarian pressure also failed and in 1194 the Byzantines met with fresh defeat at Arcadiopolis. But the Emperor did not give up the struggle. His friendly relations with the Hungarian court, which had been temporarily clouded over owing to a Hungarian attack on Serbia,[4] were renewed in order to start another campaign against Bulgaria in alliance with Hungary. But he had scarcely taken the field when, on 8 April 1195, his elder brother Alexius seized the imperial crown and had him blinded.

Alexius III (1195–1203), a weakling, possessed of a lust for power, was a typical product of this age of disintegration. As though to caricature the great Comneni emperors, he adopted the name Comnenus, since the name Angelus did not sound distinguished enough to him.[5] Under Isaac II the Empire for all its rottenness

---

[1] Jireček, *Geschichte* I, 273 f.; M. Bachmann, *Die Rede des Johannes Syropulos an Isaak II. Angelos* (1935), 68 ff.

[2] Cf. M. Laskaris, *Vizantiske princeze u srednjevekovnoj Srbiji* (Byzantine princesses in medieval Serbia), 1926, 7 ff.

[3] Cf. my study, 'Die byz. Staatenhierarchie', *Sem. Kond.* 8 (1936), 41 ff.

[4] Cf. V. Laurent, 'La Serbie entre Byzance et la Hongrie à la veille de la quatrième croisade', *Revue du Sud-Est europ.* 18 (1941), 109 ff.; N. Radojčić, 'Promena u srpsko-madjarskim odnosima krajem XII veka' (The change in Serbo-Magyar relations at the end of the twelfth century), *Glas Srpske akad. nauka* 213 (1954), 1 ff.

[5] Nic. Choniates 605.

Figure 55: (ABOVE) *The Ruins of Ephesus.* (BELOW) *The Ruins of Phila-delphia.* From 19th-century engravings in Thomas Allon and Robert Walsh, *Constantinople and . . . the Seven Churches of Asia Minor,* London, n.d.

Figure 56: *Monastery Church of the Virgin.* Studenica, Yugoslavia, 12th century. Exterior from the northeast. Photo: Bildarchiv Foto Marburg.

might have held together, but now it had lost its last chance of resistance. Year by year the internal collapse became more obvious, and even abroad the political changes of 1195 had many and far-reaching repercussions.

The result of this change of ruler particularly affected the relations between the Empire and Serbia. The father of the princess Eudocia who had married into the Serbian house was now Emperor and he no doubt used his influence to secure a change of régime in Serbia which not long after gave the throne to the imperial son-in-law the Sebastocrator Stephen. On 25 March 1196[1] the aged Nemanja abdicated in favour of Stephen and retired as monk first to the Serbian monastery of Studenica and later on to Mt. Athos, where his youngest son Sava had for some years been living the ascetic life of a monk. It might have appeared that Stephen's accession would open a new era of Byzantine influence in Serbia, but nothing of the sort occurred as the Byzantine government was too feeble to derive any benefit from the solution which it had so long sought. It was not the Byzantine father-in-law of the Serbian ruler, but the powerful Roman Church and its ally Hungary who gained decisive influence in Rascia, as well as in Bosnia, during the next few years. Nemanja's eldest son Vukan, who had to content himself with the region of Zeta and consequently felt himself slighted, declared war on his brother, relying on help from Hungary and the Roman Curia. Left in the lurch by Byzantium, Stephen also tried to save the situation by allying with Rome, and he thought Constantinople of so little account that he divorced his Byzantine wife. However, Vukan acted first, and with Hungarian support he drove his brother out of the country and took over the government himself, having first recognized the supremacy of the

---

[1] In the life of Stephen Nemanja by St. Sava, the date given is 25 March of the year 6703 (1195), though most probably the year does not come from St. Sava himself but was added later. J. Pavlović, 'Hronološke beleške sv. Save o Stevanu Nemanji (Chronological information given by St. Sava about Stephen Nemanja), *Glas. srp. uč. društva* 47 (1879), 284 ff., long ago put forward the view that Nemanja's abdication took place in 1196, a date which was accepted by almost all experts on Serbian history. On the other hand, V. Ćorović 'Pitanje o hronologiji u delima sv. Save' (Problems of chronology in the work of St. Sava), *Godišnjica N. Čupica* (49) (1940), 65 ff. and more recently R. Novaković, 'Jadan pokušaj tumačenja Savinih hronoloških podataka u Žitiju sv. Simeuna' (An attempt at an interpretation of Sava's chronology in his Life of St. Symeon), *Ist. glasnik* 3/4 (1955), 96 ff., agree in favour of the year 1195. But if the abdication of Nemanja is connected with the Byzantine *coup d'état* on 8 April 1195, as Ćorović also seems to think, the acceptance of this date raises certain difficulties. The relatively long interval between the Byzantine *coup d'état* on 8 April 1195 and Nemanja's abdication on 25 March 1196 need cause no concern. As R. Novaković, 'Kada se rodio i kada je počeo da vlada Stevan Nemanja?' (When was Stephen Nemanja born and when did his reign begin?), *Ist. glasnik* 3/4 (1958), 181, rightly points out, Nemanja's decision was certainly taken well before his official abdication.

Pope and the suzerainty of Hungary (1202). In neighbouring Bosnia events took the same course and the Ban Kulin was only able to save his throne by renouncing the Bogomil heresy and acknowledging the Roman Catholic faith and placing himself under the protection of Hungary (1203). It is true that Stephen soon regained his throne, but this was with the help of Bulgaria and not Byzantium. The attitude of the Byzantine government towards the Serbian question showed plainly how rapidly the authority of the Empire was vanishing: in 1196 Byzantium had a decisive voice in the matter of the Serbian succession, but a few years later it had fallen out of the picture and had to see the country come under papal and Hungarian influence.

Alexius III hoped to avoid a conflict with Bulgaria by concluding a peace treaty, but the Bulgarian demands were so excessive that negotiations were broken off. War began once more with the most unfortunate results for Byzantium. The district of Serres was twice ravaged by the Bulgarians in 1195 and 1196, the Byzantine army was defeated and its commander, the Sebastocrator Isaac Comnenus, taken prisoner.[1] Byzantium was too proud to come to terms and too weak to fight. There was a third course open—to support the opposition in the enemy's country. In 1196 Asen fell a victim to a conspiracy of the boyars. His murderer, the boyar Ivanko, could not hold his own in Trnovo for long, because the promised help from Byzantium failed to arrive, owing to a mutiny in the Byzantine army. He had to leave the field to Peter and he fled to Constantinople. Peter succeeded Asen on the throne, but in 1197 he also was murdered.

Ivanko was received with honour in Constantinople, and was made governor of Philippopolis. He was then given command of the imperial forces to be sent against Bulgaria, but the crafty boyar in whose hands Alexius III had placed the fate of the Byzantine war with Bulgaria soon deserted the Empire and set up a principality of his own in the district of the Rhodope. A still more important principality was founded in Macedonia where the voivode Dobromir Chrysus established himself, first of all in the district of the Strymon, and then later extended his authority and entrenched himself in the inaccessible Prosek on the Vardar. He was recognized by the Byzantine government and married one of the Emperor's relations. But Byzantium soon had to take up arms against him, for with the

[1] On what follows cf. Zlatarski, *Istorija* III, 82 ff.; Mutafčiev, *Istorija* II, 45 ff.

support of the empire of Trnovo he opened hostilities against Byzantium, took the greater part of western Macedonia, including Prilep and Bitola, and penetrated as far as central Greece. The Byzantines managed to capture their former ally Ivanko by guile and the lands he had ruled fell under imperial control once more. On the other hand, the fluctuating struggles with Dobromir Chrysus, who was joined by several high Byzantine commanders, ended with the fall of his principality to the tzar Kalojan, and a substantial portion of Macedonia was thus incorporated into Bulgaria.

Kalojan (1197-1207), the youngest brother of Peter and Asen, who had once been sent to Constantinople as a hostage, was to prove a dangerous opponent to the Byzantine Empire. Under his strong rule the new Bulgarian Empire experienced its first stormy rise to power. It became one of the most important Balkan powers and often proved the decisive factor in determining the fate of south-east Europe. His Empire had arisen in the struggle against Byzantium, and Kalojan wanted to secure legal recognition from Rome. Asen's coronation by the self-appointed Archbishop of Trnovo did not sufficiently guarantee the legitimacy of the new kingdom. The right of coronation belonged only to the two world centres, Rome and Constantinople, and the crown was only legitimate if received from either of these. It was not surprising that Kalojan turned to Rome rather than to his enemy, the rapidly disintegrating Byzantine Empire. And so on the eve of the downfall of Constantinople, Rome had brought both Serbia and Bulgaria under its sway, and had extended its influence over a considerable part of the Balkans. After lengthy negotiations Kalojan acknowledged the papal supremacy. The final act followed close on the fall of Constantinople: on 7 November 1204 a Cardinal sent by Innocent III to Trnovo consecrated the Bulgarian Archbishop Basil as Primate of Bulgaria, and the next day placed the royal crown on Kalojan's head.

The pitiful and ever-increasing ineffectiveness of Byzantine policy in the Balkans was to a large extent conditioned by the fact that the Empire was threatened by most serious dangers from the West. For some years its greatest problem was its relationship to the German Emperor Henry VI. Married to the Norman heiress Constance, Henry succeeded on the death of Barbarossa, not only to his father's heritage, but to that of William II († 1189). Sicilian opposition, which centred in William II's nephew Tancred and was supported both by the Curia and by Byzantium, lost ground with Tancred's death, and at Christmas 1194 Henry was crowned king of Sicily in Palermo. This union of the two powers constituted a deadly threat to Byzantium. The incorporation of Sicily within the German Empire provided a firm foundation for Henry's plan of world domination, and the first and most important step towards this goal was the conquest of the Byzantine Empire.[1] As heir of William II, Henry's first demand was for the surrender of the territory between Dyrrachium and Thessalonica which the Normans had conquered in 1185 and lost again, as well as the payment of a substantial tribute and the participation of the Byzantine Empire in the proposed crusade through the despatch of its fleet. The change of sovereigns in Byzantium in 1195 had made the Empire's position still worse. Henry had a dynastic interest in the throne of Constantinople because his brother Philip had married Isaac II's daughter Irene, and he justified his plans of conquest by posing as the avenger of Isaac and the protector of the family of the deposed and blinded Emperor against the usurper Alexius. The intimidated government of Alexius III made every effort to appease the German Emperor by satisfying his demands for tribute and it pledged itself to the annual payment of the huge sum of sixteen hundredweight of gold.[2] A special 'German' tax (τὸ ἀλαμανικόν) was levied on all the provinces, but the overburdened and exhausted country had already been taxed to the uttermost and it proved impossible to collect the required amount. So low had Byzantium fallen that the imperial tombs in the Church of the Holy Apostles were despoiled of their costly ornaments in order to raise the tribute and buy the favour of a dangerous rival.[3] That Henry condescended to negotiate at all with Byzantium and was for the time being content to squeeze dry and humiliate his rival, was due to the intervention of the Pope, who insisted that the German Emperor should not attack Constantinople, but as a crusader should make Jerusalem his objective. The realization of the German ambition to set up a universal Empire would not only have meant the extinction of the Byzantine Empire, but would have permanently weakened the Papacy, and for this reason the Pope was driven to take steps to preserve the schismatic Empire of Constantinople. This did not mean the abandonment of the plans for conquest, but only

---

[1] Cf. Norden, *Papsttum und Byzanz* 122 ff. On the other hand, W. Leonhardt, *Der Kreuzzugsplan Kaiser Heinrichs VI.* (1923), maintains that Henry never contemplated a conquest of the Byzantine Empire. But cf. the excellent refutation of Dölger, *Reg.* 1619.

[2] Nic. Choniates 631, 4. Originally Henry VI had demanded 50 hundredweights (ibid. 630, 16).

[3] Nic. Choniates 631 f.

their postponement. Byzantium was already in a cleft stick: king Amalric of Cyprus and Leo of Lesser Armenia had recognized the overlordship of the German Emperor. But before the decisive blow fell, Henry VI was swept away by death in September 1197.

The abolition of the 'German' tax roused great enthusiasm in Byzantium and the wretched Emperor Alexius Angelus Comnenus, who had just handed over the tribute due to the German Empire and in deadly fear torn the ornaments off the tombs of his ancestors, now considered the moment propitious for advancing his own claims to universal sovereignty and proposing to the Pope an alliance between the one Church and the one Empire, after the manner of the great Comneni.[1] Meanwhile, the death of Henry VI only brought a brief respite from the inevitable Western onslaught on the enfeebled Byzantine Empire whose very weakness invited attack. The death-blow fell from another quarter several years later.

In the West the Empire disintegrated: Italy fell away from German domination and in Germany Henry's brother Philip of Swabia had to face a rival sovereign in the person of Otto of Brunswick. The pre-eminence of the German Emperor gave way before that of the great Pope Innocent III, and this meant that the conception of a crusade once more came to the front in the eastern policy of the Western powers. The Pope did not plan the subjugation of Byzantium by force of arms, but desired its subordination to the see of St. Peter by the union of the two Churches and its participation in the crusade side by side with Western Christendom.

Next to Innocent III, the instigator of the crusade on the behalf of the Church, the central figure in the new crusading movement, the mainspring of the whole undertaking, was the mighty figure of the aged Doge Enrico Dandolo whose aim it was to direct the forces of the West against Byzantium. A great statesman, capable of making far-reaching decisions, entirely unmoved by the genuine crusading spirit, Dandolo realized that permanent security of Venetian preeminence in the East could only be obtained by destroying the Byzantine Empire. Since the time of Alexius I Venice had enjoyed extensive privileges in Byzantium both by sea and land; neither John II nor Manuel I had been able to revoke these burdensome concessions and both the Emperors from the family of the Angeli

---

[1] Cf. the answer of Innocent III of August 1198 (*Ep.* I, 353, Migne, PL 214, 327 BC); Norden, *Papsttum und Byzanz* 134.

had expressly confirmed them.[1] But the repeated attempts of the Empire to shake off the Venetian incubus which it bore with such obvious ill-will and the spontaneous outbursts of the Byzantine populace of 1171 and 1182 had created a feeling of permanent insecurity. The maritime republic had always to be on the alert, and with every change of government in Constantinople it was compelled to get fresh recognition of its claims and even to bring force to prevent their being repudiated. At the same time dangerous rivals had materialized in Pisa and Genoa, for in its difficult situation Byzantium had granted considerable privileges to the rising Italian sea powers in order to try to neutralize Venetian pre-eminence. As long as there was a Byzantine Emperor in Constantinople, Venice could never be sure that it would keep its position of monopoly. The only solution seemed to lie in the elimination of the Byzantine Empire, and the best means of achieving this was to take part in a crusade and divert it to the conquest of Byzantium. The Byzantines had allowed Venice to seize their maritime supremacy, and now were to lose their Empire to it.

The attempt to explain the diversion of the fourth crusade against Constantinople has given rise to countless theories,[2] but in actual fact it presents no problem. It was the almost inevitable result of early developments. Since the schism between the Churches, and particularly since the beginning of the crusading movement, hostility towards Byzantium had been growing in the West. With Manuel's aggressive Western policy and the provocative anti-Latin attitude of Andronicus this ill-feeling had turned to open hostility. Face to face with the obvious weakness and helplessness of the Byzantine Empire under the Angeli, Western hatred turned to thoughts of conquest. The idea of the capture of Constantinople, like an old legacy of the Normans, had been discussed in the entourage of Louis VII as early as the second crusade; during the third crusade of Frederick Barbarossa its realization seemed imminent; and it was the central pivot of the plans of Henry VI, the heir of both Barbarossa and the Norman kings. When Venice threw its commercial and political interests into the balance, the idea became a reality. The increasing secularization of the crusading spirit reached its logical conclusion: the crusade became an instrument of conquest to be

---

[1] Tafel and Thomas I, 189 ff.; Dölger, *Reg.* 1576 (cf. also 1577, 1578, 1589, 1590); Tafel and Thomas I, 248 ff.; Dölger, *Reg.* 1647.
[2] A survey of these views is given in A. Frolow, *Recherches sur la déviation de la IVe Croisade vers Constantinople*, Paris 1955.

used against the Christian East. A combination of circumstances facilitated this turn of events and contributed to the fact that the crusaders placed themselves at the service of Venice.

The crusaders assembled in Venice whence they were to be transported to Egypt in Venetian ships. As they were unable to meet the cost of the voyage, they agreed to the Doge's proposal that they should make good the deficiency by assisting Venice to recapture Zara which had deserted to Hungary. This was the first diversion from the real objective of the crusade. To serve Venetian aims the crusaders fought against Christian Hungary, though the king of Hungary had himself taken the cross, and in November 1202 Zara was stormed, despite the fact that the population of the city had fixed crucifixes on to the walls. This episode was indeed a fitting prelude to the crusade.

The second diversion soon followed on the first, and it was connected with Alexius Angelus, the son of Isaac II. The young prince had managed to escape from the dungeon where he and his blinded father were imprisoned. He hastened to the West to try to get help, and after a fruitless interview with Innocent III he reached the court of Philip of Swabia. Philip, who was attempting as far as he could to pursue the policy of Henry VI, was more than ready to support the claims of his brother-in-law to the Byzantine throne. He was prevented from direct intervention himself by troubles at home, but he entered into negotiation with the crusaders and the Venetians in the hope of getting their support for the restoration of Isaac II and his son.

Nothing could have been more welcome to the Doge than this request, and the leader of the crusade, Boniface of Montferrat, whose family had close ties with the East, was equally ready to seize the opportunity of interfering in Byzantine affairs. While the crusaders were wintering in captured Zara, messengers arrived from the German king and his protégé, and the alliance which both sides desired came into being. With all the liberality of a claimant to the throne, Alexius promised vast sums of money to the crusaders and to Venice, conciliated the Pope by holding out the possibility of the reunion of the Churches and promised that once he was restored to the imperial throne he would give his active support to the crusade, as soon as it was resumed. The great majority of the crusaders were won over by the persuasive arguments of Dandolo and Boniface: the temptation was great and consciences were satisfied by the assurance that the crusade would be continued after the expedition against Constantinople and with the added resources promised by the Byzantine claimant. Alexius joined the crusaders in Zara, and in May 1203 in Corfu the arrangements for the diversion of the crusade were agreed upon. By 24 June the crusading fleet appeared off the Byzantine capital, 'the queen of all cities'.

After the capture of Galata, the boom which barred the entry to the Golden Horn was broken and the ships of the crusaders forced their way into the harbour, and at the same time the city walls were attacked from the land side. The Byzantine garrison, and particularly the Varangian guard, offered desperate resistance, but Constantinople fell on 17 July 1203. The miserable Emperor Alexius III had fled with the imperial treasure and the crown jewels. The blind Isaac II was restored to the throne and his son Alexius IV, the crusaders' protégé, was crowned co-Emperor. A Byzantine government still existed in Constantinople, but only by the grace of the crusaders who were encamped outside the walls. This grace did not last long, for it soon became clear that Alexius IV was in no position to keep the promises which he had made in Zara and Corfu. Alexius now found himself between the devil and the deep sea: the crusaders and the Venetians demanded prompt payment and callously rejected all appeals for a respite, while the Byzantine populace turned against the Emperor who had brought the crusaders into the country and sub-jected both himself and his people to the Latins. At the end of January 1204 a revolt broke out in Constantinople and Alexius IV lost not only the throne which he had gained at such great cost, but his own life. His father died in prison soon afterwards. The imperial throne went to Alexius V Ducas Murtzuphlus, the son-in-law of Alexius III and husband of Eudocia, formerly the wife of the Serbian ruler.

Once more the anti-Latin element had won the day in Byzantium, but its triumph only hastened the final act of the tragedy. The crusaders prepared for a new battle against the Byzantine capital, with the intention of once again taking Constantinople, only this time not in order to set up another Byzantine régime, but to establish their own rule on the ruins of the Byzantine Empire. In March, beneath the walls of the Byzantine capital, the crusaders and Venice drew up a treaty with detailed provision for the partition of the conquered Empire and the foundation of a Latin Empire in

Figure 57: *Church of St. Mark's, Venice.* Exterior, west façade from above. Following the sack of Constantinople by the Fourth Crusade in 1204, much of the booty found its way to Venice, and in particular to St. Mark's, which is adorned inside and out with Byzantine spoils. Visible in this view, among later accretions, are columns, capitals, and sculptures from Constantinople, including the four gilded bronze horses above the main portal. Photo: Osvaldo Böhm, Venice.

Figure 58-A: *Ring of Admiral Michael Stryphnos.* Gold, with cloisonné enamel in pink, turquoise, green, red, and blue, Constantinople, late 12th century. On the bezel, a bust of the Virgin, with Her monogram and the inscription, "Mother of God, help thy servant," which is continued on the hoop, "Michael the Admiral Stryphnos." As Admiral of the Byzantine fleet, Stryphnos used his office for personal gain, and was blamed for the fleet's poor condition at the time of the Fourth Crusade. Diam. ⅞". Dumbarton Oaks Collections, Washington, D.C. Photo: Dumbarton Oaks Collections.

Figure 58-B: *Alabaster Paten.* White alabaster, gold, silver, and enamel, Constantinople, 11th century. This 6-lobed alabaster paten holds an enameled bust of Christ, with a metal rim adorned with cabochon jewels. Probably part of the booty from the Fourth Crusade, it is now in the Treasury of St. Mark's, Venice. Diam. 13¼". Photo: Hirmer Fotoarchiv, Munich.

Constantinople.[1] The storm then broke with the inevitable result: on 13 April 1204 the Byzantine capital fell to the superior forces of its enemy. The conquerors entered Constantinople. And so the city which had remained inviolate since the days of Constantine the Great, which had withstood the powerful onslaughts of Persians and Arabs, of Avars and Bulgars, now became the prey of the crusaders and the Venetians. For three days long pillage and massacre reigned in the city. The priceless treasures of what was then the greatest centre of civilization in the world were squandered among the conquerors and many were destroyed in sheer barbarism. 'Since the creation of the world such a vast quantity of booty had never before been taken from one city', wrote the historian of the fourth crusade.[2] 'Even the Saracens are merciful and kind' in comparison to these creatures 'who bear the cross of Christ upon their shoulders', declared a Byzantine writer.[3] The division of the booty was followed by the division of the Byzantine Empire: this set the seal on its collapse, and for more than half a century Byzantium had to undertake its work of reconstruction in the outlying provinces of the Empire.

[1] Tafel and Thomas I, 464–88.
[2] Villehardouin, *La conquête de Constantinople*, ed. E. Faral, t. II (1939), 52: 'Et bien tesmoigne Joffrois de Vilehardoin li mareschaus de Champaigne a son escient par verté, que, puis que li siecles fu estorez, ne fu tant gaainié en une ville'.
[3] Nic. Choniates 761–2. The Metropolitan of Ephesus, Nicholas Mesarites, was another eyewitness who describes the excesses of the crusaders in Constantinople in the funeral oration on his brother John, ed. Heisenberg, 'Neue Quellen' I, 41 ff.

VII

Latin Rule and the Restoration of the Byzantine Empire (1204–82)

SOURCES

NICETAS CHONIATES describes the opening years of the Latin rule to 1206.[1] The historian who really deals with the Byzantine Empire of Nicaea is George Acropolites (1217–82), who made his mark both as statesman and scholar. He was originally an older school-fellow, and then later the tutor, of the heir to the throne, Theodore II Lascaris, and in 1246 he became λογοθέτης γενικοῦ, and afterwards Grand Logothete; he attended the Council of Lyons as the representative of the Emperor and leader of the Byzantine delegation. This well-informed contemporary wrote a χρονικὴ συγγραφή in which he gives a clear description of events from the capture of Constantinople by the Latins to the Byzantine reconquest of the imperial city (1203–61).[2] Of Acropolites' other works, the funeral oration on John III Vatazes is of special historical significance.[3] The chronicle of Theodore Scutariotes of Cyzicus is a compilation made after 1282 and it extends from the creation to the reconquest of Constantinople in 1261. The pre-Comnenian period is treated quite briefly, while the main part of the work consists of excerpts from Nicetas Choniates and Acropolites, but the section which is derived from Acropolites contains many additions which give the chronicle its real value as a source.[4] The work of Acropolites is continued in the highly important history of George Pachymeres (1242 to c. 1310) who has been described by Krumbacher as the greatest Byzantine scholar of the thirteenth century. The work

---

[1] Cf. above, p. 351 f., on both the history and the occasional writings of Nicetas Choniates, which belong in part to the period after 1204, as also for the letters and writings of Michael Choniates.

[2] Critical edition by A. Heisenberg, *Georgii Acropolitae Opera* I, Leipzig 1903.

[3] ed. Heisenberg, *Opera* II, 12–29.

[4] The compilation was edited as an independent anonymous work by Sathas, Μεσαιωνικὴ βιβλ. VII (1894), 1–556, and since then has been known by scholars as the *Synopsis Sathas*. The identification with Theodore Scutariotes was made by A. Heisenberg, *Analekta, Mitt. aus. italien. Hss. byz. Chronographen* (1901), 3 ff. The additions to Acropolites are given by Heisenberg in his edition of this author, I, 275 ff.

covers the period 1255–1308 and gives the most detailed, and the only contemporary, historical picture of the stirring reign of Michael VIII Palaeologus. Pachymeres' writing is characterized by a strong emphasis on the Greek Orthodox point of view and by an uncompromising repudiation of the union with Rome, together with that tendency to indulge in theological discussion which remained a mark of later Byzantine historians in the Paleologian period. The encyclopedic scholar Nicephorus Gregoras (1295–1359) wrote a history from 1204–1359, which will be discussed more fully in the next section. It gives a brief survey of the period of the Nicaean Empire and the first decades of the restoration, and although this is not the work of a contemporary, and is only intended to be in the nature of an introduction, it contains extremely valuable material and forms a real addition to the accounts of Acropolites and Pachymeres. It would be going too far afield to cite here the Western sources for the period of the Latin Empire,[1] but the *Chronicle of the Morea* must be mentioned. This is the work of a hellenized Frank dating from the first half of the fourteenth century. It exists in verse in two vernacular Greek versions, as well as in French, Italian and Aragonese versions, and it is a mine of information on conditions in the Peloponnese under Frankish rule.[2]

The writings of Nicholas Mesarites considerably add to our knowledge of political, and particularly ecclesiastical, conditions in the early years of the Latin Empire of Constantinople and the Byzantine Empire of Nicaea; the most important of these are the funeral oration on John Mesarites († 1207), the correspondence with the imperial family, e.g. the letters before the election of Michael Autoreianus as Patriarch and the coronation of Theodore Lascaris as Emperor in 1208 and the accounts of the negotiations with the representatives of the Roman Church in 1206 and 1214–15.[3] The learned Nicephorus Blemmydes, tutor of George Acropolites and of Theodore II Lascaris, left scholarly and theoretical works, together with some writings of a more practical nature, including two autobiographies composed in 1264 and 1265. These last are full of self-

[1] Cf., for instance, the information in L. Bréhier, *L'Église et l'Orient au Moyen Âge* (1921), 1 ff. and 114 f.

[2] The Greek versions are edited by J. Schmitt, *The Chronicle of Morea*, London 1904; the Italian version, *Cronaca di Morea*, by C. Hopf, *Chroniques gréco-romanes*, Berlin 1873; the French by J. Longnon, *Livre de la Conqueste de la Princée de l'Amorée*, Paris 1911; the Aragonese by A. Morel-Fatio, *Libro de los Fechos et Conquistas del Principado de la Morea*, Geneva 1885; English trans. H. E. Lurier, New York 1964.

[3] ed. with commentary by Heisenberg, 'Neue Quellen' I–III.

appreciation with little concern for historical events in general, but all the same they are of some value as reflecting contemporary conditions in the Church and at court.[1] Blemmydes' letters to Theodore II Lascaris and the treatise on the duties of a ruler dedicated to this Emperor are also worth studying.[2] On the other hand, his poems in 'political' verse are of little value.[3] A number of Theodore II Lascaris' letters have survived and in spite of their rhetorical character provide important historical evidence.[4] Other writings of special value among the numerous literary products of this Emperor[5] are the obituary oration on Frederick II,[6] the encomium on John III Vatatzes[7] and the eulogy on the city of Nicaea.[8] The engagement of John Vatatzes to Constance-Anna and the coronation of the young Hohenstaufen princess are described in the poems of the chartophylax Nicholas Irenicus, which throw interesting light on the history of Byzantine court ceremonial.[9] The four Greek letters of Frederick II to John III Vatatzes and the Despot Michael II of Epirus are of considerable significance for Frederick's relations with Byzantium.[10] Our information about the Epirote state is unfortunately extremely inadequate and for the most part is coloured by the views of the Nicaean historians. Apart from these scanty and strongly prejudiced accounts, there are important, though sparse sources of information in the documents of the Epirote

[1] A. Heisenberg, *Nicephori Blemmydae curriculum vitae et carmina*, Leipzig 1896; the Prolegomena gives a detailed account of the life and writings of Blemmydes.

[2] ed. K. Emminger, *Studien zu den griechischen Fürstenspiegeln I. Zum* ἀνδριὰς βασιλικός *des Nikephoros Blemmydes*, Gymnasial-Programm, Munich 1906. Cf. the critical comments on this by E. Kurtz, BNJ 3 (1922), 337 ff., and S. G. Mercati, BS 9 (1948), 182 ff.

[3] A. Heisenberg, *Niceph. Blemm.* 100-19; J. B. Bury, 'An unpublished poem of Nicephorus Blemmydes', BZ 10 (1901), 418 ff.

[4] N. Festa, *Theodori Ducae Lascaris Epistolae CCXVII*, Florence 1898. His most important correspondents are George Muzalon, N. Blemmydes and Acropolites. Blemmydes' own letters are printed in Append. III, pp. 290-329 (thirty-one to Theodore II and one each to the Despot Michael II of Epirus and the Patriarch Manuel).

[5] A list of the writings of Theodore II Lascaris is given by J. B. Papadopoulos, *Théodore II Lascaris, empereur de Nicée*, Paris 1908, pp. ix ff.

[6] ed. J. B. Papadopoulos, Appendice, pp. 183-9.

[7] Some extracts are published by F. Uspenskij, 'O rukopisjach istorii Nikity Akominata v parižskoj nacion. bibl., (The manuscripts of the History of Nicetas Acominatus in the Bibliothèque Nationale, Paris), ZMNP 194 (1877), 76. The contents of the oration are expounded in detail by M. Andreeva, 'A propos de l'éloge de l'empereur Jean III Batatzès par son fils Théodore II Lascaris', *Annales de l'Inst. Kondakov* 10 (1938), 133 ff.

[8] L. Bachmann, *Theodori Ducae Lascaris imperatoris in lauden Nicaeae urbis oratio*, Rostock 1847. There is a detailed analysis of an unedited speech on the duties of subjects towards their ruler by E. Lappa-Zizicas, 'Un traité inédit de Théodore II Lascaris', *Actes du VIe Congrès Internat. d'Études Byz.* I (1950), 199 ff.

[9] ed. with commentary by Heisenberg, 'Palaiologenzeit' 97 ff.

[10] Miklosich-Müller III, 68-76; critical edition with many emendations and detailed commentary by N. Festa, 'Le lettere greche di Federigo II', *Archivio storico italiano*, ser. V, t. 13 (1894), 1-34.

rulers[1] as well as in certain collections of letters. The situation in Epirus under Michael I and Theodore Angelus Ducas Comnenus are revealed in the writings and correspondence of John Apocaucus, Metropolitan of Naupactus.[2] The rich literary remains of the learned canonist Demetrius Chomatianus, Archbishop of Ochrida,[3] provide important evidence for internal conditions in Epirus as well as on Epirote-Nicaean and Graeco-Slav relations during the first half of the thirteenth century. Two letters should be especially noted—that of 1220 in which Chomatianus vigorously protests against St. Sava's elevation to the Serbian Archbishopric, and that of 1223 when he refutes the charges brought against him by the Nicaean Patriarch Germanus in the matter of his coronation of Theodore Angelus.[4] The typicon of Michael VIII Palaeologus of 1282 for the monastery of St. Demetrius in Constantinople is prefaced by a kind of imperial autobiography.[5] In this autobiography, in which he shows some skill as an author, the Emperor lays great emphasis on the services he has rendered and the success he has achieved, while he naturally passes over in silence his failures and the darker side of his life. The work describes the events of the turbulent reign of Michael VIII from his own point of view and is of particular interest for the assessment of his personality. The typicon of Michael VIII for the monastery of the

[1] A list of the fifteen known documents (in part surviving only in a Latin trans.) of the Epirote rulers with valuable comments is given by P. Lemerle, 'Trois actes du despote d'Epire Michel II concernant Corfou', Προσφορὰ εἰς Στ.Π. Κυριακίδην (1953), 407 ff. Cf. also idem, 'Le privilège du despote d'Epire Thomas I pour le Vénitien Jacques Contareno', BZ 44 (1951), 389 ff.; M. Marković, 'Vizantiske povelje Dubrovačkog arhiva' (Byzantine documents in the archives of Dubrovnik), *Zbornik radova Viz. Inst.* 1 (1952), 205 ff.

[2] V. G. Vasiljevskij, 'Epirotica saeculi XIII', VV 3 (1896), 233–99; S. Pétridès, 'Jean Apokaukos, lettres et autres documents inédits', *Izv. Russk. Archeol. Inst. v. Konstantinopole* 14 (1909), 69–100; Papadopulos-Kerameus, Ἰωάννης Ἀπόκαυκος καὶ Νικήτας Χωνιάτης, Τεσσαρακονταετηρὶς τῆς καθηγεσίας Κ. Ε. Κόντου (1909), 379–83. Cf. also M. Wellnhofer, *Johannes Apokaukos, Metropolit von Naupaktos in Aetolien (c. 1155–1233). Sein Leben und seine Stellung im Despotate von Epiros unter Michael Dukas und Theodoros Komnenos*, Freising 1913.

[3] J. B. Pitra, *Analecta sacra et classica specilegio Solesmensi parata* VI (1891). This material has recently been excellently dealt with by D. Angelov, 'Prinos kům narodnostnite i pozemelni otnošenjia v Makedonija (Epirskija despotat) prez půrvata četvŭrt na XIII venk' (A contribution to the study of racial and agrarian conditions in Macedonia (despotate of Epirus) in the first quarter of the thirteenth century), *Izv. na kamarata na nar. kultura* IV, 3 (1947), 1–46. Cf. also M. Drinov, 'O nekotorych trudach Dimitrija Chomatiana, kak istoričeskom materiale' (On certain writings of Demetrius Chomatianus as historical evidence), VV 1 (1894), 319–40; 2 (1895), 1–23.

[4] Letter to the Patriarch Germanus in Pitra, Nr. 114, pp. 487–98; new edition of the protest to St. Sava with Serbian trans. in my study, 'Pismo Dimitrija Homatijana sv. Savi' (Demetrius Chomatianus' letter to St. Sava), *Sveto-Savski Zbornik* II (1938), 91–113.

[5] New edition, with a French translation, H. Grégoire, 'Imperatoris Michaelis Palaeologi de vita sua', B 29/30 (1959/60), 447–76.

Archangel Michael on Mt. Auxentius in Asia Minor also contains in its introduction certain details on the Emperor's life.[1] It is not possible to cite here all the numerous Greek and Latin writings on the question of ecclesiastical union. Nor can collections of documents be mentioned here in detail. On the imperial documents cf. Dölger, *Regesten* III, 1204–82 (1932), and on other documents cf. above, p. 319, note 1. Michael VIII's *prostagma* of November 1272 should, however, be specially noted; this defines the rights of Andronicus II, who had been crowned co-Emperor, and contains information of special importance for the internal history of the Byzantine Empire.[2]

1. THE DEVELOPMENT OF A NEW POLITICAL SYSTEM

General bibliography: Gerland, *Lat. Kaiserreich*; Miller, *Latins*; idem, 'The Empire of Nicaea and the Recovery of Constantinople', CMH IV (1923); idem, 'Greece and the Aegean under Frank and Venetian Domination (1204–1571)', ibid.; idem, *Essays on the Latin Orient,* Cambridge 1921; D. M. Nicol, 'The Fourth Crusade and the Greek and Latin Empires, 1204–61', CMH IV, Pt I (2nd. ed., 1966); K. M. Setton, 'The Latins in Greece and the Aegean from the Fourth Crusade to the end of the Middle Ages', ibid.; M. Dinić, 'The Balkans 1018–1499', ibid.; F. Taeschner, 'The Turks and the Byzantine Empire to the end of the thirteenth century', ibid.; Lognon, *Empire latin:* Kretschmayr, *Venedig* I and II; Diehl, *Venise*; Heyd, *Commerce du Levant* I; Gardner, *The Lascarids*; Andreeva, *Očerki*; Meliarakes, Ἱστορία; I. Romanos, Περὶ τοῦ Δεσποτάτου τῆς Ἠπείρου, Korfu 1895; D. M. Nicol, *The Despotate of Epiros,* Oxford 1957; Fallmerayer, *Geschichte des Kaisertums von Trapezunt,* Munich 1827; W. Miller, *Trebizond, the Last Greek Empire,* London 1926; F. Uspenskij, *Očerki iz istorii trapezuntskoj imperii* (Studies in the history of the Empire of Trebizond), Leningrad 1929; A. Vasiliev, 'The Foundation of the Empire of Trebizond', *Speculum* 11 (1936), 3–37; Runciman, *Crusades* III.; Setton, *Crusades,* II.

Seldom has history witnessed a proceeding so ruthlessly deliberate as the partitioning of the Byzantine Empire. A new political system had to be set up in full accordance with the treaty concluded between the crusaders and the Venetians under the walls of Constantinople in March 1204. The final decision to implement the agreement rested with the Doge Enrico Dandolo who had determined the events of recent years and had inspired the partition treaty. First,

[1] Cf. A. Dimitrievskij, *Opisanie liturg. rukopisej* (Description of liturgical manuscripts) I (1895), 769–94, and textual emendations given by Dölger, *Reg.* 2065.
[2] ed. with commentary by Heisenberg, 'Palaiologenzeit' 33 ff.; cf. also Dölger, *Reg.* 1994.

an Emperor had to be elected, and to this end an electoral college of six Franks and six Venetians assembled in accordance with the stipulations of the treaty. Everything seemed to point to the election of the Margrave Boniface of Montferrat in virtue of his earlier role as leader of the crusaders' armies, his Byzantine connections and his personal qualities. The Doge, however, preferred a less prominent figure and since the Frankish camp was rent by factions, whilst the Venetians formed a united bloc, he was able to secure the election of Count Baldwin of Flanders. The latter was crowned Emperor of the Latin Empire of Constantinople in Hagia Sophia on 16 May. Meanwhile, the Venetian Thomas Morosini became head of St. Sophia and first Latin Patriarch of Constantinople, for according to the terms of the treaty made in the previous March, if the Emperor was elected from amongst the body of knights, then the new Patriarch of Constantinople was to be chosen by the Venetians.

As Emperor of the Latin Empire Baldwin was to receive one-quarter of the entire imperial territory; of the remaining three-quarters one half was to go to the Venetians and the other half was to be distributed amongst the knights as imperial fiefs. Baldwin was assigned Thrace and the north-west region of Asia Minor, so that his territory included land both sides of the Bosphorus and the Hellespont. The Emperor also got several Aegean islands, including Lesbos, Chios and Samos. Boniface of Montferrat was to be compensated with territory in Asia Minor, but he preferred possessions in the European part. After violent quarrels and disputes, he seized Thessalonica and established a kingdom which included the neighbouring territories of Macedonia and Thessaly.

It was the Venetians who derived the greatest benefit from the undertaking and, indeed, the growing power of Venice rested on the appropriation of the most important harbours and islands. The maritime republic renounced any direct sovereignty over the territories of Epirus, Acarnania, Aetolia and the Peloponnese which had been assigned to her, and was content to occupy the ports of Coron and Modon in the Peloponnese and somewhat later Dyrrachium and Ragusa on the Adriatic coast as well (1205). Venice also took over the Ionian islands, Crete (originally granted to Boniface of Montferrat), most of the islands of the Archipelago including Euboea, Andros and Naxos, and the most important ports on the Hellespont and the Sea of Marmora, Gallipoli, Rhadestus and Heraclea, as well as Adrianople in the interior of imperial Thrace. Like the territories of the Empire, Constantinople itself was also partitioned: Venice received three-eighths, whilst five-eighths of the capital remained for the Emperor. Thus the Doge justifiably styled himself 'lord of a quarter and of a half (of a quarter) of the Roman Empire'; and whilst the Frankish princes were obliged to take an oath of fealty to the Emperor of Constantinople, Dandolo, as the treaty expressly stipulated, was exempt from any feudal obligation. A Venetian colonial empire had thus grown up in the East. The Venetians commanded the entire sea route from their own native city to Constantinople; they controlled the straits and the gateway to Constantinople, and in Constantinople itself they owned three-eighths of the city, together with Hagia Sophia.

In comparison with this vast expansion of power the weakness of the loosely co-ordinated Frankish rule seems all the more pitiful. A typical feudal structure, the Latin Empire was subdivided into numerous larger or smaller separate lordships. On the ruins of the Byzantine state there arose a complex, multiform system of fiefs.

In central and southern Greece important principalities sprang up which were only indirectly under the control of the Emperor Baldwin, for their rulers did not owe direct allegiance to the Emperor, but to the king of Thessalonica. Indeed, Boniface advanced from Thessalonica upon Athens, and transferred the suzerainty over Attica and Boeotia to the Burgundian, Otto de la Roche. The Peloponnese was similarly conquered with the support of king Boniface by William of Champlitte and Geoffrey of Villehardouin, the nephew of the historian. Here was established the French principality of Achaia or the Morea, the most remarkable of all the principalities which were set up in Byzantine territory, for it was entirely Western in its mode of life and at the same time reflected a clear-cut feudal differentiation of society. It was a part of France transplanted to Greek soil and it led its own way of life under William of Champlitte and later under the house of Villehardouin.

Although the political system of feudalism in the Western sense with its many and complex forms of vassalage was foreign to the Byzantine world, Byzantium had nevertheless sacrificed much of its former centralization, and in particular its entire economic and military systems had long rested on a feudal foundation. For centuries this process of feudalization had gradually increased in Byzantium: the economic structure and social conditions of the Byzantine Empire were no longer so very different from those of the

West, a fact which considerably facilitated the establishment of Latin control.

Much could be taken over unchanged;[1] and in actual fact there was no difference between the Byzantine *pronoia* and the Western *feudum*. The pronoiars were the important class in the country, and represented in effect the sole power with whom the conqueror had seriously to reckon. In the conquest of the Morea, about which we are best informed, opposition lasted as a rule only as long as the pronoiars resisted. They only surrendered without a struggle when confirmed in the holding of their *pronoiai*. On this condition, for the most part they readily surrendered.[2] Fundamentally, it only meant a change of suzerain. The position of the people also remained virtually the same, irrespective of whether they paid their dues to a Greek or Latin landlord.

But even so the Byzantine population tolerated the Latin dominion with extreme reluctance, not only on account of the arrogance of their conquerors, but also because of the rift between the two Churches of the victors and vanquished. The ecclesiastical subordination of the Greeks to the Papacy was formally achieved, though not by way of an agreed Church union as the Pope had hoped, but by the compulsion of conquest. Yet any real understanding between Greeks and Latins was more remote than ever. Foreign dominion served only to emphasize Byzantine awareness of their own cultural and religious way of life. Though many Byzantine feudal lords had found a place within the ruling system of their conquerors, and though the people, inwardly unreconciled, remained in their old homesteads, not a few of the Byzantine nobles left the territories in the possession of the Latins and fled to the unoccupied regions. With the support of the local population, these fugitives developed a new political life which saved Byzantium from destruction. In Asia Minor under Theodore Lascaris, a son-in-law of Alexius III Angelus, the Empire of Nicaea was established; in western Greece the principality of Epirus emerged under Michael Angelus, a cousin of the Emperors Isaac II and Alexius III.

Shortly before, but not as a result of the capture of Constantinople, the Empire at Trebizond had arisen on the south-east coast of the

---

[1] The information in the *Chronicle of the Morea* is particularly instructive in this respect. Cf. also Tafel and Thomas II, 57, 'Omnes debemus in suo statu tenere nihil ab aliquo amplius exigentes, quam quod facere consueverant temporibus graecorum imperatorum'.
[2] Cf. Ostrogorsky, *La féodalité* 55 ff.

Black Sea under the Grand Comneni Alexius and David, grandsons of Andronicus I.[1] After the fall of Andronicus I, Alexius and David were brought as children to the court of the Georgian royal house to which they were related. With effective support from the famous queen Thamar (1184-1212) they captured Trebizond in April 1204.[2] From there the younger brother, the bold and adventurous David, advanced westwards along the coast, occupied Sinope and finally brought Paphlagonia and the Pontine Heraclea under his sway. His further advance, however, was halted by Theodore Lascaris.

The Latin Empire fatally underestimated the significance of Asia Minor. When Boniface of Montferrat advanced on Thessalonica and ignored Asia Minor, it was here that the loyal Byzantine elements rallied round Theodore Lascaris. His first steps presented incredible difficulties. The former structure of the state had vanished and the formation of independent principalities was in full swing. Theodore Mancaphas had established himself as independent ruler in Philadelphia, Manuel Maurozomes in the Meander valley and Sabbas Asidenus in Sampson near Miletus.[3] David Comnenus was advancing along the coast from the east. The Latins now attempted to recover lost ground. Baldwin's brother, Henry of Flanders, and the feudal knights of Count Louis of Blois who was to have received Nicaea by the partition treaty, set out to conquer the territory of Asia Minor at the end of 1204. Before the Byzantines could establish a firm foothold here, or were in a position to organize themselves politically and militarily, they were compelled to offer battle to the superior Latin forces. Theodore Lascaris was defeated at Poimanenon, and after this most of the towns of Bithynia fell into the hands of the Latins. It looked as though the Byzantine cause was also lost in Asia Minor. At a critical moment, however, the Byzantines were unexpectedly saved by the disaster which overtook the Latin Empire in the Balkans.

---

[1] Cf. Vasiliev, 'Foundation' 3-37 (and his supplementary article 'Mesarites as a Source', *Speculum* 13 (1938), 180 ff.). On the title of the Emperors of Trebizond as Μεγάλοι Κομνηνοί cf. Dölger, BZ 36 (1936), 233, whose suggestion that it was a version of the Byzantine title of μέγας βασιλεύς is more convincing than the explanation that it was in contrast to the rulers of Epirus suggested by N. Jorga, *Revue Sud-Est europ.* 13 (1936), 176.

[2] On the role of Queen Thamar cf. Vasiliev, 'Foundation' 12 ff. His views supported by documentary evidence do not seem to me to be invalidated by the objections of Jorga, op. cit. 172 ff.

[3] On Sabbas cf. P. Orgels, 'Sabas Asidénos, dynaste de Sampson', B 10 (1935), 67 ff. On the identification of Sampson, which has been confused with Sampson (Amisus) on the Black Sea, cf. G. de Jerphanion, 'Σαμψών et Ἄμισος. Une ville à déplacer de neuf cents kilomètres', OCP 1 (1935), 257 ff.

The Byzantine landed aristocracy in Thrace had at first been prepared to recognize Latin suzerainty and to serve their new overlords, no doubt on the understanding that they retained their former possessions and their *pronoiai*. The short-sighted Latins presumptuously rejected the offer of the accommodating Greek magnates and believed, furthermore, that they could also afford to rebuff the powerful Bulgarian tzar who was ready to negotiate. The Greek aristocracy took umbrage, rebelled against Latin rule and summoned the tzar Kalojan to their aid, offering him their services and the imperial crown.[1] The revolt rapidly spread, and in the imperial Didymotichus, as well as in the Venetian Adrianople and in several other towns of Thrace, the Latin garrisons were massacred or forced to withdraw. Kalojan invaded Thrace, and made contact with the Latin forces near Adrianople. Here on 14 April 1205 the memorable battle was fought in which the Latin army of knights was routed by the Bulgarian and Cuman troops of Kalojan. The Emperor Baldwin himself was taken prisoner, never to return home again; many illustrious Frankish knights were killed, amongst them the claimant to Nicaea, Louis of Blois.[2] Thus one year after the capture of Constantinople the power of the Latins had collapsed. Theodore Lascaris now had a free hand, for the Latins withdrew from Asia Minor and only the town of Pegae remained in their possession.

In his struggle against the rival power of the Grand-Comneni and the local princes of Asia Minor, Theodore Lascaris had laid the firm foundations of his rule in western Asia Minor, and he now proceeded to organize the new Byzantine state with Nicaea as its centre. In externals he followed the pattern of old Byzantium in every detail. Administration, civil service and imperial household were revived on the old Byzantine principles.[3] The political and ecclesiastical traditions of the Byzantine Empire, which found their symbolical expression in the persons of the Emperor and Patriarch, were again renewed in Nicaea. In place of the title Despot which he had borne hitherto, Theodore assumed imperial dignity. The learned Michael Autoreianus was appointed Patriarch, and he crowned and anointed Theodore Emperor. Owing to the confused

---

[1] Nic. Choniates 791 and 808. Villehardouin II, 145 (ed. Faral). Cf. Gerland, *Lat. Kaiserreich* 41; Longnon, *Empire latin* 64 ff.; B. Primov, 'Grŭcko-bŭlgarski sŭjuz v načalo na XIII vek' (The Graeco-Bulgarian alliance at the beginning of the thirteenth century), *Istoričeski Pregled* 4 (1947), 22 ff.

[2] There is a detailed description of the battle of Adrianople in Gerland, *Lat. Kaiserreich* 46 ff., and Longnon, *Empire latin* 77 ff.

[3] On court life at Nicaea cf. Andreeva, *Očerki* 55 ff.

situation, preliminary negotiations had occupied considerable time, so that the choice of Patriarch took place only in the third week of Lent and the anointing of the Emperor during Holy Week in 1208.[1] Theodore had certainly regarded himself as Emperor before this, and had been recognized as such by his followers,[2] but only the solemn coronation and anointing by the Patriarch consecrated him and gave to his office its full imperial significance. As Basileus and Autocrator of the Romaioi, Theodore I Lascaris entered upon the succession of the Byzantine Emperors of Constantinople. He was now considered to be the sole legal Emperor of the Byzantines, and the Patriarch residing in Nicaea, who bore the title of the oecumenical Patriarch of Constantinople, was likewise considered to be the sole lawful head of the Greek Church. A Byzantine Emperor and an Orthodox Patriarch in Nicaea were now opposed to the Latin Emperor and Patriarch in Constantinople. Nicaea became the political and ecclesiastical centre of the Empire which had been driven from its age-long capital of Constantinople.

It was a matter of life and death to the Latin Empire to destroy this Greek state whose rise it had been unable to prevent. Baldwin had been replaced by his able brother Henry. First as regent, and then from 20 August 1206 as Emperor, Henry had ruled in Constantinople with considerable circumspection. To a large extent he restored Latin control over Thrace, for the Graeco-Bulgarian

---

[1] Heisenberg, 'Neue Quellen' II, 8 ff.

[2] B. Sinogowitz, 'Ueber das byzantinische Kaisertum nach dem Vierten Kreuzzuge (1204–1205)', BZ 45 (1952), 345 ff., convincingly demonstrates that it was not Theodore, but his brother Constantine Lascaris, who was proclaimed Emperor in St. Sophia on 13 April 1204 after Alexius V's flight and immediately before the entry of the crusaders into Constantinople (according to Nic. Choniates 756, 2). I had accepted the opposite interpretation of Dölger, *Reg.* III, 1, but now, like Dölger, *Deutsche Literaturzeit.* 74 (1953), 598, I agree with Sinogowitz' view which had already been put forward by earlier scholars (cf. esp. Andreeva, *Očerki* 5 f. and BS 4 (1932), 178). But unlike Dölger, op. cit., I cannot agree with Sinogowitz' hypothesis that Constantine Lascaris, whom Nicetas Choniates 756, 11, says had refused the crown, actually exercised the imperial office in Nicaea during the year 1204–5 and that Theodore Lascaris became Emperor in 1205 after the supposed death of his brother in battle against the Turks. The Greek sources give no more information about Constantine, but even Villehardouin (II, 130, ed. Faral), the only one who occasionally mentions him as fighting in Asia Minor, is very far from regarding him as the Emperor of the Greeks, and considers him rather as the faithful supporter of Theodore and 'one of the finest Greeks in Romania' (cf. also ibid. I, 168). In maintaining that Theodore Lascaris came to the throne in 1205 Sinogowitz mainly relies on Nicetas Choniates' oration on Theodore in which he mentions his anointing (Sathas, Μεσ. βιβλ. I, 113, 22). On the other hand it is known from Acropolites 11, 18 (ed. Heisenberg) that Theodore bore the title of Despot until his coronation by the Patriarch in 1208 and therefore was not proclaimed Emperor in 1205. But of course even before the coronation he was considered as the real ruler and it is perfectly natural for Acropolites 31, 22, to say that he reigned eighteen years, reckoning the commencement of his rule from 1204.

co-operation had been of short duration and Henry, in contrast to Baldwin, pursued a conciliatory policy towards the Greeks and was able to win over a section of the Greek nobility.[1]

At the end of 1206 Henry again invaded Asia Minor at the head of the Latin forces but, owing to renewed incursions by Kalojan, he was obliged to break off the struggle, and in the spring of 1207 he concluded a two-years' armistice with Theodore Lascaris. However, the Latin Empire was not threatened much longer by the Bulgar danger, for Kalojan perished in the siege of Thessalonica in October 1207. The Greek population of Thrace and Macedonia had had to suffer no less than the Latin population under the savage Bulgar attacks, and the Byzantines harboured bitter memories of the 'slayer of Romans', as Kalojan styled himself in imitation of Basil II, the 'slayer of Bulgars'. Yet the fact remains that it was Kalojan who had saved the nascent Byzantine Empire in Asia Minor from destruction.

The Nicaean Empire had not only to contend with Latin Constantinople, but also to endure a bitter struggle against the Sultanate of Iconium. The transference of the Byzantine centre to Asia Minor intensified the old Byzantine-Seljuq conflict, since it presented a serious obstacle to Seljuq penetration towards the sea coast. Through the mediation of Venice, the Sultan Ghijaseddin Kaj-Chusraw I concluded a secret treaty of alliance with the Latin Emperor in 1209.[2] On his side, Theodore Lascaris made contact with King Leo II of Lesser Armenia at Cilicia who likewise felt himself threatened by the Sultanate of Iconium.[3] A convenient excuse for making war on the young Greek Empire was provided for the Seljuqs by the former Emperor Alexius III who after a long stay on European soil now arrived at the court of Iconium. The Sultan could now disguise his plans for conquest under a veneer of legitimacy by demanding that Theodore Lascaris should abdicate in favour of his father-in-law. The battles fought round Antioch on the Meander were bitterly contested, and the extremely modest forces of the Nicaean Emperor, of which a small troop of 800 Latin mercenaries formed the core, suffered heavy casualties. None the less, he proved victorious by the spring of 1211.[4] The Sultan fell in battle, the ex-

---

[1] Cf. Gerland, *Lat. Kaiserreich* 82 ff.; Longnon, *Empire latin* 89 ff., 128 ff.

[2] The proof of this is given by Gerland, *Lat. Kaiserreich* 210 ff.

[3] Theodore I married a niece of Leo II in 1214, but the marriage was dissolved after a year. Cf. A. Heisenberg, 'Zu den armenisch-byzantinischen Beziehungen am Anfang des 13. Jahrhunderts', *S.B. d. Bayer. Akad.* 1929, fasc. 6.

[4] On the chronology cf. J. Longnon, 'La campagne de Henri de Hainaut en Asie Mineure en 1211', *Bull. de l'Acad. de Belgique* 34 (1948), 447.

Emperor Alexius III was captured and ended his days in a Nicaean monastery. The victory brought little in the way of territorial gain to the Empire of Nicaea, but its psychological effect was tremendous. The young Empire had entered the lists against the infidel in true Byzantine fashion and had won its spurs.

Next, the struggle against the Latins was renewed. Theodore Lascaris, who for some years had had a fleet at his disposal, had already been meditating an attack upon Constantinople.[1] In effect, only minor engagements in the western region of Asia Minor took place and in these the Latin Emperor was victorious. Henry won a battle on the Rhyndacus river (15 October 1211) and pushed forward to Pergamum and Nymphaeum.[2] But guerrilla warfare which occupied only small forces on each side proved indecisive. Both sides were exhausted, and at the end of 1214 a treaty which defined the frontiers between the Byzantine and Latin Empires was concluded at Nymphaeum. The Latins retained the north-west corner of Asia Minor as far as Adramyttium in the south and the rest, extending to the Seljuq frontier, was left to the Nicaean Empire.[3] So for the time being the two Emperors recognized each other's right to exist. Neither was strong enough to destroy his rival. A balance of power and relatively stable relationships were thus established.

This period of stabilization brought prosperity to the Empire of Nicaea, while after the death of Henry in 1216 Latin Constantinople increasingly declined. Meanwhile, peace was maintained between the Latins and the Nicaeans. Theodore Lascaris took as his third wife the Empress Yolande's daughter Mary, a niece of the two first Latin Emperors. In August 1219 he concluded a treaty with the Venetian podestà of Constantinople which granted freedom of trade and duty-free imports to the Venetians in the Nicaean Empire, as they had had in old Byzantium.[4] He did not hesitate to designate the Doge of Venice as 'Despot' and 'Dominator' of the quarter and the half-quarter of the Roman *imperium*, but described himself in the

---

[1] At least Henry accuses him of this intention in a letter sent to the West from the camp at Pergamon on 13 January 1212, Buchon, *Recherches et matériaux* II, 211 ff.

[2] Acropolites 27. Cf. also P. Lauer, 'Une lettre inédite d'Henri I d'Angre, empereur de Constantinople, aux prélats italiens (1213?)', *Mélanges Schlumberger* I (1924), 201; J. Longnon, op. cit. 442 ff. and *Empire latin* 127 f., though he appears to overstress the significance of Henry's victory.

[3] Acropolites 28. W. Ramsay, *Historical Geography of Asia Minor* (1890), 129 and 159; Gerland, *Lat. Kaiserreich* 218; Gardner, *The Lascarids* 84 ff.; Dölger, *Reg.* 1684; Longnon, *Empire latin* 128 and op. cit. 450 f. (who thinks the treaty was concluded at the beginning of December 1214).

[4] Zepos, *Jus* I, 481 f. (= Tafel and Thomas II, 205 ff.); Dölger, *Reg.* 1703.

inscription of this official document as 'Theodorus in Christo Deo fidelis Imperator et moderator Romeorum[1] et semper augustus Comnanus Lascarus'.

The Empire of Nicaea was also regarded by the southern Slavs as the heir of old Byzantium and the centre of Greek orthodoxy. Nemanja's son Sava, ignoring the Archbishopric of Ochrida to which the Serbian Church had hitherto been subordinated, turned to Nicaea, and in 1219 was consecrated autocephalous Archbishop of Serbia by the Patriarch of Nicaea. Two years earlier his brother Stephen the First-Crowned had received the royal crown from the hands of Rome.[2] The achievement of ecclesiastical independence was of immense advantage to the young Serbian kingdom, and it was also of equal benefit to the Empire of Nicaea. Recognition of the prerogatives of its Patriarch, who had consecrated the first Archbishop of Serbia, and the fact that his name was given the first place in the prayers of the autocephalous Serbian Church,[3] were signs of the growing prestige of the Nicaean Empire.

An important consequence of the Nicaean-Latin understanding was the collapse of the power of the Grand Comneni on the shores of the Black Sea. David Comnenus had become the vassal of the Emperor of Constantinople and had carried on the struggle against the Nicaean ruler with Latin support, but left to his own resources he was now unable to oppose the Emperor of Nicaea. In 1214 Theodore Lascaris annexed all his possessions west of Sinope, together with Heraclea and Amastris, thus establishing himself on the south coast of the Black Sea. The Seljuqs now intervened. They occupied Sinope, defeated and captured the Emperor Alexius Comnenus and then reinstated him on the throne of Trebizond as vassal of the Sultan of Iconium.[4] The Empire of Trebizond was reduced to a narrow strip of land and was cut off from western Asia Minor by the Seljuq occupation of Sinope. The political, economic and social development of the Empire of Trebizond is in

---

[1] So the *initulatio* runs; the signature gives 'Grecorum'.

[2] Cf. Jireček, *Geschichte* I, 296 ff., who cites evidence in proof of this. D. Anastasijević, 'Je li Sv. Sava krunisao Prvovenčanog?' (Did St. Sava crown Stephen the First-Crowned?), *Bogoslovlje* 10 (1935), 211 ff., assumes that Stephen having been crowned by the papal legates was then crowned again by his brother Sava which in my view does not seem very probable. But Dj. S. Radojičić, *XII Congrès Intern. des Ét. Byz., Rapports complémentaires*, Belgrade-Ochrida 1961, 102, returns to this view.

[3] Domentijan (ed. Daničić) 221. See S. Stanojević, 'Sveti Sava i nezavisnost srpske crkve' (St. Sava and the independence of the Serbian Church), *Glas Srpske akad. nauka* 161 (1934).

[4] Cf. Vasiliev, 'Foundation' 25 ff.

itself of real historical interest; but this insignificant and remote Empire had little further influence upon the general development of Byzantium. For a quarter of a millennium it survived in isolation, untouched by the struggle for Constantinople, indifferent to the restoration of the Byzantine Empire, and it survived the final downfall of Byzantium by several years.[1]

The principality of Epirus assumed far greater significance.[2] The energetic and efficient Michael Angelus had overrun the territory between Dyrrachium and the Gulf of Corinth and with Arta as his base he exercised a strict military control. The Epirote state, including Epirus, Acarnania and Aetolia, set itself up as an independent Byzantine principality in opposition to the Latin kingdom of Thessalonica in the east, to the Venetians on the Adriatic and the Slavs in the north and north-east. Like the Empire of Nicaea in Asia Minor, Epirus in the Balkan peninsula became a centre of Byzantine cultural traditions and a political rallying point. As in the case of Nicaea, a period of political development and internal consolidation was followed by an era of victorious expansion. The final goal envisaged by both these Greek centres was the re-conquest of Constantinople and the restoration of the Byzantine Empire.

About 1215, Michael Angelus, founder of the state of Epirus, was succeeded on the throne by his half-brother Theodore. After the fall of Constantinople, the latter had spent some considerable time in Nicaean territory with Theodore I Lascaris and only returned to the Epirote court in Arta at his brother's request. He had sworn— or at least so Nicaean historiography affirms—an oath of fealty to the Emperor of Nicaea, thus acknowledging his supremacy.[3] A conflict

---

[1] Cf. W. Miller, *Trebizond, the Last Greek Empire*, London 1926. F. Uspenskij, *Očerki iz istorii trapezuntskoj imperii* (Studies in the history of the Empire of Trebizond), Leningrad 1929. The documents of the monastery of Vazelon are particularly important for economic and social conditions, Th. Ouspensky et V. Bénéchévitch, *Actes de Vazélon*, Leningrad 1927.

[2] It has previously been general to speak of the 'Despotate' of Epirus, since it was generally believed that all the rulers of the Epirote state, beginning with its founder Michael Angelus, bore the title of despot, and that this title belonged to the head of the state of Epirus as such. But recently L. Stiernon, 'Les origines du despotat d'Épire' REB 17 (1959), 90 ff. (cf. also *XIIe Congrès Intern. des Ét. Byz. Resumés des Communications*, Belgrade-Ochrida 1961, 100 f.), and Ferjančić, *Despoti*, 49 ff., have independently provided compelling proof that Michael Angelus never used the title of despot (nor did his successor Theodore) and consequently cannot have founded a 'despotate'. In addition, Ferjančić's valuable book makes it clear that the title of despot was never linked with the rule of a particular region, either here or anywhere else in Byzantium, and that neither the Epirote region nor any other part of Byzantium ever possessed the particular status of a 'despotate'.

[3] Acropolites 24 f. Meliarakes, Ἱστορία 53 f. doubts the reliability of this account; Gardner, *The Lascarids*, 91, argues that it is reliable.

between these two Byzantine centres was unavoidable, for both were inspired by the same ideals and pursued the same goal. The struggle broke out with full intensity, in fact, during the reign of the powerful and ambitious Theodore, who with proud self-confidence assumed the three imperial names of Angelus, Ducas and Comnenus.[1] He even surpassed his predecessor in daring and vigour, and under his direction the western Greek principality experienced a period of stormy ascendancy.

The first act which spread his fame beyond the frontiers of the state of Epirus was his bold attack upon the crowned Latin Emperor, Peter of Courtenay, the husband of Yolande, the sister of Baldwin and Henry. Called to the throne on the death of Henry, Peter set out from France to Rome where the Pope crowned him, not, indeed, in St. Peter's where the German Emperors were crowned, but in the more modest church of San Lorenzo. From Rome, he and his entourage then reached the neighbourhood of Dyrrachium, and from here proceeded to Constantinople. He fell, however, into the hands of Theodore in the mountain passes of Albania and ended his life a prisoner in Epirus. His wife Yolande took over the regency in Constantinople, and on her death in 1219 the imperial crown of Constantinople devolved upon her feeble son Robert.

Meanwhile, Theodore Angelus Ducas Comnenus embarked upon a large-scale campaign against the Latins. First he turned his attention to the neighbouring kingdom of Thessalonica. Circumstances favoured him, as the kingdom, whose founder Boniface of Montferrat had fallen in the struggle against the Bulgars in 1207, had been paralysed by the return of many of its knights to the West, and it lacked the solid support which Latin Constantinople had provided in Henry's lifetime. Thus it fell a prey to the bold ruler of Epirus who entered Thessalonica towards the end of 1224 after a lengthy siege.[2] One of the crusader states on Byzantine territory had ceased to exist. The power of Theodore Angelus extended from the Adriatic to the Aegean and it included the original territory of the Epirote state, together with Thessaly and much of Macedonia.

[1] Michael was an illegitimate, Theodore a legitimate, son of the Sebastocrator John Angelus (on him cf. my study 'Vozvyšenie roda Angelov' (The rise of the Angeli family), *Jubil. Sbornik Russk. Archeol. Obŝt. v. Belgrade* 1936, 111 ff.). He may well have taken the name of Ducas from his mother, and he called himself Comnenus after his grandmother Theodora, the daughter of Alexius I.

[2] J. Longnon, 'La reprise de Salonique par les Grecs en 1224', *Actes du VIe Congrès Intern. d'Etudes byzantines* I (1950), 141 ff., has demonstrated from western sources that Thessalonica was not taken in 1222 or 1223, but towards the end of 1224.

After this spectacular success, Theodore assumed the imperial purple. He too now styled himself Basileus and Autocrator of the Romaioi, which meant that he claimed for himself the heritage of the Emperors of Byzantium and the leadership in the struggle for Constantinople, and thus stood in open opposition to the Empire of Nicaea. He was crowned and anointed Emperor by the learned Demetrius Chomatianus, Archbishop of Ochrida. Chomatianus had never forgiven the Nicaean Patriarchate for consecrating Sava Archbishop of Serbia, and he now proposed to pay back Nicaea in its own coin.[1]

Thus three Empires, one Latin and two Greek, had arisen on what had been Byzantine soil; in the background stood a fourth—the Empire of the Bulgarian tzars. Further developments in the Byzantine sphere were largely determined by the activities of these four powers.

2. THE RISE AND FALL OF EPIRUS: THE VICTORY OF NICAEA

General bibliography: see above, p. 422.

The downfall of the kingdom of Thessalonica had deprived the Latin Empire of its most important vassal state. The Empire of Constantinople, reduced to the territory in the neighbourhood of the capital, cut off from the Frankish principalities in Greece, internally exhausted and without a leader, was itself on the verge of collapse. On the other hand, the Byzantines were rapidly increasing in power in both Asia Minor and the Balkans, while Bulgaria was also experiencing a great revival. The life of the feeble Latin régime was only prolonged by disunity amongst its opponents—the rivalry of the two Greek Empires and the intervention of Bulgaria. Theodore I Lascaris, founder of the dynasty, bequeathed the imperial crown of Nicaea to his son-in-law John Ducas Vatazes, husband of the clever and cultured Irene. John III Vatatzes (1222-54) is undoubtedly the most important statesman of the Nicaean period and one of the most outstanding rulers of Byzantine history. In foreign and domestic politics he consolidated the work of his predecessor, thus raising the small Empire which had been almost reduced to the level of a province to the status of a great power. His achievement

[1] Cf. Chomatianus' letter of protest to Sava of May 1220, and his letter to the Patriarch Germanus in 1223 (for editions cf. above, p. 421, note 4).

was obviously facilitated by the weakness of the Latin Empire and the mistakes of his Greek and Bulgarian rivals.

In the early years of his reign the balance of power in Asia Minor had already decisively shifted in favour of Nicaea. The insurrection of the brothers of Theodore I, who attempted to deprive Vatazes of the crown, was defeated and turned to the advantage of the Emperor and his realm. At Poimanenon, where twenty years before Theodore Lascaris had succumbed to the Latins, John Vatatzes gained a victory over the Latin forces supporting the rival claimants, and thus he became master of the entire Latin territory in Asia Minor. By the treaty of 1225 the Latins lost everything in Asia Minor, except the coast opposite Constantinople together with the country round Nicomedia.[1] At the same time, the Nicaean fleet occupied the islands of Lesbos, Chios, Samos and Icaria; Rhodes also had later to acknowledge the suzerainty of the Emperor. The Nicaean Empire had thus consolidated its position on land and sea, and it began to encroach on European territory. An appeal by the population of Adrianople gave Vatatzes the excuse to despatch troops to Thrace. The imperial army occupied several coastal towns and entered Adrianople unopposed. It looked as though the restoration of Byzantine rule in Constantinople was imminent, since the Latin kingdom was not in a position to offer serious resistance. But at this point the plans of the Nicaean Emperor were scotched by his rival of western Greece.

Theodore Angelus marched from victory to victory. He not only controlled the territory of the former kingdom of Thessalonica, but by now a part of Thrace had also fallen into his hands, and he advanced on Adrianople and forced the troops of the Nicaean Emperor to withdraw. Confident of victory, he hastened towards Constantinople. He had come nearer to the coveted prize than John Vatatzes. But the Bulgarian tzar John Asen II also had the same goal in view. The reign of John Asen II (1218–41), son of Asen I, marks the zenith of the Second Bulgarian Empire. Like Symeon before him, Ivan Asen II aimed at nothing less than the foundation of a Bulgar-Byzantine *imperium* with its centre at Constantinople, and for a time he came within an ace of realizing his ambition. In 1228 the Latin Emperor Robert of Courtenay died and the imperial crown devolved upon his brother Baldwin II, a minor. In the absence of a leader and hard-pressed from without, a plan was

---

[1] Cf. Longnon, *Empire latin* 161 f.

devised in Constantinople to offer the regency to the Bulgarian ruler, for he alone seemed capable of saving the capital from Byzantine attack. The understanding between Asen II and the house of Courtenay, which sprang from their mutual kinship with the royal house of Hungary, was to be cemented by the betrothal of the young Latin Emperor to the tzar's daughter Helena. This projected marriage appeared to strengthen Asen's hand. John Asen, as a future father-in-law of an Emperor who was still a minor, already envisaged himself as the unchallenged master of Constantinople. But his plans conflicted with those of Theodore Angelus, who likewise believed Constantinople to be within his grasp. Theodore dissolved the alliance with Asen that had been directed against John Vatatzes, and he declared war on the Bulgarian ruler. His rashness proved to be his undoing. The army of the Emperor of Thessalonica was decisively defeated at Klokotnica on the Marica in the spring of 1230. Theodore himself was captured and blinded, and his swift rise to power came to a sudden end.

His brother Manuel, however, who succeeded him on the throne of Thessalonica, was able to maintain his suzerainty over Thessalonica itself and in Thessaly and Epirus, but this was only a shadow of the former power of Theodore. As claimant to Constantinople, the Empire of western Greece was now out of the running. Asen II had no difficulty in taking over the recent conquests of Theodore in Thrace and Macedonia, as well as a part of Albania, and he also supplanted the influence of the Empire of Thessalonica in Serbia, where Theodore's son-in-law Radoslav was overthrown in favour of his brother Vladislav, who had married a daughter of Asen II. It was not without reason that Asen II rightly claimed on an inscription that he had conquered all lands between Adrianople and Dyrrachium and that only Constantinople and the adjacent towns remained in the hands of the Franks. 'And even these are subject to my authority', he continued, referring to the minority of the Latin Emperor and the projected regency, 'for they have no Emperor but me, and they obey my will, for God has so ordained it.'[1]

It looked as though the battle of Klokotnica which had dashed the hopes of the Empire of western Greece was the herald of Bulgarian ascendancy. But Asen II's apparently unchallenged supremacy over

---

[1] Inscription of Asen II in the Church of the Forty Martyrs at Trnovo, reproduced in Uspenskij, *Izv. Russk. Archeol. Inst. v Konstantinopole* 7 (1901), Plate 5. Cf. also Asen II's *privilegium* to Dubrovnik, ed. G. Iljinskij, ibid. 25 ff., and I. Dujčev, *Iz starata bŭlgarska knižnina* (From Old Bulgarian literature), II, 42.

the Balkan peninsula was deceptive. It soon became clear that the real advantage from the battle went not to the Bulgarian tzar, but to the patient Nicaean Emperor, who had behaved throughout with both prudence and restraint. Asen's victory over Theodore liberated Nicaea from his rival of western Greece, but this victory did not bring the Bulgarian tzar any nearer to his goal. The prospect of Asen's regency lost its attraction for Latin Constantinople, which no longer had anything to fear from Theodore Angelus. And, indeed, with the recent increase in Bulgarian power the dangers inherent in the plan became all the more evident, and so the aged John of Brienne, titular king of Jerusalem, was elected Emperor. This led to a complete change in Asen's policy and he was forced to meet the challenge of Latin Constantinople by declaring war. He made contact with John Vatatzes and concluded with him a Graeco-Bulgarian alliance against the Latin Empire. Manuel of Thessalonica also joined the alliance, but played only a subordinate role.

Asen II's diplomatic *volte-face* necessitated a reorientation in ecclesiastical affairs. The union which Kalojan had concluded with Rome had failed to take root in Bulgaria. Yet even nominal subordination to the Roman Church was no longer acceptable to Asen as the initiator of an anti-Latin alliance of Orthodox rulers. It was essential for him to establish his own Orthodox Patriarchate in Trnovo, and to win the consent of Nicaea and the oriental Patriarchs. After lengthy negotiations, the leaders of Church and State in Nicaea agreed to sanction the establishment of the Bulgarian Patriarchate, and thus the Bulgarian Empire achieved ecclesiastical independence. The Bulgarian Patriarchate, like the autocephalous Serbian Arch-bishopric, recognized in the first instance, however, the primacy of the Patriarch of Nicaea, for it agreed to name the Byzantine Patriarch in the liturgy and to pay him church dues. The treaty of alliance was signed in the spring of 1235 in Gallipoli, recently captured by Vatatzes, and in Lampsacus the marriage was solemnized between the Emperor's son Theodore II Lascaris and the daughter of the Bulgarian tzar formerly intended for Baldwin II. Here the new authority of the head of the Bulgarian Church was also proclaimed with the consent of the eastern Patriarchs.[1]

[1] Cf. V. Vasiljevskij, 'Obnovlenie Bolgarskogo Patriaršestva pri care Ioanne Asene II v 1235 g.' (The restoration of the Bulgarian Patriarchate under the tzar John Asen II in 1235), ZMNP 238 (1885), 1–56, 206–24; P. Nikov, 'Cŭrkovnata politika na Ivan Asenja II' (The ecclesiastical policy of Ivan Asen II), *Bŭlg. istorič. bibl.* 3 (1930), 65–111. In spite of Dölger, *Reg.* 1730, it seems to me that Vasiljevskij has established that the initiative for the alliance came from Asen II. On this now cf. Zlatarski, *Istorija* III,

The allies immediately proceeded to lay siege to Constantinople by land and sea. Hostilities which had been broken off on account of the approaching winter were renewed in 1236. The invested capital held out with the support of Venetian sea power, but in spite of this the position of the Latins became so critical that Baldwin II left Constantinople to seek help from the West. Latin Constantinople was ultimately saved through disunity amongst the attackers. Once more the Bulgarian tzar changed his policy when he correctly, but belatedly, realized that the downfall of the Latin suzerainty would chiefly benefit the Nicaean Empire, which would be in reality a far greater rival to him than the exhausted Latin Empire. He therefore broke with Vatatzes, and in alliance with the Latins and the Cumans (who were pressing forward in the Balkans) he declared war on his former ally. Tzurulum, one of the main bases of Nicaean power in Thrace, was besieged by Bulgarians, Latins and Cumans. At this point, as the consequence of a severe emotional shock, Asen II's vacillating policy changed once more, but for the last time. An epidemic had broken out in Trnovo; the sudden death of his wife, of one of his sons, and of the Bulgarian Patriarch, seemed to the tzar to be a judgment of Heaven for his breach of faith with John Vatatzes. He withdrew from Tzurulum and made peace with the Nicaean Emperor at the end of 1237.[1] The temporary occupation of Tzurulum by Latin-Cuman troops made little difference to the course of events which now favoured Vatatzes. John Asen II died in 1241 and with the invasion of the Mongols Bulgarian power soon began to disintegrate.

John Vatatzes no longer had any serious rival: the reckless and excessive lust for conquest of the intrepid Emperor of Thessalonica was shattered; the strong, but spasmodic, bid for power by the Bulgarian tzar had run its course; the Latin Empire in its decline had long become a pawn in the policies of the neighbouring powers and survived only thanks to the dissension amongst its opponents. At last the Nicaean Emperor was destined to garner the fruits of his superior statesmanship, of his acumen, perseverance and circumspection. In 1242 he launched a campaign against Thessalonica where,

379 ff. St. Stanojević, 'Sv. Sava i proglas bugarske patrijaršije' (St. Sava and the establishment of the Bulgarian Patriarchate), *Glas Srpske Kralj. Akad.* 156 (1933), 173 ff., attributes the agreement of the eastern Patriarchs to the establishment of a Bulgarian patriarchate to the mediation of St. Sava, who during his second pilgrimage to the Holy Land in 1233–4 visited Jerusalem, Alexandria and Antioch and returned by way of Trnovo where he died on 14 January 1235. But cf. N. Radjočić, 'Sveti Sava', *Godišnjica* 44 (1935), 46.

[1] On the chronology cf. Dölger, *Reg.* 1758.

at the time, John ruled with the support of his father Theodore Angelus, who had been liberated by Asen II. On his victorious and rapid advance he was nearing the capital of western Greece, when the Mongol invasion of Asia Minor compelled him to withdraw and conclude peace. Though prematurely broken off, this campaign had a not unimportant consequence. The Empire of western Greece formally consented to withdraw from all further rivalry with the superior Nicaean Empire: the ruler of Thessalonica surrendered his imperial insignia and recognized the sovereign rights of the Nicaean Emperor, in return for which he was accorded the title of despot.[1]

The Mongol invasion roused the whole of eastern Europe and the Near East. Russia succumbed to the invaders and for more than two centuries was subject to the Tartars, who founded the so-called 'Golden Horde' on the lower reaches of the Volga and the Don. Poland, Silesia, Bohemia and Moravia, Hungary and the entire Danube basin, were devastated and the Tartars penetrated as far as the Adriatic coast. Withdrawing through the Balkan peninsula, they ravaged the southern Slav lands and compelled Bulgaria to pay tribute. At the same time they broke into the Near East with the same unparalleled ferocity. The very existence of the Sultanate of Iconium, the eastern neighbour of the Nicaean Empire, and of the small Empire of Trebizond was imperilled, and Nicaea itself feared for its safety. To meet the common danger John Vatatzes concluded an alliance with the Sultan of Iconium (1243).[2] But the small states of Asia Minor could not offer any serious resistance to an enemy whose power stretched from the Pacific to Central Europe. The Emperor of Trebizond, decisively defeated by the Mongols, became their tributary vassal, and even the Sultan of Iconium pledged himself to pay tribute. On these terms the Empire of Trebizond and the Sultanate of Iconium were permitted to eke out a miserable existence, for the Mongols were diverted from Asia Minor by more important ventures. The Nicaean Empire, however, emerged unimpaired, and even derived considerable benefit from the weakening of its eastern neighbours.

John Vatatzes was able to turn his attention once more to the Balkans, and with limited forces won a decisive victory over the Bulgarians and the Empire of western Greece in 1246. The Bulgarian

---

[1] Acropolites 67. Cf. Ferjančić, *Despoti* 62 f. Although John wore imperial insignia and, like Manuel, issued documents in red ink, in fact, as Ferjančić, op. cit. 58 f. and 62 f., shows, neither bore the title of Emperor.

[2] Dölger, *Reg.* 1776.

kingdom, hitherto the strongest power in the Balkans, but now a tributary of the Tartars and ruled by the sons of Asen II who were still minors, found itself in a hopeless position. The sudden death of the twelve-year-old Koloman (1241–46), who was succeeded by his still younger half-brother Michael (1246–56), served only to increase the general confusion. Unopposed, Vatatzes seized the territories which John Asen II had earlier snatched from the Empire of western Greece, and extended his sway in Thrace as far as the upper reaches of the Marica, and in Macedonia up to the Vardar. Then, with equally striking success he turned against Thessalonica where the feeble offspring of the blinded Theodore were little more than puppet-rulers on a tottering throne. Vatatzes entered Thessalonica unopposed in December 1246 with the support of a strong opposition party which eagerly looked forward to his arrival. Theodore himself was compensated with an estate near Vodena; his son Demetrius, the last ruler of Thessalonica (1244–6), was brought as a prisoner to Asia Minor. Henceforth Andronicus Paleologus was resident in Thessalonica as governor-general of the European possessions of the Nicaean Empire; his son, later the Emperor Michael Paleologus, took over command in Serres and Melnik.

Epirus, formerly the focus of the power of western Greece, had detached itself from Thessalonica shortly after the battle of Klokotnica and, together with Thessaly, preserved its independence under the Despot Michael II, an illegitimate son of Michael I Angelus. In order to avoid further complications Vatatzes concluded a treaty of friendship with Michael II and betrothed his grand-daughter Maria to Nicephorus, son and heir of Michael (1249). But under the influence of Theodore Angelus, whose restless spirit could not be curbed, Michael abandoned his ally and occupied several fortresses of the Nicaean Emperor in Macedonia. The armed conflict which followed turned out unfavourably for him; he was compelled to accept a dictated peace at the hands of the imperial ambassador in Larissa, whereby he ceded to the Nicaean Emperor not only the recently occupied cities, but also the west Macedonian territories won from the Bulgarians, together with the Albanian Kroja, and also surrendered to him his son Nicephorus. In exchange for recognition of the sovereignty of Nicaea, both father and son received from him the title of despot.[1] But Theodore Angelus was handed over, and he ended his tempestuous life in a Nicaean prison.

---

[1] Cf. Ferjančić, *Despoti* 63 ff.

John Vatatzes was in active contact with the two predominant powers of the West, the Papacy and the German Empire, and his relationship to Frederick II of Hohenstaufen, was particularly cordial. As the latter was in conflict with the Papacy and the former with the Latin Empire, the two rulers shared common ground, and finally concluded an alliance which was sealed by the marriage of John Vatatzes to Frederick's young daughter Constance after the death of his first wife Irene Lascaris. The letters of Frederick to John Vatatzes reveal sincere sympathy and admiration for the Greeks whom 'this so-called high priest (i.e. the Pope) dares to vilify as heretics, but who, in fact, have spread the Christian faith to all quarters of the earth'.[1] This alliance produced no concrete results, but doubtless enhanced the prestige of the Nicaean Empire.

Like almost every Byzantine Emperor of recent times, John Vatatzes negotiated for a union with the Church of Rome. He demanded of the Papacy the surrender of the Latin Empire as an essential preliminary. To begin with, the negotiations developed as fruitlessly as all previous attempts at union, and were further complicated by the understanding between the Greek Emperor and Frederick II. But after the death of the latter, and under the Pontificate of Innocent IV, the negotiations took a more favourable turn. As a clear-sighted politician, Innocent IV could not fail to perceive that the co-operation of the rising Byzantine Empire of Nicaea promised a richer rewaid than the maintenance of the moribund Latin *imperium*. Just as the Greek Emperor was prepared to sacrifice the independence of his Church in order to win over Constantinople, so too the Pope was prepared to abandon the Latin Empire in order to achieve a union with the Greek Church.[2] It seemed that the two parties were nearer to agreement than ever before, but again they failed to agree on the final step. As a matter of fact, there was no longer any need to purchase Rome's support at the expense of far-reaching concessions. The days of Latin Constantinople were in any case numbered, since the decisive victories of Vatatzes made the restoration of the Byzantine Empire on the Bosphorus only a matter of time.

Vatatzes had doubled the extent of the Nicaean Empire. His possessions in Asia Minor were firmly secured and the major portion of the Balkan peninsula was subject to his rule. The former rivals of Nicaea had been eliminated or weakened. The Empire of western

[1] *Le lettere greche di Federigo II*, ed. Festa, p. 22.
[2] Cf. Norden, *Papsttum und Byzanz* 359 ff.

Greece had ceased to exist, and neither remote Epirus nor enfeebled Bulgaria presented any serious danger. The Latin Empire was at its last gasp. So great was its distress that Baldwin II pledged his only son and heir, Philip, to the Venetian merchants in order to get a loan with which to relieve his perpetual need for money.[1] The territory of the Latin Empire was reduced to the country round Constantinople and was encircled by the possessions of Vatatzes. One last effort alone was needed in order to complete the work of restoration; namely, the capture of the imperial city. This final triumph, however, was reserved for another. But all the necessary steps to this end were the work of John Vatatzes, and it is he who really deserves the main credit for the re-establishment of the Byzantine Empire.

John Vatatzes' achievement in the sphere of domestic politics is no less important than his activities in the sphere of foreign policy. He strove to improve the administration of justice and to correct abuses in the administration. With the support of his wife, Irene Lascaris, he set to work to relieve the poverty and distress of the poorest sections of the population and founded many hospitals and charitable institutions.[2] His varied building activities included dignified churches to satisfy Byzantine piety, and fortifications in the frontier areas to meet military needs. In accordance with the best traditions of the Byzantine state, John Vatatzes set up small-holdings for soldiers and he added to his military resources by establishing settlements, held on condition of military service, for the Cumans who had been compelled to move on by the Tartars. These were in the frontier regions of Thrace and Macedonia, as well as in the Meander valley and in Phrygia.[3] Thus the system of frontier defences was restored, especially in the eastern regions, and the Byzantine historian George Pachymeres rightly considers this to be one of the most outstanding achievements of the Nicaean state.[4] But at the

[1] On the history of the Latin Empire cf. the important article by R. L. Wolff, 'Mortgage and Redemption of an Emperor's Son: Castile and the Latin Empire of Constantinople', *Speculum* 29 (1954), 45 ff.

[2] Nic. Gregoras I, 44.

[3] Nic. Gregoras I, 37. On the colonization of the Cumans in the east cf. also Acropolites 65 (ed. Heisenberg). Theodore II Lascaris had this settlement of the Cumans in mind when he wrote in his oration in praise of his father, 'By having the Scythians transplanted from the western territories, you made a useful subject race of them in the east, and by settling them in place of the sons of the Persians (the Turks), you have curbed their insatiable urge towards the west. . . .' Cf. the extract given from this still unpublished work in F. Uspenskij, 'K istorii krestjanskogo zemlevladenija' (On the history of peasant proprietorship), ZMNP 225 (1883), 339, and also Mutafčiev, *Vojniški zemi* 76, note 2.

[4] Pachymeres I, 16 ff. Cf. also the excellent comments on the significance of the frontier system by Wittek, *Mentesche* 9 ff.

same time *pronoia* grants were made in increasing numbers in the Nicaean Empire;[1] and indeed John Vatatzes seems in particular to have extended the granting of *pronoia* properties of more modest proportions to the lesser military aristocracy.[2]

The economic measures of John Vatatzes deserve special notice. Under his régime the Nicaean Empire enjoyed a material prosperity such as it had not known for many years.[3] The Emperor devoted particular attention to the improvement of agriculture and stock breeding and himself set an example in husbandry. The imperial estates were intended to serve as a model and to demonstrate to his subjects how careful and intelligent farming could yield profitable returns in agriculture, viticulture and stock breeding. The Emperor presented his wife with a coronet set with pearls and precious stones out of the money from the sale of eggs on his estate. This 'egg crown', as he himself called it, symbolized for him a complete programme. The first principle of his economic policy was to make the country economically self-supporting. He therefore attempted to protect his Empire from foreign imports and to break the economic monopoly of the Italian towns. He vigorously forbade his subjects to purchase foreign luxury articles. Everyone had to be content with 'the products of Roman soil and the craftsmanship of Roman hands'. Though ethical in origin, this protectionism was doubtless directed against Venice. Fiscal restrictions against Venetian imports would have led to serious complications, as they would have violated the commercial treaties which had been signed by all Byzantine Emperors from Alexius I Comnenus to Theodore I Lascaris. On the other hand, none could challenge the Emperor's right to deny his subjects excessive luxuries. None the less, precious metals and costly fabrics poured into the Empire from the neighbouring Sultanate of Iconium. The Mongol invasion, which had by-passed the Nicaean Empire but had devastated the neighbouring states, brought immense economic benefit to the Byzantines. The Turks purchased foodstuffs in the Nicaean Empire and paid high prices in gold and goods. Thus, despite frequent

[1] Cf. Ostrogorsky, *Féodalité*, 62 ff.

[2] Cf. H. Glykatzi-Ahrweiler, 'La politique agraire des empereurs de Nicée', B 28 (1958), 151 ff., 135 f.

[3] Nic. Gregoras I, 41 ff.; cf. D. Xanalatos, 'Wirtschaftliche Aufbau- und Autarkie-Maßnahmen im 13. Jahrhundert (Nikänisches Reich 1204–61)', *Leipziger Vierteljahrschr. f. Südosteuropa* 3 (1939), 129 ff., though it is a pity that his comments are weakened by a somewhat unfortunate habit of comparison with the present, or at least with recent, years.

wars, Nicaea was never short of money. The financial and economic condition of the Nicaean state under John Vatatzes was much healthier than that of the Byzantine Empire under the later Comneni and the Angeli. And, indeed, the state was in all respects much sounder, evidence enough that the vitality of the Byzantines was not exhausted and that the regeneration of the Byzantine Empire was within the bounds of possibility.

John Vatatzes, who suffered in his later years from severe epileptic fits, died on 3 November 1254.[1] His unique services to his country were accorded the highest recognition. A half-century after his death he was canonized and thenceforth until recent times the memory of the holy Emperor John the Merciful was annually commemorated in the Church of Magnesia, where he found his last resting place, and in Nymphaeum, his favourite place of residence.[2]

3. PRELUDE TO THE RESTORATION

General bibliography: see above, p. 422 ff., and also I. B. Papadopoulos, *Theodore II Lascaris, empereur de Nicée*, Paris 1908; J. Dräseke, 'Theodoros Laskaris', BZ 3 (1894), 498–515; Chapman, *Michel Paléologue*; Geanakoplos, *Michael Palaeologus*.

John Vatatzes had reunited a large part of the Byzantine lands in his victorious campaigns and built up a sound political state at home such as the Byzantine Empire had not known for many a year. His successor Theodore II Lascaris (1254–8) was to show that the Empire of Nicaea was in no way culturally inferior to the old Byzantium. John Vatatzes had actively promoted culture within the Empire and always took a keen interest in learning. His son, a pupil of the famous scholar Nicephorus Blemmydes, was himself a man of letters and a prolific writer. Before his accession he had devoted himself to learned investigations, philosophical studies and theological meditation. On succeeding to the throne, Theodore II, who took the imperial name of Lascaris from his mother, made the court of Nicaea a centre of the humanities. Nicaea was compared to ancient Athens.[3] A large number of scholars gathered round their enlightened ruler and the Empire of Nicaea experienced a

---

[1] On the date cf. Laurent, 'Notes' 162 ff.

[2] Cf. A. Heisenberg, 'Kaiser Johannes Batatzes der Barmherzige', BZ 14 (1905), 160 ff., where the fourteenth-century life of John Vatatzes is printed (pp. 193–233).

[3] Gregory of Cyprus, *Autobiography*, ed. W. Lameere, p. 179, though later Gregory, relying on his own experience, does indeed give a negative judgment on the facilities for education in Nicaea (op. cit., p. 183).

cultural revival which recalled the days of Constantine VII Porphyrogenitus. In contrast to the latter, Theodore II was not only a scholar, but also a practical man of affairs, although he was handicapped by a terrible disease which sapped his vitality, for he suffered, like his father, from epilepsy, but in an aggravated form. He had the loftiest conception of the imperial office; he directed affairs in person and as he best thought fit. Imperious and obstinate, he rebuffed the notabilities of the Empire and thus provoked their hostility. He had no use for the privileges of rank. His chief adviser was his friend George Muzalon, a man of humble origin. He strove to control the Church as he already controlled the state, and he appointed the monk Arsenius, a narrow-minded ascetic, to the patriarchal throne. Towards Rome he pursued a cautious policy and showed little enthusiasm for his father's plans for a union. He refused to countenance any submission of the Greek Church to Rome. Should any union be agreed upon, then it could only be upon a basis of equal rights, and in the event of differences of opinion he, the Emperor, was to have the casting vote as an impartial umpire.[1] This uncompromising attitude was obviously an echo of the successful foreign policy of John Vatatzes which seemed to obviate the need for papal support in the struggle for Constantinople.

The brief reign of Theodore II brought few changes in the sphere of foreign politics, nor did it bring the Byzantines perceptibly nearer to their goal—the re-conquest of Constantinople. But the Empire did at least maintain the *status quo* in face of numerous enemies whose hostility broke out anew after the death of John Vatatzes. The alliance of the Seljuqs with Michael Palaeologus threatened serious complications for the Empire, for Michael, under suspicion of high treason, had fled to the Sultan of Iconium and was supported by him in his claims. But a fresh advance of the Mongols completely changed the situation; instead of attacking the Greeks, the Sultan was constrained to ask for their support, whilst Michael Palaeologus was compelled to return in sackcloth and ashes to make his peace with the Emperor. The Byzantines now came into closer contact with the Mongols and received their ambassadors with extravagant imperial splendour in the hope of convincing the

---

[1] Cf. the characteristic comments in Theodore's work on the Holy Spirit, cited by J. Dräseke, BZ 3 (1896), 512 f. Cf. also the letters of Theodore II, ed. Festa, p. 202 ff. See also Norden, *Papsttum und Byzanz*, 380 ff.

rulers of Asia of the invincibility and the inexhaustible wealth of the Empire of Nicaea.[1]

In the Balkans the Empire was obliged to fight against Bulgaria and Epirus. The young Bulgar tzar, Michael Asen, occupied a large part of the territories in Thrace and Macedonia which had been captured by John Vatatzes. After two costly campaigns, he was, however, thrown back in 1256 and a peace treaty favourable to Nicaea was concluded.[2] The Bulgarian threat was still further lessened by the fall of Michael Asen and the outbreak of internal conflicts and by the accession of Constantine Tich (1257–77), a descendant of the Nemanjids, who had married Theodore II's daughter Irene. A matrimonial alliance, already projected under John Vatatzes, was also concluded with Epirus: Nicephorus, son of Michael II, married the Emperor's daughter Maria, and Theodore seized the opportunity to bring Dyrrachium and the Macedonian fortress Servia under his control. This advantage, however, cost him the friendship of Epirus, and from the year 1257 there was a bitter and fluctuating struggle between the two Greek states. Meanwhile, a dangerous situation had arisen during the Bulgarian, and particularly the Epirote, war, because of the increasing antagonism between the Emperor and the great families who held the most important positions of command in the army. Theodore II blamed them for his occasional failures, and the loyalty of the commanders to a ruler so hostile towards the nobility could certainly not be relied upon. But the endless indictments against members of the aristocracy, and the cruel punishments meted out by the irascible and morbidly touchy Emperor, served only to intensify the conflict. In resisting the obduracy of the aristocracy, Theodore II overreached himself, and in so doing began a conflict which was to end in the downfall of his dynasty.

When he succumbed to his hereditary malady in August 1258 at the age of thirty-six, his seven-year-old son John IV succeeded him. Theodore II, indifferent to the burning hatred which his upstart friend inspired in the aristocracy of the realm, had designated George Muzalon as regent. Even the oath which the nobility, headed by Michael Palaeologus, had sworn both to the dying Emperor and to George Muzalon could not restrain their fury.

[1] M. Andreeva, 'Priem tatarskich poslov pri nikejskom dvore' (The reception of the Tartar ambassadors at the court of Nicaea), *Recueil Kondakov* (1926), 187 ff.

[2] Dölger, *Reg.* 1883; Zlatarski, *Istorija* III, 456 ff.; Mutafčiev, *Istorija* II, 104 f.

Only nine days after the death of Theodore II, during a com-
memoration service for the deceased Emperor, George Muzalon
and his brother were set upon in church and slain in front of the
altar. The regency passed to Michael Palaeologus, the ablest and
most distinguished representative of the aristocracy. He belonged
to the old nobility, had married a grand-niece of John Vatatzes,
and counted amongst his forebears members of former imperial
families.[1] As a brilliant commander he enjoyed the confidence of
the army, particularly the Latin mercenaries; he also possessed charm
of manner and had supporters in all circles, not least amongst the
all-powerful clergy. In consequence, he was appointed Grand Duke
(*megas dux*) and later Despot: but these titles were only a stepping-
stone to the highest position; he was made co-Emperor with the
young John Lascaris and crowned at the turn of the year (1258–9).[2]

Michael Palaeologus owed his rapid rise partly to his exceptional
resourcefulness, partly to the critical situation in foreign affairs
which needed a firm hand in control. Unlike Frederick II, his son,
king Manfred of Sicily, was an enemy of the Nicaean Empire.
The increasing power of the Byzantine state had made great strides
towards recovery since the middle of the century and had restricted
the Latin Empire to the environs of Constantinople, with the consequence that Manfred resumed the anti-Byzantine policy of Henry
VI and the Norman rulers of Sicily. By 1258 he had occupied Corfu
and the most important towns of the coast of Epirus, namely,
Dyrrachium recently acquired by Theodore II, and Avlona and
Butrinto belonging to the Despot Michael II. The ruler of Epirus
was prepared to pay this price in order to win the friendship of the
Sicilian king. He gave Manfred his daughter's hand, together with
these conquered cities as a dowry, and concluded an alliance with

[1] Cf. V. Laurent, 'La généalogie des premiers Paléologues', B 8 (1933), 130 ff.

[2] The exact date of Michael's accession to the imperial throne has been much discussed. Nic. Gregoras I, 78, says he was raised on the shield on 1 December (1258)
and crowned at the end of December (quite probably at Christmas) which is accepted
by Dölger, *Reg.* III, p. 30; cf. also 'Die dynastische Familienpolitik des Kaisers Michael
Palaiologos', E. *Eichmann Festschrift* (1940), 180. Pachymeres I, 81 and 96, says that
Michael became Emperor on 1 January (1259), and he is followed by Laurent, 'Notes'
165 ff.; cf. Miller, CMH IV (1923), 508, who, unlike Laurent, rightly distinguishes
between the raising on the shield and the coronation. In any case, it is clear that Michael
did not gain the imperial throne in December 1259 (as for instance in Chapman, *Michel
Paléologue* 37) or in January 1260 (as in B. Meliarakes, Ἱστορία 509) because we have
imperial documents of Michael VIII dating from the beginning of 1259 (cf. Dölger,
Reg. 1867 ff.). The date given by Pachymeres for the accession of Michael VIII to the
imperial throne (1 January 1259) seems to be supported by the fact that, as has
been pointed out by P. Wirth, *Jahrbuch der österr. byz. Gesellschaft* 10 (1961), 87 f., the
same date is also found in the short chronicle published by B. T. Gorjanov (VV 2
(1949), 218, 18), although the day of the week is given wrongly.

him against the Empire of Nicaea. The third party in the alliance
was William of Villehardouin of Achaia, who had likewise married a
daughter of Michael II. At that time the star of the duke of Achaia
was in the ascendant; the neighbouring Latin duchy of Athens and
the three lords of Euboea recognized him as their overlord. Thus a
powerful coalition came into being, which at the last moment
threatened to destroy the Nicaean work of restoration. The rival
separatist state of Western Greece, the entire Latin strength of
Greece and the Sicilian king had joined forces in a war of annihilation
against the Empire of Nicaea. This triple alliance found further
support in the rising power of the Serbian kings Uroš I. In 1258 his
troops occupied Skoplje, Prilep and Kičevo.

The struggle against this triple alliance was a really decisive test
for Michael VIII. He emerged victorious from a challenge which
might have shaken the Empire. His brother, the Sebastocrator John
Palaeologus, led a powerful army, together with Cuman and Seljuq
levies, against the forces of the coalition.[1] In the autumn of 1259
the armies of the coalition suffered a crushing defeat in the valley of
Pelagonia.[2] The four hundred knights sent by king Manfred
perished on the battlefield and William of Villehardouin was taken
prisoner. The Epirote state seemed lost: the imperial army entered
Arta and Epirus only recovered from this blow thanks to fresh
support from Sicily. The Serbs had to evacuate the Macedonian
cities which they had recently occupied.

There was no longer any continental power capable of resisting
the recovery of Byzantium. The only power likely to intervene was
the maritime republic of Venice, the real creator of the Latin Empire
of Constantinople and chief benefactor from the situation of 1204.

---

[1] As E. Darkó, *Byzantinisch-ungarische Beziehungen in der zweiten Hälfte des 13. Jahrhunderts*
(1933), 10 ff., shows, Hungarian mercenaries are also mentioned by the *Chronicle of the
Morea*, ed. J. Schmitt, v. 2250 ff. This indicates that Hungarian mercenaries, amongst
others, fought for the Byzantines in the battle of Pelagonia, though the fact that they
are not mentioned in the Greek sources goes to show that they were few in number.
In any case, it is somewhat surprising to go on to read in Darkó (op. cit. 16 and 54)
that 'the famous battle of Pelagonia ended with the complete victory of the Nicaean and
Hungarian troops', and that 'the fortunate co-operation of the two powers (i.e. Nicaea
and Hungary) shattered the hostile alliance with all its aspiration and in so doing opened
the way to Constantinople for the Nicaeans'. It may be remarked in passing that the
triptych of Grenoble which Darkó uses (op. cit. 36-53) for the relations between
Byzantium and Hungary in the thirteenth century can hardly be older than the eighteenth
century (cf. J. Moravcsik, *Inscription grecque sur le triptyche de Grenoble* (1935); and also N.
Radojčić, *Letopis Matice Srpske* 340 (1934), 112 ff.
[2] A very detailed account of the formation of the anti-Byzantine coalition and the
battle of Pelagonia is given by D. J. Geanakoplos, 'Greco-Latin Relations on the Eve
of the Byzantine Restoration: the Battle of Pelagonia-1259', *Dumbarton Oaks Papers* 7
(1953), 99-141; see also idem, *Michael Palaeologus*, 47 ff.

To obviate this danger, Michael VIII entered into negotiations with the Genoese, the rivals of Venice. An important treaty was signed at Nymphaeum on 13 March 1261. This agreement laid the foundations of Genoese power in the East, as earlier on the treaty of 1082 had established the power of Venice. The Genoese pledged themselves to give aid to the Empire in case of war, and in return were granted extensive privileges—tax and customs concessions throughout the Empire and their own commericial quarters in the chief ports of the Empire, and also in Constantinople, once Byzantium had succeeded in recovering it.[1] In short, Genoa was to enjoy that commercial supremacy in the Levant which had been the prerogative of Venice since the end of the eleventh century. In effect, however, Byzantium became the prisoner of the two city republics and between them they steadily usurped the naval power and commercial supremacy which it had once enjoyed.

The great event, which had occupied the minds of all Byzantines for two generations and for which diplomacy and military policy had most carefully prepared the way, was at last achieved with sudden swiftness. The end of the moribund Latin Empire and the restoration of Constantinople to Byzantium occurred with surprising ease and seemed almost to be the work of chance. Despatched to Thrace with a small force for the purpose of keeping watch over the Bulgarian frontier, the imperial commander Alexius Strategopulus was reconnoitring in the near neighbourhood of Constantinople, when to his surprise he found the capital virtually unprotected. An armistice which had been concluded in August 1260 for the space of a year was still in existence, and the Venetian fleet had left with the major portion of the Frankish garrison in order to lay siege to the fortress Daphnusium, which lies on an island off the south coast of the Black Sea. Strategopulus immediately proceeded to attack the defenceless city, and captured it at dawn on 25 July 1261 almost without any opposition. Baldwin II and his followers took to flight, and thus ended the Latin dominion over Constantinople.

On 15 August the Emperor Michael VIII celebrated his entry into the city of Constantine the Great. During the fifty-seven years of Latin rule Constantinople had seen the eclipse of its splendour and wealth. The barbarous plunderings of 1204 had been followed by a systematic exploitation of Byzantine treasures: their works of art were exported to the West, for the anxious and impoverished Latin

[1] Zepos, *Jus* I, 488 ff.; Dölger, *Reg.* 1890. Cf. Heyd, *Commerce du Levant* I, 351, 427 ff.; G. J. Bratianu *Recherches sur le commerce génois dans la Mer Noire au XIIIe siècle* (1929), 81 f.

Empire saw therein a means of currying favour with the Western powers. Churches were emptied of their treasure and most venerated relics; the palace of Blachernae lay in ruins. The Byzantine population rejoiced all the more wholeheartedly at the turn of events. The entry of the Emperor into the liberated city took on the form of a religious festival. He was met by a procession bearing the icon of Hodegetria, which was believed to be a work of St. Luke the Evangelist. Then 'more as a Christian than as an Emperor', Michael VIII proceeded in solemn procession on foot to the Studite monastery, and thence to Hagia Sophia. Here in the Church of the Holy Wisdom, once more restored to the Orthodox faith, the church in which the Byzantine Emperors were traditionally crowned, the Patriarch performed the second coronation of Michael and his wife Theodora in September of the same year. This solemn act symbolized the rebirth of the Byzantine Empire in the imperial city that had now awakened to new life. At the same time, Andronicus, the Emperor's little son, then a child of three, was proclaimed Basileus as heir-presumptive to the throne, and thus a decisive step was taken towards the founding of the new dynasty.[1]

The legitimate Emperor John IV Lascaris, on the other hand, took no part in the celebrations, and a few months later Michael VIII had the unfortunate youth blinded. Following the example of Andronicus Comnenus, who had eliminated the son of Manuel, Michael Palaeologus similarly rid himself of the last Lascarid whose rights he had sworn to preserve. But while Andronicus had met with a horrible end, the adroit Michael Palaeologus managed to establish a lasting sovereignty and he founded the most long-lived dynasty of Byzantine history, the dynasty that was destined to rule the Empire until its final downfall.

4. THE RESTORATION OF BYZANTINE POWER: MICHAEL VIII

General bibliography: Chapman, *Michel Paléologue*; Geanakoplos, *Michael Palaeologus*; Norden, *Papsttum und Byzanz*; S. Runciman, *The Sicilian Vespers*, Cambridge 1958; Miller, *Latins*; Zakythinos, *Despotat* I and II; Longnon, *Empire latin*; Kretschmayr, *Venedig* II; Heyd, *Commerce du Levant* I; see also the general bibliography cited above p. 422.

[1] Andronicus (II) was made co-Emperor as early as the late summer of 1261, while Michael VIII's well-known *prostagma* of November 1272 (cf. below, p. 457 and p. 480) was on the occasion of his ceremonial coronation when the title of Autocrator was conferred on him. This is shown by F. Dölger, 'Die dynastische Familienpolitik des Kaisers Michael Palaiologos', *E. Eichmann Festschrift* (1940), 183 ff. (= *Paraspora* 182ff.)

The Byzantine Empire was already supreme in the south-east under John Vatatzes, but it was only after the capture of Constantinople that it once more became a great power. The re-conquest of the former capital was indeed simply the result of the political and military successes of the previous decades and the prize fell into the hands of the Byzantines like ripe fruit. But with the capture of the imperial city on the Bosphorus the whole position of the Byzantine Empire was changed at a blow. Byzantium once again became one of the decisive factors in European diplomacy and formed one of the centres round which the politics of the Mediterranean powers revolved.

None the less, its newly-won position as a great power was fraught with danger. In order to maintain its position, the Empire needed greater wealth and resources than it actually possessed: additional burdens and responsibilities were incurred. Expenses mounted, a larger army and fleet were required. The devastated capital was in need of reconstruction and devoured vast sums, which only increased the burden on the provinces. From the end of the twelfth century it had been clear that the Byzantines could no longer maintain their former position of authority. When they had been driven into Asia Minor, they had created a state that was internally sounder and better consolidated than the old Empire. But this provincial state had never been their ultimate goal; it was intended to serve as a stepping-stone to the attainment of their former greatness. Thus by heroic efforts the position, which had already once proved untenable, was restored.

However, the period of Latin dominion had left behind deep scars on the Byzantine body politic which the restoration was powerless to efface. Constantinople, the head, rested upon an enfeebled body, open to attack on all sides. The Italian city states controlled Byzantine waters, their colonies were scattered throughout the entire Empire and most of the islands of the eastern Mediterranean were subject to them. Greece was still under Frankish rule and even Epirus under Greek direction, together with Thessaly, elected to ignore the efforts at unification and persisted in its hostility towards the Byzantine Empire. The north of the Balkan peninsula was held by the two Slav kingdoms of the Bulgarians and Serbs which had risen to power at the expense of the Byzantine Empire. Not one of these powers was in a position to undertake any large-scale action against Byzantium, but they were all prepared to support any anti-Byzantine undertaking under Western leadership. And in the West, the restored Byzantine Empire had to face all the powers interested in the survival of the Latin Empire. An attack might therefore be expected at any moment. An alliance between the Western and Balkan powers hostile to Byzantium might well have been fatal to the restored Empire. Such a danger could only be averted by skilful manœuvring, and fortunately diplomatic finesse was Michael VIII's strong point.

Michael Palaeologus' mission was twofold—to counter the aggressive plans of the West by diplomatic means, and to restore Byzantine suzerainty in the former Byzantine provinces by eliminating the Epirote state and the last remnants of Latin rule in Greece. Realization of the latter aim depended upon success in the former.[1] The Latin base for operations against Byzantium was Sicily. As under Manfred, and later under Charles of Anjou, the policy of Michael VIII during his entire reign was therefore determined by his relationship to the Sicilian kingdom. The Sicilian plans for conquest could only be vigorously prosecuted with the Pope's support, and it was always the chief aim of Michael to prevent an alliance between the Sicilian kingdom and Rome. So long as Manfred was ruler in Sicily, this was an easy matter. It is true that there was at first a tendency on the part of Rome to adopt a negative attitude towards the restored Byzantine Empire; the Papacy could not reconcile itself to the fact that Constantinople was lost to the Roman Church and that a schismatic Greek Empire had replaced the Latin one. Urban IV (1261–4) had begun by giving moral support to the Franks in Greece in their struggle against Byzantium, and had excommunicated the Genoese who were unwilling to break their alliance with the Byzantine Emperor. But Rome's long-standing aversion to the house of Hohenstaufen had, however, prevented an alliance between the Papacy and king Manfred. Far from supporting Manfred's plans for conquest, Urban IV was actively engaged in ending Hohenstaufen rule in southern Italy and he offered the kingdom of Sicily to Charles of Anjou, the brother of the French king. Taking advantage of the conflict between the Hohenstaufen and the Papacy, Michael VIII approached the latter and successfully tempted

---

[1] I cannot agree with Norden, *Papsttum und Byzanz* 390 ff., that there is any incompatibility between Michael VIII's defensive policy towards the West and his offensive policy towards the Balkans.

the Pope by holding out the familiar Byzantine bait of a union between the Churches of Rome and Constantinople.[1]

This was all the more important as the efforts towards improving the situation in the Balkans were not wholly successful, and compelled the Empire to split its forces and fight on several fronts. At first the Emperor seemed to be in a favourable position as regards Frankish Greece, since William II of Villehardouin had been his prisoner since the battle of Pelagonia. Thus Michael VIII could dictate his own terms before permitting him to return to Achaia as ruler towards the end of 1261. William II took the oath of fealty to the Byzantine Emperor, received the title of *megas domesticus* and had to cede to Byzantium the fortresses of Monemvasia, Mistra, Maina and Hierakion.[2] The alliance was, however, short-lived. The Pope released Villehardouin from the oath sworn in Constantinople, for the *rapprochement* between the two Churches had not yet begun. He also found active support from the Venetian republic, the doughtiest opponent of the restored Byzantine Empire, whose interests seemed seriously threatened by the collapse of the Latin Empire which it had created, as well as by the pact between Byzantium and Genoa. War broke out and Michael VIII despatched a strong army including 5,000 Seljuq mercenaries to the Peloponnese under the command of his brother, the Sebastocrator Constantine, who opened hostilities with a swift and victorious Byzantine offensive. At the same time, the Genoese-Byzantine fleet attacked the Latin islands.

Fighting also took place in Epirus and Bulgaria. Intervening in the confused situation in Bulgaria, Michael VIII occupied the important seaports of Anchialus and Mesembria on the west coast of the Black Sea in 1262 and managed considerably to extend his power on land at the expense of Bulgaria. In Epirus, however, the conqueror of Constantinople, Alexius Strategopulus, a general of only moderate ability, met with little success in 1260 as in 1262. But the brother of the Emperor, the Despot John Palaeologus, won a decisive victory in the summer of 1264 and compelled the Epirote Despot Michael II to sue for peace and recognize imperial suzerainty. The son of Michael II, the Despot Nicephorus I, formerly married to the

[1] R. J. Loenertz, 'Notes d'histoire et de chronologie byzantines', REB 20 (1962), 171 ff. corrects certain details of the negotiations of Michael VIII with the Roman Curia, particularly in chronology.

[2] For details on the agreement between Michael VIII and William II cf. Zakythinos, *Despotat* I, 15 ff.; Dölger, *Reg.* 1895.

daughter of Theodore II Lascaris, now married a niece of Michael VIII.[1]

But after initial successes in southern Greece the fighting took an unfavourable turn. The war dragged on, finances were exhausted, and the Turkish auxiliaries, who had received no regular pay, went over to the Franks. In 1264[2] the victorious advance of the Byzantines ended in serious defeat at Makry-Plagi and they were compelled to withdraw. The allies of the Empire also suffered defeat at sea; in the spring of 1263 the Genoese fleet was overwhelmed by the Venetians at Settepozzi, in the Gulf of Nauplia. This defeat induced the Emperor to change his policy towards the Italian maritime republics. As the alliance with Genoa had cost the Empire great sacrifices and failed to yield the advantages anticipated, the Emperor severed relations with them, sent the Genoese ships home and opened negotiations with the more powerful republic of Venice. On 18 June 1265 a treaty was drawn up which granted the Venetians far-reaching privileges in the Empire. Meanwhile, the breach with the Genoese was only temporary. As clouds were gathering on the western horizon and as the Venetians were slow to ratify the treaty, Michael VIII once more turned to Genoa. The Genoese, who had suffered a second defeat at the hands of Venice (1266), readily accepted the Emperor's advances. The offer included free trade within the Empire, and quarters in Galata, a suburb of Constantinople on the Golden Horn (1267). They remained here until the Turkish conquest, and rapidly developed Galata into a flourishing commercial city. The return of the Genoese to Constantinople ended the procrastination of Venice: on 4 April 1268 the Byzantine-Venetian treaty was ratified, but the clause concerning the expulsion of the Genoese was omitted.[3] It was significant that the treaty was at first valid for a period of five years only. Venice introduced a new system of agreements which could be cancelled at short notice. Compared with the policy hitherto pursued, which tied Byzantium to the support of one maritime republic whilst opposing the other, this simultaneous pact with Genoa and Venice was decidedly advantageous; it diminished the risk of an alliance of the Genoese or

---

[1] Dölger, *Reg.* 1931.

[2] Like Longnon, *Empire latin* 232 f., I have kept the traditional chronology based on the information in the Chronicle of the Morea; the criticisms of Dragoumis, Χρονικῶν Μορέων τοπωνυμικά, τοπογραφικά, ἱστορικά (Athens 1921), 177, and Zakythinos, *Despotat* I, 41 ff., seem unsatisfactory.

[3] Cf. Dölger, *Reg.* 1934, 1941, 1960.

Venetian fleets with powers hostile to Byzantium, and at the same time enabled the Emperor to exploit further the rivalry between the Italian maritime cities and to play them off against each other.

Important changes had meanwhile occurred in the West. Charles of Anjou, count of Provence, had appeared in Italy in obedience to the papal summons and supplanted Manfred who had lost his life and his kingdom at the battle of Benevento. The new king of Sicily and Naples was a far more dangerous opponent of the Byzantine Empire than Manfred. Whilst the Hohenstaufen was an enemy of the Papacy, the Angevin was its protégé, and there was a grave risk of a policy of aggression against Byzantium supported by Rome.[1] Charles of Anjou, in the presence of the Pope and with his consent, had actually made a pact of friendship on 27 May 1267 in Viterbo with the Latin Emperor Baldwin II, who had been expelled from Constantinople and had concluded an agreement on the division of the Byzantine Empire which they expected to conquer. The alliance was to be sealed by a marriage between Charles' daughter Beatrice and Baldwin's son Philip. Such were the plans for conquest evolved by Charles of Anjou, only recently master of Sicily. He soon intervened in Greece, and secured for himself the Epirote possessions of Manfred and the support of William II of Villehardouin. The prince of Achaia, exhausted by his campaigns against the Byzantine troops and threatened by the hostility of the Greek population, rushed to Charles' support and placed his country under his overlordship. His daughter and heiress, Isabella, was betrothed to a son of Charles of Anjou.[2] As the hostility to the Byzantine Emperor increased, the Sicilian king, however, found further allies. Serbia and Bulgaria joined him, for both political and dynastic reasons urged the rulers of the southern Slavs to support the anti-Byzantine front: the Bulgar tzar Constantine Tich was a brother-in-law of the John Lascaris who had been dethroned and blinded by Michael VIII; the Serbian king of Uroš I was married to a French princess, and an alliance with Charles of Anjou offered the best opportunity of realizing his expansionist plans against Byzantium. Meanwhile, Charles of Anjou had finally consolidated his position in Sicily and began to despatch troops and money to Achaia.

The position of the Byzantine Empire was extremely precarious. But Michael VIII did not abandon hope: he was still confident of

---

[1] Cf. J. Gay, 'Notes sur le second royaume français de Sicile', *Mélanges Jorga* (1933), 309 ff.

[2] Cf. Longnon, *Empire latin* 236 f.

winning over the Pope, and Clement IV did in fact listen to his proposals for reopening negotiations on the question of Church union. Rome's real object was to eliminate the Greek schism and also to liberate the Holy Land, not to conquer the Byzantine Empire as the king of Sicily imagined. Events since 1204 had shown that the mere occupation of the Byzantine Empire did not advance the cause of ecclesiastical unity. A far-sighted eastern policy on the part of Rome could not be identified with Charles' plans for conquest. If Clement IV gave the impression of supporting these plans, then he did so only to bring pressure to bear on the Byzantine Emperor, and so to procure the victory of the Roman, rather than the Angevin, policy.[1] When Clement IV died in 1268, and a lengthy vacancy in the Holy See occurred, the astute Michael Palaeologus turned to the king of France for support. Following the Popes of his day, the aim of St. Louis was to liberate the Holy Land from unbelievers and to restore peace between the Churches of Christendom. Influenced by the embassies of the Byzantine Emperor, he managed to restrain his warlike brother from fighting the Greek Christians. Charles of Anjou was obliged to join him and to take part in the crusade to Tunis in the summer of 1270, so that at the crucial moment his projected attack on Byzantium was held up. In September 1271 the vacant chair of St. Peter was finally filled, and, despite the opposition of Charles of Anjou, the Italian Gregory X was elected Pope. Gregory X was an enthusiastic supporter of movements for a crusade and ecclesiastical reunion, and averse to the Angevin plans for conquest. More than ever the union with the Greek Church formed the centre of papal policy in the East.[2]

During the absence of Charles of Anjou from Europe, the situation in Frankish Greece shifted in favour of the Byzantines, who were able to consolidate once more their position in the Peloponnese. But the crusade to Tunis was only a brief interlude. Soon after his arrival in Africa, Louis IX succumbed to an epidemic, and Charles of Anjou returned to Sicily after a short and victorious campaign.

---

[1] Cf. the excellent comments in Norden, *Papsttum und Byzanz* 443 ff.

[2] V. Laurent, 'La croisade et la question d'Orient sous le pontificat de Grégoire X', *Revue hist. du Sud-Est Europ.* 22 (1945), 105, gives a detailed description of Gregory Xs' eastern policy with strong emphasis on his crusading projects. Cf. idem, 'Grégoire X et un projet de ligue anti-turque', EO 37 (1938), 257 ff., and 'Le rapport de Georges le Métochite, apocrisiaire de Michel VIII Paléologue auprès du pape Grégoire X (1275–6)', *Revue hist. du Sud-Est Europ.* 23 (1946), 233 ff.; A. Fliche, 'Le problème oriental au second concile oecuménique de Lyon (1274)', OCP 13 (1947), 475, does not in fact contribute anything new.

The despatch of reinforcements to the Morea in 1271–2 halted the advance of the Byzantines in Greece.

Meanwhile, Michael VIII was attempting to undermine the influence of Charles of Anjou in the Greek and Slav territories of the Balkans by strengthening dynastic links. The principality of western Greece had crumbled after the death of the Despot Michael II in 1271: the Despot Nicephorus, the legitimate heir, who was married to the niece of the Byzantine Emperor, succeeded to the throne in Epirus, but in Thessaly, however, Michael II's illegitimate son John took over the government. The Emperor granted him the title of Sebastocrator and married his nephew Andronicus Tarchaneiotes to the daughter of John. This safeguard proved to be unsatisfactory; the vigorous and warlike ruler of Thessaly soon became a bitter foe of the Empire and Tarchaneiotes made common cause with his father-in-law. It was, indeed, almost impossible for Byzantium to maintain cordial relations with the separatist Greek principalities, for the Emperor's real aim was the absorption of these states.

Similarly, the Emperor's plans to restore the Empire prevented any *rapprochement* with the Slav kingdoms. He considered that his control should be re-established, not only over the Balkan territory occupied by the Greeks and Latins, but also over the southern Slav lands. This is clearly revealed in the important, though ineffective, ecclesiastical decree of 1272, in which Michael VIII proposed to deprive the Serbian and Bulgarian Churches of their autocephalous position, and to subordinate the southern Slav Churches to the Greek Archbishopric of Ochrida, as Basil II had done.[1] Although negotiations for a marriage alliance with Serbia were far advanced, they finally fell through, but on the other hand Michael VIII was able to ally with Hungary and thus counterbalance an alliance between the Serbs and the Angevins. His heir to the throne, Andronicus, married the daughter of the Hungarian king Stephen V: shortly afterwards in November 1272 he was crowned co-Emperor and received at the same time far more extensive rights than had ever before been enjoyed by co-Emperors in Byzantium (cf. below, p. 480).[2] After the death of the tzarina Irene Lascaris (c. 1270) and after the marriage between the Bulgarian tzar Constatine

[1] V. N. Beneševič, *Opisanie grečeskich rukopisej sv. Ekateriny na Sinae* (A description of the Greek manuscripts of St. Catharine's monastery on Mt. Sinai), St. Petersburg 1911–17, vol. I, 3, 1, pp. 542 ff.

[2] Pachym. I, 318 f.; *prostagma* of Michael VIII of 8 November 1272, Heisenberg, 'Palaiologenzeit' 37 ff. (with detailed commentary); Dölger, *Reg.* 1994 and 1995.

and the Emperor's niece Maria, sister of the wife of the Epirote Despot, the tension in Bulgaria seemed to relax. But when Michael VIII did not surrender the seaports of Anchialus and Mesembria, in Byzantine possession since 1262, as the promised dowry, war broke out in 1272 and the Bulgarians invaded Byzantine territory. They were, however, compelled to withdraw under pressure from the Tartars, who were allied to Michael VIII, and they gave up their claim to the disputed cities.

At that time the powers to be reckoned with in the East were the Tartars of the Golden Horde in south Russia, the Mongols of the Khan Hulagu in the Near and Middle East and the Mamluks in Egypt.[1] The Mongols of Russia and those under Hulagu had parted company towards 1259 and were no longer united. Hulagu had taken possession of Baghdad, the Caliph's city, in 1258, and he had extended his sovereignty over territory ranging from India to the Mediterranean, but in 1260 he was decisively defeated by the Egyptian Mamluks. These had originally been for the most part Cumans and other peoples from the steppes of southern Russia, who had formed the bodyguard of the Egyptian Ayyūbids. In 1250 they had gained control of Egypt and had replaced the Ayyūbids by their own dynasty, which was destined to rule over Egypt down to the sixteenth century.[2] An increasing number of their compatriots from southern Russia poured in to join them, and thus the Mamluks were brought into closer relationship with the Golden Horde. Both powers were enemies of the Mongols of the Near East and therefore the only means of communication open to them was by sea, and since the key to this situation was in the hands of Byzantium it became imperative for them to come to terms with the Byzantine Emperor. This is a clear proof of the extent to which their reinstatement in Constantinople had increased the international prestige and authority of the Byzantines. But to begin with Michael VIII was on good terms with Hulagu and the Mongols of the Near East, since this enabled him to bring pressure to bear on the neighbouring Sultanate of Iconium. For this reason he was not disposed to ally

[1] Cf. F. Uspenskij, 'Vizantijskie istoriki o mongolach i egipetskich mamljukach' (Byzantine historians on the Mongols and Egyptian Mamluks), VV 24 (1923–6), 1 ff.; G. Vernadskij, 'Zolotaja Orda, Egipet i Vizantija v ich vzaimootnošenijach v carstvovanie Michaila Paleologa' (The Golden Horde, Egypt and Byzantium and their relations in the reign of Michael Palaeologus), *Sem. Kond.* 1 (1927), 73 ff.

[2] Cf. Stanley Lane-Poole, *A History of Egypt in the Middle Ages* (1901), 242 ff.; A. Poliak, 'Le caractère colonial de l'État Mamelouk dans ses rapports avec la Horde d'Or', *Revue des Études islamiques* 1935, 231 ff.

with the Mongols of Russia and the Mamluks. The Tartars of southern Russia, in alliance with the Bulgarians, therefore made a fierce attack upon the Empire in 1264. The Byzantine army was heavily defeated, Michael VIII himself came within an ace of losing his life and the territory of Thrace was so completely devastated far and wide, that 'neither ox nor husbandman was to be seen'.[1] In response to the appeal of John of Thessaly and Andronicus Tarchaneiotes, the Tartars made a second devastating attack in 1271. These inroads, together with the complications in Bulgaria, induced Michael VIII to settle his disputes with the south Russian Tartars. In 1272 he concluded a treaty of friendship with the famous Tartar leader Nogaj, who exercised decisive influence in the Golden Horde and was in a position to counter any anti-Byzantine action on the part of the Bulgarians, as he soon demonstrated.[2] The Emperor married him to his illegitimate daughter Euphrosyne and loaded him with gifts. From that moment the relations of the Byzantine Emperor with the Golden Horde and the Mamluks remained untroubled, and the exchange of embassies between Byzantium and Egypt grew more and more frequent. Michael VIII encircled the ring of powers hostile to Byzantium with a further ring intended to hold the enemies of the Empire in check. The Tartars of Nogaj brought pressure to bear upon Bulgaria, just as the Mongols of Hulagu had done upon the Sultanate of Iconium; in the rear of the Serbs stood the Empire's ally Hungary, while Charles of Anjou, the arch-enemy of Byzantium, was restrained from attacking the Byzantine Emperor by the Papacy, which still cherished hopes of a union.

But Gregory X was, however, no longer satisfied with the vague promises of union with which Michael VIII had already beguiled Rome for more than a decade. He gave the Emperor an ultimatum —either the Greek Church was to submit, in which case he guaranteed the full support of the Catholic powers, otherwise he declared that he could no longer restrain the persistent demands of Charles of Anjou.[3] The expiration of the Byzantine-Venetian treaty gave the

---

[1] Nic. Gregoras I, 101.

[2] Chronological indications in the sources are very infrequent. Cf. Dölger, *Reg.* 1969, 1976, 1977. The chronology given here is based on the connection between the various events described: the alliance with Nogaj cannot have been before 1272 since it was preceded by the Tartar attack invoked by John of Thessaly which occurred in 1271 at the earliest and the Bulgar-Byzantine war which could hardly have broken out before the spring of 1272, as between the death of the tzarina Irene Lascaris in 1270 and this war the tzar's marriage with the Emperor's niece Mary and the subsequent birth of a son has to be fitted in.

[3] Cf. Norden, *Papsttum und Byzanz* 489 ff.

Pope an opportunity to bring the strongest pressure to bear upon Michael VIII from this quarter, and he warned the Venetians not to renew the treaty before the union was completed. Charles of Anjou, for his part, also made every effort to win Venice over to the anti-Byzantine camp. At the same time, he took active steps in the Balkans and Greece. He concluded a pact of friendship with the violently anti-imperial ruler of Thessaly and in 1273 despatched still larger forces to the Morea. He had already gained a footing in Albania, the gateway to Byzantium, and the Catholic section of the country acknowledged him as their lord. He strengthened his alliance with Serbia and Bulgaria, and in 1273 the ambassadors of the Bulgarian tzar and the Serbian king arrived at his court.[1] All the enemies of the Empire, Latins and Greeks, Slavs and Albanians, united under the leadership of Charles of Anjou. Bound by treaties and by ties of marriage to the titular Emperor of Constantinople, as well as to the ruler of Frankish Greece, Charles now coveted the Byzantine imperial crown.

Under these circumstances the threats of Gregory X exercised virtual compulsion and the Emperor had no choice but to submit to the papal will. Despite the obstinate opposition of the Byzantine clergy, Michael VIII came to terms with the papal legate in Constantinople and ultimately was even able to persuade a section of the clergy to accept the union. The historic act was concluded at the Council of Lyons on 6 July 1274. In the name of the Emperor, the Grand Logothete George Acropolites swore to acknowledge, not only the papal primacy, but the Roman faith, and the ecclesiastical members of the Byzantine legation, the former Patriarch Germanus and the Metropolitan Theophanes of Nicaea, also signed the imperial declaration. The union of the Churches, for more than two centuries one of the principal aims of Rome's policy, and the object of endless and consistently fruitless negotiations, had at last been realized.

The political advantages which Michael VIII anticipated from the submission of the Church were in fact soon realized. Under papal pressure, Charles of Anjou was obliged to abandon his projected conquest of Byzantium and he pledged himself to cease hostilities until 1 May 1276. Venice, too, renewed her treaty with the Byzantine Emperor in March 1275,[2] but only for the space of two years.

---

[1] Cf. Jireček, *Geschichte* I, 323.

[2] And not on 19 March 1277 when the treaty was renewed for a further two years. Cf. Norden, *Papsttum und Byzanz* 540, note 1. But Chapman, *Michel Paléologue*, 132 and also Geanakoplos *Michael Palaeologus*, 301, place the conclusion of this treaty in 1277.

Byzantium, which had recently been driven to bay, now seized the initiative and went over to the offensive. Even while the Council of Lyons was still sitting, the Angevin troops in Albania were being hard pressed by the Byzantines, who captured the important towns of Berat and Butrinto, and began to lay siege to Dyrrachium and Avlona. In 1275 the Emperor despatched his brother John with a powerful army to Thessaly, which had become a centre of anti-imperial disturbances under the Sebastocrator John Angelus. The campaign opened victoriously and brought the imperial troops to the walls of the Thessalian capital Neopatras, but failed before the personal bravery and skill of the Sebastocrator John, who at the decisive moment brought up reinforcements from the neighbouring Frankish duchy of Athens. A second campaign against Thessaly in 1277 also proved inconclusive. On the other hand, the Empire won signal successes at sea. The naval operations of the Italian Licario, promoted *megas dux*, were particularly fortunate: Euboea and a considerable number of the Aegean islands fell into his hands, with the result that the Byzantine fleet was again master of the Aegean.

In the Peloponnese an important change took place; William II of Villehardouin died in 1278 and in consequence the principality of the Morea fell under the direct rule of Charles of Anjou. At first sight this change seemed to spell danger to Byzantium, but in reality it portended a weakening of the Frankish rule and so benefited the Emperor. The difficulties with which William II had had to contend were too much for the governors appointed by Charles of Anjou. The country was exhausted by continual wars and the Greek population increasingly opposed the foreign domination of the Latins. Under these circumstances Byzantium was able to extend its territories as far as Arcadia, and this, together with the recent successes in the Archipelago, indicated a considerable strengthening of the imperial position.

This improvement of its position abroad was, however, purchased at the cost of a severe internal crisis. The Byzantine people and the majority of the clergy repudiated the union and offered bitter opposition to the Emperor. The relations between Michael VIII and the Greek Church had already seriously deteriorated. After the blinding of the young John Lascaris, the Patriarch Arsenius had outlawed Michael Palaeologus and it was with considerable difficulty that the Emperor finally succeeded in deposing the fanatical ascetic (1266). He was granted a dispensation by his second successor on the patriarchal throne, Joseph, but a section of the Church and the people remained loyal to the exiled Arsenius. These formed the party of the so-called Arsenites, which obstinately opposed the Emperor and the new leaders of the Church. When Michael VIII submitted to the Pope and demanded that his Church should recognize Roman supremacy, a storm broke out which swept through the entire population. The difficulties were increased by Joseph's refusal to accept the union, thus necessitating another violent change in ecclesiastical leadership. The Chartophylax John Beccus, a gifted and versatile man who had been won over to the cause of reunion after initial opposition, was appointed Patriarch. The country was now divided into two hostile camps and an authoritative order to end the Graeco-Roman schism had only created a deep rift within the Byzantine Empire. The Byzantine people, to whom orthodoxy had ever been sacred and whose hatred for the Latins had become second nature, defied the Emperor who had betrayed the faith of their fathers. The Emperor, however, ignored their protests and adhered to the union which, in his eyes, was alone able to save his Empire. Cruel persecutions followed against high and low alike. The prisons were crowded with clergy and laity, humble folk and princes of imperial descent, for the schism affected all sections of the population and the imperial family was itself divided.[1]

Even beyond the Byzantine frontiers, the Emperor's policy of Church union created serious complications. Michael's favourite sister Eulogia (Irene),[2] an active opponent of the union, joined her daughter Maria, the Bulgarian tzarina, whereupon the two women turned the Bulgarian court into a nest of anti-imperial intrigue. In this direction, however, the tension was soon relieved, if only temporarily. In the prostrate Empire of Trnovo, ravaged by Mongolian depredations and torn by social conflicts, a violent popular revolt broke out, accompanied by severe internal struggles. By armed intervention in the Bulgarian disorders in opposition to the victorious popular leader Ivajlo, the Byzantines succeeded in setting up a Hellenized descendant of the Asenids, who was married to the Emperor's daughter Irene, and they raised him to the tottering throne of the tzars as Ivan Asen III (1279).

---

[1] Cf. H. Evert-Kappesova, 'La société byzantine et l'Union de Lyon', BS 10 (1949), 28 ff. Cf. also idem., 'Une page des relations byzantino-latines. Le clergé byzantin et l'union de Lyon (1274–82), ibid. 13 (1952/53), 68 ff., and 'Byzance et le St. Siège à l'époque de l'union de Lyon', ibid. 16 (1955), 297 ff.; Geanakoplos, *Michael Palaeologus*, 265 ff.

[2] Papadopulos, *Genealogie d. Palaiologen* Nr. 29.

In the separatist Greek principalities hatred of the Emperor's policy of union had particularly disastrous results. Even the peace-loving Nicephorus of Epirus was moved to launch an attack against Michael Palaeologus; he occupied the seaport of Butrinto, recently captured by the Byzantines, only to surrender it later (1279) to Charles of Anjou. Michael's arch-enemy John of Thessaly, who for years had fought against the Byzantine Empire with the support of the Western powers, now proclaimed himself the leader of the orthodox Greeks and gathered round him the ever increasing numbers of Byzantines who were opposed to the union. In 1278 he even held a council which condemned the Emperor as a heretic.[1]

Meanwhile, the Papacy, as well as the Emperor, had to make strenuous efforts to maintain the union between Rome and Byzantium. After the death of Gregory X (1276) this co-operation came to a standstill as the influence of the Sicilian king increased in Rome. Nicholas III (1277–80) once again tried to uphold the Roman conception of a universal Church and therefore did his best to further the policy of union. He also sought to establish a balance of power between Rudolf of Habsburg and Charles of Anjou in the West and between the Angevin and the Byzantine Emperor in the East, in order to set the universal power of the Roman Church above all temporal authorities. During the period of Nicholas' pontificate Michael VIII felt secure in the West, and this accounts for the outstanding Byzantine successes in the Morea and the Archipelago at this time (cf. above, p. 461). At the next papal election the influence of Charles of Anjou was, however, decisive, and the situation was completely transformed. On 22 February 1281 the Frenchman Martin IV, a willing tool of the powerful Sicilian king, ascended the papal throne. The Curia abandoned its position as sovereign arbitrator and obediently fell into line with the Angevin policy of aggression. Under the patronage of the Pope, Charles of Anjou and the Latin titular Emperor Philip, son of Baldwin II, concluded a treaty with the Venetian republic at Orvieto on 3 July 1281 'for the restoration of the Roman *imperium* usurped by the Palaeologus'.[2] Martin IV went even further, and so completely renounced the policy of his predecessors in his blind subservience to Charles of Anjou that he condemned the Byzantine Emperor as a schismatic, even though he had supported the union and in so doing had therefore incurred the

[1] Cf. V. Grumel, 'En Orient après le concile de Lyon', EO 24 (1925), 321 ff.
[2] Tafel and Thomas I, 287 ff.

hostility of his own people; he also declared him deposed and prohibited all Christian princes from communicating with him.

This meant the complete collapse of Michael VIII's policy of union, which had indeed been abandoned even by Rome herself. The Western powers united against Byzantium: Venice lent its fleet to Charles of Anjou and the Pope gave his moral support. The Balkan rulers joined the anti-Byzantine front, and in co-operation with Charles of Anjou, John of Thessaly and the new Serbian king, the energetic Milutin (1282–1321) invaded Macedonia in 1282. The Serbian king occupied the important town of Skoplje which the Byzantines were never to recover. In Bulgaria the Byzantine puppet Ivan Asen III had already lost the crown in 1280. His successor and opponent George I Terter (1280–92), a descendant of the Cumans, who as leader of the Bulgarian boyars had wrested the power from him, turned against Byzantium as anticipated and allied himself with the Angevin and John of Thessaly. Never before had Charles of Anjou been so near to his goal, nor had Michael ever been in so critical a situation: it looked as though the days of the Byzantine Empire were numbered.

But at the height of the crisis the tide of fortune changed: a terrible catastrophe overwhelmed Charles of Anjou in his most confident moment and the skilled diplomacy of Michael Palaeologus celebrated its greatest triumph. A conspiracy on a vast scale against Angevin rule in Sicily, in which John of Procida, a learned doctor who had emigrated from southern Italy and later became Chancellor of Aragon, played the part of a mediator, had been in preparation for several years.[1] Through his agency Michael Palaeologus had come to an understanding with King Peter III of Aragon, the son-in-law of Manfred, during the pontificate of Nicholas III. Peter was to attack Charles of Anjou in the rear and recapture the kingdom that Charles had snatched from king Manfred in 1266. The Byzantine Emperor placed at his disposal funds for building a fleet. At the same time imperial plenipotentiaries, amply supplied with money, stirred up revolt in Sicily against the foreign domination of the Angevin. The country, exhausted and embittered by incessant preparations for war and the abuses of the local officials, was seething with discontent. But it was Byzantine gold that brought the latent crisis to a head, as it had also been responsible for assisting the king of Aragon with his war preparations. 'Should I dare to claim',

[1] Cf. S. Runciman, *The Sicilian Vespers*, Cambridge 1958, 201 ff. and App. 288 ff. for the disputed role of John of Procida.

so runs Michael VIII's autobiography, 'that I was God's instrument to bring freedom to the Sicilians, then I should only be stating the truth.'[1] At the moment when Michael Palaeologus was in direst straits, rebellion broke out in Palermo on 31 March 1282. The rising spread like wildfire over the entire island and Angevin rule in Sicily met with a bloody end in the famous Sicilian Vespers. In August Peter of Aragon appeared with his fleet. He was crowned in Palermo with the crown of Manfred and became ruler of Sicily, while it was only with the greatest difficulty that Charles of Anjou was able to save his possessions on the Italian mainland. A campaign against Byzantium was now out of the question; the kingdom of southern Italy had disintegrated, Charles of Anjou abandoned the struggle after this unparalleled disaster, the Pope was heavily involved in the catastrophe, the titular Latin Emperor Philip was ignored by all and Venice made advances to the Byzantine Emperor and the king of Aragon. The avalanche which for twenty years had threatened to overwhelm the restored Byzantine Empire had thus been arrested by the diplomatic genius of Michael Palaeologus.

[1] ed. Grégoire, B 29/30 (1959/60), 461.

VIII

The Decline and Fall of the Byzantine Empire (1282–1453)

SOURCES

THE first group of historians of this period consists of George Pachymeres, Nicephorus Gregoras and John Cantacuzenus. For the history of the period up to 1308 by George Pachymeres see above, p. 418; this work is as important for the early period of the reign of Andronicus II as it was for the preceding reign of Michael VIII. It describes among other things the Turkish conquest of Asia Minor, Byzantino-Serbian relations during the period of the resurgence of Serbia under King Milutin, and contains detailed information on the eventful campaigns of the Grand Catalan Company which should however be compared with the divergent account of the Catalan Muntaner who participated in the expedition.[1] On a still higher level is the great work of Nicephorus Gregoras entitled Ῥωμαϊκὴ ἱστορία, a title that significantly reveals Byzantine awareness of its Roman tradition. This *Roman History* deals with the period between 1204 and 1359 in thirty-seven books; the period up to about 1320 is compressed into seven books, whilst the period in which Gregoras was active is treated in greater detail in thirty books. Nicephorus Gregoras (1290/91–1360)[2] is one of the outstanding figures of the fourteenth century and one of the most remarkable and prolific scholars of Byzantium who wrote on all aspects of contemporary knowledge.[3] His history is full of information and throws considerable light on constitutional, administrative and economic questions often neglected in historical works of the middle ages. His presentation is graphic and in general reliable. Only in the treatment of the hesychast controversy in which Gregoras, as leading anti-hesychast, took an active part in the fifties of the fourteenth century, does the history lose all objectivity and degenerate into a diffuse and

---

[1] On this cf. A. Rubió i Lluch, 'Paquiemeres y Muntaner', *Sec. hist. arqueol. de l'Institut d'Estudis Catalans. Mémoires* I (1927), 33 ff.

[2] On the date of his birth cf. V. Grecu, *Bull de l'Acad. Roumaine* 27 (1946), 56 ff.

[3] On the life and writings of Nicephorus Gregoras cf. R. Guilland, *Essai sur Nicéphore Grégoras*, Paris 1926.

disquietingly tendentious account, overloaded with official documents. Apart from his history, it is the letters of Gregoras which, of all his extensive literary remains, are of the greatest value as a source.[1] The famous history of Emperor John VI Cantacuzenus (1341-54) begins with the rising of Andronicus III in 1320 and ends a few years after the abdication of the author, and is the apologia of a retired statesman in the form of memoirs. Cantacuzenus attempts to present his activities in the most favourable light and suppresses or glosses over inconvenient facts, and his statements must therefore be treated with caution. On the whole, his facts are reliable and it is his interpretation which is often tendentious. This account of an experienced statesman, based on his diary and often on documents, offers a mine of important information, and ranks high, both for its literary qualities and as a historical source.

The second group consists of the historians who wrote after the collapse of the Byzantine Empire—Laonicus Chalcocondyles, Ducas, George Sphrantzes and Critobulus. The Athenian Laonicus Chalcocondyles, a pupil of the humanist Gemistus Plethon, who took Herodotus and Thucydides as his models, gives a brief survey of world history from the Assyrians to the beginnings of the Ottoman kingdom and then describes the period of the Turkish conquest and the downfall of the Byzantine Empire.[2] The work ends with the capture of Lemnos in 1463, but was apparently written in the eighties of the fifteenth century. The account is skilful, and bears witness to the literary gifts, as well as to the historical insight, of the author, in spite of some chronological confusion. In accordance with the contemporary historical situation, the centre of the stage is occupied, not by Byzantium, but by the Ottoman Empire, whose rapid rise to power forms the real theme of Chalcocondyles, a theme that was

---

[1] Bezdeki, 'Nicephori Gregorae epistolae XC', *Ephemeris Dacoromana* 2 (1925), 239–377; R. Guilland, *Correspondance de Nicéphore Grégoras*, Paris 1927, where some of the 161 extant letters of N. Gregoras are printed with French trans., but for the majority only a very brief summary is given. The careful notes, pp. 291–389, on N. Gregoras' correspondents are useful; but on the text and trans. cf. H. Grégoire, B 3, 468 ff.

[2] ed. J. Darko, *Laonici Chalcocandylae historiarum demonstrationes* I, II 1 and 2, Budapest 1922, 1923 and 1927; Rumanian translation, V. Grecu, *Laonic Chalcocondil: Expuneri istorice*, Ed. Acad. Rep. Pop. Romine 1958. Cf. also K. Güterbock, 'Laonikos Chalkondyles', *Zeitschr. f. Völkerrecht* 4 (1910), 72 ff.; Darko, 'Zum Leben des Laonikos Chalkonkondyles', BZ 24 (1923), 29 ff.; idem, 'Neue Beiträge zur Biographie des Laonikos Chalkokondyles', ibid. 27 (1927), 275 ff.; idem, 'Neue Emendationsvorschläge zu Laonikos Chalkokondyles', ibid. 32 (1932), 2 ff. W. Miller, 'The Last Athenian Historian: Laonikos Chalkondyles', JHS 42 (1922), 36 ff. Δ. Καμπουρογλοῦ, Οἱ Χαλκοκονδύλαι, Athens 1926, pp. 104–71. A. Nimet, *Die türkische Prosopographie bei Laonikos Chalkokandyles*, Diss. Hamburg 1933; further bibliography in Moravcsik, *Byzantinoturcica* I, 2nd ed., 396 ff.

entirely new in Byzantine historical writings. He had spent many
years at the court of the Despot of the Morea, and gives a detailed
account of the events in the Peloponnese which were so decisive for
the history of the Byzantine Empire in the fifteenth century. Ducas
who had long been in the service of Genoa has a different approach.[1]
In contrast to the humanist Chalcocondyles, Ducas writes in the
Greek vernacular. His work, covering the period to 1462, is
characterized by reliability and vivid description. Moreover, the
narrative is sustained by real dramatic power, as his detailed
description of the capture of Constantinople illustrates. Like
Chalcocondyles, Ducas prefaces his work with a brief survey of
world history and his main account does not begin until the outbreak of civil war in 1341, and goes into fuller detail with Sultan
Bajezid's accession in 1389.[2] The work also survives in an old
Italian edition, which fills in a few of the lacunae of the original
text (printed in CB after the Greek text). A more circumscribed
period of Byzantine history is examined in the work of George
Sphrantzes,[3] which in the original version covers the period from
1413-77, but in the later and enlarged version begins with the dynasty
of the Palaeologi.[4] As a friend of the imperial family and a high

[1] His first name has not been preserved. V. Grecu, 'Pour une meilleure connaissance
de l'historien Doukas', *Mémorial L. Petit* (1948), 128 ff., argues that he was called
Michael like his grandfather but this is so far only a suggestion.

[2] New critical edition with an introduction and Rumanian translation: V. Grecu,
Ducas, Istoria turco-bizantină (1341-1462), Ed. Acad. Rep. Pop. Romine 1958.

[3] On his name cf. V. Laurent, 'Σφραντζῆς et non Φραντζῆς', BZ 44 (1951) (*Dölger-
Festschrift*), 373 ff., and 'Sphrantzès et non Phrantzès à nouveau', REB 9 (1951), 170 f.

[4] There is a new edition of the first two books by J. B. Papadopoulos, *Georgii Phrantzae
Chronikon* I, Leipzig (Teubner) 1935. As he had already stated elsewhere (cf. *Bulletin de
l'Inst. Archéol. Bulgare* 9, 177 ff.), he did not consider that Sphrantzes was the author of
the *Chron. Maius* which he was editing, but thought that this was based on the shorter
Chron. Minus (Migne, PG 156, 1025-80) which he regarded as the genuine work of
Sphrantzes, while the *Maius* was produced in 1573-5 by Macarius Melissenus. F. Dölger,
Otto-Glauning-Festschrift (1936), 29 ff., and BZ 37 (1937), 502 f., thinks that the *Minus* was
Sphrantzes' diary which he himself expanded and revised when he wrote his history
(i.e., the *Chron. Maius*) which was subsequently falsified by Macarius with various
additions. This view was then supported by Papadopoulos, 'Über "Maius" und "Minus"
des Georgios Phrantzes', BZ 38 (1938), 323 ff. Cf. also Dölger, ibid. 489 ff. On the
other hand, V. Grumel, EO 36 (1937), 88 f., and H. Grégoire, B 12 (1937), 389 ff.,
consider that the *Maius* was the real work of Sphrantzes and the *Minus* an extract made
later; Moravcsik, *Byzantinoturcica* I, 152, also inclines towards this view. Meanwhile,
those who attack the genuineness of the *Maius* have received fresh support from the
investigations of R. J. Loenertz, 'La date de la lettre θ' de Manuel Paléologue et l'inauthenti-
cité du "Chronicon Maius" de Georges Phrantzès', EO 39 (1940), 91 ff., and especially
his 'Autour du Chronicon Maius attribué à Georges Phrantzès', *Miscellanea G. Mercati*
III (1946), 273 ff., where he maintains that the *Maius* is a compilation made by Macarius
Melissenus from the genuine *Minus*, as well as also from Chalcocondyles and the
chronicle of Dorotheus of Monemvasia. This conclusion is based on weighty and in

official of the Byzantine state under the three last Palaeologi, Sphrantzes differs in maintaining a traditional Byzantine outlook in contrast to both Chalcocondyles and Ducas, the friend of the Genoese; unlike Ducas, who was a supporter of Church union, he was an uncompromising opponent of the Latins. His account is factual and sets great store on chronological accuracy, and his method of presentation lies midway between the artificial archaism of Chalcocondyles and the intentional journalese of Ducas. The three almost contemporary historians supplement each other in subject matter and in interpretation, though the most accurate of them is probably Ducas.[1] As a supplement to the writings of Chalcocondyles, Ducas and Sphrantzes, the account of Critobulus of Imbros should be consulted. Chalcocondyles had gone as far as to make the Turkish state the centre of his story, but Critobulus, an aristocratic Greek, who tried to reconcile himself to the Turkish domination and to please his new masters, went even further and wrote a history of the Sultan Muhammed II. The full account of the capture of Constantinople, which occupies a large part of his work, covering the years 1451 to 1467,[2] is especially important for students of Byzantine history. In contrast to Sphrantzes, Critobulus, like Chalcocondyles and Ducas, did not himself witness the fateful event.[3] In addition, there are many extant reports on the fall of

the main entirely convincing arguments; its accuracy is made increasingly certain by further research into this period, so that the dispute may now be regarded as concluded. The view of Loenertz is now also shared by Moravcsik, *Byzantinoturcica* I, 2nd ed., 287 ff. cf. Dölger's agreement, BZ 43 (1950), 63.

[1] Cf. E. Černousov, 'Duka, odin iz istorikov konca Vizantii' (Ducas, one of the historians of the Byzantine downfall), VV 21 (1914), 171 ff.; W. Miller, 'The Historians Doukas and Phrantzes', JHS 46 (1926), 63 ff.; V. Grecu, 'Pour une meilleure connaissance de l'historien Doukas', *Mémorial L. Petit* (1948), 128 ff. Further bibliography in Moravcsik, *Byzantinoturcica* I, 2nd ed., 250 ff.

[2] Müller, FHG, *v* (1870), 40–161; English translation, C. T. Riggs, *History of Mehmed the Conqueror by Kritovoulos*, Princeton; 1954; a critical edition of Critobulus, with an introduction and translation in Rumanian has been published by V. Grecu, *Critobuli Imbriotae De rebus per annos 1451–1467 a Mechemete II gestis*, Editio Acad. Reip. Pop. Romaniae, 1963. On Critobulus and his work see J. Radonić, 'Kritovul, vizantijski istorik XV v.' (Critobulus, a Byzantine historian of the fifteenth century), *Glas Srpske Kralj Akad.* 138 (1930), 59 ff.; Z. V. Udalcova, 'Vizantijskij istorik Kritovul o južnych slavjanach i drugich narodach Balkanskogo poluostrova v XV v.' (The Byzantine historian Critobulus on the southern Slavs and other Balkan peoples in the XVth century), VV 4 (1951), 91 ff. See also Moravcsik, *Byzantinoturcica* I, 2nd ed., 434 ff.

[3] The account of the fall of Constantinople given by the four Byzantine historians is to be found printed all together with an introduction in N. Tomadakes, Δούκα—Κριτοβούλου—Σφραντζῆ—Χαλκοκονδύλον Περὶ ἁλώσεως τῆς Κωνσταντινουπόλεως (1453). Συναγωγὴ κειμένων μετὰ προλόγου καὶ βιογραφικῶν μελετημάτων περὶ τῶν τεσσάρων ἱστοριογράφων, Athens, 1953. A German translation of the account from the *Chronicon Maius* attributed to Sphrantzes, with introduction and commentary, is given by E. v. Ivanka, *Die letzten Tage von Konstantinopel* in *Byz. Geschichtsschreiber* I, Graz-Vienna-Cologne, 1954. For a Russian translation of the accounts of pseudo-Sphrantzes and

Constantinople by foreign eye-witnesses. The description of the Venetian Nicolo Barbaro is especially important by reason of its accuracy.[1] Even isolated events of the late Byzantine period which deeply stirred the minds of contemporaries found their historians in Byzantium. As John Cameniates had formerly described the capture of Thessalonica by the Arabs, so John Anagnostes gave an eye-witness account of the capture of this city by the Turks in 1430, and John Cananus the attack of Murad II upon Constantinpole in 1422 (both in CB after G. Sphrantzes).

We are thus relatively well informed on the period up to about 1360, and also on the last decades of Byzantine history; on the other hand, information on the intermediary period is not well provided for, as Nicephorus Gregoras and John Cantacuzenus do not touch upon it, and the historians of the fifteenth century, Chalcocondyles, Ducas and Sphrantzes, only treat it briefly and with inadequate knowledge. The anonymous short chronicles provide considerable help here, for though very meagre in content they are chronologically accurate.[2]

Ducas see A. A. Stepanov, 'Vizantijskie istoriki Duka i Frandzi o padenii Konstantino-polja' (The Byzantine Historians Ducas and Phrantzes on the Fall of Constantinople), VV 7 (1953), 385–430.

An extensive chronicle of the Turkish Sultans up to 1512, written in the Greek vernacular and preserved in the Codex Barberinus gr. 111, has been published by G. Zoras, Χρονικὸν περὶ τῶν Τούρκων Σουλτάνων· Athens, 1958. But, as has been shown by E. A. Zachariadou, Τὸ Χρονικὸ τῶν Τούρκων Σουλτάνων καὶ τὸ ἰταλικό του πρότυπο, Ἑλληνικά, Παράρτημα 14 (1960), this chronicle goes back to an Italian original.

[1] Nicolo Barbaro, *Giornale dell'assedio di Constantinopoli* 1453, ed. E. Cornet, Vienna 1856. Special attention should be given to the account which Leonard of Chios sent on 16 August 1453 to Pope Nicholas V; cf. Gy. Moravcsik, 'Bericht des Leonardus Chiensis über den Fall von Konstantinopel in einer vulgärgriechischen Quelle', BZ 44 (1951) (*Dölger-Festschrift*), 428 ff. There is also the interesting account of the Russian Nestor Iskander who took part in the battle for Constantinople on the Turkish side; cf. N. A. Smirnov, 'Istoričeskoe značene russkoj 'Povesti' Nestora Iskandera o vzjatii turkami Konstantinopolja v 1453 g.' (The historical significance of the Russian 'Relatio' of Nestor Iskander about the capture of Constantinople by the Turks in 1453), VV 7 (1953), 50 ff. For other accounts of the fall of Constantinople by non-Greek eye-witnesses cf. the list in Gibbon-Bury. VII, 332 ff., and Vasiliev, *History* (1952), 649. On the accounts of the Turkish sources cf. A. Moschopoulos, 'Le siège et la prise de Constantinople selon les sources turques', *Le Cinq-centième anniversaire de la prise de Constantinople*, Athens 1953, 23 ff.

[2] An important chronicle stretching to 1391, published by J. Müller, 'Byzantinische Analekten', *S.B. d. Wiener Akad.* IX, 1852, 389 ff. This chronicle is given in a shortened form (omitting the beginning covering the years 1204 to 1282 which is practically value-less) by Lampros-Amantos, Βραχέα Χρονικά Nr. 52, pp. 88 ff.; cf. also Nr. 15, pp. 31 ff. This collection contains a number of other chronicles which give information of great importance on the chronology of the Palaeologian period. Valuable critical comments on this edition are given by P. Wittek, B 12 (1937), 309 ff. Charanis, 'Short Chronicle', gives a useful historical commentary on the Βραχέα Χρονικά. A similar chronicle of significance going to 1352 has been published from a Moscow manuscript by B. Gorjanov, VV 2 (1949), 276 ff., with a Russian trans. It is prefaced by an introduction which unfortunately shows no acquaintance with the many other known sources of this type, while the edition of the text and the translation leave much to be desired. A further short chronicle with interesting information on the second half of the fourteenth and

Additional information can be found in a Bulgarian chronicle covering the period from 1296 to 1413.[1] The most important historical work of old Serbian literature is the biography of Stephen Lazarević (1389–1427) written in 1431–32 by Constantine the Philosopher who belonged to the circle of the Patriarch Euthymius of Trnovo.[2] This account, rich in historical detail and set in a wider historical framework, is important for the Byzantine history of the first three decades of the fifteenth century. A history of Epirus in the second half of the fourteenth century is found in the chronicle wrongly ascribed to the monks Comnenus and Proclus.[3] The history of the Empire of Trebizond during the period 1204–1426 is described in the meagre chronicle of Michael Panaretus.[4]

In addition the various occasional writings and letters, rhetorical and theological works, so abundant during the productive literary period of the Palaeologi, provide a supplement to the purely historical writings. Research into, and the editing of, this literature is still in its infancy. Only sources considered to have historical value are briefly listed here. The learned Patriarch Gregory (George) of Cyprus (1283–9) left behind, in addition to an extensive correspondence, a clear and straightforward autobiography which in its lucid and simple presentation compares favourably with that of Nicephorus Blemmydes. The encomiums of Michael VIII and Andronicus II, on the other hand, are couched in the language of conventional

the first half of the fifteenth centuries has recently been published by R. J. Loenertz, 'Chronicon breve de Graecorum imperatoribus, ab anno 1341 ad annum 1453 codice Vaticano Graeco 162', EEBS 28 (1958), 204 ff. Cf. also the 'Chronicon breve Thessalonicense' published by Loenertz in *Démétrius Cydonès, Correspondence* I, Studi e Testi 186 (1956), 174, and his article, 'Chroniques breves byzantines', OCP 24 (1958), 158 ff.

[1] ed. I. Bogdan, *Archiv f. slav. Philol.* 13 (1891), 526–35; cf. the important comments of K. Jireček, 'Zur Würdigung der neuentdeckten bulgarischen Chronik', ibid. 14 (1892), 235 ff.

[2] ed. V. Jagić, *Glasnik* 42 (1875), 223–8, 372–7; cf. St. Stanojević, 'Die Biographie Stephan Lazarevićs von Konstantin dem Philosophen als Geschichtsquelle', *Archiv f. slav. Philol.* 18 (1896), 409–72.

[3] ed. G. Destunis, St. Petersburg 1858 (with Russian trans.); J. Avramović, *Glasnik* 14 (1862), 233–75 (with Serbian trans.); also I. Bekker in CB, *Epirotica*, Fragmentum II, 209–39. As part of an extensively planned work, which arose out of the investigations of a reliquary of Epirote provenance now preserved in the cathedral treasure of Cuenca in Spain, a new edition of this chronicle with detailed commentary has been produced by S. Cirac Estopañan, *Bizancio y España. El legato de la basilissa Maria y de los déspotas Thomas y Esaú de Joannina*, I–II, Barcelona 1943. He also gives by way of an appendix a very cursory history of Epirus. On the Epirote chronicles, cf. L. Vranusis, Χρονικὰ τῆς μεσαιωνικῆς καὶ τουρκοκρατουμένης Ἠπείρου, Joannina, 1962. A critical edition of the text is to follow this comprehensive and fundamental preliminary work. See also the important discussion by G. Schirò, 'Struttura e contenuto della Cronaca dei Tocco', B 32 (1962), 203–50, 343 f.

[4] Critical edition with introduction and commentary by O. Lampsides, Μιχαὴλ τοῦ Παναρέτου περὶ τῶν Μεγάλων Κομνηνῶν, Athens 1958.

panegyrics.[1] Nicephorus Chumnus, a pupil of Gregory of Cyprus, belonged to the circle of distinguished scholars in Byzantium under Andronicus II and held high office in the service of the state; he was for a time the μεσάζων, or first minister, and was himself related to the imperial family (his daughter Irene was married to the Despot John Palaeologus, a son of Andronicus II). He wrote several theological and philosophical works in which he supported Aristotelian doctrine. He also produced mathematical and astronomical treatises, and many rhetorical writings, amongst them a fulsome encomium of Andronicus II.[2] As ὁ ἐπὶ τοῦ κανικλείου he drafted several official documents on behalf of the Emperor; of particular interest is the edict of 1296 for the reform of the legal system and a chrysobull of 1313 whose preface mentions the help given to the Byzantines against the Turks by the Serbian king Milutin. The correspondence of this influential personality is also of great historical importance.[3] The distinguished philologist Thomas (Theodulus) Magister, the author of many philological, rhetorical and theological treatises, also wrote two works on the imperial power (περὶ βασιλείας) and on the state (περὶ πολιτείας) which contain valuable information on the imperial administration in the period of Andronicus II and do not attempt to conceal its defects.[4] Theodore Metochites, the leading statesman and most outstanding scholar of the time of Andronicus, who succeeded Chumnus in the office of μεσάζων, published philosophical and purely scientific works, and a number of rhetorical treatises and poems, which often contain valuable historical information. Metochites' account of his embassy to the Serbian court, for the purpose of arranging a peace treaty and a marriage between

---

[1] Detailed research into the manuscript tradition of the correspondence has been done by W. Lameere, *La tradition manuscrite de la Correspondance de Grégoire de Chypre*, Brussels-Rome 1937; the text of the autobiography with a French trans. is also given here (pp. 176–91), but unfortunately Lameere has not done a new edition of the letters. The edition of Σ. Εὐστρατιάδης, Γρηγορίου τοῦ Κυπρίου οἰκουμενικοῦ πατριάρχου ἐπιστολαὶ καὶ μῦθοι (1910) is inaccessible to me, but as Lameere, 7 ff., shows, it is very incomplete and based on inadequate examination of the manuscripts. The two orations eulogizing Michael VIII and Andronicus II were published by Fr. Boissonade, *Anecdota Graeca* I, 313–93. The collected works are in Migne, PG 142, 20–469, where the theological works against the Latin doctrine and the supporters of the ecclesiastical union are printed together with the autobiography and the panegyrics.

[2] On his life, his political activity and his literary work cf. the detailed study of J. Verpeaux, *Nicéphore Choumnos, homme d'État et humaniste byzantin (c. 1250/5–1327)*, Paris 1959.

[3] Most of the known writings of Nicephorus Chumnus can be found in Fr. Boissonade, *Anecdota Graeca* I, II, III, V. The documents mentioned are also in Zepos, *Jus* I, 558 ff. and 549 ff. Cf. also 'Actes de l'Athos' 17 Nr. 26. Cf. the full information, including a list of his works in manuscript in J. Verpeaux, op. cit., 17 ff.

[4] Migne, PG 145, 447–548.

king Milutin and the Emperor's daughter Simonis, deserves close attention.[1] The poems of Manuel Holobolus[2] and his panegyric on Michael VIII,[3] and the poems of Manuel Philes, e.g. the account of his journey as ambassador to Russia, and various occasional poems to the members of the ruling house and high officials of Church and state, as well as his epigrams which contain descriptions of works of art, are all of some value for the history of the first Palaeologi.[4]

Among the most important historical sources for the age of the Palaeologi are the writings of Demetrius Cydones of Thessalonica, one of the most fertile and interesting writers of the fourteenth century. Throughout a long life he had occupied high office in the service of the state under several Emperors. As a neoplatonist he played a leading part in the development of philosophical thought; as a supporter of Church union and opponent of the hesychasts he influenced theological development. As the translator of several Latin works, including the *Summa Theologiæ* of Thomas Aquinas, he did much to promote a cultural understanding between Byzantium and the West which he had often visited. His extensive correspondence[5] and his rhetorical writings are of the greatest value,

---

[1] The report of the embassy is given in Sathas, Μεσ. βιβλ. I (1872), 154–93. Most of the rhetorical works are still unedited, but there is, however, a eulogy on Nicaea in Sathas I, 139–53. The *Miscellanea*, the main work of Metochites, is in the old edition of Chr. G. Müller and Th. Kiessling, *Th. Metochitae Miscellanea philosophica et historica*, Leipzig 1821. Of the twenty poems so far known, only three have been edited by M. Treu, *Dichtungen d. Grosslogotheten Theodoros Metochites*, Gymnasial-Progr. Potsdam 1895 (the first poem giving detailed information on Metochites' life is particularly important), and by R. Guilland, 'Le palais de Théodore Métochite', *Rev. des Études grecques* 35 (1922), 82. On the unedited poems cf. R. Guilland, 'Les Poésies inédites de Théodore Métochite', B 3 (1926), 265 ff.; idem, *Correspondance de Nicéphore Grégoras* 358 ff.; An evaluation of Metochites and his work as a whole is made by H. G. Beck, *Theodore Metochites. Die Krise des byzantinischen Weltbildes in 14. Jahrhundert*, Munich 1952. Of equal importance both for Metochites and for Chumnus, as well as for the intellectual life of the period, is the penetrating study by I. Ševčenko, *Études sur la polémique entre Théodore Métochite et Nicéphore Choumnos*, Brussels, 1962.

[2] Fr. Boissonade, *Anecdota Graeca* V, 159–82; M. Treu, BZ 5 (1896), 546 f.

[3] L. Previale, 'Un panegirico inedito per Michele VIII Paleologo', BZ 42 (1942), 1 ff.

[4] E. Miller, *Manuelis Philae carmina*, 2 vols., Paris 1855–7; A. Martini, *Manuelis Philae carmina inedita*, Naples 1900.

[5] G. Cammelli, *Démétrius Cydonès, Correspondance*, Paris 1930, gives a selection of fifty letters, with French trans. and a valuable biographical introduction. Cf. the important comments of G. Mercati, 'Per l'epistolario di Demetrio Cidone', *Studi bizant. e neoell.* 3 (1931), 203 ff., and his extremely valuable work, *Notizie di Procoro e Demetrio Cidone . . . ed altri appunti* (Studi e testi 56, Vatican 1931), containing several other letters and important writings. The autobiography of Demetrius Cydones published in this collection (359 ff.), has been translated by H. G. Beck, *Ostkirchliche Studien* 1 (1952), 208–25; 264–82. Cf. also the successful treatment of Loenertz, 'M. Paléologue et D. Cydonès', and particularly Loenertz, *Lettres de D. Cydonès*, where there is a very thorough investigation into the whole manuscript tradition as the preliminary to a complete edition of the correspondence, as well as an edition of five more letters and two minor writings. Now cf. the edition that has recently been published by R. J. Loenertz, *Démétrius Cydonès, Correspondence* I, II, Studi e Testi 186 (1956) and 208 (1960).

particularly the two addresses to John VI Cantacuzenus, the address to John V Palaeologus,[1] his Μονωδία ἐπὶ τοῖς ἐν Θεσσαλονίκῃ πεσοῦσιν (a sombre picture of the Zealot rule in Thessalonica) and his two exhortations (συμβουλευτικοί) urging the Byzantine people to unite with the Latins and to resist the Turks and giving a clear and historically accurate picture of the hopeless position of the Byzantine Empire about the year 1370.[2] Cydones also drew up several prefaces to the chrysobulls of John V.[3] The correspondence of Demetrius Cydones' pupil Manuel Calecas is also of considerable interest: he favoured the ecclesiastical union and opposed the hesychasts, and he ended his life in a Dominican house in 1410.[4] Apart from the historical works of Nicephorus Gregoras and John Cantacuzenus, our information on the hesychast controversy is found in the writings of the founder of the hesychast movement, Gregory Sinaites, its famous leader Gregory Palamas, the Patriarch Philotheus, the opponents of the hesychasts, Barlaam of Calabria and Gregory Acindynus, the well-known mystic Nicholas Cabasilas and also in the records of the councils summoned to settle the conflict.[5] Besides theological writings and letters[6] Nicholas Cabasilas is also the author of two interesting treatises, on usury and against the taking of usury,[7] and of a significant account of the alienation of church property.[8] Of great importance from the point of view of

[1] G. Cammellii, 'Demetrii Cydonii orationes tres, adhuc ineditae', BNJ 3 (1922), 67 ff. and 4 (1923), 77 ff., 282 ff.

[2] Migne, PG 109, 640 ff.; 154, 961 ff., 1009 ff.

[3] Zachariä von Lingenthal, 'Prooemien zu Chrysobullen von D. Cydones', S.B. d. Preuss. Akad. 1888, 1409 ff. Cf. also Sp. Lampros, 'Ein Proömium zu einem Chrysobull von D. Kydones', BZ 5 (1896), 339 f.

[4] Edited by R.-J. Loenertz, *Correspondance de Manuel Calécas* (Studi e Test 152, 1950), with detailed biographical introduction and very useful prosopographical information on M. Calecas' correspondents.

[5] An important part of the hesychast and anti-hesychast writings still remains unedited. What has so far been published is available for the most part in Migne, PG 150 and 151. Three important writings of Gregory Palamas have been published and translated by J. Meyendorff, *Grégoire Palamas, Défense des saints hésychastes*, Louvain 1959. A closer insight into both the edited and unedited hesychast and anti-hesychast works is given by the important work of Meyendorff, *Palamas*. Cf. also Beck, *Kirche*, 712 ff.

[6] P. Enepekides, 'Der Briefwechsel des Mystikers Nikolaos Kabasilas', BZ 46 (1953), 18 ff. Cf. the interesting observations on this in I. Ševčenko, 'Nicolaus Cabasilas' Correspondance and the Treatment of Late Byzantine Literary Texts', BZ 47 (1954), 49 ff.

[7] R. Guilland, 'Le traité inédit 'Sur l'usure' de Nicolas Cabasilas', Εἰς μνήμην Σ. Λάμπρου (1935), 269–77; Migne, PG 150, 727–50. On this cf. Zakythinos, *Crise monétaire* 120 ff.

[8] Until recently, this work was only known in the form of extracts published by Tafrali, *Thessalonique*, 261 ff. It is now available in full in the edition by I. Ševčenko, 'Nicolas Cabasilas' "Anti-Zealot" Discourse. A Reinterpretation', DOP 11 (1957), 81–171, who also makes it the subject of an important study which goes deep into the problems of Byzantine social history. Ševčenko shows that Cabasilas' discourse was

social history is the recently published 'Dialogue between the Rich and the Poor' by Alexius Makrembolites, which is a burning protest against social inequality and the economic misery of the Byzantine population.[1]

Of those Byzantine rulers who have left works, Manuel II Palaeologus (1391–1425) is one of the most outstanding. In addition to theological treatises, this cultured and gifted Emperor was the author of several rhetorical works and occasional writings, as well as a fairly large number of letters of considerable historical value which provide a vivid picture of the personality of the Emperor himself.[2] A still unedited work by John Chortasmenus, celebrating Bajezid's defeat at the battle of Angora (1402) as a miracle of the Mother of God, contains important information about the desperate situation of the Empire before the turn in events that took place in 1402.[3] We possess a particularly large number of rhetorical writings of the last decades of Byzantium which throw light upon the situation in the crumbling Empire and especially upon the conditions in the Peloponnese now recaptured by the Greeks, as well as many theological and polemical works on the burning question of union which had been much to the fore since the Council of Florence. Of primary importance are the writings of George Gemistus Plethon, philosopher and humanist, who dreamed of a renaissance of ancient Greece in the Peloponnese, the works of Bessarion, the learned leader of the union party and later Cardinal in the Church of Rome, of Mark Eugenicus, the famous champion of

not written against the rule of the Zealots in Thessalonica as was previously supposed, but against the imperial government's measures of secularization for military purposes, i.e. by granting monastic lands in *pronoia*. In a further article he examines a number of texts from the MS. Parisinus gr. 1276, which seem to represent the earlier redactions of the work with corrections and additions in Cabasilas' own hand: I. Ševčenko, 'The Author's Draft of Nicolas Cabasilas' "Anti-Zealot" Discourse in Parisinus graecus 1276', DOP 14 (1960) 179 ff. Since by reason of its watermarks this MS. must be dated to the later decades of the fourteenth century, Cabasilas' discourse was not produced in the fifth decade of this century, as Ševčenko had believed in his first article, and consequently was not directed against the government of Anne of Savoy but against the very extensive alienations of monastic properties and their distribution to pronoiars after the battle of Marica in 1371, which seems much more convincing (see below, p. 541). This later dating is undoubtedly a strong argument in favour of Ševčenko's thesis that Cabasilas' discourse has nothing to do with the Zealots.

[1] Published, with an English translation and commentary, by I. Ševčenko, 'Alexius Makrembolites and his "Dialogue between the Rich and the Poor"', ZRVI 6 (1960), 187–228

[2] E. Legrand, *Lettres de l'empereur Manuel Paléologue*, Paris 1893; Migne, PG 156, 82 ff.

[3] A translation of part of this work, from the Vienna MS. Suppl. gr. 75 is given by H. Hunger, *Byzantinische Geisteswelt*, Baden-Baden 1958, 282–6. For the other writings and correspondence of John Chortasmenus cf. idem, 'Zeitgeschichte in der Rhetorik des sterbenden Byzanz', *Wiener Archiv f. Gesch. des Slawentums u. Osteuropas* 3 (1959), 152 ff.

the Orthodox Church, and his brother John Eugenicus, of the rhetorician John Docianus and finally of Gennadius Scholarius, the first Patriarch of Constantinople after the collapse of the Empire.[1] The historian can sometimes glean important information from the poetry of the fifteenth century. This is particularly true of a poem ascribed in one version to Zoticus Paraspondylus and in the other to George Argyropulus, which describes the battle of Varna (1444) in the vernacular and adds many details to the accounts given in histories.[2]

Of vital importance for research into the administration and court affairs of late Byzantium is the work wrongly attributed to the Curopalates George Codinus on secular and ecclesiastical offices (περὶ τῶν ὀφφικίων τοῦ παλατίου Κωνσταντινουπόλεως καὶ τῶν ὀφφικίων τῆς μεγάλης ἐκκλησίας), which was compiled under John VI Cantacuzenus or soon after his reign. The work of the Pseudo-Codinus has a similar significance for the late Byzantine period as the *De cerimoniis* of Constantine VII and the *Cletorologion* of Philotheus for the middle Byzantine Empire. It gives information about the customs at court festivals, describes the rite of imperial coronation and other important state ceremonies, provides lists of the order of rank of both ecclesiastical and civil office-holders and dignitaries, together with particulars of their functions and the insignia of their various ranks. The occasional mention of the date when a procedure or an office was first instituted enhances the value of the work for the history of Byzantine court life and administration.

The most important work on jurisprudence in the late Byzantine period is that of the Nomophylax of Thessalonica, Constantine Harmenopulus, produced in 1345.[3] It is called the *Hexabiblos* on account of its division into six books, and it includes both civil and criminal law and provides a compendium of the legal manuals and codification of earlier times. It was based on the *Procheiron* and was supplemented by the *Synopsis Major* and *Synopsis Minor*, the *Epanagoge*, the *Ecloga*, the novels, the *Peira* and so on. Harmenopulus' legal compendium was very popular and was widely used even outside the frontiers of the Byzantine Empire. The same applies to the *Syntagma*

[1] Cf. the collection of texts in Sp. Lampros, Παλαιολόγεια καὶ Πελοποννησιακά, 4 vols., Athens 1912–30. The important new edition of G. Scholarius by E. Petit, H. A. Siderides and M. Jugie, Paris 1928 ff., is not accessible to me.
[2] ed. Gy. Moravcsik, Ἑλληνικὸν ποίημα περὶ τῆς μάχης τῆς Βάρνης, Οὑγγροελληνικαὶ Μελέται I, Budapest 1935.
[3] ed. G. E. Heimbach, Leipzig 1851. On the occasion of the 600th anniversary of the *Hexabiblos* the Law Faculty of the University of Thessalonica published a number of important historical and legal papers in their Τόμος Κωνσταντίνου Ἁρμενοπούλου, Thessalonica 1951.

of Matthew Blastares written in 1335, which presents a nomo-canonical collection (i.e. both secular and ecclesiastical rulings) in alphabetical order, and shortly after its publication was translated into Serbian by order of Stephen Dušan.[1] These works of compilation should be used with extreme caution as sources for the working legal practice of the fourteenth century, since it is well known that they contain much material that is out of date and no longer valid.

The many surviving monastic records of the age of the Palaeologi are an invaluable source for the study of the internal conditions of the late Byzantine Empire. The numerous documents of the monasteries of Mt. Athos are particularly important during this period, and they provide copious information upon the administrative and financial systems and the economic and social conditions of late Byzantium. Although much of the existing material in monastic archives is not yet available in print, our knowledge of this important type of source material has, however, been considerably enriched by the publications of recent years.[2]

For the relations between the Western powers, particularly the Italian maritime republics, and the East, N. Jorga has compiled a full record of material in archives.[3] A useful aid to study is the collection of rulings of the Venetian senate relating to the Byzantine lands for the period 1329–1463, published by F. Thiriet.[4] The recently discovered 'Book of Accounts' of the Venetian Giacomo Badoer, who was in the Byzantine capital from 1436–40 and kept records of his business, is of particular importance for the study of economic life in Constantinople before its fall.[5]

[1] ed. Rhalles and Potles, Σύνταγμα τῶν θείων καὶ ἱερῶν κανόνων VI, Athens 1859; Serbian trans. ed. St. Novaković, *Matije Vlastara Sintagmat* (The Syntagma of Matthew Blastares), Belgrade 1907.

[2] Cf. especially F. Dölger, *Aus den Schatzkammern des Heiligen Berges*, Munich 1948; P. Lemerle, *Actes de Kutlumus*, Paris 1945; A. Guillou, *Les Archives de Saint-Jean-Prodrome sur le mont Ménécée*, Paris 1955; F. Dölger, *Sechs byzantinische Praktika des 14. Jahrhunderts für das Athoskloster Iberon*, Abh. d. Bayer. Akad. d. Wissensch. N.F. 28, 1949; V. Mošin, 'Akti iz svetogorskih arhiva' (Documents from the archives of the Holy Mountain), *Spomenik Srpske Akad. Nauka* 91, 1939; V. Mošin-A. Sovre, *Supplementa ad acta Chilandarii*, Ljubljana 1948. Cf. above, p. 282, note 2, for details of the most important older publications. A collection of the Greek documents of Serbian rulers is given by A. Solovjev and V. Mošin, *Grčke povelje srpskih vladara* (Greek charters of the Serbian rulers), Belgrade 1936, with a valuable commentary on technical terms.

[3] N. Jorga, *Notes et extraits pour servir à l'histoire des croisades au XVe siècle*, 6 vols., Paris 1899–1916.

[4] F. Thiriet, *Régestes des délibérations du Sénat de Venise concernant la Romanie* I–III, Paris-La Haye, 1958–61.

[5] *Il libro dei conti di Giacomo Badoer*, ed. U. Dorini and T. Bertelè, Rome, 1956. An interesting source for economic conditions and the currency of the late Byzantine period is to be found in *Ein byzantinisches Rechenbuch des 15. Jahrhunderts*, ed. H. Hunger and K. Vogel, Denkschriften der Österr. Akad. d. Wissensch. Philos.-hist. Kl., vol. 78, pt. 2. Vienna 1963.

1. BYZANTIUM AS A MINOR STATE:
ANDRONICUS II

General bibliography: Stein, 'Untersuchungen'; Zakythinos, *Crise moné-taire*; Ostrogorsky, *Féodalité*; idem., *Paysannerie*; idem, 'The Palaelogi', CMH IV, Pt I (2nd. ed., 1966); G. Schlumberger, *Expedition des 'Almu-gavares' ou routiers catalons en Orient*, Paris 1902; A. Rubió i Lluch, *La Expedición y Dominación de los Catalanes en Oriente, Memor. de la R. Acad. de buenas letras de Barcelona* 4 (1883); idem, *Atenes en temps dels Catalans, Anuari de l'Inst. d'Estudis Catal.* 1 (1907); K. M. Setton, *Catalan Domination of Athens* 1311–88, Cambridge, Mass. 1948 (with detailed bibliography); idem, 'The Latins in Greece and the Aegean from the Fourth Crusade to the end of the Middle Ages', CMH IV, Pt I (2nd. ed., 1966); F. Taeschner, 'The Otto-man Turks to 1453', ibid.; I. v. Hammer-Purgstall, *Geschichte des osmanischen Reiches,* 10 vols., Pest 1827–35; Jorga, *Geschichte* I; E. Oberhummer, *Die Türken und das osmanische Reich,* Leipzig-Berlin 1917; H. Gibbons, *The Foun-dation of the Ottoman Empire,* Oxford 1916; W. L. Langer and R. P. Blake, 'The Rise of the Ottoman Turks and its Historical Background', *Am. Hist. Rev.* 37 (1932), 468–505; Wittek, *Mentesche*; idem, *The Rise of the Ottoman Empire,* London 1938; G. Georgiades Arnakis, Οἱ πρῶτοι Ὀθωμανοί, Athens 1947; Jireček, *Geschichte* I; Mutafčiev, *Istorija* II; M. Dinić, 'The Balkans 1018–1499', CMH IV, Pt I (2nd. ed., 1966); Miller, *Latins*; Kretschmayr, *Venedig* II; Heyd, *Commerce du Levant* I; G. I. Bratianu, *Recherches sur le commerce génois dans la Mer Noire au XIIIᵉ siècle,* Paris 1929; E. Č. Skržinskaja, 'Genuezcy v Konstantinopole v XIVv.'. (The Genoese in Constantinople in the fourteenth century), VV 1 (1947), 215–34.

Michael VIII emerged victorious from his defensive war against Western aggression, but in spite of most strenuous efforts he met with little success in his attempts to take the offensive and regain the lost Byzantine provinces. The Slavs maintained their hold on the northern half of the Balkan peninsula and though Michael VIII was able to win territory from a weakened Bulgaria, the rising power of the Serbian kingdom threatened him with further loss of territory. The Italian city republics still controlled the sea routes. By a supreme effort the Byzantine Empire had recovered part of the Peloponnese, but the greater portion was still in the hands of the Franks. Attica, together with Boeotia and the adjacent islands, also remained under Frankish rule. Thessaly and Epirus with Aetolia and Acarnania were subject to the Angeli and obstinately resisted the Emperor's authority, and it was in these separatist Greek states that the attempts at reoccupation by Michael VIII met with least success. Just as earlier on the disintegration of Byzantium from within had prepared the ground for the catastrophe of 1204, so now it was the separatist Greek forces which strongly resisted imperial efforts at unification,

Figure 59: *The So-Called Palace of Constantine Porphyrogenitus.* Constantinople, 12th or 13th century. Originally an annex to the Blachernae Palace, it stands by the Land Walls on a hill overlooking the Golden Horn. Although popularly known as the Palace of Constantine Porphyrogenitus, scholars assign it to the early Palaeologan period. Photo: Hirmer Fotoarchiv, Munich.

Figure 60: *St. John the Baptist*. Miniature icon, gold leaf ground on a limewood panel, 13th century. Ht. 7⅝", w. 5⅞". Virginia Museum Collections, Richmond. Photo: Virginia Museum.

and it was Thessaly, with its important Greek landowners, which played a leading part in opposing the Emperor's attempts at recovering control over the Balkan peninsula.

Yet continuous wars in the Balkans, and the exhausting defensive struggle against the expansionist drive of the Angevins, had completely drained the energy of the Byzantine Empire. Michael VIII's policy has a certain amount in common with that of Manuel I, particularly in its principles and method, its boldness and grandeur of conception, in its predominantly Western orientation, as well as in its positive achievements and negative results. It was an imperial policy on the grand scale which influenced world events from Egypt to Spain. But it imposed an intolerable burden on the Byzantine state. Michael Palaeologus' attempt to achieve the status of a great power exhausted the Empire in the same way as Manuel Comnenus' ambition to create a universal Empire had done a century before. In Asia, as on the previous occasion, the defensive capacity of the Byzantine Empire was undermined, and the consequences were now far more serious. The Empire was likewise drained of its military and financial resources, and once again there was a marked change of fortune. The Byzantine Empire began to decline without hope of recovery. There was a vast difference between the proud Empire of Michael VIII and the wretched state of his successors. In their hands Byzantium sank to the level of a second-rate power and finally became a mere pawn in the politics of its neighbours.

A simple explanation is usually offered for this transformation: Michael VIII had been a gifted statesman, while his successor Andronicus II was a feeble and incompetent ruler. In reality there were more deep-seated reasons to account for the rapid decline of Byzantine power which had set in by the close of the thirteenth century. The internal weaknesses of the state were incurable and increasing external pressure drove Byzantium irretrievably towards catastrophe. The health of the body politic was undermined and after the excessive demands made upon the Empire by Michael VIII the inevitable reaction set in. At the same time the Ottomans and Serbs, who were to exercise a decisive influence over future events, began their rapid rise to power, and the Byzantine state, militarily and financially exhausted, was powerless against the dual threat from the East and the Balkans. It is, therefore, these momentous factors in foreign and domestic politics, and not the personal qualities of its rulers, which really account for the decline of Byzantium.

Andronicus II (1282–1328) was certainly no great statesman; at the same time he was by no means the incompetent weakling often portrayed in modern histories. His policy was not free from serious blunders, but to his credit it must be admitted that he undertook many important and wise measures which show that he was fully conversant with the needs of the state. It was no fault of his that any attempts at reorganization could only have a very limited effect in so hopeless a situation and that they were invalidated by later events. Furthermore, he was a highly cultured man and showed marked interest in learning and literature, and men of high intellectual ability, such as Theodore Metochites and Nicephorus Gregoras, were amongst his closest advisers and collaborators. It is to the credit of the much abused Andronicus that the age of the Palaeologi was distinguished by its culture, and that Constantinople, despite its political decline, remained an intellectual centre of the world.

Under his father's rule Andronicus II had already taken part in affairs of government as co-Emperor.[1] Under him his son and co-Emperor, Michael IX († 1320), was destined to play an even more important political role. The growing importance of the position of co-Emperor is a characteristic feature of the era of the Palaeologi; it finds formal expression in the titular equality of the senior Emperor and co-Emperor, for henceforth not only the reigning Emperor himself, but also, with his consent, the first co-Emperor as the next heir-presumptive (but not any other co-Emperors) might bear the title of Basileus and Autocrator.[2] Here are the first steps towards the transformation of a centralized autocracy into the joint rule by members of the imperial house over the various parts of the Empire with their strongly separatist tendencies.

The idea of partitioning the Empire soon emerged, though to begin with it was only an offshoot of alien Western conceptions. It was Irene (Yolande) of Montferrat, the second wife of the Emperor Andronicus II, who demanded in the interest of her own sons that the imperial territory should be divided between all the imperial princes. But the decisive rejection of the Empress's plan was significant. Andronicus II refused the demands of his wife and a violent quarrel ensued: the Empress left the capital and went to

---

[1] Information on the rights and authority of the co-Emperor is given in Michael VIII's *prostagma* of November 1272; cf. above, pp. 422 and 457.

[2] Pseudo-Codinus 86. On this cf. F. Dölger, BZ 33 (1933), 141, Ostrogorsky, 'Avtokrator' 108 ff., 117 ff., and *Annales de l'Institut Kondakov* 10 (1938), 179 ff., where it is shown that the title of Autocrator was not applied to co-Emperors before the Palaeologian period.

Thessalonica, made contact from there with her son-in-law, the Serbian king Milutin, and attempted to secure the succession to the Serbian throne for one of her sons. But her plans failed to materialize as the primitive life in Serbia did not suit the fastidious princeling.[1] In this conflict the clash between the Romano-Byzantine and the Western conceptions of the state came to a head: what the Empress's demands amounted to was a confusion of the concepts of public law and private law. All this was well understood in Byzantium. 'Incredible as it may seem', wrote Nicephorus Gregoras, 'it was her wish that the sons of the Emperor should not rule as sovereigns in accordance with old Roman custom, but should partition Roman towns and lands after the Latin fashion. Thus each of her sons was to administer a particular part which was to be his own personal possession, and these individual portions were to be subject to the law of private property, as though they were inherited from their parents and could be passed on to their children and their children's children. This Empress', explained Nicephorus Gregoras, 'was of Latin origin and she took over this new custom from the Latins and attempted to introduce it among the Romans.'

Byzantium still clung to its imperial unity, but the structure of the state steadily disintegrated and the relationship between the centre and the provinces grew rapidly looser. In effect, the provinces were henceforth connected with the central power only through the person of the governor and for this reason relatives of the Emperor, or courtiers from his immediate circle, were normally given appointments of this kind. They were rapidly replaced since confidence in them was short-lived, but should this last slender link snap then it only remained for provinces to come under the control of local landowners.[2] The administrative system, the glory and backbone of the Byzantine state, was thus losing its strong centralization and its clear-cut hierarchical structure.

The establishment of the dynasty of the Palaeologi on the imperial throne signified a victory for the higher Byzantine nobility. The process of feudalization revived and reached its climax from the fourteenth century onwards. The secular and ecclesiastical landlords enlarged their estates, added to the number of their *paroikoi*, demanded increasingly extensive privileges and were frequently

[1] Nic. Gregoras I, 243 ff. On this see M. Laskaris, *Viz. princeze* 73, and M. Dinić 'Odnos izmedju kralja Milutina i Dragutina' (Relations between King Milutin and Dragutin) ZRVI 3 (1955), 77 ff. who places this episode in the period around 1315.
[2] Cf. the excellent comments of Stein, 'Untersuchungen' 20 ff.

granted complete immunity.[1] Amidst the general distress they lived a favoured life apart, more and more withdrawn from the state control. In marked contrast, the position of the small freeholder continually deteriorated, as also did that of the small landed nobility, whose holdings did not possess the same privileges and who lost both land and labour to the great estates. This was all the more so, in that only large estates with capital reserves were in a position to survive the terrible devastations caused by enemy inroads.

This development weakened the state politically, as well as seriously affecting its financial and military resources. The great landowners increasingly evaded their tax obligations and in addition absorbed property of the tax-paying peasant proprietors and the lesser gentry, so that the revenues of the state rapidly declined, all the more so since the revenue was further reduced by increasing misappropriations among those responsible for the administration of taxation. As well as the large private estates, the lands granted as *pronoia* were given new privileges. Originally the *pronoia* estates were held conditionally on lease, and could not be inherited, but now the pronoiars were increasingly permitted to transmit to their heirs the grant and revenues. On his accession Michael VIII allowed the *pronoia* grants of his supporters to become heritable; in the figurative language of Pachymeres, he invested their *pronoia*, granted for life only, with immortality.[2] In the course of time, the imperial government was increasingly prepared to agree to the request of a pronoiar for this concession. But as before the *pronoia* grant still represented property of a particular kind, for even a heritable *pronoia* estate could not be alienated and carried with it the obligation to render service, which was inherited together with the property.[3] However, though the heritable *pronoia* grant continued to be a non-transferable property entailing specific obligations, the increasing hereditary transmission of such properties indicated considerable modification of the original system, and pointed to the growing weakness of the central

[1] Cf. especially P. Charanis 'On the Social Structure and Economic Organization of the Byzantine Empire in the Thirteenth century and Later' BS 12 (1951), 94 ff.; A. P. Každan, *Agrarnye otnošenija v Vizantii XIII–XIV vv.* (Agrarian relations in Byzantium in the thirteenth and fourteenth centuries), Moscow 1952; G. Rouillard, *La vie rurale dans l'Empire byzantin*, Paris 1953; Ostrogorsky, *Paysannerie*; B. T. Gorjanov, Pozdnevizantijskij immunitet (Late Byzantine immunity), VV 11 (1956), 177 ff., 12 (1957), 97 ff.; G. A. Ostrogorsky, 'K istorii immuniteta v Vizantii', VV 13 (1958), 55 ff. (tr. 'Pour l'histoire de l'immunité à Byzance', B 28 (1958), 165 ff.); D. Angelov, *Agrarnite otnošenija v severna i sredna Makedonija prez XIV vek* (Agrarian relations in northern and central Macedonia in the fourteenth century), Sofia 1958.

[2] Pachymeres I, 97.

[3] Ostrogorsky, *Féodalité*, 92 ff.

power and its progressive acquiescence in the demands of the powerful feudal nobility.

The inadequacy of the *pronoia* system during the age of the Palaeologi is clearly revealed in the fact that the Byzantine army which, as early as the Comneni, had been largely composed of foreign mercenaries, now consisted almost entirely of them. This placed a heavy financial burden upon the state, and it was the maintenance of large bodies of mercenaries, essential to the foreign policy of Michael VIII, and his innumerable military undertakings, which brought financial ruin to the Empire. The Byzantine forces under Michael VIII undoubtedly numbered several tens of thousands, for in the year 1263 six thousand mounted troops alone were required to police the Peloponnese[1] and no less than ten thousand soldiers took part in a Bulgarian campaign in 1279.[2] These figures are modest when compared to the middle Byzantine period, or even the age of the Comneni, but for the impoverished state of the later period this army with its host of mercenaries meant a crushing burden.[3] Radical reductions had to be made, and this Andronicus II did. But to begin with he was too drastic. He thought that by relying on the naval strength of his Genoese allies he could completely do without the maintenance of a fleet with its particularly heavy expenditure.[4] To the burden of economic dependence upon Genoa he thus added the burden of naval dependence. The land army, too, was severely reduced and the Byzantine forces had reached such a low level, that in the opinion of contemporaries they were 'a laughing stock' and were virtually 'non-existent'.[5] Such judgments are no doubt grossly exaggerated, but they reflect the impression created amongst the population by the necessary, but all too rapid, reduction in Byzantine military strength. The contrast between the imposing forces of Michael VIII and the more than modest military resources of his successor was most striking, and, indeed, from the end of the thirteenth century armies of more than a few thousand warriors were rarely met with in Byzantium. This would be sufficient to explain why Byzantium surrendered its position as a great power and

---

[1] *Chronicle of the Morea* 4657 ff.

[2] Pachymeres I, 466.

[3] Chapman, *Michel Paléologue* 154, appears to accept a total strength at 20,000 men, assuming a mobile force of 15,000 with 5,000 garrisoning the towns. But no doubt the 15,000 soldiers fighting in the Peloponnese from about 1263-5 (according to Hopf, followed by Chapman) were only part of the available troops, since fighting was going on at the same time in other districts.

[4] Nic. Gregoras I, 174; 20.

[5] Nic. Gregoras I, 223, 20 and 158, 10.

was unable to resist the advance of the vastly superior forces of the Ottomans.

An important symptom of the financial crisis was the depreciation of the Byzantine gold coin which was debased by inferior alloys. The serious depreciation of the Byzantine *nomisma* from the mid-eleventh century onwards recovered under the later Comneni, since improved conditions permitted the minting of coins of considerably higher gold content. Thus at the beginning of the thirteenth century the gold coin appears to have had about 90 per cent of its face value.[1] Then the *hyperpyron*, as the Byzantine gold piece had come to be called, probably as early as the time of Alexius I,[2] depreciated further in value, and as a result confidence abroad in its stability was finally destroyed. From the middle of the thirteenth century, the Byzantine gold coin which once had held undisputed sway in international trade was increasingly replaced by the new gold coin, 'la buona moneta d'oro' of the Italian city republics.[3] In fact, under John Vatatzes, the gold content of the Byzantine *hyperpyron* amounted to sixteen carats, or two-thirds of its face value; after the recapture of Constantinople under Michael Palaeologus it was fifteen carats, and during the first years of Andronicus II only fourteen carats. During the period of distress at the beginning of the fourteenth century the *hyperpyron* sank to a half of its original value.[4] This led to a rapid rise in prices and the high cost of food meant widespread famine for the majority of the population, many of whom were reduced to penury.[5]

The malady could not be cured. In the following years the value of Byzantine currency fell with the increasing deterioration in the general situation, and to the growing economic distress was added the increasingly difficult problem of feeding the population. In order to remedy the rapid deterioration in the state's financial position, Andronicus introduced measures of taxation which resulted in a considerable increase in revenue, which rose to 1,000,000 *hyperpyra* a year.[6] This necessitated an increased burden of taxation which

[1] Cf. Stein, 'Untersuchungen' 11 ff.; Zakythinos, *Crise monétaire* 6 and 23.

[2] Cf. Dölger, 'Zur Textgestaltung der Lavra-Urkunden und zu ihrer geschichtlichen Auswertung', BZ 39 (1939), 64 f.; Zakythinos, *Crise monétaire* 2.

[3] Cf. Bratianu, *Études byz.* 221 ff.

[4] Pachymeres II, 493 f. On this cf. Zakythinos, *Crise monétaire* 8 ff., who correctly interprets the information given by Pachymeres and points out where earlier interpretations have gone wrong.

[5] Pachymeres II, 494. Graphic details of the misery and hunger of the Byzantine population are given in the letters of Athanasius Patriarch of Constantinople; cf. the extracts in R. Guilland, 'La correspondance inédite d'Athanase, Patriarche de Constantinople (1289–93; 1304–10)', *Mélanges Diehl* I (1930), 138 f. Cf. also Bratianu, *Études byz.* 162 ff.; Zakythinos, *Crise monétaire* 109 f.   [6] Nic. Gregoras I, 317.

further aggravated the already impoverished condition of the population, all the more so as extra payments in kind were increased by the introduction of a new tax, the so-called σιτόκριθον. This demanded that every agricultural labourer should deliver to the State a portion of his harvest *in natura*, in the form of six *modioi* of wheat and four *modioi* of barley *pro zeugarion*.[1] But Andronicus II managed to increase revenue, not only by higher taxes, but also by restricting the rights of tax exemption enjoyed by the big landowners —certain kinds of tax, particularly the land tax, were frequently excepted from exemption and had to be paid even by holders of deeds granting immunity.[2] Although the Emperor often found himself forced to relax this rule in favour of the most powerful feudal lords and the most influential monasteries, yet these measures must have been responsible for a considerable addition to the state revenue.

The desperate impoverishment of Byzantium is revealed by the fact that Andronicus' contemporaries adjudged the target achieved to be extremely high. The annual revenue of the Byzantine state in the early middle ages amounted to some seven to eight million *nomismata* of full value.[3] Now it was only with the greatest difficulty that taxation brought in one million gold pieces, though the gold coin carried only half of its original value. Before the tax reforms of Andronicus, revenue returns were obviously much smaller. Taxation did not, of course, provide the only source of revenue,[4] but it no doubt made up the major part of the budget, particularly as most of the customs dues were diverted from the Empire to the Italian maritime republics.

The increased receipts were intended to cover current administrative expenditure, payments to powerful neighbours and the maintenance of a fleet of twenty triremes and a standing army of 3,000 cavalry: 2,000 of the latter were to be stationed in Europe, 1,000 in Asia.[5] Thus the Emperor endeavoured to make amends for the drastic reduction of the forces which he had proposed on his accession under pressure of financial necessity. But the very programme

---

[1] Pachymeres II, 493.
[2] Cf. G. Ostrogorsky, 'Pour l'histoire de l'immunité à Byzance', BZ 28 (1958), 211 ff.
[3] Stein, *Studien* 142 ff.
[4] Stein, 'Untersuchungen' 10, considers that the sum of 1,000,000 *hyperp.* given by Nic. Gregoras was the state's total revenue from all sources, which can hardly be true. But, allowing for the depreciation in value of the *hyperpyron*, he is probably not exaggerating when he estimates that the revenue towards the end of the thirteenth century before the tax reforms of Andronicus was 'at most an eighth of that of the iconoclast Emperors'.
[5] Nic. Gregoras I, 317, 23.

he envisaged was lamentable. Small wonder that the disbursements to powerful neighbours became one of the major items of expenditure in the budget. Since Byzantium lacked the military strength to defend herself against her enemies, peace had to be purchased by means of hard-won savings set aside for this express purpose. Nicephorus Gregoras caustically compared this behaviour to that of a man 'who attempts to purchase the friendship of wolves by opening the veins in various parts of his body and allowing them to drain his blood until they are satisfied'.[1] Byzantium had become a minor state living on reputation. It collapsed because it could no longer fulfil its inherited responsibilities nor could it defend itself any longer in its present geographical position.

On the ecclesiastical problem, as on many other issues, the policy of Andronicus II differed radically from that of his father. Here as elsewhere circumstances demanded a complete reorientation. It was meaningless to pursue the idea of union, for this issue had been a dead letter, if not from the time of Martin IV's elevation to the pontificate, then at least since the days of the Sicilian Vespers. Immediately after his accession Andronicus had solemnly repudiated the idea of a union in order to follow a strictly orthodox course. John Beccus was compelled to relinquish the patriarchal see of Constantinople, and the office of Patriarch was once again bestowed on Joseph, who had been deposed after the Council of Lyons, and then, after his early death, upon the scholar Gregory of Cyprus. The serious spiritual crisis had been surmounted and the Empire was relieved of the anxiety which had caused such disquiet since the days of the Council of Lyons. But it was a long while before the Byzantine Church returned to normal. The old quarrel flared up between the radical ascetic party of the Zealots and the moderates, the so-called 'politicians', who were in sympathy with the government. The Zealots still proclaimed their loyalty to the Patriarch Arsenius, long dead, and they opposed both the government and the ecclesiastical authority. The disputes, violent though they were, ultimately came to nothing, and at the beginning of the fourteenth century the Arsenites, with the exception of a few isolated fanatics, resumed communion with the ruling powers of the Church.

During the reign of the most orthodox Emperor Andronicus II the importance of the Church and its influence on the entire spiritual life of the Empire reached its climax. The influence of monasticism

[1] Nic. Gregoras I, 317, 12.

Figure 61: *Church of St. George.* Staro Nagoricino, Yugoslavia. Exterior, west façade. Built by King Milutin of Serbia in 1312–1313. Photo: Cyril Mango.

Figure 62: *Monastery Church of Chilandari.* Mount Athos. Built for the Serbian Monastery on Mount Athos by King Milutin of Serbia, circa 1300.

grew particularly powerful. After the long crisis during the period of Latin rule and the severe trials during the period of ecclesiastical reunion, an era began in which Byzantine monasticism was distinguished for its spirituality and enjoyed material well-being. This was the golden age of Byzantine monasticism, especially the venerable monasteries of Mt. Athos; they increased both their spiritual influence and their lands. In addition, the monasteries of Mt. Athos, which had been directly subject to imperial jurisdiction since the time of Alexius I Comnenus, were subordinated to the Patriarch of Constantinople by a chrysobull of November 1312. In future, the *protos* of the Holy Mountain, who presided over the council of abbots from all the houses of Mt. Athos, was to be appointed by the Patriarch and not by the Emperor.[1] This was an important concession, for Mt. Athos exercised a growing influence on the entire spiritual life of the Empire. Andronicus also reorganized the dioceses and drew up a new order of precedence for individual sees in order to bring ecclesiastical administration up to date, for except for isolated instances it had remained unmodified since the time of Leo VI.[2] The disparity between the Byzantine Church's sphere of influence and the dwindling territory of the Byzantine state became increasingly apparent. While the state was disintegrating the Patriarchate of Constantinople remained the centre of the Orthodox world, with subordinate metropolitan sees and archbishoprics in the territories of Asia Minor and the Balkans now lost to Byzantium, as well as in the Caucasus, Russia and Lithuania. The Church remained the most stable element in the Byzantine Empire.

Owing to the military and financial weakness of the Empire, Andronicus II followed a policy of moderation abroad. He tried to guarantee his frontiers on all sides by concluding treaties of peace and friendship, even approaching the Western powers who were interested in Byzantium, though they had threatened no serious danger since the days of the Sicilian Vespers. After the premature death of his first wife, Anna of Hungary, he married Irene, daughter of the Margrave of Montferrat, in 1284. By this marriage the house of Montferrat lost its claims to the crown of Thessalonica, for the Margrave, who was then titular king of Thessalonica, surrendered his shadowy claim in favour of his daughter, the present Empress

[1] Ph. Meyer, *Die Haupturkunden für die Geschichte der Athosklöster* (1894), 190 ff.; Porf. Uspenskij, *Istorija Afona* III, 2 (1892), 140 ff.
[2] H. Gelzer, 'Ungedruckte und ungenügend veröffentlichte Texte der *Notitiae episcopatuum*', *Abh. d. Bayer. Akad. d. Wiss.* 21, Abh. 3 (1903), 595 ff. On the *Notitiae episcopatuum* now see the comprehensive survey of Beck, *Kirche*, 148 ff.

of Byzantium. With a like aim in view, the Emperor attempted to marry his son and successor Michael IX to the daughter of Philip and grand-daughter of Baldwin II, Catherine of Courtenay, who was regarded in the West as the titular Empress of Constantinople. Although negotiations for the projected marriage had been in progress for several years from 1288 onwards, they fell through, and in 1296 Michael IX married an Armenian princess.[1] The West still harboured hostile intentions towards Byzantium and was unwilling to throw overboard any tool that might help to realize them. The main support for these plans came from France and the kingdom of Naples; their most active protagonists were Philip of Tarentum, son of Charles II, king of Naples, and Charles of Valois, brother of the French king, Philip the Fair. The aim of both princes were feeble imitations of the expansionist policy of Charles of Anjou and only attained a certain measure of importance because of the weakness of the Byzantine Empire. Philip of Tarentum, to whom Charles II transferred the rights and properties of the house of Anjou in Romania in 1294, administered the Angevin inheritance in Epirus and claimed suzerainty over the Frankish dominions in Greece, and even over Thessaly, in place of the king of Naples. He secured for himself the possessions in Epirus by marrying Thamar, daughter of the Despot Nicephorus, and in 1295 the Epirotes ceded to him in addition the towns in Aetolia.

The power of the separatist Greek states collapsed even more rapidly than that of the Byzantine Empire. In addition, relations between Epirus and Thessaly were severely strained and armed conflict repeatedly broke out. In 1290 Byzantium took advantage of the situation to intervene successfully. The Byzantine army marched through Thessaly, penetrated deeply into Epirote territory and laid siege to Jannina. Dyrrachium also fell to the Byzantines, and for a brief period the Empire once again stretched to the shores of the Adriatic.

The alliance of Epirus with Philip of Tarentum cost the principality a portion of its territory without strengthening its position, and in the end widened the rift with Thessaly, where Philip's claim to over-lordship roused great resentment. In 1295 the sons of the Sebasto-crator John made war on Epirus; the Epirotes were defeated and appealed to the Byzantine Empire for support. The course of

---

[1] Cf. G. Bratianu, 'Notes sur le projet de mariage entre l'empereur Michel IX Paléo-logue et Catherine de Courtenay', *Revue du Sud-Est europ.* 1 (1924), 59 ff. Cf. Pia Schmid, 'Zur Chronologie von Pachymeres, Andronikos L. II–VII', BZ 51 (1958), 84.

events in the separatist Greek states seemed therefore to favour Byzantium, especially as the Despot Nicephorus of Epirus and the old enemy of the Byzantines, the Sebastocrator John of Thessaly, both died in 1296. Thereupon the Byzantine princess Anna, a niece of Michael VIII,[1] took over the regency in Epirus for her son Thomas, a minor, and with her the pro-Byzantine party gained control. At this point, however, Serbia intervened with superior forces and occupied Dyrrachium which had only recently been recaptured by the Byzantines.[2]

Serbian penetration southwards towards Byzantium had begun under Nemanja and it now reached a decisive stage. Since the days when Milutin (1282–1321) had seized Skoplje from the Byzantines in the first years of his reign (cf. above, p. 464), there had been continuous Serbian attacks upon the frontiers of Macedonia. In 1297 Byzantium, under its most able general, Michael Glabas, made a counter-attack, but this final effort was unsuccessful. The exhausted Empire had no chance in the field against the unimpaired vigour of the young Slav state. Andronicus II therefore decided to make a lasting peace with the Serbian king and offered him the hand of his sister Eudocia, widow of the Emperor John of Trebizond. This alliance with Byzantium offered Milutin welcome support in his struggle against his elder brother Dragutin.[3] A marriage with a Byzantine princess born in the purple meant an increase in prestige that was not to be underestimated, for even though the might of the Byzantine Empire was a thing of the past, the old traditions still lived on and the imperial house had lost none of its standing in the eyes of the neighbouring peoples. Milutin's displeasure was the more deeply roused when Eudocia flatly refused his hand. Byzantium was inextricably committed and, in view of the threatening attitude of the Serbian king, Andronicus II decided to offer him his little five-year-old daughter Simonis as wife.[4] He overruled the scruples of his clergy who opposed the marriage of the young princess with the Serbian king, already married for the third time to a Bulgarian spouse. Milutin, for his part, had to allay the protests of the nobility who were against concluding any peace with Byzantium,[5] for it was indeed the great Serbian magnates who had been the chief

---

[1] Daughter of his sister Eulogia, cf. Papadopulos, *Genealogie der Palaiologen* Nr. 30.
[2] Cf. Jireček, *Geschichte* I, 339.
[3] Cf. M. Laskaris, *Viz. princeze*, 55 ff., M. Dinić, 'Odnos izmedju kralja Milutina i Dragutina' (Relations between king Milutin and Dragutin) ZRVI 3 (1955), 57 ff.
[4] Cf. M. Laskaris, *Viz. princeze*, 58.
[5] See Theodore Metochites' account of the embassy, Sathas, Μεσ. βιβλ. I, 166.

beneficiaries from the recent conquest of Byzantine territory and the real driving force in the wars against Byzantium.[1] After protracted negotiations conducted with the Serbian court by the imperial plenipotentiary, Theodore Metochites, peace was signed in spring 1299 and the marriage was celebrated between Milutin and the young Simonis. The conquered lands north of the Ochrida-Prilep-Štip line were given as dowry to Milutin.

The peace treaty and the marriage of Milutin considerably increased Byzantine influence in Serbia. An intensive Hellenization of Serbian court life and administration now began and reached its climax in the Empire of Dušan.[2] The political orientation frequently changed, but the impregnation of the Serbian kingdom with Byzantine culture continued and was even intensified as it extended its frontiers at the expense of Byzantium and penetrated more deeply into the old Byzantine territories.

The weakness of Byzantium in the Balkans was determined partly by its internal military and financial exhaustion and partly by decisive external events in Asia Minor, as well as the complications of the Genoese-Venetian war in which Byzantium was involved to its detriment. Michael VIII had endeavoured to prevent either the Genoese or the Venetians from gaining the upper hand, but Andronicus committed the fatal political blunder of giving unilateral and unreserved support to Genoa. Though Venice commanded the southern part of the Aegean, Genoa had built up a strong position in the northern Archipelago, in the Sea of Marmora and in the Pontus, and from Galata she controlled the sea passage from the Mediterranean to the Black Sea with its hinterland.[3] The increase of Genoese power revived the longstanding rivalry between Venice and Genoa. In 1294 war broke out between them and the Empire was soon implicated. As the Emperor afforded shelter behind the walls of the capital to the Genoese who were under attack in Galata, the Venetians made reprisals in the suburbs outside the walls of Constantinople. The Byzantines then replied with counter reprisals against the Venetians resident in Constantinople, and the war between Venice and Genoa resolved itself into a war between Venice

[1] Cf. G. Ostrogorsky, 'Dušan i njegova vlastela u borbi sa Vizantijom' (Dušan and his nobles in the struggle against Byzantium), *Zbornik u čast šeste stogodišnjice Zakonika cara Dušana*, I (1951), 79 ff.

[2] Cf. V. Mošin, 'Vizantiski uticaj u Srbiji u XIV v.' (Byzantine influence in Serbia in the fourteenth century), *Jugosl. Istoriski Časopis* 3 (1937), 147 ff.

[3] Cf. G. J. Bratianu, *Recherches sur le commerce génois dans la Mer Noire au XIIIe siècle*, Paris 1929, 250 ff.

and Byzantium. The Genoese calmly left their allies in the lurch, withdrew from the fighting and concluded with Venice the 'eternal peace' of 1299.[1] Byzantium, without a fleet, found itself in a most precarious position; however firmly the Empire, from motives of prestige, resisted the Venetian demands for compensation, it was ultimately compelled, under the threat of Venetian ships in the Golden Horn, to bow to superior force and make the payments demanded. The ill-fated war was terminated in 1302 by a ten years' armistice; the Venetians were confirmed in their old commercial privileges and were awarded a number of new colonies in the Archipelago. The Genoese, however, profited from their experience gained in the war to build a strong wall round Galata. Thus a strong Genoese fortress arose next to the Byzantine capital. To crown all, the Genoese commander Benedetto Zaccaria of Phocaea, who had distinguished himself as an admiral in the service of the French king Philip the Fair and had amassed fabulous wealth from the alum mines of Phocaea, seized the Byzantine island of Chios in 1304.[2] Thus both maritime republics emerged from the war with increased strength, while the Empire reaped only fresh sacrifices and humiliations from a war into which it had been unwittingly drawn.

But the most decisive events took place in Asia Minor and it was here that the Empire was hit hardest. The Mongol invasion which had stirred up the whole of the Near East towards the middle of the thirteenth century had driven many Turkish tribes towards Asia Minor. Fresh hordes streamed towards the Byzantine-Seljuq frontier and the new influx soon descended upon the Byzantine territories of western Asia Minor in search of land and booty. In the course of time, the Turkish incursions became increasingly violent, while Byzantine resistance was extremely feeble. The system of frontier defences erected in the Nicaean days had fallen into decay and the country was defenceless against foreign invasion. Without a shadow of doubt the restoration of 1261 had considerably weakened Byzantine powers of resistance in Asia Minor. Since that time the central authority had been withdrawn farther from the eastern frontier and the whole centre of gravity of imperial policy had shifted towards the west. The new tasks awaiting the restored Empire in the Balkans and the dangers threatening from the west necessitated the full concentration of its forces in its European lands, and financial and

[1] Tafel and Thomas III, 391 ff.
[2] Hopf, *Geschichte* I, 372 ff.; Heyd, *Commerce de Levant* I, 445 ff. 461 ff.; Miller, *Essays* 283 ff.

military resources alike were insufficient to defend the territories in Asia. Under Michael VIII the situation was such that the *akritai* (border troops) on the Seljuq frontier were without pay and drifted away,[1] or that the troops assigned to frontier defence in Asia were recalled to the European theatres of war. 'In this way', wrote a contemporary, 'the defences of the eastern territory were weakened, whilst the Persians (Turks) were emboldened to invade lands which had no means of driving them off.'[2] In addition, the increasing feudalization of the Palaeologian Empire hastened the decay of the military freeholdings which had been established in the frontier districts during the Nicaean period. Thus financial, social and general political causes combined to undermine the defensive system in Asia Minor.

The entire territory succumbed to the Turkish conquest and, though a few Byzantine towns offered isolated resistance, in the open country generally speaking the collapse was complete. By 1300 practically the whole of Asia Minor was in Turkish hands. Soon only a few fortresses stood out above the Turkish flood— Nicaea, Nicomedia, Brusa, Sardes, Philadelphia, Magnesia and isolated seaports such as Heraclea on the Pontus, Phocaea and Smyrna.[3] The Turkish leaders divided up the conquered territory amongst themselves, with the result that western Asia Minor was split up into a number of Turkish principalities. What used to be Bithynia fell to Osman, founder of the Ottoman dynasty which was destined to unite all Turkish tribes under its sceptre and to subdue Byzantium as well as the southern Slav kingdoms.

Byzantium was helpless in face of the catastrophe because of its military impotence. Asia Minor, once the backbone of Byzantine power, was lost to the Empire for ever. Andronicus II had vainly counted on the support of the Alans, who volunteered to serve against the Turks in return for permission to settle in the Empire. They arrived 10,000 strong with women and children, in accordance with the agreement, but the result was entirely negative. Under the leadership of the co-Emperor Michael IX the Alan troops advanced upon Asia Minor, but suffered a heavy defeat in their first engagement with the Turks and hastily withdrew, plundering and pillaging the Byzantine population.

In this critical situation a fresh possibility of help presented itself

[1] Nic. Gregoras I, 138.
[2] Pachymeres I, 310. Cf. also the excellent comments of Wittek, *Mentesche* 16 ff., 24 ff.
[3] Cf. Wittek, *Mentesche* 18.

to the Emperor. Roger de Flor, the illustrious leader of the Catalan Grand Company, offered his services and those of his men in the struggle against the Turks. The Catalan Grand Company was well versed in warfare. It had supported king Frederick of Sicily in the struggle against the Angevin attempts at reconquest, and after the peace of Caltabellota, which ended the Angevin-Aragon war and established the independence of Sicily under the house of Aragon, the Catalan soldiers were out of employment and were looking for new spheres of action. The Byzantine Emperor gladly accepted their offer, and towards the end of 1303 Roger de Flor arrived in Constantinople with 6,500 men.[1] Andronicus II, who staked all on the Catalans, agreed to advance four months' pay, gave Roger de Flor the hand of his niece Maria Asen in marriage,[2] appointed him *megas dux* and later even conferred on him the title of Caesar. At the beginning of 1304 the Catalans crossed over to Cyzicus and in the spring advanced upon Philadelphia, which was besieged by the Turks. The Turks were decisively beaten and Roger de Flor made a victorious entry into the liberated town. This victory proves that a small but reliable army could suffice to save the situation. The tragedy was that the Byzantine Empire possessed no such army and could only raise one by recruiting mercenaries. But an army of alien stock was a double-edged weapon, particularly as it was an autonomous body and could withdraw at any moment from the control of the Empire which had no means of enforcement or compulsion at its disposal.

After their victory the Catalans embarked on pillaging expeditions, made the entire neighbourhood on sea and land unsafe, preyed indiscriminately upon Byzantines and Turks and finally, instead of making war on the Turks, attacked Byzantine Magnesia. There was a feeling of relief in Constantinople when the Catalans were induced to withdraw to Europe. They passed the winter of 1304–5 in Gallipoli and were to return again to Asia early in the following year. But tension between the imperial government and the Catalan Grand Company increased. In Byzantium there was rising indig-

[1] A. Rubió y Lluch has done particularly valuable research on the history of the Catalans in the East; his numerous works are cited and commented on by K. M. Setton, p. 286 ff. (cf. below). Cf. also G. Schlumberger, *Expédition des 'Almugavares' ou routiers catalans en Orient*, Paris 1902; Miller, *Latins* 211 ff.; L. N. d'Olwer, *L'expansio de Catalunya en la Mediterrània oriental*, Barcelona 1926; and especially K. M. Setton, *Catalan Domination of Athens* 1311–88, Cambridge, Mass. 1948.

[2] She was a daughter of the Bulgarian tzar Ivan III Asen (1279–80) who fled to Constantinople and of Irene Palaeologina, a sister of Andronicus II; cf. Papadopulos, *Genealogie der Palaiologen* Nr. 44.

nation with these arrogant mercenaries and the co-Emperor Michael IX was particularly ill-disposed towards them. The Catalans, too, were disgruntled at the irregularity of their pay which they blamed for any excesses on their part. In April 1305 Roger de Flor was assassinated in the palace of Michael IX. In this way it was hoped that the country would get rid of the troublesome mercenaries, but in reality the worst was yet to come. The indignant Catalans started a campaign against the Byzantines to avenge their leader and open war broke out. The heterogeneous army of Michael IX, reinforced with Alans and Turks, was decisively defeated at the fortress of Aprus; the heir to the throne who had fought with great bravery in the vanguard was wounded and only escaped by fleeing to Didymotichus. The most he could hope for was the defence of the important towns in Thrace, for the open country was ravaged by the enemy. For two whole years the Catalans, whose reduced forces had been strengthened by reinforcements from home and by the addition of Turkish contingents, mercilessly plundered and ravaged the countryside of Thrace.

The situation was the more urgent as at the same time Bulgarian pressure from the north increased. Bulgaria, which had been split into several small principalities and appeared to have succumbed to the Tartars in the last years of the thirteenth century, had now shaken off the Tartar yoke in consequence of the complications in the Golden Horde after the downfall of Nogaj (1299), and it once again embarked upon the road to recovery under Theodore Svetoslav (1300–22). Taking advantage of the desperate position of the Byzantine Empire, the Bulgarian tzar extended his frontiers south of the Balkan chain of mountains and occupied several important fortresses and seaports on the shores of the Black Sea, including the much disputed bases of Mesembria and Anchialus. The Byzantine government had no option but to put up with the loss and concluded a peace treaty with the Bulgarian tzar by the terms of which he retained all his conquests (1307).[1] Meanwhile, the Catalans, after ravaging Thrace, crossed the mountains of Rhodope and took possession of Cassandria in the autumn of 1307. From here they continued their plundering expeditions, and even the monasteries of Mt. Athos did not escape their fury, though their attack

[1] F. Dölger, 'Einiges über Theodora, die Griechin, Zarin der Bulgaren (1308–30)', *Mélanges Grégoire* I (1949), 215 f., note 2 (= *Paraspora* 225 f., note 8) considers that it was in connection with this peace treaty that Theodora, the daughter of Michael IX, was given in marriage to the tzar Theodore Svetoslav (i.e. as early as 1308 and not 1320, as used to be thought).

upon the stronghold of Thessalonica in the spring of 1308 was beaten off.

During this period of acute distress the anti-Byzantine plans of the West revived again. Philip of Tarentum, hoping to extend his position in the area of Epirus and Albania, joined forces with the Catholic Albanians and seized Dyrrachium. His campaign against the pro-Byzantine Despina Anna of Epirus proved a failure (1306). More dangerous to Byzantium than the 'Despot of Romania and ruler of the kingdom of Albania', as Philip now styled himself, was the energetic Charles of Valois. This prince without a principality, who had married the titular Empress Catherine of Courtenay, formerly sought after by Byzantium, made great efforts to revive the expansionist plans of Charles of Anjou, and now that Byzantium seemed plunged in chaos he aspired to the imperial crown of Constantinople. In 1306 he concluded an agreement with the Venetian republic which could not resist the temptation to revert once more to the policy of the fourth crusade. In 1308 a treaty was signed with the Serbian king Milutin who never seems to have broken completely with Byzantium; involved in a lengthy war (1301–12) with his brother Dragutin, he could not intervene effectively against Byzantium nor renew the conquests in Macedonia.[1] Pope Clement V lent his moral support to the undertaking by pronouncing anathema upon the Byzantine Emperor (1307). Charles of Valois also found supporters amongst the Byzantine nobility, a circumstance that reveals the degree of disintegration in Byzantium. The governor of Thessalonica, John Monomachus, and the commandant of Sardes, Constantine Ducas Limpidaris, declared themselves ready to accept the French prince as their sovereign. In the existing circumstances the most decisive factor was the winning over of the Catalan Grand Company which was, in effect, master of the situation in the Byzantine East. In this Charles of Valois was successful, although king Frederick of Sicily tried hard to assert his suzerainty over the Catalans. In 1308 Charles' plenipotentiary, Theobald of Cepoy, arrived in Euboea with eleven Venetian vessels; from there he proceeded to Cassandria and accepted in the name of his master an oath of fealty from the Catalan Grand Company.

He was soon undeceived. The Catalans, completely indifferent to the plans and intentions of Charles of Valois, moved from Cassandria

---

[1] Cf. M. Dinić, 'Odnos izmedju kralja Milutina i Dragutina' (Relations between king Milutin and Dragutin), ZRVI 3 (1955), 62 ff. where in many respects he casts new light on the events of this period in Serbia.

to Thessaly, where John II (1303-18), a grandson of the Sebasto-crator John, was ruling. He was a sickly youth who had first been placed under the tutelage of Guy II de la Roche, duke of Athens, but after the latter's death had gone over to the Byzantine Emperor and had become engaged to his illegitimate daughter Irene. The land was entirely controlled by the great feudal lords and as a state Thessaly was at its last gasp. The commanding position which it had once held under the Sebastocrator John I was now a distant memory and any resistance to the Catalans was out of the question. For a year the Grand Company led a carefree existence, living on the rich gifts of the fertile soil. Then in the spring of 1310, supplied with Thessalian money, they repaired to central Greece and entered the service of Walter, duke of Athens. But they clashed with the Franks, as they had previously quarrelled with the Byzantines, and war resulted. On 15 March 1311 at Cephissus in Boeotia the Catalans won a decisive victory over the numerically superior forces of the Franks, and duke Walter of Brienne and the majority of his knights were slain in the battle. Frankish power in Thebes and Athens was broken and was replaced by a Catalan principality. Athens, which had been under French rule for a century, now fell to the Catalans for a period of over seventy years.[1]

Such was the strange outcome of the extraordinary Catalan expedition. A handful of warlike adventurers from the West had forced its way from Constantinople and Philadelphia to Athens, and there, in the oldest and most illustrious centre of culture, had established its own principality. The adventurous exploits of the Catalans in Asia Minor, Thrace and Macedonia, in northern and central Greece and their victories over Turks, Byzantines and Franks serve to underline the weakness of the Byzantine Empire and the dissident Greek and Latin states at that time. The Catalans made their appearance in the East at an opportune moment, when Byzantine power had already declined and Turkish power was still in its infancy.

The withdrawal of the Catalans to Frankish Greece had brought the Byzantine Empire a measure of relief. The aggressive plans of Charles of Valois were left high and dry. In Thessaly, Cepoy broke away from the Catalans from whom neither he nor his master had anything further to expect. At the same time the legal claim of the Valois to the imperial crown of Constantinople had vanished with the death of his wife, the titular Empress Catherine of Courtenay, in

---

[1] Cf. K. M. Setton, *Catalan Domination of Athens*, 1311-88, Cambridge, Mass. 1948.

1308. The right of succession passed to her daughter Catherine of Valois. As a child she was married in 1313 to Philip of Tarentum who considered an alliance with the titular Empress of such importance that he dissolved his marriage with Thamar of Epirus. Though supported by France and Naples, Philip's plans for conquest did not, however, advance beyond the preparatory stages. Thus the schemes of Charles of Valois and Philip of Tarentum—pale shadows of the policy of Charles of Anjou—disappeared in smoke. Western efforts at a restoration were finished. In 1310 Venice signed a twelve year armistice with the Byzantine Emperor. The king of Serbia once again established close relations with Byzantium. He sent the Emperor reinforcements, to the number of some two thousand mounted troops.[1] When his son Stephen rose against him in 1314, he was overthrown and blinded and sent to the Byzantine court.[2]

The Byzantine position in the Peloponnese was also strengthened. In 1308 Andronicus II had made an important change in the administration of the Morea by ending the unfortunate system by which the Byzantine governors of the Morea were changed each year. After this, Cantacuzenus, father of the future Emperor John VI, governed the Byzantine lands in the Morea until his early death in 1316. His period of office marked the beginning of the revival of Byzantine power in the Peloponnese. His work was continued by Andronicus Asen (1316–21), a son of the former Bulgarian tzar Ivan III Asen and of the Emperor's sister Irene Palaeologina, who by a successful campaign against the Franks managed to consolidate and expand Byzantine power in the Morea. In addition, Constantinople granted Monemvasia, the most important Byzantine seaport in the Morea, considerable trade privileges in order to establish a Byzantine commercial centre in the Peloponnese to counterbalance the Venetian centres of Coron and Modon.[3]

[1] Nic. Gregoras I, 268. Cf. also Andronicus II's chrysobull to Chilandari of October 1213, 'Actes de l'Athos' 17, Nr. 26.

[2] Jireček, *Geschichte* I, 346 ff. M. Dinić, 'Odnos izmedju kralja Milutina i Dragutina', ZRVI 3 (1955), 77 ff.

[3] A chrysobull, no longer extant, was granted to the city by Michael VIII, probably soon after the reconquest of Constantinople (Dölger, *Reg.* 1897). It received a further chrysobull from Andronicus II in 1284: Miklosich-Müller V, 154/55 (*Reg.* 2102). The date of the very important chrysobull, only preserved in the *Chronicon Maius* of Sphrantzes (ed. Bonn, 400–4), which lists the privileges of the merchants of Monemvasia with great detail and accuracy, is uncertain. Zachariae, *Jus* III, 634–8 (= Zepos, *Jus* I, 538–41), and Miklosich-Müller V, 165–8, treat it as a chrysobull of Andronicus II of Nov. 1317 (more correctly 1316). F. Dölger (*Facsimiles byz. Kaiserurk.*, Sp. 34, *Reg.* 1897 and BZ 34 (1934), 126 f.) has several times put forward the view that it is a chrysobull of Andronicus III of 1336 but in his *Reg. IV* he refers to it as a chrysobull of Andronicus II of Nov. 1316, abandoning his earlier view, and giving detailed reasons for his change of opinion

An important change also took place in the two separatist Greek states. In the year 1318 the dynasty of the Angeli in Epirus and Thessaly became extinct; the Despot Thomas was murdered by his nephew Nicholas Orsini of Cephalonia. The latter, an enemy of the Angevins, went over to the Greek Orthodox faith and established himself in Epirus as successor to the murdered Thomas and married his widow, Anna, the daughter of Michael IX. A year later he received the title of despot from Byzantium.[1] Jannina as well as other strongholds in the country came under the control of the Byzantine Emperor. Still more decisive was the change of events in Thessaly, for after the death of John II it ceased to exist as an independent state. The Byzantine Emperor claimed the province as a vacant imperial fief. But only the northern portion of the country recognized his suzerainty, and even this part only submitted nominally.[2] The most powerful of the Thessalian magnates attempted to make themselves independent and founded principalities of their own, in particular the old Byzantine noble family of the Melisseni. In addition, vast numbers of Albanians broke into Thessaly; this was the beginning of the Albanian migration which poured over the whole of Greece during the following decades. However, the greater part of the former principality with its capital Neopatras was seized by the Catalan duchy of Athens, while the Venetians occupied the port of Pteleon. Byzantium had once again to shoulder the burden, and even the modest attempts at improvement, which made themselves felt during the decade after the removal of the Catalan plague, were soon wiped out by the unfortunate feud between the old Emperor and his grandson Andronicus III which plunged the Empire into prolonged civil war.

(*Reg.* 2383). However, it follows from Miklosich-Müller V, 166, 5, that this is the first time that the person granting this chrysobull has given a privilege to Monemvasia. Therefore—quite apart from other by no means minor difficulties—this chrysobull cannot have been granted by Andronicus II, the author of the chrysobull of 1284, but should be dated to Andronicus III, if not to Andronicus IV in 1376. It is true that its peculiarities fit neither the one nor the other in evey respect and one would also have to make certain corrections to the date that is attached to it—quite considerable corrections in the case of Andronicus III. But in any case there is no question as to the authenticity of this valuable document.

[1] Cf. Ferjančić, *Despoti*, 47 f.

[2] Nic. Gregoras I, 229 ff., 278 f. Cf. I. Sokolov, 'Krupnye i melkie vlasteli v Fessalii' (Great and lesser nobles in Thessaly), VV 24 (1923–6), 35 ff.; A. Solovjev, 'Fessalijskie archonty v XIV v.' (The magnates of Thessaly in the fourteenth century), BS 4 (1932), 159 ff.

2. THE PERIOD OF CIVIL WARS:
SERBIAN ASCENDANCY IN THE BALKANS

General bibliography: V. Parisot, *Cantacuzène homme d'État et historien*, Paris 1845; Florinskij, *Andronik i Kantakuzin*; idem, *Južnye Slavjane i Vizantija vo vtoroj četverti XIV v.* (The South Slavs and Byzantium in the second quarter of the fourteenth century), St. Petersburg 1862; D. Muratore, *Una principessa Sabauda sul trono di Bisanzio*, Chambéry 1905; F. Dölger, 'Johannes VI. Kantakuzenos als dynastischer Legitimist', *Annales de l'Inst. Kondakov* 10 (1938), 19–30 (= *Paraspora* 194–207); Lemerle, *L'Émirat d'Aydin*; Tafrali, *Thessalonique*; Ševčenko, 'Nicolas Cabasilas'; Meyendorff, *Palamas*; R. Guilland, *Essai sur Nicéphore Grégoras*, Paris, 1926; Zakythinos, *Despotat*, I and II; Jiriček, *Geschichte I*; S. Stanojević, *Istorija srpskoga naroda* (History of the Serbian people), 3rd ed. Belgrade, 1926; V. Ćorović, *Istorija Jugoslavije*, Belgrade 1933; *Istorija naroda Jugoslavije* (History of the peoples of Yugoslavia), I, Belgrade 1953; S. Novaković, *Srbi i Turci XIV i XV veka* (Serbs and Turks in the fourteenth and fifteenth centuries), new edition, with corrections and additions by S. Ćirković, Belgrade 1960; Mutafčiev, *Istorija* II; A. Burmov, 'Istorija na Bûlgarija prez vremeto na Šišmanovci' (History of Bulgaria under the Šišmanovs), *Godišnik na Sofijskija Univ.*, Ist.-filol. fak. 43, Sofia 1947; Stein, 'Untersuchungen'; see also the general bibliography cited above, p. 478.

The quarrels between the old and the young Andronicus began a long succession of civil wars which hastened the internal collapse of the Byzantine Empire. This dynastic family rivalry inaugurated a period of severe internal crises which exhausted the Empire and ultimately left it defenceless against the expansion of the Turks and Serbs. The conflict between grandfather and grandson arose to begin with for personal reasons. Andronicus III, the eldest son of Michael IX, an attractive and gifted youth of handsome appearance, had once been the favourite of the old Emperor. The rank of co-Emperor had been bestowed upon him when he was still young and he was regarded as the second heir-presumptive in succession to his father. In the course of time mutual ill-feeling arose. The frivolous behaviour of young Andronicus, his extravagance and dissipation, sorely tried the patience of the austere old Emperor, while, for his part, the young prince found the tutelage of his father and grandfather increasingly irksome. The unhappy outcome of one of his love affairs precipitated the breach. Andronicus' followers plotted the assassination of their master's rival and then found that it was his brother Manuel whom they had murdered in tragic error. The terrible news hastened the death of Michael IX who was lying seriously ill in Thessalonica († 12 October 1320), and so infuriated the old Emperor that he decided to exclude Andronicus from the succession.

The young Andronicus, however, had many supporters, particularly among the younger Byzantine nobility, and the unpopular old Emperor met with powerful opposition led by John Cantacuzenus, a young and wealthy magnate and close friend of Andronicus III, and the ambitious adventurer Syrgiannes, of Cuman descent on his father's side though his mother's family was related to the imperial house. A leading part in the conspiracy was also played by Theodore Synadenus and the upstart Alexius Apocaucus who both held important commands in Thrace and Macedonia. Syrgiannes and Cantacuzenus secured for themselves governorships in Thrace on payment of considerable sums. The abuse of the sale of offices was widespread in the Empire of the Palaeologi; even the enlightened Logothete Theodore Metochites seems to have assented to the practice.[1] On this occasion it was destined to cost the government dear, for Syrgiannes and Cantacuzenus used their newly-acquired administrative districts as a centre for organizing resistance. Exploiting the discontent of the overtaxed province, the Byzantine aristocracy unleashed a powerful movement against the government of Constantinople. At Easter 1321, Andronicus III left the capital to join the army which his friends had raised near Adrianople. In the impending struggle he had a decisive psychological advantage over the old Emperor, whose reign had cost the Empire severe losses and privations. Under the pressure of financial necessity, Andronicus II had been compelled to resort to stringent measures of economy, a step which was hardly conducive to imperial popularity. Andronicus III, however, was not burdened by any responsibility, and he was in a position to make the most extravagant promises and adopt any demagogic expedient. In order to win supporters, he made gifts of land or granted privileges with the greatest lavishness. He is said to have exempted Thrace from any obligation to pay taxes.[2] Such expedients were more decisive for the outcome of the civil war than the military strength of the opponents. It is not surprising that the population of Thrace supported the generous young Emperor. When his army under the command of Syrgiannes began its march on Constantinople, the old Emperor, fearing an insurrection in the capital, hastened to conclude peace.

Andronicus III was assigned Thrace and certain districts in Macedonia which he had already awarded to his supporters; the rest, including the capital, was retained by Andronicus II. Thus the

---

[1] Nic. Gregoras I, 302, 3 and 426, 3.
[2] Nic. Gregoras I, 319, 14.

Figure 63: *Theodore Metochites*. Detail of mosaic panel over the central door, inner narthex, Church of St. Savior in Chora (Kariye Djami), Constantinople, circa 1310. One of the great statesmen and scholars of his time, Theodore Metochites restored and enlarged the church between 1303 and 1320. He is shown here presenting the church to Christ enthroned. (See also Figures 64, 65, 66.) Photo: Byzantine Institute, Inc., Washington, D.C.

Figure 64: *Church of St. Savior in Chora (Kariye Djami)*. Exterior, west
façade, Constantinople, restored and enlarged, 1303–1320. This small church,
now in the process of restoration by the Byzantine Institute of America, is perhaps the best surviving example in the style of the so-called Byzantine Revival of
the 14th century. At that time Theodore Metochites enlarged and enriched the
church, adding the exonarthex on the west façade and the Pareccleseion (mortuary chapel) on the south flank (right). The minaret is a Turkish addition.
(See also Figures 63, 65, 66.)   Photo: Robert L. Van Nice.

imperial territory was partitioned after all, though a short time before such a measure had been entirely unacceptable to Byzantines. In order to preserve a semblance of unity in external affairs, Andronicus II reserved to himself the right to treat with foreign powers. But this principle was soon abandoned; each of the two Emperors pursued his own foreign policy, at variance with, or even directed against, the policy of his rival. Peace did not last for long and in 1322 civil war again broke out. Rivalry between the *megas dux* Syrgiannes and the *megas domesticus* Cantacuzenus created dissension in the camp of the young Andronicus. As Andronicus III took the side of his friend Cantacuzenus, Syrgiannes, who up to now had been the real leader of the enterprise, went over to the old Emperor and in his service directed the struggle against his former master and protégé. In the Empire sympathies increasingly favoured the young Andronicus. After several cities in the immediate neighbourhood of Constantinople had gone over to him, the old Emperor again gave in and peace was restored on the earlier terms.

A longer interval of peace then followed and on 2 February 1325 Andronicus III was crowned as co-Emperor with his grandfather. Though the civil war had been brought to an end without serious fighting, its consequences both at home and abroad were serious enough. Owing to hostilities, agriculture, particularly in Thrace, was interrupted by continual troop movements and normal economic life was everywhere brought to a standstill. The authority of the central government was exceedingly insecure even in those areas which remained in the old Emperor's hands by the terms of the treaty. The governor of Thessalonica, the *panhypersebastus* John Palaeologus, a nephew of Andronicus II and son-in-law of the Grand Logothete Theodore Metochites,[1] decided to secede from the Empire. He was supported in his intention by the two sons of the Grand Logothete who commanded Strumica and Melnik. A particularly dangerous situation arose when the *panhypersebastus* appealed for aid to his son-in-law, the Serbian king Stephen Dečanski, and appeared at his court in Skoplje. In its alarm the imperial government hurriedly offered him the title of Caesar, but he died while he was at the Serbian court (1327). In Asia Minor the Turkish conquests continued; Brusa was starved out and had to surrender on 6 April 1326[2] to Orchan, the son of Osman, who made it his capital, and as

---

[1] Cf. Papadopulos, *Genealogie der Palaiologen* Nr. 38.

[2] On the date cf. Charanis, 'Short Chronicle' 341 f., who uses the anonymous chronicle of 1391 (Lampros-Amantos, Βραχέα Χρονικά Nr. 52, 5).

the burial-place of Osman it came to be regarded as a holy city by the Ottomans.

Meanwhile, in the spring of 1327 war broke out for a third time between the two Emperors and on this occasion the southern Slav kingdoms intervened more actively in the internal conflicts of Byzantium. The Serbo-Bulgarian conflict was associated with the rivalry which divided the imperial house and with it the Empire. Thanks to his long-standing connections with the ruling house of Serbia, Andronicus II allied himself with Serbia, whilst Andronicus III made a pact with the Bulgarian tzar Michael Šišman, who had repudiated his wife, the sister of the Serbian king, and had married Theodora, widow of his predecessor and sister of the young Andronicus. Fortune again favoured Andronicus III; the desperate situation increased the discontent in the Empire and at the same time brought added support to the young Emperor. The counter-attack undertaken by the partisans of the old Emperor in Macedonia was nipped in the bud before the help of the Serbian king could reach them. The whole of Byzantine Macedonia acknowledged the authority of the young Andronicus and Thessalonica itself recognized him. Andronicus III then left his army, which was by now already encamped not far from Constantinople under the command of Synadenus, and went with Cantacuzenus to Thessalonica, where he was solemnly received as Emperor (January 1328). Even in the capital itself, the opposition was growing alarmingly and Andronicus II was thinking of the possibility of new peace negotiations when suddenly the Bulgarian tzar Michael Šišman changed his attitude and sent Bulgar and Tartar reinforcements to his aid. This inspired new hope in the old Emperor, but at the same time it stirred up the young Andronicus to more vigorous action. By threats and negotiations he managed to persuade the Bulgarian tzar to recall the armed forces which had been despatched, and he simultaneously got into touch with his partisans in Constantinople. On 24 May 1328 he forged his way into the capital and without any bloodshed took control of affairs. He made his grandfather abdicate, but allowed him for the time being to remain in the imperial palace; it was only after two years that the supporters of the young Andronicus forced the old Emperor to enter a monastery, where he died on 13 February 1332 as the monk Anthony.

With Andronicus III (1328–41) a new generation came to power, a generation whose typical representative was John Cantacuzenus.

He had been the real leader of the rebellious movement of the last few years, and now it was he who took control of the government. In political acumen he was head and shoulders above all his contemporaries, including the chivalrous and brave, but unstable, Emperor. Andronicus III played the general with great energy and not without success, but it was Cantacuzenus who directed the policy of state. With the end of the civil war the time of demagogic promises was past, and in many respects Andronicus III and Cantacuzenus, who with the attainment of power had assumed its responsibilities, continued the policy of the fallen government. In any case, the results of the civil war were in many ways beyond repair. Financial needs had become even more pressing and during the years of internal dissension the value of the *hyperpyron* had fallen again. The new government, however, showed to better advantage in its legal reforms.

The corruption of the Byzantine law courts had become proverbial, and for this reason Andronicus II had already attempted a reform of the judicial system. In 1296 he set up in Constantinople a court consisting of twelve judges, either high ecclesiastics or laity of senatorial rank, which, as the supreme court of appeal, was to ensure the safe course of justice. The results were, however, disappointing. The newly-created law court was discredited and its activities suspended. In 1329 Andronicus III therefore set up a new board of judges which was composed of four members, two ecclesiastics and two laymen. These four 'Supreme Justices of the Romans' (καθολικοὶ κριταὶ τῶν ῾Ρωμαίων) had exceedingly far-reaching powers and they were to supervise the judicial system of the whole Empire. Their judgments were final and irrevocable. Nevertheless, Andronicus III was destined to suffer a bitter disappointment over his supreme judges. As early as 1337 three of them were proved guilty of corruption, deprived of their office and exiled. However, the institution of chief justices continued, and even survived up to the end of the Empire, although in the course of time it underwent many changes in response to the practical needs of the day. Naturally all four judges could not always be present at judicial proceedings in the provinces, and it was soon considered sufficient to have the judgment of one of them who would give his decision in the name of all four. Disunity between the different parts of the Empire became more and more apparent from the mid-fourteenth century onwards, and this meant that the over-centralized structure of the judicial system had to be further modified in order to make it more flexible. In addition to the supreme judges of the Romans in Constantinople, local chief justices were instituted: later on, Thessalonica, the Morea and Lemnos, each had their own supreme judges, as well as Serres under Serbian domination. The extensive participation of the clergy in the administration of justice was characteristic of the age of the Palaeologi. The influence of the Church on the judicial system of the Empire was further increased by the fact that in addition to the imperial court of the chief justices, two of whom were normally clerics, there was also an ecclesiastical law court under the Patriarch which co-operated with the imperial court of law, usually supporting it and working with it, but also on occasion opposing it; in times of crisis it could even completely replace the imperial court.[1]

The external situation was marked by the steady advance of the Ottomans in Asia Minor, and of the Serbs in Macedonia, as well as by the further weakening of the Greek and Latin separatist states. Byzantium stood helpless against the Ottomans and the Serbs though it was able to achieve a certain amount of success in both northern Greece and the Aegean, largely owing to the help of the Seljuqs. The factor which particularly characterized the policy of the new régime and gave it its individual note was the co-operation of Cantacuzenus with the Seljuq emirs, who, like the Byzantine Empire, were threatened by the Ottoman expansion. On the other hand, the government tried to break off its alliance with Genoa, in order to regain its independence in maritime and commerical policy. The strengthening of the imperial navy was an essential preliminary to this, and so shipbuilding became one of the most important tasks which the Emperor Andronicus and his Grand Domestic John Cantacuzenus had to face. As the revenues of the state were inadequate for this, Canatcuzenus and other magnates came forward and contributed their own wealth to help strengthen the fleet.[2] Consequently, the state and its military and naval forces became financially dependent on the great men of the Empire.

---

[1] Cf. Zachariä, *Geschichte* 385 ff., and L. Petit, 'La réforme judiciaire d'Andronic Paléologue (1329), EO 9 (1906), 134 ff., and above all the important contributions of Lemerle who has done really detailed work on this subject for the first time. Cf. P. Lemerle, 'Le Juge général des Grecs et la réforme judiciaire d'Andronic III', *Mémorial L. Petit* (1948), 292–316; 'Recherches sur les institutions judiciaires à l'époque des Paléologues. I: Le tribunal impérial', *Mélanges Grégoire* I (1949), 369–84; 'Recherches sur les institutions judiciaires à l'époque des Paléologues. II: Le tribunal du patriarcat ou tribunal synodal', *Mélanges Peeters* (1950), 320–3. Cf. also I. Ševčenko, 'Léon Bardalès et les juges généraux ou la corruption des incorruptibles', B 19 (1949), 247 ff.

[2] Cantacuzenus II, 58 ff., expressly maintains this for 1341.

The increased power of the Serbian kingdom drove Byzantium and Bulgaria into one another's arms again. The discord which had arisen between Andronicus III and his Bulgarian brother-in-law towards the end of the Byzantine civil war had indeed resulted in frontier raids and plundering expeditions on both sides. Peace, however, was soon restored and an alliance against Serbia was concluded. Even so, this did not lead to combined Byzantine and Bulgarian action. It is true that Andronicus III moved into the Serbian frontier district, but, before he could really attack, the decisive battle between Serbia and Bulgaria took place on 28 July 1330 at Velbužd (Küstendil), and on hearing the news of his ally's defeat the Emperor withdrew. The Bulgarian army was destroyed, the tzar Michael Šišman was himself fatally wounded in the battle. The victorious king of Serbia restored his sister Anna and her son Ivan Stephen to the throne of Trnovo, and Andronicus' sister Theodora was forced to take flight.[1]

The battle at Velbužd marks a turning-point in the history of the Balkans. It decided the struggle for Macedonia and laid the foundation of the Serbian hegemony under whose aegis the development of south-east Europe went forward during the following decades. Andronicus III tried to ensure that in at least one respect his Empire should profit from the defeat of his Bulgarian ally. Under the pretence of avenging his sister Theodora, he occupied several fortresses in the Bulgaro-Byzantine frontier region and also seized the hotly contested ports of Mesembria and Anchialus. Meanwhile, there was a change in Bulgaria, and shortly afterwards another in Serbia. The Bulgarian boyars expelled the tzarina Anna with her son and placed Michael Šišman's nephew Ivan Alexander (1331–71) on the throne. In Serbia the nobles rose against the king Stephen Dečanski and gave the throne to his son Stephen Dušan (1331–55). The two Slav rulers then made a lasting peace and Dušan married Helena the tzar's sister. Ivan Alexander took the offensive against Byzantium and was able to regain the cities which Andronicus had seized and to secure his former frontiers by means of a treaty (1332). Meanwhile, led by their new king, the Serbian nobles at once began their conquest of Byzantine Macedonia.

From the very outset and throughout his triumphant reign Dušan was the exponent of the vigorous expansionist drive of the Serbian

[1] Jireček, *Geschichte* I, 361 ff.; A. Burmov, 'Istorija na Bŭlgarija prez vremeto na Šišmanovci' (History of Bulgaria in the time of the Šišman dynasty), *Godišnik na Sofijskija Univ.* 43 (1947), 40 ff.

nobility which succeeded in winning new land from the decaying Byzantine Empire.[1] In so doing, he was increasingly helped by the internal difficulties of Byzantium. Early in 1334 a distinguished Byzantine deserter went over to the service of the Serbian ruler: Syrgiannes, who had played the role of leader in both camps during the civil war, had fled from Constantinople, and after lingering some time in Galata, Euboea and Albania, finally appeared at the court of Dušan. This energetic man, a veteran in war, rendered valuable services to the Serbian king in his struggle against the Byzantine Empire. By then several important Byzantine strongholds in Macedonia were falling into enemy hands, Ochrida, Prilep, Strumica, Castoria and Vodena, and the victorious Serbian advance was only halted by the solid walls of Thessalonica. Finally, one of the Emperor's supporters succeeded in eliminating Syrgiannes, and in August 1334 Dušan accepted Byzantine overtures of peace, as his kingdom was being threatened from the north by Hungary. At a personal meeting between Dušan and Andronicus III in August 1334 a peace treaty was concluded, by which the Serbs retained the greater part of their conquests in Macedonia, including Ochrida, Prilep and Strumica.[2]

While in Europe the catastrophe had only just begun, the last act of the tragedy was being played out in Asia. Yet Andronicus III and John Cantacuzenus continually strained every effort to avert their fate. As early as 1329 they had despatched a force of 2,000 troops against the Ottomans in order to raise the siege of Nicaea. But the unequal struggle was lost to the Byzantines when their more powerful enemy won the battle of Philocrene, and on 2 March 1331[3] Orchan captured the city which had been the centre of Byzantium two generations ago. Six years later, Nicomedia also fell into the hands of the Ottomans;[4] all that was left of the Empire in Asia Minor was an isolated town here and there, such as Philadelphia or Heraclea on the Black Sea. It was, indeed, remarkable that the Byzantines could manage to hold out here for several decades,

[1] Cf. G. Ostrogorsky, 'Dušan i njegova vlastela u borbi sa Vizantijom' (Dušan and his nobles in the struggle with Byzantium), *Zbornik . . . cara Dušana* I (1951), 79 ff.

[2] Jireček, *Geschichte* I, 367 ff. M. Dinić, 'Za hronologiju Dušanovih osvajanja, vizantiskih gradova' (On the chronology of Dušan's conquest of Byzantine towns), ZRVI 4 (1956), 7.

[3] On the date cf. Sp. Lampros, Νέος Ἑλληνομνήμων 7 (1910), 154 = Lampros-Amantos, Βραχέα Χρονικά Nr. 26, 4. It is given as 1 March 1331 in the chronicle published by Gorjanov, VV 2 (1949), 283, 86; on this cf. V. Laurent, REB 7 (1950), 209.

[4] On the capture of Nicomedeia in 1337 cf. G. Arnakis, Οἱ πρῶτοι Ὀθωμανοί Athens 1947, 197, and V. Laurent, REB 7 (1949), 211.

completely surrounded by the Turkish flood, but it was a feat which had no effect on the course of events. After conquering the coast of Bithynia the Ottomans, who in the course of time had considerably increased their power at the expense of neighbouring Turkish tribes, began to take to the sea and made incessant attacks on the European coastal areas of the Empire. Andronicus III was able to drive off these attacks, but they spelt great danger for the future.

Just as the Ottomans had made their way across the northern part of the Aegean Sea, so the Seljuqs of the coastal emirates of Asia Minor attacked the southern part. Their onslaught fell largely upon the Latins, who dominated this area, and did not much affect the Byzantines whose possessions were limited to the islands off the coasts of Thrace and Asia Minor. In these circumstances it was not surprising that the Seljuqs and Byzantines came to an understanding. With the support of the Seljuq emirate, which was just as hostile to the Ottomans and Latins as the Empire itself, Andronicus and Canta-cuzenus tried to strengthen the Byzantine position at sea with their newly-built fleet. In 1329 the imperial navy sailed against the island of Chios, which was under the control of the Genoese family of the Zaccaria; it had recognized imperial suzerainty to begin with, but had afterwards completely broken away from the Empire. This important island was now regained and remained an imperial possession until 1346. With the active support of the neighbouring Seljuq emirs the Emperor also managed to force another Genoese dependency, Phocaea, to recognize Byzantine supremacy, and finally he rescued Lesbos from its attempted conquest by the Western powers. In fact, the whole drama of 1204 was repeated here on a smaller scale: the league of Christian powers, formed to combat the Turkish pirates, attacked a Byzantine island, even though the Byzantine Emperor himself had been formally enrolled as a member. The Emperor was now forced to call in Seljuq aid to defend his possession against his Christian brethren, and after a dramatic battle he succeeded in doing so.

It was, however, in Thessaly and Epirus that the Empire achieved its great successes. After the death of the most powerful of the Thessalian princes, Stephen Gabrielopulus Melissenus († 1333), the country fell into complete chaos. The imperial governor of Thessalonica, John Monomachus, at once intervened, followed by the Emperor himself, and soon the northern half of Thessaly up to the Catalan frontier had been incorporated into the Byzantine Empire.

The despot of Epirus, John Orsini (1323-5), who had tried to seize the western part of Thessaly for himself, was driven back and forced to evacuate the territory. Even the Albanian tribes who had migrated into Thessaly and who had so far been able to keep their independence,[1] now recognized the imperial authority.

With the annexation of Thessaly, the problem of Epirus became of first importance. As the result of unending internal dissension and the conflicting claims on the country, as well as the incessant attacks of neighbouring powers, the whole territory of Epirus was in a state of ferment and the final collapse of the enfeebled separatist state was now merely a question of time. The victory of the Byzantine party at Arta hastened its end. The Despot John was poisoned by his wife, and the Despina Anna, who with her son Nicephorus II had taken over the government, entered into negotiation with the Emperor. Andronicus and Cantacuzenus marched through Thessaly at the head of a strong army, whose nucleus consisted mainly of Turkish troops, and after quelling a revolt which had broken out in Albania they proceeded to receive the submission of the despotate (1337). Without any bloodshed Epirus and also Acarnania were added to the Empire. The Despina Anna had badly miscalculated: she had hoped that having once recognized Byzantine suzerainty she would be able to continue to rule the country in the name of her son, but the Emperor would not hear of a government from the old dynasty of Despots which was so closely linked with the tradition of Epirote independence. The administration of the land was entrusted to an imperial governor, the *protostrator* Synadenus, while Anna and Nicephorus had to move to Thessalonica.

Meanwhile, the Western powers who had interests in Epirus tried to deprive the Empire of the gains of its all too easy victory. They used the slighted Nicephorus as a tool to play off against the Palaeologi. At the instigation of the titulary Latin Empress Catherine of Valois, at that time ruler of the principality of Achaia, the Angevin governor of Dyrrachium stirred up a revolt in favour of the deposed Despot. Nicephorus II was proclaimed in Arta, and the *protostrator* Synadenus thrown into prison. But only a few towns joined the movement, most of the country remaining loyal to the Greek Emperor, and when Andronicus III and Cantacuzenus appeared with a small army early in 1340,[2] the rebellious movement at once

---

[1] Cantacuzenus I, 474, describes them as ἀβασίλευτοι.

[2] This chronology follows Florinskij, 'Andronik i Kantakuzin', vol. 204, 241 f., note 3.

collapsed. Nicephorus returned to honourable exile in Thessalonica and had to content himself with the title of *panhypersebastus* and the privilege of betrothal to a daughter of Cantacuzenus as a substitute for the royal dignity which he had forfeited. John Angelus was appointed governor of Epirus as a reward for his services in suppressing the revolt, while Synadenus took over the governorship of Thessalonica. It now looked as though one of the most serious consequences of the Byzantine collapse of 1204 had been finally removed. It is true that there were still Latin principalities in Greece, but there were no longer any independent Greek states in the Balkans, for these had now been reincorporated into the Empire as provinces. Cantacuzenus praises this success in most glowing terms, a success which, for all their exertions, previous governments had failed to achieve.[1]

This achievement was, however, not so much the result of Byzantine force of arms as of the internal disintegration of the separatist states, which had once been able to defy the imposing might of Michael VIII, but now yielded almost without a struggle to the enfeebled Empire. However, the Byzantines were not destined to enjoy their success for long. There is something tragic in the fact that just when these lost territories had been regained for the Empire, the expansionist drive of the Serbs should be turned on these very districts. Dušan conquered the Albanian territory in the following years, and soon afterwards, before they had really been assimilated into the Empire once more, Epirus and Thessaly also fell into the hands of the great Serbian king (see below, p. 524). Given favourable circumstances Byzantium was still capable of achieving a measure of success by means of clever statesmanship and astute diplomatic manoeuvring, but it was clear that it no longer had the strength to retain its gains for any length of time. The Empire had barely recovered from the civil wars of the twenties sufficiently to be able to attend to important duties of state and to make headway, if not against the Serbs and the Ottomans, at least against weaker opponents, when the collapse came. The reign of Andronicus III was only a breathing space in the middle of a period of internal strife. After his death, a new civil war flared up again, bringing a state of chaos far more bloody and deadly than the confusions of the twenties and of far graver consequence. And from this civil war the Empire was never to recover.

When Andronicus III died on 15 June 1341, his son John V was

---

[1] Cantacuzenus I, 504.

only nine years old.[1] The Grand Domestic John Cantacuzenus, who had been the real ruler even during Andronicus III's lifetime, asserted his claim to the regency as the nearest friend of the late Emperor. He was confronted with a strong opposition centred in the Dowager Empress Anne of Savoy and the Patriarch John Calecas. The most dangerous opponent of Cantacuzenus was his former supporter, the cunning Alexius Apocaucus, who had distinguished himself in the last civil war as a supporter of Andronicus III, and then, thanks to Cantacuzenus, had risen to rank and wealth. The life of the Byzantine capital was permeated with court intrigue and the struggles of contending factions. Before long there were external dangers to be faced: the Turks were plundering the Thracian coast, the Serbs had once again pressed forward as far as Thessalonica and the Bulgarians were also threatening war. Cantacuzenus met these enemies of the Empire with troops recruited at his own private expense and he soon managed to restore peace. He even saw the possibility of strengthening the imperial position in Greece. The feudal lords of Achaia despatched an embassy to the Grand Domestic announcing their readiness to accept Byzantine overlordship, for the country was in chaos and the French barons preferred to submit to the Byzantine Emperor rather than to the representatives of the Florentine banking house of the Acciajuoli, who had recently taken over the government of the principality for the titular Empress Catherine. Cantacuzenus was filled with high expectations and in a speech to the war council he declared, 'Should we succeed with God's help in bringing the Latins living in the Peloponnese under the control of the Empire, then the Catalans in Attica and Boeotia will acknowledge us, either voluntarily or by compulsion. And the power of the Romans will stretch from the Peloponnese to Byzantium as it used to, and it is obvious that it will then be easy to demand satisfaction from the Serbs and the other neighbouring barbarian peoples for all the insults that they have heaped upon us for so long.'[2]

But nothing came of these hopes. The outbreak of civil war dispelled any idea of an extension of Byzantine power, and in addition it destroyed what little strength Byzantium still possessed. Cantacuzenus' absence from the capital gave his enemies the opportunity to stage a *coup d'état*. The Grand Domestic, who was devoting

---

[1] On the date of John V's birth (November 1331) cf. Charanis, 'Short Chronicle' 344, based on Lampros-Amantos, Βραχέα Χρονικά Nr. 47, 11.

[2] Cantacuzenus II, 80.

himself to great patriotic plans, was declared an enemy of his country, his house was destroyed, his estates plundered and such of his supporters who had not succeeded in escaping from Constantinople in time were thrown into prison. The Patriarch John placed himself at the head of the regency, and Apocaucus, now created *megas dux*, became governor of the capital and of the neighbouring towns and islands, while all his supporters received high honours and important positions. Cantacuzenus took up the challenge and on 26 October 1341 he had himself proclaimed Emperor at Didymotichus. But he held strictly to the principle of legitimate succession, as he continued to do throughout the civil war, and he had the names of the Empress Anne and of the legitimate Emperor John V proclaimed first, and only after them his own name and that of his wife Irene.[1] He was determined to emphasize that he was not fighting against the legitimate imperial house, but against the usurpation of Apocaucus who had quickly assumed dictatorial powers in Constantinople. As Andronicus III had done in his struggle against his grandfather, Cantacuzenus relied above all on the support of the magnates of Thrace in his fight against the regency in Constantinople and once again the province was to be victorious over the capital.

Byzantium was on the threshold of one of the gravest crises it had ever experienced. The civil war of the twenties had considerably weakened the Empire, the civil war of the forties drained it of its last vestige of strength. Foreign powers took a more prominent part than ever in the internal quarrels of the Byzantines which were now intensified by social and religious differences. Byzantium was experiencing a grave social, as well as a political, crisis. The movement of the Zealots brought into prominence certain powerful social forces of a revolutionary character, and inextricably bound up with this turmoil of political and social strife was the most important religious conflict of the late Byzantine age—the hesychast controversy.

From the very earliest days there had been monks who had lived a strict hermit life in holy silence (ἐν ἡσυχίᾳ) and in Byzantium these were called hesychasts. In the fourteenth century hesychasm became particularly important by reason of mystical and ascetical developments which can be traced back indirectly to the great eleventh-

---

[1] Apparently for a time the Empress-mother Anna was formally recognized as senior sovereign in Constantinople. Cf. the seals and coins in T. Bertelè, *Monete e sigilli di Anna di Savoia, imperatrice di Bisanzio* (Rome 1937), and the comments on these by F. Dölger, BZ 38 (1938), 195 f. Cf. also Dölger, 'Johannes VI. Kantakuzenos als dynastischer Legitimist', *Annales de l'Inst. Kondakov* 10 (1938), 19 ff. (*Paraspora*, p. 194 ff.).

century mystic, Symeon the New Theologian, whose teaching and practice had much in common with those of the hesychasts.[1] It arose, however, as a direct result of the influence of Gregory of Sinai, who travelled in Byzantium in the thirties of the fourteenth century. His mystical and ascetical teaching was most enthusiastically received in Byzantine monasteries, particularly by the monks of Mt. Athos, and this most venerated stronghold of Byzantine orthodoxy became the centre of the hesychast movement. The highest goal of the hesychasts was the vision of the Divine Light. Special ascetical techniques were used in striving to attain this illumination. In solitude and retirement the hesychast had to repeat the so-called Jesus prayer ('Lord Jesus Christ, Son of God, have mercy on me'), holding his breath while he did so. Gradually the supplicant felt a sense of unspeakable ecstasy and saw himself surrounded by rays of supernatural Divine Light, the same uncreated Light which had appeared to the disciples of Jesus on Mt. Tabor.

This belief in the perpetual visibility of the Light on Tabor met with opposition, and the methods employed by the hesychasts were particularly criticized and ridiculed. The attack on hesychasm was opened by the Calabrian monk Barlaam, a man of considerable learning, but dogmatic and quarrelsome, a restless soul who combined Western pride with genuine Greek love of disputation. He had come to Constantinople to pit his brains against the leaders of Byzantine learning, but he had been worsted in a public debate by the encyclopaedic scholar Nicephorus Gregoras, as his rationalistic and Aristotelian approach found no response with the Byzantine public. The Calabrian therefore relieved his wounded self-esteem in a violent spate of polemic directed against the mysticism of the monks on Athos, which appeared to him to reek of the blackest superstition. The defender of hesychast mysticism was the great theologian Gregory Palamas[2] and he entered the arena against Barlaam. A heated controversy flared up: the question of the

---

[1] Cf. K. Holl, *Enthusiasmus und Bussgewalt beim griechischen Mönchtum. Eine Studie zu Symeon dem neuen Theologen*, Leipzig 1898; further bibliography in Beck, *Kirche*, 585 ff.

[2] On the theology of Gregory Palamas cf. Monach Vasilij (Krivošein), 'Asketičeskoe i bogoslovskoe učenie sv. Grigorija Palamy' (The ascetical and theological teaching of St. Gregory Palamas), *Sem. Kond.* 8 (1936), 99–154, where a detailed account of the older literature is given; trans. into German, Mönch Wassilij, 'Die asketische und theologische Lehre des hl. Gregorius Palamas', *Das östl. Christentum*, Heft 8 (1939); trans. into English, *Eastern Churches Quarterly* 3 (1938; reprinted separately 1954); and especially Meyendorff, *Palamas*, 173 ff.; Beck, *Kirche*, 323 ff., 712 ff. Cf. also H. G. Beck, 'Palamismus und Humanismus', *XIIe Congrès Intern. des Études byz. Rapports III*, Belgrade-Ochrida 1961, and also the suppl. papers of G. Schirò and J. Meyendorff, ibid., *Rapports complémentaires*, 35 ff., 39 f.

Figure 65: *Pareccleseion* (*Mortuary Chapel*). Interior, looking east toward the apse, Church of St. Savior in Chora (Kariye Djami), Constantinople, circa 1310. Completely decorated with wall-paintings, the Pareccleseion was added to the church by Theodore Metochites. It consists of a long rectangular room ending in a semicircular apse, with a dome over the center. The paintings, all related to the themes of death and resurrection, have recently been cleaned by the Byzantine Institute of America. (See also Figures 63, 64, 66.) Photo: Byzantine Institute, Inc., Washington, D.C.

Figure 66: *The Anastasis*. Detail of the wall-painting in the apse conch, the Pareccleseion, Church of St. Savior in Chora (Kariye Djami), Constantinople, circa 1310. Appropriate to a mortuary chapel, the apse painting depicts the Anastasis, in which Christ descends into Hell and raises Adam and Eve from the dead. Satan lies bound at His feet, among the fragments of the shattered gates of Hell. (See also Figures 63, 64, 65.) Photo: Byzantine Institute, Inc., Washington, D.C.

ascetical methods used by the hesychasts, which had originally provided a target for Barlaam's sarcasm, was soon completely over-shadowed by the problem of the philosophical and theological fundamentals of the hesychast doctrine. Barlaam denied the possi-bility of seeing the Light of Tabor, arguing that as it was not identical with God it could not enjoy eternal existence, but was temporal like every creation of God. The acceptance of the existence of an uncreated light meant that this must be nothing less than the Godhead itself, which alone is eternal and unchanging, but it would then be impossible to see this light, since God is invisible. On the other hand, Palamas differentiated between the transcendental divine substance (οὐσία) and divine energies (ἐνέργειαι or δυνάμεις) which are active in this world and are manifested to men, but which are not created, but rather manifestations of an endless operation of God. If there were no such manifestation of the divine substance, there could be no relationship between the immanent world and the transcenden-tal Godhead. He maintained that the divine energies were manifested in the wisdom, the love, the grace of God, and the light seen by the apostles on Mt. Tabor, and eternally made visible to the mystically illumined, was another such divine energy. Where Barlaam had drawn a definite dividing line between the eternal and the temporal, Gregory Palamas saw an intermediary and a mediating power between God and man, which proceeded from God and revealed itself to mankind. Hesychast doctrine therefore expressed the funda-mental longing of Greek spirituality, which had already influenced the attitude of the Byzantine Church in the Christological disputes and during the iconoclast controversy: the longing to bridge the gulf between this world and the next. For this reason the hesychast teaching, which was so strongly rejected by Rome, was warmly accepted by the Byzantine Church.

Yet even in Byzantium hesychasm was only accepted after a long struggle, for in the Byzantine Church itself there was at first keen opposition to the new teaching, even though it had such strong links with the older tradition. It is true that at a council held on 10 July 1341 under the presidency of Andronicus III, Palamas obtained a clear victory.[1] After the death of the Emperor a few days later, Barlaam renewed his attacks, while George Acindynus from the Slav city of Prilep, who at first had tried to mediate between the two opponents, also turned against the Palamite doctrine. He too

---

[1] Cf. Meyendorff, *Palamas*, 77 ff.

was condemned by a council held in the presence of the Grand Domestic John Cantacuzenus (August 1341). But the political upheaval which followed soon afterwards brought about a change. The Patriarch John Calecas, an avowed opponent of Palamas, adopted an increasingly anti-hesychast position. Palamas fell into disgrace, and was later imprisoned and even excommunicated. Though by no means all the adherents of Cantacuzenus supported hesychasm, and not all his opponents were opposed to the doctrine of Palamas,[1] yet nevertheless the closer the link between the hesychasts and the rival Emperor John Cantacuzenus, the more deeply the religious dispute became involved with the political conflict which was dividing the Empire into two hostile camps.

The social rift went even deeper, and it was indeed the social conflict within the Empire which was the really grave problem during the civil war, and it is this which accounts for its widespread and devastating result. Increasing economic poverty had only served to sharpen conflicts between different classes. As the Empire became weaker and more impoverished, the misery of the great masses in the countryside and in the cities became almost unbearable. Both in the country and in the towns all the wealth was concentrated in the hands of a small aristocratic class, and against them was directed the bitterness of the destitute masses.

At the height of its power Byzantine absolutism had built up a powerful bureaucratic system on the ruins of the old municipal administration and urban life had been compelled to come under the yoke of its all-embracing centralization. When the central power grew weaker, local influence had begun to gain ground once more and independent town life seemed to revive again.[2] This revival of urban self-government was not due to the rise of new social forces, but rather to the weakening of the central power which was undermined by feudal elements; town life in Byzantium therefore produced in the late Byzantine period no flourishing class of merchants and craftsmen, as in the West, but was dominated by the local landed aristocracy.[3] This difference must be borne in mind, even

---

[1] This has previously been overlooked, but is made quite clear by Meyendorff, *Palamas*.

[2] Cf. the important comments by Bratianu, *Privilèges* 101 ff.; Bréhier, *Institutions* 208 ff.

[3] Cf. E. Frances, 'La féodalité et les villes byzantines aux XIIIe XIVe siècles', BS 16 (1955), 76 ff.; E. Kirsten, 'Die byzantinische Stadt', *Berichte zum XI Intern. Byzantinisten-Kongress*, Munich 1958, 34 ff.; N. V. Pigulevskaja—E. E. Lipšic—M. J. Sjuzjumov—A. P. Každan 'Gorod i derevnja v Vizantii v IV–XIIe vv.' (Town and Country in Byzantium from the fourth to the twelfth centuries), *XIIe Congrès Intern. des Études byz.* *Rapports I*, Belgrade-Ochrida 1961, 35 ff., and the suppl. paper of D. Angelov, ibid. *Rapports complémentaires*, p. 18 ff.

though the events which revolutionized the Byzantine city life about the middle of the fourteenth century have many parallels in the corresponding history of the Italian and Flemish towns, and fit into the general framework of the urban social struggles in Europe at this time.[1] It is this fundamental difference which explains why the once dominant economic position of Byzantium was so quickly and so completely undermined, in the end to be replaced by the Italian trading cities.

The dispute between the regency in Constantinople and Cantacuzenus, the leader of the aristocracy, brought the smouldering social divisions of the Empire to the surface. In his armed struggle against Cantacuzenus, Alexius Apocaucus relied on the support of the masses and stirred up the spirit of social hatred against his opponent's aristocratic supporters. The highly inflammable material burst into flame. In Adrianople an insurrection broke out against the local aristocracy, and this soon spread to other towns in Thrace. Members of the aristocratic and wealthy classes, the supporters of the magnet Cantacuzenus, were everywhere downed.

The greatest excesses and the greatest bitterness of the class war took place in Thessalonica, the great port with its heterogeneous population where excessive wealth existed side by side with extreme poverty. Thessalonica, which had always had its own unique position in the Empire, had been a forum where every aspiration of freedom was expressed and it had a strong popular party, well organized and professing a fairly well defined political ideology— the party of the Zealots. Here the anti-aristocratic movement was expressed not merely in a violent outburst of popular feeling, but after the Zealots had seized power in 1342 it became for some time the dominant system. After the supporters of Cantacuzenus had been driven from the town, the Zealots set up their own government in Thessalonica.

The governor Synadenus had to leave the city. Other representatives of the aristocracy sought their safety in flight. Their possessions were confiscated. The Zealots, who were regarded in conservative ecclesiastical circles as disciples of Barlaam and Acindynus, were also violently opposed to the hesychasts, who supported Cantacuzenus. The political Zealots were enemies of the church Zealots. And yet the Zealots combined their revolutionary social politics with a certain legitimacy. As opponents of Cantacuzenus they

[1] Bratianu, *Privilèges* 119 ff.

recognized the legitimate Emperor John Palaeologus and the most prominent members of this anti-aristocratic party were members of the house of Palaeologus. A governor sent from Constantinople and the leader of the Zealots shared the responsibility of administration. As the latter had the greater influence, the city virtually lived according to its own will and enjoyed almost complete independence of any other authority. For seven years the second city of the Empire remained under the control of a revolutionary anti-aristocratic party, which asserted its power with great determination and ruthlessly eliminated its opponents.[1]

From Thessalonica to Constantinople the power of the aristocracy was everywhere crushed. It looked as though Cantacuzenus' cause was lost, and his nearest friends, including even Synadenus, broke away from him, as being the only way of saving their lives and their property. Deprived by the revolution of any support in the Empire itself, Cantacuzenus withdrew with some 2,000 men to the Serbian frontier and appealed to Stephen Dušan for help. Intervention in the Byzantine civil war suited the Serbian king's policy of expansion and provided an outlet for the Serbian nobles who were thirsting for conquest. The king and queen of Serbia received the Byzantine rival Emperor in Priština with great honour (July 1342), and Cantacuzenus remained for some time in Serbia. His negotiations with Dušan and with the Serbian nobles led to the conclusion of an

[1] Contemporaries of the Zealot rule describe it in the gloomiest terms, but all extant accounts come from embittered opponents of the Zealots. The information that they give about the measures taken by the Zealots and their intentions is unfortunately very scanty. Accounts in specialist works and also in earlier editions of this book were based in the main on a *Logos* of Nicholas Cabasilas. But Ševčenko, *Nicolas Cabasilas*, 81 ff., has shown that this work does not describe Zealot rule, but certain measures taken by the imperial government, and very probably refers to a later period (cf. p. 478, n. 8 above). The usual view of the Zealot régime and its measures must therefore be revised. Thus for example the reproaches of Cabasilas against the sale of state offices and episcopal sees do not refer to the Zealots. Similarly his tirade against the alienation of monastic lands—which forms the main object of his sermon and has consequently been regarded as the main item in the Zealot programme—does not prove, without support from other sources, that the Zealots instituted measures of secularization. As far as I can see, Nicephorus Gregoras II, 796, 15, only says that they deprived the rich of their goods (καὶ τῶν πλουτούντων ἀφαιρούμενοι τὰς οὐσίας). Cantacuzenus II, 234, 7, reports that they broke into and destroyed the houses of the aristocrats who had fled, and robbed them of their goods (καὶ τὰς οὐσίας διήρπαξον). This was obviously not a question of the appropriation of landed property, but of the confiscation of their possessions in the city of Thessalonica, to which Zealot control properly speaking was limited. Thus the basis of our knowledge about the character of the Zealot régime, and the measures taken by their government, has become narrower, but consequently a good deal more certain. The feeling that must have inspired the Zealot movement can be seen in the recently published work of Alexius Makrembolites, which takes the form of a dialogue between the rich and the poor and breathes a spirit of deep social embitterment. Cf. I. Ševčenko, 'Alexios Makrembolites and his "Dialogue between the Rich and the Poor" ', ZRVI 6 (1960), 187 ff.

alliance by means of which both parties were trying to suit their own ends. The assaults of the allies on the strongly defended Serres in 1342 and 1343 were, however, unsuccessful. Cantacuzenus' following had dwindled away to scarcely 500 men, when he learnt that Thessaly had recognized him as Emperor. Thus the country of the great landed magnates joined the leader of the Byzantine aristocracy. Cantacuzenus made his old friend and relation John Angelus governor of the province for life. The latter now ruled semi-independently, but with loyal recognition of his master's rights of suzerainty, over Epirus with Acarnania and Aetolia, as well as over Thessaly, and he was soon in a position to extend his already considerable domain at the expense of the Catalan possessions in Thessaly. So although Cantacuzenus had been expelled from the old imperial territory, he still retained his hold over recently reconquered Greek districts, which had always been in the forefront of his mind and whose reunion with the Empire had been largely his work.

These successes of the rival Byzantine Emperor hastened the breach between him and the Serbian ruler. It was by no means Dušan's intention to allow either of the Byzantine parties to gain the upper hand, so he dropped Cantacuzenus and joined hands with the regency in Constantinople, which was only too eager to court his favour. His son and heir to the throne, Uroš, was betrothed to the sister of the young Emperor John Palaeologus (in the summer of 1343). Cantacuzenus now found in Dušan not an ally, but a powerful enemy. But it was still possible for Cantacuzenus to look elsewhere, for even in Andronicus III's reign he had had particularly close ties with the Emir Omur.[1] By the end of 1342 Omur had come to his assistance, and from then onwards Cantacuzenus received continual support from the Turks, first the Seljuqs and then the Ottomans, which gave him the superiority over his opponents, and indeed, from the military point of view, finally turned the Byzantine civil war in his favour. But even with Omur's support he was unable to capture Thessalonica. The city resisted him most fiercely, and the threatening external danger only increased the radicalism of the Zealot government.[2] Cantacuzenus had therefore to renounce

---

[1] Omur is the principal hero of the most important part of the work of the Turkish chronicler Enveri, who describes in detail his campaigns and victories in Byzantine territory. This part has been published and translated into French by I. Mélikoff–Sayar, *Le destān d'Umūr Pacha*, Paris 1954. A close study of this important source has been made by Lemerle, *L'Émirat d'Aydin, Byzance et l'Occident. Recherches sur "La geste d'Umur Pacha"*, Paris 1957.

[2] Cantacuzenus II, 393 f.

Thessalonica and abandon the rest of Macedonia to Dušan. But with the aid of the Seljuqs he began to conquer Thrace, and by the beginning of 1343 Omur had forced his way into Didymotichus.[1] This success was, however, only won at the cost of allowing the regained land to be devastatingly plundered by the Turkish troops.

Meanwhile, the regency in Constantinople was relying on the support of the southern Slavs, and had won over to its side not only Dušan, but also the Bulgarian tzar Ivan Alexander, and then the former ally of Omur and Cantacuzenus, the daring Hajduk Momčilo, who had settled along the Byzantine and Bulgarian borders with his own troops.[2] But the friendship of the Slav ruler did not help the legitimate Emperor to any great extent and had cost the Byzantine state great sacrifices. The situation steadily deteriorated, while Cantacuzenus' allies were pillaging Byzantine territory. Apocaucus' allies were appropriating vast tracts of the Empire. In the course of the year 1343 Dušan captured Voden, Castoria and Lerin and concluded the conquest of Albania, which, with the exception of the Angevin town of Dyrrachium, now came under his control.[3] The Bulgarian tzar was paid for his friendship by the cession of a large stretch of territory on the upper Marica with Philippopolis and Stanimachus, but he gave no assistance whatsoever to the government which had so recklessly agreed to these concessions. After changing sides more than once Momčilo settled as an independent ruler in southern Rhodope. From this base the bold adventurer, to whom Cantacuzenus had given the title of Sebastocrator and the Empress Anne that of Despot, terrorized the whole district until at last Omur in the service of Cantacuzenus destroyed his power and had him executed (1345).

By the summer of 1345 Cantacuzenus had subdued practically the whole of Thrace, and in Constantinople itself his opponents had suffered a severe reverse. Their most prominent supporter, the *megas dux* Alexius Apocaucus, met his end on 11 June 1345, for while inspecting the dungeons in the imperial palace he was attacked by the inmates and killed. Even in Thessalonica there were signs of the first reaction against the rule of the Zealots, which to begin with only led to a stronger outburst of the revolutionary forces.

[1] Cf. Lemerle, *L'Émirat d'Aydin*, 144 ff.

[2] Interesting information about Momčilo is given in the Turkish chronicle mentioned above, ed. Mélikoff-Sayar, 101, 124.

[3] Cf. M. Dinić, 'Za hronologiju Dušanovih osvajanja vizantiskih gradova' (On the chronology of Dušan's conquest of Byzantine towns), ZRVI 4 (1956), 1 ff.

Significantly enough, the attempted reaction was led by the imperial governor, who was none other than the Grand Primicerius John Apocaucus, a son of the dictator of Constantinople. It is true that he was supposed to be supporting the anti-aristocratic régime in Thessalonica, but he soon fell out with the Zealot party and with its leader Michael Palaeologus, who had made himself master of the city. He had the leader of the Zealots murdered, took complete control of the government and after his father's assassination in Constantinople he openly declared for Cantacuzenus.[1] Then the Zealots led by Andrew Palaeologus prepared their counterstroke. John Apocaucus was overpowered and together with some hundred of his followers perished by a cruel death: one after another the prisoners were hurled from the walls of the citadel and hacked to pieces by the mob of the Zealots assembled below. Then followed a hunt for all the members of the upper classes: they were 'driven through the streets like slaves, with ropes round their necks—here a servant dragged his master, there a slave his purchaser, while the peasant struck the *strategus* and the labourer beat the soldier (i.e. the pronoiar)'.[2] The Zealot government was restored and for several years maintained itself in almost complete independence. Thus the ties between Thessalonica and the rest of the Empire were further loosened.

Despite these setbacks, with the fall of the *megas dux* Alexius Apocaucus, Cantacuzenus could now be certain of victory. Backed by the strongest economic and political elements, he marched towards his goal unhindered, while the authority of the regency in Constantinople visibly declined. It is true the rival Emperor no longer enjoyed the support of his friend Omur to the same extent, and was soon to lose it altogether. Omur was diverted by war with the confederacy of Western powers who had become active again and had occupied Smyrna in 1344. This struggle, which dragged on with varying fortune, made increasing demands on Omur and was eventually responsible for his death in 1348.[3] Meanwhile, Cantacuzenus had found an even more powerful ally in the Ottoman

---

[1] R. J. Loenertz, 'Note sur une lettre de Démétrius Cydonès à Jean Cantacuzène', BZ 44 (1951) (*Dölger-Festschrift*), 405 ff., has admirably shown how a letter of Demetrius Cydones probably written in Berrhoia in the summer of 1345 expresses the rejoicing which was felt by Cantacuzenus' followers at this passing change. But Cydones' joy was rapidly turned to sorrow as is shown by the passage quoted immediately afterwards.

[2] Demetrius Cydones, PG 109, 648 f.

[3] A thorough account of the activity of the western league in the forties of the fourteenth century is given by Gay, *Clemént VI* 32 ff. Cf. also Lemerle, *L'Émirat d'Aydin*, 180 ff., 218 ff.

Sultan Orchan (1346). He did not hesitate to give his daughter
Theodora in marriage to the Sultan.[1] The times had indeed changed:
once the greatest rulers in Christendom had not been considered
worthy of the hand of a Byzantine princess, and now a Byzantine
princess was to grace the harem of a Turkish Sultan.

Confident of victory, Cantacuzenus was crowned Emperor in
Adrianople on 21 May 1346. This coronation, which was performed
by the Patriarch of Jerusalem, was intended to give legitimate
sanction to the proclamation at Didymotichus which had marked the
beginning of the civil war in 1341. The Empress Anne's power was
now limited to the capital and its immediate vicinity. The ambitious
woman would not, however, give up the struggle. Her negotiations
with the Turks were at last successful and in the summer of 1346
6,000 Seljuqs came from the emirate of Saruchan, but, instead of
attacking Cantacuzenus, they invaded Bulgaria where they hoped to
find richer booty than in devastated Thrace, and on their way home
they ravaged and plundered the surroundings of Constantinople. It
was in vain that the Empress made last-minute overtures to the
hesychasts, such as the deposition of the Patriarch John Calecas on
2 February 1347,[2] or the release of Palamas from prison, while his
supporter Isidore was placed on the Patriarchal throne. On 3 February 1347 the gates of Constantinople were opened to Cantacuzenus.
The garrison of the city went over to his side and soon the Empress
Anne was forced to give up the struggle. Cantacuzenus was recognized as Emperor. He was destined to rule the Empire for ten years
before the legitimate ruler John V was allowed to take his share in
the government. Cantacuzenus married his daughter Helena to
John.

On 13 May there was another coronation ceremony: this time
Cantacuzenus received the imperial crown from the hands of the
Patriarch of Constantinople, since only coronation performed by the
metropolitan of the capital conferred complete and indisputable
validity. A spiritual bond of relationship was established between
Cantacuzenus and the family of the Palaeologi which was designed
to legitimize the position of the new ruler. Cantacuzenus, so to
speak, took the place that the dead Andronicus III had occupied; he
was regarded as the latter's 'spiritual' brother and the 'common

---

[1] According to Enveri, who gives a long and amusing account of the matter, he had
already offered her to Omur (ed. I. Mélikoff-Sayar, p. 106 ff.).

[2] Cf. Laurent, 'Notes' 170.

The Serbian Empire of the Nemanjids (from St. Stanojević, *Istoriski Atlas*)

father' of John Palaeologus and of his own children, and therefore as the head of the ruling house.[1]

The victory of Cantacuzenus brought the civil war to an end for the time being. The Zealots still held Thessalonica, and obstinately refused to acknowledge Cantacuzenus, repudiating all orders which arrived from Constantinople. But their downfall was now only a question of time. They were aware of this themselves, and opened negotiations with Stephen Dušan, preferring to hand the city over to the Serbian ruler rather than to Cantacuzenus. But at the end of 1349 their rule collapsed. Their leader, Andrew Palaeologus, fled to the Serbs, while the governor Alexius Metochites sent an appeal to Cantacuzenus. Towards the end of the year Cantacuzenus, accompanied by John Palaeologus, made a triumphal entry into the city which had defied him so long and so obstinately, and Gregory Palamas, who had been appointed Archbishop of Thessalonica, but refused entry by the Zealots, was now received into the city of St. Demetrius.

The installation of Cantacuzenus on the throne of Constantinople confirmed the victory of the hesychast movement, though this did not mean the end of the religious controversy, for the learned Nicephorus Gregoras, who earlier on had challenged Barlaam in a public debate, now came forward as the leader of the anti-hesychasts. However, in 1351 a council in the Blachernae palace solemnly recognized the orthodoxy of the hesychasts and Barlaam and Acindynus were excommunicated. Although controversy continued for some time to come, hesychasm was recognized from then on as the official doctrine of the Greek Orthodox Church. Gregory Palamas was canonized soon after his death († 1357/8),[2] and hesychast ideas were to form an essential element in later developments in the Greek Church. The important mystic Nicholas Cabasilas, the learned canonist Symeon of Thessalonica, and Mark Eugenicus, the champion of orthodoxy against the union with Rome in the fifteenth century, were all followers of this teaching. For the Byzantine Empire the acceptance of hesychasm had a cultural as well as a religious significance. After the strong Latin influence in the twelfth and thirteenth centuries the conservative Greek tradition in Byzan-

---

[1] Cf. the important study by F. Dölger, 'Johannes VI. Kantakuzenos als dynastischer Legitimist', *Annales de l'Inst. Kondakov* 10 (1938), 19 ff., esp. 25 and 30 with the references to the sources.
[2] Cf. N Βέης, 'Τὸ ἔτος τῆς τελευτῆς τοῦ Γρ. Παλαμᾶ', 'Ἀθηνᾶ 16 (1904), 638 and 18 (1905), 39 f.

Figure 67: *John VI Cantacuzenus Enthroned*. Illuminated miniature painting on parchment, Manuscript of John VI Cantacuzenus, 1370–1375. The first of 4 full-page illustrations in the manuscript, it shows the emperor enthroned, in full regalia, surrounded by bishops, monks, and retainers. (See also Figure 70.) Ht. 13″, w. 9¾″. Bibliothèque Nationale, Paris, *Cod. gr. 1242*, f. 5ᵛ. Photo: Hirmer Fotoarchiv, Munich.

Figure 68: (ABOVE) *Land Walls and Citadel of Thessalonica.* View of the massive city fortifications, from the east. (BELOW) *Church of St. Catherine.* Thessalonica, probably early 14th century. Exterior view of the apse and south flank. Photos: (above) Boissonas, Geneva; (below) Cyril Mango.

tium came into its own in the first half of the fourteenth century, and it was diametrically opposed to Western culture as well as to the Roman Church. If Manuel I Comnenus and Michael VIII Palaeologus represented the latinophile outlook, then Andronicus II and John VI Cantacuzenus (who, though an opponent of the elder Andronicus, was in many respects his real follower), appeared as the exponents of the orthodox conservative Byzantine outlook.

It was the Serbian ruler who reaped the benefit from the Byzantine civil war. The internal struggles which crippled and ruined the Byzantine Empire made Dušan great. Except for Thessalonica, the whole of Macedonia was under his rule, for after repeated attacks the strongly fortified Serres fell on 25 September 1345,[1] whereupon the rest of the region, as far as the Mesta (Nestos), came under his control. Soon afterwards Dušan took the imperial title, styling himself from now on Emperor of the Serbs and Greeks,[2] which was a clear indication that the old Byzantine Empire was to disappear to make room for a new Serbo-Greek Empire. As the Bulgarian tzar Symeon had once done, so now Dušan saw the real climax of his struggle with Byzantium in his claim to the title of Emperor, the highest symbol of the political and spiritual pre-eminence of Byzantium. And as in Bulgaria, there was now an independent patriarchate in Serbia side by side with the tzardom and closely linked with it. On Easter Sunday, 16 April 1346, he was solemnly crowned Emperor at Skoplje by the newly-created Serbian Patriarch. Constantinople

---

[1] On the date cf. A. Solovjev, 'Car Dušan u Serezu' (tzar Dusan at Serres), *Jugosl. Istor. Časopis* 1 (1935), 474. On the question of the south-eastern frontier of Dušan's kingdom cf. the observations of K. Jireček, *Archiv f. Slav Phil.* 17 (1892), 262 f., who disagrees with the view of S. Novaković that the Serbian border extended as far as the Marica. Cf. also Lemerle, *Phillipes*, 197 ff. The question has recently been studied by G. Škrivanić, 'O južnim i jugoistočnim granicama srpske države za vreme cara Dušana i posle njegove smrti' (*Istor. Časopis* 11 (1960), 1 ff.).

[2] For a closer determination of the date when Dušan assumed the title of Emperor (end of November or December 1345) cf. M. Laskaris, 'Povelje srpskih vladalaca u grčkim publikacijama' (Charters of Serbian rulers in Greek publications), *Prilozi za književnost* 8 (1928), 185 ff. In his Greek charters Dušan calls himself after the Byzantine style Στέφανος ἐν Χριστῷ τῷ Θεῷ πιστὸς βασιλεὺς καὶ αὐτοκράτωρ Σερβίας καὶ Ῥωμανίας. On the other hand, the Serbian title, which has many minor variations, runs: 'Stefan v Christa Boga verni car Srbliem i Grkom' (Stephen in Christ our God the devout tzar of Serbs and Greeks). Cf. St. Stanojević, 'Studije o srpskoj diplomatici' (Studies in Serbian diplomatic), *Glas Srpske Akad.* 106 (1923), 40 ff., and Ostrogorsky, 'Avtokrator' 154 ff. On the ethnical re-interpretation of the Roman imperial conception by Dušan and the tzars of the Second Bulgarian Empire cf. Ostrogorsky, 'Die byzantinische Staaten-hierarchie', *Sem. Kond.* 8 (1936), 47, note 9. There is an interesting contribution to the history of Dušan's title of tzar and its recognition or non-recognition by foreign powers by M. Dinić, 'Dušanova carska titula u očima savremenika' (The title of the tzar Dušan in the eyes of contemporaries), *Zbornik u čast šeste stogodišnjice Zakonika cara Dušana*, I (1951), 87 ff. Cf. also idem, 'Srpska vladarska titula za vreme Carstva' (The title of the Serbian ruler in the days of the tzardom), ZRVI 5 (1958), 9 ff.

could naturally not be expected to consent to this coronation and it was witnessed by the Patriarch of Trnovo, by the autocephalous Archbishop of Ochrida and by representatives from the monasteries of Athos. Mt. Athos happened to be within the territory now controlled by the Serbian tzar, who did everything he could to win the favour and recognition of the most venerated centre of Greek orthodoxy. He himself made a lengthy visit to the Holy Mountain and showered rich gifts of lands and privileges on the ancient monasteries.[1] The monasteries of Athos never enjoyed such extensive rights of immunity as under the rule of Stephen Dušan.[2] Three years after his coronation, in May 1349, at a council at Skoplje, and then again in a more complete form in Serres in 1354, Dušan promulgated the legal code which was to give a sound foundation to his new empire.[3]

The lull in the Byzantine civil wars did not hold up the advance of the Serbs. On the contrary, in the first years of Cantacuzenus' reign Dušan completed the conquest of Epirus, and also seized Thessaly as well (1348). It is true that after the crushing of the Zealots in Thessalonica Cantacuzenus advanced into Macedonia and succeeded in occupying Berrhoia and Voden (1350), but the strongholds he regained soon fell to Dušan again.

With very slight expenditure of energy and without fighting a single major pitched battle, Dušan had seized from Byzantium more than half its remaining territory, and had almost doubled the size of his empire. The only military operations had been for the most part the siege of various single towns which did not resist the Serbian ruler for long.[4] His realm now stretched from the Danube to the Gulf of Corinth and from the Adriatic to the Aegean coast. His empire was indeed half Greek, largely consisting of Greek and Greek-speaking territory, and, in fact, the focal point of the new empire was in the Greek lands. As Emperor of the Serbs and the Greeks, Dušan took over direct control of the predominantly Greek southern half of his empire, while he entrusted the administration of the Serbian lands in the north to his son, king Uroš.[5] In the development of his court and of his administrative and legal systems Dušan

---

[1] His Greek deeds of gift are modelled in all respects on the Byzantine imperial charters. Cf. the texts given by A. Solovjev-V. Mošin, *Grčke povelje srpskih vladara* (Greek charters of Serbian rulers), Belgrade 1936.

[2] Cf. G. Ostrogorsky 'K istorii immuniteta v Vizantii', VV 13 (1958), 87 ff.

[3] A detailed survey of the extensive literature on the code of Dušan is given by N. Radojčić in *Zbornik u čast šeste stogodišnjice Zakonika cara Dušana*, I (1951), 207 ff.

[4] Cf. Jireček, *Geschichte* I, 369.

[5] Nic. Gregoras I, 747.

borrowed a good deal from the Byzantine Empire, particularly in his new southern acquisitions, which had been part of the Empire. Here Byzantine organs of administration and courts continued their work undisturbed and not infrequently Greek archons entered the service of the Serbian ruler. But even in the conquered Greek districts, the important administrative offices were held by members of the Serbian nobility, rewarded with Byzantine honorary titles; Dušan's comrades in arms were the chief beneficiaries of his successful wars of conquest.[1] For the most part life went on under the same law, only the ruling class had changed.

Thus, although after a period of bitter civil war the Greek aristocracy had been able to assert its supremacy over what was left of the Byzantine Empire, it had been defeated in its struggle against a foreign enemy and had to a very great extent been forced to cede its position and its lands to the victorious Serbian nobility. And now the remaining portion of the Byzantine Empire was also threatened. The Serbian ruler, who called himself 'fere totius Imperii Romani dominus',[2] seemed within an ace of his final goal. Only one last effort seemed necessary to enter Constantinople and his ambitious plans would be completed by the capture of the capital. But like Symeon before him, Dušan was now denied this final triumph. For he too lacked a fleet, without which the conquest of Constantinople was impossible. Every attempt on his part to win over Venice to his side failed: the Venetians had no intention of replacing the weak Byzantine Empire by that of the powerful Serbian tzar.

The civil war had also inflicted new losses on the Empire at sea. The Genoese had recaptured Chios in 1346 and the island soon became the main base of the trading company of the Giustiniani, which held it until the middle of the sixteenth century.[3] Byzantine naval power, revived under Andronicus III at such great sacrifice, had been destroyed again during the years of the civil war. At sea the Empire was hemmed in between Venice and Genoa in complete and humiliating impotence, just as it was on land between the Ottomans and the Serbs. The Byzantine sphere of influence was limited to Thrace and the islands in the northern part of the Aegean, to

---

[1] Cf. Jireček, *Geschichte* I, 386. A. Solovjev, 'Grečeskie archonty v serbskom carstve XIV v.' (Greek nobles in the Serbian Empire in the fourteenth century), BS 2 (1930), 275 ff.; G. Ostrogorsky, 'Dušan i njegova vlastela u borbi sa Vizantijom' (Dušan and his nobility in the struggle with Byzantium), *Zbornik cara Dušana* I (1951), 83 ff.

[2] In a document to Venice (15 October 1345) issued from the conquered Serres; S. Ljubić, *Monum. hist. Slav. mer.* II, 278.

[3] Cf. Miller, *Essays* 298 ff.

Thessalonica, now cut off by the victorious advance of Dušan, and to its possessions in the distant Peloponnese.

But far worse than its territorial losses was the economic and financial ruin of the Byzantine state. The population was no longer able to pay its taxes, for in Thrace, the chief possession of the Empire, agriculture had been completely suspended during the years of the civil war, and this countryside which had had to endure the horrors of social struggles, followed by the devastating ravages of Turkish troops, was like a desert.[1] Byzantine trade was ruined: while the Genoese customs officials in Galata were collecting 200,000 *hyperpyra* a year, the annual customs revenue of Constantinople had sunk to a bare 30,000 *hyperpyra*.[2] The *hyperpyron* itself had no fixed value and contemporaries affirm that its purchasing power grew daily smaller.[3] The revenue of the Byzantine state at the beginning of the fourteenth century had been only a small part of its former budget (see above, p. 484), but now the imperial revenue was nothing more than a fraction of the modest receipts of the time of Andronicus II. In fact there was no longer any question of a balanced budget, and for anything involving considerable outlay the government had to have recourse to special means of raising revenue, either by appealing to the generosity of the wealthy classes or by relying on foreign loans and gifts. At the beginning of the civil war the Empress Anna had pawned the crown jewels in Venice for a loan of 30,000 ducats; and although the Venetians reminded the Empire of this debt whenever trade treaties were renewed, they never succeeded in getting it repaid and the imperial jewels remained in the treasury of St. Mark's.[4] About 1350 the Grand Duke of Moscow sent money for the restoration of Hagia Sophia, and as though it was not bad enough to have to receive foreign gold for such a purpose, this pious gift of the Russian prince was immediately confiscated and passed over to the infidel, for it was spent on enlisting Turkish mercenaries.[5] All this goes to show the depths to which Byzantium had sunk. Even in the imperial palace, once the scene of magnificence and splendour, there was such poverty that on the occasion of a feast to celebrate the coronation of John Cantacuzenus the goblets were no longer of gold and silver, but

[1] Nic. Gregoras II, 683; Cantacuzenus II, 302 ff.
[2] Nic. Gregoras II, 842.
[3] Nic. Gregoras III, 52.
[4] Miklosich-Müller III, 124 and 140; Hopf, *Geschichte* I, 444; Zakythinos, *Crise monétaire* 92, 99.
[5] Nic. Gregoras III, 199 f.

had been replaced by lead and earthenware.[1] And the crowning misfortune came in 1348 when the Empire was visited by the plague, which more than decimated the capital and then spread throughout the whole of Europe.[2]

It is a curious fact that as the size of the Empire diminished, so the demand for division of the supreme authority grew. The remaining fragments of territory left could no longer be governed from a single centre and the imperial autocracy was replaced by the joint control of individual members of the ruling dynasty. Under John Cantacuzenus the principle of division of authority among the imperial house became the general practice. Cantacuzenus transferred the Byzantine dependency of Morea to his second son Manuel.[3] His elder son, Matthew, received territory of his own in western Thrace, a district stretching from Didymotichus to Christopolis, on what was then the Serbian frontier. In this way Cantacuzenus undoubtedly meant to strengthen his own new dynasty at the expense of the legitimate ruling house of the Palaeologi, but he was also strongly influenced by the fact it was only by the creation of a firm system of family control that the various parts of the Empire could be prevented from breaking away.[4] This method of government had already been foreshadowed during the preceding period and it was preserved and extended by the Palaeologi who succeeded Cantacuzenus. The ruler had to rely on members of his own family for support against the great feudal lords, for in a feudal state the ruling dynasty was really only the strongest of many rival families of magnates.

Cantacuzenus' foreign policy shows remarkable continuity. As Grand Domestic under Andronicus III, as rival Emperor during the civil wars, and as the acknowledged ruler, he consistently followed the same policy. This is illustrated both by his co-operation with

[1] Nic. Gregoras II, 788. Under Cantacuzenus the imperial table was only allotted a tenth of what it used to have, Nic. Gregoras II, 811.

[2] According to a Western chronicle (*Chron. Estense*, Muratori 15, 448) eight-ninths of the population of Constantinople perished; in any case, the number of the victims was exceedingly high, Cantacuzenus III, 49 ff.

[3] The idea has been widely accepted that the Byzantine dependency in the Morea formed a 'despotate' from this period on. According to Ferjančić, *Despoti*, this view must be abandoned. It is true that the sons of the Emperor who reigned in the Morea mostly bore the title of despot, but they did so not as governors of the region of the Morea, but as sons of the Emperor, or as his brothers. The granting of the title of despot has no relation in time or in fact to their despatch to the Peloponnese. The dependency of the Morea represented their apanage, similar to the other areas of the Empire which were bestowed on members of the ruling house as apanages at this period. Cf. also p. 432, n. 2 above.

[4] Cf. Stein, 'Untersuchungen' 25 f.

the Turks, which he maintained to the end, and by his hostile attitude to Genoa, which, in spite of occasional vacillation, remained a characteristic feature of his policy. But it was impossible to oppose the all-powerful Genoese without an independent navy, and so once more the first and most urgent consideration was the problem of getting together a fleet. As the state treasury was empty, the Emperor made an appeal to the private owners. But the terrible years of the civil wars had greatly reduced private resources and the propertied class had little inclination to make sacrifices. With the utmost difficulty 50,000 *hyperpyra* were collected and spent on ship-building.[1] Moreover, the Emperor was not prepared to accept the fact that almost 87 per cent. of the customs dues of the Bosphorus went to the Genoese, and he attempted to put an end to this disgraceful situation. He lowered Constantinople's tariffs for the majority of imports, with the result that incoming merchant ships were increasingly diverted to the Byzantine port and avoided the Genoese Galata.[2] As was to be expected, the Genoese, hard hit by these measures, took up arms and, in spite of all the preparations that had been made, the Empire lost the unequal struggle. The Byzantine fleet was destroyed early in 1349 and all the sacrifices and exertions were proved useless: the Empire was not destined to shake off the Genoese yoke.

Scarcely was the war between Byzantium and Galata over than a new war between Venice and Genoa flared up in Byzantine waters. This was provoked by Genoa's attempt to establish control over the entire trade of the Black Sea; they tried to block the passage of foreign ships and went as far as confiscating several Venetian merchantmen in Caffa for evading this control (1350). Venice allied with Peter IV of Aragon, and Cantacuzenus finally joined the alliance, although he had at first held back through uncertainty as to the outcome of the struggle. On 13 February 1352 a great battle was fought in the Bosphorus: on the one side were the Genoese, and on the other the Venetian and Aragonese ships together with a small detachment of fourteen ships which the Emperor had managed to equip with Venetian help. The fight lasted until nightfall and the result was indecisive, so that both sides could claim the victory. The struggle was continued in Western waters, until in 1355 sheer exhaustion forced the protagonists to make peace. The departure of the Venetian and Aragonese fleets after the battle on the Bosphorus

[1] Cantacuzenus III, 80.
[2] Cantacuzenus III, 68 ff. Cf. Heyd, *Commerce du Levant* I, 498 ff.

left Cantacuzenus in an awkward position. Thus isolated he was forced to come to terms with the Genoese, especially as they had made an alliance with Orchan. As a result of these enforced diplomatic changes the Venetians came to an understanding with John V. The Palaeologian Emperor received a loan of 20,000 ducats from Venice to subsidize his fight against Cantacuzenus and in return he promised to cede the island of Tenedos to the republic. He was also urged by the powerful Serbian tzar to break with Cantacuzenus, and so Byzantium once again stood on the threshold of a new civil war.

From the very beginning all Cantacuzenus' enemies had gathered round the person of the legitimate Emperor, and as he grew older John V himself had begun to rebel against the extent to which he was ignored. Cantacuzenus tried to avoid conflict by a clever manœuvre: the territory in the Rhodope ruled by Matthew Cantacuzenus was handed over to John V, while Matthew received a new and even more important governorship in the district of Adrianople. But this arrangement did not last long, and when the inevitable break came, hostilities took the unusual form of a war between the autonomous principalities of John Palaeologus and Matthew Cantacuzenus. In the autumn of 1352 John V, supported by Venetian money, invaded his brother-in-law's territory at the head of a small army. He met with no opposition and even Adrianople itself opened its gates to the legitimate Emperor, while Matthew retired to the acropolis of the city. John Cantacuzenus hastened to his rescue with Turkish troops and restored the *status quo*. Adrianople and other cities which had deserted the Cantacuzeni had to submit to the savage plundering of the Turks as punishment. At this point the hard-pressed Palaeologus appealed to the Serbs and Bulgarians for help and received from Stephen Dušan a cavalry division of 4,000 men in exchange for his brother, the Despot Michael, as hostage.[1] However, Orchan did not desert his friend Cantacuzenus and sent him a fresh consignment of troops of at least 10,000 men under the command of his son Suleiman.[2] Thus the outcome of the quarrel between the two Byzantine Emperors lay in the hands of the Ottomans and the Serbs. The day was won by the superior Turkish forces, for while the Bulgarians were retreating at the approach of the

[1] The figure given by Nic. Gregoras III, 181, but 7,000 according to the obviously exaggerated account of Cantacuzenus III, 246. On the Despot Michael Palaeologus cf. Papadopulos, *Genealogie der Palaiologen* Nr. 74.

[2] Cf. Cantacuzenus III, 248. Gregoras III, 181, says the Turks actually numbered 12,000 men.

Ottoman hordes the Serbian troops and the Greek forces of John V were utterly defeated near Didymotichus (at the end of 1352).

Cantacuzenus, although he had actually been carrying on his feud with the Palaeologi for more than a decade, had tried to support the principle of legitimacy. He now felt that the moment had come for establishing the power of his house on a surer foundation and finally eliminating the legitimate Emperor. In 1353 Matthew Cantacuzenus was proclaimed co-Emperor with his father and his successor, while the name of John V Palaeologus was no longer to be included in the prayers of the Church or in the acclamations at public festivals.[1] John Cantacuzenus swept aside the protest of the Patriarch Callistus, and had the obstinate prelate deposed by a synod and replaced by Philotheus. In 1354 in the Church of the Blachernae Matthew received the imperial crown from the hands of the Emperor and the new Patriarch.

The triumph of the house of Cantacuzenus was, however, of short duration. The swing over of opinion in the Empire was already clearly shown during the course of the war between John Palaeologus and Matthew Cantacuzenus. Thanks to the Ottomans, John Cantacuzenus had once again triumphed over his opponents, but Turkish help was a two-edged weapon. The time of the sporadic Turkish plundering raids was coming to an end, the period of the definite settlement of the Ottomans in Europe was beginning. By 1352 they had already taken possession of the fortress of Tzympe near Callipolis (Gallipoli) and in March 1354, after a terrible earthquake, which drove the Byzantines from the district, Orchan's son Suleiman occupied Callipolis itself.[2] It was useless for Cantacuzenus to appeal to the friendship of Orchan, or, in spite of the extreme poverty of the state, to offer him great sums of money to evacuate the captured

---

[1] According to Cantacuzenus III, 33, Matthew originally had no special titular dignity but held a rank which was 'higher than that of a Despot and immediately below that of the Emperor'. This rank between Basileus and Despot, for which there was no special designation, was first held by the son of Michael VIII, Constantine Palaeologus (Cantacuzenus, ibid.). This was the strange culmination of the increasing debasement and differentiation of titles: the scale of precedence among the highest honours had become so complicated that it could no longer be defined in concise terms.

[2] On the chronology cf. Charanis, 'Short Chronicle' 347 ff., based on Lampros-Amantos, Βραχέα Χρονικά Nr. 52, 22. Cf. also Jireček, *Archiv f. slav. Philol.* 14 (1892), 259. G. Georgiades Arnakis, 'Gregory Palamas among the Turks and Documents of his Captivity as Historical Sources', *Speculum* 26 (1951), 111 f. and 'Gregory Palamas, the Χιόνες and the Fall of Gallipoli' B 22 (1952), 310 ff., attempts to put the capture of Gallipoli in March 1355 on the ground of indirect evidence, but this is not possible since it is well established that the city fell to the Turks during John Cantacuzenus' reign. Cf. Charanis, 'On the Date of the Occupation of Gallipoli by the Turks', BS 16 (1955), 113 ff., who rightly argues that the city was captured in March 1354.

Figure 69: *Emperors of the Palaeologan House.* Pen and wash drawing on parchment, 15th century. Top row, Andronicus III, John VI Cantacuzenus, John V; center row, Andronicus IV, John VII, Manuel II; bottom row, John VIII, Constantine XI, and a stylized bust of Constantine the Great to complete the pattern. Biblioteca Estense, Modena. *Cod. αS.5.5 (=Gr. 122),* f. 294^{v}. Photo: U. Orlandini, Modena.

Figure 70: *John VI Cantacuzenus as Emperor and as the Monk Ioasaph.* Illuminated miniature painting on parchment, Manuscript of John VI Cantacuzenus, 1370–1375. The last of 4 illustrations in the manuscript, it portrays John as emperor in full regalia and, following his abdication, as the monk Ioasaph; 3 angels above symbolize the Trinity. (See also Figure 67.) Ht. 13″, w. 9¾″. Bibliothèque Nationale, Paris. *Cod. gr. 1242, f. 123ᵛ.* Photo: Bibliothèque Nationale.

town. The Ottomans had no intention of giving up the fortress, which provided them with an excellent base for future attacks on Thrace. In Constantinople the population was seized by acute panic, and everybody thought that the city was in immediate danger from the Turks.[1] The position of Cantacuzenus became untenable and the time was ripe for his overthrow.

Meanwhile, John V had approached the Genoese, the old enemies of Cantacuzenus, and had easily gained their support and alliance. A Genoese corsair, Francesco Gattilusio, the master of two galleys, in which he had crossed the Aegean in search of booty and adventure, was to bring the Palaeologus to the throne of his fathers. In return for this service John V promised him the hand of his sister Maria, with the island of Lesbos, the largest and most important island left to the Empire, as dowry.[2] In November 1354 the conspirators forced their way into Constantinople. John Cantacuzenus was forced to abdicate and enter a monastery.[3] As the monk Joasaph he lived on for nearly thirty years, without completely renouncing the world. He not only wrote his famous history and composed theological writings defending the doctrines of the hesychasts, but he repeatedly intervened in political affairs both in Constantinople and in the Morea. His influence in the declining Empire and in the imperial house, torn apart by ceaseless disputes, ended only with his death. He died on the 15 June 1383 in the Peloponnese.[4]

The authority and the historical role of the house of Cantacuzenus also survived the fall of John VI. The rival Emperor Matthew held out for some time in the Rhodope district. From here he even attacked the Serbs in the neighbouring district, but was captured by them at Philippi and handed over to John V Palaeologus. He was then forced to renounce his claims to the throne (1357). On the other hand, the attempt to deprive Manuel Cantacuzenus of his control over the Morea was a failure and in the end this astute Despot was recognized by the government of John V. Manuel governed the Byzantine possessions in the Peloponnese until his death in 1380; he was then succeeded (up to 1382) by his elder brother Matthew, who had gone to the Morea after his own downfall

[1] Demetrius Cydones, Migne PG 154, 1013.

[2] On the rule of the Gattilusio in Lesbos which lasted until the Turkish conquest in 1462 cf. Miller, *Essays* 313 ff.

[3] On the date of the fall of John Cantacuzenus (22 November 1354) cf. Loenertz, *Lettres de D. Cydonès* 109.

[4] Cf. J. Meyendorff, 'Projet de Concile Oecuménique n 1367: um dialogue inédit entre Jean Cantacuzène et le légat Paul', DOP 14 (1958) 149 ff.

in the north. During the course of his long rule Manuel Cantacuzenus put the affairs of the Morea in order and strengthened Greek
rule by successful resistance to Turkish inroads. At this time of the
hopeless decay of Byzantine power revival of the Greek supremacy
in the Morea shone out like a solitary beacon. But the country was
for a considerable time under the autonomous rule of the house of
Cantacuzenus, and was therefore practically cut off from the central
government of the Palaeologi.

Byzantine sovereignty was, in fact, more impotent now than it
had been when Cantacuzenus had ascended the throne of Constantinople; the disintegration of imperial territory had proceeded apace
and its economic and financial position was still more hopeless. The
Byzantine Empire had had to endure three civil wars in a generation
and nothing could save it now. The two mainstays of the former
power of the Byzantine state had been its monetary wealth and its
excellent administrative system. But the Byzantine treasury gaped
empty and the administrative system was completely dislocated. The
currency had depreciated, all sources of revenue had dried up and
most of the former treasures had already been squandered. The
themes and the departments of the logothetes, the foundation-stones
of Byzantine provincial and central administration, were now mere
names. The most important offices were empty titles, and even the
memory of their former functions had been lost: the Pseudo-Codinus
states that it was no longer known what the offices of the λογοθέτης
γενικοῦ and the λογοθέτης τοῦ Δρόμου had once represented.[1] If
we recall the earlier significance of these offices and remember that
as late as the twenties of the fourteenth century Theodore Metochites
had served under Andronicus II, first as λογοθέτης γενικοῦ, and then
as μέγας λογοθέτης,[2] we cannot fail to realize the extent and rapidity
of the dissolution of the Byzantine state during the fateful decades
of the civil wars. The collapse of the financial position and the disintegration of the machinery of government took away the firm
foundation of the Byzantine Empire's very existence. The process
of disintegration still went on for some time, for to the very end

[1] Codinus, 34 and 36. In the same way, the offices of the other logothetes, and even
the once highly important office of City eparch, became empty titles, ibid. 35 and 39 f.
[2] Nic. Gregoras I, 271, 303 and 305. It is therefore not possible to agree with Dölger,
Finanzverwaltung 20, that the office of the λογοθέτης γενικοῦ had disappeared as early as
1204. Cf. the opposite view of Stein, 'Untersuchungen' 33; V. Laurent, EO 38 (1939),
'368 ff.; P. Lemerle, *Actes de Kutlumus* No. 34, p. 131, J. Verpeaux, 'Le cursus honorum
de Théodore Métochite', REB 18 (1960), 195 ff.; I. Sevčenko, *Études sur la polémique entre
Théodore Métochite et Nicéphore Choumnos*, Brussels 1962, 272 ff. Cf. also Andreeva,
Očerki 39.

Byzantium displayed an amazing tenacity. Nevertheless, the history of the last century of Byzantium is nothing but the history of an inevitable decline.

3. THE OTTOMAN CONQUEST OF THE BALKAN PENINSULA: BYZANTIUM AS A TURKISH DEPENDENCY

General bibliography: Halecki, *Un empereur*; Dölger, 'Johannes VII'; G. T. Kolias, 'Η ἀνταρσία 'Ιωάννου Z'; Charanis, 'Palaeologi and Ottoman Turks'; Loenertz, 'M. Paléologue et D. Cydonès'; idem, 'Péloponèse'; idem, *Lettres de D. Cydonès*; Gay, *Clément VI*; Silberschmidt, *Das oriental. Problem*; N. Jorga, *Philippe de Mézières et la croisade au XIV siècle*, Paris 1896; G. Ostrogorsky, 'Byzance État tributaire de l'Empire turc', ZRVI 5 (1958), 49-58; M. Viller, 'La question de l'Union des églises entre Grecs et Latins depuis le concile de Lyon jusqu'à celui de Florence', *Revue d'hist. eccl.* 17 (1921), 261-305, 515-32; 18 (1922), 20-60. On the history of the Ottomans, the South Slavs, the Italian maritime republics and Frankish Greece see above, p. 478 f. and p. 499.

As early as 6 August 1354 the Bailo, the Venetian ambassador in Constantinople, had informed the Doge, Andreas Dandolo, that the Byzantines, threatened by the Turks and Genoese, were ready to submit to any power—Venice, or the Serbian ruler, or the King of Hungary.[1] On 4 April 1355 Marino Faliero advised the republic simply to annex the Empire, as otherwise in its miserable condition it would fall a victim to the Turks.[2] It was an open secret that Byzantium was on the verge of collapse, and the only question appeared to be whether the remains of the Empire were to fall to the Turks or to a Christian power.

Meanwhile, one of the most likely candidates for the Byzantine inheritance soon fell out of the race: on 20 December 1355 Stephen Dušan died in his prime and his life's work sank with him into the grave. The young tzar Uroš (1355-71) had neither the authority nor the energy of his father and was unable to hold together the loosely knit and heterogeneous elements of his Empire, which had been forged together all too hastily by Dušan's strong hand, and now disintegrated. Everywhere independent or half-independent principalities sprang up and from the ruins of Dušan's Greco-Serbian

[1] Ljubić, *Monum. hist. Slav. merid.* III, 266; Šafarik, *Glasnik srpskog učenog društva* 12 (1860), 13.
[2] Hopf, *Geschichte* I, 448.

Empire there arose a medley of small states. But the decay of the Serbian realm brought no real relief to the Byzantines. It is true that Dušan's death relieved them of a powerful enemy, but Byzantium was so enfeebled that it was incapable of deriving any advantage from the dissolution of the Serbian Empire and did not even make any effort to recapture the former Byzantine territories. It is true that the Grand Stratopedarch Alexius and the Grand Primcerius John in the service of John V occupied the coastal area round the mouth of the Strymon up to Chrysopolis, but the offensive led by the two brothers rapidly came to a halt; they held the coastal towns, while the hinterland remained firmly in the hands of the Serbs.[1] The deposed Nicephorus II of Epirus undertook an extensive campaign to win back his lost inheritance. He had considerable success both in Epirus and in Thessaly, but perished in 1358 fighting against the Albanians. On the other hand, the danger of Turkish conquest became even more imminent after the death of Dušan, for there was no longer any power in the Balkans capable of withstanding the Ottoman advance.

It is to John V's credit that he certainly did not underestimate the gravity of the situation, though any illusions on this score would hardly have been possible. The Turks already stood on the threshold of Thrace, the only province still left to the Empire. In an attempt to ward off the threatening danger the Emperor seized upon the well-tried method of opening negotiations for a union between Rome and Constantinople, a card which the founder of the Palaeologian dynasty had once played with great finesse. But there was a vast difference between the situation then and now: under Michael VIII the Empire had been threatened by a Western power, upon whom the Pope could exert moral pressure, but now John V was faced by the infidel who could only be influenced by force of arms; moreover, recent experiences in the Aegean with the league of Christian powers sponsored by the Papacy were not exactly encouraging. The promise of Church union was a trump card in the political game which the Byzantine court played at regular intervals. After the failure of the union of Lyons negotiations with Rome had been shelved for some forty years, but even Andronicus II had made a temporary move in this direction during the difficult years of the civil war. Further attempts to negotiate a union were also made by

[1] Cf. the full discussion by Lemerle, *Phillipes*, 206 ff. who is the first to have given a clear account of the activities of the two brothers.

Andronicus III, and even more decisively by the Empress Anne, as well as in the most difficult hours of John Cantacuzenus' rule, though without any tangible results.[1] John V, however, took the matter seriously. With great enthusiasm and genuine devotion he worked to bring about the Church union, inspired by the early influence of his Catholic mother. On 15 December 1355, just a year after his accession, he sent a detailed and delightfully naive letter to Avignon asking the Pope to despatch him five galleys and fifteen transport vessels with 1,000 foot and 500 horsemen. In return he promised to convert his subjects to the Roman faith within six months and offered the Pope such far-reaching guarantees for the fulfilment of this promise as even the direst needs of the Empire could not excuse. Among other things, his second son Manuel, then a child of five or six years, was to be sent to the papal court to be educated by the Pope; moreover, should he not fulfil his promises, the Emperor was prepared to abdicate, leaving control of the Empire to the papal pupil Manuel, or if he was still a minor to the Pope himself as his adopted father.[2] Apparently Innocent VI did not take these extravagant promises too seriously; at any rate, in his reply to John V he made no reference to his detailed proposals, but contented himself with praising the Emperor's sentiments in warm but general terms and despatching his legate to Byzantium. The Emperor was soon obliged to inform Rome that at the moment he was not in a position to win over the entire Byzantine population to accept the union, since the papal embassy, not being accompanied by armed galleys, did not carry the necessary conviction and many of his subjects would not listen to his directives. After this negotiations for a union were at a standstill for several years.

In actual fact the opposition referred to in the Emperor's letter was of considerable strength. It is true that there was in Byzantium a fairly strong party friendly to the union whose most distinguished representative was at this time the famous rhetorician Demetrius Cydones, but the overwhelming majority of the Byzantine clergy and laity held firmly to the old traditional belief as they had done in former negotiations over the union. The Patriarch Callistus was a personal enemy of Cantacuzenus who had regained the patriarchal throne of Constantinople after the accession of John V; he was

[1] Halecki, *Un empereur* 17 ff., seems to overestimate the significance of the negotiations carried out under John Cantacuzenus; Gay, *Clément VI* 111 ff., to whom Halecki refers, is far more reserved. Cf. also M. Viller, 'La question de l'union des églises', *Revue d'hist eccl.* 18 (1922), 26 ff.

[2] There is a detailed analysis of the letter in Halecki, *Un empereur* 31 ff.

imbued with an exceedingly conservative outlook and he was most tenacious of the privileges of his Patriarchate. The Greek Church knew how to preserve its rights far better than did the debilitated Empire. During his first Patriarchate, Callistus had already excommunicated the upstart independent Serbian Patriarchate,[1] and he had obtained from the Bulgarian Patriarchate the recognition of the supremacy of the see of Constantinople, so that in future at Trnovo the name of the Patriarch of Constantinople was placed first in the prayers of the liturgy. The conflict with the Serbian Church was to be settled on similar lines. Thus while the Byzantine state was being forced to cede one position after another, the Byzantine Church was regaining its former authority.

Soon after Suleiman's occupation of Gallipoli, the systematic Turkish conquest of the Balkan lands began. In the year 1359 the Ottoman hordes were seen for the first time beneath the walls of Constantinople.[2] The exhausted Empire was in no condition to offer resistance and although no immediate danger threatened the strongly fortified capital, the rest of Thrace, whose last strength had been drained by the civil war, fell a prey to the enemy. One town after another was captured: by 1361 Didymotichus had fallen finally to the Turks and probably a year later Adrianople.[3]

Under Murad I (1362-89), the conquest of the Balkans, and not only of the Greek territory, but especially of the southern Slav lands, entered a decisive phase. Like Byzantium, these could not repulse the advance of the more powerful enemy. After the death of Dušan,

[1] Between autumn 1352 and spring 1354, according to V. Mošin, 'Sv. patrijarh Kalist i srpska crkva' (The blessed Patriarch Callistus and the Serbian Church), *Glasnik srpske prav. crkve* 27 (1946), 202.

[2] Matteo Villani, Muratori 14, 567.

[3] The chronology of the Turkish conquests is very uncertain. According to M. Villani, *Muratori* 14, 567 f., Didymotichus was taken for a time as early as 1359 and then finally fell in November 1361. According to Panaretus of Trebizond, ed. O. Lapsidis (1958), 74, 15, Adrianople appears to have been last in Byzantine hands in 1362. Cf. Jireček, *Archiv f. slav. Philol* 14 (1892), 260 and BZ 18 (1909) 582 f. Babinger, *Beiträge* 46 f., would like to put back the capture of Didymotichus to 1360, and of Adrianople to 1361, but this seems to me impossible in view of the sources just quoted. R. J. Loenertz, 'Études sur les chroniques brèves byzantines', OCP 24 (1958) 155 ff., now actually places the fall of Adrianople in the year 1360 (p. 159), basing his view on a Venetian chronicle and on the Short Chronicle Lampros-Amantos, No. 36. But both sources obviously contain errors and confusions. Loenertz himself notes this with respect to the Short Chronicle No. 36; with regard to the Venetian source cf. the observations of S. Ćirković in S. Novaković, *Srbi i Turci XIV i XV veka* (Serbs and Turks in the fourteenth and fifteenth centuries), Belgrade 1960, 445 f. The suggestion of A. Burmov, 'Koga e zavladjan Odrin ot turcite?' (When was Adrianople captured by the Turks?) *Izv. na Bǎlg. istor. družestvo* 21 (1945), 23 ff., that Adrianople did not fall until after the battle of the Marica in 1371, is wide of the mark. This suggestion, which is largely based on later Serbian sources, is rightly rejected by M. Tichmirov, *Voprosy istorii* 1948, 691 f. and Babinger, REB 7 (1950), 205.

the Serbian Empire was in process of complete dissolution, but conditions in Bulgaria were even worse, since the country was split up and was utterly crippled by extreme economic poverty and ecclesiastical troubles. In 1363 the skilful general Lala Šahin entered Philippopolis and took up his residence there as the first Beylerbey (governor) of Rumelia. And the Sultan himself soon transferred his residence to the Balkans, setting up his court first in Didymotichus and then (from about 1365) in Adrianople.[1] Thus the Ottomans firmly established themselves in Europe, especially as the Turkish advance was accompanied by systematic measures for colonization: the native population was removed in great numbers to slavery in Asia Minor, while Turkish colonists were settled in the conquered districts, and the Turkish nobles, in particular the Sultan's generals, were rewarded with generous gifts of land.[2]

Intimidated by the Turkish advance, Bulgaria sought safety by throwing in its lot with the powerful conquerors, which led to a clash with both Hungary and Byzantium.[3] In 1364 an armed conflict between Byzantium and Bulgaria broke out, and the Byzantine Emperor succeeded in occupying Anchialus. So this most inopportune war at least brought the Byzantines the satisfaction of knowing that there was at any rate one state which was even weaker than their own unfortunate Empire.

Disappointed in his hopes of help from Rome, the Byzantine Emperor looked around for other allies against the advancing Turks. The Patriarch Callistus himself went to Serres, where he met Dušan's widow, but he died soon after, the victim of a sudden illness. Nor did negotiations with the Italian maritime republics have any tangible result. So the Emperor turned once more to Avignon. At the moment there were serious preparations in the West for a crusade, and in the autumn of 1365 an expedition actually set out under the leadership of king Peter of Cyprus; but its objective was Egypt, and so once more John V saw his hopes shattered. But he certainly did not lack energy and in the spring of 1366 he journeyed in person to Hungary in order to beg king Louis the Great for help.

For the first time a Byzantine Emperor entered a foreign country, not as a general at the head of his army, but as a petitioner seeking

[1] Cf. Babinger, *Beiträge* 48 ff.
[2] Cf. Nikov, 'Turskoto zavladevane' (The Turkish conquest), 46 ff.; Babinger, *Beiträge* 48 f., 57 ff.
[3] According to Nikov, 'Turskoto zavladevane' 55 ff.

help. But all in vain—the Roman principle was observed—first conversion, and then assistance. And in fact the Hungarian king demanded not only that the Emperor of Byzantium adopt the Roman faith, but also that he be rebaptized according to the Roman rite.[1] Empty-handed, John V turned home again, only to meet with a fresh misfortune. Having arrived in the Hungarian-occupied Vidin, he was forced to interrupt his journey, as the Bulgarians would not allow him to pass. It is most unlikely that this could have happened without the knowledge of his son Andronicus, who was married to a daughter of the Bulgarian tzar. At any rate, the son did nothing to liberate his father and only the intervention of the 'Green Count', Amadeo of Savoy, saved the unfortunate ruler from his plight. The 'Green Count', a cousin of the Emperor, had appeared with a crusading army in Byzantine waters in the summer of 1366. In his first onslaught he seized Gallipoli from the Turks, after which he turned against the Bulgarians, and he not only forced them to liberate the Emperor, but also to cede Mesembria and Sozopolis, which once more gave the Byzantines a firm footing on the western coast of the Black Sea.

Meanwhile, in Amadeo of Savoy's mind the crusade was inextricably bound up with the plans for union. At the request of Amadeo, the papal legate, Paul, who accompanied him, was received in June 1367 by the members of the Byzantine ruling house in the presence of high ranking representatives of Church and State for a discussion about Church reunion. The interlocutor on the Greek side was none other than the dethroned Emperor John Cantacuzenus, the 'father' of the reigning Emperor, whose forceful personality completely dominated the whole assembly. Cantacuzenus demanded that an oecumenical Council be summoned at Constantinople and contrived to wring agreement from the papal legate.[2] But his demand aroused no response in Rome. A direct agreement with John, who was prepared to be converted, meant more to the Pope, and this was the ultimate outcome. In August 1369 John V reached Rome by

[1] This is made clear from the text recently published by J. Meyendorff mentioned in the note that follows.
[2] Cf. J. Meyendorff, 'Projet de Concile Decuménique en 1367; un dialogue inédit entre Jean Cantacuzène et le légat Paul', DOP 14 (1960), 147–77, who makes known a contemporary account of these discussions and gives an excellent introductory commentary. This interesting and important account comes of course from an adherent of Cantacuzenus. Cf. also idem, 'Jean-Joasaph Cantacuzène et le projet de Concile Oecuménique en 1367, *Akten des XI. Int. Byzantinisten-Kongresses*, Munich 1960, 363 ff.

way of Naples. He was accompanied by many state dignitaries, but by not a single representative of the Byzantine clergy. After the rejection of the demand put by Cantacuzenus, the Byzantine Church adopted an attitude of extreme caution. And while in Rome the Emperor was renouncing the faith of his fathers, the Patriarch Philotheus, who had once more been called to the see of Constantinople after the death of Callistus, was seeking to strengthen the loyalty of the Orthodox to their faith, issuing letters and admonitions not only to the Byzantine population, but also to all the Orthodox Christians beyond the Empire's frontiers, in Syria and Egypt, in the southern Slav lands and in Russia.[1] Thus John V's conversion to the Roman faith which took place with great ceremony in October 1369 remained an individual act applying to the Emperor's person alone. There was no union of the two Churches,[2] and their relations to each other remained unaltered. The political results of the journey were however completely negative, for all the Emperor's hopes of Western help for his Empire were only a snare and a delusion.

Thus the real purpose of the journey failed and his change of faith was in vain. But John V did not return home at once, and early in 1370 went to Venice. He was driven to this by urgent financial need. He was no longer seeking military aid for his Empire, but was trying at least to obtain some money. His long stay in Venice, however, brought him fresh disappointments and further severe humiliations. An agreement was however made. John V was prepared to give the Venetian republic the island of Tenedos which they urgently wanted, while in return the Venetians promised to return the Byzantine crown jewels pawned thirty years earlier by his mother and to give him in addition six transport ships and twenty-five thousand ducats in cash. The matter seemed to be settled and the Emperor received on request an advance payment of four thousand ducats. But Andronicus, who during his absence was acting as regent in Constantinople, refused to hand over Tenedos to the Venetians, for on account of its position at the entry to the Dardanelles, the island was also sought by his friends the Genoese. Thus the Emperor John V found himself in an extremely precarious position. He had no money for his journey home and was also

---

[1] Cf. Halecki, *Un empereur* 235 ff.

[2] This is rightly stressed by Halecki, *Un empereur* 205, while the opposite view is incorrectly taken by A. Vasiliev, 'Il viaggio di Giovanni V Paleologo in Italia e l'unione di Roma del 1369', *Studi bizantini e neoellenici* 3 (1931), 153–92.

unable to repay his debts and the advance payment he had received. His urgent appeal for help was coolly rejected by Andronicus. He alleged that the people would not let the Church treasure be touched (it was public knowledge that there was no other treasure available). John V could now be thankful that his plans of 1355 had not been put into effect, and that he had not sent the boy Manuel to Avignon as a hostage as he had then intended. For Manuel, who was ruling Thessalonica, hurried to his father's aid and rescued him in his hour of need.[1] In October 1371[2] the sorely tried Emperor finally returned, after being absent for two years, without having accomplished anything. He appears to have made no attempt in these hopeless circumstances to induce his country to accept the reunion of the Churches. According to Demetrius Cydones, who had accompanied the wretched Emperor on this ill-fated journey, it had been 'a vain trouble of no use whatsoever to our country'.[3]

John V had failed to get help, but the urgency of his need was brought home by another devastating Turkish victory. After the establishment of the Ottomans in Thrace, Macedonia seemed the most seriously threatened province. The despot John Uglješa who ruled in Serres was the first 'to take up arms against the godless Muslims'.[4] He wished to organize a greater counter-offensive against the conqueror and he called on Byzantium to join 'the common struggle against the common enemy'.[5] He went so far as to meet the Byzantines by condemning in the strongest terms the

[1] R. J. Loenertz, 'Jean V Paléologue à Venise' (1370–71), REB 16 (1953), 1217 ff., gives an excellent reconstruction of the story of John V in Venice and has thus resolved a much disputed problem. Halecki, *Un empereur*, 335 ff. and B 17 (1944/45), 313 ff., has asserted that the arrest of John V in Venice as a debtor was a later legend and that he remained a year in Venice of his own free will. Dölger, 'Johannes VII.', 22 ff., BZ (1933), 134 and 43 (1950), 441 and Charanis, 'Palaeologi and Ottoman Turks' 286 ff., have pointed out that this view is untenable and have argued that John V was in fact held in Venice as an insolvent debtor. With the exhaustive study of Loenertz, Halecki's thesis has finally been repudiated, while the opinion held by Dölger and Charanis (which I adopted in earlier editions of this book), has been shown to need more precise definition, although admittedly this does not affect the essence of the matter but only certain nuances. As Loenertz himself says: 'He (John V) was virtually a prisoner in Venice; not a prisoner for debt, as has been wrongly stated, but all the same a prisoner of his debts, or at least, of his lack of money' (p. 218). And again: 'The Signoria, in order to prevent the Emperor from leaving, had no need to put his feet in the stocks, for since he had neither money or credit, he could not provision his galleys for the return journey' (p. 225).
[2] Lampros-Amantos, Βραχέα Χρονικά No. 47, 32, for the dating; on this cf. Charanis, 'Short Chronicle' 340 and 'Palaeologi and Ottoman Turks' 292.
[3] D. Cydonès, *Correspondance*, ed. Loenertz, I, No. 37, 5.
[4] Solovjev-Mošin, 'Grčke povelje srpskih vladara' (Greek charters of Serbian rulers), No. 38, 6.
[5] Demetrius Cydones, Migne PG 154, 1034.

elevation of Dušan to the rank of Emperor and the setting up of the Serbian patriarchate, and by recognizing the jurisdiction of the patriarchate of Constantinople within his own territory.[1] Nevertheless, only his brother, king Vukašin, joined him. The brothers led their army against Adrianople and clashed with the enemy at Černomen on the Marica. Here their forces were destroyed by the Turks on 26 September 1371. Both Uglješa and Vukašin were killed and thus the two strongest personalities of the time in the Balkans disappeared from the scene. After this catastrophe Macedonia lost its independence. The local princes, including Vukašin's son, Kraljević Marco, the hero of the Serbian folk-songs, had to recognize the suzerainty of the Sultan and pledge themselves to pay tribute and perform military service. The final subjection of their principalities, as of the other Balkan countries, was now only a matter of time.

The Ottoman victory on the Marica, the greatest and most far-reaching in its effects before that of 1453, was a body blow against Byzantium, in spite of the fact that the Empire had not taken part in the battle. It was small consolation and only a passing success that Manuel from his base in Thessalonica occupied the territory of the fallen Despot Uglješa and entered Serres (November 1371).[2] The situation of the Byzantine Empire had become so critical that the imperial government, as Manuel records in a later document, decided at that very time, 'immediately after the death of the despot of Serbia, the late Uglješa', to deprive the Byzantine monasteries of half their lands in order to grant them out as *pronoia* estates, and thus to stregthen the country's defences against the 'exceedingly serious and long drawn out' Turkish invasion.[3] Nor was this all: shortly after the battle of the Marica, Byzantium itself sank into formal dependence on the Ottoman overlord and pledged itself to pay him tribute and perform military service.[4] About the same time Bulgaria

---

[1] Solovjev-Mošin, No. 35.

[2] Cf. the text published from the Protaton MS. Nr. 21 by P. N. Papageorgiou, BZ 3 (1894), 316, note 2. Cf. also Loenertz, 'M. Paléologue et D. Cydonès' 278; Lemerle, *Philippes* 214 ff. The government of Thessalonica and the conquests in Macedonia were then solemnly passed to Manuel for his life; cf. the prooemium to the chrysobull drawn up by D. Cydones, ed. Zachariä von Lingenthal, *S.B. d. Preuss. Akad. d. Wiss.* 1888, II, 1417 ff.

[3] Cf. Manuel II's very informative *prostagma* of December 1408, published by V. Mošin, 'Akti iz svetogorskih arhiva' (Documents of the archives of the Holy Mountain), *Spomenik* 91 (1939), 165 ff. On further information on the secularization of the lands of the Byzantine monasteries and their distribution as *pronoia* estates cf. Ostrogorsky, *La féodalité* 161 ff.

[4] Cf. G. Ostrogorsky, 'Byzance, État tributaire de l'Empire turc', ZRVI 5 (1958), 49 ff.

also recognized Turkish suzerainty. And so barely twenty years after the first Ottoman settlement on European soil, both the Byzantine Empire and its once powerful rival, the Empire of the Bulgarian tzar, had become Turkish dependencies.

In the spring of 1373 the Emperor John V was already fulfilling his new duty as vassal by accompanying the Sultan on a campaign in Asia Minor. Andronicus, however, made use of his father's absence from Constantinople to raise an open revolt against him. He joined forces with the Ottoman prince Saudži Čelebi, and the result was a curious double rebellion of the Byzantine and Ottoman princes against their respective fathers (May 1373). Murad speedily crushed the revolt, had Saudži's eyes put out and demanded that John V should punish his own son in the same manner. The Emperor did not dare disobey the Sultan's order, but whereas Saudži succumbed to the severity of his wounds, the execution of the punishment was carried out in a milder form on Andronicus and his little son John, so that they did not completely lose their eyesight and were both later on able to play an important role again, though once more to the detriment of the Empire. In place of the rebel, who had been arrested and deprived of his rights as successor to the throne, Manuel was recognized as the heir of John V and on 25 September 1373 he was crowned co-Emperor.[1]

The feud in the Byzantine ruling house was exploited by the Venetians and Genoese in their struggle for Tenedos. Since John V had promised it to the Venetians, the Genoese at once decided to bring about a change of government in Constantinople, and thus to prevent Venice from gaining possession of a base which had obvious economic and strategic advantages. They therefore helped the imprisoned Andronicus to escape to Galata in order that he might take up arms against John V, as rival claimant, though in reality he was being used against Venice. On 12 August 1376 Andronicus IV, supported by the Turks, forced his way into Constantinople after a siege which had lasted thirty-two days, and he then imprisoned his father and brother. A few days later he ceded Tenedos to the Genoese, while he returned Gallipoli, which had been recaptured

---

[1] Cf. Charanis, 'Palaeologi and Ottoman Turks' 293 ff., with references to the sources; R. J. Loenertz, 'La première insurrection d'Andronic IV Paléologue (1373)', EO 38 (1939), 340 ff.; F. Dölger, 'Zum Aufstand des Andronicus IV gegen seinen Vater Johannes V. im Mai 1373', REB 19 (1961), 328 ff.

by Amadeo of Savoy ten years before, to the Turks.[1] But the Genoese were unable to take possession of Tenedos. The island remained faithful to John V and in October 1376 it was occupied by the Venetians. But the Genoese could not tolerate this and a year later war broke out over the disputed island.[2]

However, John V and Manuel II were able to escape from prison with Venetian help, and then with Turkish approval they set about regaining the lost throne. Public opinion seems to have been on their side, but this was a factor of little significance, for internal forces no longer had any influence in determining the fortunes of the Empire, and everything depended entirely on the attitude of external factors. Byzantium was now only a pawn in the political game of the great powers who had interests in the East—the two Italian republics and the Ottoman empire. In their struggle for the imperial crown John V and Andronicus IV were in fact the mere exponents of the conflicting interests of Genoa and Venice. But it was the will of the Sultan which decided the issue: with Turkish support John V and Manuel II re-entered the capital on 1 July 1379. The price was the pledge to pay the Sultan tribute and to give him military aid. Manuel had to present himself every year at the Sultan's court with the fixed tribute and to accompany his Ottoman overlord on campaign whenever he ordered.[3]

The struggle between Venice and Genoa for Tenedos was, however, continued, and was indeed carried on by both sides with increasing bitterness, until the exhausted opponents finally came to terms with each other on 8 August 1382 in Turin, thanks to the mediation of Count Amadeo of Savoy. A compromise was reached: Tenedos was to be given to neither Venice nor Genoa, its fortifications were to be razed to the ground, its population transplanted to Crete and Euboea and the demilitarized island handed over to the plenipotentiary of the Count of Savoy. Byzantium was completely ignored in all this, as though the island had never belonged to the Empire. Meanwhile, the Venetian Bailo of Tenedos, delayed handing

---

[1] D. *Cydonès, Correspondance,* ed. Loenertz II, no. 167, 15. Charanis, 'Palaeologi und Ottoman Turks', 296 ff., thinks that Gallipoli was only handed over at the beginning of 1377, relying on the information in a chronicle of sixteenth-century origin (Lampros-Amantos no. 45, 6); but how little weight can be placed on evidence from this chronicle is shown by its statement that Murad also took Serbia at the same time. Loenertz, *Lettres de D. Cydonès* 114, places the surrender of Gallipoli in September 1376.

[2] Cf. F. Thiriet, 'Venise et l'occupation de Ténédos au XIVe siècle', *Mélanges d'Archéologie et d'Histoire* (1953), 219 ff.

[3] According to Chalcocondyles (ed. Darkó, I, 57, 13 and 58, 1), the tribute payments were fixed at 30,000 gold coins a year, while according to Sphrantzes (ed. Papadopulos p. 60, 21), the Byzantine military aid amounted to 12,000 men in cavalry and infantry.

over this important island, so that the treaty was not put into effect until the winter of 1383–84, and even after this Venice continued for some time to use it as a maritime base.[1]

After his restoration, John V, in spite of recent events, had to recognize Andronicus IV and his son John VII as his legitimate heirs and to cede to them Selymbria, Heraclea, Rhaedestus and Panidus. This recognition, which meant that Manuel had been set aside and brought fresh dissension into the ruling house, was confirmed on 2 November 1382 by a formal treaty.[2] Thus the remains of the Byzantine Empire were divided into several principalities, governed by members of the ruling house: John V ruled in Constantinople; Andronicus IV, now more dependent on the Sultan than on his father, held the cities which the Empire still possessed on the Sea of Marmora; the dispossessed Manuel II now arbitrarily took over authority in his former domain of Thessalonica;[3] in the Morea Theodore I, the third son of the Emperor, had been ruling since 1382.

The Palaeologi had managed to seize the Byzantine possessions in the Peloponnese from the Cantacuzeni. This was the only success which the Palaeologian dynasty had to its credit in these grim times. Theodore I (1382–1406) had to recognize the suzerainty of the Turks, and as an obedient vassal he then enjoyed Turkish support against his adversaries at home and abroad.[4] In his struggle against the local aristocracy and the neighbouring small Latin principalities he succeeded in doing a good deal to consolidate Byzantine rule in the Morea. He brought new blood into the country by settling in it a considerable number of Albanians, who were then migrating southwards.[5] At the centre of the Byzantine Empire, on the other hand, the situation continued to go from bad to worse. External pressure was increased, and the apparent reconciliation between the Emperor and his eldest son did not last. Andronicus took up arms again, and tried to seize a fortress between Selymbria and Constantinople. John V was only able to beat back this attack after a hard struggle which almost cost him his life. Soon afterwards Andronicus IV died (June 1385).[1]

---

[1] Cf. Thiriet, op. cit., 228 ff.

[2] Cf. Loenertz, 'M. Paléologue et D. Cydonès', 287, 477. Cf. also idem, 'Fragment d'une lettre de Jean V Paléologue à la commune de Gênes 1387–1391', BZ 51 (1958), 37 ff.

[3] Cf. Dennis, *Manuel II*, 46 ff.

[4] Cf. Loenertz, 'Péloponèse 166 ff.

[5] Cf. Zakythinos, *Despotat* II, 31 ff.

Figure 71: (ABOVE) *Mistra.* General view of the hillside capital of the Despots of the Morea, near Sparta. (BELOW) *Palace of the Despots, Mistra.* Viewed from above, the throne room is seen at left, with the forecourt to its right. Photos: (above) from Gabriel Millet, *Monuments byzantins de Mistra*, Paris, 1910; (below) Ljubica Popović, 1961.

Figure 72: *Church of the Virgin and Church of the Apostles.* The Patriarchate, Peć, Yugoslavia, 1250–1330. Exterior view of the apses, from the east-southeast. Photo: Bildarchiv Foto Marburg.

In the Balkans the struggle between the Christians and the Ottomans was approaching its climax. Serbia was still capable of putting up a stiff resistance. Among the rulers who had seized the remnants of Dušan's empire, the strongest and most distinguished was prince Lazar, who had gained control of the government in Rascia after the death of tzar Uroš († 1371), the last direct descendant of the Nemanići. He managed to win over some of the local lords to his own side, and to bring others under his influence by force. But the most important factor in the coming struggle was Lazar's alliance with Tvrtko of Bosnia, whose power was rapidly growing.[2] As the descendant of a side branch of the house of Nemanja, Tvrtko had assumed the royal crown in 1377, and when Louis of Hungary died in 1382 he began his rapid and powerful advance into Croatia and Dalmatia, which resulted in the emergence of a large, though short-lived, south Slav realm, thus making him the most powerful Christian ruler in the Balkans at the time. Tvrtko's incorporation of Serbian territory into his kingdom did not hinder the co-operation between the two princes. Even relations with Byzantium became more friendly, thanks to Lazar's diplomatic skill, for in 1375 the ecclesiastical dispute provoked by the setting up of an independent Serbian Patriarchate at Peć had been allayed by a compromise in 1375, by which the ban of excommunication laid upon the Serbian Church was raised and its head accorded the rank of Patriarch.[3]

The Ottomans were continually becoming more bold in their attacks and were a terrible menace to both Greek and Slav. It is true that in 1382, Manuel II mounted an offensive against the Turks, based on Thessalonica.[4] This was an open revolt against his Ottoman overlords and a bold provocation which was in direct conflict with the policy of his father in Constantinople. But his offensive

[1] Lampros-Amantos, Βραχέα Χρονικά No. 15, 23 ff.; Loenertz, 'M. Paléologue et D. Cydonès', 477 ff. and 'Fragment d'une lettre de Jean V à la commune de Gênes', BZ 51 (1958), 39 ff.
[2] Cf. V. Ćorović, *Historija Bosne* (History of Bosnia), Belgrade 1940, 276 ff.; *Istorija naroda Jugoslavije* (History of the peoples of Yugoslavia) I, 1953, 530 ff.
[3] *Životi kraljeva i arhiepiskopa srpskih* (Lives of Serbian Kings and Archbishops), ed. Daničić (1866), 381 ff.; M. Lascaris, 'Le patriarcat de Peć a-t-il été reconnu par l'Eglise de Constantinople en 1375?' *Mélanges Diehl* I (1930), 171 ff., wrongly doubts Byzantine recognition of the Serbian patriarchate in 1375; cf. my comments in *Sem. Kond.* 5 (1932), 323 f., and now cf. also V. Laurent, 'L'archevêque de Peć et le titre de patriarche après l'union de 1375', *Balcania* 7 (1944), 303 ff.
[4] The credit for pointing this out belongs to Dennis, in his interesting work, *Manuel II.* But Dennis seems to overestimate the success of the Byzantine counter-offensive. The accounts referring to it in the correspondence of Demetrus Cydones—the only source to mention it—are full of spirited rhetoric, but do not contain a single concrete fact about what was achieved.

could not have any significant or lasting results. The Turks held the upper hand and on 19 September 1383 Serres finally fell to them.[1] Shortly afterwards the siege of Thessalonica began. The well-defended seaport held out for more than three years, but finally had to open its gates to the Ottomans in April 1387.[2] Manuel left the city shortly before it fell and fled to Lesbos.

Meanwhile Sofia in about 1385[3] and Niš in 1386 had fallen. After the fall of Niš Lazar had however wiped out Murad's force at Pločnik, and in 1388 a Turkish army that had penetrated into Bosnia was defeated by the Bosnian voivode Vlatko Vuković at Bileća. But then Murad advanced with a large army to seek a decisive battle with the South Slavs. The first blow was struck at the Bulgarian tzar who, encouraged by Lazar's resistance, had dared to defy the Sultan and had refused the payment of tribute. The Ottomans broke into Bulgaria, overcame the resistance of the tzar and forced him into subjection (1388). Then the Sultan turned against the Serbs.

Prince Lazar, with his Serbian and Bosnian troops, met Murad on the field of Kosovo ('the field of the Blackbirds') and here on 15 June 1389 took place the historic battle which after the catastrophe on the Marica is the most decisive event in the Ottoman conquest of the Balkan peninsula, and which lives on in the national consciousness as the central point in the history of medieval Serbia. At first fortune seemed to favour the Serbs. The Sultan himself was killed, but under the leadership of the heir to the throne, Bajezid, the superior

---

[1] According to F. Taeschner and P. Wittek, 'Die Vezirfamilie der Ğandarlyzāde and ihre Denkmäler', *Der Islam* 18 (1929), 71 ft., the Turks took Serres for a short period as early as 1373. So also Loenertz 'M. Paléologue et D. Cydonès', 278 (date: 1372); Lemerle, *Philippes* is more cautious and so indeed is Dennis, *Manuel* II, 66 f. The view that the Turks occupied the city temporarily in 1372 or 1373 is based on the statements made in the Turkish chronicle of Sa'eddin and especially on a document of Murad I, extant in a Greek translation, which has been preserved in the Prodromos monastery at Serres and assures this monastery (?—it speaks of the monks τῆς ἐκκλησίας Μαργαρίτου) of the Sultan's protection. Cf. the text itself in A. Guillou, *Les archives de St-Jean-Prodrome sur le mont Ménécée*, Paris 1955, p. 155, in which this document is dated to 1372, while Taeschner and Wittek, and the communication of J. H. Mordtmann which they quote, op. cit., 72 n. 1, place it in 1373. But it is in any case remarkable that the Byzantine documents of this period, which often refer to Serbian rule before 1371 (cf. especially, Lemerle, *Actes de Kutlumus* No. 33 of August 1375 and No. 34 of October 1375), do not contain a single word of any subsequent occupation by the Turks.

[2] On the chronology of the capture of Thessalonica cf. Charanis, 'Short Chronicle', 359 ff., Loenertz 'M. Paléologue et D. Cydonès', 478 ff., Dennis *Manuel* II, 151 ff. Apparently Thessalonica was again freed from the Turks and, as Loenertz, op. cit. 483, shows, was then stormed by Bajezid I on 12 April 1394. New evidence that Thessalonica was still in Byzantine hands in January 1394 is given by M. Laskaris, Τόμος Κ. 'Αρμενοπούλου (1951), 331 ff.

[3] On the chronology cf. Babinger, *Beiträge*, 65 ff.

Ottoman forces won the day.[1] Prince Lazar was taken prisoner and was executed together with his nobles. His successors had to submit to the conqueror and recognize Ottoman suzerainty. The last centre of resistance was crushed and the Turkish conquest now swept rapidly over the Balkans.

Like the Byzantine Emperor and the Bulgarian tzar, the Serbian feudal lords had also, each in their turn, to pledge themselves to perform military service and pay tribute to the Sultan. The Turkish tax was levied on the whole population, both in Byzantium and throughout the South Slav lands. Imposed on the whole country and on every landowner, regardless of previous privileges, the Turkish *charadj* represented a most important and at the same time a most severe financial obligation from which not even the ruler of a country could grant exemption, short of making the payment himself on behalf of anyone for whom the tax was remitted.[2]

After the victory at Kosovo and the accession of Bajezid I, still more Ottoman pressure was brought to bear on Byzantium. The position of the Empire rapidly grew worse, its dependence on the Sultan increased, and not only the surrounding countryside, but even Constantinople itself was controlled by him and any tendency to independent action at once nipped in the bud. Bajezid used as his tool the young John VII, who as a true son of Andronicus IV continued to assert his claim to the throne, thereby playing into the Sutlan's hands. Bajezid gave him his support, and on the 14 April 1390 John VII seized the capital and the imperial throne.[3] While Genoa and Venice had played the leading role during the usurpation of Andronicus IV in 1376, the possession of the throne of Constantinople was now entirely at the disposal of the Sultan. The influence of the Italian maritime republics had declined, for they were exhausted by the war over Tenedos, and Genoa was further weakened by

[1] There is little certain information about the course of the battle, since contemporary accounts of it are inadequate and legends soon grew up round the events. Cf. the critical survey by S. Ćirković in S. Novaković, *Srbi i Turci* (Serbs and Turks) (1960), 453 ff. For recent literature on the battle of Kosovo see ibid., 470. On the accounts given by Byzantine sources cf. especially N. Radojčić, 'Die griechischen Quellen zur Schlacht am Kosovo Polje', B 6 (1931), 241 ff. Cf. also M. Braun, *Kosovo, die Schlacht auf dem Amselfeld in geschichtlicher und epischer Überlieferung*, Leipzig 1937.

[2] Cf. I. Bozić, *Dohodak carski*, Belgrade 1956, 54 ff. G. Ostrogorsky, 'Byzance, État tributaire de l'Empire turc', ZRVI 5 (1958), 53 ff.

[3] In addition to Dölger, 'Johannes VII' and Charanis, 'Palaeologi and Ottoman Turks', G. Kolias, Ἡ ἀνταρσία ''Ιωάννου Ζ' ἐναντίον 'Ιωάννου Ε' Παλαιολόγου (1390)', Ἑλληνικά 12 (1951), 36–64, has now produced an authoritative investigation into the history for John VII's *coup d'état*, which for the first time makes thorough use of the important eye-witness account of Ignatius of Smolensk.

internal troubles. It is however worth noticing that John VII had supporters in Constantinople, which facilitated his entry into the city and assumption of control.[1]

John VII's elevation to the throne was the Sultan's first step towards the occupation of Constantinople. At that time the Venetian senate was preparing to send an embassy to that city and its plenipotentiaries were given special instructions in case they happened to find 'the son of Murad' already in possession of the capital.[2] John VII's government did not, however, last long. Manuel, who had escaped to Lemnos, prepared for a counterblow. After two unsuccessful attempts, on 17 September 1390 he succeeded in entering Constantinople, driving out his rival and recovering the sovereignty for himself and his father.[3] But it was all too plain in Constantinople that no one could occupy the imperial throne who was not prepared to submit unreservedly to the will of the powerful Sultan and to perform his every wish. John V continued to reign as a puppet-ruler in Constantinople, but Manuel now lived at the Sultan's court as a submissive vassal, putting up with every humiliation. He and his father had already had to accompany Murad I on campaign, and then to fight at his side against the Seljuqs. But Manuel was now forced to accompany Bajezid against Byzantine Philadelphia, and to assist him with Byzantine troops when he captured this last Byzantine city in Asia Minor.[4] At the same time, humiliations no less hard to bear were being inflicted on the old Emperor in Constantinople, and

---

[1] This is clear from the account of Ignatius of Smolensk; cf. Kolias, op. cit. 39 f., 43 ff.

[2] Cf. the 'commisio' for the Venetian ambassadors cited by Silberschmidt, *Das oriental. Problem* 68.

[3] Lampros-Amantos, Βραχέα Χρονικά No. 52, 44. Cf. Kolias, op. cit. 41 and 49 ff.; Dölger, 'Johannes VII' 28; Charanis, 'Palaeologi and Ottoman Turks' 304.

[4] Chalcocondyles I, 58. Cf. Wittek, *Mentesche* 78 ff., on the capture of Philadelphia in 1390 (not in 1379 as often given in the older works). From the sequence of events described above, it is clear that this event occurred after the reinstatement of John V and Manuel when the Sultan exacted recognition of their dependence on him in particularly oppressive forms and it was notorious that Manuel had to stay in Bajezid's camp. Charanis, 'Palaeologi and Ottoman Turks' 304 ff., also reaches this conclusion, and rightly stresses that the conquest of the city in any case fell between 17 September 1390 and 16 February 1391, and in all probability was before the end of 1390. Cf. also Babinger, *Beiträge* 9, note 37. H. Hunger, *Byzantinische Geisteswelt von Konstantin dem Grossen bis zum Fall Konstantinopels*, Baden-Baden, 1958, 282 ff., translates an interesting extract from an unedited work of John Chortasmenus, who describes the pitiable condition of the Empire before the battle of Angora. In order to illustrate the 'monstrous enslavement' of the Roman Empire at that time, he recalls how 'the barbarians as it were, hardly let our most pious Emperor breathe freely for a single hour, but chased him up and down the whole world and with his help brought under their control cities which had not been previously subjected' (p. 285).

by Bajezid's orders he had to raze to the ground the new fortifications which he had erected in the knowledge of the perils which now threatened the imperial city itself.[1] John V's life of trials and suffering came to an end on 16 February 1391.[2]

On hearing the news of his father's death Manuel escaped from Brusa and hurried to Constantinople to secure possession of the throne before it was seized by his ambitious nephew, John VII.[3] Manuel II (1391–1425) was an enlightened and widely-gifted ruler, who appreciated art and learning and was an adept with the pen. In character he was one of the most sympathetic figures of later Byzantine history. Fate had inflicted upon him a most humiliating position at the Sultan's court, but, in spite of this, his whole bearing won the respect even of the Turks themselves. Bajezid is said to have remarked about him: 'If anyone did not know that he was an Emperor, they would certainly have deduced it from his appearance'.[4] And this was the ruling sovereign in the city on the Bosphorus in one of the darkest hours of its history.

The imperial city was now identical with the imperial Empire, for apart from the principality in the Morea, the Byzantines had no possessions on the mainland except their old capital which had only managed to prolong its existence, isolated as it was in a sea of Turkish conquests, by reason of the strength of its walls.[5] But even so it was impoverished and deserted, and the number of inhabitants had sunk to 40–50,000.[6] The exploitation and humiliation of his intimidated vassals in Constantinople and the Morea did not satisfy Bajezid for long, and he soon turned to open hostility. This change was announced at a dramatic meeting which he ordered his Byzantine and Slav vassals to attend in the winter of 1393–4 at Serres.[7] From

[1] Ducas 77, 11 ed. Grecu (CB, 48). Silberschmidt, *Das oriental. Problem*, entirely misunderstands the situation when he speaks of a Byzantino-Turkish 'union' ('alliance' or 'entente') at this time and enlarges on the Emperor's 'Turkish policy', regarding the Turks as the Emperor's weapon against all his enemies and attributing to the Venetian senate anxiety lest 'a Greek Empire of the Turkish nation' should develop (pp. 52, 68, 70, 79 and passim).
[2] On the date cf. Charanis, 'Short Chronicle' 357 f., based on Lampros-Amantos, Βραχέα Χρονικά Nr. 52, 47; cf. also Nr. 29, 23.
[3] Cf. Dölger, 'Johannes VII' 28.
[4] Sphrantzes (ed. Papadopoulos) I, 120.
[5] According to Ducas, 77, 26, ed. Grecu (CB, 49), Bajezid, angered at Manuel's flight, sent him a message which concluded with the words: 'If you will not do and give me what I command, shut the gates of the city and rule within it, for everything outside is mine.'
[6] Cf. A. M. Schneider, 'Die Bevölkerung Konstantinopels im XV. Jahrhundert', *Nachr. d. Akad. d. Wiss. in Göttingen*, Philol.-Hist. Kl. 1949, no. 9, 236 ff.
[7] Cf. Zakythinos, *Despotat* I, 153 f., and esp. Loenertz, 'Péloponese' 172 ff. Cf. also V. Laurent, 'Un acte grec inédit du despote serbe Constantin Dragas', REB 5 (1947), 180.

now on Constantinople was in a state of blockade, and the city was cut off from all approach on the land side.[1] The Byzantine capital was in a pitiful condition and the problem of provisioning it, which had steadily grown more acute during the last decades, now reached its climax. The Morea was also faced with plundering Turkish inroads.

In 1393 the great general Evrenoz-bey captured Thessaly, and then the Ottomans turned to the rest of Greece where conquest was facilitated by dissension among the various rulers. Catalan rule in Greece was already a thing of the past and by 1379 the Navarre Company had deprived them of Thebes. Attica was at present controlled by the duke of Athens, Nerio I Acciajuoli (1388-94), a member of the Florentine merchant family that had played an important role in Greece from the mid-fourteenth century onwards and had long ruled over Corinth.[2] There was a close friendship between Nerio and the Despot Theodore Palaeologus, his son-in-law. But both of them were frequently at loggerheads with Venice, while the Byzantine Despot of Mistra was in almost perpetual conflict with the Navarrese in Achaia. Nerio died in September 1394 and practically all his lands went to his second son-in-law count Carlo Tocco of Cephalonia, whereupon Theodore, who felt himself slighted, quarrelled violently with him and tried to seize Corinth by force from the fortunate heir. At this point Carlo Tocco appealed to the Ottomans for help and Evrenoz-bey's forces defeated the Palaeologus beneath the walls of Corinth, broke into the Byzantine Morea and with the enthusiastic support of the Navarrese occupied the Byzantine fortresses of Leontarion and Akova at the beginning of 1395.[3]

With equal rapidity the Ottoman conquest spread to the northern Balkans. In 1393 the Bulgarian Empire was finally subjugated. Trnovo, the capital of the tzars, fell on 17 July after a severe siege and was given over to the ruthless devastation of its conquerors. The rest of the country was soon in the hands of the Turks[4] and for nearly

---

[1] Cf. the comments of Jireček, BZ 18 (1909), 584 f., on the beginning of the blockade in 1394.

[2] Cf. K. M. Setton, *Catalan Domination of Athens*, Cambridge, Mass. 1948, 125ff; and also Miller, *Essays* 135 ff.; Longnon, *Empire latin* 323 ff.

[3] Cf. Zakythinos, *Despotat* I, 155 ff.: Loenertz, 'Péloponèse' 185 f.

[4] Nikov, 'Turskoto zavladevane' 69, note 1, had already rightly stressed that there appeared to be some confusion in the accounts of the Turkish sources, i.e. the duplication of the events of 1388 and 1393. Cf. the thorough comments of Babinger, *Beiträge* 29 ff., who seems, however, to go too far in wishing entirely to eliminate the Bulgarian campaign of 1388.

five hundred years Bulgaria remained a province of the Ottoman Empire.

Meanwhile, prince Mircea the Elder of Wallachia, who had strong support from Hungary, put up vigorous opposition to the Turks and on 17 May 1395 a particularly fierce battle was fought with great loss of life on the plain of Rovine. In fulfilment of their obligations as vassals, a number of Christians fought on the side of the Ottomans, including the Serbian prince Stephen Lazarević, son and heir of the hero of Kosovo, Vukašin's son Marko who ruled a small area round Prilep, and Constantine Dragaš, the father-in-law of Manuel II, who governed in eastern Macedonia. King Marko and Constantine Dragaš were killed in the battle. From the military point of view Mircea seems to have been the victor, but all the same he had to recognize the Sultan's authority and pay tribute.[1] The Dobrudja, which had been for the last decades a Bulgarian principality and shortly before had fallen within Mircea's sphere of influence, was now seized by the Ottomans and the crossings over the Danube were garrisoned by Turkish troops.

These latest Ottoman successes made a great impression in the West. The occupation of Bulgaria meant that Hungary was directly threatened, and the Latin principalities in Greece also felt the heavy hand of Turkish aggression in the immediate neighbourhood. Up to now Byzantine appeals for help and papal warnings had fallen on deaf ears, but now men felt that combined action by the Christian powers against the Ottoman threat was imperative. The appeal by the Hungarian king Sigismund was answered by the chivalry of several European countries, and in particular by the knighthood of France spurred on by the thought of a crusade. After considerable

[1] Earlier scholars considered that the Turks suffered military defeat at the battle of Rovine. This view was abandoned, but it appears to have a very strong element of probability according to the striking arguments of Dj. Radojičić, 'Jedna glava iz "života Stefana Lazarevića" od Konstantina Filozofa' (A chapter from Constantine the Philosopher's Life of Stephen Lazarević), *Hrišćanski život* 6 (1927), 138 ff., and M. Dinić, 'Hronika sen-deniskog kaludjera kao izvor za bojeve na Kosovu i Rovinama' (The chronicle of the monks of St. Denis as a source for the battles of Kosovo and Rovine), *Prilozi za književnost, jezik, istoriju i folklor* 17 (1937), 51 ff. Babinger, *Beiträge* 3 ff., relying on Turkish sources, considers that the outcome of the battle was indecisive. It has been established beyond doubt that the date of the battle of Rovine was not on 10 October 1394 (as formerly held) but on 17 May 1395, since this is the date of the death of Constantine Dragaš who fell in the fight; cf. Dj. Radojičić, op. cit., and 'La chronologie de la bataille de Rovine', *Revue hist. du Sud-Est europ.* 5 (1928), 136 ff. This inescapable conclusion is strengthened by the arguments of M. Dinić, op. cit., and is in no way weakened by the comments of Babinger, *Beiträge* 3 ff., who supports the year 1393. Radojičić's chronology is rightly followed by Zakythinos, *Despotat* I, 153, note 3, and Loenertz, 'Péloponèse' 175 and passim. Cf. also V. Laurent, REB 5 (1947), 180, note 3, and 6 (1948), 282.

hesitation even Venice joined the coalition and despatched a small fleet to the Dardanelles to patrol the straits and keep open the line of communication between Byzantium and the crusading forces assembling in Hungary. The expedition seemed full of promise, but it was a complete failure. At the battle of Nicopolis on 25 September 1396 the large but motley host was routed by the Turks, largely because of the lack of cohesion between the Hungarian and French contingents.[1] King Sigismund escaped capture by flight, and in company with the Grand Master of the Knights of St. John and several German knights he reached Constantinople by sea, and from there he returned home by way of the Aegean and Adriatic. His passage through the Dardanelles was made to the sound of the piteous cries of the Christian captives, whom the Sultan had ordered to be lined up on both shores of the straits in order to humiliate the defeated king.[2]

After this fresh catastrophe the situation in the Balkans became even more hopeless. The principality of Vidin, the last remaining Bulgarian district, now fell to the Ottomans. Even in Greece the effects were felt. In 1397 Athens was temporarily occupied by the Turks[3] and the Byzantine Morea experienced a new and devastating invasion. The Muslim crossed the Isthmus, stormed Venetian Argos, defeated the forces of the Byzantine Despot and penetrated Byzantine territory as far as the south coast, burning and plundering.[4] The plight of Constantinople had reached its lowest depths and the capture of the blockaded imperial capital seemed imminent.

4. THE FINAL DOWNFALL

General bibliography: Berger de Xivrey, *Mémoires sur la vie et les ouvrages de l'empereur Manuel Paléologue*, Mémoires de l'Inst. de France, Acad. des Inscriptions et Belles-Lettres 19, 2, Paris 1853; A. Mompherratos, Διπλωματικαὶ ἐνέργειαι Μανουὴλ Β', Athens 1913; Vasiliev, 'Putešestvie Manuila';

[1] Cf. G. Kling, *Die Schlacht bei Nikopolis im Jahre* 1396, Diss. Berlin 1906; A. S. Atiya, *The crusade of Nicopolis*, London 1934; R. Rosetti, 'The Battle of Nicopolis (1396)', *Slavonic Review* 15 (1937), 629 ff.

[2] Cf. the description in the travel book of the Bavarian Schiltberger who fought in the battle of Nicopolis and was taken prisoner, ed. V. Langmantel (Tübingen 1885), 7.

[3] Cf. J. H. Mordtmann, 'Die erste Eroberung von Athen durch die Türken zu Ende des 14. Jahrhunderts', BNJ 4 (1923), 346 ff.

[4] Cf. Zakythinos, *Despotat* I, 156 ff., with references to the sources.

Norden, *Papsttum und Byzanz*; Zakythinos, *Despotat* I and II; J. Radonić, *Zapadna Evropa i balkanski narodi prema Turcima u prvoj polovini XV veka* (Western Europe and the Balkan peoples and their relation with the Turks in the first half of the fifteenth century), Novi Sad 1905; Jireček, *Geschichte* II; Jorga, *Geschichte* I and II; E. Pears, *The Destruction of the Greek Empire and the Story of the Capture of Constantinople by the Turks*, London 1903; idem, 'The Ottoman Turks to the Fall of Constantinople', CMH IV (1923), 633–705; *Le Cinq-centième anniversaire de la prise de Constantinople*: 1453–1953, Athens 1953; F. Babinger, *Mehmed der Eroberer und seine Zeit*, Munich 1953; see also the general bibliography cited above, p. 533.

Byzantine sovereignty was profoundly shaken by the events of the last decades: it was no longer a factor in international politics, nor could its Emperor maintain his position as head of the hierarchy of Christian rulers. Even Moscow, faithful as it was to tradition, refused to recognize the vassal of the Turk as the heir of Constantine the Great and the spiritual overlord of the Orthodox world. The Grand Duke Basil I, the son of Demetrius Donskoj, the powerful conqueror of the Tartars, forbad the mention of the Byzantine Emperor's name in Russian churches and coined the phrase: 'We have a Church but no Emperor'. The sovereign rights of the Greek Church remained sacred to the ruler of the expanding Russian state, but he could no longer support the conception of the supremacy of the pitiful Byzantine Emperor. It was clear, as often before during the last years of Byzantine history, that the prestige of the Byzantine Church stood far higher in Orthodox countries than that of the Byzantine state. The Byzantine protest to Moscow was not long in coming, but it was made by the Patriarch of Constantinople and not by the Emperor. There was a time when the Byzantine Church had relied on the authority of a strong secular power to give it backing in the eyes of the outside world, but now the diminishing international prestige of the Byzantine Empire had to be bolstered up by the Patriarch of Constantinople. Their roles were reversed: it was not the state which stood behind the Church, but the Church which supported the state. 'It is not a good thing, my son', so the Patriarch Antony wrote to the Grand Duke Basil, 'for you to say "We have a Church, but no Emperor". It is not possible for Christians to have a Church without an Emperor, for the imperial sovereignty and the Church form a single entity and they cannot be separated from each other. . . . Hear what the prince of the Apostles, Peter, says in his first epistle: "Fear God, honour the Emperor." He did not say "the emperors" for he was not referring to the so-called "emperors" of various different countries, but he said "the Emperor" in order to emphasize that there was only one Emperor in the world. . . . If other Christian rulers have appropriated to themselves the name of Emperor this has been done against nature and law by tyranny and force. Which of the fathers, which Councils, which canonical rulings speak of these "emperors"? They one and all proclaim a single Emperor whose laws, ordinances and decrees hold throughout the world, who alone, with none other, is revered by all Christians.'[1] The doctrine of one oecumenical Emperor had never been laid down more forcibly or with more fiery eloquence than in this letter which the Patriarch of Constantinople sent to Moscow from a city blockaded by the Turks. To the very end and in spite of all trials the Byzantines held fast to their belief that their ruler was the only true Emperor and as such the rightful overlord of Christendom. 'And if by God's decree the infidel has encircled the realm of the Emperor, he still receives today from the Church the same consecration, the same honour and the same prayers and is anointed with the same holy oil and is consecrated Emperor and Autocrator of the Romans, that is, of all Christians.'[2] Byzantium clung tenaciously to the conception which had once given it political and spiritual predominance in the Eastern world. But such tenets were now ruthlessly shattered by hard reality. After the battle of Nicopolis the position of Byzantium had still further deteriorated, and by 1398 the various Russian princes, and in particular the same Basil of Moscow, were receiving appeals for help and alms for their Christian brethren in Constantinople who 'were besieged by the Turk and languishing in need and misery'.[3]

During the last few years of the fourteenth century Byzantium was indeed reduced to such straits that all the Emperor could do was to send out fresh appeals for help to the outside world. Manuel II begged for assistance not only from Russia, but from the Pope, the Doge of Venice, and the kings of France, England and Aragon. An equally illuminating sidelight on the condition of the Empire was the fact that, while Manuel was appealing for help, John VII was negotiating the sale of his claims on the Byzantine throne to the French king in return for a castle in France and an annual income

[1] Miklosich-Müller, II, 191 f. The end of this exhortation of the Patriarch Antony (1388–90; 1391–7) is mutilated, and it therefore bears no date; it has usually been assigned to the year 1393, but it more probably belongs to the period 1394–7 because it speaks of the encirclement of Constantinople, and it was not until 1394 that Bajezid's blockade commenced (cf. above, p. 550).

[2] Miklosich-Müller, II, 190.

[3] *Polnoe Sobr. Russk. Letopisej* (Complete Collection of Russian Chronicles), 11 (1897), 168.

to 25,000 florins.[1] Charles VI, however, did not appear to be seriously tempted by this proposed bargain, but he answered Manuel's appeal and sent Byzantium a body of 1,200 picked troops under the command of the marshal Boucicaut, who valiantly managed to fight his way through to Constantinople, attacking the Turks with great bravery. But as was only to be expected, his little force, whatever good luck it had, could not free the Empire from the Ottoman danger. Manuel therefore determined to set out for the West himself in order to supplicate in person for help for his unfortunate Empire. Boucicaut had encouraged him in this resolve and had also been skilful enough to bring about an understanding between the two rival claimants to the Byzantine throne. It was arranged that John VII was to rule as Emperor in Constantinople during Manuel's absence. Yet Manuel had no illusions as to the state of affairs in the capital, and in spite of the recent reconciliation he did not trust his nephew whom he was leaving as regent, so that he thought it safer to leave his wife and children with his brother Theodore in the Morea.

Manuel set out on 10 December 1399 and he was accompanied by Boucicaut.[2] He began by visiting Venice and several other Italian cities and he then went on to Paris, and from there to London. Everywhere he was paid great honour, and the very fact of his visit, as well as his commanding presence, made a deep impression. The thoughts and sentiments which his coming aroused are well expressed in the pathetic words of a contemporary English scholar and historian, who wrote: 'I thought in my heart how cruel it was that this great Christian prince from the distant east had been compelled by the threats of the infidel to visit the far-off isles of the west to supplicate for help against them. My God! Where art thou, ancient glory of Rome? Today the splendour of thy Empire is laid low and it can indeed be said of thee in the words of Jeremias, "She that was a princess among the heathen and a queen among the nations, is now enslaved". Who would have believed that thou wouldst sink into such utter misery, that after having once governed the whole world from thy throne of eminence, thou art now quite powerless to help the Christian faith!'[3] The visit of the Emperor and his followers to

---

[1] The authorization which he had drawn up for this purpose for his French negotiators on 15 August 1397 has been printed with a commentary by Sp. Lampros, Νέος Ἑλληνομνήμων 10 (1913), 248 ff.

[2] The best and most detailed account of this famous journey with numerous references to the sources is by Vasiliev, 'Putešestvie Manuila'. Cf. also G. Schlumberger, *Un empereur de Byzance à Paris et à Londres*, in *Byzance et les croisades* (1927), 87-147, 361-2.

[3] *Chronicon Adae de Usk.*, ed. E. M. Thompson (1904), 57. Cf. Vasiliev, 'Putešestvie Manuila' 272 and *History* 634.

West European centres was of considerable significance from the cultural point of view, and facilitated closer relationships between Byzantium and the Western world during the period of the early renaissance. But from a practical point of view Manuel's journey and his appeals achieved little, for he obtained nothing but vague promises which remained unfulfilled. He stayed away from his Empire for an astonishing length of time during which his rival John VII ruled as he wished, though in increasing dependence upon the Sultan. It almost looked as though Manuel felt that he could not face the return, for he broke his journey in Paris and stayed there for nearly two years, although he could have no illusions about the possibility of getting any help. But then came the saving news that the forces of Bajezid had been defeated by the Mongols of Timur and that Byzantium was freed from the Turkish peril.

Timur was the most powerful Mongol ruler since Jenghis Khan's time and one of the greatest conquerors in the world's history. He came from a branch of a minor Turkish noble family in Turkestan, and after long and relentless fighting he achieved his aim of rehabilitating the vast empire of Jenghis Khan.[1] When he had subdued central Asia and the Golden Horde in southern Russia, he undertook in 1398 a gigantic expedition to India, and then he overran Persia, Mesopotamia and Syria, and ended by attacking the Ottoman empire in Asia Minor. His campaigns were accompanied by rape and pillage of the cruellest nature and wherever his hordes went they reduced the country to the state of a barren desert 'where there was neither the bark of a dog nor the chirp of a bird nor the cry of a child'.[2] This irresistible Juggernaut now crushed the might of Bajezid. In the decisive battle of Angora on 28 July 1402,[3] after a long and bitter struggle, Timur routed the Ottoman forces. The great Sultan fell into the hands of the victor and ended his life in Mongol captivity. Timur, however, withdrew from Asia Minor in the spring of 1403, and two years later the aged conqueror died during an expedition to China.[4] His violent intervention in the

---

[1] Cf. W. Barthold, *Zwölf Vorlesungen über die Geschichte der Türken Mittelasiens* (1935), 209 ff.; R. Grousset, *L'empire des Steppes* (1939), 486 ff.

[2] Ducas, 109, 20, ed. Grecu (CB, 77).

[3] On the date cf. Vasiliev, 'Putešestvie Manuila' 285, note 3.

[4] G. Roloff, 'Die Schlacht bei Angora', HZ 161 (1940), 244 ff., thinks that Timur's retreat and abandonment of the attempt to control Asia Minor was due to the fact that the forces at his command had been so reduced by their heavy losses that they were no longer adequate; the sources greatly exaggerate his initial strength at Angora, which Roloff would estimate, as he would that of the Ottoman army, at about 20,000 men at most.

affairs of Asia Minor was brief, but had the most momentous consequences. He had struck down the power of the Ottomans, and in so doing had prolonged the existence of the Byzantine Empire by half a century.

In the stricken Ottoman empire there was utter confusion,[1] but the internal weakness of Byzantium was such that it was utterly incapable of taking advantage of this breathing space in order to build up its own strength. Even so the situation in the East had been completely transformed and this in itself brought a measure of relief to Byzantium. Bajezid's eldest son, Suleiman, had established himself on the European side and was at war with his brothers who had control in Asia Minor. He signed a treaty in 1403[2] with Byzantium, with the Serbian Despot Stephen Lazarević[3] and the maritime powers of Venice, Genoa and Rhodes. Byzantium was relieved of the duties of vassal to the Turks and ceased to pay tribute. In fact Thessalonica was also regained, with considerable surrounding territory, as was Chalcidice with Mount Athos, and also the group of islands consisting of Skiathos, Skopelos and Skyros, with important strips of coast on the Black Sea and the Sea of Marmara.[4]

On the other hand, the alliance with Suleiman meant that the Byzantines would be involved in the internal struggle against the rival claimants to the Turkish throne, and the Serbian princes were likewise involved in this conflict which affected the whole course of events in the Balkans. In 1411 Suleiman was defeated by his brother Musa and his fall threatened the Empire with a new and serious crisis. Musa took a cruel revenge on Suleiman's allies and began the siege of Constantinople. It was, however, Muhammed who emerged

[1] There is a detailed and thorough treatment of this period in Jorga, *Geschichte* I, 325 ff.

[2] On the chronology cf. Heyd, *Commerce du Levant* II, 286; G. Ostrogorsky, 'Byzance, État tributaire de l'Empire turc', ZRVI 5 (1958), 53, n. 20.

[3] John VII granted him the title of Despot when he visited Constantinople after the battle of Angora in which he had to take part as the vassal of Bajezid. Cf. the recent comments of Ferjančić, *Despoti*, 182 ff.

[4] In a document of which little note has been taken, Manuel II sends instructions to Demetrius Buliotes, whom he sent as his plenipotentiary to Athos after it had been liberated (published by Arcadius of Vatopedi in: Γρηγόριος Παλαμᾶς 2 (1918), 449–52). This informative document shows that Manuel handed over the region of Thessalonica to John VII and signed a formal treaty with him on the matter. We learn from the same document that the suspension of the Turkish tax did not mean a complete liberation from the payment of the *haradj*. The Emperor 'donated' to the monasteries of Athos and also to other landowners only two-thirds of the sum which 'in the time of the late Emir Bajezid bey' was demanded as *haradj*, while a third was still exacted by, and from now on flowed into, the Byzantine treasury under its original name *haradj*. Cf. G. Ostrogorsky, 'Byzance, État tributaire de l'Empire turc', ZRVI 5 (1958, 54 ff.).—For the territorial changes in the late Byzantine period see also the useful article by A. Bakalopoulos, 'Les limites de l'Empire byzantin depuis la fin du XIVe siècle, jusqu'à la chute (1453)', BZ 55 (1962), 56 ff.

as victor from this struggle between the Ottoman princes. With the support of the Emperor Manuel and the Despot Stephen Lazarević he defeated Musa in 1413 and took over the sovereignty of the Ottoman Empire as Sultan. This put an end to the civil war, the gravest crisis which had threatened the Ottomans was removed, and the way prepared for a revival of Muslim power. Muhammed I (1413–21) devoted his energies chiefly to the internal consolidation of his Empire and the strengthening of his position in Asia Minor. He maintained his understanding with the Byzantine Emperor and throughout his reign good relations between the two powers remained practically undisturbed.

Byzantium was so sure of the Sultan's friendship that soon after Muhammed I's accession it was felt possible for Manuel II to leave his capital. He spent some time in Thessalonica and then in the spring of 1415 he went to the Peloponnese, where Mistra was flourishing, in contrast to the capital which was slowly withering away, even though external pressure had been greatly diminished. Here in Mistra the humanist George Gemistus Plethon hoped to see his Utopia come into being; he dreamed of the rebirth of Hellenism in southern Greece and he had evolved a new constitution modelled on Plato's republic. In various treatises addressed to the Emperor and the Despot of Mistra the neoplatonic statesman also expounded practical suggestions for the simplification of taxation and the establishment of a national army to replace mercenaries.[1] Here in the Byzantine Peloponnese the urge of Hellenism to live and to build up a new political organism found its expression on the very eve of the collapse of the Byzantine Empire. The Morea became the stronghold of Greek life, which not only took root here, but seemed to be able to expand. To defend this precious possession the Emperor had a long and stout wall rebuilt across the Isthmus of Corinth, called the Hexamilion. Manuel's visit to the Peloponnese also had some influence in shaping the internal affairs of the country, for his presence helped to keep in check the centrifugal tendencies of

[1] Sp. Lampros, Παλαιολόγεια καὶ Πελοποννησιακά III (1926), 246–65; IV (1930), 113–35; Migne, PG 160, 821–66. On Plethon's ideas cf. H. F. Tozer, 'A Byzantine Reformer', JHS 7 (1886), 353 ff.; J. Dräseke, 'Plethons und Bessarions Denkschriften über die Angelegenheiten im Peloponnes', *N. Jahrb. f. das klass. Altertum* 27 (1911), 102 ff.; Zakythinos, *Despotat* I, 175 ff. (with further bibliography), and II, 322 ff.; M. V. Anastos, 'Pletho's Calendar and Liturgy', DOP 4 (1948), 183–305; I. P. Mamalakes, Γεώργιος Γεμιστὸς-Πλήθων, Athens, 1939; and especially F. Masai, *Pléthon et le platonisme de Mistra*, Paris 1956; further bibliography in Moravcsik, *Byzantinoturcica* I, 2nd ed., 478 ff. *Mazaris' Journey to Hades*, ed. Boissonade, *Anec. gr.* III (1831), 122–86 is also important for a picture of contemporary conditions in the Peloponnese.

the local nobility and to invoke a greater respect for the authority of the government. In March 1416 the Emperor left the Peloponnese and his place was taken by his eldest son John who shortly afterwards travelled to the Morea, by way of Thessalonica, in order to help his young brother, the Despot Theodore II, with the administration of the country.[1] Under the command of John the Byzantine forces carried out a successful campaign against Latin Achaia. The prince Centurione Zaccaria lost most of his territory and only the intervention of Venice postponed the final collapse of his authority.[2]

With the death of Muhammed I and the accession of his son Murad II (1421–51) the breathing space which fate had granted to Byzantium came to an end. The Ottomans had built up their power again and the new Sultan resumed the aggressive policy of Bajezid. The situation was similar to that before the battle of Angora. The Emperor's son John, who had been crowned co-Emperor on 19 January 1421,[3] tried in vain to play off the pretender Mustafa, who made the most tempting promises to the Byzantines in the event of his success, against Murad II.[4] The attempt failed and only incited the anger of the Ottoman ruler. Murad II crushed the pretender and with youthful impetuosity he turned against Constantinople. On 8 June 1422 a real siege of the city began. Once more the strength of the defences saved the Byzantine capital, and as Murad was faced at this point with a new rival to his throne in his young brother Mustafa, he had to leave this purpose unachieved for the time being. The decisive blow did not fall for another thirty years, but with the attack on Constantinople in 1422 it is true to say that the last death struggle of the Byzantine Empire had begun.

In the spring of 1423 the Turks again broke into southern Greece. The Hexamilion wall which Manuel had built across the Isthmus at great cost was destroyed and the whole of the Morea devastated. Eventually the imperial government succeeded in making a treaty with Murad II in 1424 by which Byzantium agreed to renew its payment of tribute. Thus Byzantium relapsed once again into the position of a dependent vassal state, from which she had been freed for a while after the battle of Angora. She was never again to break away from this state of dependence, in which she remained until the end.

[1] On John VIII's stay in Thessalonica in 1416 cf. M. Lascaris, Τόμος Κ. Ἀρμενοπούλου (1951), 440 ff.
[2] Cf. Zakythinos, *Despotat* I, 180 ff.
[3] Cf. Dölger, 'Die Krönung Johanns VIII. zum Mitkaiser', BZ 36 (1936), 318 f.
[4] Cf. Jorga, *Geschichte* I, 378 ff.

Soon afterwards Thessalonica also had to meet its fate. Manuel's third son Andronicus was ruling as the last Despot of the threatened starving city. The position was so hopeless and the pressure so great that in the summer of 1423 he handed the city over to the Venetians. The maritime republic pledged itself to respect the rights and customs of the citizens and undertook to defend and provision the city.[1] As was to be expected, this transaction roused the resentment of the Ottoman ruler who had regarded the city as his certain prey. The Venetians tried to come to an understanding with him and their proposals became more lavish from year to year, with Turkish pressure outside the city constantly on the increase and starvation threatening within its walls. They began by taking over with some hesitation the annual payment of 100,000 *aspra* which the Byzantine Despot had already been paying to the Ottoman, but in the course of further discussions this sum was raised to 150,000 *aspra* and finally as much as 300,000 *aspra*.[2] In the end all this negotiation and bargaining proved useless, and after a brief rule of seven years the Venetians again lost Thessalonica. Murad II appeared in person under the walls of the city and after a rapid assault he took possession of it on 29 March 1430.

Soon after his son had been crowned co-Emperor, Manuel II had withdrawn from affairs of state. Broken in mind and body, the aged Emperor died on 21 July 1425 as the monk Matthew. John VIII (1425–8) was now to reign over Constantinople and the surrounding country as Basileus and Autocrator of the Romans. The remaining districts of the Byzantine Empire on the Black Sea and in the Peloponnese were governed by his brothers as independent rulers. Economically and financially, the dismembered and enfeebled Empire lay in complete ruin. Even under Manuel II gold coins were seldom minted, and under John VIII the Byzantine gold coinage completely ceased, and silver was normally used.[3]

The one bright spot in the Byzantine world was the Morea whose government at that time was shared between the Emperor's three

---

[1] K. Mertzios, Μνημεῖα Μακεδονικῆς Ἱστορίας, Thessalonica 1947, 34 ff., has communicated important documents from the Venetian Archives showing that the often-repeated account (also in the first German edition of this book) which makes Andronicus sell the city to the Venetians for 50,000 ducats is a myth. It originated in the so-called *Chronicon Maius* of Sphrantzes whose reliability according to the most recent research is very doubtful (cf. above, p. 468, note 4). Cf. also P. Lemerle, 'La domination vénitienne à Thessalonique', *Miscellanea G. Galbiati* III (*Fontes Ambrosiani* 27) (1951), 219 ff.

[2] K. Mertzios, op. cit. 66 ff.

[3] Cf. Wroth, *Byz. Coins* I, pp. LXVIII f.; A. Blanchet, 'Les dernières monnaies d'or des empereurs byzantins', *Revue numism.* 14 (1910), 78 ff.; Stein, 'Untersuchungen' 113 f.; Zakythinos, *Crise monétaire* 17 ff.

Figure 73: *Manuel II Palaeologus.* Illuminated miniature painting on parchment, early 15th century. Manuel is shown in full imperial regalia; this is the only illustration in a manuscript of his *Funeral Oration for His Brother Theodore.* Bibliothèque Nationale, Paris, *Cod. Suppl. gr. 309,* f. VI. Photo: Bibliothèque Nationale.

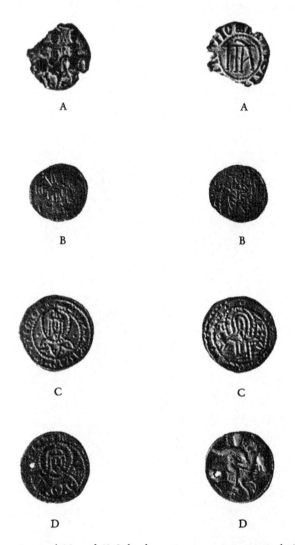

Figure 74: *Coins of Manuel II Palaeologus* (1391–1425). Actual size. Coins A and B are bronze; coins C and D are silver. (Compare with gold coins in Figures 2, 3, 4.) Dumbarton Oaks Collections, Washington, D.C. Photo: Wallace Lane, Dumbarton Oaks.

brothers Theodore, Constantine and Thomas. Undeterred by the Turkish inroads of 1423, the Byzantine Morea continued its successful attacks on the small neighbouring Latin principalities. Count Carlo Tocco, who was defeated in a naval battle in 1427, came to an agreement with the Byzantines, and in 1428 he gave the Despot Constantine the hand of his niece with his remaining possessions in the Peloponnese as her dowry. In early 1430 Constantine entered Patras after a long siege, and two years later the Latin principality of Achaia came to an end.[1] With the exception of the Venetian colonies of Coron and Modon in the south-west and Nauplia and Argos in the east, the whole of the Peloponnese was now under Greek rule. The struggle between Greeks and Franks, which had begun here in the days of Michael VIII and continued almost without interruption, had now been brought to an end with the victory of the Greeks, but only on the eve of the Turkish conquest. The final success was mainly due to the work of the young Constantine, who some twenty years later was to end his life in the fight for Constantinople as the last Emperor of Byzantium. The contrast between the dying capital and the rapidly expanding province of southern Greece was even more striking than in Manuel II's day.

Meanwhile, the Emperor John VIII was hard pressed by the Turks, and in despair he resolved to try once more to negotiate a union between the two Churches and to obtain the frequently promised Western help against the infidel at the cost of ecclesiastical submission to Rome. It is true that previous attempts of this kind did not offer much encouragement for discussions between Rome and Constantinople, and usually ended where they had begun in mutual hoodwinking and self-deception. The Byzantine Empire looked to Rome for rescue from the Turkish danger and promised in return ecclesiastical union which it was unable to put into effect in view of Byzantine popular feeling; Rome demanded recognition of her supremacy as a first essential and promised in return help against the Turks which she was not even capable of supplying to the Roman Catholic powers in the East, except to a very limited extent. The Emperor Manuel with all his experience had regarded the possibility of union with quiet scepticism, and on his death-bed he is said to have expressly warned his son against placing any hope in this: a reconciliation between Greek and Latin was out of the question and attempts to achieve this would only aggravate the schism.[2] But

[1] Zakythinos, *Despotat* I, 204 ff.
[2] Sphrantzes (ed. Papadopoulos) I, 178.

however strong Byzantine feeling in general might be against the union, there was always an influential circle in Constantinople who favoured this policy, seeing agreement with Rome as their only hope in the hour of danger. And the Emperor John VIII now put himself at the head of this party. After the siege of Constantinople in 1422, when he was still heir to the throne, he had visited Western courts in his attempts to get help, and from 1431 onwards fresh negotiations had been in progress with a view to concluding the union. Owing to the differences between Eugenius IV and the Council of Basle these negotiations were protracted, until finally it was agreed to call a council in Italy which the Emperor was to attend in person. For the period of his absence he summoned his brother Constantine to Constantinople as regent, thus incidentally putting an end to the unpleasant quarrels which had broken out amongst the imperial brothers governing the Morea.

On 24 November 1437 John VIII left his capital and journeyed to the West as his father had done some forty, and his grandfather some seventy, years before. He did not go merely to ask for help like Manuel, but, like John V, he went to be received into the Roman Church and, moreover, to bring his people and the Greek clergy into union with Rome. His brother Demetrius, the Patriarch Joseph, several metropolitans and many bishops and abbots went with him, and early in 1438 they reached Ferrara where the council was opened on 9 April. In view of the unfortunate position of the Greeks the outcome was a foregone conclusion, but in spite of this the debates in Ferrara, and then in Florence, were very prolonged,[1] and were repeatedly accompanied by violent disputes, largely due to the bitter opposition which Mark Eugenicus, Metropolitan of Ephesus, displayed towards members of the Roman Church and the pro-union party of Byzantium. It was not until 6 July 1439 that the union was proclaimed in the Greek and Latin tongues by the Cardinal

---

[1] A detailed description of the conciliar negotiations is given by G. Hofmann, 'Die Konzilsarbeit in Ferrara', OCP 3 (1937), 110–40, 403–55; 'Die Konzilsarbeit in Florenz', ibid. 4 (1938), 157–88, 372–422. There is fresh material for the preliminaries of the Council in Hofmann's study, 'Roderigo, Dekan von Braga; Kaiser Johann VIII. Palaiologos. Zwei Briefe aus Konstantinopel, 13. Oktober und 18. November 1437, zur Vorgeschichte des Konzils von Florenz', ibid. 9 (1943), 171 ff. For the history of the events leading up to the Council of Florence, cf. also V. Laurent, 'Les préliminaires du concile de Florence: Les neuf articles du Pope Martin V et la réponse du patriarche Joseph II (octobre 1422)', REB 20 (1962), 5–60. The most important publication of sources for the history of the Council is also by G. Hofmann, *Epistolae pontificiae ad Concilium Florentinum spectantes*, I–III, Rome 1940–6. Cf. also J. Gill, *The Council of Florence*, Cambridge 1958, and 'Greeks and Latins in a Common Council: the Council of Florence', OCP 25 (1959), 265 ff.

Julian Cesarini and the Archbishop Bessarion of Nicaea in the cathedral of Florence.[1] It is true that the statement about papal primacy was named in deliberately vague terms and that the Greeks were allowed to keep their own Church ritual, but all controversial questions were decided from the point of view of Rome.

On the surface the pro-union party seemed to have gained a still greater victory than in the days of the Council of Lyons, for on this occasion the Emperor had appeared before the Council in person and together with the highest representatives of the Byzantine Church had openly professed the Roman faith. But in reality the decisions taken at the Council of Florence were of no effect. The warning that negotiations on the question of union would only serve to widen the breach proved true. The Byzantine people protested against the decrees of Ferrara and Florence with passionate fanaticism, and, while all the exhortations of the pro-unionists were ignored, the fiery sermons of Mark Eugenicus found everywhere a most enthusiastic response. The union of Florence had far less influence than that of the Council of Lyons, when the founder of the Palaeologian dynasty was in a stronger position and better able to impose his will on the opposition than John VIII. Moreover, the union of 1274 had a more practicable political aim, in that it sought to defend Byzantium from Western aggression, while the purpose of the union of 1439 was to free it from the Turkish danger which Rome was in no position to undertake.

Instead of bringing help against the external enemy the union only precipitated internal dissension in Byzantium, sowing hatred and strife amongst the Byzantine people, while it robbed the Empire of what prestige remained to it in the Slav world beyond its borders. The Muscovite realm, far removed from the troubles which harassed Byzantium, but brought up by it in hatred of Rome, regarded the conversion of the Emperor and the Patriarch of Constantinople as an incredible act of treachery. The Greek Isidore who had been appointed Metropolitan of Russia was a prominent member of the pro-union party; on his return from Florence he was deposed by the Grand Duke Basil II and was thrown into prison. From now on Russia chose its Metropolitan itself and turned its back on apostate Byzantium, which had forfeited all claims to leadership in the Orthodox world by its betrayal of the true faith. So Russia was lost and

[1] Cf. A. Mercati, 'Il decreto d'unione del 6 luglio 1439 nell' Archivio Vaticano', OCP 11 (1945), 3 ff. The text of the act proclaiming the union (in Latin and Greek) is published in G. Hofmann's collection of sources, op. cit. II, Nr. 176, pp. 68–79.

bitter dissension provoked within Byzantium itself, while practically nothing was gained. The expected assistance from the West did not materialize and in Constantinople the union was a failure. The Roman Catholic and the Greek Orthodox Churches were still in opposition. And while the Byzantine people held fast to their faith, the most prominent supporters of the pro-union party followed their views to their logical conclusion and went over to Rome altogether. The leader of the Greek unionists, the learned Bessarion,[1] and Isidore, who had escaped from a Russian prison, became Cardinals in the Roman Church. The negotiations at Ferrara and Florence had no positive political results, but they did rouse the suspicion of Murad II, and John VIII had to pacify the Sultan by explaining that they were of a purely religious nature.

The Ottoman power was experiencing genuine difficulties from another quarter. The Muslim advance in the Balkans had provoked the resistance of Hungary, as it had done in the days of Bajezid. The heroic voivode of Transylvania, John Corvinus-Hunyadi, roused great enthusiasm and fresh hopes by his brilliant victories over the Turks in Serbia and Wallachia. The Pope called all Christian peoples to a crusade and in southern Hungary a motley force of about 25,000 men soon assembled under the leadership of king Vladislav III, the young Jagellon who had united the crowns of Poland and Hungary, together with Hunyadi and the Serbian Despot George Branković who had been driven out of his lands by the Turks. While Murad II was occupied in Asia Minor with war against the emir of Caramania, the crusade set out at the beginning of October 1443[2] from Semendria (Smederevo) across the Danube. It quickly passed through Serbian territory where Hunyadi, who was leading the van, once more won a decisive victory over the forces of the Turkish governor of Rumelia on the heights above Niš. Unopposed, the crusaders entered Bulgaria and took Sofia in order to pass on towards Thrace. Here they met with more effective opposition from the Turks, and the unbearable cold of the winter compelled the Christian army to retreat. During its return journey it attacked the Ottomans in the mountains of Kunovica to the south-east of Niš, and again heavily defeated them at the very beginning of 1444.

It looked as though the tide was turning, and the Ottoman army,

[1] L. Mohler, *Kardinal Bessarion als Theologe, Humanist und Staatsmann*, Paderborn 1923; further bibliography and sources in Beck, *Kirche*, 767 ff.

[2] Cf. B. Krekić, 'Učešće Dubrovnika u rativima protiv Turaka 1443 i 1444 g.' (The participation of Dubrovnik in the war against the Turks in 1443 and 1444), *Zbornik radova Viz. Inst.* 2 (1953), 148 (with English summary).

which until recently had always known success, was forced to take the defensive and on more sides than one. In Albania rebellion had been brewing for some time and now the fight for freedom assumed alarming proportions under the leadership of the valiant Scanderbeg (George Castriota). As 'Captain of Albania' for many years (1443–68) he carried on a heroic war against the Ottoman which Christendom watched in enthusiastic amazement.[1] In southern Greece, the Despot Constantine assumed the offensive. He had exchanged his apanage on the Black Sea for Theodore's territory in the Peloponnese and he ruled from 1443 onwards over the most important part of the Morea, with Mistra as his centre, while Thomas still governed his smaller and less important part. His first task was to rebuild the Hexamilion wall across the Isthmus which the Turks had destroyed in 1423. He then pushed forward into central Greece and occupied Athens and Thebes. The duke Nerio II Acciajuoli, who had been a Turkish vassal, was now forced to acknowledge the suzerainty of the Despot of Mistra and promised to pay him tribute.[2]

It was this changed situation which induced Murad II to try to come to terms with his opponents. In June 1444 he met the ambassadors of king Vladislav, George Branković and Hunyadi in Adrianople, and a ten years' truce was negotiated. The Serbian Despot was to receive his territory back, and the Ottomans were to exercise less control over Wallachia. The Sultan pledged himself to the agreed terms and then withdrew to Asia Minor, while his plenipotentiaries were sent to Hungary to get Vladislav to ratify the agreement. At the end of July 1444 at Szegedin he too signed the treaty. There is no doubt that this arrangement meant a considerable limitation of Turkish power in the Balkans and it promised the Christians a breathing space for ten years. At the same time, disappointment was felt in Christendom, particularly by the Roman Curia, which in view of the recent victories and the naval help promised by Venice had hoped that the Turks would be completely expelled from Europe and the war pressed home to a successful conclusion. Cardinal Julian Cesarini absolved the hesitating young king from the oath which he had just taken, and by September the crusading army was again on the march. But its forces were already greatly diminished and in particular it was without Serbian help, as George Branković

---

[1] Full details of all the original and secondary material on Scanderbeg are given by J. Radonić, *Djuradj Kastriot Skenderbeg i Albanija u XV veku* (George Castriota Scanderbeg and Albania in the fifteenth century), Belgrade 1942.

[2] Cf. Zakythinos, *Despotat* I, 226 ff.

was satisfied with his peace terms and therefore completely withdrew from the undertaking. In the hope that they would receive support from the Venetian fleet, the crusaders set out towards the Black Sea and after a difficult journey through Bulgarian territory they reached the coast. But the Venetian fleet, joined by two galleys from Dubrovnik,[1] was unable to prevent the movement of Turkish troops from Asia Minor. Murad II now hastened to the scene of action, and on 10 November 1444 a fiercely-contested battle was fought at Varna which dashed to the ground all the proud hopes of Christendom. After a bitter struggle the Christian army was wiped out. King Vladislav fell on the field and Cardinal Cesarini, the real instigator of this unfortunate crusade, also lost his life.[2] This defeat of the Christians had even more serious effects than that of Nicopolis; it had shattered the last attempt at concerted Christian action against Turkish aggression. Despair in the Christian camp was deeper than ever before, and the unfortunate Emperor of Constantinople had to welcome the victor with congratulations and gifts.

But Constantine carried on his campaign in Greece even after the disaster of Varna. He again appeared in Boeotia and extended his control over Phocis and up to the Pindus. It looked as though at the last moment a new Greece would arise on the soil of ancient Hellas as the heir of dying Byzantium. It was not long, however, before the Despot felt the avenging hand of the victor of Varna. In 1446 Murad II invaded Greece with a large force and rapidly overran the

---

[1] Cf. Krekić, op. cit. 149 ff.

[2] The letters of the humanist Ciriaco of Ancona throw completely new light on the events of 1444 and particularly on the agreement at Adrianople. These have been made available by F. Pall, 'Ciriaco d'Ancona e la crociata contro i Turchi', *Bull. hist. de l'Acad. Roumaine* 20 (1938), 9–68, and O. Halecki, *The Crusade of Varna. A Discussion of Controversial Problems*, New York 1943, has reprinted them in a new sequence. Both scholars are, however, in complete disagreement in their evaluation of the circumstances which led to the catastrophe of Varna. Supporting a thesis put forward before in Polish historiography, Halecki attempts to show that king Vladislav never signed a peace treaty with the Sultan, so that the treaty of Szegedin is only a legend and the young Jagellon was not guilty of breaking his oath. Halecki, pp. 67 ff., is not, however, successful in his attempts to explain away a number of well-informed and independent sources which are in agreement in offering evidence to the contrary. The very opposite to the account which he would like to maintain is given by a number of contemporaries from different countries and in different positions, as for instance Muhammed II, Aeneas Silvio Piccolomini (afterwards Pope Pius II), the Polish historian Długosz and the scholar Gałka, the Burgundian Walerand of Wawrin, the Byzantines Ducas and Chalcocondyles. Pall is therefore justified in rejecting any doubts about the historicity of the treaty of Szegedin and the fact of the breach; cf. F. Pall, 'Autour de la croisade de Varna: la question de la paix de Sceged et de sa rupture', *Bull. hist. de l'Acad. Roumaine* 22 (1941), 144 ff., and 'Un moment décisif de l'histoire du Sud-Est européen: la croisade de Varna', *Balcania* 7 (1944), 102 ff. A full account of the dispute is given by F. Babinger, 'Von Amurath zu Amurath. Vor- und Nachspiel der Schlacht bei Varna', *Oriens* 3 (1950), 229 ff. Cf. also idem, *Mehmed der Eroberer und seine Zeit*, Munich 1953, 28 ff.

lands of central Greece. The Byzantine Despot made his first serious stand at the Hexamilion wall, but this barrier was destroyed by the Turkish cannon and on 10 December 1446 the wall was stormed and the issue decided. The Turks poured into the Morea, ravaged Byzantine towns and villages and carried off more than 60,000 prisoners.[1] The Despot was, however, granted peace terms in return for a promise to pay tribute, for the Sultan still had Scanderbeg and Hunyadi to deal with. Like an echo of the battle of Varna, Murad II and Hunyadi met in October 1448 on the field of Kosovo. Here, where once the fate of Serbia had been decided, Hunyadi was forced to yield to the superior strength of the Turks after a long and fierce battle. Scanderbeg held out in the Albanian mountains where he remained invincible for many years.

Meanwhile, soon after the failure of his plans for a united Greece the Despot Constantine was called to the throne of Constantinople. On 31 October 1448 the Emperor John VIII died childless and, as Theodore had died shortly before, he was succeeded by the valiant Despot Constantine Dragases—so called after his mother Helen who belonged to the Serbian dynasty of Dragaš in east Macedonia.[2] On 6 January 1449 Constantine was crowned Emperor in the Morea and two months later he entered the capital. The sovereignty of the Morea was divided between Thomas and Demetrius. The latter had repeatedly tried to gain the imperial throne with the help of the Turks, and now, once again relying on Turkish aid, he soon came into fierce conflict with his brother Thomas in the Morea.

Neither the courage nor the statesmanlike energy of the last Emperor of Byzantium could save the Empire from certain destruction. After the death of Murad II in February 1451, his son Muhammed II ascended the throne and Constantinople's last hour had come. Byzantine Constantinople lay in the heart of Ottoman territory, separating the European and Asiatic possessions of the Turks. The first aim of the new Sultan was to eliminate this foreign body and to give the growing Ottoman Empire a strong centre in Constantinople. With considerable energy and circumspection he prepared

---

[1] Cf. Zakythinos, *Despotat* I, 235, with references to the sources.

[2] A detailed account of the life of this Empress is given by D. Anastasijević 'Jedina vizantijska carica Srpkinja' (The only Byzantine Empress of Serbian origin), *Brastvo* 30 (1939), 26 ff. Cf. also ibid. 31 (1950), 78 ff., and 32 (1941), 50 ff. She was the daughter of the 'lord' Constantine Dragaš, who in the last decades of the fourteenth century ruled in eastern Macedonia, first with his brother, the Despot John Dragaš, and then as sole ruler, and who fell in 1395 at the battle of Rovine (cf. p. 551 above, with n. 2). That only Constantine XI and not his brother bore the name Dragaš is probably explained by the fact that he bore his grandfather's Christian name.

to capture the imperial city and thus carry the work of his predecessors to its logical conclusion. The Byzantine court could have no illusions as to Muslim intentions, especially as the Sultan had had a strong outer fortification (Rumili Hissar) constructed in the immediate vicinity of the capital.

Like his brother, Constantine XI placed all his hopes on help from the West, even though there was little likelihood of this, for there was indeed nothing else left to hope for. At the last moment he tried to revive the wrecked plans for the union of the two Churches. Cardinal Isidore, who had once been Metropolitan of Russia, came to Constantinople as papal legate, and on 12 December 1452, five months before the city fell, he proclaimed the union in Hagia Sophia and celebrated Roman mass. The Byzantine populace was furiously indignant, for the more desperate their need the more tenaciously they clung to their faith and resented more passionately than ever this violation of their religious feelings. Their mood of despair and their irreconcilable hatred of the Latins was expressed at the time in the trenchant words of one of the Emperor's highest officials—'I would rather see the Muslim turban in the midst of the city than the Latin mitre'.[1] The closer the moment of the downfall of Byzantium, the stronger the movement which favoured reconciliation with the Turks and regarded the rule of the Ottomans as a lesser evil than subjection to Rome.

It was not, however, the hostility of the Byzantine populace to the union which ruled out the possibility of Western help for Constantinople. Any effective co-operation in aid of Byzantium was doomed at the outset by reason of the conflicting interests and ambitions of the Western rulers. Alphonso V of Aragon and Naples, who was then the most powerful prince in the Mediterranean, pursued the same policy towards the Byzantine Empire in the last years of its existence as his Norman, German and French predecessors in South Italy had done earlier on. He attempted to found a new Latin empire in Constantinople with himself as emperor. The very modest resources which Pope Nicholas V (1447–55) had meant to use for the defence of Constantinople against the Turks were swallowed up by the aggressive policy of the king of Naples, whose continual demands for money from Rome were met without a protest.[2] Even if the

---

[1] Ducas 329, 11, ed. Grecu (CB, 264).

[2] Cf. Norden, *Papsttum und Byzanz* 731 ff.; Fr. Cerone, 'La politica orientale di Alfonso di Aragona', *Archivio Storico per le provincie Napoletane* 27 (1902), 3 ff., 380 ff., 555 ff., 774 ff., and 28 (1903), 153 ff.; C. Marinescu, 'Le pape Nicolas V et son attitude envers l'Empire byzantin', *Bull. de l'Inst. Archéol. Bulgare* 9 (1935), 331 ff.; idem, 'Contribution

West had actively intervened in Constantinople, its aim would not in any case have been to rescue the Byzantine Empire. But neither was there any possibility of founding a new Latin Empire in the East. It is true that there was once a time when it was a question as to whether Byzantium would fall into Turkish or Latin hands. This had been decided by the developments of the last century, though Byzantium itself had taken little share in the determination of events. Its fate had been settled by decisive events which were outside its control and without its co-operation, for it had long been merely a pawn in the political moves of other powers. Internally exhausted and crippled, it was now only a city state and fell an easy prey to the Turks.

In the early days of April 1453 Muhammed II assembled a powerful army beneath the walls of the city.[1] It was faced on the Byzantine side by only 500 Greeks and about 2000 foreign troops. The main contingent of the Westerners consisted of 700 Genoese, who just before the siege began had reached Constantinople in two galleys under the command of Giustiniani, to the great joy of the Byzantines. It would be safe to assume that the superiority in numbers of the attacking force over the defence was more than ten to one. The strength of Constantinople did not lie in her brave but totally inadequate defending force, but in the unique position of the city and in the stout walls which John VIII and Constantine XI had both done their best to keep in good repair.

In the past Byzantium had often been saved by her advantageous strategical position and by the strong fortifications, but at the same time also by her superiority over other countries in military technique. Now this technical superiority was on the side of the Turks. Muhammed II had got together vast equipment and, with the help of Western engineers, was particularly well supported by artillery. In storming Constantinople the Turks used this new weapon to an extent undreamt of before and in the words of a Greek contemporary

à l'histoire des relations économiques entre l'Empire byzantin, la Sicile et le royaume de Naples de 1419 à 1453', *Studi biz. e neoell.* 5 (1939), 209 ff. Cf. also R. Guilland, Aἱ πρὸς τὴν Δύσιν ἐκκλήσεις Κωνσταντίνου ΙΑ' τοῦ Δράγασση πρὸς σωτηρίαν τῆς Κωνσταντινουπόλεως, *EEBS* 22 (1952), 60 ff.

[1] On the fight for Constantinople cf. E. Pears, *The Destruction of the Greek Empire and the Story of the Capture of Constantinople by the Turks*, 1903 (G. Schlumberger, *Le siège, la prise et le sac de Constantinople par les Turcs en 1453* (1915) has no independent value). Cf. also E. Pears, CMH IV (1923), 693 ff., and the excellent bibliography, idem 883 ff.; cf. now C. Amantos, 'La prise de Constantinople' in *Le Cinq-centième anniversaire de la prise de Constantinople*, Athens 1953, 9 ff.; F. Babinger, *Mehmed der Eroberer und seine Zeit*, Munich 1953, 88 ff.

'the cannons decided the whole issue'.[1] The small cannons which the defenders were using could not compete with the great Turkish ordnance.

The actual siege began on 7 April. The main attack was launched against the city walls from the land side and particularly against the Pempton Gate which the Turks had rightly judged to be the weakest point in the Byzantine defences. The Golden Horn was barred by a heavy chain which all Turkish efforts had failed to break, and it was as a result of such an attempt that a naval battle broke out on 20 April in which the imperial fleet won the day. This victory roused great enthusiasm in Constantinople and gave fresh courage to the defenders, even though it brought no relief to the invested city. On the other hand, on 22 April Muhammed II managed to drag a considerable number of ships over land to the Golden Horn and the city was now bombarded by sea as well as by land. The handful of defenders held out with desperate courage to stave off the inevitable end. The Emperor's unquenchable resolution in battle set a magnificent example to his subjects. He remained at his post to the last as if determined not to survive defeat.[2] Many severe attacks were beaten back and the confidence of the besiegers began to be undermined, but after seven weeks of onslaught the walls of the beleaguered city showed serious breaches. The final issue could not be long delayed.

Muhammed II decided to make the general attack on 29 May. While the Sultan was marshalling his troops for the fight on the evening before, the Christians, Greeks and Latins together, joined in their last service in Hagia Sophia. When they had finished their devotions, the defenders returned to their posts and the Emperor went round inspecting the fortifications until late into the night. The assault began in the early hours of dawn and the city was attacked simultaneously from three sides. For a long time the courageous defenders resisted every onslaught and beat back their opponents. The Sultan then threw in his main reserve, the janissaries who were the picked troops of the Ottoman army, and after a bitter struggle they succeeded in scaling the walls. At the decisive moment Giustiniani, who was fighting side by side with the Emperor, was fatally wounded and had to be carried away. This loss spread confusion in the ranks of the defenders and hastened the Turkish break-through.

[1] Critobulus, ed. Müller, F.H.G. V, 80.
[2] Cf. G. Kolias, 'Constantin Paléologue, le dernier défenseur de Constantinople', in *Le Cinq-centième anniversaire de la prise de Constantinople*, Athens 1953, 41 ff.

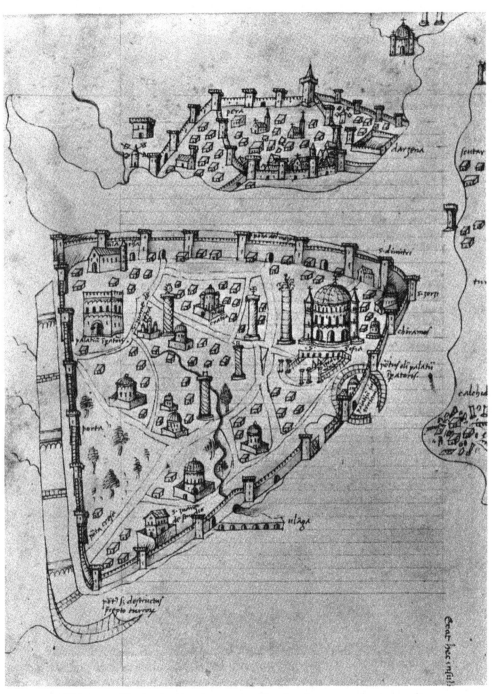

Figure 75: *Constantinople, circa 1420.* Pen drawing on parchment, 15th century. This stylized bird's-eye view is one of many drawn to illustrate the treatise *Liber insularum*, by the 15th-century traveler, Cristoforo Buondelmonti. Biblioteca Apostolica Vaticana, Rome, *Cod. Rossianus 702*, f. 32ᵛ. Photo: Biblioteca Apostolica Vaticana.

Figure 76: (ABOVE) *The Land Walls of Constantinople.* The area between the Gate of St. Romanus and the Gate of Adrianople, where the Turkish armies penetrated the city on May 29, 1453. From a 19th-century engraving in Thomas Allon and Robert Walsh, *Constantinople and . . . the Seven Churches of Asia Minor,* London, n.d. (BELOW) *Constantinople in the 17th Century.* A bird's-eye view of the city as the capital of the Turkish Empire. Engraving from Guillaume Joseph Grelot, *Relation nouvelle d'un voyage de Constantinople,* Paris, 1680.

The city was soon in their hands. Constantine XI fought on to the end and was killed fighting, as he had desired. For three days and three nights the Sultan's troops were allowed to plunder the city as they had been promised just before the final assault to raise their flagging morale. Property of priceless value, works of art, precious manuscripts, holy icons and ecclesiastical treasure were all destroyed. Muhammed II made his solemn entry into the conquered city and Constantinople became the capital of the Ottoman Empire. The Byzantine Empire had ceased to exist.

It was with Constantine the Great's foundation of the imperial city on the Bosphorus that the Byzantine Empire had come into being, and it had perished with the fall of this city under the last Constantine. It is true that the Morea in southern Greece and the Empire of Trebizond survived the fall of Constantinople for a few years. But their subjugation presented no problem to the Turks. The conquest of Constantinople provided the Ottomans with a bridge between their European and Asiatic possessions; it gave unity to the Ottoman Empire and provided a fresh impetus to its policy of expansion. The mighty Muslim Empire rapidly absorbed what remained of Greek as well as Latin and Slav possessions in the Balkans. In 1456 Athens was captured by the Turks and the Parthenon, for a thousand years a church dedicated to the Mother of God, became a Turkish mosque. In 1460 Byzantine rule in the Morea came to an end; Thomas fled to Italy, while Demetrius, who was hostile to the Latins, found his way to the Sultan's court. In September 1461 the Empire of Trebizond also fell,[1] and thus the last remaining Greek territory came under Turkish rule. The Serbian despotate had succumbed in 1459, to be followed in 1463 by the kingdom of Bosnia, and before the end of the century the remaining Slav and Albanian districts up to the Adriatic were in the hands of the Muslim. Once more there had come into being an Empire extending from Mesopotamia to the Adriatic with its centre in Constantinople—this was the Turkish Empire, risen from the ruins of the Byzantine Empire and for several centuries destined to reunite the old Byzantine territories into a single polity.

Byzantium fell in 1453, but her spiritual and political traditions lived on and their influence was felt, not only in those lands which had once been Byzantine, but beyond the old frontiers of the Empire, acting as a stimulus to the civilization and political development of

[1] Cf. F. Babinger, 'La date de la prise de Trébizonde par les Turcs', REB 7 (1949), 205 ff.

European nations. The Christian religion in its specifically Greek form as the personification of Byzantine spirituality and the antithesis of Roman Catholicism was regarded as a holy of holies both by the Greeks and by the southern and eastern Slavs. During the centuries of Turkish rule the Greeks, Bulgarians and Serbians regarded the Orthodox faith as the expression of their spiritual and national individuality, and it was indeed the Orthodox Church which preserved the people of the Balkans from being engulfed in the Turkish deluge and so made possible their national revival in the nineteenth century. Orthodoxy was also the spiritual standard beneath which the Russian countries found their unity and the realm of Moscow became a great power. Soon after the fall of Byzantium and the southern Slav kingdoms, Moscow shook off the Tartar yoke once and for all, and as the only independent Orthodox principality it naturally became the centre of the Orthodox world. Ivan III, the great liberator and consolidator of the Russian lands, married the daughter of the Despot Thomas Palaeologus, the niece of the last Emperor of Byzantium. He assumed the imperial Byzantine two-headed eagle in his arms, introduced Byzantine ceremonial into Moscow and soon made Russia the leader of the Christian East as Byzantium had once been. If Constantinople was the New Rome, Moscow was to become the 'Third Rome'. The great traditions of Byzantium, its faith, its political ideas, its spirituality, lived on through the centuries in the Russian Empire.

The influence of Byzantine culture was even more penetrating and affected both East and West. It was not so marked in Roman and Germanic countries as in Slav lands, but all the same, the cultural contribution of Byzantium to the West is by no means negligible. The Byzantine state was the instrument by means of which Graeco-Roman antiquity survived through the ages, and for this reason Byzantium was the donor, the West the recipient. This was particularly true at the time of the renaissance, when there was such passionate interest in classical civilization and the West found that it could satisfy its longing to explore the treasures of antiquity from Byzantine sources. Byzantium had preserved the heritage of the ancient world and in so doing had fulfilled its mission in world history. It had saved from destruction Roman law, Greek literature, philosophy and learning, so that this priceless heritage could be passed on to the peoples of western Europe who were now ready to receive it.

GENEALOGICAL TABLES
LISTS OF RULERS AND DESPOTS
LISTS OF PATRIARCHS AND POPES
INDEX

GENEALOGICAL TABLES OF THE BYZANTINE DYNASTIES

The following tables are intended to help the general reader. They do not claim to be complete but confine themselves to the more important names mentioned in this book. The names of Emperors are given in heavy type. Fuller genealogical tables can be found in Grumel, *Chronologie*, p. 360 ff.

1. Dynasty of Heraclius 610-711

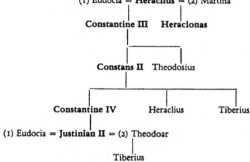

2. Syrian Dynasty 717-802

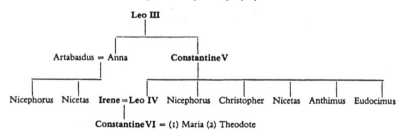

3. Amorian Dynasty 820-867

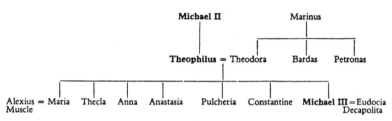

4. Macedonian Dynasty 867-1056

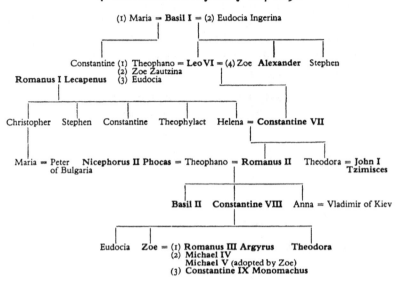

```
                        (1) Maria = Basil I = (2) Eudocia Ingerina
                                      |                |
            ┌─────────────────────────┘    ┌───────────┼──────────────┐
            |                               |           |              |
       Constantine (1) Theophano = Leo VI = (4) Zoe  Alexander     Stephen
                    (2) Zoe Zautzina           |
Romanus I Lecapenus (3) Eudocia               |
            |                                  |
 ┌──────────┼──────────┬────────────┬─────────┴──────┐
 |          |          |            |                |
Christopher Stephen Constantine Theophylact  Helena = Constantine VII
 |                                                       |
 |                                          ┌────────────┴──────────┐
Maria = Peter  Nicephorus II Phocas = Theophano = Romanus II   Theodora = John I
        of Bulgaria                                    |                  Tzimisces
                                       ┌───────────────┼────────────┐
                                       |               |            |
                                    Basil II    Constantine VIII  Anna = Vladimir of Kiev
                       ┌───────────────┼────────────────────────┐
                       |               |                        |
                    Eudocia         Zoe = (1) Romanus III Argyrus    Theodora
                                          (2) Michael IV
                                          Michael V (adopted by Zoe)
                                          (3) Constantine IX Monomachus
```

5. Dynasty of the Ducas 1059-1078

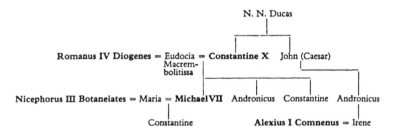

```
                                    N. N. Ducas
                                        |
                            ┌───────────┴──────────┐
                            |                      |
Romanus IV Diogenes = Eudocia = Constantine X   John (Caesar)
                      Macrem-  |                      |
                      bolitissa|                      |
                          ┌────┴────┬──────────┬──────┴──────┐
                          |         |          |             |
Nicephorus III Botaneiates = Maria = Michael VII  Andronicus Constantine Andronicus
                          |                              |
                     Constantine              Alexius I Comnenus = Irene
```

6. Dynasty of the Comneni 1081-1185

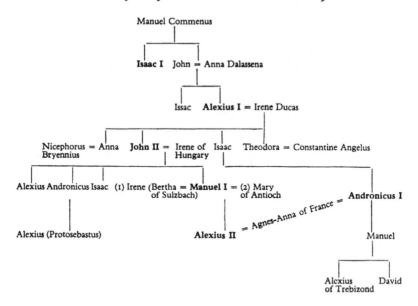

7. Dynasty of the Angeli 1185-1204

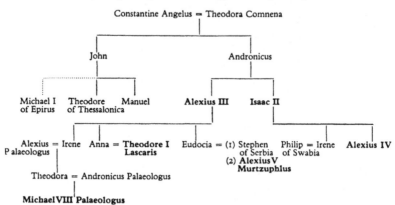

8. Dynasty of the Lascarids 1204-1261

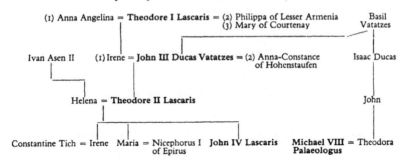

(1) Anna Angelina = **Theodore I Lascaris** = (2) Philippa of Lesser Armenia
(3) Mary of Courtenay

Basil Vatatzes

Ivan Asen II   (1) Irene = **John III Ducas Vatatzes** = (2) Anna-Constance of Hohenstaufen   Isaac Ducas

Helena = **Theodore II Lascaris**   John

Constantine Tich = Irene   Maria = Nicephorus I of Epirus   **John IV Lascaris**   **Michael VIII Palaeologus** = Theodora

9. Dynasty of the Palaeologi 1261-1453

Andronicus Palaeologus = Theodora Palaeologina

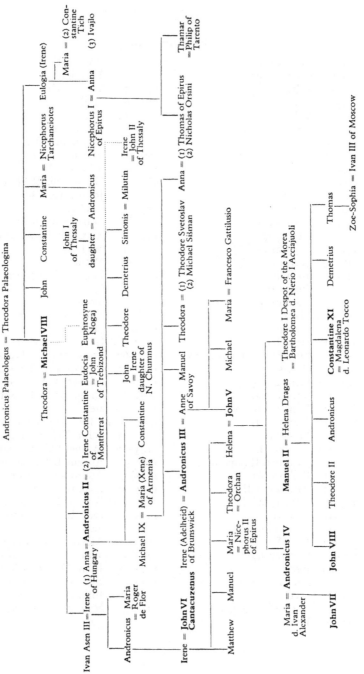

1. Byzantine Empire

324–37	Constantine I	820–9	Michael II
337–61	Constantius	829–42	Theophilus
361–3	Julian	842–67	Michael III
363–4	Jovian	867–86	Basil I
364–78	Valens	886–912	Leo VI
379–95	Theodosius I	912–13	Alexander
395–408	Arcadius	913–59	Constantine VII
408–450	Theodosius II	920–44	Romanus I Lecapenus
450–7	Marcian	959–63	Romanus II
457–74	Leo I	963–9	Nicephorus II Phocas
474	Leo II	969–76	John I Tzimisces
474–5	Zeno	976–1025	Basil II
475–6	Basiliscus	1025–28	Constantine VIII
476–91	Zeno (again)	1028–34	Romanus III Argyrus
491–518	Anastasius I	1034–41	Michael IV
518–27	Justin I	1041–2	Michael V
527–65	Justinian I	1042	Zoe and Theodora
565–78	Justin II	1042–55	Constantine IX Monomachus
578–82	Tiberius I Constantine		
582–602	Maurice	1055–6	Theodora (again)
602–10	Phocas	1056–7	Michael VI
610–41	Heraclius	1057–9	Isaac I Comnenus
641	Constantine III and Heraclonas	1059–67	Constantine X Ducas
		1068–71	Romanus IV Diogenes
641	Heraclonas	1071–8	Michael VII Ducas
641–68	Constans II	1078–81	Nicephorus III Botaneiates
668–85	Constantine IV		
685–95	Justinian II	1081–1118	Alexius I Comnenus
695–8	Leontius	1118–43	John II Comnenus
698–705	Tiberius II	1143–80	Manuel I Comnenus
705–11	Justinian II (again)	1180–3	Alexius II Comnenus
711–13	Philippicus	1183–5	Andronicus I Comnenus
713–15	Anastasius II	1185–95	Isaac II Angelus
715–17	Theodosius III	1195–1203	Alexius III Angelus
717–41	Leo III	1203–4	Isaac II (again) and Alexius IV Angeli
741–75	Constantine V		
775–80	Leo IV	1204	Alexius V Murtzuphlus
780–97	Constantine VI	1204–22	Theodore I Lascaris
797–802	Irene	1222–54	John III Ducas Vatatzes
802–11	Nicephorus I	1254–8	Theodore II Lascaris
811	Stauracius	1258–61	John IV Lascaris
811–13	Michael I Rangabe	1259–82	Michael VIII Palaeologus
813–20	Leo V		

1282–1328	Andronicus II Palaeologus	1376–9	Andronicus IV Palaeologus
1328–41	Andronicus III Palaeologus	1390	John VII Palaeologus
		1391–1425	Manuel II Palaeologus
1341–91	John V Palaeologus	1425–48	John VIII Palaeologus
1347–54	John VI Cantacuzenus	1449–53	Constantine XI Palaeologus

2. Latin Empire of Constantinople

1204–5	Baldwin I of Flanders	1217–19	Yolande
1206–16	Henry of Flanders	1221–8	Robert of Courtenay
1217	Peter of Courtenay	1228–61	Baldwin II
		(1231–37	John de Brienne)

3. Epirote Principality

1204–15 Michael I
1215–24 Theodore
(end of 1224 entered Thessalonica
and crowned Emperor)

Thessalonica	*Epirus*	*Thessaly*
1224–30 Theodore, Emperor	c. 1231–71 Michael II	1271–96 John I
1230–c. 1237 Manuel	1271–96 Nicephorus I	1296–1303 Constantine
c. 1237–44 John	1296–1318 Thomas	1303–18 John II
1244–6 Demetrius	(Anna Palaeologina-Cantacuzena was regent to c. 1313)	1318 dissolved
1246 conquered by John Vatatzes of Nicaea	1318–23 Nicholas Orsini	1348 conquered by Stephen Dušan
	1323–35 John Orsini	
	1335–40 Nicephorus II (regent Anna Palaeologina)	

(1340 conquered by Byzantium, 1348 by Stephen Dušan)

4. Bulgaria

First Bulgarian Empire			
681–702	Asparuch	767–72	Toktu
702–18	Tervel	772	Pagan
718–25	unknown	c. 772–77	Telerig
725–39	Sevar	777–c. 803	Kardam
739–56	Kormisoš	c. 803–14	Krum
756–62	Vinech	814	Dukum, Dicevg
762–5	Teletz	814–31	Omurtag
765–7	Sabin	831–6	Malomir
767	Umar	836–52	Presiam (perhaps identical with the preceding)

852–89 Boris I Michael
889–93 Vladimir
893–27 Symeon
927–69 Peter
969–71 Boris II

Macedonian Empire

976–1014 Samuel
1014–15 Gabriel Radomir
1015–18 John Vladislav

Second Bulgarian Empire

1186–96 Asen I
1196–7 Peter
1197–1207 Kalojan

1207–18 Boril
1218–41 Ivan Asen II
1241–6 Koloman Asen
1246–56 Michael Asen
1257–77 Constantine Tich
1278–9 Ivajlo
1279–80 Ivan Asen III
1280–92 George I Terter
1292–8 Smiletz
1299 Čaka
1300–22 Theodore Svetoslav
1322–3 George II Terter
1323–30 Michael Šišman
1330–1 Ivan Stephen
1331–71 Ivan Alexander
1371–93 Ivan Šišman
c. 1360–96 in Vidin: Ivan Stracimir

5. Serbia

mid-9th century John Vlastimir
to 891 Mutimir
891–2 Prvoslav
892–917 Peter Gojniković
917–20 Paul Branović
920–*c.* 924 Zacharias Prvoslavljević
927–after 950 Časlav Klonimirović

Zeta

end of the 10th century to 1016
John Vladimir
c. 1040–*c.* 1052 Stephen Voislav
c. 1052–1081 Michael, from 1077
king
1081–*c.* 1101 Constantine Bodin
....

Rascia

c. 1083–*c.* 1114 Vukan
The chronology of the following Grand
Župans is not known with certainty.
The most important are:

Uroš I, Uroš II, Desa, Tichomir
(brother of Nemanja)
c. 1166–96 Stephen Nemanja
1196–*c.* 1228 Stephen the First-
Crowned, king from 1217
c. 1228–*c.* 1234 Stephen Radoslav
c. 1234–1243 Stephen Vladislav
1243–76 Stephen Uroš I
1276–82 Stephen Dragutin
1282–1321 Stephen Uroš II Milutin
1321–31 Stephen Uroš III Dečanski
1331–55 Stephen Dušan, tzar from
1345
1355–71 Tzar Stephen Uroš
(1365–71 King Vukašin)
1371–89 Prince Lazar
1389–1427 Stephen Lazarević, Despot from 1402
1427–56 George Branković, Despot from 1429
1456–8 Lazar Branković, Despot

6. Muslim Rulers

(I am indebted for this list to Dr. Hans Georg Beck, Munich)

(a) *the direct descendants of the Prophet*

632-4 Abu Bekr
634-44 Omar I
644-56 Othman
656-61 Ali

(b) *the Umayyads*

661-80 Muawija I
680-3 Jezid I
683-4 (?) Muawija II
684-5 Merwan I
685-705 Abdalmalik
705-15 Walid I
715-17 Suleiman
715-20 Omar II
720-4 Jezid II
724-43 Hischam
743-4 Walid II
744 Jezid III
744-50 Merwan II
744 Ibrahim

(c) *the Abbasids*

750-4 as-Saffach
754-75 al-Mansur
775-85 al-Machdi
785-6 al-Hadi
786-809 Harun al-Raschid
809-13 al-Amin
813-33 al-Mamun
833-42 al-Mutasim
842-7 al-Wathik
847-61 al-Mutawakkil
861-2 al-Muntasir
862-6 al-Mutazz
866-9 al-Muchtadi
869-92 al-Mutamid
892-902 al-Mutadid
902-8 al-Muktafi
912-32 al-Muktadir
932-4 al-Kahir
934-40 al-Radi

940-3 al-Muttaki
943-6 al-Mustakfi
946-74 al-Muti
974-91 at-Tai
991-1031 al-Kadir
1031-75 al-Kaim

The remaining Abbasid Caliphs are not of importance for Byzantine history. The last Abbasid died in 1258.

(d) *the Seljuk Sultans of Rum (Iconium)*

1077/8-86 Suleiman I
1092-1107 Kilij Arslan I
1107-16 Malik-Shah
1116-56 Masud I
1156-92 Kilij Arslan II
1192-96 Kaikosru I
1196-1204 Suleiman II
1204 Kilij Arslan III
1204-10 Kaikosru I (again)
1210-20 Kaikaus I
1220-37 Kaikubad I
1237-45 Kaikosru II
1246-57 Kaikaus II
1248-65 Kilij Arslan IV
1249-57 Kaikubad II
1265-82 Kaikosru III
1282-1304 Masud II
1284-1307 Kaikubad III
1307-8 Masud III

(e) *the Ottoman Sultans to the fall of Constantinople*

1288-1326 Osman
1326-62 Orchan
1362-89 Murad I
1389-1402 Bajezid I
1402-21 Muhammed (Mehmed) I (from 1413 sole ruler)
1402-10 Suleiman
1411-13 Musa
1421-51 Murad II
1451-81 Muhammed II (Mehmed) the Conqueror

GREEK DESPOTS OF THE MOREA (MISTRA)

I. Under the Cantacuzeni

Manuel Cantacuzenus, son of John VI Cantacuzenus	1348–1380
Matthew Cantacuzenus, brother of Manuel	1380–1383
Demetrius Cantacuzenus, son of Matthew	1383

II. Under the Palaeologi

Theodore I, youngest son of John V Palaeologus	1383–1407
Theodore II, son of Manuel II Palaeologus	1407–1443
Sole reign	1407–1428
With his brothers Constantine and Thomas	1428–1443
Constantine and Thomas	1443–1449
Constantine becomes Emperor in 1449	
Thomas and his son Demetrius	1449–1460
Mistra falls to the Turks in 1460	

315–327?	Metrophanes	675–677	Constantine I
327?–340	Alexandros	677–679	Theodoros I
340–341	Paul I	679–686	Georgios I
341–342	Eusebios	686–687	Theodoros I
342–344	Paul I (again)		(again)
342–348	Makedonios I	688–694	Paul III
348–350	Paul I (again)	694–705	Kallinikos I
350–360	Makedonios I (again)	705–712(?)	Kyros
360–369	Eudoxios	712(?)–715	John VI
369–379	Demophilos	715–730	Germanos I
369–370	Euagrios	730–754	Anastasios
379–381	Gregorios I	754–766	Constantine II
381	Maximos	766–780	Niketas I
381–397	Nektarios	780–784	Paul IV
398–404	John I Chrysostom	784–806	Tarasios
404–405	Arsakios	806–815	Nikephoros
405(406?)–425	Attikos	815–821	Theodotos (Melis-
426–427	Sisinnios I		senos Kassiteras)
428–431	Nestorios	821–834	Antonios I (Kas-
431–434	Maximianos		simatas)
434–447	Proklos	834–843	John VII Moroch-
447–449	Phlabianos		arzanios (Gram-
449–458	Anatolios		matikos)
458–471	Gennadios I	843–847	Methodios I
471–489	Akakios	847–858	Ignatios (Niketas)
489–490	Phrabitas	858–867	Photios
490–496	Euphemios	867–878	Ignatios (again)
496–511	Makedonios II	878–886	Photios (again)
511–518	Timotheos I	886–893	Stephanos I
518–520	John II Kappadokes	893–901	Antonios II
520–536	Epiphanios		Ka(u)leas
536	Anthimos I	901–907	Nikolaos I
536–552	Menas		Mystikos
552–565	Eutychios	907–912	Euthymios
565–577	John III Antiocheus	911–925	Nikolaos I
577–582	Eutychios (again)	925–928	Stephanos II
582–595	John IV Nesteutes	928–931	Tryphon
595–606	Kyriakos	933–956	Theophylaktos
607–610	Thomas I	956–970	Polyeuktos
610–638	Sergios	970–974	Basileios I Skam-
638–641	Pyrrhos I		andrenos
641–654	Paul II	974–980	Antonios III
655	Pyrrhos I (again)		Studites
655–666	Peter	984–995	Nikolaos II Chrys-
667–669	Thomas II		oberges
669–675	John V	995–998(?)	Sisinnios II

999–1019	Sergios II Manuelites	1215–1222	Manuel I Sarantenos
1019–1025	Eustathios		(Charitopulos)
1025–1043	Alexios Studites	1222(?)–1240	Germanos II
1043–1058	Michael I Kerullarios	1240	Methodios
		1244–1255	Manuel II
1059–1063	Constantine III Leichudes	1255–1260	Arsenios (Autoreianos)
1064–1075	John VIII Xiphilinos	1260–1261	Nikephoros II
		1261–1267	Arsenios
1075–1081	Cosmas I Hierosolymites	1267	Germanos III (Lazos Markutzas)
1081–1084	Eustratios Garidas	1268–1275	Joseph I
1084–1111	Nikolaos III Kyrdiniates Grammatikos	1275–1282	John XI Bekkos
		1282–1283	Joseph I (again)
1111–1134	John IX Agapetos	1283–1289	Gregorios II
1134–1143	Leon Styppes		(Georgios) Kyprios
1143–1146	Michael II Kurkuas (Oxeites)	1289–1293	Athanasios I
		1294–1303	John XII
1146–1147	Cosmas II Attikos		(Cosmas)
1147–1151	Nikolaos IV Muzalon	1303–1311	Athanasios I (again)
1151–1153	Theodotos (Theodosios?)	1311–1315	Nephon I
		1316–1320	John XIII Glykys
1153	Neophytos I	1320–1321	Gerasimos I
1154–1156	Constantine IV Chliarenos	1323–1334	Jesaias
		1334–1347	John XIV Aprenos
1156–1169	Lukas Chrysoberges	1347–1349	Isidoros I
1169–1177	Michael III	1350–1354	Callistos I
1177–1178	Chariton Eugeneiotes	1354–1355	Philotheos
		1355–1363	Callistos I (again)
1178–1183	Theodosios Boradiotes	1364–1376	Philotheos (again)
		1376–1379	Makarios
1183–1187	Basileios II Kamateros (Phylakopulos)	1380–1388	Neilos
		1389–1390	Antonios IV
		1390–1391	Makarios (again)
1187–1190	Niketas II Muntanes	1391–1397	Antonios IV (again)
1190–1191	Leontios Theotokites	1397	Callistos II
		1397–1410	Matthaios I
1191–1192	Dositheos (Theodosios?)	1410–1416	Euthymios II
		1416–1439	Joseph II
1192–1199	Georgios II Xiphilinos	1440–1443	Metrophanes II
		1443–1450	Gregorios III
1199–1206	John X Kamateros		(Mammas) Melissenos Strategopulos
1206–1212	Michael IV Autoreianos	1450	Athanasios
1212–1215	Theodoros II Eirenikos (Kopas)	1453–1459	Gennadios II (Georgios Kurtesios) Scholarios
1215–?	Maximos II		

POPES OF ROME, 314-1455

314–335	Sylvester	657–672	Vitalian
336	Mark	672–676	Deodatus II
337–352	Julius I	676–678	Domnus I
352–366	Liberius	678–681	Agatho
366–384	Damasus I	682–683	Leo II
384–399	Siricius	684–685	Benedict II
399–401	Anastasius I	685–686	John V
401–417	Innocent I	686–687	Conon
417–418	Zosimus	687–701	Sergius I
418–422	Boniface I	701–705	John VI
422–432	Celestine I	705–707	John VII
432–440	Sixtus III	708	Sisinnius
440–461	Leo I, "The Great"	708–715	Constantine
461–468	Hilarius	715–731	Gregory II
468–483	Simplicius	731–741	Gregory III
483–492	Felix III (II)	741–752	Zacharias
492–496	Gelasius I	752	Stephen II
496–498	Anastasius II	752–757	Stephen III (II)
498–514	Symmachus	757–767	Paul I
514–523	Hormisdas	768–772	Stephen IV (III)
523–526	John I	772–795	Hadrian I
526–530	Felix IV (III)	795–816	Leo III
530–532	Boniface II	816–817	Stephen V (IV)
533–535	John II	817–824	Paschal I
535–536	Agapetus I	824–827	Eugenius II
536–537	Silverius	827	Valentine
537–555	Vigilius	827–844	Gregory IV
556–561	Pelagius I	844–847	Sergius II
561–574	John III	847–855	Leo IV
575–579	Benedict I	855–858	Benedict III
579–590	Pelagius II	858–867	Nicholas I
590–604	Gregory I, "The Great"	867–872	Hadrian II
604–606	Sabinianus	872–882	John VIII
607	Boniface III	882–884	Marinus I
608–615	Boniface IV	884–885	Hadrian III
615–618	Deodatus I	885–891	Stephen VI (V)
619–625	Boniface V	891–896	Formosus
625–638	Honorius I	896	Boniface VI
640	Severinus	896–897	Stephen VII (VI)
640–642	John IV	897	Romanus
642–649	Theodore I	897	Theodore II
649–655	Martin I	898–900	John IX
654–657	Eugenius I	900–903	Benedict IV

903	Leo V	1130–1143	Innocent II
904–911	Sergius III	1143–1144	Celestine II
911–913	Anastasius III	1144–1145	Lucius II
913–914	Lando	1145–1153	Eugenius III
914–928	John X	1153–1154	Anastasius IV
928	Leo VI	1154–1159	Hadrian IV
928–931	Stephen VIII (VII)	1159–1181	Alexander III
931–935	John XI	1181–1185	Lucius III
936–939	Leo VII	1185–1187	Urban III
939–942	Stephen IX (VIII)	1187	Gregory VIII
942–946	Marinus II	1187–1191	Clement III
946–955	Agapetus II	1191–1198	Celestine III
955–964	John XII	1198–1216	Innocent III
963–965	Leo VIII	1216–1227	Honorius III
964–966	Benedict V	1227–1241	Gregory IX
965–972	John XIII	1241	Celestine IV
973–974	Benedict VI	1243–1254	Innocent IV
974–983	Benedict VII	1254–1261	Alexander IV
983–984	John XIV	1261–1264	Urban IV
985–996	John XV	1265–1268	Clement IV
996–999	Gregory V	1271–1276	Gregory X
999–1003	Sylvester II	1276	Innocent V
1003	John XVII	1276	Hadrian V
1004–1009	John XVIII	1276–1277	John XXI
1009–1012	Sergius IV	1277–1280	Nicholas III
1012–1024	Benedict VIII	1281–1285	Martin IV
1024–1032	John XIX	1285–1287	Honorius IV
1032–1044	Benedict IX	1288–1292	Nicholas IV
1045	Sylvester III	1294	Celestine V
1045	Benedict IX (again)	1294–1303	Boniface VIII
1045–1046	Gregory VI	1303–1304	Benedict XI
1046–1047	Clement II	1305–1314	Clement V
1047–1048	Benedict IX (again)	1316–1334	John XXII
1048	Damasus II	1334–1342	Benedict XII
1049–1054	Leo IX	1342–1352	Clement VI
1055–1057	Victor II	1352–1362	Innocent VI
1057–1058	Stephen X (IX)	1362–1370	Urban V
1059–1061	Nicholas II	1370–1378	Gregory XI
1061–1073	Alexander II	1378–1389	Urban VI
1073–1085	Gregory VII	1389–1404	Boniface IX
1086–1087	Victor III	1404–1406	Innocent VII
1088–1099	Urban II	1406–1415	Gregory XII
1099–1118	Paschal II	1417–1431	Martin V
1118–1119	Gelasius II	1431–1447	Eugenius IV
1119–1124	Calixtus II	1447–1455	Nicholas V
1124–1130	Honorius II		

355–365	Felix II	1080;	Clement III
366–367	Ursinus	1084–1100	
418–419	Eulalius	1100	Theodoric
498;	Laurentius	1102	Albert
501–505		1105–1111	Sylvester IV
530	Dioscorus	1118–1121	Gregory VIII
687	Theodore	1124	Celestine II
687	Paschal	1130–1138	Anacletus II
767–768	Constantine	1138;	Victor IV
768	Philip	1159–1164	
844	John	1164–1168	Paschal III
855	Anastasius	1168–1178	Calixtus III
903–904	Christopher	1179–1180	Innocent III
974;	Boniface VII	1328–1330	Nicholas V
984–985		1378–1394	Clement VII
997–998	John XVI	1394–1423	Benedict XIII
1012	Gregory	1409–1410	Alexander V
1058–1059	Benedict X	1410–1415	John XXIII
1061–1072	Honorius II	1439–1449	Felix V

INDEX

Aachen (Aix-la-Chapelle), town 198
Abasgi 102, 370
Abbasid, dynasty of Caliphs at Baghdad 167, 182, 276
Abdalmalik, Caliph of Damascus 129
Abd-ar-Rahman III, Umayyad Caliph of Cordova 283
Absolutism 67, 77, 82, 114, 245, 514f.
Abul Kasim, Turkish emir of Nicaea 360
Abydus, town in Asia Minor on the Hellespont 181, 189, 257, 303
Acacius, Patriarch of Constantinople (472–488) 64
Acarnania 423; part of the kingdom of Epirus 432, 478; Byzantine 508, 517
Acciajuoli, Nerio I, duke of Athens 550
Acciajuoli, Nerio II, duke of Athens 565
Acciajuoli, Florentine family in Greece 510
Achaemenids, old Persian dynasty 44, 95
Achaia, Frankish duchy in the Peloponnese 424f., 448, 453, 455, 508, 510; under the Navarrese Company 550, 559, 561
Achelous, river near Anchialus on the Black Sea, battle (917) 263
Acindynus, Gregory, opponent of the hesychasts 474, 513, 515, 522
Acre, see Akkon
Acroinon, town in Phrygia, battle (740) 157
Acropolites, George, historian and statesman 418f., 460
Adana, town in Cilicia 365, 379
Adramyttium, town in Asia Minor 430
Adrianople, town in Thrace 196, 333, 348, 361; battle against the West Goths (378) 52, 196; besieged by Krum 201; by Symeon 263; by Samuel 309; taken by Frederick I 407; under Venetian rule 423; victory of Kalojan over the Latins 427; controlled by Theodore Angelus 435; social revolution 515; Cantecuzenus crowned in 520; under governorship of Matthew Cantacuzenus 529; taken by Ottomans 536, 565
Adriatic sea 93, 206, 236, 303, 346, 357, 367, 423, 432, 433, 439, 488, 571
Aegean sea 45, 93, 257, 313, 377, 490, 504, 534; Aegean islands 158, 423, 461
Aetius, eunuch, Irene's minister 181
Aetius, general in the western half of the Roman Empire 57
Aetolia 423; part of the kingdom of Epirus 432, 478; Byzantine 488, 517

Africa 35; under the Vandals, 58, 61; reconquered by Belisarius 70, 79; monothelete controversy 118; conquered by Arabs 140f.
Agathias, historian 6, 25, 211
agentes in rebus 37
Agnes-Anna, daughter of Louis VII, wife of Alexius II and of Andronicus I 396
Akkon (Acre), town in Palestine 297
Akova, town in the Peloponnese 550
Alamanni 52
Alans 61–2, 370, 492, 494
Alaric, leader of the Visogoths 55, 63
Albania and Albanians 301; Asen II takes part of 436; entry of Charles of Anjou 460; Philip of Tarentum 495; settlement in Thessaly 498; under Andronicus III 508; under Dušan 518, 534; Scanderbeg's opposition to the Turks 565
Albigensians 269; *see also* Bogomils
Alemannus, Nicolaus 2
Aleppo, town in Syria 276, 284, 308
Alexander, Emperor (912–913) 210; co-Emperor with Basil I 233, 240; with Leo VI 241; government of 261f.
Alexandria, occupied by the Arabs 115, 167; patriarchate of 58f.
Alexiad, by Anna Comnena 351f., 377
Alexius I Comnenus, Emperor (1081–1118), general under Michael VII 348f.; accession to the throne 349f.; government of 356–375, 376f., 381, 386, 400, 401, 413, 443, 484, 487
Alexius II Comnenus, Emperor (1180–1183) 394–6
Alexius III Angelus, Emperor (1195–1203) 408, 410–16, 425, 429
Alexius IV Angelus, co-Emperor with Isaac II (1203–1204) 415–16
Alexius V Ducas Murtzuphlus, Emperor (1204) 416
Alexius I Comnenus, Emperor of Trebizond (1204–1222) 426, 431
Alexius, *strategus* of the Armeniakon theme under Constantine VI 180
Ali, Caliph, son-in-law of Muhammed 117
Allatius, Leo 2, 3
allelengyon (τὸ ἀλληλέγγυον) 137, 188, 307, 322
Almus, brother of Stephen II of Hungary 378
Alopus, Leo, *proedrus* 338
Alp Arslan, Seljuq Sultan (1063–1072) 343, 348

Metochites, Theodore, statesman and scholar under Andronicus II 472, 490, 500, 501, 532

Mersius, Johannes 2

Mezezius, usurper 123

Michael I Rangabe, Emperor (811–813) **197–200**, 221

Michael II, Emperor (820–829) **203–6**

Michael III, Emperor (842–867) 210, **222–32**, 233, 234, 249

Michael IV, Emperor (1034–1042) **323–6**, 336

Michael V, Emperor (1041–1042) 316, 326

Michael VI, Emperor (1056–1057) 338–9

Michael VII Ducas, Emperor (1071–1078) 130³, 316, 344, **345–8**, 376

Michael VIII Palaeologus, Emperor 213, 419, 421, 471, 473; commander in Serres and Melnik 440; at the court of the Sultan of Iconium 445; Grand Duke, Despot, co-Emperor 447; his rule **448–65**, 478f., 489, 509, 523, 534, 561

Michael IX Palaeologus, co-Emperor with Andronicus II (1294–1320) 480, 488, 494, 498, 499

Michael I Angelus, ruler of Epirus (1204–c. 1215) 421, 425, 432, 440

Michael II Angelus, Despot of Epirus (1237?–1271) 420, 440, 446, 453, 457

Michael of Anchialus, *hypatus* of the philosophers, Patriarch of Constantinople 355

Michael Asen, Bulgarian tzar (1246–1256) 440, 446

Michael Autoreianus, Patriarch of Constantinople in Nicaea (1208–1212) 419, 427f.

Michael Cerularius, Patriarch of Constantinople (1043–1058) 319; ecclesiastical schism 336f.; under Isaac I 338–41

Michael Šišman, Bulgarian tzar (1323–1330) 502, 505

Michael the Syrian, chronicler 90

Michael of Thessalonica, heretic, rhetorician 354

Michael of Zachlumia 268

Michael of Zeta, receives crown from Rome (1077) 346

Miklosich, Franz 15

Miletus, town in Asia Minor 426

miliaresion, Byzantine silver coin 188, 190¹

Military holdings 43; development in seventh century 97f., 133; under Nicephorus I 190; government's measures to protect in the tenth century 272–6, 280f., 286f., 306; to assert state rights over 294f.; decay in the eleventh century 322f., 329f., 331f., 349; revival

under the Comneni 391f.; in the Nicaean Empire 442; collapse 492; *see also* Soldiers (*stratiotai*) and soldiers' property

Miller, William 11

Milutin, Serbian king (1282–1321) 466, 472, 473, 481; conquers Byzantine territory 464; marriage with Simonis 489f.; alliance with Charles of Valois 495; with Andronicus II 497

Miraculi Sancti Demetrii 90

Mircea the Elder, Wallachian prince 551

Mistra, town in the Peloponnese 558, 565; despot of 550, 558; *see also* Morea

Modon, town in the Peloponnese, Venetian 423, 497, 561

Moechian controversy 180f., 187, 197

Moesia, Slavs occupy 93, 126

Momčilo, Hajduk 518

Mommsen, Theodor 6

Monasticism, in the seventh century 138; opposition to iconoclasm 174f., 209; after the victory of orthodoxy 178f., 180f.; under Nicephorus II Phocas 285, 287f.; under Basil II 306f.; hesychasm 511–13; *see also* Zealots, 'Politicians', Mt. Athos

Monemvasia, town in the Peloponnese 453, 497; *Chronicle* of 148

Mongols, break into Europe and the Near East 439, 443; of Khan Hulagu 458f.; of Timur 556; *see also* Tartars

Monnier, Henri 7f.

Monomachus, John, governor of Thessalonica 495, 507

Monophysitism 58f.; and the Council of Chalcedon 59f.; under Basiliscus and Zeno 64; Anastasius I 66, 68; Justinian I 69, 78; Heraclius 107–9; and Iconoclasm 152, 161, 172

Monotheletism, under Heraclius 107–9; Constans II 118; condemned by the sixth oecumenical Council 127; reaction under Philippicus 153

Montesquieu 5

Montfaucon, Bernard de 4

Monutes, Theophanes 165f.

Mopsuestia (Mamistra), town in southeast Asia Minor 290, 365, 379

Morava, river in the Balkans, battle (1190) 408

Moravcsik, Gyula 1, 21

Moravians, Constantine and Methodius' mission to 228, 229f.; Methodius' followers expelled 236; Tartar attacks 439

Morea, under Frankish rule 424f.; wars under Michael VIII 457, 460f., 463; reorganization under Andronicus II

CPSIA information can be obtained at www.ICGtesting.com
Printed in the USA
BVOW06s2139290915

420260BV00002B/3/P

9 780813 511986